Index of American Periodical Verse: 1978

by
Sander W. Zulauf
and
Edward M. Cifelli

The Scarecrow Press, Inc.
Metuchen, N.J. & London
1980

Library of Congress Catalog Card No. 73-3060

ISBN 0-8108-1301-7

Copyright © 1980 by Sander W. Zulauf and Edward M. Cifelli

Manufactured in the United States of America

CONTENTS

PREFACE

The Index of American Periodical Verse: 1978 is the eighth annual volume in the series which Sander Zulauf and Irwin Weiser originated in 1971. It conveniently locates the poems that were published in nearly 200 magazines in 1978. When used in conjunction with the seven earlier volumes, it offers a clear idea of the work of individual poets in the past decade, as well as a clear indication of the abundance of contemporary poetry. The series suggests the vitality of the publishing of poetry in the United States in that it records the contents of the quarterlies and the occasionally-published journals with the smallest circulations as well as the major national and international magazines which publish poetry.

The Index continues to record the successes and failures of poets and editors as the eighties begin. It will continue to offer a representative selection of magazines that regularly publish poetry; it is a unique, reliable reference book that is useful to anyone with an interest in contemporary poetry.

The format of the Index this year follows that of its predecessors. The first section lists the title abbreviation of each publication indexed, the complete name of the magazine, the names of the editors, the editorial addresses, and the latest available subscription and single copy prices.

The main section of the Index is the alphabetical listing of poets and their published poems. Under each poet's name there is an alphabetical list of poem titles. Following each title there is a reference citation which locates the poem. This citation includes the underlined title abbreviation for the magazine--"OhioR" (for Ohio Review); the volume and number of the issue in parentheses--"(3:2)" signifying volume 3, number 2; "Sum 78" for an issue dated summer 1978; and the page number--"p."--on which the poem appears or begins.

More noticeable this year than in previous years in this decade is the fact that there is a marked increase in poets using rhyme, meter, and form. Little Magazine devoted an issue to formal poetry. Poetry, thriving under the editorship of John Frederick Nims, published many formal poems, including Tom Disch's wonderfully definitive answer to Joyce Kilmer entitled "Poems."

We humbly thank the people who helped us make this volume. Mrs. Marion Zulauf again helped us alphabetize the Index. The librarians who helped us this year were Mrs. Dorothy Souchack and the periodicals staff at the Sherman H. Masten Learning Resources Center at County College of Morris, Randolph, N. J.; Mrs. Constance Lane, Director of the Roxbury Public Library, Succasunna, N. J. The editors of all the magazines listed here continue to make the Index possible annually through their cooperation. We also add our special thanks to those editors who announce the Index in each issue they publish. We again thank the people at Scarecrow Press who help us make this an accurate record of contemporary poetry. And we add our thanks with love to our families: Bobbi, Lisa and Laura Cifelli, Madeline and Scott Zulauf, and Michael and Mary Beth Stoddard.

Succasunna, N. J.   S. W. Z.
August, 1979   E. M. C.

ABBREVIATIONS

ad.	adaptation
arr.	arrangement
Back:	back-issue copy price
Ed. (s.)	Editor(s)
Exec.	Executive
(ind.)	price for individuals
(inst.)	price for institutions
(lib.)	price for libraries
p.	page
pp.	pages
Po. Ed.	Poetry Editor
Pub.	Publisher
Sing:	single copy price
SI	Special Issue
(stud.)	price for students
Subs:	subscription price or address
tr.	translation
U	University
w.	with
$8/yr	eight dollars per year
(19)	number 19
(7:8)	volume 7, number 8

Months

Ja	January	Jl	July
F	February	Ag	August
Mr	March	S	September
Ap	April	O	October
My	May	N	November
Je	June	D	December

Seasons

Aut	Autumn, Fall	Spr	Spring
Wint	Winter	Sum	Summer

PERIODICALS ADDED

Bachy

Durak

Little Magazine

Missouri Review

New England Review

North Stone Review

Pikestaff Forum

Smudge

Telephone

Tendril

PERIODICALS DELETED

The American Review

Broadside Series

Dragonfly

Esquire

Horizon

Icarus

Lynx

Marilyn

Mark Twain Journal

Mississippi Review

Montana Gothic

New

Phylon

Poets in the South

Quartet

Seventies

Transatlantic Review

Yardbird Reader

PERIODICAL TITLE CHANGES

Bleb became The Ark with issue (14).

Boxspring became Norwuttuck with issue (8).

Rapport became Slow Loris Reader with issue (11).

PERIODICALS INDEXED

AAR
ANN ARBOR REVIEW
Fred Wolven, Ed.
Washtenaw Community College
Ann Arbor, MI 48106
(28)
Subs: $6/3
Sing: $2

AAUP
AAUP BULLETIN
R. K. Webb, Ed.
Suite 500
One Dupont Circle, N. W.
Washington, DC 20036
(64:1-4)
Subs: $10/yr

Agni
AGNI REVIEW
Sharon Dunn
Askold Melnyczuk, Eds.
Box 349
Cambridge, MA 02138
(8-9)
Subs: $7/2 yrs
$4/yr
Sing: $2.50

Aieee
AIEEE
Jack Grady
Orlan Cannon, Eds.
Alphaville
Box 3424
Charlottesville, VA 22903
(-)
Sing: $2

AmerPoR
AMERICAN POETRY REVIEW
Stephen Berg, et al. , Eds.

Temple U Center City
1616 Walnut St. Room 405
Philadelphia, PA 19103
(7:1-6)
Subs: $16/3 yrs
$11/2 yrs
$6/yr
Sing: $1.25

AmerS
THE AMERICAN SCHOLAR
Joseph Epstein, Ed.
1811 Q St. , N. W.
Washington, DC 20009
(47:1-4)
Subs: $20/3 yrs
$14.50/2 yrs
$8/yr
Sing: $2

AndR
THE ANDOVER REVIEW
William H. Brown, Ed.
Erica Funkhouser, Po. Ed.
Phillips Academy
Andover, MA 01810
(4:2) (5:1-2)
Subs: $6/yr
Sing: $3

Antaeus
ANTAEUS
Daniel Halpern, Ed.
1 West 30th St.
New York, NY 10001
(28-30/31)
Subs: $12/yr
Sing: $3.50

AntR
ANTIOCH REVIEW
Robert S. Fogarty, Ed.

1

Sally Frye
Ethan Thomas, Po. Assistants
Box 148
Yellow Springs, OH 45387
 (36:1-4)
  Subs: $10/yr
  Sing: $2.50

Aphra
APHRA
Elizabeth Fisher, et al., Eds.
Box 893
Ansonia Station
New York, NY 10023
 (-)
  Subs: $5.50
  Sing: $1.50
  Back: $1.75

AriD
ARION'S DOLPHIN
Stratis Haviaras, Ed.
Box 313
Cambridge, MA 02138
 (-)
  Subs: $4
  Sing: $1

ArizQ
ARIZONA QUARTERLY
Albert Frank Gegenheimer, Ed.
U of Arizona
Tucson, AZ 85721
 (34:1-4)
  Subs: $5/3yrs
        $2/yr
  Sing: $.50

ArkRiv
THE ARK RIVER REVIEW
Jonathan Katz
Anthony Sobin, Eds.
Box 14
Wichita State U
Wichita, KS 67208
 (4:2)
  Subs: $5

Ascent
ASCENT

Daniel Curley, et al., Eds.
English Dept.
U of Illinois
Urbana, IL 61801
 (3:3) (4:1)
  Subs: $3
  Sing: $1.50

Aspect
ASPECT
Ed Hogan, et al., Eds.
1105 Broadway
Somerville, MA 02144
 (71:72/73)
  Subs: $6
  Sing: $1.50

Aspen
ASPEN ANTHOLOGY
J. D. Muller, Ed.
Bruce Berger
Virginia Slachman, Po. Eds.
Box 3185
Aspen, CO 81611
 (5-6)
  Sing: $2.50

Atl
THE ATLANTIC
Robert Manning, Ed.
Peter Davison
Phoebe-Lou Adams, Po. Eds.
8 Arlington St.
Boston, MA 02116
  Subs: Box 1857
        Greenwich, CT 06830
 (241:1-6) (242:1-6)
  Subs: $35/3 yrs
        $27/2 yrs
        $15/yr
  Sing: $1.50

Bachy
*BACHY
Bob Mehlman
Leland Hickman, Eds.
11317 Santa Monica Blvd.
West Los Angeles, CA 90025
 (11-13)

---

*New titles added to the Index in 1978.

Subs: $7.50/yr
Sing: $3

BallSUF
BALL STATE UNIVERSITY
FORUM
Merrill & Frances M. Rippy,
  Eds.
Ball State U
Muncie, IN 47306
  (19:1-4)
  Subs: $5/yr
  Sing: $1.50

BelPoJ
THE BELOIT POETRY
JOURNAL
Robert H. Glauber, et al., Eds.
Box 2
Beloit, WI 53511
  (28:3/4) (29:1/2)
  Subs: $11/3 yrs
         $4/yr
  Sing: $1.50

BerksR
BERKSHIRE REVIEW
Michael Davitt Bell, et al.,
  Eds.
Williams College
Box 633
Williamstown, MA 02167
  (13:2)
  Subs: $1/yr
  Sing: $.50

BigD
BIG DEAL
Barbara Baracks, Ed.
Box 830
Peter Stuyvesant Sta.
New York, NY 10009
  (-)
  Subs: $21/6 (inst.)
         $18/6 (ind.)
  Sing: $3.50 (inst.)
         $3 (ind.)

BirdE
BIRD EFFORT
Robert Long
Josh Dayton, Eds.
25 Mudford Ave.

East Hampton, NY 11937
  (-)
  Sing: $1

Bits
BITS
Dennis Dooley, et al., Eds.
Gutenberg Annex
Dept. of English
Case Western Reserve U
Cleveland, OH 44106
  (7-8)

BlackF
BLACK FORUM
Revish Windham, Ed.
Horace Mungin
Zandra Holmes, Po. Eds.
Box 1090
Bronx, NY 10451
  (2:2)
  Subs: $3/yr
  Sing: $2

Bleb/Ark
BLEB/THE ARK
Geoffrey Gardner, Ed.
Box 322
Times Square Sta.
New York, NY 10036
  (13)
  Subs: $2/yr
  Sing: $1

BosUJ
BOSTON UNIVERSITY JOURNAL
Paul Kurt Ackermann, Ed.
704 Commonwealth Ave.
Boston, MA 02215
  (26:1-2)
  Subs: $9/yr (inst.)
         $6/yr (ind.)
  Sing: $2

Bound
BOUNDARY 2
William V. Spanos
Robert Kroetsch, Eds.
SUNY--Binghamton
Binghamton, NY 13901
  (6:2) (6:3/7:1)
  Subs: $15/yr (inst.)
         $10/yr (ind.)
  Sing: $4

Box
BOXSPRING
Suzanne P. Bernard, et al.,
　Eds.
Hampshire College
Amherst, MA　01002
　(6-7)
　(8), as Norwottuck
　Subs:　$3/yr
　Sing:　$2

CalQ
CALIFORNIA QUARTERLY
Elliot L. Gilbert, Ed.
100 Sproul Hall
U of California
Davis, CA　95616
　(13/14)
　Subs:　$5/yr
　Sing:　$1.50

CarlMis
CARLETON MISCELLANY
Keith Harrison, Ed.
Carleton College
Northfield, MN　55057
　(-)
　Subs:　$10/2 yrs
　　　　$5.50/yr
　Sing:　$2

CarolQ
CAROLINA QUARTERLY
Katherine Kearns
Margaret Ketchum, Eds.
Michael McFee, Po. Ed.
U of North Carolina
Greenlaw Hall　066-A
Chapel Hill, NC　27514
　(30:1-3)
　Subs:　$6/yr
　Sing:　$2
　Back:　$2

CarouselQ
CAROUSEL QUARTERLY
Jay B. Isaacs
Box 111
Mt. Laurel, NJ　08054
　(3:1-4)
　Subs:　$10/yr

CEACritic
CEA CRITIC

Elizabeth W. Cowan, Ed.
English Dept.
Texas A&M U
College Station, TX　77843
　(40:2-4) (41:1)
　Subs:　$20/2 yrs
　　　　$12/yr

CentR
CENTENNIAL REVIEW
David Mead, Ed.
Linda Wagner, Po. Ed.
110 Morrill Hall
Michigan State U
East Lansing, MI　48824
　(22:1-4)
　Subs:　$5/2 yrs
　　　　$3/yr
　Sing:　$1

Chelsea
CHELSEA
Sonia Raiziss, Ed.
Box 5880
Grand Central Station
New York, NY　10017
　(37)
　Subs:　$5
　Sing:　$3

ChiR
CHICAGO REVIEW
Cheryl Glickfield, Ed.
Catherine Mouly
Mara Anne Tapp, Po. Eds.
Faculty Exchange
Box C
U of Chicago
Chicago, IL　60637
　(29:4) (30:1-3)
　Subs:　$27/3 yrs
　　　　$18.50/2 yrs
　　　　$10/yr
　Sing:　$2.85

Chomo
CHOMO-URI
Annette Townley, et al., Eds.
Box 1057
Amherst, MA　01002
　(4:3) (5:1-2)
　Subs:　$10/3 yrs
　　　　$7/2 yrs

$4/yr
Sing: $1.50

Chowder
CHOWDER REVIEW
Ron Slate, Ed.
1720 Vilas Ave.
Madison, WI   53711
(10/11)
Subs: $5.50/yr
Sing: $2

ChrC
THE CHRISTIAN CENTURY
James M. Wall, Ed.
407 S. Dearborn St.
Chicago, IL   60605
(95:1-43)
Subs: $34/3 yrs
        $25/2 yrs
        $15/yr
Sing: $.50

CimR
CIMARRON REVIEW
Clinton C. Keeler, Ed.
208 Life Sciences East
Oklahoma State U
Stillwater, OK   74074
(42-45)
Subs: $10/yr
Sing: $4

ColEng
COLLEGE ENGLISH
Donald Gray, Ed.
Brian O'Neill, Po. Consultant
Dept. of English
Indiana U
Bloomington, IN   47401
Subs: NCTE
        1111 Kenyon Rd.
        Urbana, IL   61801
(39:5-8) (40:1-4)
Subs: $20/yr
Sing: $2.50

Columbia
COLUMBIA
Meryl Johnson, Ed.
Allison Funk
Robert Farnsworth, Po. Eds.
404 Dodge

Columbia U
New York, NY   10027
(2)
Sing: $3

Comm
COMMONWEAL
James O'Gara, Ed.
John Fandel, Po. Ed.
232 Madison Ave.
New York, NY   10016
(105:1-25)
Subs: $32/2 yrs
        $18/yr
Sing: $.75

ConcPo
CONCERNING POETRY
Ellwood Johnson, Ed.
Robert Huff, Po. Ed.
Dept. of English
Western Washington U
Bellingham, WA   98225
(11:1-2)
Subs: $4/yr
Sing: $2
Back: $2

Confr
CONFRONTATION
Martin Tucker, Ed.
English Dept.
Brooklyn Center of
    Long Island U
Brooklyn, NY   11201
(16-17)
Subs: $10.50/3 yrs
        $7/2 yrs
        $3.50/yr
Sing: $2
Back: $2

CornellR
CORNELL REVIEW
Baxter Hathaway, Ed.
108 North Plain St.
Ithaca, NY   14850
(3-4)
Subs: $25/3 yrs
        $18/2 yrs
        $10/yr
Sing: $3.50

CutB
CUTBANK
Art Homer
Rick Robbins, Eds.
Kathy Callaway, et al., Po.
Consultants
Dept. of English
U of Montana
Missoula, MT 59812
(10-11)
Subs: $6.50/2 yrs
      $3.50/yr
Sing: $2

DacTerr
DACOTAH TERRITORY
Mark Vinz, Ed.
Moorhead State U
Box 775
Moorhead, MN 56560
(15)
Sing: $2.50

DeKalb
DeKALB LITERARY ARTS
JOURNAL
William S. Newman, Ed.
DeKalb Community College
555 N. Indian Creek Drive
Clarkston, GA 30021
(11:1-4)
Sing: $3/double issue
      $1.50

DenQ
DENVER QUARTERLY
Leland H. Chambers, Ed.
U of Denver
Denver, CO 80208
(13:1-4)
Subs: $14/2 yrs
      $8/yr
Sing: $2

Durak
*DURAK
Robert Lloyd
D. S. Hoffman, Eds.
1219 Landsburn Circle
Westlake Village, CA 91361
or
RD 1 Box 352
Joe Green Rd.

Erin, NY 14838
Note: Publishes solicited manu-
      scripts only.
(1)
Subs: $5/2 yrs
      $3/yr
Sing: $1.50

EngJ
ENGLISH JOURNAL
Stephen J. Judy, Ed.
Richard Calisch, Po. Ed.
Box 112
East Lansing, MI 48823
Subs: 1111 Kenyon Rd.
      Urbana, IL 61801
(67:5) Poetry published in
      May issue only.
Subs: $20/yr
Sing: $3

EnPas
EN PASSANT
James A. Costello
1906 Brant Road
Wilmington, DE 19810
(7)
Subs: $6
Sing: $1.75

Epoch
EPOCH
Walter Slatoff
James McConkey, Eds.
245 Goldwin Smith Hall
Cornell U
Ithaca, NY 14853
(27:2-3) (28:1)
Subs: $4/yr
Sing: $1

Epos
EPOS
Evelyn Thorne
Jean West MacKenzie, Eds.
Rollins College
Winter Park, FL 32012
(27:1-2)
Final issue.

Esq
ESQUIRE

Esquire discontinued publishing
poetry in January, 1978.

Falcon
THE FALCON
W. A. Blais, Ed.
Belknap Hall
Mansfield State College
Mansfield, PA   16933
  (16-17)
  Subs: $4/yr
  Sing: $2
  Note: "The editors regret
that they can no longer con-
sider unsolicited poetry or fic-
tion. "

Field
FIELD
Stuart Friebert
David Young, Eds.
Rice Hall
Oberlin College
Oberlin, OH   44074
  (18-19)
  Subs: $8/2 yrs
         $5/yr
  Sing: $2. 50

Focus
FOCUS/MIDWEST
Charles L. Klotzer, Ed.
Dan Jaffe, Po. Ed.
928a N. McKnight
St. Louis, MO   63132
  (12:78) (13:79)
  Subs: $11. 50/2 yrs
         $7/yr
  Sing: $1. 25

FourQt
FOUR QUARTERS
John Christopher Kleis, Ed.
Richard Lautz, Po. Ed.
English Department
LaSalle College
20th & Olney Aves.
Philadelphia, PA   19141
  (27:2-4) (28:1)
  Subs: $7/2 yrs
         $4/yr
  Sing: $1

GeoR
GEORGIA REVIEW
Stanley W. Lindberg, Ed.
U of Georgia
Athens, GA   30602
  (32:1-4)
  Subs: $10/2 yrs
         $6/yr
  Sing: $2

Glass
GLASSWORKS
Betty Bressi, Ed.
Box 163
Rosebank Station
Staten Island, NY   10305
  (3:1/2/3)
  Subs: $4. 50
  Sing: $3

Gravida
GRAVIDA
Ina Chadwick Wilde, et al.,
  Eds.
Box 76
Hartsdale, NY   10530
  Subs: Box 118
         Bayville, NY   11709
  (-)
  Subs: $4
  Sing: $1. 25

GreenfieldR
THE GREENFIELD REVIEW
Joseph Bruchac III, Ed.
Greenfield Center, NY   12833
  (6:3/4) (7:1/2)
  Subs: $4/yr
  Sing: $2

GRR
GREEN RIVER REVIEW
Raymond Tyner, Ed.
SVSC Box 56
University Center, MI   48710
  (9:1-3)
  Subs: $6/yr

Hand
HAND BOOK
Susan Mernit
Rochelle Ratner, Eds.

184 West North Broadway
Columbus, OH   43214
or
50 Spring St.
New York, NY   10013
  (2)
  Subs: $6
  Sing: $4

HangL
HANGING LOOSE
Robert Hershon, et al., Eds.
231 Wyckoff St.
Brooklyn, NY   11217
  (32-34)
  Subs: $6
  Sing: $1.50

Harp
HARPER'S MAGAZINE
Lewis H. Lapham, Ed.
Two Park Ave.
New York, NY   10016
  Subs: 1255 Portland Place
        Boulder, CO   80323
  (256:1532-1537)
  (257:1538-1543)
  Subs: $11.98/yr
  Sing: $1.50

HarvAd
HARVARD ADVOCATE
Richard V. Nalley, President
Owen Andrews, Po. Ed.
21 South St.
Cambridge, MA   02138
  (111:3-4) (112:1)
  (111:5) not printed.
  Subs: $5
  Sing: $1.25

Hills
HILLS
Bob Perelman, Ed.
1220 Folsom
San Francisco, CA   94103
  (5)
  Sing: $2

HiramPoR
HIRAM POETRY REVIEW
David Fratus
Carol Donley, Eds.

Box 162
Hiram, OH   44234
  (24-25)
  Subs: $2
  Sing: $1

HolCrit
THE HOLLINS CRITIC
John Rees Moore, Ed.
Box 9538
Hollins College, VA   24020
  (15:1-5)
  Subs: $10/3 yrs
        $7/2 yrs
        $4/yr

Hudson
THE HUDSON REVIEW
Frederick Morgan
Paula Deitz, Eds.
65 East 55th St.
New York, NY   10022
  (31:1-4)
  Subs: $26/3 yrs
        $18/2 yrs
        $10/yr
  Sing: $3

Humanist
HUMANIST
Paul Kurtz, Ed.
SUNY at Buffalo
Amherst, NY   14260
  Subs: 7 Harwood Dr.
        Amherst, NY   14226
  (38:1-6)
  Subs: $27/3 yrs
        $20/2 yrs
        $12/yr
  Sing: $2

Iowa
IOWA REVIEW
David Hamilton
Fredrick Woodard, Eds.
308 EPB
The U of Iowa
Iowa City, IA   52242
  (9:1-4)
  Subs: $7
  Sing: $2

JnlONJP
JOURNAL OF NEW JERSEY
POETS
Walter Cummins, Ed.
Dept. of English
Fairleigh Dickinson U
Madison, NJ 07940
(2:1-2) (3:1)
(2:3) not printed.
Subs: $3
Sing: $1

JnlOPC
JOURNAL OF POPULAR
CULTURE
Ray B. Browne, Ed.
Bowling Green U
Bowling Green, OH 43403
(11:1) (11:3-4) (12:1-3)
Subs: $25/2 yrs
$15/yr
Sing: $4

Juice
JUICE
Stephen S. Morse
Judy L. Brekke, Eds.
5321 Cole St.
Oakland, CA 94601
Note: (6) could not be in-
dexed because authors of poems
were not identified.
Subs: $4/yr
Sing: $2.50

KanQ
KANSAS QUARTERLY
Harold Schneider
Ben Nyberg, Eds.
Dept. of English
Kansas State U
Manhattan, KS 66506
(10:1-4)
Subs: $16/2 yrs
$9/yr
Sing: $2.50
Back: $2.50

Kayak
KAYAK
George Hitchcock, Ed.
Marjorie Simon, Associate Ed.
325 Ocean View Ave.

Santa Cruz, CA 95062
(47-49)
Subs: $4/4
Sing: $1

LaB
Là-BAS
Douglas Messerli, Ed.
Box 431
College Park, MD 20740
(9) included in 1977 Index.
(10-11)

LadHJ
LADIES' HOME JOURNAL
Lenore Hershey, Ed.
641 Lexington Ave.
New York, NY 10022
Subs: Box 1697
Des Moines, IA 50306
(95:1-12)
Subs: $7.97
Sing: $1.25

LitR
THE LITERARY REVIEW
Martin Green
Harry Keyishian, Eds.
Fairleigh Dickinson U
285 Madison Ave.
Madison, NJ 07940
(21:3-4) (22:1-2)
Subs: $9/yr
Sing: $3.50

LittleM
*THE LITTLE MAGAZINE
Carolyn Kirkpatrick, Ed.
Box 207
Cathedral Station
New York, NY 10025
(11:3-4)
Subs: $7/4
Sing: $1.50

LittleR
THE LITTLE REVIEW
John McKernan, Ed.
Dept. of English
Marshall U
Huntington, WV 25701
(-)

Subs: $2.50
Sing: $1.25

Madem
MADEMOISELLE
Edith Raymond Locke, Ed.
Mary Elizabeth McNichols, Po.
  Ed.
Conde Nast Building
350 Madison Ave.
New York, NY 10017
  (84:1-12)
  Subs: $10/yr
  Sing: $1.25

Madrona
MADRONA
Charles Webb, Ed.
4730 Latona, N.E.
Seattle, WA 98105
  (15/16)
  Subs: $5/3
  Sing: $2

MalR
THE MALAHAT REVIEW
Robin Skelton, Ed.
Box 1700
Victoria, B.C.
Canada V8W 2Y2
  (45-48)
  Subs: $10/yr
  Sing: $3 & $5

MassR
THE MASSACHUSETTS REVIEW
Lee Edwards, et al., Eds.
Memorial Hall
U of Massachusetts
Amherst, MA 01002
  (19:1-4)
  Subs: $9/yr
  Sing: $2.50

MichQR
MICHIGAN QUARTERLY REVIEW
Laurence Goldstein, Ed.
3032 Rackham Bldg.
The U of Michigan
Ann Arbor, MI 48109
  (17:1-4)
  Subs: $22/3 yrs
         $16/2 yrs

$9/yr
Sing: $2.50
Back: $3

MidwQ
THE MIDWEST QUARTERLY
V. J. Emmett, Jr., Ed.
Michael Heffernan, Po. Ed.
Pittsburg State U
Pittsburg, KS 66762
  (19:2-4) (20:1)
  Subs: $4/yr
  Sing: $1.50

MinnR
THE MINNESOTA REVIEW
Roger Mitchell
Susan Scott Thompson, Eds.
Box 211
Bloomington, IN 47401
  (NS10-NS11)
  Subs: $12/2 yrs (inst.)
         $9/2 yrs (ind.)
         $7/yr (inst.)
         $5/yr (ind.)
  Sing: $2.50

MissouriR
*MISSOURI REVIEW
Marcia Southwick
Larry Levis, Eds.
Dept. of English
231 A & S
U of Missouri--Columbia
Columbia, MO 65211
  (1:1) (2:1)
  Subs: $10/2 yrs
         $6/yr
  Sing: $2.25

ModernPS
MODERN POETRY STUDIES
Gerald O'Grady, Ed.
Robert Mattern, Po. Ed.
207 Delaware Ave.
Buffalo, NY 14202
  (9:1-3)
  Subs: $9/3 (inst.)
         $7.50/3 (ind.)

ModR
MODULARIST REVIEW
R. C. Morse, Ed.

Wooden Needle Press
65-45 Yellowstone Blvd.
Forest Hills, NY 11375
(-)
Subs: $3/yr
Sing: $3

Montra
MONTEMORA
Eliot Weinberger
The Montemora Foundation
Box 336 Cooper Station
New York, NY 10003
(4)
Subs: $12/3 (inst.)
      $10/3 (ind.)
Sing: $4

MoonsLT
MOONS AND LION TAILES
H. Schjotz-Christensen, Ed.
The Permanent Press
Lake Street Station
Box 8434
Minneapolis, MN 55408
(2:4)
Subs: $12/4 (inst.)
      $10/4 (ind.)
Sing: $2.50

Mouth
MOUTH OF THE DRAGON
Andrew Bifrost, Ed.
342 E. 15th St.
New York, NY 10003
(-)
Subs: $18/5 (inst.)
      $13/5 (ind.)
Sing: $3

Mund
MUNDUS ARTIUM
Rainer Schulte, Ed.
U of Texas at Dallas
Box 688
Richardson, TX 75080
(-)
Subs: $10/yr (inst.)
      $8/yr (ind.)
Sing: $4.50

Nat
THE NATION

Victor Navasky, Ed.
Grace Schulman, Po. Ed.
333 Sixth Ave.
New York, NY 10014
(226:1-24) (227:1-23)
Subs: $45/2 yrs
      $25/yr
      $17/yr (stud.)
Sing: $1

NegroHB
NEGRO HISTORY BULLETIN
J. Rupert Picott, Ed.
1401 14th St., N.W.
Washington, DC 20005
(41:1-6)
Subs: $8/yr
Sing: $1.50
Bound: $12/yr

NewC
NEW COLLAGE
A. McA. Miller, Ed.
5700 North Trail
Sarasota, FL 33580
(-)
Subs: $3/yr
Sing: $1

NewEngR
*NEW ENGLAND REVIEW
Sydney Lea
Jay Parini, Eds.
M. Robin Barone, Managing Ed.
Box 170
Hanover, NH 03755
(1:1-2)
Subs: $25/12
      $18/8
      $10/4

NewL
NEW LETTERS
David Ray, Ed.
U of Missouri--Kansas City
5346 Charlotte
Kansas City, MO 64110
(44:3-4) (45:1-2)
Subs: $40/5 yrs (lib.)
      $25/5 yrs (ind.)
      $18/2 yrs (lib.)
      $12/2 yrs (ind.)
      $8/yr

Sing: $2.50
Back: Prices on request.

NewOR
NEW ORLEANS REVIEW
Dawson Gaillard, Ed.
Loyola U
New Orleans, LA 70118
(5:4) (6:1)
Subs: $14/12
$10/8
$6/4
Sing: $1.50

NewRena
THE NEW RENAISSANCE
Louise T. Reynolds, Ed.
Stanwood Bolton, Po. Ed.
9 Heath Road
Arlington, MA 02147
(10)
Subs: $6/3
Sing: $2.85

NewRep
THE NEW REPUBLIC
Martin Peretz, Ed.
Robert Pinsky, Po. Ed.
1220 19th St., N.W.
Washington, DC 20036
Subs: Subs Service Dept.
Box 705
Whitinsville, MA
01588
(178:1-25) (179:1-26/27)
Subs: $24/yr
$17/yr (stud.)
Sing: $1

NewRivR
NEW RIVER REVIEW
Charles L. Hayes, Ed./Pub.
Philip Pierson, Po. Ed.
Highlands Press
Radford, VA 24142
(2:2)
Sing: $2

NewWR
NEW WORLD REVIEW
Marilyn Bechtel, Ed.
Jessica Smith, Chairman,
Editorial Board

Suite 308
156 Fifth Ave.
New York, NY 10010
(46:1-6)
Subs: $5/yr
Sing: $1

NewYRB
THE NEW YORK REVIEW OF
BOOKS
Robert B. Silvers
Barbara Epstein, Eds.
250 W. 57th St.
New York, NY 10019
Subs: Subs Service Dept.
Box 940
Farmingdale, NY
11737
(25:1-21/22)
Subs: $14.50/yr
Sing: $.85

NewYorker
THE NEW YORKER
Howard Moss, Po. Ed.
25 W. 43rd St.
New York, NY 10036
(53:46-52) (54:1-45)
Subs: $24/yr
Sing: $1

Nimrod
NIMROD
Francine Ringold, Ed.
U of Tulsa
Tulsa, OK 74104
(22:2)
Subs: $4/yr
Sing: $2.25

NoAmR
NORTH AMERICAN REVIEW
Robley Wilson, Jr., Ed.
Peter Cooley, Po. Ed.
U of Northern Iowa
Cedar Falls, IA 50613
(263:1-4)
Subs: $8/yr
Sing: $2

Nor
NORWOTTUCK
See Boxspring

NorthSR
*NORTH STONE REVIEW
James Naiden, Ed.
Allen Topper, Associate Ed.
U Station
Box 14098
Minneapolis, MN 55414
  (8)
  Subs: $7. 50/3 (inst.)
         $6. 50/3 (ind.)
  Sing: $3

Northeast
NORTHEAST
John Judson, Ed.
Juniper Press
1310 Shorewood Dr.
La Crosse, WI 54601
  (3:5-6)
  Subs: $13/yr (includes four
         chapbooks)
  Sing: $2

NowestR
NORTHWEST REVIEW
Michael Strelow, Ed.
John Ackerson, Po. Ed.
U of Oregon
Eugene, OR 97403
  (17:1)
  Subs: $5/yr
  Sing: $2

Obs
OBSIDIAN
Alvin Aubert, Ed. / Pub.
Wayne State U
Detroit, MI 48202
  (4:1-2)
  Subs: $5. 50/yr
  Sing: $2

OhioR
OHIO REVIEW
Wayne Dodd, Ed.
Jack Matthews, Advisory Ed.
Ellis Hall
Ohio U
Athens, OH 45701
  (19:1-3)
  Subs: $10/yr
  Sing: $3. 50

OP
OPEN PLACES
Eleanor M. Bender, Ed.
Box 2085
Stephens College
Columbia, MO 65201
  (25-26)
  Subs: $7/2 yrs
         $4/yr
  Sing: $2

Paint
PAINTBRUSH
Ben Bennani, Ed.
Dept. of English
Northeastern U
Boston, MA 02115
  (7/8-9/10)
  Subs: $13/3 yrs
         $9/2 yrs
         $5/yr
  Sing: $5

Pan
PANACHE
David Lenson, Pub.
Candice Ward, Po. Ed.
Box 77
Sunderland, MA 02144
  (19)
  Sing: $2

ParisR
THE PARIS REVIEW
George A. Plimpton, Ed.
Jonathan Galassi, Po. Ed.
45-39 171 Place
Flushing, NY 11358
Poetry Mss. :
541 E. 72nd St.
New York, NY 10021
  (72-74)
  Subs: $20/12
         $11/6
  Sing: $2. 25

PartR
PARTISAN REVIEW
William Phillips, Ed.
John Ashbery, Po. Ed.
Boston U
19 Deerfield St.

Boston, MA 02215
or
522 Fifth Ave.
New York, NY 10036
(45:1-4)
  Subs: $25/3 yrs
       $17.50/2 yrs
       $9/yr
  Sing: $2.50

Paunch
PAUNCH
Arthur Efron, Ed.
123 Woodward Ave.
Buffalo, NY 14214
(50/51-52)
  Subs: $7/yr (lib.)
       $4/yr (ind.)
       $3/yr (stud.)
  Sing & Back: Prices on
    request.

Peb
PEBBLE
Greg Kuzma, Ed.
The Best Cellar Press
118 South Boswell Ave.
Crete, NE 68333
(-)
  Subs: $10/4 (lib.)
       $8/4 (ind.)
  Sing: $4/double issue
       $2

Pequod
PEQUOD
David Paradis
Mark Rudman, Eds.
Box 491
Forest Knolls, CA 94933
Poetry Mss.:
Mark Rudman
817 West End Ave.
New York, NY 10025
(2:4)
  Subs: $12/3 yrs
       $9/2 yrs
       $5/yr
  Sing: $3

Perspec
PERSPECTIVE
Washington U

Box 1122
St. Louis, MO 63130
(-)
  Subs: $4/yr
  Sing: $1

Pig
PIGIRON
Jim Villani, Ed./Pub.
Print Media Arts
Box 237
Youngstown, OH 44501
(4-5)
  Subs: $12/3 yrs
       $9/2 yrs
       $5/yr
  Sing: $3

PikeF
*PIKESTAFF FORUM
James R. Scrimgeour
Robert D. Sutherland, Eds.
Box 127
Normal, IL 61761
(1)
  Subs: $5/6

Playb
PLAYBOY
Hugh M. Hefner, Ed./Pub.
919 N. Michigan Ave.
Chicago, IL 60611
(25:1-12)
  Subs: $16/12
  Sing: Varies.

Ploughs
PLOUGHSHARES
DeWitt Henry
Peter O'Malley
Directors
Box 529
Cambridge, MA 02139
(4:2-4)
  Subs: $8
  Sing: $3.50

Poem
POEM
Robert L. Welker, Ed.
Box 1247
West Station
Huntsville, AL 35807

Subs: The Huntsville Literary
Assn.
Box 919
Huntsville, AL 35804
(32-34)
Subs: $5/yr

PoetC
POET AND CRITIC
David Cummings, Ed.
203 Ross Hall
Iowa State U
Ames, IA 50010
Subs: Iowa State U Press
South State St.
Ames, IA 50010
(10:2)
Subs: $7/2 yrs
$4/yr
Sing: $2

PoetL
POET LORE
Miriam Andrews, Exec. Ed.
Heldref Publications
4000 Albemarle St., N.W.
Washington, DC 20016
(-)
Subs: $10/yr
Sing: $2.50

Poetry
POETRY
John Frederick Nims, Ed.
601 S. Morgan St.
Box 4348
Chicago, IL 60680
(131:4-6) (132:1-6) (133:1-3)
Subs: $18/yr
Sing: $2
Back: $2.25

PoetryNW
POETRY NORTHWEST
David Wagoner, Ed.
4045 Brooklyn Ave. NE
U of Washington
Seattle, WA 98105
(19:1-4)
Subs: $5/yr
Sing: $1.50

PoNow
POETRY NOW

E. V. Griffith, Ed./Pub.
3118 K Street
Eureka, CA 95501
(19-20)
Subs: $12.50/18
$9/12
$5/6
Sing: $1.25
Back: Bicentennial Issue, $5.

PortR
PORTLAND REVIEW
Art Homer, Ed.
Katherine Prunty, Managing Ed.
Portland State U
Box 751
Portland, OR 97207
(-)
Subs: $5/2 yrs
$3/yr
Sing: $3

PraS
PRAIRIE SCHOONER
Bernice Slote, Ed.
201 Andrews Hall
U of Nebraska
Lincoln, NE 68588
(52:1-4)
Subs: $12/yr (lib.)
$24/3 yrs (ind.)
$16.50/2 yrs (ind.)
$9/yr (ind.)
Sing: $2.50

QRL
QUARTERLY REVIEW OF LIT-
ERATURE
T. Weiss & R. Weiss, Eds.
26 Haslet Ave.
Princeton, NJ 08540
(-)
Subs: $20/2 (cloth)
$10/2 (paper)
Sing: $6.50

QW
QUARTERLY WEST
Andrew Grossbardt, Ed.
Richard Iacovoni, Managing Ed.
312 Olpin Union
U of Utah
Salt Lake City, UT 84112
(5)

Subs: $5/3
Sing: $2

Rapp
RAPPORT
Title change--see
SLOW LORIS READER

RemR
REMINGTON REVIEW
Dean Maskevich, Po. Ed.
Joseph A. Barbato, Fiction Ed.
505 Westfield Ave.
Elizabeth, NJ 07208
   (-)
   Subs: $3/yr
   Sing: $2.50

RusLT
RUSSIAN LITERATURE TRI-
QUARTERLY
Carl R. Proffer
Ellendea Proffer, Eds.
Ardis Publishers
2901 Heatherway
Ann Arbor, MI 48104
   (15)
   Subs: $25/3 (inst.)
          $16.95/3 (ind.)
          $13.95/3 (stud.)
   Back: Prices on request.
   Cloth: Add $10 to each rate.

St. AR
ST. ANDREWS REVIEW
William Loftus, Managing Ed.
Ronald H. Bayes, Ex. Ed.
St. Andrews Presbyterian Col-
   lege
Laurinburg, NC 28352
   (4:3/4) (5:1)
   Missing (4:1-2)
   Subs: $12/2 yrs
          $6/yr
   Sing: $3

Salm
SALMAGUNDI
Robert Boyers, Ed.
Peggy Boyers, Ex. Ed.
Skidmore College
Saratoga Springs, NY 12866
   (40-43)

Subs: $20/2 yrs (inst.)
       $12/yr (inst.)
       $10/2 yrs (ind.)
       $6/yr (ind.)
Sing: Varies.
Back: Prices on request.

Sam
SAMISDAT
Merritt Clifton
Robin Michelle Clifton, Eds.
Box 231
Richford, VT 05476
or
Box 10
Brigham, Quebec
Canada J0E 1J0
   (63-70)
   Missing (68).
   Subs: 3¢ per printed page.
          $15/500pp.

SeC
SECOND COMING
A. D. Winans, Ed.
Second Coming Press
Box 31249
San Francisco, CA 94131
   (5:2)
   Subs: $5.75/yr (lib.)
          $4/yr (ind.)

SenR
SENECA REVIEW
James Crenner
Bob Herz, Eds.
Hobart & William Smith Col-
   leges
Geneva, NY 14456
   (9:1-2)
   Subs: $5/yr
   Sing: $3

SewanR
SEWANEE REVIEW
George Core, Ed.
U of the South
Sewanee, TN 37375
   (86:1-4)
   Subs: $26/3 yrs (inst.)
          $19/2 yrs (inst.)
          $11/yr (inst.)
          $22/3 yrs (ind.)
          $16/2 yrs (ind.)

$11/yr (ind.)
Back: $4

Shen
SHANANDOAH
James Boatwright, Ed.
Richard Howard, Po. Ed.
Box 722
Washington and Lee U
Lexington, VA 24450
(29:2-4)
Subs: $8/2 yrs
       $5/yr
Sing: $1.50
Back: $2.50

Sky
SKYWRITING
Martin Grossman, Ed.
511 Campbell St.
Kalamazoo, MI 49007
(7/8)
Subs: $6/3
Sing: $2 & $4

SlowLR
SLOW LORIS READER
(formerly RAPPORT)
Patricia Petrosky, Ed.
923 Highview St.
Pittsburgh, PA 15206
(1/2)
Subs: $3.50/2
Sing: $2

SmF
SMALL FARM
Jeff Daniel Marion, Ed.
Box 563
Jefferson City, TN 37760
(-)
Subs: $4/yr (lib.)
       $3/yr (ind.)
Sing: $2

SmPd
SMALL POND
Napoleon St. Cyr, Ed./Pub.
10 Overland Drive
Stratford, CT 06497
(42-44)
Subs: $3.75/yr
Sing: $1.50

Smudge
*THE SMUDGE
Douglas Mumm, Ed.
Box 19276
Detroit, MI 48219
(1-3) (Supplement)
Subs: $8/yr
Sing: $2
Back: Prices on request.

Some
SOME
Alan Ziegler, et al., Eds.
309 W. 104th St.
Apt. 9D
New York, NY 10025
(9)
Subs: $9/yr (inst.)
       $5/yr (ind.)
Sing: $2.50

SoCaR
SOUTH CAROLINA REVIEW
Richard J. Calhoun, Ed.
Dept. of English
Clemson U
Clemson, SC 29631
(10:2) (11:1)
Subs: $3.50/2 yrs
       $2/yr
Sing: $1.50

SoDakR
SOUTH DAKOTA REVIEW
John R. Milton, Ed.
Box 111
U Exchange
U of South Dakota
Vermillion, SD 57069
(16:1-4)
Subs: $10/2 yrs
       $6/yr
Sing: $1.50

SouthernHR
SOUTHERN HUMANITIES RE-
VIEW
Barbara A. Mowat
David K. Jeffrey, Eds.
9088 Haley Center
Auburn U
Auburn, AL 36830

(12:1-4)
Subs: $6/yr
Sing: $2

SouthernPR
SOUTHERN POETRY REVIEW
Robert Waters Grey, Ed.
English Dept.
U of North Carolina
Charlotte, NC 28223
(18:1-2)
Subs: $4/yr
Sing: $2

SouthernR
SOUTHERN REVIEW
Donald E. Stanford
Lewis P. Simpson
Coeditors
Drawer D
U Station
Baton Rouge, LA 70893
(14:1-4)
Subs: $13/3 yrs
$9/2 yrs
$5/yr
Sing: $1.50

SouthwR
SOUTHWEST REVIEW
Margaret L. Hartley, Ed.
Southern Methodist U
Dallas, TX 75275
(63:1-4)
Subs: $12/3 yrs
$9/2 yrs
$5/yr
Sing: $1.50

Sparrow
SPARROW
Felix and Selma Stefanile
Sparrow Press
Vagrom Chap Books
103 Waldron St.
West Lafayette, IN 47906
(35-37)
Subs: $6/3
Sing: $2

Spirit
THE SPIRIT THAT MOVES US
Morty Sklar, Ed.
Box 1585

Iowa City, IA 52240
(-)
Subs: $3.75/yr
Sing: $3.50 & $1

Stand
STAND
Jon Silkin, Ed.
Robert Ober, U.S. Ed.
59 Clarendon St.
Boston, MA 02116
Subs: 19 Haldane Terr.
Newcastle upon Tyne
England NE2 3AN
(18:4) (19:1-4)
Subs: $11.75/2 yrs
$6/yr
Sing: $1.50

StoneC
STONE COUNTRY
Judith Neeld, Ed.
20 Lorraine Rd.
Madison, NJ 07940
(78:1-3)
Subs: $4/3
Sing: $1.75

Stonecloud
STONECLOUD
Dan Ilves
Rick Smith, Eds.
Pacific Perceptions, Inc.
1906 Parnell Ave.
Los Angeles, CA 90025
(7)
Suspended publication.
Sing: $1.75
Set: $10.50/(1-7)

SunM
SUN & MOON
Douglas Messerli
Howard Fox, Eds.
4330 Hartwick Rd. #418
College Park, MD 20740
(5-6/7)
Subs: $15/4 (inst.)
$10/4 (ind.)
Sing: $3 & $4.50

Tele
*TELEPHONE

Maureen Owen, Ed.
Box 672 Old Chelsea Sta.
New York, NY 10011
(13-14)
Subs: $4/yr
Sing: $2

Tendril
*TENDRIL
George E. Murphy, Jr., et al.,
Eds.
Box 512
Green Harbor, MA 02041
(1-3)
Subs: $5/3
Sing: $2

TexQ
TEXAS QUARTERLY
Miguel González-Gerth, Ed.
Box 7517
U Station
Austin, TX 78712
(21:1)
Subs: $10/yr
Sing: $4

13thM
13th MOON
Ellen Marie Bissert, Ed.
Box 3
Inwood Station
New York, NY 10034
(4:1)
Subs: $6/3
Sing: $2.25

Thought
THOUGHT
G. Richard Dimler, S.J., Ed.
Fordham U Press
U Box L
Bronx, NY 10458
(53:208-211)
Subs: $12/yr
Sing: $4

ThRiPo
THREE RIVERS POETRY
JOURNAL
Gerald Costanzo, Ed.
Three Rivers Press
Box 21

Carnegie-Mellon U
Pittsburgh, PA 15213
(11/12)
Subs: $5/4
Sing: $1.50

TriQ
TRIQUARTERLY
Elliott Anderson, Ed.
1735 Benson Ave.
Northwestern U
Evanston, IL 60201
(41-43)
Subs: $30/3 yrs
$20/2 yrs
$12/yr
Sing: Varies; usually $4.25.

UnmOx
UNMUZZLED OX
Michael Andre, Ed.
Box 840
Canal Street Station
New York, NY 10013
(-)
Subs: $10/12
$8/8
$5/4
Sing: $2.25

US1
U.S. 1 WORKSHEETS
U.S. 1 Poets' Cooperative
21 Lake Drive
Roosevelt, NJ 08555
(11)
Subs: $4/8
Sing: $.50
Back: Prices on request.

UTR
UT REVIEW
Duane Locke, Ed.
UT Review
U of Tampa
Tampa, FL 33606
(5:3-4)
Sing: $2.50

Vaga
VAGABOND
John Bennett, Ed.
1610 N. Water St.

Ellenburg, WA 98926
(27-28)
Subs: $6
Sing: $2

VirQR
VIRGINIA QUARTERLY REVIEW
Staige D. Blackford, Ed.
Gregory Orr, Po. Consultant
One West Range
Charlottesville, VA 22903
(54:1-4)
Subs: $15/3 yrs
$12/2 yrs
$7/yr

Waters
WATERS
Rocky Karlage, Ed.
Box 19341
Cincinnati, OH 45219
(-)
Subs: $5/4
Sing: $2

WebR
WEBSTER REVIEW
Nancy Schapiro, Ed.
Jerred Metz, Po. Ed.
Webster College
Webster Groves, MO 63119
(4:1-2)
Subs: $5/yr
Sing: $1.25

WestHR
WESTERN HUMANITIES REVIEW
Jack Garlington, Ed.
U of Utah
Salt Lake City, UT 84112
(32:1-4)
Subs: $10/yr (inst.)
$6/yr (ind.)
Sing: $2

Wind
WIND
Quentin R. Howard, Ed.
RFD Route 1
Box 809K
Pikeville, KY 41501
(28-31)
Subs: $6/yr (inst.)

$5/yr (ind.)
Sing: $1.50

WindO
THE WINDLESS ORCHARD
Robert Novak, Ed.
English Dept.
Indiana-Purdue U
Fort Wayne, IN 46805
(31-33)
Subs: $20/3 yrs
$7/yr
$4/yr (stud.)
Sing: $2

Women
WOMEN/POEMS
Celia Gilbert
Pat Rabby, Eds.
23 Merriam St.
Lexington, MA 02173
(-)
Sing: $1.50

WorldO
WORLD ORDER
Firuz Kazemzadeh, et al., Eds.
2011 Yale Sta.
New Haven, CT 06520
Subs: 415 Linden Ave.
Wilmette, IL 60091
(12:1-4)
Subs: $11/2 yrs
$6/yr
Sing: $1.60

WormR
WORMWOOD REVIEW
Marvin Malone, Ed.
Ernest Stranger, Art Ed.
Box 8840
Stockton, CA 95204
(67-72)
Subs: $6/4 (inst.)
$4.50/4 (ind.)
Patron: $12/yr

Xa
XANADU
George William Fisher, Ed.
1704 Auburn Rd.
Wantagh, NY 11793
(-)

Subs: $2.50/2
Sing: $1.50

YaleLit
YALE LIT
Elizabeth Grossman, Ed.
243-A Yale Sta.
New Haven, CT   06520
   (147:3)
   Subs: $18/3 yrs
           $14/2 yrs
           $7.50/yr
   Sing: $2

YaleR
THE YALE REVIEW
J. E. Palmer, Ed.
250 Church St.
1902A Yale Sta.
New Haven, CT   06520
   (67:3-4) (68:1-2)
   Subs: $12/yr (inst.)
           $10/yr (ind.)

Sing: $3
Back: Prices on request.

YellowBR
YELLOW BRICK ROAD
Robert Matte, Jr.
Paul H. Cook, Eds.
Emerald City Press
Box 40814
Tucson, AZ   85717
   (10)
   Subs: $5.50/3 (inst.)
           $4/3 (ind.)
   Sing: $1.50

Zahir
ZAHIR
Diane Kruchkow, Ed.
Box 715
Newburyport, MA   01950
   (9)
   Subs: $3/yr
   Sing: $1.50

THE INDEX

AAL, Katharyn Machan
"The Making of Bread." <u>Paint</u> (9/10) Spr-Aut 78, p. 8.

AARON, Howard
"Chandelier." <u>NowestR</u> (17:1) 78, p. 61.

AARON, Jonathan
"A Dog." <u>NewYorker</u> (54:38) 6 N 78, p. 178.
"Memories of the Dictator." <u>NewYorker</u> (54:9) 17 Ap 78, p. 40.

ABBOTT, Nell
"Across the Partners Desk." <u>HiramPoR</u> (25) Aut-Wint 78, p. 11.

ABISSI, Colette E.
"Empathy." <u>Paint</u> (9/10) Spr-Aut 77, p. 10.
"Slow Suicide." <u>Paint</u> (9/10) Spr-Aut 78, p. 11.

ABRAMS, Doug
"The Confines." <u>GreenfieldR</u> (6:3/4) Spr 78, p. 79.
"From One to Another." <u>Wind</u> (28) 78, p. 2.
"The Irreducible." <u>GreenfieldR</u> (6:3/4) Spr 78, p. 78.
"Quorum." <u>Wind</u> (28) 78, p. 1.
"The Retention Principle." <u>BallSUF</u> (19:4) Aut 78, p. 53.
"Severence." <u>Wind</u> (28) 78, p. 1.

ABRASH, Merritt
"A Northeast Fabulary." <u>Kayak</u> (49) O 78, p. 3.

ABSHER, Tom
"Harvest." <u>Nat</u> (227:13) 21 O 78, p. 417.
"Love Poem." <u>Nat</u> (226:18) 13 My 78, p. 576.

ACKERMAN, Diane
"Canto Vaquero" (for Merejildo "Mettie" Guitierrez, Tequesquite
    Ranch, Albert, N.M.). <u>SenR</u> (9:2) Aut-Wint 78, p. 53.
"Upstate." <u>PoNow</u> (19) 78, p. 31.

ACKERSON, John
"May." <u>CalQ</u> (13/14) Spr-Sum 78, p. 67.

ACKROYD, Graham
"Lament of an Exile" (tr. of Mu'tamid). <u>Kayak</u> (48) Je 78, p. 68.

23

ADAMO, Ralph
"Bravado of Halloween, The." NewOR (5:4) 78, p. 305.

ADAMS, Betsy
from In Antarctica: "Off Ice." Pig (5) 78, p. 17.
from In Antarctica: "With Some Woman I Adore." Pig (5) 78,
p. 16.
"Losing the Moon-1." DacTerr (15) Wint-Spr 77-78, p. 16.
"Losing the Moon-2. (Politics and the Disc)." DacTerr (15)
Wint-Spr 77-78, p. 16.
"Losing the Moon-3. (Irreverence)." DacTerr (15) Wint-Spr
77-78, p. 17.
"Losing the Moon-4. (Marry Me, My Lord)." DacTerr (15)
Wint-Spr 77-78, p. 18.
"the tapestry: 1." Chomo (5:1) Sum 78, p. 4.
"the tapestry: 3." Chomo (5:1) Sum 78, p. 5.

ADAMS, David
"Golfers." KanQ (10:1) Wint 78, p. 9.

ADAMS, David A.
"Four Panel Screen: A Chinese Tale Painted in the Ancient
Manner." WormR (69) 78, p. 10.

ADAMS, Holiday
"Trying to Poet." CarouselQ (3:4) Wint 78, p. 30.

ADCOCK, Betty
"At Least." SoCaR (11:1) N 78, p. 119.
"Extinctions." SoCaR (11:1) N 78, p. 118.

ADY, Endre
Eleven poems (tr. by Joseph Grosz). LitR (21:4) Sum 78,
p. 490.

AESCHYLUS
from The Oresteia: "From Agamemnon" (tr. by Robert Lowell).
AmerPoR (7:5) S-O 78, p. 22.
from The Oresteia: "From the Furies" (tr. by Robert Lowell).
AmerPoR (7:5) S-O 78, p. 23.

AGEE, Jonis
"The Man Who Clears." NewRivR (2:2) 78, p. 26.

AGUILA, Pancho
"To Francois Villon (1431-1463)." PikeF (1) Spr 78, p. 26.

AHARONI, Ada
"The Bus Station" (tr. of Yehuda Amichai). WebR (4:2) Aut 78,
p. 36.
"The Man" (tr. of Shin Shalom). WebR (4:2) Aut 78, p. 35.

AI
"The Gilded Man." Antaeus (30/31) Sum-Aut 78, p. 51.

"Guadalajara Hospital. " VirQR (54:4) Aut 78, p. 704.
"Ice. " ChiR (29:4) Spr 78, p. 4.
"Killing Floor. " ParisR (74) Aut-Wint 78, p. 186.
"Nothing But Color" (for Yukio Mishima). ParisR (74) Aut-Wint
    78, p. 184.
"The Singers. " Antaeus (30/31) Sum-Aut 78, p. 49.
"Sleep Like a Hammer. " ChiR (29:4) Spr 78, p. 6.
"Talking to His Reflection in a Shallow Pond" (for Yusunari
    Kawabata). MichQR (17:4) Aut 78, p. 505.
"The Wake. " VirQR (54:4) Aut 78, p. 703.

AIKEN, James Douglas
"The Third Night. " Epos (27:2) 77, p. 20.

AJAY, Stephen
"The Bodies. " PoNow (20) 78, p. 19.
"Elephant Lover. " PoNow (20) 78, p. 19.
"Winter Delicacies. " PoNow (20) 78, p. 19.

ÅKESSON, Sonia
"In Hässelby" (tr. by Joanna Bankier). AmerPoR (7:2) Mr-Ap
    78, p. 12.

AKHMATOVA, Anna
"Alone" (tr. by Stephen Berg). NewYRB (25:12) 20 Jl 78, p. 3.
"Dante" (tr. by Lyn Coffin). MichQR (17:4) Aut 77, p. 461.
"Fragment, 1959" (tr. by Stephen Berg). NewYRB (25:3) 9 Mr
    78, p. 20.
"It Was Frightful ... " (tr. by Liza Tucker). Field (18) Spr 78,
    p. 21.
"January, 1917" (tr. by Stephen Berg). Nat (226:11) 25 Mr 78,
    p. 348.
"M. B. (Mikhail Bulgakov)" (tr. by Lyn Coffin). MichQR (17:4)
    Aut 78, p. 460.
"The Muse" (tr. by Lyn Coffin). MichQR (17:4) Aut 78, p. 459.
"1914" (tr. by Stephen Berg). Nat (226:9) 11 Mr 78, p. 284.
"Northern Elegies" (tr. by Liza Tucker). Field (18) Spr 78,
    p. 15.
"Poems" (tr. by Judith Hemschemeyer and Anne Wilkinson).
    Pequod (2:4) 78, p. 16.
"Voronezh" (to Osip Mandelstam) (tr. by Lyn Coffin). MichQR
    (17:4) Aut 78, p. 461.

AKIKO, Yosano
Eleven poems (tr. by Kenneth Rexroth). GreenfieldR (6:3/4) Spr
    78, p. 9.

ALAMIA, Judith Rhoads
"At the Forks. " WorldO (12:2) Wint 77-78, p. 30.

ALANIZ, Silvia Bertha
"I Expect So Little. " CarouselQ (3:4) Wint 78, p. 18.

ALBERT, Alan
"The Star." KanQ (10:4) Aut 78, p. 4.

ALDAN, Daisy
"The Bay." Poetry (131:6) Mr 78, p. 326.
"I Was an Ox." Bits (8) Jl 78.
"Under the Marble Arches." Poetry (131:6) Mr 78, p. 325.

ALEIXANDRE, Vicente
"After Love" (tr. by Lewis Hyde). ParisR (74) Aut-Wint 78,
      p. 37.
"The Comet" (tr. by Lewis Hyde). MoonsLT (2:4) 78, inside
      front cover.
"The Eagles" (tr. by Lewis Hyde). ParisR (74) Aut-Wint 78,
      p. 31.
Eight poems (tr. by Stephen Kessler). Iowa (9:1) Wint 78,
      p. 53.
"Guitar or Moon" (tr. by Lewis Hyde and David Unger). ParisR
      (74) Aut-Wint 78, p. 33.
"The Hands" (tr. by Lewis Hyde). ParisR (74) Aut-Wint 78,
      p. 34.
"Llueve." ChiR (30:2) Aut 78, p. 18.
from Poemas de la consumación: "A Few Words" (tr. by Willis
      Barnstone and David Garrison). Nat (226:8) 4 Mr 78,
      p. 248.
from Poemas de la consumación: "The Poet Remembers His
      Life" (tr. by Willis Barnstone and David Garrison). Nat
      (226:8) 4 Mr 78, p. 248.
"We Feed on Shadow" (tr. by Lewis Hyde). ParisR (74) Aut-
      Wint 78, p. 35.
"The Young and the Old" (tr. by Lewis Hyde). ParisR (74) Aut-
      Wint 78, p. 39.

ALENIER, Karren L.
"Procreation." Tele (14) 78.

ALESHIRE, Joan
"Exhibition of Women Artists (1790-1900)." 13thM (4:1) 78,
      p. 71.
"Vermont: Winter, 1890's." 13thM (4:1) 78, p. 73.

ALEXANDER, Bonnie
"Mother." Pan (19) 77, p. 27.
"Nightsong." Pan (19) 77, p. 27.

ALEXANDER, Lonny
"Death Race." CarouselQ (3:4) Wint 78, p. 19.

ALEXANDER, Paul
"A Going." SlowLR (1/2) 78, p. 96.
"History." Bits (8) Jl 78.
"The House." Poem (32) Mr 78, p. 16.

ALLARDT, Linda
  "For Taxes." PoNow (20) 78, p. 1.
  "Forgotten." PoNow (20) 78, p. 1.
  "Long Dry." PoNow (20) 78, p. 1.
  "Prospecting." PoNow (20) 78, p. 1.
  "Road Closed." PoNow (20) 78, p. 45.
  "Three-Legged." PoNow (20) 78, p. 1.

ALLEN, Deborah
  "For My Mother." BelPoJ (29:1) Aut 78, p. 1.

ALLEN, Dick
  "Alfresco." YaleR (68:2) Wint 79, p. 259.
  "One More for Miss Marple." CarolQ (30:2) Spr-Sum 78,
      p. 107.
  "Stanzas." Bits (7) Ja 78.
  "World War II Child." CarolQ (30:2) Spr-Sum 78, p. 108.

ALLEN, Elizabeth
  "London: Cockneys and Aristocrats." PikeF (1) Spr 78, p. 16.

ALLEN, Frank
  "Pylons." DeKalb (11:3/4) Spr-Sum 78, p. 30.

ALLEN, Harriette Bias
  "Do-Gooder." CarouselQ (3:4) Wint 78, p. 1.

ALLEN, James
  "Neighbor." StoneC (78:1) Wint 78, p. 31.
  "Playground." StoneC (78:1) Wint 78, p. 31.
  "Summit Morning." Wind (30) 78, p. 14.

ALLEN, Margerie Goggin
  "Contradiction." Pan (19) 77, p. 23.

ALLEN, Michael
  "In China, Sleep Is Green." ColEng (40:2) O 78, p. 164.

ALLEN, Paul Edward
  "At the Lake House." SouthernPR (18:1) Spr 78, p. 9.

ALLEN, R. D.
  "Children's Games." Wind (31) 78, p. 1.

ALLEN, R. H.
  "Three Watches of the Night." Poem (34) N 78, p. 7.

ALLMAN, John
  "A Dream of 1918." Chowder (10/11) Aut-Wint 78-79, p. 13.
  "His Cremation." PoetryNW (19:3) Aut 78, p. 16.
  "The Soul Plays You Bet Your Life." PoNow (19) 78, p. 46.
  "The Soul Walks Out." PoNow (19) 78, p. 46.
  "The Ward Wife." PoetryNW (19:3) Aut 78, p. 14.

ALMON, Bert
  "Breakfast at Angelo's." <u>NewOR</u> (5:4) 78, p. 349.
  "Inland Commerce." <u>Poem</u> (34) N 78, p. 48.

ALMQUIST, Norma
  "How Everything Keeps Its I." <u>Epos</u> (27:2) 77, p. 17.
  "My Old Woman." <u>Epos</u> (27:2) 77, p. 17.

ALONSO, Nina Rubinstein
  "At the Chapel" (for C. D.). <u>AmerPoR</u> (7:4) Jl-Ag 78, p. 21.

ALONSO, Ricardo
  "Changó/Thunder." <u>Obs</u> (4:1) Spr 78, p. 94.
  "Cimarrón" (for Esteban Montejo). <u>Obs</u> (4:1) Spr 78, p. 96.
  "Dance of the Ancestors 1/1/76." <u>Obs</u> (4:1) Spr 78, p. 97.
  "Morning Coming." <u>Obs</u> (4:1) Spr 78, p. 99.
  "Song of the Drum" (for Les Wood). <u>Obs</u> (4:1) Spr 78, p. 95.

ALPERS, Richard
  "Scenes of Wealth and Peace" (from <u>Georgics,</u> Book II, by
      Vergil). <u>Northeast</u> (3:5) Spr-Sum 78, p. 3.

ALPERT, Barry
  "For O Magel Serene Intensity" (homage à Ernie Gehr). <u>SunM</u>
      (5) Aut 78, p. 42.
  "Long Term Projects" (homage à Bruce Nauman). <u>SunM</u> (5) Aut
      78, p. 39.
  "Manny Farber at OK Harris, Clockwise." <u>SunM</u> (5) Aut 78,
      p. 41.
  "A Scenario for Robert Rauschenberg." <u>SunM</u> (5) Aut 78, p. 40.

ALTER, Richard L.
  "Poetry." <u>GRR</u> (9:2) 78, p. 151.
  "Worst Days Have Yet to Come." <u>GRR</u> (9:2) 78, p. 151.

ALTIZER, Nell
  "The Solemn Songs." <u>LittleM</u> (11:3) Aut 77, p. 78.

ALWAN, Ameen
  "At the Station" (tr. of Jaime Sabines). <u>AmerPoR</u> (7:2) Mr-Ap
      78, p. 29.
  "Here's What's Happening" (tr. of Jaime Sabines). <u>AmerPoR</u>
      (7:2) Mr-Ap 78, p. 28.
  "I'm Happy" (tr. of Jaime Sabines). <u>AmerPoR</u> (7:2) Mr-Ap 78,
      p. 28.
  "Like Lost Birds" (tr. of Jaime Sabines). <u>AmerPoR</u> (7:2) Mr-
      Ap 78, p. 28.
  "Poem: It's said ... " (tr. of Jaime Sabines). <u>AmerPoR</u> (7:2)
      Mr-Ap 78, p. 29.
  "Something About the Death of Major Sabines" (tr. of Jaime
      Sabines). <u>AmerPoR</u> (7:2) Mr-Ap 78, p. 29.

ALWAN, Georgia
  "The Nest." <u>Bound</u> (6:2) Wint 78, p. 542.

AMADEO, JoAnn
  "Nightshades." CarouselQ (3:2) Sum 78, p. 1.

AMAJ (J. D. Williams)
  "Biko." BlackF (2:2) Aut-Wint 78, p. 36.

AMICHAI, Yehuda
  "The Bus Station" (tr. by Ada Aharoni). WebR (4:2) Aut 78,
      p. 36.

AMMONS, A. R.
  "The Brook Has Worked Out the Prominences of a Bend."
      Poetry (133:2) N 78, p. 80.
  "Country Music." MichQR (17:4) Aut 78, p. 457.
  "Density." Hudson (31:4) Wint 78-79, p. 588.
  "I Went Back." BelPoJ (28:4) Sum 78, p. 4.
  "Immortality." BelPoJ (28:4) Sum 78, p. 4.
  "Persistences." Poetry (132:2) My 78, p. 88.
  "Poverty." Hudson (31:4) Wint 78-79, p. 588.
  "Response." Hudson (31:4) Wint 78-79, p. 590.
  "The Role of Society in the Artist." Epoch (27:2) Wint 78,
      p. 167.
  "Room Conditioner." Tendril (2) Spr-Sum 78.
  "Strolls." Poetry (133:2) N 78, p. 81.
  "Sunday at McDonald's." Hudson (31:4) Wint 78-79, p. 589.
  "Vehicle." Hudson (31:4) Wint 78-79, p. 590.
  "Warming Trend." BelPoJ (28:4) Sum 78, p. 5.
  "Weather-Bound." Hudson (31:4) Wint 78-79, p. 587.

AMOROSI, Ray
  "Caves." AmerPoR (7:4) Jl-Ag 78, p. 30.
  "Night in Garland, Maine." Tendril (1) Wint 77-78.
  "Night of September First." AmerPoR (7:4) Jl-Ag 78, p. 30.
  "Only a Saint Levitates." AmerPoR (7:4) Jl-Ag 78, p. 30.

AMPRIMOZ, Alexandre L.
  "Death of a Tropical General." BallSUF (19:1) Wint 78, p. 70.

AMSTER, Andy
  "A Southern Scene." Wind (29) 78, p. 9.

ANCRUM, Nancy
  "almonds are." Tele (13) 77.
  "Beaufort." Tele (13) 77.
  "Frank O'Hara." Tele (13) 77.
  "Passage." Tele (13) 77.
  "Science Fiction." Tele (13) 77.

ANDAY, Melih Cevdet
  "The Death of the Vessel" (tr. by Talat Halman and Brian
      Swann). St. AR (4:3/4) 77-78, p. 100.

ANDERSEN, Benny
  "Atmosphere" (tr. by Alexander Taylor). MoonsLT (2:4) 78,

p. 81.
"The Last Poem in the World" (tr. by Alexander Taylor).
   MoonsLT (2:4) 78, p. 79.
"Women" (tr. by Alexander Taylor).   MoonsLT (2:4) 78, p. 76.

ANDERSON, Barbara
"Dust." PoetryNW (19:2) Sum 78, p. 26.
"Rilke: Valmont, Switzerland." Antaeus (30/31) Sum-Aut 78,
   p. 53.
"Whirlwind of the Lord." AntR (36:4) Aut 78, p. 467.

ANDERSON, Carolyn
"Food Essay." WormR (69) 78, p. 9.
"Free Form." WormR (69) 78, p. 9.
"Layover." WormR (69) 78, p. 9.

ANDERSON, Cathy
"Amelia (1898-1937)." AntR (36:3) Sum 78, p. 366.

ANDERSON, David
"From an American Dictionary." Pig (4) 78, p. 20.
"Plowing." Pig (4) 78, p. 1.
"Training for Uncertainty." Pig (5) 78, p. 18.
"Woman." Pig (5) 78, p. 15.

ANDERSON, Jack
"The Clouds of That Country." LittleM (11:4) Wint 78, p. 14.
"Ode to the Electric Chair." LittleM (11:3) Aut 77, p. 18.
"The Pastoral Mode." LittleM (11:4) Wint 78, p. 12.
"Richie and Ruthie." PoNow (19) 78, p. 32.
"The Rotation of the Earth." Hand (2) 78, p. 163.
"Where You Are." Some (9) 78, p. 13.
"Winter Twilight." Some (9) 78, p. 12.

ANDERSON, Jack L.
"The Conversation: Part II." GreenfieldR (7:1/2) Aut 78, p. 71.

ANDERSON, Jon
"Camouflage." Iowa (9:1) Wint 78, p. 25.
"The Face of Dürer" (for Gail Orlen). AntR (36:4) Aut 78,
   p. 466.
"Tucson: A Poem about Wood." Iowa (9:1) Wint 78, p. 24.
"Winter Light." Antaeus (30/31) Sum-Aut 78, p. 56.
"Witness." Antaeus (30/31) Sum-Aut 78, p. 54.

ANDERSON, Kemmer
"Mount Carmel Man." ChrC (95:5) 15 F 78, p. 156.

ANDERSON, Kenneth L.
"Savannah." Poem (33) Jl 78, p. 30.

ANDERSON, Maggie
"Daphne." 13thM (4:1) 78, p. 47.

ANDERSON, Mark
  "Cliches. " Zahir (9) 77, p. 26.
  "Getting By. " Wind (28) 78, p. 3.
  "Song for My Twenty-fifth Birthday. " Wind (28) 78, p. 3.

ANDRADE, Jorge Carrera
  "Biography for the Use of Birds" (tr. by Donald D. Walsh).
      AmerPoR (7:4) Jl-Ag 78, p. 20.

ANDRE, Michael
  "Thanks Day. " Tele (13) 77.
  "Torrid Tauna. " Tele (13) 77.

ANDREA, Marianne
  "Familiar Graveyard" (for Anna Akhmatova, after her "Poem
      Without a Hero"). Confr (16) Spr-Sum 78, p. 13.

ANDREJCAK, Dawna Maydak
  "I Liked the Lemon-Yellow of Sundays Best" (to V. Y. and A. Y.).
      EngJ (67:5) My 78, p. 65.

ANDRESEN, Sophia de Mello Breyner
  "The Photographs" (tr. by Alexis Levitin). LitR (21:4) Sum 78,
      p. 456.
  "The Young Girl and the Beach" (tr. by Alexis Levitin). LitR
      (21:4) Sum 78, p. 456.

ANDREWS, Bruce
  "Caramel. " Tele (14) 78.
  from Love Songs: "Song No 94. " SunM (5) Aut 78, p. 63.
  from Love Songs: "Song No 165. " SunM (5) Aut 78, p. 59.
  "New York. " Hills (5) 78, p. 66.
  "Song No 58. " Tele (14) 78.
  "Washes. " Tele (14) 78.

ANDREWS, Jenne
  "Exultations in Late Summer. " SenR (9:1) Spr-Sum 78, p. 99.

ANDREWS, Michael
  "& Before That. " Stonecloud (7) 78, p. 145.
  "When Someone Gives You the Pink Slip & It Doesnt Run There
      Is Always Spain. " Stonecloud (7) 78, p. 91.

ANDREWS, Nancy
  "Boat Man at Mombasa. " BallSUF (19:4) Aut 78, p. 36.

ANDREWS, Owen
  "Man with a Portrait in Mind. " HarvAd (112:1) D 78, p. 20.
  "Weather Changes. " HarvAd (112:1) D 78, p. 20.

ANGELI, Mary Louise
  "The Empty Skin of a Cicada Nymph. " BallSUF (19:2) Spr 78,
      p. 34.

ANGELL, Roger
"Greetings, Friends!" NewYorker (54:45) 25 D 78, p. 37.

ANGLIM, John R.
"Invalid." Tendril (3) Aut 78, p. 9.
"The Operation." Tendril (3) Aut 78, p. 8.

ANGOFF, Charles
"Seven and Nine." StoneC (78:2) Spr 78, p. 16.
"Stella Whispers to Jonathan Swift." Zahir (9) 77, p. 61.

ANGUIANO, Carla
"Poetry." SeC (5:2) 78, p. 37.

ANGULO, Mario
"Happy Ballads to Greet Rafael Alberti in My Absence" (tr. of
    José López-Pacheco). MalR (47) Jl 78, p. 98.
"On a Photograph of Machado, Thinking of Pablo, for Rafael"
    (tr. of Roberto Sanesi). MalR (47) Jl 78, p. 114.
"A Postcard for Rafael Alberti" (tr. of Pere Quart). MalR (47)
    Jl 78, p. 154.

ANONYMOUS
"The Boss's Wife." Playb (25:5) My 78, p. 165.
"Conversation with My Lover's Wife." JnlONJP (2:2) 77, p. 11.
"The girls' hearts soften" (tr. by Terese Svoboda). Antaeus (28)
    Wint 78, p. 205.
"Go heap dung on the hearth" (tr. by Terese Svoboda). Antaeus
    (28) Wint 78, p. 204.
"I Know God's Alright." LadHJ (95:12) D 78, p. 105.
"I wish everybody was like me." NewL (45:1) Aut 78, p. 62.
"I'm afraid of the dark." NewL (45:1) Aut 78, p. 61.
from Man'yōshū: Twenty poems. Montra (4) 78, p. 143.
"The old-fashioned girls" (tr. by Terese Svoboda). Antaeus (28)
    Wint 78, p. 206.
"An Original Song in Favor of Trades Union" (1829 NYC).
    NewWR (46:2) Mr-Ap 78, p. 26.
"Revelation" (tr. by Richard O'Connell). Playb (25:4) Ap 78,
    p. 157.
"Umbilical cord." NewL (45:1) Aut 78, p. 61.

ANSON, John S.
"Black-Shadow-Giving Chestnut" (tr. of Conrad Ferdinand Meyer).
    Poetry (131:6) Mr 78, p. 322.
"'Grieve No More.'" PoNow (20) 78, p. 2.
"Huss's Prison" (tr. of Conrad Ferdinand Meyer). Poetry
    (131:6) Mr 78, p. 324.
"The Lamppost." PoNow (20) 78, p. 2.
"A Little Dirt." PoNow (20) 78, p. 2.
"Sheet Lightning" (tr. of Conrad Ferdinand Meyer). Poetry
    (131:6) Mr 78, p. 323.

ANTIPATER of Thessalonica
"Stiff" (tr. by Richard O'Connell). Playb (25:4) Ap 78, p. 157.

ANTONAZZI, Frank J., Jr.
 "The Lovers." JnlONJP (2:2) 77, p. 17.
 "Poem, for Karen." JnlONJP (2:2) 77, p. 17.
 "Poem: I'm an actor in a grey French movie." JnlONJP (2:2)
     77, p. 17.
 "Poem: Once more." JnlONJP (2:2) 77, p. 17.

ANTONELLI, Alfred
 "The gray merky mud." Tele (13) 77.
 "It is not the young that inherit the earth." Tele (13) 77.
 "Only failure knows the humble soul." Tele (13) 77.

APONICK, Kathleen
 "Asylum Spring." Aspect (71) Ap-Je 77, p. 45.
 "Bottled Fireflies." Aspect (71) Ap-Je 77, p. 44.

APPLEGATE, Tim
 "A Dream of Horses." Poem (32) Mr 78, p. 37.

APPLEMAN, Marjorie
 "Displaced Person." SouthernPR (18:1) Spr 78, p. 48.
 "On the Bowery." SouthernPR (18:1) Spr 78, p. 48.

APPLEMAN, Philip
 "Mr. Extinction, Meet Ms. Survival." Poetry (133:3) D 78,
     p. 151.
 "Petals on a Wet, Black Bough." ColEng (39:8) Ap 78, p. 944.
 "State of Nature." Poetry (132:2) My 78, p. 68.

APPLETON, Sarah
 "From Within the Wheel Looking Down." Hand (2) 78, p. 84.

APPLEWHITE, James
 "Beginning with Egypt." SoCaR (10:2) Ap 78, p. 14.
 "Christian Daughter." SoCaR (10:2) Ap 78, p. 12.
 "Drinking Music." SoCaR (10:2) Ap 78, p. 15.
 "An Erased Window." SoCaR (10:2) Ap 78, p. 12.
 "Following the River." CarolQ (30:1) Wint 78, p. 80.
 "From As Far Away As Dying." SoCaR (10:2) Ap 78, p. 12.
 "Outside Cleeve Abbey." SoCaR (10:2) Ap 78, p. 13.
 "Reanimations." SouthernR (14:2) Spr 78, p. 341.
 "Royal Hospital." SoCaR (10:2) Ap 78, p. 14.
 "Some Words for Fall." CarolQ (30:1) Wint 78, p. 79.

APRILL, Arnold
 "Financial Considerations." Tele (14) 78.
 "Greatness." Tele (14) 78.
 "Tar Babies." Tele (14) 78.

APTER, Ronnie
 "Driving in New England." JnlONJP (2:1) 77, p. 21.
 "A Good Intention." JnlONJP (2:1) 77, p. 20.
 "Poem: I have spent years still." JnlONJP (2:1) 77, p. 20.
 "Wedding Night." JnlONJP (2:1) 77, p. 21.

ARAGON, Louis
"Les Lilas et les Roses." CalQ (13/14) Spr-Sum 78, p. 110.

ARENAL, Electa
"Biography, Poetry and Destiny" (tr. of León Felipe). WebR
(4:2) Aut 78, p. 15.
"Like a Flea" (tr. of León Felipe). AmerPoR (7:4) Jl-Ag 78,
p. 15.
"Like You" (tr. of León Felipe). WebR (4:2) Aut 78, p. 16.
"XXIII Caption for the Child of Vallecas by Velázquez" (tr. of
León Felipe). AmerPoR (7:4) Jl-Ag 78, p. 15.

ARENELLA, Roy
"Begin." Glass (3:1/2/3) 78, p. 77.
"Moon." Glass (3:1/2/3) 78, p. 78.
"Seed." Glass (3:1/2/3) 78, p. 79.

ARGÜELLES, Ivan
"Another Life." Bleb/Ark (13) 78, p. 9.
"Daedalus." Bleb/Ark (13) 78, p. 8.
"Death of Brian Jones." Confr (16) Spr-Sum 78, p. 66.
"Death of Mussolini." Bleb/Ark (13) 78, p. 5.
"España: Alma Y Derrota" (for césar vallejo, miguel hernández,
león felipe, y pablo neruda). Bleb/Ark (13) 78, p. 6.
"'In the Colonies.'" PoNow (20) 78, p. 2.
"Interrogation." Bleb/Ark (13) 78, p. 3.
from The Latin Anthology: "can it be that suffering." MinnR
(NS 11) Aut 78, p. 36.
"Mohammad's Bride." Bleb/Ark (13) 78, p. 2.
"The Seven Kings." Bleb/Ark (13) 78, p. 1.

ARIDJIS, Homero
Ten poems (tr. by Eliot Weinberger). Montra (4) 78, p. 184.

ARMANTROUT, Rae
"One." Hills (5) 78, p. 6.
"Textron." Hills (5) 78, p. 7.
"Travels." Tele (14) 78.
"Universe." Hills (5) 78, p. 5.
"View." Tele (14) 78.
"Xenophobia." Hills (5) 78, p. 8.

ARMITAGE, Barri
"And the Wind Returneth Again According to Its Circuits." Wind
(28) 78, p. 4.
"When Time Forgot to Look." Wind (28) 78, p. 5.

ARNDT, Walter
"The Czar's Cadets at Peterhof" (tr. of Mikhail Lermontov).
Playb (25:1) Ja 78, p. 198.

ARNOLD, Bob
"On Building a Stonewalk in November." Hand (2) 78, p. 45.

ARNOLD, Kenneth
    "Letter to Ernesto Cardenal in Exile." WebR (4:2) Aut 78,
       p. 17.

ARPIN, Roger C.
    "The Sixtieth Day of Winter." BallSUF (19:4) Aut 78, p. 49.

ARREOLA, J. J.
    "Among the Urdos" (tr. by Brian Swann). WebR (4:2) Aut 78,
       p. 14.

ARSENAULT, Joel
    "Watching You Go Down the Road at Dawn." CarolQ (30:3) Aut
       78, p. 78.

ARTHUR, Thomas C.
    "Our Angel Is Late." ChrC (95:1) 4-11 Ja 78, p. 14.

ARVEY, Michael
    "Follower." MichQR (17:2) Spr 78, p. 212.
    "The Ornithologist." Poem (32) Mr 78, p. 24.
    "Poem: As starlight plunges onto the hill's antlers." Poem
       (32) Mr 78, p. 25.
    "The Wind in the Woods." Poem (32) Mr 78, p. 23.
    "A Woman Called Bloom." Poem (32) Mr 78, p. 22.

ASHBY-DAVIS, Claire
    "A 'W' Poem." EngJ (67:5) My 78, p. 53.

ASHLEY, Nova Trimble
    "A Found Poem." KanQ (10:4) Aut 78, p. 48.
    "Humiliation Revisited." BallSUF (19:4) Aut 78, p. 37.

ASKLEPIADES
    "Here lies Archeanassa" (tr. by Frederick Morgan). GreenfieldR
       (6:3/4) Spr 78, p. 5.
    "I played once with Hermione" (tr. by Frederick Morgan).
       GreenfieldR (6:3/4) Spr 78, p. 5.

ASTOR, Susan
    "Demons" (for Isaac Bashevis Singer). ParisR (72) Wint 77,
       p. 48.
    "Grandpa P." ParisR (72) Wint 77, p. 49.
    "In the Laboratory" (for George J. Honecker). Shen (29:4) Sum
       78, p. 51.
    "Now." PoNow (20) 78, p. 2.

ATCHITY, Kenneth John
    "Coming Up This Morning." Stonecloud (7) 78, p. 104.
    "Informing Dreams" (for Pearl S. Buck). Poem (32) Mr 78,
       p. 52.
    "Late December." BallSUF (19:4) Aut 78, p. 23.

"A Melancholic Moment." Poem (32) Mr 78, p. 51.
"Why I Didn't Stop." Stonecloud (7) 78, p. 104.

ATKINS, Ron
　"Special Bookcase." EngJ (67:5) My 78, p. 62.

ATKINS, Russell
　"'Divinely Sensuous,' She Said." PoNow (19) 78, p. 39.
　"It's Here in the." PoNow (19) 78, p. 39.
　"Where There's Water." PoNow (19) 78, p. 39.

ATWOOD, Margaret
　"Dust." Field (18) Spr 78, p. 80.
　"Five Poems for Grandmothers." OP (26) Aut-Wint 78, p. 3.
　"Nasturtium." Field (18) Spr 78, p. 78.
　"The Woman Makes Peace with Her Faulty Heart." Field (18)
　　Spr 78, p. 76.
　"The Woman Who Could Not Live with Her Faulty Heart." Field
　　(18) Spr 78, p. 74.
　"You Are Happy." MoonsLT (2:4) 78, p. 64.

AUBERT, Alvin
　Eight poems. Obs (4:2) Sum 78, p. 94.
　"Johnson's Ezekiel." Obs (4:1) Spr 78, p. 90.
　"Johnson's Street Musicians." Obs (4:1) Spr 78, p. 89.
　"Not a Tree at All." Obs (4:1) Spr 78, p. 88.
　"Reverie in 3 Riffs." Obs (4:1) Spr 78, p. 87.
　"Ringo, the Four Legged Dolphin." Paint (9/10) Spr-Aut 78,
　　p. 12.
　"Whirl High." Paint (9/10) Spr-Aut 78, p. 13.

AUER, Eric
　"1225 224 223 222 221." Tele (13) 77.
　"Testament." Tele (13) 77.
　"western." Tele (13) 77.

AUG, Ellen Wendy
　"to herman aldridge cohen." Tele (14) 78.

AUGUSTINE, Jane
　"Cragmont Avenue Childhood." Montra (4) 78, p. 126.
　"Meeting a Beggar." Montra (4) 78, p. 129.

AULT, Leslie F.
　"The Unknown Poem." JnlONJP (2:2) 77, p. 13.

AUSTIN, F. A.
　"And Truth to Tell." Aspect (71) Ap-Je 77, p. 51.
　"The Conquest of Space." Aspect (71) Ap-Je 77, p. 50.

AWAD, Joseph
　"First Communion." SmPd (42) Wint 78, p. 18.
　"The Funeral." Wind (30) 78, p. 1.

"The Listener." Epos (27:2) 77, p. 13.
"Nocturne." Poem (33) Jl 78, p. 8.
"When We Came to Chicago." Wind (30) 78, p. 1.

AXELROD, David
  "The Buffalo to Chicago Grey Great Lakes Blues." SunM (5)
      Aut 78, p. 94.

AXELROD, Roberta
  "Ashes-of-Roses." Zahir (9) 77, p. 12.
  "Winter's Ride." Zahir (9) 77, p. 10.

AYERS, Noreen
  "Hollows" (for Dr. James Caillouette). Stonecloud (7) 78, p. 70.

AYRES, Elizabeth
  "I am a mountain lion." HangL (33) Sum 78, p. 3.
  "A Long Story." HangL (34) Wint 78-79, p. 3.
  "Smoke and Fire." HangL (33) Sum 78, p. 10.

AZZARA, T.
  "Calendar Girl." Pan (19) 77, p. 60.

BACA, Jimmy Santiago
  "Letters Come to Prison." GreenfieldR (7:1/2) Aut 78, p. 35.

BACCHUS, Tom
  "Culling the Deer." SmPd (44) Aut 78, p. 26.

BACH, Toby
  "My Father's Eyes." Epos (27:2) 77, p. 26.

BACKHURST, Paul
  "Andy." Poetry (131:4) Ja 78, p. 197.

BACON, Barbara
  "The Day We Went to Pull." AAR (28) 78, p. 16.
  "Edges of Childhood." AAR (28) 78, p. 19.
  "In Between the Curve." AAR (28) 78, p. 18.
  "The Quiltmaker." AAR (28) 78, p. 16.

BADAWI, M. M.
  from Rasa'il min London: (I, II). Paint (7/8) Spr-Aut 77,
      p. 29.

BAGG, T. R.
  "Les Petits Ages" (Hommage à Couperin, VIIe Ordre). Shen
      (29:3) Spr 78, p. 74.
  "Le Tombeau de Charles Baudelaire." Humanist (38:1) Ja-F 78,
      p. 60.

BAILEY, Jane
  "Deja Vu." PoNow (20) 78, p. 19.

"Facing Wind." Columbia (2) Aut 78, p. 42.
"The Open Field." PoNow (20) 78, p. 19.
"Peacock." PoNow (20) 78, p. 19.
"Ripening." PoNow (20) 78, p. 19.

BAILEY, Larry
"hard to love a black chile." NewRena (10) 78, p. 79.
"this ain't no dream world." NewRena (10) 78, p. 81.

BAIRD, Andrew
"Carolina Prime." SouthernR (14:4) Aut 78, p. 755.
"Father Romulus, Speaking by Invitation, at Lumpkin County
    Baptist Church." SouthernR (14:4) Aut 78, p. 756.
"Yeats in Criticism." SouthernR (14:4) Aut 78, p. 757.

BAIRD, Ansie
"About Long Days in October." SoDakR (16:3) Aut 78, p. 28.
"Much Later to the Poet." SoDakR (16:3) Aut 78, p. 29.
"Poem: He was the golden man come down." PoNow (20) 78,
    p. 3.

BAKER, Corrinne
"The Catalpa Tree." QW (5) Wint 78, p. 25.
"Grandpa and Me, Killing Chickens." QW (5) Wint 78, p. 26.

BAKER, Peter
"The American Friend." HarvAd (111:4) My 78, p. 22.
"Anxiety." HarvAd (111:3) Ap 78, p. 18.

BAKER, Thomas
"Naivete." Zahir (9) 77, p. 22.

BAKER, Will
"Adultery." PoNow (20) 78, p. 3.
"Death Is Surely a Woman." NewL (45:2) Wint 78, p. 92.
"Memo to Happy Warriors." NewL (45:2) Wint 78, p. 92.
"Post-Romanticism." PoNow (20) 78, p. 3.

BALAKIAN, Peter
"Approaching the Summer Solstice" (for Helen). CutB (10) Spr-
    Sum 78, p. 4.
"Facing the Remains." CutB (10) Spr-Sum 78, p. 9.
"Father Fisheye." CarolQ (30:2) Spr-Sum 78, p. 112.
"Night-Catch." Nat (227:16) 11 N 78, p. 516.
"Ocean Markings/The New Year" (for Lucille). PoetryNW (19:1)
    Spr 78, p. 27.
"A Sequence of Wind Between Seasons." SouthernPR (18:1) Spr
    78, p. 27.

BALAZS, Mary
"An Autumn Mountain Speaks." GRR (9:2) 78, p. 145.
"For Eliot, Ending His First Year." Wind (29) 78, p. 2.
"In the Campground." Wind (29) 78, p. 1.

"Interior: A Metaphor." StoneC (78:2) Spr 78, p. 7.
"Not on This Green Island." GRR (9:3) 78, p. 212.
"Still Life." Wind (29) 78, p. 1.
"The Tree's Summer." Wind (29) 78, p. 3.

BALCOFF, Sophie
"Our Neighbor, Seen from the Bathroom Window on the Day His
    Wife Left Him." 13thM (4:1) 78, p. 9.

BALDERSTON, Jean
"Iceland Air" (In Memoriam, W. H. Auden). Wind (28) 78, p. 6.
"Mail." Bits (8) Jl 78.
"The Sphinx." Wind (28) 78, p. 6.

BALDWIN, Bill
"Soldier's Pay." SouthernPR (18:2) Aut 78, p. 57.

BALDWIN, Jim
"Mary Paduchak." SouthernR (14:1) Wint 78, p. 106.

BALDY, Gary Daniel
"Junction." CarouselQ (3:4) Wint 78, p. 25.

BALLARD, Rae
"Mary Remembers the Annunciation." ChrC (95:42) 20 D 78,
    p. 1237.

BALLERINI, Luigi
from Denomisegninatura: "Destinegation" (tr. of Mario Diacono,
    w. Richard Milazzo). Chelsea (37) 78, p. 57.

BALLINGER, Franchot
"Loving the Moonstruck" (for Father). EnPas (7) 78, p. 18.

BALLOWE, James
"Ritual Descent in Spring." Bound (6:2) Wint 78, p. 548.
"Starved Rock." Bound (6:2) Wint 78, p. 551.

BANGS, Carol Jane
"Suggested Bike Route." PoNow (20) 78, p. 3.

BANKIER, Joanna
"In Hässelby" (tr. of Sonja Åkesson). AmerPoR (7:2) Mr-Ap 78,
    p. 12.

BANKS, Dorothy
"If It Be Your Will." BlackF (2:2) Aut-Wint 78, p. 27.

BARAKA, Amiri
"Clay." Bound (6:2) Wint 78, p. 326.
"A Conference of 'Socialists' at Brown University." Bound (6:2)
    Wint 78, p. 324.
"Das Kapital." NewOR (6:1) 78, p. 10.

"Literary Statement on Struggle!" Bound (6:2) Wint 78, p. 322.
"A Poem for Deep Thinkers." NewOR (6:1) 78, p. 9.
"Reprise of one of A. G.'s Best Poems!" Bound (6:2) Wint 78,
    p. 327.
"Revolutionary Love." Bound (6:2) Wint 78, p. 325.
"Revolutionary Love." NewOR (6:1) 78, p. 11.

BARALE, Michéle
"Falling Through." KanQ (10:2) Spr 78, p. 98.
"Falls." Wind (28) 78, p. 5.

BARBARESE, J. T.
"An American Chemist to His Friend, a Poet." KanQ (10:2) Spr
    78, p. 78.
"On Becoming Twenty-Eight." Nimrod (22:2) Spr-Sum 78, p. 8.

BARBER, Ben
"cherokee run." Tele (13) 77.
"hari rama hari rama." Tele (13) 77.
"Plough and Stars." Tele (14) 78.
"Stove." Tele (13) 77.
"What a beautiful silence." Tele (13) 77.

BARBER, X. T.
"The Shaman of Marmora." HarvAd (111:4) My 78, p. 10.

BARBU, Ion
"Dioptric" (tr. by Thomas A. Perry). Paint (7/8) Spr-Aut 77,
    p. 61.

BARG, Barbara
"Tree Verse." Tele (14) 78.
"Whole Poem." Tele (14) 78.

BARGEN, Walter
"Bunker, Mo." SoDakR (16:2) Sum 78, p. 44.
"September." SoDakR (16:2) Sum 78, p. 43.

BARKER, David
Eight poems. WormR (68) 77, p. 85.

BARKER, Wendy
"Lady Bess." 13thM (4:1) 78, p. 76.
"My Father's Living Room." Chomo (5:1) Sum 78, p. 36.
"Practice." CalQ (13/14) Spr-Sum 78, p. 135.

BARLOW, George
"America Plethora: MacCorporate MacDream." BelPoJ (29:2)
    Wint 78-79, p. 44.
"Facing the Prairie" (for Nancy Fast). BelPoJ (29:2) Wint 78-
    79, p. 43.

BARNA, Ed
"'In fourteen hundred and ninety-two Columbus sailed the ocean

41   BARNARD

blue' isn't going to make the carburetor work. " Agni (9) 78,
    p. 110.
"The Unbearable Sensation. " Agni (9) 78, p. 109.

BARNARD, Jane
    "The Abnormal Labor" (tr. of Benjamin Peret, w. Albert Frank
        Moritz). MalR (48) O 78, p. 78.

BARNES, Jim
    "Circus Poster. " NewL (45:2) Wint 78, p. 78.
    "Domain. " Nat (226:7) 25 F 78, p. 221.
    "Floating the Big Piney. " Nat (226:14) 15 Ap 78, p. 438.
    "Old Soldiers Home at Marshalltown, Iowa. " NewL (45:2) Wint
        78, p. 79.
    "On Blue Mountain Tower. " Nat (226:17) 6 My 78, p. 543.

BARNES, Tim
    "Mother and Henry. " CutB (10) Spr-Sum 78, p. 50.
    "Oaklined Streets" (for the Waverly house). PikeF (1) Spr 78,
        p. 21.

BARNETT, Anthony
    "IX, X, and XI. " PartR (45:3) 78, p. 431.

BARNSTONE, Willis
    from Poemas de la consumación: "A Few Words" (tr. of Vicente
        Aleixandre, w. David Garrison). Nat (226:8) 4 Mr 78,
        p. 248.
    from Poemas de la consumación: "The Poet Remembers His
        Life" (tr. of Vicente Aleixandre, w. David Garrison). Nat
        (226:8) 4 Mr 78, p. 248.
    "Raining" (tr. of Vicente Aleixandre). ChiR (30:2) Aut 78,
        p. 19.

BARON, Mary
    "Abortion Clinic. " SouthernR (14:1) Wint 78, p. 122.
    "Christening. " SouthernR (14:1) Wint 78, p. 124.
    "I Dream of Elizabeth R. " SouthernR (14:1) Wint 78, p. 123.
    "Souvenir. " PoNow (19) 78, p. 21.

BARON, Virginia Olsen
    "Snowstorm. " ChrC (95:7) 1 Mr 78, p. 206.

BARONE, Bruce Daryl
    "Please Forward if B Is Not Home. " Tele (13) 77.
    "Turquoise. " Tele (13) 77.

BARONE, Patricia
    "The wild geese seem flung. " Tendril (2) Spr-Sum 78.

BARRAX, Gerald W.
    "He Goes Around His World. " GeoR (32:2) Sum 78, p. 369.

BARROWS, Anita
"The Equations" (for Richard). Montra (4) 78, p. 106.

BARTH, R. L.
"The New Poetry." ConcPo (11:1) Spr 78, p. 25.
"Rereading Notebooks." ConcPo (11:1) Spr 78, p. 25.
"To Walter Savage Landor, for the Young Poets." ConcPo
    (11:1) Spr 78, p. 25.

BARTKOWECH, R.
"Passing On." Pig (4) 78, p. 29.

BARTLETT, Elizabeth
"Ambivalent." Wind (29) 78, p. 7.
"Bitter Sweet." ConcPo (11:2) Aut 78, p. 39.
"From a Notebook." Glass (3:1/2/3) 78, p. 69.
"Mental Bars." Wind (29) 78, p. 6.
"Petition." Wind (29) 78, p. 6.

BARWELL, Jay
"A Formal Worry." Glass (3:1/2/3) 78, p. 43.
"Witness." Pan (19) 77, p. 55.

BASHAM, Kate
"Impersonations: The Failure of Excuses." DacTerr (15) Wint-
    Spr 77-78, p. 2.

BASS, Madeline Tiger
"On the Meaning of Names" (for Robin Hirsch). Glass (3:1/2/3)
    78, p. 83.

BATKI, John
"Biographical Note." GreenfieldR (6:3/4) Spr 78, p. 163.
"Human Affairs." GreenfieldR (6:3/4) Spr 78, p. 163.
"In Fog, In Silence" (tr. of Attila Jozsef). Hand (2) 78, p. 20.
"Sleep Quietly Now" (tr. of Attila Jozsef). Hand (2) 78, p. 19.
"Tail of the Tiger." Hand (2) 78, p. 52.

BATTIN, Wendy
"The Revolution." Madem (84:3) Mr 78, p. 86.

BAUDELAIRE
"Recueillement" (tr. by R. Sieburth and S. W. DeRachewiltz).
    St.AR (5:1) Aut-Wint 78, p. 61.
"Tableaux Parisiens XCIX." SouthernR (14:2) Spr 78, p. 330.

BAUER, Cheryl
"Rites for a Nightmare." MalR (45) Ja 78, p. 310.

BAUMANN, Susan
"The Dictionary under Mountain Fringe." Shen (29:2) Wint 78,
    p. 55.
"The Other Is." Stonecloud (7) 78, p. 96.

BAUMEL, Judith
  "To a Friend in Asia." NewRep (179:5) 29 Jl 78, p. 26.

BAXTER, Charles
  "Anecdote." Kayak (48) Je 78, p. 59.
  "Cantata at Midnight." Shen (29:3) Spr 78, p. 35.

BAXTER, E. R.
  "fragment P." Pig (5) 78, p. 35. Concrete poem.
  "Ghost n in a block of A's & P's." Pig (5) 78, p. 36. Con-
      crete poem.
  "the R runs thru the night, head full of nothing." Pig (5) 78,
      p. 37. Concrete poem.

BAYLES, Martha
  "The Refinery." MinnR (NS10) Spr 78, p. 68.

BEACHAM, Walton
  "Blinders." SouthernPR (18:2) Aut 78, p. 18.

BEARDSLEY, Doug
  "Barkley Sound." MalR (45) Ja 78, p. 281.
  "Black Gold, Blue Mountains" (for Rosie). MalR (45) Ja 78,
      p. 282.
  "Chesterman Bay." MalR (45) Ja 78, p. 280.
  "Exchange" (for Carl Beam). MalR (45) Ja 78, p. 279.

BEARN, Pierre
  "La Mesange et Le Chat." GRR (9:2) 78, p. 120.
  "Une Mouche Inopportune." GRR (9:2) 78, p. 122.
  "Noël Marin." GRR (9:2) 78, p. 124.

BEASLEY, W. Conger, Jr.
  "Notice." Focus (13:79) Ja-F 78, p. 30.
  "Train Trip Through Hungary." Focus (13:79) Ja-F 78, p. 30.

BEAVER, Bruce
  from Death's Directives: (V). Antaeus (30/31) Sum-Aut 78,
      p. 270.

BECHTEL, Charles W.
  "At Reading." SouthernPR (18:2) Aut 78, p. 67.

BECK, Art
  "Acid Freaks." Vaga (28) Aut 78, p. 52.
  "Broken April." Vaga (28) Aut 78, p. 53.
  "The Insane Girl--International Settlement, 1969." Vaga (28)
      Aut 78, p. 54.
  "The Last Man." Vaga (28) Aut 78, p. 56.
  "The Nun." Vaga (28) Aut 78, p. 51.
  "Variations." Vaga (27) Spr 78, p. 5.

BECK, Regina
  "Clay." Tele (14) 78.

"I sit peacefully in the office. " Tele (14) 78.
"my back yard. " Tele (14) 78.
"the slippery eel. " Tele (14) 78.
"unwind. " Tele (14) 78.

BECKER, Carol
"Back for the Summer. " StoneC (78:1) Wint 78, p. 9.

BECKER, Robin
"Art & the Artist. " Aspect (71) Ap-Je 77, p. 30.
"Letters to Michael. " Pan (19) 77, p. 25.
"Lighthouse" (for Lennie). Aspect (71) Ap-Je 77, p. 28.

BEDARD, Brian
"The Assiniboin Hear about a Speech Clinic. " SoDakR (16:2)
    Sum 78, p. 68.

BEECHER, John
"The Face You Have Seen. " MinnR (NS10) Spr 78, p. 69.
"A Veteran's Day of Recollection. " MinnR (NS10) Spr 78, p. 71.

BEHLEN, Charles
"Matney Dryer. " PoNow (20) 78, p. 3.

BEHN, Robin
"Atlantis" (tr. of Wislawa Szymborska, w. Claudia Johnson).
    ThRiPo (11/12) 78, p. 69.
"Seen from Above" (tr. of Wislawa Szymborska, w. Claudia John-
    son). ThRiPo (11/12) 78, p. 71.

BEINING, Guy R.
"Circulation One. " EnPas (7) 78, p. 19.
"Circulation Two. " EnPas (7) 78, p. 19.
"Dew as Inprint. " Stonecloud (7) 78, p. 11.
"Discovery 160. " Zahir (9) 77, p. 58.
"the era begins to look absorbing. " Stonecloud (7) 78, p. 28.
"Hourglass Fragments. " Zahir (9) 77, p. 54.
"Pigiron. " Pig (5) 78, p. 1.
"Ruins 98. " Zahir (9) 77, p. 59.
"Sweet Miss Misery 51, 139. " Zahir (9) 77, p. 57.
"to this crazy lady that thinks i am asexual. " Stonecloud (7) 78,
    p. 32.
"unlock the court of heart. " Zahir (9) 77, p. 58.

BELEDIAN, Krikor
"The Chimney" (tr. by Diana Der Hovanessian). StoneC (78:2)
    Spr 78, p. 21.

BELIVEAU, Judith
"A Way to Die. " Zahir (9) 77, p. 41.

BELL, Jason
"The Invisible Child. " ParisR (74) Aut-Wint 78, p. 190.

BELL, Roni
"Freedom." CarouselQ (3:3) Aut 78, p. 22.

BELLAMY, Joe David
"Mile Run." OP (26) Aut-Wint 78, p. 35.
"Not Unlike the Runner." OP (26) Aut-Wint 78, p. 40.
"Real Blood." OP (26) Aut-Wint 78, p. 39.
"Running My Heart Up." OP (26) Aut-Wint 78, p. 36.
"Solar Eclipse." PoetryNW (19:4) Wint 78-79, p. 10.
"The Space Around the Runner." OP (26) Aut-Wint 78, p. 37.
"Track Practice." OP (26) Aut-Wint 78, p. 38.

BELLI, Giuseppe Gioachino
"La Bellezza." SouthernR (14:3) Sum 78, p. 460.
"E ciò li Tistimoni." SouthernR (14:3) Sum 78, p. 464.
"Er Giorno der Giudizzio." SouthernR (14:3) Sum 78, p. 462.
"Marta e Madalena." WestHR (32:4) Aut 78, p. 314.

BELOTE, Suzanne
"Elegy." EngJ (67:5) My 78, p. 63.

BENAGE, Marlene
"The Beasts." CarouselQ (3:4) Wint 78, p. 33.
"Eyes Touch Eyes." CarouselQ (3:1) Spr 78, p. 22.
"Joy." CarouselQ (3:2) Sum 78, p. 4.
"Lightswitch." CarouselQ (3:3) Aut 78, p. 27.

BENBOW, Margaret
"The Kosher Grocer's Daughter." BelPoJ (29:1) Aut 78, p. 2.

BENDA, Jan
"Elegy on the Death of a Friend" (tr. of Milan Exner, w. Clayton Eshleman). Montra (4) 78, p. 12.

BENDER, Robert J.
"Architectures." Poem (32) Mr 78, p. 33.
"My Father Was a Nail Driver." Poem (32) Mr 78, p. 34.

BENEDETTI, David
"Nature." Hills (5) 78, p. 79.

BENEDIKT, Michael
"Before You Do." PoNow (19) 78, p. 14.
"A Double Dose of Blue Volkswagens." Agni (9) 78, p. 39.
"The Same Thing." Agni (9) 78, p. 38.
"Styles of Orgasm." Agni (9) 78, p. 41.
"To His Feminine Self." Ploughs (4:2) 78, p. 24.
"The Upper Hand." PoNow (19) 78, p. 14.
"Vermont." Tele (14) 78.
"Who Wants." Tele (14) 78.

BENJAMIN, Saul Hillel
"Aeneas to His Father." YaleR (67:3) Spr 78, p. 420.

BENN
"Chopin" (tr. by R. Sieburth and S. W. DeRachewiltz).   St. AR
   (5:1) Aut-Wint 78, p. 54.

BENNANI, Ben
"Stranger in a Distant City" (tr. of Mahmud Darwish).   Paint
   (9/10) Spr-Aut 78, p. 37.

BENNETT, Bruce
"Curious." Poetry (132:2) My 78, p. 92.
"Ready or Not." Poetry (132:2) My 78, p. 92.
"The Rendezvous." Poetry (132:2) My 78, p. 93.

BENNETT, John
"Brown Funk." Vaga (27) Spr 78, p. 88.
"End of the Line for Sherlock." Vaga (27) Spr 78, p. 54.
"Punch-drunk Fighter." Vaga (28) Aut 78, p. 30.

BENNETT, Karen
"Ink." FourQt (27:4) Sum 78, p. 23.

BENSON, Steve
"Dance--it is the phenomena of light." Hills (5) 78, p. 63.
"The Right Way." Hills (5) 78, p. 64.
"vanity." Hills (5) 78, p. 55.

BENTLEY, Beth
"Then." Nat (226:19) 20 My 78, p. 608.

BENTLEY, Sean
"Joints." WindO (33) Aut-Wint 78-79, p. 3.

BENVENISTE, Rachelle
"Two Lovers Discussing Marriage in a Seaside Room." Stonecloud (7) 78, p. 96.

BENVENUTO, Joyce
"The Man Who Knows How." Nimrod (22:2) Spr-Sum 78, p. 9.
"Words Itch at My Ear: I Think I Understand Them." Nimrod
   (22:2) Spr-Sum 78, p. 10.

BERG, Eric Ivan
"My River Fraser" (for Red). MalR (45) Ja 78, p. 223.
"Old Cariboo Wagon Road North" (for Pat Lane). MalR (45) Ja
   78, p. 222.

BERG, Stephen
"Alone" (tr. of Anna Akhmatova). NewYRB (25:12) 20 Jl 78,
   p. 3.
"Fragment, 1959" (tr. of Anna Akhmatova). NewYRB (25:3) 9
   Mr 78, p. 20.
"A Free Variation of Anna Akhmatova's Bezhetsk." Iowa (9:4)
   Aut 78, p. 85.

"A Free Variation of Anna Akhmatova's Lines. " Iowa (9:4) Aut
    78, p. 84.
"In Our Life. " Antaeus (30/31) Sum-Aut 78, p. 60.
"January, 1917" (tr. of Anna Akhmatova). Nat (226:11) 25 Mr
    78, p. 348.
"1914" (tr. of Anna Akhmatova). Nat (226:9) 11 Mr 78, p. 284.
"Things. " Antaeus (30/31) Sum-Aut 78, p. 58.

BERGAMIN, José
    "Sonnet to Rafael Alberti" (tr. by Lucia Graves). MalR (47) Jl
    78, p. 181.

BERGE, Carol
    "Mississippi Woman. " SenR (9:2) Aut-Wint 78, p. 77.

BERGH, Kent
    "Among Walls with Windows. " DacTerr (15) Wint-Spr 77-78,
    p. 59.

BERGIE, Sigrid
    "Because of Windows. " Tele (14) 78.
    "Franklin Brainard" (1920-1976). DacTerr (15) Wint-Spr 77-78,
    p. 7.
    "Late October Slow. " DacTerr (15) Wint-Spr 77-78, p. 8.
    "Minneapolis at Dusk. " Tele (14) 78.
    "Rain Yoga. " NorthSR (8) Aut-Wint 78-79, p. 70.
    "Typewriter Keys. " Tele (14) 78.

BERGIN, Thomas G.
    "Calypso. " SewanR (86:4) Aut 78, p. 513.

BERGMAN, David
    "Blind Insight. " CimR (45) O 78, p. 28.
    "Eclogue. " MichQR (17:2) Spr 78, p. 210.
    "Gout. " WindO (31) Wint-Spr 78, p. 11.
    "I Dream of Old Men. " HangL (33) Sum 78, p. 17.
    "The Medium to Her Lover. " Confr (17) Aut-Wint 79, p. 97.
    "Ruffled Pride. " WindO (31) Wint-Spr 78, p. 11.

BERGMAN, Roger
    "In My House" (for Bea Haskins). KanQ (10:2) Spr 78, p. 96.

BERGSTROM, Vera
    "in the clearing. " Wind (31) 78, p. 3.
    "In the Downing. " CarouselQ (3:4) Wint 78, p. 35.

BERKE, Nancy
    "Poem to a Stranger. " Tele (13) 77.
    "Stranded. " Tele (13) 77.

BERLIND, Bruce
    "Fragment. " NewL (45:2) Wint 78, p. 77.

BERLINER, Tom G.
"a friend." Tele (13) 77.

BERNARD, April
"Advice." HarvAd (111:4) My 78, p. 26.
"Apology." HarvAd (111:4) My 78, p. 26.
"Meditation." HarvAd (111:4) My 78, p. 26.

BERNARD, Suzanne P.
"To a Photograph of Myself at Ten." Box (7) Spr 78, p. 1.

BERNHEIMER, Alan
"Amarillo." Hills (5) 78, p. 48.
"Lionel." Hills (5) 78, p. 53.
"Or Something." Hills (5) 78, p. 47.

BERNSTEIN, Carole
"As hard as you tried." HangL (32) Spr 78, p. 56.
"Message." HangL (33) Sum 78, p. 61.
"poem for aug." HangL (33) Sum 78, p. 60.

BERNSTEIN, Charles
"Dodgem." Tele (14) 78.
"of a form, etc." Hills (5) 78, p. 46.
"of a sort." Hills (5) 78, p. 44.
"Poem: here. Forget." Hills (5) 78, p. 45.
"Space and Poetry." SunM (5) Aut 78, p. 54.

BERRETT, Jean
"A Walk Down Franklin St. at Dusk, After the First Snow."
    SmPd (44) Aut 78, p. 27.
"Willow at Dawn." SmPd (44) Aut 78, p. 28.

BERRY, Kevin
"if she makes me write." SeC (5:2) 78, p. 39.
"That's Entertainment." SeC (5:2) 78, p. 38.

BERRY, Skip
"Like Icarus, Rising." WindO (32) Sum-Aut 78, p. 45.
"Migration." WindO (32) Sum-Aut 78, p. 46.

BERRY, Wendell
"The Dark Lantern." AmerPoR (7:4) Jl-Ag 78, p. 40.
"The Long Night." SouthernR (14:4) Aut 78, p. 726.
"Ripening." Nat (227:13) 21 O 78, p. 413.
"Two Kentucky River Poems." AmerPoR (7:4) Jl-Ag 78, p. 40.
"The Wheel." GeoR (32:2) Sum 78, p. 281.

BERRYHILL, Michael
"Recent Items A Comment." HolCrit (15:2) Ap 78, p. 14.

BERSSENBRUGGE, Mei-mei
"Assonance." Hand (2) 78, p. 103.

"Spring Street Bar." <u>PartR</u> (45:3) 78, p. 436.
"The Translation of Verver." <u>PartR</u> (45:3) 78, p. 436.

BERTAGNOLLI, Olivia
  "Uprooting." <u>SouthernPR</u> (18:2) Aut 78, p. 41.

BERTOLINO, James
  "Brilliance." <u>Paint</u> (9/10) Spr-Aut 78, p. 15.
  "The Eleventh <u>Hour</u> Poem." <u>Epoch</u> (27:3) Spr 78, p. 284.
  "Late Mother." <u>Paint</u> (9/10) Spr-Aut 78, p. 14.
  "Sparrows." <u>Epoch</u> (27:3) Spr 78, p. 285.

BEST, Zoe
  "Contraception of Their Plan." <u>Chomo</u> (4:3) Spr 78, p. 31.

BETTS, Leonidas J.
  "Encounter." <u>EngJ</u> (67:5) My 77, p. 67.

BEUM, Robert
  "A House on the Freeway." <u>Comm</u> (105:8) 14 Ap 78, p. 246.

BEVER, Bernard
  "River Water." <u>Zahir</u> (9) 77, p. 68.

BEYER, William
  "Night Meeting." <u>Wind</u> (29) 78, p. 46.

BIASOTTI, Raymond
  "Cartwell Street." <u>SmPd</u> (43) Spr 78, p. 6.
  "City." <u>SmPd</u> (44) Aut 78, p. 11.
  "Poets." <u>SmPd</u> (43) Spr 78, p. 4.
  "Win, Place and Show" (for me and you). <u>SmPd</u> (44) Aut 78,
      p. 10.

BICKLEY, Paul
  "Another King Richard Winter Morning." <u>WindO</u> (31) Wint-Spr
      78, p. 31.

BIDER, Djemma
  "Who Will Drive Me Home?" (tr. of Vladimir Nabokov).
      <u>NewYorker</u> (54:37) 30 O 78, p. 40.

BIHLER, Penny
  "The Animals Are Cleaning Themselves." <u>JnlONJP</u> (2:1) 77,
      p. 26.
  "Hiking the Crevasse." <u>JnlONJP</u> (2:1) 77, p. 26.
  "In Your Dream." <u>JnlONJP</u> (2:1) 77, p. 27.
  "Love Song." <u>EngJ</u> (67:5) My 78, p. 55.
  "The Pigeon Man (and the Pigeon Lady)." <u>JnlONJP</u> (2:2) 77,
      p. 18.

BIJOU, Rachelle
  "The Poet's Leg." <u>Tele</u> (13) 77.
  "Sans Serif." <u>Tele</u> (13) 77.

BILOFSKY, Fred
"Untitled." CarouselQ (3:4) Wint 78, p. 6.

BINGHAM, Sallie
"George Rogers Clark or A Use for Old Houses." Shen (29:3)
    Spr 78, p. 77.

BIRBECK, Joe
"Earth Spun Illusion." CarouselQ (3:4) Wint 78, p. 4.

BIRK, Daniel
"Atlantic Dreams." CarouselQ (3:1) Spr 78, p. 17.

BISHOP, Elizabeth
"North Haven" (In Memoriam: Robert Lowell). NewYorker
    (54:43) 11 D 78, p. 40.
"Santarém." NewYorker (54:1) 20 F 78, p. 40.

BISHOP, Wendy
"Frankenstein." WindO (33) Aut-Wint 78-79.
"Quesuychatatata: The 120 Year Old Man Named 'Give Me the
    Cheese.'" WindO (33) Aut-Wint 78-79.
"The Summer Season." WindO (33) Aut-Wint 78-79.

BIZZARO, Patrick
"Manassas." FourQt (27:3) Spr 78, p. 9.
"The Taste of Rope." FourQt (27:3) Spr 78, p. 10.
"Virginia Summer" (for William Heyen). FourQt (27:3) Spr 78,
    p. 11.
"Waiting for the Show to Begin." NewRivR (2:2) 78, p. 8.

BJORKLUND, Beth
"'Let's Celebrate'" (tr. of Doris Mühringer). Paint (9/10) Spr-
    Aut 78, p. 39.
"Questions and Answers" (tr. of Doris Mühringer). Paint (9/10)
    Spr-Aut 78, p. 38.

BLACK, Charles
"The Man of Order in Hope." SouthernR (14:3) Sum 78, p. 499.
"The Prophet without Honor." SouthernR (14:3) Sum 78, p. 498.

BLACK, Isaac J.
"The Assassin's Poem." BelPoJ (29:2) Wint 78-79, p. 2.
"Burying Bones: At the Van Dyke Site (1953)." Obs (4:2) Sum
    78, p. 64.
"The Days of the Casualaires" (or: Section from an Autobiogra-
    phy in Progress) (1954-1962). Obs (4:2) Sum 78, p. 66.
"The Dream." Obs (4:2) Sum 78, p. 66.
"The Killing of the Sparrow: 1951." Obs (4:2) Sum 78, p. 64.
"Our Story." BelPoJ (29:2) Wint 78-79, p. 2.
"Poopie's Note." BelPoJ (29:2) Wint 78-79, p. 3.
"The Ring." BelPoJ (29:2) Wint 78-79, p. 4.

"Shooting Ourselves before Breakfast." Obs (4:2) Sum 78, p. 65.
"The Untouchables: 1959." Obs (4:2) Sum 78, p. 65.

BLACK, John
"Chiaroscuro." SouthernHR (12:2) Spr 78, p. 99.
"Holding Pattern." SouthernHR (12:2) Spr 78, p. 98.

BLACKWELL, Will H.
"Dawn." Epos (27:2) 77, p. 16.
"Impressions." Epos (27:1) 77, p. 20.
"Priest." Epos (27:1) 77, p. 19.

BLAETTNER, Norbert
"Heaven." WindO (31) Wint-Spr 78, p. 32.

BLANKENBURG, Gary
"Light." EngJ (67:5) My 78, p. 59.

BLASING, Randy
"Rubaiyat: Second Series" (tr. of Nazim Hikmet, w. Mutlu
     Konuk). LitR (21:4) Sum 78, p. 423.
"Rubaiyat: Third Series" (tr. of Nazim Hikmet, w. Mutlu
     Konuk). AntR (36:3) Sum 78, p. 371.

BLAUNER, Laurie
"Once White." CutB (11) Aut-Wint 78, p. 32.

BLAZEK, Douglas
"Foraging." Aspen (5) Spr 78, p. 79.
"Shadow Work at Dawn." Aspen (5) Spr 78, p. 80.

BLESSING, Richard
"The Boy with the Sad Fingers." SewanR (86:2) Spr 78, p. 261.
"The Clowns." Iowa (9:3) Sum 78, p. 83.
"Elegy for Elvis." PoetryNW (19:3) Aut 78, p. 42.
"Keeping a Roof Over Your Head" (for Lisa). Iowa (9:3) Sum 78,
     p. 84.
"The Poet's Dream the Night after His Son Scores 36 in a Little
     Dribbler's Game." PoetryNW (19:3) Aut 78, p. 41.

BLISS, S. W.
"One Day." CarouselQ (3:2) Sum 78, p. 18.
"Untitled." CarouselQ (3:1) Spr 78, p. 5.

BLOCH, Chana
"Deep Calleth Unto Deep" (tr. of Dahlia Ravikovitch). ChiR
     (30:2) Aut 78, p. 51.
"Firewood." SouthernHR (18:1) Spr 78, p. 5.
"Yom Kippur." SouthernPR (18:1) Spr 78, p. 6.

BLOCKLYN, Paul
"The Days." BallSUF (19:4) Aut 78, p. 41.

BLOK, Alexander
  "She Came In Out of the Cold" (tr. by Guy Daniels). Pequod
    (2:4) 78, p. 11.

BLOSSOM, Laurel
  "Doomed. " Poetry (132:6) S 78, p. 327.
  "Leaving. " Poetry (132:6) S 78, p. 328.
  "Next Time. " Poetry (132:6) S 78, p. 332.
  "Skate. " Poetry (132:6) S 78, p. 329.

BLOTTER, Nancy
  "Trophies. " YellowBR (10) 78, p. 38.

BLOUNT. Roy, Jr.
  "Don't Be So Rambunctious Around Your Grandma, She's a Little
    Tired This Morning. " BosUJ (26:1) 78, p. 68.

BLUM, Etta
  "Dawn Lake. " Nat (226:16) 29 Ap 78, p. 514.
  "I Could Walk Widely. " Nat (227:23) 30 D 78, p. 742.

BLY, Robert
  from Book for the Hours of Prayer: "2" (tr. of Rainer Maria
    Rilke). Field (18) Spr 78, p. 95.
  from Book for the Hours of Prayer: "7" (tr. of Rainer Maria
    Rilke). Field (18) Spr 78, p. 96.
  from Book for the Hours of Prayer: "11" (tr. of Rainer Maria
    Rilke). Field (18) Spr 78, p. 97.
  from Book for the Hours of Prayer: "18" (tr. of Rainer Maria
    Rilke). Field (18) Spr 78, p. 98.
  from Book for the Hours of Prayer: "20" (tr. of Rainer Maria
    Rilke). Field (18) Spr 78, p. 99.
  "An Evening When the Full Moon Rose as the Sun Set. " GeoR
    (32:3) Aut 78, p. 512.
  "The Farallones Islands. " OhioR (19:3) Aut 78, p. 49.
  "Moon on a Pasture near Ortonville. " GeoR (32:2) Sum 78,
    p. 332.
  "A Moth with Black Eyes. " OhioR (19:3) Aut 78, p. 50.
  "No Name for It" (tr. of Harry Martinson). MoonsLT (2:4) 78,
    p. 42.
  "A Ramage of the Man Who Is Alone. " OhioR (19:3) Aut 78,
    p. 51.
  "Walking the Mississippi Shore at Rock Island, Illinois. "
    MissouriR (1:1) Spr 78, p. 5.
  "Walking Where the Plows Have Been Turning. " GeoR (32:3)
    Aut 78, p. 513.
  "Women We Never See Again. " GeoR (32:2) Sum 78, p. 333.

BOBROWSKI, Johannes
  "Elder Blossoms" (tr. by Silvia Scheibli). Stonecloud (7) 78,
    p. 119.
  "Gertrud Kolmar" (tr. by Silvia Scheibli). Stonecloud (7) 78,
    p. 118.

"Home of the Painter, Chagall" (tr. by Silvia Scheibli). Stone-
     cloud (7) 78, p. 119.
"Memorial for a Fisherman" (tr. by Don Bogen). Antaeus
     (30/31) Sum-Aut 78, p. 64.
"The Wood House over the Wilia" (tr. by Don Bogen). Antaeus
     (30/31) Sum-Aut 78, p. 62.

BOCK, Frederick
   "Grasshoppers." Poetry (132:2) My 78, p. 97.

BOE, Deborah
   "Body of a Man." Kayak (49) O 78, p. 37.
   "Defense to One's Mother for Loving a Bad Man." US1 (11) Aut
       78, p. 8.
   "Doing Nothing." US1 (11) Aut 78, p. 10.
   "He Finds His Voice." SmPd (44) Aut 78, p. 27.
   "Insomnia." US1 (11) Aut 78, p. 9.
   "Nightmares." Kayak (49) O 78, p. 36.
   "Offering the Flowers." Kayak (49) O 78, p. 35.
   "The Red Sea." Columbia (2) Aut 78, p. 18.
   "Spring in the Big House." Kayak (49) O 78, p. 36.
   "These Swans." US1 (11) Aut 78, p. 8.
   "Tiresias." US1 (11) Aut 78, p. 9.
   "The Unwanted Gifts." US1 (11) Aut 78, p. 4.
   "A Woman." Kayak (49) O 78, p. 37.

BOETTCHER, Frances
   Ten poems. WormR (69) 78, p. 8.

BOGAN, Louise
   "From the Journals of a Poet." NewYorker (53:50) 30 Ja 78,
       p. 39. Journal excerpts.

BOGART, Cliff
   "Black's Out. A Note to the Remaining Guests." Tele (14) 78.

BOGEN, Don
   "On the Retirement of a Secretary of State." Kayak (48) Je 78,
       p. 24.
   "Memorial for a Fisherman" (tr. of Johannes Bobrowski).
       Antaeus (30/31) Sum-Aut 78, p. 64.
   "A Postcard from St. Petersburg." ParisR (73) Spr-Sum 78,
       p. 32.
   "To All the Tired Children." Kayak (48) Je 78, p. 25.
   "The Wood House over the Wilia" (tr. of Johannes Bobrowski).
       Antaeus (30/31) Sum-Aut 78, p. 64.

BOGIN, George
   "The Initiate." KanQ (10:4) Aut 78, p. 83.
   "The Moon over Munsey Park." KanQ (10:4) Aut 78, p. 82.
   "Stranger." GreenfieldR (6:3/4) Spr 78, p. 110.

BOHM, Robert
   "Gettysburg, Pennsylvania." Pan (19) 77, p. 36.

BOIARSKI, Phil
  "Dziadek." <u>MinnR</u> (NS11) Aut 78, p. 5.
  "Dziadek." <u>ParisR</u> (73) Spr-Sum 78, p. 35.

BOLAND, Eavan
  "Anorexic." <u>LitR</u> (22:2) Wint 79, p. 248.
  "Anorexic." <u>Stand</u> (19:2) 78, p. 17.
  "Degas's Laundresses." <u>LitR</u> (22:2) Wint 79, p. 252.
  "The Gorgon Child." <u>LitR</u> (22:2) Wint 79, p. 250.
  "In Her Own Image." <u>LitR</u> (22:2) Wint 79, p. 256.
  "In His Own Image." <u>LitR</u> (22:2) Wint 79, p. 255.
  "It's a Woman's World." <u>Stand</u> (19:2) 78, p. 18.
  "Monotony." <u>LitR</u> (22:2) Wint 79, p. 253.

BOND, Harold
  "Falling in Love with Dorothy Malone." <u>NewRep</u> (178:9) 4 Mr
     78, p. 32.

BOND, Pearl
  "Jewish Mother" (for Della). <u>YellowBR</u> (10) 78, p. 43.

BONNEFOY, Yves
  "The River" (tr. by Susanna Lang). <u>ChiR</u> (29:4) Spr 78, p. 88.
  "Summer of Night" (tr. by Marc Elihu Hofstadter). <u>MalR</u> (46)
     Ap 78, p. 84.

BOOK, M. K.
  "Marvin Milton Visits Hell." <u>WormR</u> (70) 78, p. 52.

BOOTH, Martin
  "Killing a Rat on 28th February." <u>PraS</u> (52:3) Aut 78, p. 258.
  "The Potter." <u>MalR</u> (48) O 78, p. 110.
  "Tracks in Nebraska." <u>PraS</u> (52:3) Aut 78, p. 260.
  "View from the Hen Run." <u>PraS</u> (52:3) Aut 78, p. 259.

BOOTH, Philip
  "Carrier." <u>GeoR</u> (32:2) Sum 78, p. 408.
  "Dragging." <u>NewRep</u> (178:9) 4 Mr 78, p. 30.
  "Fall." <u>NewEngR</u> (1:1) Aut 78, p. 82.
  "Falling Apart." <u>Shen</u> (29:2) Wint 78, p. 78.
  "Flinching." <u>MissouriR</u> (2:1) Aut 78, p. 41.
  "Gathering Greens." <u>NewYorker</u> (54:37) 30 O 78, p. 134.
  "Lichens." <u>Antaeus</u> (30/31) Sum-Aut 78, p. 65.
  "Old Man." <u>AmerPoR</u> (7:3) My-Je 78, p. 48.
  "Snapshot." <u>ThRiPo</u> (11/12) 78, p. 19.
  "Stove." <u>MoonsLT</u> (2:4) 78, p. 25.
  "Still Life." <u>AmerPoR</u> (7:3) My-Je 78, p. 48.
  "Syntax." <u>Atl</u> (242:4) O 78, p. 104.
  "Tools." <u>Antaeus</u> (30/31) Sum-Aut 78, p. 66.
  "Words for the Room." <u>PoetryNW</u> (19:2) Sum 78, p. 47.

BORAWSKI, Walta
  "Harvard has no class these days; nothing does." <u>PoNow</u> (20)
     78, p. 46.

BORCK, Jim Springer
  "'Bodily worship is only the token to others or ourselves of men-
    tal adoration.'--Dr. Johnson to Boswell, March 15, 1774."
    SouthernR (14:3) Sum 78, p. 496.
  "Cold Snap." SouthernR (14:3) Sum 78, p. 497.
  "Thinking About It." SouthernR (14:3) Sum 78, p. 495.

BORGES, Jorge Luis
  "A History of Night" (tr. by Alastair Reid). NewYRB (25:21/22)
    25 Ja 79, p. 26.

BORGSTADT, Elvira
  "Moonstruck the old woman rises." GRR (9:3) 78, p. 220.
  "A woman whose name I don't know." GRR (9:3) 78, p. 221.

BORGZINNER, Yadira
  "Dark Love." SeC (5:2) 78, p. 12.
  "What Is Poetry?" SeC (5:2) 78, p. 11.

BORICH, Michael
  "The Girl." ParisR (73) Spr-Sum 78, p. 142.

BORING, Janet Joel
  "We Come to Watch." CarouselQ (3:3) Aut 78, p. 26.

BORSON, Roo
  "Eucalyptus." MalR (45) Ja 78, p. 62.
  "Path." NewOR (6:1) 78, p. 15.
  "What the Darkness Said." CalQ (13/14) Spr-Sum 78, p. 89.

BOSLEY, Keith
  "The Man-Fish." Nat (226:3) 28 Ja 78, p. 94.

BOSS, Laura
  "Billy 'Balloon.'" JnlONJP (2:2) 77, p. 12.

BOSWORTH, M. E.
  "Pentecost." ChrC (95:17) 10 My 78, p. 493.

BOTTOMS, David
  "Calling Across Water at Lion Country Safari." Poetry (133:2)
    N 78, p. 87.
  "The Catfish." Poetry (133:2) N 78, p. 85.
  "Coming Back from Pinelog Mountain." SouthernPR (18:1) Spr
    78, p. 72.
  "Crawling Out at Parties" (for Carl Sagan). Poetry (132:2) My
    78, p. 81.
  "Smoking in an Open Grave." NewL (44:3) Spr 78, p. 39.
  "The Traveler." SouthwR (63:4) Aut 78, p. 338.
  "Watching Gators at Ray Boone's Reptile Farm." Poetry (133:2)
    N 78, p. 86.

BOUDREAU, Jean
  "Bicycles Know the Streets." CarouselQ (3:1) Spr 78, p. 11.

"Glass House. " StoneC (78:1) Wint 78, p. 30.

BOUISE, Oscar A
   "John Brown Pleads. " NegroHB (41:1) Ja-F 78, p. 786.

BOURNE, Louis M.
   Nine poems (tr. of José Hierro). AmerPoR (7:2) Mr-Ap 78,
      p. 30.
   "This Particular Moment" (tr. of Angel González). AmerPoR
      (7:2) Mr-Ap 78, p. 35.

BOWDEN, Michael
   "Coyotes. " Tendril (2) Spr-Sum 78.
   "Morning Camp at Rustlers' Pass. " Tendril (2) Spr-Sum 78.
   "Owl. " Tendril (2) Spr-Sum 78.

BOWEN, James K.
   "The Edge. " AmerS (47:4) Aut 78, p. 514.
   "Pumpkins and Root Crops. " PoNow (20) 78, p. 4.
   "Row Crops. " SouthernPR (18:2) Aut 78, p. 81.

BOWERING, Marilyn
   "Blooding the Earth. " MalR (45) Ja 78, p. 20.
   "Ghost Story. " MalR (45) Ja 78, p. 19.
   "The Lady's Blue Cloak. " MalR (45) Ja 78, p. 23.
   "Learning the Bomb. " MalR (45) Ja 78, p. 22.

BOWIE, Robert
   "All the Days After. " GreenfieldR (6:3/4) Spr 78, p. 165.
   "Awakening. " Epos (27:1) 77, p. 25.

BOWMAN, P. C.
   "A Mobile by Alexander Rutsch. " Poetry (132:1) Ap 78, p. 17.
   "Syntheses of Love. " Poetry (132:1) Ap 78, p. 18.

BOYCHUK, Bohdan
   Eight poems (tr. of Boris Pasternak, w. Mark Rudman).
      VirQR (54:4) Aut 78, p. 601.
   "How Life Lulls Us" (tr. of Boris Pasternak, w. Mark Rudman).
      Pequod (2:4) 78, p. 12.

BOYER, Tammy
   "I am facing the dawning sun. " HangL (33) Sum 78, p. 64.
   "Spring Cleaning. " HangL (33) Sum 78, p. 62.
   "The Sun Worshipper. " HangL (34) Wint 78-79, p. 56.

BOZANIC, Nick
   "The Call. " SouthernPR (18:2) Aut 78, p. 20.
   "Inside. " SouthernPR (18:2) Aut 78, p. 20.
   "Nocturne. " Wind (31) 78, p. 5.

BOZOIAN, Paula M.
   "The Horticulturist. " KanQ (10:1) Wint 77, p. 87.

"Worlds in Conjunction." KanQ (10:1) Wint 78, p. 88.

BRADBURY, Ray
"Telephone Friends, in Far Places." Tendril (2) Spr-Sum 78.

BRADEN, Dennis
"The Leaving." DacTerr (15) Wint-Spr 77-78, p. 21.

BRADLEY, George
"Christ Pantocrator in San Giorgio dei Greci." NewYorker
    (54:42) 4 D 78, p. 2.
"Filippo Brunelleschi, Florence, 1425." Shen (29:2) Wint 78,
    p. 76.
"Lights of Assisi." AmerPoR (7:2) Mr-Ap 78, p. 13.

BRADLEY, Sam
"At the Marshalling Yard." GreenfieldR (6:3/4) Spr 78, p. 70.
"The Child Comes, God's Witness." ChrC (95:42) 20 D 78,
    p. 1233.
"A Peace to the Irish." SouthernHR (12:1) Wint 78, p. 18.

BRADY, Daniel P.
"The Book Jacket Spiel to End all Spiels--the Ultimate Best
    Seller!" PikeF (1) Spr 78, p. 25.

BRADY, Jean
"Weather for a Morning." StoneC (78:3) Aut 78, p. 24.

BRAIDA, Darold D.
"the children." WindO (32) Sum-Aut 78, p. 4.

BRALOWER, Paul
"Salt Peanuts." Tele (13) 77.
"Yellow Blinkers." Tele (13) 77.

BRAMAN, Sandra
"Address Electricity." Hills (5) 78, p. 38.
"philosophy from descartes to hume." SunM (5) Aut 78, p. 142.
"The scaling/relief." Hills (5) 78, p. 38.
"to my psychoanalyst." SunM (5) Aut 78, p. 143.

BRAMBACH, Rainer
"Beyond Rjeka" (tr. by Stuart Friebert). Field (18) Spr 78,
    p. 34.
"Going Home" (tr. by Stuart Friebert). Field (18) Spr 78,
    p. 34.
"Poor Prospects for Drinkers" (tr. by Stuart Friebert). Field
    (18) Spr 78, p. 32.
"Sung Landscape" (tr. by Stuart Friebert). Field (18) Spr 78,
    p. 33.
"Under Appletrees" (tr. by Stuart Friebert). Field (18) Spr 78,
    p. 33.

"Lumberjack's Bar" (tr. by Stuart Friebert).   Tendril (2) Spr-
Sum 78.

BRANCH, M. D.
"Misconception." BlackF (2:2) Aut-Wint 78, p. 24.
"Your Galaxy." BlackF (2:2) Aut-Wint 78, p. 24.

BRANDT, Kathleen
"Moonshine Blues." Glass (3:1/2/3) 78, p. 52.

BRANHAM, Robert
"Recluse Unfound" (tr. of Chia Tao, w. Daniel Stevenson).
Nimrod (22:2) Spr-Sum 78, p. 108.
"Staying with Wang Ch'ang-Ling" (tr. of Ch'ang Chien, w. Daniel
Stevenson). Nimrod (22:2) Spr-Sum 78, p. 109.
"Untitled" (tr. of Liu Shen-hsu, w. Daniel Stevenson). Nimrod
(22:2) Spr-Sum 78, p. 108.

BRANIN, Jeff
"Hawksbill Summit." WindO (31) Wint-Spr 78, p. 34.
"I Love You, Dammit: Long Distance." Wind (30) 78, p. 2.
"Pony Express." WindO (31) Wint-Spr 78, p. 35.

BRAUDE, Michael
"The Children of Greenwich." ChiR (30:1) Sum 78, p. 30.

BRAUN, Richard Emil
"Amphitrite." ModernPS (9:3) Wint 79, p. 226.
"Mazzaro." ModernPS (9:3) Wint 79, p. 211.

BRAVERMAN, Diane
"Leaning" (For my parents). SouthernPR (18:1) Spr 78, p. 26.

BRAVERMAN, Kate Ellen
"Ends." Bachy (13) Aut-Wint 78-79, p. 83.
"Estimates." Stonecloud (7) 78, p. 137.
"Fall Rain, Fall Wind and Leaf." Bachy (13) Aut-Wint 78-79,
p. 82.
"In the Plague Zone." Bachy (13) Aut-Wint 78-79, p. 81.
"Meeting the Palm Reader." Bachy (13) Aut-Wint 78-79, p. 80.
"Reconstruction." Bachy (13) Aut-Wint 78-79, p. 82.
"Vow." Bachy (13) Aut-Wint 78-79, p. 80.
"Winter Rain." Bachy (13) Aut-Wint 78-79, p. 81.

BRAVERMAN, Madelyn
"Memo: To All Teachers." EngJ (67:5) My 78, p. 66.
"Warning: To All Teachers." EngJ (67:5) My 78, p. 66.

BRECHT, Stefan
"One morning, shaving." Confr (16) Spr-Sum 78, p. 40.

BREEDON, A. D.
"Poems on Reading The Three Marias' New Portuguese Letters."
Stand (18:4) 77, p. 52.

BREMER, C. R.
"Milk and Meat." DeKalb (11:1/2) Aut-Wint 77-78, p. 43.

BREMSER, Bonnie
"Life Is Just a One Night Stand." Tele (14) 78.
"Still Life with Wild Apples and Grapes." Tele (14) 78.

BRENNAN, Joseph Payne
"Darkness." Comm (105:16) 18 Ag 78, p. 519.

BRENNAN, Matthew
"Baseball's Structure." JnlOPC (12:2) Aut 78, p. 375.

BRETT, Peter
"Gambler." Wind (28) 78, p. 7.
"julio." Zahir (9) 77, p. 38.
"Love." Tele (14) 78.
"Meals." Tele (14) 78.
"Mission District." GRR (9:2) 78, p. 132.
"Sunday." GRR (9:2) 78, p. 134.
"Wife of Gonzales." GRR (9:2) 78, p. 133.

BREWER, Kenneth
"The Barn." DeKalb (11:3/4) Spr-Sum 78, p. 31.

BREWSTER, Marty
"Suckers." CarouselQ (3:2) Sum 78, p. 14.

BRIDGES, Lee
"A Pilgrim's Song of Nigeria." NegroHB (41:3) My-Je 78,
    p. 841.

BRIDGES, Monte
"The Strip Search." GreenfieldR (7:1/2) Aut 78, p. 78.

BRIGHAM, Besmilr
"Before Stars Have Come Out." OP (25) Spr-Sum 78, p. 10.
"A Christmas, the Mask We Live With." OP (25) Spr-Sum 78,
    p. 14.
"In My Dream the Children Remeber" (to the children of Bryan,
    Texas). OP (25) Spr-Sum 78, p. 4.
"The Old Writers, Their Liberties." OP (25) Spr-Sum 78, p. 7.
"The Run Through Rock, Why It Quivers." OP (25) Spr-Sum 78,
    p. 12.
"The Second Child." OP (25) Spr-Sum 78, p. 3.
"Under the Same Light: The Poet and the Clown (reading in
    Albuquerque)." OP (25) Spr-Sum 78, p. 8.
"The Wasps." Confr (16) Spr-Sum 78, p. 115.

BRINGHURST, Robert
"Death By Water." MalR (45) Ja 78, p. 127.
"The Heart Is Oil." MalR (45) Ja 78, p. 126.
"Spell for White Sandals." MalR (45) Ja 78, p. 128.
"The Stonecutter's Horses." MalR (45) Ja 78, p. 130.

BRINK, D. B.
"Hurricane, the Stallion" (tr. of Rykardo Rodriguez Rios). <u>Paint</u>
    (9/10) Spr-Aut 78, p. 46.
"Litany to Levu" (tr. of Rykardo Rodriguez Rios). <u>Paint</u> (9/10)
    Spr-Aut 78, p. 47.

BRINKMANN, Rolf Dieter
"The African" (tr. by Hartmut Schnell). <u>NewL</u> (45:1) Aut 78,
    p. 37.
"Journey to the Northern Gardens" (tr. by Hartmut Schnell).
    <u>NewL</u> (45:1) Aut 78, p. 38.

BRISBY, Stewart
"Concert at Auburn Prison." <u>GreenfieldR</u> (7:1/2) Aut 78, p. 69.
"Conversation with a Man Who Said He Was from Jamaica; or,
    Your Daughters Are Safe in Guadalajara But They'll Cut Off
    Your Arm for Your Watch." <u>GreenfieldR</u> (7:1/2) Aut 78,
    p. 22.
"The Poet." <u>GreenfieldR</u> (7:1/2) Aut 78, p. 70.

BRISSENDEN, R. F.
"The Death of Damiens, or l'Après-midi des Lumières."
    <u>Antaeus</u> (30/31) Sum-Aut 78, p. 257.
"She remembers the first Aeroplane to fly from the North to the
    South of Britain." <u>Antaeus</u> (30/31) Sum-Aut 78, p. 259.

BRISTOW, Joseph
"Gifts." <u>Stand</u> (19:1) 77-78, p. 65.

BRITTON, Coburn
"A Chronology at the Frick Collection." <u>Shen</u> (29:2) Wint 78,
    p. 56.

BRITTON, Donald
"The Certain Body." <u>LaB</u> (11) 78, p. 9.
"Non Piangere, Donald!" <u>LaB</u> (11) 78, p. 7.
"La Plus Belle Plage." <u>LaB</u> (11) 78, p. 6.
"Signs." <u>LaB</u> (11) 78, p. 4.
"We Loved the Inexact." <u>LaB</u> (11) 78, p. 3.

BRIZENDINE, Nancy
"guess who moved next door & drives a truck." <u>Tele</u> (14) 78.
"A Poem, Too Late." <u>Tele</u> (13) 77.
"slowly beat six eggs." <u>Tele</u> (14) 78.

BROADBENT, Ken
"The Death Camas." <u>QW</u> (5) Wint 78, p. 117.
"The Dream of a New Life." <u>QW</u> (5) Wint 78, p. 116.

BROCK, Randall
"those." <u>CarouselQ</u> (3:3) Aut 78, p. 29.
"you." <u>SmPd</u> (44) Aut 78, p. 34.

BROCK, Van K.
  "In the Manner of V. B." (for George Seferis).   SouthernR (14:4)
      Aut 78, p. 751.

BRODEY, Jim
  "At Peace." Tele (13) 77.
  "In Bliss" (for Frank Lima). Tele (13) 77.
  "Uninspired." Tele (13) 77.

BRODINE, Karen
  "gardening at night." HangL (32) Spr 78, p. 3.
  "Girlfriends." HangL (33) Sum 78, p. 20.
  "Selling the House." HangL (32) Spr 78, p. 4.
  "Singing for Your Supper" (for my stepmother). HangL (33) Sum
      78, p. 18.
  "Visiting." HangL (32) Spr 78, p. 5.
  "Walking the Shark." HangL (32) Spr 78, p. 6.

BRODSKY, Joseph
  "Autumn in Norenskaya" (tr. by Daniel Weissbort, w. the author).
      Iowa (9:4) Aut 78, p. 2.
  "Brighton Rock" (tr. by Alan Myers). NewYorker (53:51) 6 F
      78, p. 30.
  "December 24, 1971" (tr. by Alan Myers). NewYRB (25:20) 21
      D 78, p. 4.
  "East Finchley" (tr. by Alan Myers). NewYorker (54:14) 22 My
      78, p. 42.
  "A Grand Elegy for John Donne" (tr. by Andrei Navrozov).
      YaleLit (147:3) 78, p. 9.
  "Lithuanian Divertissement" (to Thomas Ventslova) (tr. by Alan
      Myers). NewYRB (25:15) 12 O 78, p. 11.
  "Mexican Divertimento" (for Octavio Paz) (tr. by Alan Myers).
      NewYRB (15:19) 7 D 78, p. 10.
  "Part of Speech" (tr. by Daniel Weissbort). Poetry (131:6) Mr
      78, p. 311.
  "The Rustle of Acacias" (tr. by Daniel Weissbort, w. the author).
      Iowa (9:4) Aut 78, p. 1.
  "To a Tyrant" (tr. by Alan Myers). NewYorker (54:22) 17 Jl 78,
      p. 26.
  "(To E. R.)" (tr. by George L. Kline). Paint (7/8) Spr-Aut 77,
      p. 27.
  "Torso" (tr. by Howard Moss). NewYorker (54:32) 25 S 78,
      p. 42.
  "York: In Memoriam W. H. Auden" (tr. by Alan Myers).
      NewYorker (54:18) 19 Je 78, p. 34.

BRODSKY, Louis Daniel
  "A Sky Filled with Trees." AmerS (47:1) Wint 77-78, p. 23.
  "My Flying Machine." FourQt (27:2) Wint 78, p. 13.

BROMIGE, David
  "Seeing that you asked." Hills (5) 78, p. 117.

BROMLEY, Anne
"Dog Dag." Pan (19) 77, p. 29.
"Wild Man in a Small Town." Pan (19) 77, p. 29.

BROMWICH, David
"Mad Song." Poetry (131:4) Ja 78, p. 216.

BRONK, William
"Life Supports." Montra (4) 78, p. 5.

BROOK, Donna
"Thinking of Jack Spicer." AntR (36:4) Aut 78, p. 472.

BROOKHOUSE, Christopher
"For Stephen." CarolQ (30:2) Spr-Sum 78, p. 82.

BROOKS, David
"The One Place." Antaeus (30/31) Sum-Aut 78, p. 255.

BROOKS, James
"Let the Sun." AmerPoR (7:6) N-D 78, p. 35.

BROOKS, Paul
"Epilogue." Bachy (11) Spr 78, p. 40.
"Notes from a Political Exile." Bachy (11) Spr 78, p. 36.

BROOKS, Randy
"Five Haiku." WindO (31) Wint-Spr 78, p. 7.
"Mommy High/Coo." YellowBR (10) 78, p. 41.
"Mommy Tanka." YellowBR (10) 78, p. 41.

BROSMAN, Catharine Savage
"Abiding Winter." SouthernR (14:3) Sum 78, p. 508.
"A Hollow Where Love Lasts." SouthernHR (12:1) Wint 78,
    p. 57.
"The Loft." SouthernR (14:3) Sum 78, p. 509.
"New Orleans Sketchbook." SouthernR (14:3) Sum 78, p. 506.

BROUGHTON, T. Alan
"Fear." Poetry (133:1) O 78, p. 31.
"First Snow, Deep Sleep, as Always." VirQR (54:3) Sum 78,
    p. 491.
"Grace." Poetry (133:1) O 78, p. 27.
"Happiness." Poetry (133:1) O 78, p. 29.
"Inhibition." Poetry (133:1) O 78, p. 28.
"Loneliness." Poetry (133:1) O 78, p. 30.
"A Reply, Perhaps Christian" (for mikal). Confr (16) Spr-Sum
    78, p. 44.
"Restlessness." VirQR (54:3) Sum 78, p. 491.
"Three Voices: Delphi." BelPoJ (28:3) Spr 78, p. 4.
"Three Weddings." ThRiPo (11/12) 78, p. 20.

BROWN, Elizabeth
"Searching a Field after a Snowfall." SmPd (44) Aut 78, p. 12.

BROWN, Harry
"The Nature of Surprise." Wind (30) 78, p. 52.

BROWN, J. William
"Driving: West Texas." SouthwR (63:4) Aut 78, p. 366.

BROWN, Jae
"The Album." StoneC (78:3) Aut 78, p. 28.

BROWN, Judy
"Song for an Old Friend." Stonecloud (7) 78, p. 97.

BROWN, Kurt
"Falling." BallSUF (19:4) Aut 78, p. 51.

BROWN, Matt
"Glitter Town." DeKalb (11:3/4) Spr-Sum 78, p. 91.

BROWN, Matthew R.
"The Katydid's Song." GRR (9:2) 78, p. 142.
"Lone Tree." GRR (9:3) 78, p. 219.
"You Are Not Yours." GRR (9:2) 78, p. 141.

BROWN, Michael R.
"The Bookworm." WormR (72) 78, p. 127.

BROWN, Rebecca
"Elegy for a Sister" (for B. R. W.). LittleM (11:3) Aut 77, p. 40.

BROWN, Robert W.
"Anger: A Letter." PikeF (1) Spr 78, p. 6.
"Untitled." PikeF (1) Spr 78, p. 6.

BROWN, Russell M.
"The Poet Dreams of Himself as Magician." LitR (21:3) Spr 78,
    p. 344.

BROWN, Stephen Ford
"Fishing Trip." PoNow (20) 78, p. 4.
"French Provincial." PoNow (20) 78, p. 4.

BROWN, Terry W.
"Memorial Day." KanQ (10:1) Wint 78, p. 124.
"My Uncle." Tele (13) 77.

BROWNE, Colin
"The Crow in the Oak Tree: His Memory." MalR (45) Ja 78,
    p. 261.

BRUCE, Debra
"At the Drive-In." OP (25) Spr-Sum 78, p. 48.
"From a Window." OP (25) Spr-Sum 78, p. 45.
"I Haven't Been Able to Get Anything Done Since I Met You" (for
    Douglas). PraS (52:2) Sum 78, p. 189.

"Insomnia." PraS (52:2) Sum 78, p. 188.
"Morning News: Iowa." OP (25) Spr-Sum 78, p. 47.
"My Father's House." OP (25) Spr-Sum 78, p. 50.
"Poem to a Field Rat." OP (25) Spr-Sum 78, p. 46.

BRUCHAC, Joseph
"Deer Song." Tendril (3) Aut 78, p. 12.
"Drinking from the Maple Buckets." Hudson (31:2) Sum 78,
    p. 303.
"Four Entrances." Tendril (3) Aut 78, p. 10.
"A Mockingbird." Nat (227:4) 5-12 Ag 78, p. 124.
"One Hot Summer Night, 1947." OhioR (19:3) Aut 78, p. 72.

BRUMM, Anne-Marie
"Pavan for a Dead Princess" (for the world-weary). AAUP
    (64:2) My 78, p. 89.

BRUNER, Mark
"Finn Sjoblom." CarouselQ (3:2) Sum 78, p. 17.
"The Partridge." CarouselQ (3:4) Wint 78, p. 13.

BRUNING, Michael J.
"The End Results." DeKalb (11:3/4) Spr-Sum 78, p. 92.
"Feelings." DeKalb (11:3/4) Spr-Sum 78, p. 92.

BRUNNQUELL, Don
"Blackthorn." Epoch (27:2) Wint 78, p. 148.

BRUSH, Thomas
"Christmas." PoNow (19) 78, p. 45.
"Don't Cry." PoetryNW (19:4) Wint 78-79, p. 32.
"Heaven." DacTerr (15) Wint-Spr 77-78, p. 38.
"In a Classroom at Night." DacTerr (15) Wint-Spr 77-78, p. 39.
from The Pike Place Market Musical: "Floating." NoAmR
    (263:4) Wint 78, p. 30.
from The Pike Place Market Musical: "Let Go." NoAmR
    (263:4) Wint 78, p. 34.
"Sleep, Child." PoetryNW (19:4) Wint 78-79, p. 32.
"Sleeping in a Cabin Built by My Grandfather in 1916."
    PoetryNW (19:2) Sum 78, p. 20.

BRYAN, Sharon
"Big Sheep Knocks You About." Ploughs (4:2) 78, p. 40.
"Seeing It." Nat (227:13) 21 O 78, p. 421.

BRYANT, Mavis
"A Theory of Love." TexQ (21:1) Spr 78, p. 53.

BRYER, Sally
"Ingrid Jonker." MalR (45) Ja 78, p. 152.

BUCHANAN, E. Clay, III
"Who Will Love You." Wind (30) 78, p. 59.

BUCKLEY, Catherine
 "Call from a Stranger. " EngJ (67:5) My 78, p. 63.

BUCKLEY, Christopher
 "At 30. " SlowLR (1/2) 78, p. 29.
 "Dear Diane. " Stonecloud (7) 78, p. 7.
 "Looking Up" (for Christian Charles Schiefen). SenR (9:1) Spr-
    Sum 78, p. 49.
 "On Modigliani's 'Daughter of the People.'" SenR (9:1) Spr-Sum
    78, p. 52.
 "Somewhere in Ohio. " CutB (10) Spr-Sum 78, p. 86.

BUCKNER, Sally
 "Photographer. " ChrC (95:8) 8 Mr 78, p. 240.

BUDBILL, David
 "Bobbie. " PoNow (20) 78, p. 20.
 "Conrad. " Bleb/Ark (13) 78, p. 71.
 from From Down to the Village: "Flossie. " Bleb/Ark (13) 78,
    p. 69.
 "Old Man Pike. " PoNow (20) 78, p. 20.

BUDENZ, Julia
 "Crockery. " FourQt (27:2) Wint 78, p. 15.
 "Encounter. " Bits (7) Ja 78.
 "Flora Baum, Typed. " Epos (27:1) 77, p. 8.
 "Flora Baum, Typist. " Epos (27:1) 77, p. 8.

BUDIN, Sue
 "Search. " AAR (28) 78, p. 63.
 "Sonafu. " AAR (28) 78, p. 62.

BUFFLER, Esther
 "Red Is the Color. " HarvAd (112:1) D 78, p. 13.

BUKOWSKI, Charles
 "The Deathly Bravo. " WormR (72) 78, p. 153.
 "fat head poem. " Vaga (28) Aut 78, p. 38.
 "59 Cents a Pound. " NowestR (17:1) 78, p. 19.
 "A 56 Year Old Poem. " WormR (72) 78, p. 154.
 "It's Strange. " WormR (68) 77, p. 118.
 Legs, Hips and Behind. WormR (71) 78. Entire issue.
 "The Veryiest. " WormR (68) 77, p. 118.

BULL, Lon
 "Cloud Cuckoo Land. " AmerPoR (7:6) N-D 78, p. 34.
 "Passage. " AmerPoR (7:6) N-D 78, p. 34.
 "Red. " AmerPoR (7:6) N-D 78, p. 34.

BULLIS, Jerald
 "Am I Gathering My Days. " NoAmR (263:3) Aut 78, p. 65.
 "Buck It. " Epoch (28:1) Aut 78, p. 65.
 "Every Day. " Epoch (28:1) Aut 78, p. 66.

"Gathering." BelPoJ (28:4) Sum 78, p. 21.
"I Say the Soul &." BelPoJ (28:4) Sum 78, p. 20.
"Vision Is a Looking Out." Epoch (28:1) Aut 78, p. 64.

BULMAN, Aaron E.
"A Regional Accent." SmPd (43) Spr 78, p. 16.

BUNDALIAN, Maribeth
"No One Cares." SeC (5:2) 78, p. 40.

BUNDY, Joan Wolf
"Infertility." Northeast (3:5) Spr-Sum 78, p. 14.
"Sweeping." Northeast (3:5) Spr-Sum 78, p. 15.
"Winter Morning." Northeast (3:5) Spr-Sum 78, p. 14.

BUNGAY, Ray
"After the Ball Blues." JnlONJP (2:1) 77, p. 23.
"A Harmonica without Teeth." JnlONJP (2:2) 77, p. 11.

BURCH, Edward
"If Spring Should Come." KanQ (10:2) Spr 78, p. 76.
"Seaman and Moon." KanQ (10:2) Spr 78, p. 75.

BURDEN, Jean
"On Coming Upon an Old Snapshot of Peter DeVries." Poetry
    (133:3) D 78, p. 149.
"Photograph of My Mother at Eighteen." Salm (42) Sum-Aut 78,
    p. 123.
"Portrait of My Father at Four." Salm (40) Wint 78, p. 93.
"Premonition in the Midst of Plenty." Poetry (132:5) Ag 78,
    p. 259.

BURDOINE, Michael N.
"Enough." Wind (28) 78, p. 12.

BURGESS, Anthony
"For Un Omaggio a Rafael Alberti" (tr. of Eugenio Montale).
    MalR (47) Jl 78, p. 113.

BURKARD, Michael
"Gin. White Out" (for Carl Hughes). AmerPoR (7:4) Jl-Ag 78,
    p. 46.
"Praise." OhioR (19:3) Aut 78, p. 25.
"A Sideways Suicide." AmerPoR (7:4) Jl-Ag 78, p. 47.

BURKE, Carol
"Commission" (for Marcelle Toor). NorthSR (8) Aut-Wint 78-79,
    p. 52.

BURKE, Daniel
"Ash Wednesday." FourQt (27:2) Wint 78, p. 2.

BURKE, Herbert
"Encounter." GRR (9:3) 78, p. 204.

"Out of Thrace." GRR (9:3) 78, p. 200.
"The Performer." GRR (9:3) 78, p. 202.
"The Way Is the Dream." GRR (9:3) 78, p. 199.

BURKE, Mark
"Daughter of Moonlight." MalR (48) O 78, p. 89.
"Divorced Child." MalR (48) O 78, p. 88.
"English Sixth Lesson." MinnR (NS10) Spr 78, p. 66.

BURLINGAME, Robert
"In a New England Attic." OhioR (19:2) Spr-Sum 78, p. 47.
"Indescribable." SouthwR (63:3) Sum 78, p. 280.
"Late Winter in West Texas" (for Karl and Jane Kopp). OhioR
    (19:1) Wint 78, p. 93.

BURNETT, Edward L.
"The Punishment of Oedipus." AmerS (47:2) Spr 78, p. 236.

BURNHAM, Deborah
"Poem: God, my sons were right, they scorned religion, said
    it's a death." BelPoJ (29:1) Aut 78, p. 6.
"Speaking of Tongues." BelPoJ (29:1) Aut 78, p. 5.

BURNS, R. A.
"The Toad That Ate Los Angeles." PoNow (19) 78, p. 24.

BURR, Gray
"Mr. Thoben." Poetry (132:3) Je 78, p. 145.
"A Ramble." Poetry (132:3) Je 78, p. 146.
"Sunday at the Beach." Poetry (132:3) Je 78, p. 144.
"The Unseen." PoNow (19) 78, p. 12.

BURRISS, William S.
"Our Old Lady of the Cycles." Pan (19) 77, p. 74.

BURROWS, E. G.
"After the Overcast." PoetryNW (19:3) Aut 78, p. 45.
"A Circle of Standing Stones." MichQR (17:3) Sum 78, p. 365.
"The Geology of Spring." GRR (9:1) 78, p. 33.
"The House of August." Sky (7/8) Spr 78, p. 5.
"Passengers." PoetryNW (19:3) Aut 78, p. 45.
"Railroad." Sky (7/8) Spr 78, p. 9.
"Song Sung for a Wedding." Sky (7/8) Spr 78, p. 11.
"The Unearthlings." PoNow (19) 78, p. 22.

BURSK, Christopher
"Able Bodied Seamen." WindO (31) Wint-Spr 78, p. 5.
"Diseases of the Blood." Epoch (28:1) Aut 78, p. 87.
"Ensjuntar." Pig (5) 78, p. 19.
"Gravity." ParisR (74) Aut-Wint 78, p. 194.
"Handymen." AAR (28) 78, p. 94.
"Infidelities." WindO (31) Wint-Spr 78, p. 3.
"The Museum in Hagerty's Boarded-Up Stable" (for Loren Eisley).
    Sam (65) 78, p. 58.

"The One We Made Leap First, Swing from the Old Rafters."
    WindO (31) Wint-Spr 78, p. 4.
"Recess." PoNow (19) 78, p. 37.
"Squaring Off." Pig (5) 78, p. 72.
"Thieves, Arabs of the Tall Grass" (for Herb Fredericks).
    ParisR (74) Aut-Wint 78, p. 193.
"Tying My Wrists." Epoch (28:1) Aut 78, p. 88.

BURT, John
    "Hengest's War." WebR (4:2) Aut 78, p. 24.

BURT, Lucille
    "Portrait." Tendril (3) Aut 78, p. 13.

BURTIS, William
    "Dawn Comes to the All Night Diner" (for John Bowie). Aspen
    (5) Spr 78, p. 92.
    "Midnight Special." Aspen (5) Spr 78, p. 94.
    "1967." Aspen (5) Spr 78, p. 93.

BURWELL, Martin
    "It's a new world, Chris." Wind (28) 78, p. 8.

BURWELL, Rex
    "Christi Fuller in the Novel Ball Street." CalQ (13/14) Spr-Sum
    78, p. 60.
    "Depression" (for Virginia, who knows). CalQ (13/14) Spr-Sum
    78, p. 61.
    "Poet, You Should Learn from Coleridge." CimR (42) Ja 78,
    p. 63.

BUSH, Clive
    "Lament for Sir Thomas Wyatt and Others" (for Janet Floyd).
    AmerPoR (7:3) My-Je 78, p. 46.

BUSHA, Gary C.
    "Big Game Hunters on the Serengeti Plain." PoNow (20) 78,
    p. 4.
    "To a Young Woman Conscious Only of Her Beauty." Wind (31)
    78, p. 8.

BUSHMAN, Naomi
    "Judging Distance." HangL (32) Spr 78, p. 7.

BUTCHER, Grace
    "Another Gracchi Slain." Northeast (3:6) Wint 78-79, p. 17.
    "Burying the White Cat." Northeast (3:6) Wint 78-79, p. 16.
    "Man." Northeast (3:6) Wint 78-79, p. 15.
    "New and Old Beginnings." HiramPoR (24) Spr-Sum 78, p. 6.
    "One Friday in October When the Farm Stopped." HiramPoR
    (24) Spr-Sum 78, p. 5.
    "The Others." PoNow (19) 78, p. 24.
    "Woman." Northeast (3:6) Wint 78-79, p. 16.

BUTLER, Jack
"The Buzzard." NewYorker (53:49) 23 Ja 78, p. 26.
"Concerto for Wall-Eyed Weary Women." NewOR (6:1) 78,
    p. 58.
"Fall Now, and All the Little Poets." PoetryNW (19:1) Spr 78,
    p. 7.
"Notes Toward an Aubade." PoetryNW (19:1) Spr 78, p. 9.

BUTLER, Madeleine
"Okra." NewOR (5:4) 78, p. 358.

BUTRICK, L. H.
"On the North Forty." SouthernPR (18:2) Aut 78, p. 80.
"The Stray." SouthernHR (12:1) Wint 78, p. 56.

BUTTERWORTH, Keen
"The Jack Pot." SouthernHR (12:2) Sum 78, p. 109.

BUVAL, Antonio
"Things Go Better for Blacks (In Alabama Bars)." NewOR (5:4)
    78, p. 329.

BUYCK, Kathy
"My father and I are prisoners." HangL (33) Sum 78, p. 65.
"A silly dream." HangL (33) Sum 78, p. 66.
"A Weird Dream." HangL (33) Sum 78, p. 67.

BYNUM, Edward B.
"C. B. (1906-1976)." Obs (4:2) Sum 78, p. 81.
"New Entry." Obs (4:2) Sum 78, p. 80.
"Spring." Obs (4:2) Sum 78, p. 81.
"XVI." Obs (4:2) Sum 78, p. 80.

BYNUM, Kay Hays
"Balance Due." Tele (14) 78.
"Body Language" (for R). Tele (14) 78.

CADNUM, Michael
"The Death of Chairman Mao." CarolQ (30:2) Spr-Sum 78,
    p. 80.
"Empire." MichQR (17:1) Wint 78, p. 24.
"Taxidermists." MichQR (17:1) Wint 78, p. 25.

CADOU, René Guy
"Antonin Artaud" (tr. by Charles Guenther). Bleb/Ark (13) 78,
    p. 19.
"Behind the Curtains" (tr. by Charles Guenther). Bleb/Ark (13)
    78, p. 18.
"I Think about That Little Room" (tr. by Charles Guenther).
    Bleb/Ark (13) 78, p. 17.
"Poetic Art" (tr. by Charles Guenther). Bleb/Ark (13) 78,
    p. 20.

CADY, Joseph
"Finding Ireland." Shen (29:2) Wint 78, p. 72.

CAFFYN, Lois
"Nightlights." KanQ (10:1) Wint 78, p. 65.

CAGNONE, Nanni
from CLAUDIO COSTA sintomi di un lavoro: "'a', in altre
parole 'b'." Chelsea (37) 78, p. 116.
from Indicta, Desunt: "entrambi avrebbe detto apparizione."
Chelsea (37) 78, p. 134.

CAHILL, Patricia
"The Sentry." Pan (19) 77, p. 64.

CAIN, Cristy
"Old Age." SeC (5:2) 78, p. 41.

CAIN, John
"Upon the Bible Belt." NewL (45:2) Wint 78, p. 58.

CAIN, Seymour
"Holy Safad." ChrC (95:17) 10 My 78, p. 499.

CAISTOR, Nick
"Of Lizards and Grandmothers." Stand (19:3) 78, p. 64.

CALDARA, Anna Maria
"Backs of Buildings." JnlONJP (2:2) 77, p. 5.
"Out of the Garden." JnlONJP (2:2) 77, p. 5.

CALEB, J. Rufus
"Great-Uncles." PoNow (10) 78, p. 4.

CALITRI, Robin
"No Words." CutB (10) Spr-Sum 78, p. 82.

CALK, Heather
"america the beautiful." SeC (5:2) 78, p. 42.
"Maybe he had one too many." SeC (5:2) 78, p. 44.
"Through My Eyes." SeC (5:2) 78, p. 43.

CALLAWAY, Kathy
"Animal Crackers." Nat (221:8) 16 S 78, p. 248.
"The Dolorosa Drowns in Normal Brilliance." CutB (11) Aut-
Wint 78, p. 33.
"How to Love Mountains." Nat (227:11) 7 O 78, p. 353.
"Piling Up Rocks." CutB (11) Aut-Wint 78, p. 35.
"Stealing the Photographs." CutB (11) Aut-Wint 78, p. 34.

CALLIS, Dan
"Friends." CarouselQ (3:4) Wint 78, p. 11.

CALVIN, Ritchie
"The Wind and I." CarouselQ (3:1) Spr 78, p. 9.

CALVO, Igor
"A Fable" (tr. by Roberto Márquez). Iowa (9:4) Aut 78, p. 76.

CAMP, James
"After the Philharmonic." OP (25) Spr-Sum 78, p. 36.
"Humanism" (For Lana, Washoe and Koko and those that will
    come after). OP (25) Spr-Sum 78, p. 34.
"Infans ex Machina." OP (25) Spr-Sum 78, p. 33.
"Landscape Like a Quilt." OP (25) Spr-Sum 78, p. 32.
"Sing-Along Story." OP (25) Spr-Sum 78, p. 36.

CAMPBELL, D. G.
"Interlude." StoneC (78:2) Spr 78, p. 10.

CAMPBELL, David
"A Fragile Affair." Antaeus (30/31) Sum-Aut 78, p. 260.

CAMPBELL, Deborah
"Qualms." SouthernPR (18:2) Aut 78, p. 22.

CAMPBELL, Larry
"We Knew by Black Fire." BlackF (2:2) Aut-Wint 78, p. 26.

CAMPBELL, Loretta
"Marian Anderson" (for a Black Poet). BlackF (2:2) Aut-Wint
    78, p. 27.

CAMPBELL, Marybelle
"An Elegy for Ezra Pound." St. AR (5:1) Aut-Wint 78, p. 138.

CAMPBELL, Tim
"The Telephone." SeC (5:2) 78, p. 13.

CANDELARIA, Frederick
"Canadian Passport." MalR (45) Ja 78, p. 314.
"Impasse." MalR (45) Ja 78, p. 315.

CANICK, Michael
"Solitaire: A Piano Movement in Two Movements." Pig (4) 78,
    p. 98.

CANNON, Maureen
"Widow." LadHJ (95:6) Je 78, p. 70.

CANNON, Melissa
"Coma." Tendril (2) Spr-Sum 78.
"Hand Game for an Irish Child." Tendril (3) Aut 78, p. 15.
"Raped Girl." Chomo (5:2) Aut-Wint 78, p. 70.
"A Tree Falls Unseen in the Forest" (for Russell Riepe, 1906-

1976).   Tendril (3) Aut 78.
"Vulture Song."   Tendril (2) Spr-Sum 78.

CANNON, William
"To Write if Nothing More."   CarouselQ (3:2) Sum 78, p. 28.

CANTRELL, Charles
"The Film, the Lightning."   EnPas (7) 78, p. 38.
"Howchie."   Northeast (3:5) Spr-Sum 78, p. 58.
"Not Scared, Reaching."   SouthernPR (18:1) Spr 78, p. 13.
"Poem: Sun going down."   Tele (13) 77.

CAPAROSO, Fred
"kansas storm."   PoetryNW (19:3) Aut 78, p. 25.
"magician."   PoetryNW (19:3) Aut 78, p. 24.

CARAM, Eve
"A Winter Visit at Bard."   GreenfieldR (6:3/4) Spr 78, p. 57.

CARBONI, Richard
"the red starlet."   Zahir (9) 77, p. 17.

CARCO, Vincent
"Children at the Planetarium."   ChiR (30:1) Sum 78, p. 55.

CARDOZO, Nancy
"The Difficulties."   SouthernR (14:1) Wint 78, p. 110.

CARISIO, Justin
"Death of the Aerialist."   FourQt (27:4) Sum 78, p. 18.

CARLILE, Henry
"The Burned Girl."   Antaeus (30/31) Sum-Aut 78, p. 67.
"The Camera."   MalR (48) O 78, p. 94.
"Depression."   Iowa (9:1) Wint 78, p. 33.
"The Face in the Painting" (for Carl Morris).   MalR (48) O 78,
    p. 91.
"Flood Control."   Antaeus (28) Wint 78, p. 136.
"Giant Ocean Sunfish."   Antaeus (28) Wint 78, p. 138.
"Havana Blues."   Iowa (9:1) Wint 78, p. 34.
"In the More Recent Past."   OhioR (19:3) Aut 78, p. 69.
"Incomplete Description of 'The World's Smallest Church Grotto.'"
    PoetryNW (19:3) Aut 78, p. 10.
"Leda and the Swan."   MalR (48) O 78, p. 96.
"Listening to Beethoven on the Oregon Coast."   Antaeus (30/31)
    Sum-Aut 78, p. 68.
"Song."   MalR (48) O 78, p. 90.
"Take the Bass for Example."   PoetryNW (19:3) Aut 78, p. 9.
"To Write a Sestina."   MalR (48) O 78, p. 92.

CARLIN, Ritchie
"a poem for Jack."   Hand (2) 78, p. 177.

CARLISLE, C. R.
  "The Exile" (tr. of Hugo Rodriguez-Alcala). Nimrod (22:2) Spr-
    Sum 78, p. 95.
  "Farewell" (tr. of Guido Rodriguez-Alcala). Nimrod (22:2) Spr-
    Sum 78, p. 94.
  "I Have" (tr. of Elsa Wiezell). Nimrod (22:2) Spr-Sum 78,
    p. 102.
  "Small Account" (tr. of Elsa Wiezell). Nimrod (22:2) Spr-Sum
    78, p. 102.

CARLISLE, Susan
  "Fish Stories." Epoch (27:2) Wint 78, p. 145.
  "Tracking." AndR (4:2) Aut 77, p. 18.

CARLISLE, Thomas John
  "Immune to Clemency." ChrC (95:15) 26 Ap 78, p. 444.

CARLSON, Catherine Anne
  "The Temperance River Madness." Focus (12:78) N-D 77, p. 31.

CARLSON, Karen
  "Health Department Man." AntR (36:2) Spr 78, p. 193.
  "Rat House." AntR (36:2) Spr 78, p. 192.
  "Rat Purge." AntR (36:2) Spr 78, p. 194.

CARLSON, Penny L.
  "Wells County" (for my father). DacTerr (15) Wint-Spr 77-78,
    p. 31.

CARLSON, R. S.
  "Episode: September 1971." NowestR (17:1) 78, p. 68.

CARLSON, Thomas
  "Mrs. Freake and Baby Mary." WindO (32) Sum-Aut 78, p. 20.
  "Sins of the Fathers." WindO (32) Sum-Aut 78, p. 21.

CARMEN, Marilyn
  "Dislocated Thoughts." CarouselQ (3:2) Sum 78, p. 16.

CARMI, T.
  "Alone" (tr. by Marcia Falk). Hand (2) 78, p. 134.

CARMODY, Lawrence M.
  "'American Indian, Circa A. D. ,' in the Museum of Natural His-
    tory." NewOR (5:4) 78, p. 348.
  "I'll Nominate Bones." NewOR (5:4) 78, p. 345.
  "Letter." NewOR (5:4) 78, p. 346.
  "Letter in the Second Month." NewOR (5:4) 78, p. 347.
  "Of a Rabbit by the Road." NewOR (5:4) 78, p. 346.

CARNAHAN, Peter
  "Getting Somewhere. Benching in Suburban Station, Philadelphia."
    ParisR (72) Wint 77, p. 149.

CARPENTER, John R.
"The Burning." SouthwR (63:3) Sum 78, p. 281.

CARREGA, Gordon
"Uncle." ParisR (72) Wint 77, p. 115.

CARSON, Ciarán
"The Patchwork Quilt." LitR (22:2) Wint 79, p. 266.
"The Rosary Rally." LitR (22:2) Wint 79, p. 269.
"Smithfield." LitR (22:2) Wint 79, p. 268.
"Twine." LitR (22:2) Wint 79, p. 265.
"Visitors." LitR (22:2) Wint 79, p. 265.

CARTER, Jared
"The Birdstone." Chowder (10/11) Aut-Wint 78-79, p. 53.
"Dans la Foret de Fontainebleau" (pour Michel et Jacqueline).
    Ascent (3:3) 78, p. 27.
"Geodes." PraS (52:4) Wint 78-79, p. 378.
"Hard Water." Wind (29) 78, p. 8.
"Spring Night." Wind (29) 78, p. 8.

CARVER, Raymond
"Distress Sale." Kayak (49) O 78, p. 16.
"Rogue River Jet-Boat Trip Gold Beach, Oregon, July 4, 1977."
    AntR (36:3) Sum 78, p. 372.

CARY, Carl
"Impromptu #3." Wind (30) 78, p. 4.
"Rut Season." Wind (30) 78, p. 5.

CASANOVA, Beth
"Embers Everlasting." CarouselQ (3:4) Wint 78, p. 18.

CASCIO, Nina
"Imaginary Bath" (For Dulce) (tr. of Cecília Meireles). Paint
    (9/10) Spr-Aut 78, p. 45.
"Sketches" (tr. of Cecília Meireles). Paint (9/10) Spr-Aut 78,
    p. 44.

CASEY, Michael
"The Owner." BosUJ (26:2) 78, p. 39.

CASH, Nancy
"The Sun, Wonder Bread, and a Thin Slice of Moon." Stone-
    cloud (7) 78, p. 33.
"The Professor: Ten Years After." EngJ (67:5) My 78, p. 52.

CASHORALI, Peter
"me and my friend aleida." Bachy (12) Aut 78, p. 127.
"My Father." Pig (4) 78, p. 94.
"snider poem." Bachy (12) Aut 78, p. 129.
"tangalakis poem." Bachy (12) Aut 78, p. 127.

CASS, Michael
"Georgia Preacher." ChrC (95:31) 4 O 78, p. 918.

CASSIDY, John
"The Scholar Speaks, in Her Retirement." Stand (19:3) 78,
     p. 63.

CASSITY, Turner
"The Garden and the Gods." ChiR (30:1) Sum 78, p. 53.
"Relics." ChiR (30:1) Sum 78, p. 52.

CASTANO, Wilfredo Q.
"Coyote Caller." GreenfieldR (6:3/4) Spr 78, p. 86.
"Ethnic Diagnosis." GreenfieldR (6:3/4) Spr 78, p. 86.

CASTELLANO, Susan
"Rope." CarouselQ (3:3) Aut 78, p. 25.

CASTRO, Michael
"The Dust & the Sun & the Many & the One." Hand (2) 78,
     p. 34.

CASWELL, Donald
"Sketching the Cormorant." Wind (30) 78, p. 7.

CATENACCI, Edward N.
"Parallel." JnlONJP (2:1) 77, p. 8.
"Power Failure." JnlONJP (3:1) 78, p. 22.
"Return." JnlONJP (2:1) 77, p. 8.
"Those Life after Death Studies All Over TV and Reader's
     Digest." JnlONJP (2:1) 77, p. 9.

CATHERS, Ken
"Blue Heron." MalR (45) Ja 78, p. 151.
"Origin." MalR (45) Ja 78, p. 146.
"Petroglyphs." MalR (45) Ja 78, p. 150.
"Shaman." MalR (45) Ja 78, p. 147.
"Touch." MalR (45) Ja 78, p. 144.
"Way Things Are." MalR (45) Ja 78, p. 148.

CATTAFI, Bartolo
"Bormann" (tr. by Brian Swann and Ruth Feldman). MalR (46)
     Ap 78, p. 145.
"From Nyhavn" (tr. by Brian Swann and Ruth Feldman). Falcon
     (17) 78, p. 11.
"Interior" (tr. by Brian Swann and Ruth Feldman). Falcon (17)
     78, p. 12.
"A New World" (tr. by Brian Swann and Ruth Feldman).
     Columbia (2) Aut 78, p. 80.
"Peace" (tr. by Brian Swann and Ruth Feldman). MalR (46) Ap
     78, p. 144.
"Something Precise" (tr. by Lawrence R. Smith). ParisR (74)
     Aut-Wint 78, p. 110.

"Stalk" (tr. by Brian Swann and Ruth Feldman).   MalR (46) Ap
      78, p. 144.
"Wingspan" (tr. by Lawrence R. Smith).   ParisR (74) Aut-Wint
      78, p. 109.

CATTONAR, Joanna
    "Calligraphy." Hand (2) 78, p. 166.

CATULLUS
    "Carmen Ci" (tr. by Frederick Morgan).   GreenfieldR (6:3/4)
      Spr 78, p. 4.
    "Carmen LXXV." SouthernR (14:2) Spr 78, p. 330.
    "Carmina Catulli IV, V, VI" (tr. by Peter Laurie).   St. Ar (5:1)
      Aut-Wint 78, p. 123.

CAUBLE, Don
    "The Big Iron Gate." PoNow (19) 78, p. 46.

CAVALIERO, Glen
    "In Cromwell's County." Stand (19:2) 78, p. 2.

CECIL, Richard
    "Addenda to Schedual C Form 1040." Epoch (27:3) Spr 78,
      p. 226.
    "Almost a Love Poem in Winter!" Epoch (27:3) Spr 78, p. 228.
    "Apology." AmerPoR (7:4) Jl-Ag 78, p. 48.
    "California Drive." Epoch (27:3) Spr 78, p. 227.
    "Love Poem with One True Thing In It." Sam (65) 78, p. 56.
    "The Secret." Epoch (27:3) Spr 78, p. 229.

CEDRINS, Inara
    "Let Me Give You Some Black Fur." Nimrod (22:2) Spr-Sum 78,
      p. 11.
    "White Nights" (tr. of Herta Krauja). FourQt (27:4) Sum 78,
      p. 35.

CELAN
    from Schneepart (tr. by R. Sieburth and S. W. DeRachewiltz).
      St. AR (5:1) Aut-Wint 78, p. 55.

CELAYA, Gabriel
    "Many Thanks" (to Rafael Alberti for the gift of Ora Maritima)
      (w. Amparo Gastón, tr. by Lucia Graves). MalR (47) Jl 78,
      p. 110.

CERVO, Nathan
    "The Bicyclist." EnPas (7) 78, p. 28.
    "Under the Motionless Chandelier." EnPas (7) 78, p. 26.

CHACE, Sarah
    "Spring in Philadelphia." HarvAd (111:4) My 78, p. 18.

CHADWICK, Jerah
    "The Country of Water." CutB (11) Aut-Wint 78, p. 72.

"From an Album." CutB (11) Aut-Wint 78, p. 71.
"From the Gypsy." CutB (10) Spr-Sum 78, p. 30.

CHAET, Eric
     "Another Cafe." Vaga (28) Aut 78, p. 36.
     "Training." Vaga (28) Aut 78, p. 37.

CHAFFIN, Lillie D.
     "Faith." Poem (32) Mr 78, p. 12.
     "Inflated by the Need." Poem (32) Mr 78, p. 10.

CHAMBERS, Craig
     "Conversion." Wind (30) 78, p. 47.

CHAMBERS, Leland H.
     "The Cave (To Donald Sutherland) (tr. of Octavio Paz).   DenQ
          (13:3) Aut 78, p. 4.
     "Cleopompus and Heliodemus" (tr. of Rubén Darío).   DenQ (13:4)
          Wint 79, p. 54.

CHANDONNET, Ann
     "Snow." WormR (68) 77, p. 113.

CHANDRA, G. S. Sharat
     "The Ghost of Meaning." ModernPS (9:2) Aut 78, p. 121.
     "Let Us Not List." ModernPS (9:2) Aut 78, p. 121.
     "The New Church." PartR (45:4) 78, p. 588.
     "Preparations." PartR (45:4) 78, p. 589.

CH'ANG Chien
     "Staying with Wang Ch'ang-Ling" (tr. by Robert Branham and
          Daniel Stevenson). Nimrod (22:2) Spr-Sum 78, p. 109.

CHANG, Diana
     "Farming." NewL (45:2) Wint 78, p. 96.
     "Through a Narrow Window." NewL (45:2) Wint 78, p. 95.
     "Transfiguration." NewL (45:2) Wint 78, p. 97.

CHANTIKIAN, Kosrot
     "The Poet & the Crow." Bleb/Ark (13) 78, p. 29.

CHAPMAN, Diane
     "Snake." Smudge (1) Spr 78, p. 13.
     "The Spite Wall." CarouselQ (3:3) Aut 78, p. 3.

CHAPPELL, Fred
     "The Autumn Bleat of the Weathervane Trombone." SouthernPR
          (18:2) Aut 78, p. 45.
     "The Peaceable Kingdom of Emerald Windows." Epoch (27:2)
          Wint 78, p. 118.
     "Remembering Wind Mountain at Sunset." CarolQ (30:3) Aut 78,
          p. 36.

CHASE, Joel
"Snowbound. " Epos (27:1) 77, p. 9.
"The Waitress. " Epos (27:1) 77, p. 9.

CHASIN, Helen
"Before the Power Failure, New York, July 1977. " Poetry
(133:2) N 78, p. 78.
"Changes. " Poetry (133:2) N 78, p. 77.
"Poem Incorporating a Phrase from a Poem by Tom Lux Begin-
ning with a Random Phrase from Coleridge. " Poetry (132:2)
My 78, p. 90.

CHATAIN, Robert
"In Amundson's Tent. " LittleM (11:3) Aut 77, p. 63.

CHATFIELD, Hale
"Cruising at about Forty. " PoNow (19) 78, p. 45.
"Essai. " Epos (27:2) 77, p. 4.
"Pseudopoem. " HiramPoR (24) Spr-Sum 78, p. 8.

CHATTERTON, Valerie
"Miniature from the Life of Ambrose Hobbs. " MalR (46) Ap 78,
p. 105.

CHAVES, Anna Caraveli
Eight Greek Songs (tr.). Montra (4) 78, p. 68.

CHAVES, Jonathan
"I Get Up from My Sickbed and Sit by Myself" (tr. of Yüan Hung-
tao). VirQR (54:2) Spr 78, p. 335.
"Mid-Autumn Moon" (tr. of Su Shi Su Tung-P'o). VirQR (54:2)
Spr 78, p. 333.
Nine poems (tr. of Yün Shou-p'ing). Hudson (31:4) Wint 78-79,
p. 605.
"On Hearing That a Girl" (tr. of Yüan Hung-tao). VirQR (54:2)
Spr 78, p. 336.
"Pei-Ming Cemetery" (tr. of Yüan Hung-tao). VirQR (54:2) Spr
78, p. 335.
"A Record of My Trip to Mount Shê" (tr. of Yüan Hung-to).
VirQR (54:2) Spr 78, p. 337.
Ten poems and a letter (tr. of Yuan Hung-tao). Montra (4) 78,
p. 43.
"Twenty-First Day of the Seventh Month" (tr. of Yüan Hung-tao).
VirQR (54:2) Spr 78, p. 334.

CHERNER, Anne
"The Gymnast. " PoetryNW (19:3) Aut 78, p. 27.

CHERNOFF, Maxine
"The Boat. " ChiR (30:1) Sum 78, p. 32.
"Kill Yourself with an Objet d'Art. " Sky (7/8) Spr 78, p. 66.
"The Meaning of Anxiety. " ChiR (30:1) Sum 79, p. 33.

CHERRY, Kelly
"God Slang." FourQt (28:1) Aut 78, p. 38.
"Heartwood: A Diary." SouthernR (14:3) Sum 78, p. 500.
"The Lonely Music." SouthernR (14:3) Sum 78, p. 502.
"Night Air." Chowder (10/11) Aut-Wint 78-79, p. 42.
"On a Sunny Slope." FourQt (28:1) Aut 78, p. 40.
"Plans for a House in Latvia." Chowder (10/11) Aut-Wint 78-
    79, p. 43.
"Resurrection Quatrain." FourQt (27:4) Sum 78, p. 43.
"The Rose." SouthernR (14:3) Sum 78, p. 501.
"Triplet of the Poet's Longing." FourQt (28:1) Aut 78, p. 40.
"Voices." FourQt (28:1) Aut 78, p. 40.

CHIA Tao
"Recluse Unfound" (tr. by Robert Branham and Daniel Stevenson).
    Nimrod (22:2) Spr-Sum 78, p. 108.

CHILDRESS, William
"The Werewolf." PoNow (19) 78, p. 24.

CHIN, David P.
"Anima." StoneC (78:3) Aut 78, p. 10.

CHINMOY, Sri
"The Boat of Silver Light." Stonecloud (7) 78, p. 142.
"The Boat of Silver Light." Wind (28) 78, p. 17.
"O My Poem." Stonecloud (7) 78, p. 10.

CHOYCE, Lesley W.
"The Only Poem I Ever Wrote about Paris." JnlONJP (3:1) 78,
    p. 20.

CHRISTENSEN, Paul
"The Clothes." CEACritic (40:4) My 78, p. 25.
"Everyday I Wake...." CEACritic (40:4) My 78, p. 25.
"Lunch." CEACritic (40:4) My 78, p. 24.
"The Simple Is More Difficult." CEACritic (40:4) My 78, p. 25.
"The Sun Shines...." CEACritic (40:4) My 78, p. 26.
"The Thrill of Doing Something Twice." CEACritic (40:4) My
    78, p. 24.
"When Will I Ever Go Down Again to Live in My Life?"
    CEACritic (40:4) My 78, p. 26.

CHRISTENSON, Kathryn
"Dark Advent." ChrC (95:41) 13 D 78, p. 1204.
"Sarah Speaks." ChrC (95:15) 26 Ap 78, p. 438.

CHRISTINA, Martha
"Delivery." Tendril (3) Aut 78, p. 17.
"Ektachrome." Tendril (3) Aut 78.
"The Etiquette of Clay." YellowBR (10) 78, p. 17.
"First of the Year." Tendril (3) Aut 78, p. 16.

"For Rachel, Late in August." Tendril (2) Spr-Sum 78.
"Listen." Tendril (2) Spr-Sum 78.

CHRISTMAN, Berniece Bunn
"Night Train." Comm (105:11) 26 My 78, p. 327.
"Sewing Kit." LadHJ (95:9) S 78, p. 184.

CHURCHILL, Marilyn
"Harvest." AAR (28) 78, p. 87.
"Scroll Painting." AAR (28) 78, p. 88.
"Witch's Complaint." AAR (28) 78, p. 87.

CHURRY, Craig
"Letter to Bernheimer from Back Scottsbluff." MidwQ (19:4)
    Sum 78, p. 370.
"My Cousin Who Dies Quick in the Night" (for William Ebling,
    in memoriam). MidwQ (19:4) Sum 78, p. 371.
"Swapping Oranges." MidwQ (19:4) Sum 78, p. 372.

CIARDI, John
"Censorship." Poetry (132:2) My 78, p. 101.
"For Instance." Poetry (132:5) Ag 78, p. 271.
"The Lungfish." Poetry (132:5) Ag 78, p. 269.
"Machine." Poetry (132:5) Ag 78, p. 272.

CICCONE, James
"The Other Day...." GreenfieldR (6:3/4) Spr 78, p. 69.

CIROCCO, William
"Headlong." Paunch (52) O 78, p. 79.
"On a Mother and Child by Picasso." Paunch (52) O 78, p. 81.
"A Song of DNA." Paunch (52) O 78, p. 80.

CITINO, David
"Breathmaker." GRR (9:2) 78, p. 127.
"Challenging Situation No. 33: The Feast." HolCrit (15:5) D 78,
    p. 15.
"The Flight Back." Epos (27:1) 77, p. 29.
"Knots." SouthernPR (18:1) Spr 78, p. 36.
"Mario Lanza Defeats Luciano Pararotti in a Tenor Competition
    Held on a Turntable in My Father's Living Room." Aspen
    (5) Spr 78, p. 57.
"The Poem Trap." PoNow (20) 78, p. 5.
"Two." Box (6) Aut 77, p. 13.
"The Vigil: A Folk Tale." GRR (9:2) 78, p. 128.
"Voyeurs." PoNow (20) 78, p. 5.
"When Clichés Collide: or, the Galaxy from Outer Space,
    Chapter One." KanQ (10:2) Spr 78, p. 120.

CLAIRE, William
"Late in the Century." Confr (17) Aut-Wint 79, p. 36.

CLAMPITT, Amy
"The Sun Underfoot among the Sundews." NewYorker (54:26) 14
Ag 78, p. 32.

CLAMURRO, William
"Five Poems for Rachel." Pan (19) 77, p. 51.

CLARE, Josephine
"Afternoon." Tele (13) 77.
"Alone with Double Bed." Tele (13) 77.
"Call Any Tree by Any Name You Want." NewL (45:2) Wint 78,
p. 37.
"Elevenses." Tele (13) 77.
"Fine Body." NewL (44:3) Spr 78, p. 74.
"Flying, First Time, into Mother's Arms." NewL (44:3) Spr 78,
p. 73.
"I Have Written to California." NewL (45:2) Wint 78, p. 38.
"In Anticipation & Delight." NewL (45:2) Wint 78, p. 36.
"Is the Grass Biased." NewL (45:2) Wint 78, p. 35.
"Morning." Tele (13) 77.
"once I wore leaves." Tele (13) 77.
"The Party." Tele (13) 77.
"Very Much So." Tele (13) 77.

CLARK, Carole
"Williams Bay." EngJ (67:5) My 78, p. 56.

CLARK, Gerald
"desperation." AAR (28) 78, p. 93.
"she wanted me." AAR (28) 78, p. 92.

CLARK, Kevin
"Berkeley Rose Garden." WindO (33) Aut-Wint 78-79.

CLARK, Martha
"Cheerleader." Aspect (71) Ap-Je 77, p. 42.

CLARK, Melissa
"The Trees Above Town." Pig (4) 78, p. 84.

CLARK, Patricia
"Holding On." CutB (11) Aut-Wint 78, p. 53.

CLARK, Tom
"The Big Cigars." PoNow (19) 78, p. 29.
"So Long." PoNow (19) 78, p. 29.

CLAUSEN, Christopher
"Four Carolina Elegies" (In Memory of Paul Chernin, M.D.,
1942-1974). CarolQ (30:2) Spr-Sum 78, p. 61.

CLAUSEN, Jan
"The Transplant." GreenfieldR (6:3/4) Spr 78, p. 118.

CLEWELL, David
   "The Hardrock Kid." Stonecloud (7) 78, p. 49.
   from Heroes: "The Distance." Chowder (10/11) Aut-Wint 78-
      79, p. 66.
   "Losing My Voice." Chowder (10/11) Aut-Wint 78-79, p. 64.

CLIFTON, Merritt
   "Heritage." Sam (69) 78, p. 39.
   "I Said, Love Thy Neighbor." Sam (69) 78, p. 49.
   "Old Profession." Zahir (9) 77, p. 14.

CLIFTON, Harry
   "Ordinands." Stand (19:2) 78, p. 19.

CLINE, Charles
   "Plums." Wind (29) 78, p. 10.

CLINTON, D.
   from Inca Memoris/Book 6. MinnR (NS10) Spr 78, p. 63.

CLINTON, Dorothy Randle
   "Ascending Line." CarouselQ (3:3) Aut 78, p. 11.

CLINTON, Robert
   "Frog Song." BelPoJ (28:3) Spr 78, p. 18.

CLOCKADALE, Jill
   "Anniversary." CentR (22:2) Spr 78, p. 182.
   "The Archivist." CentR (22:2) Spr 78, p. 183.
   "Change of Venue." 13thM (4:1) 78, p. 31.

CLOSSON, Kay
   "it's your birthday." SmPd (42) Wint 78, p. 25.

CLOUTIER, David
   "The Birth of Fire." Bleb/Ark (13) 78, p. 54.
   from Dieu Transparent: "Less the Bird" (tr. of Claude Esteban).
      Durak (1) 78, p. 50.
   from Dieu Transparent: "Free the Path, Leave" (tr. of Claude
      Esteban). Durak (1) 78, p. 49.
   from Dieu Transparent: "Stone" (tr. of Calude Esteban). Durak
      (1) 78, p. 48.
   "Eagle Song." Bleb/Ark (13) 78, p. 54.
   "Wives of the Wind" (tr. of Jean Follain). WebR (4:1) Spr 78,
      p. 32.

COAKLEY, William Leo
   "The Marriage of Dionysus and Apollo." ParisR (72) Wint 77,
      p. 111.

COBIN, Susan
   "Wandering Jew." CimR (42) Ja 78, p. 28.

COCCIMIGLIO, Vic
"Conception." ParisR (73) Spr-Sum 78, p. 41.

CODRESCU, Andrei
"A Human Touch Misunderstood." Tele (13) 77.
"The Life on Film of St. Theresa." Tele (13) 77.

COE, Elizabeth
"Going Home Round-About." AmerPoR (7:3) My-Je 78, p. 41.
"Mountain Lady." AmerPoR (7:3) My-Je 78, p. 41.
"Rodin's Balzac in the Museum of Modern Art Garden."
    AmerPoR (7:3) My-Je 78, p. 41.

COFFIN, Lyn
"Dante" (tr. of Anna Akhmatova). MichQR (17:4) Aut 77, p. 461.
"M. B. (Mikhail Bulgakov)" (tr. of Anna Akhmatova). MichQR
    (17:4) Aut 78, p. 460.
"The Muse" (tr. of Anna Akhmatova). MichQR (17:4) Aut 78,
    p. 459.
"Voronezh" (to Osip Mandelstam) (tr. of Anna Akhmatova).
    MichQR (17:4) Sum 78, p. 461.

COGGESHALL, Rosanne
"After Reading Holy the Firm for Annie Dillard." Epoch (28:1)
    Aut 78, p. 37.
"March 2." Epoch (28:1) Aut 78, p. 39.

COHEN, Gerald
"Hinging." BallSUF (19:4) Aut 78, p. 40.
"Sabbatical." BallSUF (19:4) Aut 78, p. 27.

COHEN, Marc
"Stairway Beach." PartR (45:3) 78, p. 442.

COHEN, Marty
"Doing 55." LittleM (11:3) Aut 77, p. 10.

COHEN, Marvin
"Inside the Head." Hand (2) 78, p. 139.

COHEN, Richard
"White Cranes." Wind (29) 78, p. 11.
"To the Muse: Our Lady of the Highways." Wind (29) 78, p. 11.

COHEN, Stephen P.
"Friends and Strangers." Box (6) Aut 77, p. 15.

COLBERT, Alison
"He Said He Was Leaving for Phoenix." Zahir (9) 77, p. 29.
"Walker Evans" (for Robert Moskowitz). Zahir (9) 77, p. 30.

COLBY, Joan
"The Beaten Woman." PikeF (1) Spr 78, p. 26.

"Black and Silver." WindO (31) Wint-Spr 78, p. 30.
"The Blue Dress of Water." EnPas (7) 78, p. 30.
"Clio Invents Her Textbook." HolCrit (15:3) Je 78, p. 15.
"DreamLand." NewRena (10) 78, p. 14.
"An Ecclesiastical Visit." Stonecloud (7) 78, p. 69.
"The Fairy Tale." NewRena (10) 78, p. 13.
"Fractures." NewRivR (2:2) 78, p. 43.
"Getting Out." Stonecloud (7) 78, p. 72.
"Immigrants" (for C. Z.). Epoch (27:2) Wint 78, p. 176.
"Inscape." Pan (19) 77, p. 45.
"The Loss of Rich Stones." StoneC (78:2) Spr 78, p. 12.
"Manual for Dexterity." Tendril (2) Spr-Sum 78.
"The Mint." ColEng (40:3) N 78, p. 293.
"My Aunt's Room." Tendril (2) Spr-Sum 78.
"Octopus Lady." Zahir (9) 77, p. 8.
"What You Remember of Me." Nor (8) Aut 78, p. 28.

COLE, B. H.
"The Scandal." SoDakR (16:4) Wint 78, p. 61.

COLE, E. R.
"Later-Day Rites at Remembrance Rock, Galesburg." Wind (30)
    78, p. 3.

COLE, James
"Junkyard." SouthernPR (18:2) Aut 78, p. 27.
"Sonic Boom: Cape Hatteras." SouthernPR (18:2) Aut 78, p. 27.

COLE, Peter
"Reason for Revolution." Box (7) Spr 78, p. 9.
"The Young Priest." Box (7) Spr 78, p. 8.

COLEMAN, E. L. (see Jabari MWENEA)

COLEMAN, Wanda
"Central Avenue Soul Train Shuffle." Bachy (11) Spr 78, p. 97.
"Frustrations (Poem 1)." Bachy (11) Spr 78, p. 97.
"The Lady with Bougainvillea in Her Eyes" (for Kate Braverman).
    Bachy (11) Spr 78, p. 94.
"Male Order Catalog." Bachy (11) Spr 78, p. 93.
"The Silver Satin Nigga' Rides--" (for Al & Pete who never see
    anymore). Bachy (11) Spr 78, p. 97.
"Sometimes I Have a Song for My Mommy and Daddy." Bachy
    (11) Spr 78, p. 95.
"Stephen & Lady as Seen Thru Windows." Bachy (11) Spr 78,
    p. 94.

COLICCHIO, Joe
"Sweet Sleep." Aspect (71) Ap-Je 77, p. 39.

COLLIER, Michael
"Marriage Story." PoetryNW (19:4) Wint 78-79, p. 12.
"Rodin." NewOR (5:4) 78, p. 319.

COLLINGWOOD, Harris
"Flight." HarvAd (112:1) D 78, p. 5.

COLLINS, Billy
"All Ears." Field (19) Aut 78, p. 54.
"The Books of Boyhood." Field (19) Aut 78, p. 54.
"The Games." ParisR (72) Wint 77, p. 147.
"Names." WormR (68) 77, p. 109.
"RCA Victor." ParisR (72) Wint 77, p. 148.
"Silver Dollars." WormR (68) 77, p. 110.
"The Sphere." Field (19) Aut 78, p. 56.

COLLINS, Denise
"Lilacs Every Spring." US1 (11) Aut 78, p. 5.

COLLINS, Martha
"First Words" (for A. W. Essick [1871-1945]). Agni (8) 78,
    p. 99.
"Joanie." PoetryNW (19:3) Aut 78, p. 36.
"Retreat." MichQR (17:2) Spr 78, p. 195.
"Trees in Night Rain." Bits (8) Jl 78.
"We Come to New Hampshire and Look What Happens." Comm
    (105:2) 20 Ja 78, p. 54.
"When She Thinks of It." AndR (5:2) Spr 78, p. 88.

COLLOM, Jack
"joe namath leaves the stadium." Tele (14) 78.
"Robert Schumann lying on a blue-covered couch" (w. John
    Moulder and Mara Meshak). Tele (14) 78.

COLT, George Howe
"Over the Rainbow." Shen (29:4) Sum 78, p. 41.

COLVER, Russell
"Post Operative." SewanR (86:2) Spr 78, p. 263.

COMPTON, Gayle
"Nearing Richwood, W. Va.--U. S. 39." Wind (31) 78, p. 6.
"Walking Ties in Late Summer." Wind (31) 78, p. 6.

CONANT-BISSELL, Jane
"The Lilacs and the Roses" (tr. of Louis Aragon). CalQ (13/14)
    Spr-Sum 78, p. 111.
"Milton's Wife on Her Twenty-Third Birthday." CalQ (13/14)
    Spr-Sum 78, p. 106.

CONNAH, Roger
"The Extraterritorial Beard." PartR (45:4) 78, p. 590.
"The Opera: alfresco." PartR (45:4) 78, p. 590.

CONNELLAN, Leo
"Scott Huff." PoNow (19) 78, p. 42.

CONNER, Shirley
"Living in the Woods." QW (5) Wint 78, p. 37.

CONNOLLY, J. F.
"The Young Girl Who Came with Poems." Tendril (1) Wint 77-
78.

CONNOR, Tony
"An Anonymous Painting." ColEng (39:5) Ja 78, p. 545.
"In Crumpsall Library." ColEng (39:5) Ja 78, p. 543.
"A Late Caller." ColEng (39:5) Ja 78, p. 546.
"A Photograph of My Mother with Her Favourite Lodger."
ColEng (39:5) Ja 78, p. 542.
"A Picture of R. C. in a Prospect of Blossom." ColEng (39:5)
Ja 78, p. 541.
"Things Divested." ColEng (39:5) Ja 78, p. 547.

CONOVER, Roger L.
"Knowing Your Goats." Epoch (27:2) Wint 78, p. 132.
"Windfall." SoDakR (16:2) Sum 78, p. 19.

CONSTANTINE, David
"The belly: a big craw." Stand (18:4) 77, p. 10.
"In Memoriam 8571 Private J. W. Gleave who was at Montauben,
Trônes Wood and Guillemont." Stand (19:4) 78, p. 12.

CONTOSKI, Victor
"Anonymous Voice" (tr. of Tadeusz Rozewicz). Hand (2) 78,
p. 91.
"Cardinals." HangL (33) Sum 78, p. 25.
"Chanute, Kansas." ThRiPo (11/12) 78, p. 24.
"The Constellations of Autumn." PoNow (19) 78, p. 23.
"The Enemy." PoNow (19) 78, p. 41.
"Hatred." ThRiPo (11/12) 78, p. 23.
"Meadowlark." HangL (33) Sum 78, p. 26.
"Night on the Prairie" (for Harley Elliott). HangL (33) Sum 78,
p. 23.
"November 26." NewL (45:2) Wint 78, p. 90.
"Teddy Bear." NewL (45:2) Wint 78, p. 91.
"Unhappy Couple." NewL (45:2) Wint 78, p. 90.
"Wherever I go in the world." HangL (33) Sum 78, p. 24.

COOK, Paul H.
"The Gangsters." WormR (72) 78, p. 147.
"Illusion." Agni (9) 78, p. 101.
"Jody Clone." Zahir (9) 77, p. 28.
"One More Time." Tendril (2) Spr-Sum 78.
"Pique." WormR (72) 78, p. 147.
"Things to Do with a Woman: #2 The Laundry." WormR (72)
78, p. 146.
"Uncle Jerry." Tendril (1) Wint 77-78.

COOKE, Robert
"At the Pensao Magestic, Brazil." SouthernPR (18:2) Aut 78, p. 53.

COOLEY, Peter
"Another August." Nowest (17:1) 78, p. 31.
"Aravat." GeoR (32:3) Aut 78, p. 571.
"Calling." OP (25) Spr-Sum 78, p. 59.
"Drinker's Song." ConcPo (11:1) Spr 78, p. 46.
Eight poems. ThRiPo (11/12) 78, pp. 10-16.
"Engorgement." PoNow (19) 78, p. 37.
"Entering Radiance." OP (25) Spr-Sum 78, p. 60.
"Little Love Letter." ConcPo (11:1) Spr 78, p. 45.
"Locales." SouthernPR (18:1) Spr 78, p. 73.
"Mid-Point." OP (25) Spr-Sum 78, p. 66.
"Mute's Song." PoetryNW (19:2) Sum 78, p. 14.
"The Poem." WebR (4:2) Aut 78, p. 58.
"Saint-Breaking: The Process of Bronze." SouthwR (63:1) Wint
      78, p. 41.
"Song of the Hermit." PoetryNW (19:2) Sum 78, p. 15.
"Song of the Idiot." MissouriR (2:1) Aut 78, p. 31.
"Touching It." GreenfieldR (6:3/4) Spr 78, p. 53.
"Waking In It." OP (25) Spr-Sum 78, p. 63.
"The Word Continuing." OP (25) Spr-Sum 78, p. 61.
"You Know This." OP (25) Spr-Sum 78, p. 62.

COONEY, Bill
"I Dream Against Reality." JnlONJP (3:1) 78, p. 21.
"Idyll." JnlONJP (2:2) 77, p. 24.

COOPER, Charles
"Janitor." SouthernPR (18:1) Spr 78, p. 58.

COOPER, Dennis
Fifteen poems. Bachy (13) Aut-Wint 78-79, p. 74.
"High School Basketball" (for Danny Wilde). PoNow (20) 78,
      p. 5.

COOPER, Jane
"The Flashboat." NewYorker (53:47) 9 Ja 78, p. 34.

COOPER, M. Truman
"In the Name of Peace." Zahir (9) 77, p. 15.
"I've Got These Old Shoes God." WormR (69) 78, p. 36.
"Thigh Women." WormR (69) 78, p. 36.

COOPER, T. D.
"Glorious Morning." CarouselQ (3:1) Spr 78, p. 21.

CORDING, Robert
"Conjuring." AmerS (47:2) Spr 78, p. 190.

COREY, Chet
"We Travel Both Ways Now." KanQ (10:4) Aut 78, p. 84.

COREY, Stephen
"Gifts." Bleb/Ark (13) 78, p. 63.
"Nude Man Tosses Meat from Truck." Bleb/Ark (13) 78, p. 60.

"The Poetry of American Political Tracts" (for E. D. and W. W.).
Bleb/Ark (13) 78, p. 62.
"Praying Mantises. " AmerPoR (7:6) N-D 78, p. 35.
"Understanding King Lear. " AmerPoR (7:6) N-D 78, p. 35.

CORN, Alfred
"Alcaics: Remembering Mykinai. " Poetry (131:5) F 78, p. 270.
"Audience. " Poetry (131:5) F 78, p. 267.
"Moving: New York-New Haven Line. " Shen (29:4) Sum 78,
p. 82.
"Prime Minister in Retirement. " Poetry (131:5) F 78, p. 268.
"Repertory. " Poetry (131:5) F 78, p. 269.
"Shores. " Nat (227:10) 30 S 78, p. 314.
"Tanagra. " Poetry (131:5) F 78, p. 271.
"The Village" (For James Merrill). Nat (226:7) 25 F 78, p. 220.
"Winter Stars. " NewYorker (53:48) 16 Ja 78, p. 29.

CORNELL, Tad
"On Safari for Clitoris. " Aspen (5) Spr 78, p. 10.
"Panic on White. " Aspen (5) Spr 78, p. 10.

CORNWALL, S. E.
"Memories of the Peach, or Before I Got to the Pit. " CarouselQ
(3:4) Wint 78, p. 22.

CORRENTE, Linda
"Sacraments. " LittleM (11:3) Aut 77, p. 66.

CORRIGAN, M. T.
"The Hunchback of California. " PoNow (20) 78, p. 46.

CORRIGAN, Paul
"At the Grave of the Unknown Riverdriver. " PoetryNW (19:4)
Wint 78-79, p. 38.
"Katahdin Falls at Night. " Tendril (1) Wint 77-78.
"Notes on Thoreau's Maine Journals. " SoDakR (16:3) Sum 78,
p. 12.

COSTAKIS, Tony
"Crazy John died. " SeC (5:2) 78, p. 45.
"Duane. " SeC (5:2) 78, p. 46.

COSTELLO, James
"Of Man and Bird. " EnPas (7) 78, p. 24.

COSTELLO, Karen L.
"The Crush. " CarouselQ (3:4) Wint 78, p. 31.

COSTLEY, Bill
from War Stories: "09/17/75 rev 1. " Aspect (71) Ap-Je 77,
p. 24.
from War Stories: "Soldiers (2) 09/29/75. " Aspect (71) Ap-Je
77, p. 26.

from War Stories: "Soldiers (6) 11/06/75." <u>Aspect</u> (71) Ap-Je
77, p. 27.

COTRELL, Gretchen
"Barabbas the Revolutionary and the Cleft-Palate Orphan."
<u>Stonecloud</u> (7) 78, p. 99.
"Los Angeles Moon, Patent Pending." <u>Stonecloud</u> (7) 78, p. 30.
"Whiteblackbird" (to R. B.). <u>Stonecloud</u> (7) 78, p. 67.

COTTER, Holland
"Etruscan Tomb Painting." <u>Agni</u> (9) 78, p. 97.

COUNCILMAN, Emily Sargent
"After Golgotha." <u>ChrC</u> (95:11) 29 Mr 78, p. 332.

COURSEN, Herb
"Below Hope Farm: 5 July." <u>SmPd</u> (44) Aut 78, p. 31.
"Maine: 4th of July." <u>SmPd</u> (43) Spr 78, p. 8.

COURT, Wesli
"Spring Song." <u>CimR</u> (45) O 78, p. 17.

COUTERMASH, John H.
"Writer." <u>Smudge</u> (1) Spr 78, p. 7.

COWING, Sheila
"August." <u>StoneC</u> (78:3) Aut 78, p. 9.
"Bread Tins." <u>StoneC</u> (78:3) Aut 78, p. 8.

COWLEY, Malcolm
"Prayer on All Saint's Day." <u>SewanR</u> (86:4) Aut 78, p. 563.

COX, Elizabeth
"The Roosting Tree." <u>SouthernPR</u> (18:2) Aut 78, p. 42.

CRAMER, Steven
"A Cold Day in July." <u>Agni</u> (9) 78, p. 44.
"Pentimento." <u>Poetry</u> (131:6) Mr 78, p. 327.

CRASE, Douglas
"The Day Line." <u>Poetry</u> (131:5) F 78, p. 279.
"Gunpowder Morning in a Gray Room." <u>Poetry</u> (131:5) F 78,
p. 280.
"The House at Sagg." <u>Poetry</u> (131:5) F 78, p. 281.
"There Is No Real Peace in the World." <u>AmerPoR</u> (7:2) Mr-Ap
78, p. 48.

CRAVEN, Robert Liddell
"Lines." <u>Poem</u> (33) Jl 78, p. 52.
"Nothing the Same." <u>Poem</u> (33) Jl 78, p. 49.
"Which Point of View." <u>Poem</u> (33) Jl 78, p. 50.

CRAWFORD, Jack, Jr.
"'Good Day' to Killers." <u>PoetryNW</u> (19:2) Sum 78, p. 45.

CRAWFORD, Tom
"Aunt Mary." NewL (45:1) Aut 78, p. 13.
"Count Us" (For Gary Thompson). NewL (45:1) Aut 78, p. 13.

CRECELIUS, Bruce
"When a poet walks through a docile wood." EngJ (67:5) My 78,
p. 50.

CREELEY, Robert
"Thirty poems." Bound (6:3/7:1) Spr-Aut 78, p. 80.

CREIGHTON, Dean
"Bullshit of the Mostly-Likely." Smudge (1) Spr 78, p. 10.

CREIGHTON, John
"Invocation/Lines to the Wind." Wind (30) 78, p. 8.
"On Criticizing a Farmer for His Lack of Imagination." NewOR
(6:1) 78, p. 68.

CREWE, Jennifer
"Growing." OhioR (19:3) Aut 78, p. 100.
"Houses." OhioR (19:3) Aut 78, p. 101.

CRIPPS, Jo
"April's Mouth." NorthSR (8) Aut-Wint 78-79, p. 41.
"The Garden." NorthSR (8) Aut-Wint 78-79, p. 40.
"The Mothers' Clinic." NorthSR (8) Aut-Wint 78-79, p. 41.

CROBAUGH, Emma
"Hear the New Sounds." CarouselQ (3:3) Aut 78, p. 1.

CROW, Mary
"Forgetfulness" (tr. of Alfonsina Storni, w. Marion Hodapp).
WebR (4:1) Spr 78, p. 12.
"Loneliness" (tr. of Alfonsina Storni, w. Marion Hodapp). WebR
(4:1) Spr 78, p. 11.
"The Moment" (tr. of Alfonsina Storni, w. Marion Hodapp).
WebR (4:1) Spr 78, p. 10.
"On the Other Hand." Aspen (6) Aut 78, p. 77.
"The Pyramid at Cuernavaca." Aspen (6) Aut 78, p. 78.
"Words to My Mother" (tr. of Alfonsina Storni, w. Marion
Hodapp). WebR (4:1) Spr 78, p. 9.

CROWE, Ronald
"Inventory." ParisR (73) Spr-Sum 78, p. 151.

CRUM, Shutta
"Lightning Storm." AAR (28) 78, p. 38.
"wild hyacinths." AAR (28) 78, p. 37.

CSOORI, Sándor
"A Föltámadás elsö Pillanatai." ChiR (30:2) Aut 78, p. 16.
"Afternoon of Grand Old Men" (tr. by Jascha Kessler). Nimrod

(22:2) Spr-Sum 78, p. 101.
"Anniversary" (tr. by Nicholas Kolumban). GreenfieldR (6:3/4)
     Spr 78, p. 6.
"A Bullet" (tr. by Nicholas Kolumban). GreenfieldR (6:3/4) Spr
     78, p. 7.
"The First Moments of Resurrection" (tr. by Nicholas Kolumban).
     ChiR (30:2) Aut 78, p. 17.
"Imploring Words of Friendship to the Second Person" (tr. by
     Nicholas Kolumban). NewL (45:1) Aut 78, p. 40.
"My Beast" (tr. by Nicholas Kolumban). AntR (36:2) Spr 78,
     p. 195.
"Wait Until It's Evening" (tr. by Nicholas Kolumban). NewL
     (45:1) Aut 78, p. 41.

CULBERTSON, Nancy
"Lemminkainen's Journey." StoneC (78:2) Spr 78, p. 23.

CULLEN, John C.
"Living in the Blue Room." Wind (29) 78, p. 13.

CULLEN, Paula B.
"Acrobatics." Poem (32) Mr 78, p. 44.
"A Case of Museum Anxiety." CimR (43) Ap 78, p. 21.
"The Embalmer." CimR (43) Ap 78, p. 28.
"4½ Friends." Poem (32) Mr 78, p. 45.
"Papa in the Field." Poem (32) Mr 78, p. 43.
"Photo Snap." JnlONJP (2:2) 77, p. 15.
"Possession." JnlONJP (2:2) 77, p. 14.

CULLINANE, R. H.
"Satin Tufts and Survivors." JnlONJP (2:2) 77, p. 20.
"Water Fountain." JnlONJP (2:2) 77, p. 20.

CUMMING, Robert
"Home Again." SouthernPR (18:1) Spr 78, p. 37.

CUMMINGS, Dede
"Poem Written at Home on My Mother's Typewriter." Madem
     (84:11) N 78, p. 136.

CUMMINGS, Melissa
"Cats + Sand." DeKalb (11:3/4) Spr-Sum 78, p. 32.
Nine poems. Bachy (12) Aut 78, p. 131.

CUMMINGS, Peter
"Bicycle Poem Six: Instantology." GreenfieldR (6:3/4) Spr 78,
     p. 144.

CUNNINGHAM, J. V.
"The Metaphysical Amorist." NewRep (178:6) 11 F 78, p. 38.
     Correction.
Nine poems. NewRep (178:4) 28 Ja 78, p. 30.

CURRIE, John
"Old Woman's Morning Through the Yard." GreenfieldR (6:3/4)
Spr 78, p. 112.
"The Still Life...." GreenfieldR (6:3/4) Spr 78, p. 112.

CURRY, David
"Abiding." Northeast (3:5) Spr-Sum 78, p. 6.
"Ars Poetica (overheard)." GreenfieldR (6:3/4) Spr 78, p. 63.
"At Howard Johnson's." Northeast (3:5) Spr-Sum 78, p. 6.
"Child in the World." Northeast (3:5) Spr-Sum 78, p. 8.
"From Childhood." Northeast (3:5) Spr-Sum 78, p. 8.
"Spring, 1975." Northeast (3:5) Spr-Sum 78, p. 7.
"Unfinished." GreenfieldR (6:3/4) Spr 78, p. 62.

CURTIS, Jack
"Pico Blanco." Epos (27:1) 77, p. 23.
"Wife." StoneC (78:3) Aut 78, p. 4.

CURTIS, Tony
"At Abercanaid" (with Denise Levertov and Michael Harper).
SoDakR (16:4) Wint 78-79, p. 24.
"At the Hutterites in South Dakota." SoDakR (16:4) Wint 78-79,
p. 23.
"My Father." SoDakR (16:4) Wint 78-79, p. 21.
"My Father in Pembrokeshire." SoDakR (16:4) Wint 78-79,
p. 22.

CUSACK, A.
"Lucien Samaras' Corridor No. 2: Interpretation I." Hand (2)
78, p. 148.

CUSACK, Anne E.
"Factory." Chomo (4:3) Spr 78, p. 21.
"Hatshepsut." 13thM (4:1) 78, p. 29.
"Sickroom." Chomo (4:3) Spr 78, p. 20.
"Starry Room." Chomo (4:3) Spr 78, p. 22.
"Wedding." Chomo (4:3) Spr 78, p. 24.

CUSH, Catherine
"Hearbreaker." JnlONJP (2:2) 77, p. 18.

CUTLER, Bruce
from The Doctrine of Selective Depravity: "A Hit." KanQ (10:4)
Aut 78, p. 112.
from The Doctrine of Selective Depravity: "Song of Innocence."
BelPoJ (28:3) Spr 78, p. 9.

CYNDIAN, Charles London
"Excessive Women & Crazy Men." Wind (29) 78, p. 15.
"Sex with Father." YellowBR (10) 78, p. 18.
"Unique." Wind (29) 78, p. 15.

CZERNIAWSKI, Adam
"Chestnut" (tr. of Tadeusz Rózewicz). Stand (18:4) 77, p. 8.

"Prayer of Mr. Cogito-Traveller" (tr. of Zbigniew Herbert).
    Stand (18:4) 77, p. 6.
"Whoever Sees" (tr. of Tadeusz Rózewicz).   Stand (18:4) 77,
    p. 8.

DACEY, Florence
"Pretend." DacTerr (15) Wint-Spr 77-78, p. 63.

DACEY, Philip
"The Bar-Girl (Altea, Spain)." ThRiPo (11/12) 78, p. 25.
"The Coal-Furnace." Agni (9) 78, p. 99.
"A Dream of Hopkins." LitR (21:3) Spr 78, p. 304.
"Getting Caught in a Rainstorm." MassR (19:3) Aut 78, p. 460.
"He Goes to a Costume Party Dressed as Gerald Manley Hop-
    kins." Hudson (31:1) Spr 78, p. 120.
"Hopkins to Whitman: From the Lost Correspondence."
    PoetryNW (19:2) Sum 78, p. 5.
"Hopkins under Ether." Poetry (132:2) My 78, p. 73.
"Instructions Toward a Nude." ThRiPo (11/12) 78, p. 26.
"Letter: A Family Man Explains His Adultery." GeoR (32:3)
    Aut 78, p. 528.
"Love on a Waterbed." KanQ (10:4) Aut 78, p. 55.
"The Man with Red Suspenders." BallSUF (19:4) Aut 78, p. 31.
"Men-Strual." KanQ (10:4) Aut 78, p. 56.
"The Mermaid Crashed upon the Mind." Chowder (10/11) Aut-
    Wint 78-79, p. 10.
"The Palmer Method." HiramPoR (25) Aut-Wint 78, p. 12.
"The Poem As Striptease." Bits (7) Ja 78.
"Rhymes With." NewRivR (2:2) 78, p. 67.
"Rondel" (for James McMichael). ColEng (39:8) Ap 78, p. 948.
"A Simple Garden Ladder: From the Lost Correspondence of
    Gerald Manley Hopkins to Robert Bridges." NoAmR (263:3)
    Aut 78, p. 66.

DAGLARCA, Fazil Husnu
"Night of the Amnesty" (tr. by Clarence Major). Aspen (6) Aut
    78, p. 37.

DAIGON, Ruth
"Lists." Tendril (1) Wint 77-78.

DAILEY, Joel
"Absurd Flies." WormR (69) 78, p. 5.
"Clientelle" (for Len Durso). WormR (69) 78, p. 6.
"Directions for the West Coast." WormR (69) 78, p. 6.
"Humid Paper." WormR (69) 78, p. 5.
"Midnight in Marlon Brando's Bedroom." PoNow (20) 78, p. 5.
"A Real Hotdog." WormR (69) 78, p. 5.

DALE, Carolee
Two poems. MalR (45) Ja 78, p. 64.

DALLMAN, Elaine
"Girls Are Sugar and Spice, Women Are a Sweet Mystery."
    13thM (4:1) 78, p. 21.

DALTON, Dorothy
"Undulation." StoneC (78:1) Wint 78, p. 34.

DALY, William F.
"Emily." KanQ (10:4) Aut 78, p. 38.
"Landscape." KanQ (10:4) Aut 78, p. 20.

D'AMBOISE, Jacqueline
"Aide-Mémoire." MalR (48) O 78, p. 127.
"I've Tried to Take the Quicksand." MalR (48) O 78, p. 126.

DANA, Robert
"Angels and Deaths in St. Augustine" (for my daughter, Arden).
    PoNow (19) 78, p. 20.
"Heavy Weather." PoNow (19) 78, p. 20.
"Ninety-One in the Shade." NoAmR (263:3) Aut 78, p. 62.
"Wherever You Are Now." Stand (18:4) 77, p. 37.

DANEY, Stephen
"Audience." Tele (14) 78.
"Between Two Eyes." Tele (14) 78.
"Whispers of Decay." Tele (14) 78.

DANIEL, Marky
"Flying West, October." PoetryNW (19:3) Aut 78, p. 23.

DANIEL, Thom
"Sanity." GreenfieldR (6:3/4) Spr 78, p. 133.

DANIELS, Guy
"At the Glass-Blowing Factory" (tr. of Andrei Voznesensky).
    Pequod (2:4) 78, p. 25.
"She Came In Out of the Cold" (tr. of Alexander Blok). Pequod
    (2:4) 78, p. 11.

DANIELS, Jim
"Advice to a Friend Entering the Factory." Northeast (3:6) Wint
    78-79, p. 5.

DANISH, Barbara
"Looking Up Suddenly to See." HangL (33) Sum 78, p. 27.
"28:1." HangL (33) Sum 78, p. 28.

DANKLEFF, Richard
"Livery Stable." AmerS (47:3) Sum 78, p. 382.
"South of the Smoky Hill." KanQ (10:3) Sum 78, p. 109.

DANON, Ruth
"Alaska." NewEngR (1:2) Wint 78, p. 196.
"Grief." Poetry (19:4) Wint 78-79, p. 28.

DANTI, Marie
"The Mask of Metaphor." CarouselQ (3:3) Aut 78, p. 17.

DARIO, Rubén
"Cleopompus and Heliodemus" (tr. by Leland H. Chambers).
   DenQ (13:4) Wint 79, p. 54.

DARLING, Angela
"Vapors. " CarouselQ (3:2) Sum 78, p. 12.

DARLINGTON, Andrew
"Shedding Strangeness. " Wind (28) 78, p. 9.
"The Winter Journey/Ballet in Mud. " Wind (28) 78, p. 9.
"Wintercourse. " Wind (28) 78, p. 9.

DARMSTADT, A. E.
"Perspective Shift Upon an Evolutionary Plain. " CarouselQ (3:3)
   Aut 78, p. 30.
"Toy Maker. " CarouselQ (3:3) Aut 78, p. 30.

DARR, Ann
"Friends. " Bits (7) Ja 78.

DARRAGH, Tina
"'A' is for 'ox.'" LaB (11) 78, p. 11.
"'K' is for 'palm of the hand.'" LaB (11) 78, p. 13.

DARWISH, Mahmud
"Stranger in a Distant City" (tr. by Ben Bennani).   Paint (9/10)
   Spr-Aut 78, p. 37.

DASH, Tony
"For the Keeper of the Long House. " WormR (69) 78, p. 2.
"Three Women Running in the Country. " WormR (69) 78, p. 1.

DASKOVSKY, David
"Pile of Ash. " ParisR (73) Spr-Sum 78, p. 109.

D'AUBIGNE, Agrippa
Eight Sonnets and an Ode. Montra (4) 78, p. 16.

DAUENHAUER, William
"Cocktail Talk. " Smudge (1) Spr 78, p. 26.
"Metamorphosis/Transformation. " Smudge (1) Spr 78, p. 19.

DAUER, Rosamond
"The House of the Heart. " Glass (3:1/2/3) 78, p. 89.

DAVENPORT, Guy
One hundred and twenty-four poems (tr. of Herakleitos).
   AmerPoR (7:1) Ja-F 78, p. 14.

DAVID, Almitra
"Custody Case. " Chomo (5:2) Aut-Wint 78, p. 64.

DAVIDSON, David M.
"Summer Work." DacTerr (15) Wint-Spr 77-78, p. 42.
"Then." CarouselQ (3:3) Aut 78, p. 15.

DAVIES, Alan
from Life Studies: "Muriel; Alain Resnais (France, 1922-). "
Tele (13) 77.
from Life Studies: "A Shortened Life of Mahler." Tele (13) 77.
from Life Studies: "Tchaikovsky's Temper, His Mood." Tele
(13) 77.

DAVIES, Bob
from Timber: (13). Northeast (3:5) Spr-Sum 78, p. 50.

DAVIES, Nancy
"Lullaby." BallSUF (19:4) Aut 78, p. 11.
"The Sea Serpent." DeKalb (11:3/4) Spr-Sum 78, p. 33.

DAVIS, Glover
"Telescope/Kaleidescope." Poetry (132:1) Ap 78, p. 11.

DAVIS, Paul
"Ministerial Secrets." ChrC (95:11) 29 Mr 78, p. 324.

DAVIS, Susan
"fever." NewL (45:1) Aut 78, p. 15.
"parting gesture." NewL (45:1) Aut 78, p. 16.

DAVIS, Thadious M.
"For Papa (And Marcus Garvey)." Obs (4:1) Spr 78, p. 91.
"'Honeysuckle Was the Saddest Odor of All, I Think.'" Obs (4:1)
Spr 78, p. 93.
"Strong Women Survive Hurricane Season." Obs (4:1) Spr 78,
p. 92.

DAVIS, William Virgil
"A Bucket of Water." MoonsLT (2:4) 78, p. 31.
"The Hunting Dark." PoetC (10:2) 78, p. 24.
"A Late Elegy for John Berryman." SewanR (86:2) Spr 78,
p. 262.
"Mountain Dream." MalR (46) Ap 78, p. 40.
"No Echo." MoonsLT (2:4) 78, p. 34.
"One Way to Reconstruct the Scene." Atl (241:3) Mr 78, p. 98.
"A Room." MoonsLT (2:4) 78, p. 33.
"Some Day in Spring." PoNow (19) 78, p. 21.
"The Stopped Clock." MoonsLT (2:4) 78, p. 32.
"A Triptych for My Father." SewanR (86:2) Spr 78, p. 265.

DAVISON, Peter
"New Year's Eve." NewEngR (1:1) Aut 78, p. 28.
"On Ithaka." NewEngR (1:2) Wint 78, p. 191.
"The Ram Beneath the Barn." NewYorker (54:7) 3 Ap 78, p. 38.

DAVLIN
"The Beach. " Smudge (3) Aut 78, p. 8.

DAWSON, Hester Jewell
"Art Gallery. " JnlONJP (2:2) 77, p. 12.

DAWSON, Leven
"Marriage and the Stream. " NewOR (5:4) 78, p. 306.

DAWSON, Melinda
"Dragonfly. " CutB (11) Aut-Wint 78, p. 4.

DAY, Ann
"Insider. " SoDakR (16:2) Sum 78, p. 56.
"Zen on C Street. " SoDakR (16:2) Sum 78, p. 57.

DAY, Lucille
"Self-Planting Seeds. " Epos (27:2) 77, p. 11.
"Tumor. " Epos (27:2) 77, p. 10.

DAYTON, Irene
"New Year. " Wind (31) 78, p. 8.

DEAL, Kathryn
"Golden Wedding Anniversary. " WindO (32) Sum-Aut 78, p. 4.
"Zen and Building a Treehouse. " WindO (32) Sum-Aut 78, p. 4.

DEAL, Susan Strayer
"It Is True. " PraS (52:4) Wint 78-79, p. 366.
"On the Plains of Nebraska. " DeKalb (11:1/2) Aut-Wint 77-78,
    p. 44.

DEAN, John
"Edward Hopper's American Mid-Afternoon Nausea. " PikeF (1)
    Spr 78, p. 21.
"Petrified Cézanne. " PikeF (1) Spr 78, p. 21.

DEAN, Robert
"The Child. " PartR (45:3) 78, p. 433.
"Conscience. " PartR (45:3) 78, p. 433.
"Verisimilitude. " PartR (45:3) 78, p. 434.

DeANDRADE, Carlos Drummond
"Song to the Man of the People: Charlie Chaplin" (tr. by John
    Nist). AmerPoR (7:2) Mr-Ap 78, p. 23.

DEANE, Seamus
"A Distant Beach. " SewanR (86:1) Wint 78, p. 33.
"Epiphany. " LitR (22:2) Wint 79, p. 227.
"Middle Kingdom. " LitR (22:2) Wint 79, p. 229.
"'Send War in Our Time, O Lord' (John Mitchell). " Stand
    (19:2) 78, p. 16.
"The Victim. " LitR (22:2) Wint 79, p. 228.

DeANGELIS, Jacqueline
"Jack and Mary." Pig (5) 78, p. 82.

DeARAUJO, Virginia
"Emerita (1903-1978)." PoetryNW (19:4) Wint 78-79, p. 14.

DEBLINGER, Paul M.
"Glide Chokes." FoNow (20) 78, p. 6.

DeBOLT, William Walter
"Alternative." ChrC (95:31) 4 O 78, p. 908.
"Atheist." CarouselQ (3:1) Spr 78, p. 6.
"Back to the Angels." CarouselQ (3:1) Spr 78, p. 6.
"Good Christmas." ChrC (95:42) 20 D 78, p. 1230.
"Origin of Genius." ChrC (95:34) 25 O 78, p. 1012.
"Why Spring Returns." ChrC (95:18) 17 My 78, p. 527.

DeBRUYN, Nellie L.
"Cape Cod Evening: 1939." DacTerr (15) Wint-Spr 77-78, p. 44.
"Morning in a City: 1944." DacTerr (15) Wint-Spr 77-78, p. 44.

DECAVALLES, Andonis
Eleven poems (tr. of Yannis Ritsos). Falcon (16) 78, p. 32.
"A Stele." LitR (21:3) Spr 78, p. 346.
"The Third Year" (tr. by Kimon Friar). LitR (21:4) Sum 78,
    p. 392.
"To the Master-Builder" (to Pandelis Prevelakis) (tr. by Kimon
    Friar). LitR (21:4) Sum 78, p. 389.
"Zoophoros" (tr. by Kimon Friar). LitR (21:4) Sum 78, p. 391.

DECKER, Michael
"In the Lighthouse." Shen (29:2) Wint 78, p. 74.

DECKER, Theo
"for: Icarus the Moth." SouthernPR (18:1) Spr 78, p. 54.

DEETER, Kay
"Before and After Hours." HiramPoR (25) Aut-Wint 78, p. 13.

DeFOE, Mark
"Interviewing a Center-Fold." HolCrit (15:1) F 78, p. 13.
"13 Ways of Eradicating Blackbirds." Epoch (27:3) Spr 78,
    p. 281.

DeFORD, Sara
"The Loss." ChrC (95:37) 15 N 78, p. 1100.
"To an Indian Schoolboy." ChrC (95:42) 20 D 78, p. 1239.

DeFREES, Madeline
"Imaginary Ancestors: The Woman with Fabled Hair." Iowa
    (9:2) Spr 78, p. 79.
"Plum Rain." PoetryNW (19:2) Sum 78, p. 28.

DEHLAVI, Amir Khusrow
 "Last night I dreamt you brought me wine" (tr. by Omar Pound).
  Montra (4) 78, p. 41.

DeJESUS, Teresa
 "Curfew" (tr. by Maria A. Proser, Arlene Scully, and James
  Scully). MinnR (NS11) Aut 78, p. 6.
 "'I Am a Small Woman'" (tr. by Maria A. Proser, Arlene
  Scully, and James Scully). MinnR (NS11) Aut 78, p. 8.
 "It Makes Me Furious!" (tr. by Maria A. Proser, Arlene Scully,
  and James Scully). MinnR (NS11) Aut 78, p. 7.
 "Mistrust" (tr. by Maria A. Proser, Arlene Scully, and James
  Scully). MinnR (NS11) Aut 78, p. 9.

DEKIN, Timothy
 "Anxiety. " SouthernR (14:1) Wint 78, p. 99.
 "Down on the Farm. " SouthernR (14:1) Wint 78, p. 100.

DELANEY, John
 "Fingerprints. " StoneC (78:3) Aut 78, p. 16.
 "Meaning Is Extension. " HolCrit (15:2) Ap 78, p. 13.
 "Notes from a Playground. " SmPd (43) Spr 78, p. 12.

DELAVAN, Holly
 "Cars as Celebrants. " ChrC (95:20) 31 My 78, p. 587.

DELGADO, Holly
 "Rio Grande Passage. " CarouselQ (3:1) Spr 78, p. 4.

DelGRECO, Robert
 "Dakota Poem. " SoDakR (16:2) Sum 78, p. 37.
 "Divining. " SoDakR (16:2) Sum 78, p. 39.
 "Listening. " SoDakR (16:2) Sum 78, p. 38.

DELP, Michael
 "Homebound. " Zahir (9) 77, p. 45.
 "Poem for Myself. " GreenfieldR (6:3/4) Spr 78, p. 111.

DeMARIS, Ron
 "Campus at Night. " Epos (27:2) 77, p. 22.
 "Cover Girl. " Epos (27:1) 77, p. 27.

DEMARS, Douglas
 "The Deadly Chrome Plated Cap Pistol. " EnPas (7) 78, p. 37.

DeMELLO, Agustin Eastwood
 "Volcano. " Wind (29) 78, p. 21.

DeMOTT, Robert
 "From the Poetry Manual. " HiramPoR (25) Aut-Wint 78, p. 14.
 "Waiting Out the Gathering Season" (for James Magner). FourQt
  (28:1) Aut 78, p. 11.

DEMPSTER, Barry
"Boys." Confr (16) Spr-Sum 78, p. 24.
"Confessions of a Husband." BallSUF (19:4) Aut 78, p. 26.
"England 77." SmPd (42) Wint 78, p. 5.
"Jonah." WindO (32) Sum-Aut 78, p. 22.
"Laurier Avenue" (for my mother). WindO (32) Sum-Aut 78,
      p. 24.
"Love Story." Wind (28) 78, p. 11.
"Nana." WindO (32) Sum-Aut 78, p. 23.
"Prison Poem." SouthernPR (18:2) Aut 78, p. 30.
"Reunion with an Old Lover." Nimrod (22:2) Spr-Sum 78, p. 13.
"Wild Memory." Wind (28) 78, p. 11.

DenBOER, D.
"Clancy Indifferent." Zahir (9) 77, p. 52.

DENISON, John
"Itinerary." DenQ (13:2) Sum 78, p. 57.
"Motorcade." DenQ (13:2) Sum 78, p. 55.
"A Story without an Ending." DenQ (13:2) Sum 78, p. 58.
"Why Can't I Be Carefree Like Everyone Else?" DenQ (13:2)
      Sum 78, p. 56.
"Your Mother." PoNow (20) 78, p. 6.

DENNING, Steve
"Steps" (for Stan Denning 1929-1971). SlowLR (1/2) 78, p. 13.

DENNIS, Carl
"At the Corner." Salm (41) Spr 78, p. 118.
"Over There." NewEngR (1:2) Wint 78, p. 195.
"The Plum Tree." Salm (41) Spr 78, p. 118.
"The Pure in Heart." Salm (41) Spr 78, p. 117.

DENSON
"my sister is retarded...." HiramPoR (25) Aut-Wint 78, p. 15.

DENT, Peter
"By Fingertips." KanQ (10:1) Wint 78, p. 64.

DEPTA, Victor M.
"The Embroidery." GeoR (32:3) Aut 78, p. 631.
"The Four Mice." WebR (4:2) Aut 78, p. 26.

DeRACHEWILTZ, S. W.
"Angst" (tr. of Mallerme, w. R. Sieburth). St.AR (5:1) Aut-
      Wint 78, p. 62.
"Canto XLVII" (tr. of Pound, w. R. Sieburth). St.AR (5:1) Aut-
      Wint 78, p. 66.
"Chopin" (tr. of Benn, w. R. Sieburth). St.AR (5:1) Aut-Wint
      78, p. 54.
from Drafts and Fragments (tr. of Holderlin, w. R. Sieburth).
      St.AR (5:1) Aut-Wint 78, pp. 41-48.
"From Peace Poems" (tr. of Eluard, w. R. Sieburth). St.AR

(5:1) Aut-Wint 78, p. 63.

"The Lover" (tr. of Eluard, w. R. Sieburth). St.AR (5:1) Aut-Wint 78, p. 62.

"Make Room" (tr. of Supervielle, w. R. Sieburth). St.AR (5:1) Aut-Wint 78, p. 65.

"Morning" (tr. of Theophile de Viau, w. R. Sieburth). St.AR (5:1) Aut-Wint 78, p. 60.

"Movement" (tr. of Supervielle, w. R. Sieburth). St.AR (5:1) Aut-Wint 78, p. 64.

"New Wilderness" (tr. of Junger, w. R. Sieburth). St.AR (5:1) Aut-Wint 78, p. 52.

"Night" (tr. of Supervielle, w. R. Sieburth). St.AR (5:1) Aut-Wint 78, p. 64.

"Nike" (tr. of Rilke, w. R. Sieburth). St.AR (5:1) Aut-Wint 78, p. 53.

"Other America" (tr. of Supervielle, w. R. Sieburth). St.AR (5:1) Aut-Wint 78, p. 65.

"Perspective" (tr. of Eluard, w. R. Sieburth). St.AR (5:1) Aut-Wint 78, p. 63.

"Psalm" (tr. of Trakl, w. R. Sieburth). St.AR (5:1) Aut-Wint 78, p. 51.

"Recuillement" (tr. of Baudelaire, w. R. Sieburth). St.AR (5:1) Aut-Wint 78, p. 61.

"Remembrance" (tr. of Holderlin, w. R. Sieburth). St.AR (5:1) Aut-Wint 78, p. 68.

from Schneepart (tr. of Celan, w. R. Sieburth). St.AR (5:1) Aut-Wint 78, p. 55.

"To Childe Elis" (tr. of Trakl, w. R. Sieburth). St.AR (5:1) Aut-Wint 78, p. 51.

Two poems (tr. of Montale, w. R. Sieburth). St.AR (5:1) Aut-Wint 78, p. 66.

"Untitled" (tr. of Supervielle, w. R. Sieburth). St.AR (5:1) Aut-Wint 78, p. 64.

DerHOVANESSIAN, Diana

"Balancing Act." LadHJ (95:1) Ja 78, p. 111.

"The Bottomless Eye." ParisR (72) Wint 77, p. 136.

"The Chimney" (tr. of Krikor Beledian). StoneC (78:2) Spr 78, p. 21.

"The Choosing." LadHJ (95:11) N 78, p. 90.

"Cock Robin." AndR (5:1) Spr 78, p. 38.

"Facing the Silence" (tr. of Artem Haroutiounian). CarolQ (30:2) Spr-Sum 78, p. 83.

"Gazel for Semiramis" (tr. of Hovaness Shiraz). Nimrod (22:2) Spr-Sum 78, p. 86.

"The Spanish Dancer." NewRep (179:20) 11 N 78, p. 28.

"The Unlikely Pair." LitR (21:3) Spr 78, p. 374.

DeROUS, Peter

"Body Burnt." WormR (69) 78, p. 37.

"Fear." WormR (69) 78, p. 37.

"If." WormR (69) 78, p. 37.

"Reference I." WormR (69) 78, p. 37.

D'EVELYN, Thomas
"Hell's Angels" (for Breck Caldwell). SouthernR (14:1) Wint 78,
    p. 105.
"In Memoriam." SouthernR (14:1) Wint 78, p. 103.
"Morning Air." SouthernR (14:1) Wint 78, p. 104.
"My Neighbor." SouthernR (14:1) Wint 78, p. 104.

DeYOUNG, Robert
"The Organization." Epos (27:2) 77, p. 34.

DIACONO, Mario
from Denomisegninatura: "Destinegazione." Chelsea (37) 78,
    p. 56.
from Mysticficaction: "Ang/Water Loo St." Chelsea (37) 78,
    p. 72.
from Mysticficaction: "Holympic." Chelsea (37) 78, p. 69.
from Mysticficaction: "Iperscriptio: M'Other." Chelsea (37) 78,
    p. 65.
from Mysticficaction: "M'." Chelsea (37) 78, p. 63.
from Mysticficaction: "Word in Progress." Chelsea (37) 78,
    p. 67.

DiCICCO, Pier Ciorgio
"The Bartender Speaks." ThRiPo (11/12) 78, p. 28.

DICKEY, Paul
"Square Root of -1." KanQ (10:1) Wint 78, p. 78.

DICKEY, William
from The Rainbow Grocery: "Alligators and Paris and North
    America" (for Adrianne on her birthday). MassR (19:3) Aut
    78, p. 511.
from The Rainbow Grocery: "Killing to Eat." MassR (19:3) Aut
    78, p. 509.

DICKINSON, Simonne
"Birthday Card." Wind (29) 78, p. 16.
"A Boy's Room." Wind (29) 78, p. 16.
"Melancholiage." Wind (29) 78, p. 16.

DICKSON, John
"The Bartender's Widow." StoneC (78:3) Aut 78, p. 21.
"The Dashing Figure." Epos (27:1) 77, p. 5.
"The Mortality of Stone." Epos (27:1) 77, p. 4.

DICKSON, L. L.
"Image #41." BelPoJ (28:4) Sum 78, p. 1.

DIENSTFREY, Patricia
"Newspaper Story 2." HangL (33) Sum 78, p. 29.

DIETER, Dwight
"'And Now, Center Stage....'" CarouselQ (3:4) Wint 78, p. 31.

"Punctuation." CarouselQ (3:3) Aut 78, p. 5.
"This Morning's Cream." CarouselQ (3:3) Aut 78, p. 5.

DIGBY, John
"Then and Only Then." Durak (1) 78, p. 54.
"Van Gogh at Saint Rémy." Kayak (49) O 78, p. 68.

DiGRANDI, Diana
"Life's Mirage." CarouselQ (3:4) Wint 78, p. 8.

DILE, Robin
"Untitled." CarouselQ (3:3) Aut 78, p. 24.

DILLARD, Annie
"Metaphysical Model with Feathers." Atl (242:4) O 78, p. 82.

DIONYSIUS of Andros
"Two Against One" (tr. by Richard O'Connell). Playb (25:4) Ap
    78, p. 157.

DiPALMA, Ray
"Birthday Notation" (for Tom & Val Raworth). NorthSR (8) Aut-
    Wint 78-79, p. 29.
"Lady Lady." PartR (45:3) 78, p. 432.
"a machine reaches." Hills (5) 78, p. 77.
"No Shepherds." Hills (5) 78, p. 78.
"Poem: The day out of the green world." NorthSR (8) Aut-Wint
    78-79, p. 28.

DiPASQUALE, Emanuel
"every flower blooms." Wind (31) 78, p. 21.
"For My Mother." Poem (33) Jl 78, p. 23.
"A Genital Chant." JnlONJP (2:1) 77, p. 22.
"A Half Sleep, Sicilian Childhood." SewanR (86:3) Sum 78,
    p. 366.
"Love Song for Mari." JnlONJP (2:1) 77, p. 22.
"Melody and Roots." Poem (33) Jl 78, p. 24.
"News for T. S. Eliot." JnlONJP (3:1) 78, p. 6.
"Night is a rhapsody." Wind (31) 78, p. 19.
"Nightmare." JnlONJP (3:1) 78, p. 6.
"Nights" (to Mari on her 23rd birthday). JnlONJP (2:1) 77,
    p. 22.
"Per Mia Madre." Poem (33) Jl 78, p. 23.
"The Poet Wishes He Were Water." JnlONJP (3:1) 78, p. 6.

DiPRIMA, Diane
from Loba, Part IV: "Dream: The Loba Reveals Herself."
    Hand (2) 78, p. 120.
from Loba, Part IV: "Four Poets Speak of Her." Hand (2) 78,
    p. 117.
from Loba, Part IV: "I am a shadow crossing ice." Hand (2)
    78, p. 115.
from Loba, Part IV: "A Painting of the Loba." Hand (2) 78,

p. 119.
from Loba, Part IV: "Some Lies about the Loba." <u>Hand</u> (2) 78,
  p. 116.
from Loba, Part IV: "'There the Goddess in Amber Robes Rules
  Over Those Who Have Passed Out of History.'" <u>Hand</u> (2) 78,
  p. 118.

DiPRISCO, Joseph
  "Firing Squad." <u>PoetryNW</u> (19:1) Spr 78, p. 34.
  "In the Movie." <u>PoetryNW</u> (19:1) Spr 78, p. 33.

DiSANTO, Grace
  "Nightmare." <u>CarouselQ</u> (3:2) Sum 78, p. 14.

DISCH, Donna
  "A Fresh Snowfall Is Predicted." <u>Aspen</u> (5) Spr 78, p. 78.

DISCH, Tom
  "Abecedary." <u>Poetry</u> (133:3) D 78, p. 140.
  "A Bookmark." <u>LittleM</u> (11:3) Aut 77, p. 32.
  "Concerto for Piano and Orchestra." <u>LittleM</u> (11:3) Aut 77,
    p. 30.
  "High Purpose in Poetry: A Primer" (for A. R. Ammons).
    <u>Poetry</u> (132:2) My 78, p. 84.
  "Just Before the Cops Arrive." <u>ParisR</u> (Spr-Sum 78, p. 91.
  "Luxe, Calme, et Desespoir." <u>Poetry</u> (133:3) D 78, p. 143.
  "The Ocean." <u>ParisR</u> (73) Spr-Sum 78, p. 89.
  "Poems" (For Joyce Kilmer). <u>Poetry</u> (133:3) D 78, p. 142.
  "The Problem of Safety: a Manifesto." <u>ParisR</u> (73) Spr-Sum 78,
    p. 87.
  "Selected Quirks." <u>LittleM</u> (11:3) Aut 77, p. 33.
  "The Thirty Nine Articles." <u>LittleM</u> (11:3) Aut 77, p. 28.
  "To Our Christmas Tree." <u>Poetry</u> (133:3) D 78, p. 139.

DISCHELL, Stuart
  "After Cheyenne." <u>PoNow</u> (20) 78, p. 6.
  Ten poems. <u>Agni</u> (9) 78, p. 67.

DISTLER, Ann Goette
  "Teresa." <u>SouthernR</u> (14:3) Sum 78, p. 504.

DISTLER, Bette
  "Hospital Journal." <u>13thM</u> (4:1) 78, p. 88.

DiSUVERO, Victor
  "Robert Lowell, Dead This September 12th, 1977." <u>Kayak</u> (47)
    F 78, p. 66.

DITSKY, John
  "The Bus Called Benin." <u>Paint</u> (9/10) Spr-Aut 78, p. 9.
  "Canadian Mean." <u>Smudge</u> (2) Sum 78, p. 27.
  "Catafalque." <u>ChrC</u> (95:6) 22 F 78, p. 185.
  "Fit." <u>StoneC</u> (78:2) Spr 78, p. 15.

"A Pirandellian Episode." NewRena (10) 78, p. 50.
"Scratch." StoneC (78:2) Spr 78, p. 15.
"Taking Exception." NewRivR (2:2) 78, p. 63.

DIVERS, Greg
"Selections from Life, Auto, Fire." SouthernPR (18:2) Aut 78,
    p. 74.

DIVOK, Mario
"Simplicity." CarouselQ (3:1) Spr 78, p. 1.

DIXON, D.
"Big John Milton in North Platte, Nebraska." CalQ (13/14) Spr-
    Sum 78, p. 107.

DIXON, Melvin
"Chill" (for Didier). BelPoJ (29:2) Wint 78-79, p. 21.
"Etymology: A Father's Gift." BelPoJ (29:2) Wint 78-79, p. 20.
"Getting Rocks." BelPoJ (29:2) Wint 78-79, p. 17.
"Grandmother: Crossing Jordan." BelPoJ (29:2) Wint 78-79,
    p. 19.
"Hungry Travel." BelPoJ (29:2) Wint 78-79, p. 18.

DiZAZZO, Raymond
"Sea Storm" (for my son). Stonecloud (7) 78, p. 10.
"2056." Stonecloud (7) 78, p. 32.

DJANIKIAN, Gregory
"Abel." ThRiPo (11/12) 78, p. 28.
"Lot's Complaint." ThRiPo (11/12) 78, p. 29.
"Rowing on Eaton-Brook Lake at Twilight." AmerS (47:3) Sum
    78, p. 326.

DLUGOS, Tim
"White Petals." FourQt (27:4) Sum 78, p. 20.

DOBBIE, T. A.
"In Control." MalR (45) Ja 78, p. 117.
"Lost Faith/Fallen Idols." MalR (45) Ja 78, p. 117.

DOBBS, Jeannine
"Music Lesson." YellowBR (10) 78, p. 35.

DOBBS, Mitchell
"On Not Reading Yeats' 'Among School Children.'" EngJ (67:5)
    My 78, p. 63.

DOBRIN, Arthur
"A Lack of Privacy." PoetC (10:2) 78, p. 14.

DOBSON, Rosemary
"The Three Fates." Antaeus (30/31) Sum-Aut 78, p. 254.

DOBYNS, Stephen
"Fragments." Iowa (9:4) Aut 78, p. 30.
"Getting Through Winter." NewYorker (54:45) 25 D 78, p. 47.
"Morning Song." Poetry (132:4) Jl 78, p. 216.
"A Separate Time." Poetry (132:4) Jl 78, p. 215.
"Song for Making the Birds Come" (For Shirley Stark). Poetry
    (132:4) Jl 78, p. 217.
"Song for Putting Aside Anger." Poetry (132:4) Jl 78, p. 218.
"Song of the Wrong Response." Iowa (9:4) Aut 78, p. 29.

DODD, Wayne
"Essay in Three Parts: On Poetry." MissouriR (2:1) Aut 78,
    p. 34.
"Night Poem." GeoR (32:2) Sum 78, p. 265.
"Prologue to a Longer Story." GeoR (32:2) Sum 78, p. 263.

DOLAN, John
"Japanese Horror Movie." BallSUF (19:4) Aut 78, p. 56.

DOMINA, Lynn
"memories, conclusions, and rebellions." GRR (9:2) 78, p. 140.

DOMINGO, Sandy
"crazy john wanted." SeC (5:2) 78, p. 47.

DONAHUE, George Michael
"The Effect of the Catechism." JnlONJP (2:1) 77, p. 25.
"One More Thing." StoneC (78:3) Aut 78, p. 14.
"St. Gideon and the Mammonburger." JnlONJP (2:1) 77, p. 25.
"San Gazpacho del Frio Y Acebuche." JnlONJP (2:1) 77, p. 24.

DONAHUE, Jack
"The Sparrow." Confr (17) Aut-Wint 79, p. 67.

DONAVEL, David F.
"Alewives." KanQ (10:4) Aut 78, p. 97.
"Approaching Boston from the North." Wind (31) 78, p. 9.
"Reflections on the El." Wind (31) 78, p. 10.

DONEGAN, Ann Warner
"Note Found under the Eaves." Tendril (1) Wint 77-78.
"Windfall." Tendril (1) Wint 77-78.

DONKER, Anthonie
"Een Breughel." GRR (9:2) 78, p. 110.

DONLEY, Carol
"Tour of a Remodeled House." HiramPoR (24) Spr-Sum 78,
    p. 10.

DONNELLY, Dorothy
"Spiderwork." NewRep (179:20) 11 N 78, p. 28.

DONOVAN, Brad
"A Bright Thing Too Far." Aspen (5) Spr 78, p. 81.
"A Letter from Mt. Pleasant, Michigan." Aspen (6) Aut 78,
    p. 35.
"Pasternak." Aspen (6) Aut 78, p. 34.

DONOVAN, Rhoda
"No Signal for a Crossing." BelPoJ (28:3) Spr 78, p. 1.

DONZELLA, D. W.
"The World Turns Wide to Winter." DacTerr (15) Wint-Spr 77-
    78, p. 69.

DORAN, Donna
"The Eclipse." Columbia (2) Aut 78, p. 13.

DORBIN, Sandy
"Hero." Pan (19) 77, p. 34.

DORESKI, William
"Thanksgiving, Growing Older." GeoR (32:3) Aut 78, p. 540.
"Wanting to Be Superman." Tendril (1) Wint 77-78.

DORFMAN, Richard
"The Scream." Zahir (9) 77, p. 9.

DORMAN, Sonya
"Explaining." LittleM (11:4) Wint 78, p. 29.
"Hammer and Nail." Northeast (3:6) Wint 78-79, p. 4.
"A Holiday Passes." Northeast (3:6) Wint 78-79, p. 3.
"Retreating Inland" (for Iris Owens). LittleM (11:4) Wint 78,
    p. 28.
"The Terms of the Lease." PoNow (19) 78, p. 26.
"Vespers at the Buena Vista Apartments." Northeast (3:6) Wint
    78-79, p. 4.

DORN, Edward
"Bumpersticker." ChiR (30:3) Wint 79, p. 112.
"The Country Awards." ChiR (30:3) Wint 79, p. 112.
"De Characteristic do git inflated." ChiR (30:3) Wint 79, p. 112.
"Name for an early american punk group." ChiR (30:3) Wint 79,
    p. 112.

DORNEY, Dennis M.
"Orioles." PoNow (20) 78, p. 6.

DORSET, Gerald
"Haole Sets Foot in Hawaii." Tele (13) 77.
"Strong Convictions & Men of Action." Wind (28) 78, p. 32.
"To Marry and to Breathe." Wind (28) 78, p. 41.

DORSETT, Robert
"Mary on the Wards." SouthernPR (18:2) Aut 78, p. 83.
"Squatter Area, Kowloon." Wind (30) 78, p. 31.

DORSETT, Thomas
"Clouds." Wind (29) 78, p. 18.
"The Guard." CarouselQ (3:4) Wint 78, p. 3.
"To an Eyelash." Wind (29) 78, p. 18.

DOTY, Cat
"Nun." HangL (32) Spr 78, p. 9.
"Wearing Out the House." HangL (32) Spr 78, p. 8.

DOTY, M. R.
"Because the Channel." Chowder (10/11) Aut-Wint 78-79, p. 61.
"Town in the Farmlands." Epos (27:2) 77, p. 32.

DOUGHERTY, Kate
"Poet's Child." YellowBR (10) 78, p. 35.

DOUGHERTY, Sister Mary Ellen, S. S. N. D.
"Exhibit." SouthernHR (12:3) Sum 78, p. 212.
"What Grandfather Knew." Comm (105:16) 18 Ag 78, p. 530.

DOUSKEY, Franz
"Cold Like No Other World." Tele (13) 77.
"It's the Prayers." YellowBR (10) 78, p. 16.

DOVE, Rita
"The Bird Frau." OhioR (19:2) Spr-Sum 78, p. 18.
"Robert Schumann, or: Musical Genius Begins with Affliction."
    GeoR (32:3) Aut 78, p. 643.

DOW, Philip
"Ducks of the Heart." ModernPS (9:3) Wint 79, p. 186.
"Elegy." Bound (6:2) Wint 78, p. 471.

DOWD, Jeanne
"Old Farmer." AAR (28) 78, p. 79.
"To the Barmaid in Manet's Painting, 'A Bar at the Folies-
    Bergere.'" AAR (28) 78, p. 79.

DOWNES, Gwladys
"Animus, Anima." MalR (47) Ja 78, p. 40.
"Astronomical Bearing." MalR (45) Ja 78, p. 39.
"Five-finger Exercises." MalR (45) Ja 78, p. 42.
"'L'Habitant de mes Pensees'" (à P. Valéry). MalR (45) Ja 78,
    p. 46.
"Rune." MalR (45) Ja 78, p. 45.
"Words for a High Dark Trail." MalR (45) Ja 78, p. 48.

DOWNS, Stuart
"Bedposts." Epos (27:1) 77, p. 24.

DOWNS, Virginia
"'Going Up Fool's Hill.'" HiramPoR (25) Aut-Wint 78, p. 16.

DOXEY, William S.
 "At the Snail Museum." GreenfieldR (6:3/4) Spr 78, p. 115.
 "Bristlecone." KanQ (10:1) Wint 78, p. 108.
 "Cathedrals." Atl (242:1) Jl 78, p. 46.
 "The Man Who Slept with Death" (for Erica Jong). StoneC (78:2)
     Spr 78, p. 22.
 "The Sisters." HolCrit (15:2) Ap 78, p. 13.

DOYLE, Dennis
 "Indications of the Internal." FourQt (27:4) Sum 78, p. 22.

DOYLE, James
 "The State Fair." PoNow (20) 78, p. 6.

DOYLE, Mike
 "Goodbye." MalR (45) Ja 78, p. 264.
 "November Incident." MalR (45) Ja 78, p. 264.
 "Outside the Garden." MalR (45) Ja 78, p. 262.
 "Spring Balance." MalR (45) Ja 78, p. 264.

DRACHLER, Rose
 "The Enduring Beast" (for Miriam Beerman). Hand (2) 78,
     p. 16.
 "Lament for the Quiet Girl." Hand (2) 78, p. 15.
 "Who Is This Stilled." Hand (2) 78, p. 14.

DRAKE, Albert
 "Reality Sandwich." PikeF (1) Spr 78, p. 25.

DRAKE, Barbara
 "Amelia." WormR (72) 78, p. 125.
 "Bus Fare." WormR (72) 78, p. 124.
 "Earthquakes." HangL (34) Wint 78-79, p. 14.
 "First Confession." Bits (8) Jl 78.
 "Garbage." ThRiPo (11/12) 78, p. 30.
 "Listen Doctor." WormR (72) 78, p. 123.

DRESBACH, D. P.
 "Debut." Wind (28) 78, p. 13.
 "November Poem." Wind (28) 78, p. 13.
 "December Prayer." Wind (28) 78, p. 14.

DREW, George
 "Ming." HolCrit (15:2) Ap 78, p. 14.
 "Nelson, 2." Wind (31) 78, p. 11.
 "A Short Unhappy History of Uncle Frank." DacTerr (15) Wint-
     Spr 77-78, p. 58.

DRISCOLL, Jack
 "Hit and Run." PoetryNW (19:1) Spr 78, p. 19.
 "The Meeting." Wind (31) 78, p. 45.
 "The Police Photographer." ThRiPo (11/12) 78, p. 31.
 "Sleeping in the Same Poem." KanQ (10:1) Wint 78, p. 123.

DRURY, John
   "Bamboo" (for Ruth McClure).   Epoch (28:1) Aut 78, p. 54.
   "Bridge of the Carousel" (tr. of Rainer Maria Rilke).   DenQ
      (13:4) Wint 79, p. 52.
   "My Life Is Not This Steep and Turning Hour" (tr. of Rainer
      Maria Rilke).   DenQ (13:4) Wint 79, p. 53.
   "The Stunt Man."   Shen (29:3) Spr 78, p. 78.
   "To Jonathan, Who Enlisted."   PoNow (20) 78, p. 7.

DUBIE, Norman
   "Cockaigne" (Homage to Pieter Bruegel, the Elder).   NewYorker
      (54:27) 21 Ag 78, p. 28.
   "The Composer's Winter Dream:"   Field (18) Spr 78, p. 22.
   Eight poems.   AmerPoR (7:4) Jl-Ag 78, p. 3.
   "The Fox Who Watched for the Midnight Sun."   NewYorker
      (54:24) 31 Jl 78, p. 32.
   "French Pilgrims and a Motorcycle with Sidecar: 1953."   Salm
      (42) Sum-Aut 78, p. 125.
   "Grand Illusion."   Antaeus (30/31) Sum-Aut 78, p. 69.
   "The Great Wall of China."   MissouriR (2:1) Aut 78, p. 29.
   "In the Beginning There Was the End of Solitude, Beginning Again:"
      Agni (8) 78, p. 117.
   "Inverse Chinese Characters above Cleator, Arizona."   QW (5)
      Wint 78, p. 6.
   "The Late Halcyon Days Between Wars: 1932" (for Dave Smith).
      Columbia (2) Aut 78, p. 77.
   "The Obituaries of Caryatids."   ParisR (72) Wint 77, p. 44.
   "The Scrivener's Roses" (For Marvin Fisher).   Poetry (133:2) N
      78, p. 93.
   "The World Isn't a Wedding of the Artists of Yesterday."   Poetry
      (132:2) My 78, p. 66.

DUBIE, William
   "Late Snow on Condemned Cars."   Tendril (3) Aut 78, p. 19.
   "Our Stone Walls of Water."   PoNow (20) 78, p. 7.
   "Scarecrow in the Killing Frost."   CarouselQ (3:2) Sum 78, p. 4.
   "Spring."   Tendril (3) Aut 78, p. 20.

DuBOIS, Constance
   "Adam and Eve."   Poem (34) N 78, p. 55.

DUDIS, Ellen Kirvin
   "August 1939."   LittleM (11:3) Aut 77, p. 54.
   "Water Babies."   ColEng (40:1) S 78, p. 28.

DUEMER, Joseph
   "Letter to the Naturalist."   PoetryNW (19:4) Wint 78-79, p. 21.
   "Whisky Bottle Found on the Beach."   PoetryNW (19:2) Sum 78,
      p. 34.

DUFAULT, Peter Kane
   "Equinoctial."   Atl (241:1) Ja 78, p. 85.

"Equinoctial." Atl (241:2) F 78, p. 86.
"Goshawk." Atl (242:4) O 78, p. 56.

DUFF, Gerald
    "A History of Windows." SouthernPR (18:2) Aut 78, p. 32.

DUGAN, Lawrence
    "At the Ninth Street Market." Comm (105:23) 24 N 78, p. 759.
    "The Microscope." NewRep (178:9) 4 Mr 78, p. 32.

DUGGAN, Devon Miller
    "The Names of Quilts." CutB (11) Aut-Wint 78, p. 13.
    "Swallowing the Salt." Shen (29:4) Sum 78, p. 39.

DUKES, Norman
    "Bullseye." Agni (8) 78, p. 102.

DuMARIS, Ron
    "He Who Would Give Each Beast a Name." EnPas (7) 78, p. 13.

DUNBAR, Sybil J.
    "... Fair Play." Obs (4:1) Spr 78, p. 84.
    "In My Mood." Obs (4:1) Spr 78, p. 84.

DUNMORE, Helen
    "Breakfast." Stand (18:4) 77, p. 65.

DUNN, Sharon
    "Mail Order." CutB (11) Aut-Wint 78, p. 79.

DUNN, Stephen
    "Autumn Montage." NorthSR (8) Aut-Wint 78-79, p. 10.
    "A Circus of Needs." Chowder (10/11) Aut-Wint 78-79, p. 9.
    "A Common Blessing." Chowder (10/11) Aut-Wint 78-79, p. 6.
    "Creating the Conditions." PoetryNW (19:2) Sum 78, p. 10.
    "Danse Manhattanique." ThRiPo (11/12) 78, p. 33.
    "I Am So Embarrassed by My Lies I Try to Make Them Come
        True." Chowder (10/11) Aut-Wint 78-79, p. 8.
    "In the Monastery of Work and Love." PoetryNW (19:2) Sum 78,
        p. 12.
    "Instead of You." PraS (52:1) Spr 78, p. 73.
    "Modern Dance Class." Iowa (9:1) Wint 78, p. 36.
    from The Monastery of Work and Love. Poetry (133:3) D 78,
        p. 153.
    "Mouths." PoetryNW (19:2) Sum 78, p. 11.
    "On the Coast." NorthSR (8) Aut-Wint 78-79, p. 9.
    "The Photograph Album." NorthSR (8) Aut-Wint 78-79, p. 8.
    "This Late in the Century." AmerPoR (7:5) S-O 78, p. 34.
    "The Trial." PoetryNW (19:2) Sum 78, p. 13.
    "The Weatherman." ThRiPo (11/12) 78, p. 34.

DUNNE, Carol
    "Augur." Tendril (1) Wint 77-78.

"Big Snow." Tendril (3) Aut 78, p. 21.
"Dog." Tendril (2) Spr-Sum 78.

DUNNING, Stephen
"Against the Silence." SouthernPR (18:2) Aut 78, p. 72.
"Cutting In." HiramPoR (24) Spr-Sum 78, p. 12.
"Driving West on 96." SlowLR (1/2) 78, p. 77.
"Glass Eyes, Patches." HiramPoR (25) Aut-Wint 78, p. 17.
"In Little Rock." HiramPoR (25) Aut-Wint 78, p. 19.
"A Little Visit." Nimrod (22:2) Spr-Sum 78, p. 16.
"Love, the Circus, Near Seattle." Nimrod (22:2) Spr-Sum 78,
    p. 18.
"My father as angel." SouthernPR (18:2) Aut 78, p. 71.
"Poem for Nose." HiramPoR (25) Aut-Wint 78, p. 18.
"Sarah, Late from Camp." MichQR (17:3) Sum 78, p. 364.
"Through the Wax." ConcPo (11:1) Spr 78, p. 37.
"To Montana, the Center of Light." Nimrod (22:2) Spr-Sum 78,
    p. 14.
"Walking Bear." NewL (44:3) Spr 78, p. 36.

DuPLESSIS, Rachel Blau
"Flower." Montra (4) 78, p. 9.
"Painting." Montra (4) 78, p. 10.
"A Poem of Myself." Montra (4) 78, p. 11.
"Pomegranate." Montra (4) 78, p. 8.
"Undertow." Montra (4) 78, p. 6.

DuPRIEST, Travis
"Experimental Religion" (for Cynthia Campbell). ChrC (95:4)
    1-8 F 78, p. 99.
"The Gift." ConcPo (11:2) Aut 78, p. 31.

DUREN, Francis
"Covetousness." SouthernHR (12:3) Sum 78, p. 211.
"How I Feel When I Get a Rejection Slip." SouthernHR (12:3)
    Sum 78, p. 250.
"Murderer." SouthernHR (12:3) Sum 78, p. 204.
"My Mother in February." SouthernHR (12:3) Sum 78, p. 212.
"Rift." SouthernHR (12:2) Spr 78, p. 122.
"Sloth." SouthernHR (12:3) Sum 78, p. 230.
"Spring Poem." SouthernHR (12:2) Spr 78, p. 122.

DURHAM, Sukey
"For a Friend." HangL (33) Sum 78, p. 30.
"Two Love Poems." HangL (33) Sum 78, p. 33.

DUVAL, Quinton
"Camping." CalQ (13/14) Spr-Sum 78, p. 141.
"The Wind from the South." CarolQ (30:2) Spr-Sum 78, p. 22.

DWYER, David
"A Love Letter." SoDakR (16:2) Sum 78, p. 31.

DWYER, Frank
  "Apology." __Salm__ (40) Wint 78, p. 95.
  "Family Happiness." __PraS__ (52:2) Sum 78, p. 175.

DYBEK, Stuart
  "At the Monet Exhibit." __Stonecloud__ (7) 78, p. 14.
  "Don't Forget Tonight." __Stonecloud__ (7) 78, p. 144.
  "Gambler." __Stonecloud__ (7) 78, p. 14.
  "Hester the Jester." __Pig__ (4) 78, p. 9.
  "Milkweed." __Comm__ (105:5) 3 Mr 78, p. 149.
  "Orchids." __Stonecloud__ (7) 78, p. 14.
  "Salome." __Pig__ (4) 78, p. 9.
  "Sea Horses." __PoetryNW__ (19:3) Aut 78, p. 44.

DYCK, Edward
  "Turnhill." __NorthSR__ (8) Aut-Wint 78-79, p. 26.

DYGERT, Ann
  "Accident." __CarouselQ__ (3:4) Wint 78, p. 38.

DYSON, Adelaide
  "We Are the Children." __KanQ__ (10:1) Wint 78, p. 76.

EADES, Joan
  "April Fools." __KanQ__ (10:1) Wint 78, p. 38.
  "Meeting the Man." __JnlONJP__ (3:1) 78, p. 21.

EAKINS, Patricia
  "Cup." __OP__ (26) Aut-Wint 78, p. 49.
  "Dress." __OP__ (26) Aut-Wint 78, p. 52.
  "(for Elizabeth)." __Stonecloud__ (7) 78, p. 71.
  "Lamp." __OP__ (26) Aut-Wint 78, p. 50.
  "Leaving Here IV." __SmPd__ (43) Spr 78, p. 3.
  "Mirrors." __OP__ (26) Aut-Wint 78, p. 55.
  "My Mother Flew Around You Like/Bees Around/Zinnias."
      __Stonecloud__ (7) 78, p. 93.
  "Peach." __OP__ (26) Aut-Wint 78, p. 53.
  "Third-Story Window." __OP__ (26) Aut-Wint 78, p. 51.
  "Umbrella." __OP__ (26) Aut-Wint 78, p. 54.

EARLEY, Beth
  "The Bees at Night." __Glass__ (3:1/2/3) 78, p. 30.
  "Trio." __Glass__ (3:1/2/3) 78, p. 31.

EATON, Charles Edward
  "The Avocado Connection." __ConcPo__ (11:2) Aut 78, p. 40.
  "The Chandelier." __Salm__ (42) Sum-Aut 78, p. 130.
  "The Enfabled Nude." __ColEng__ (39:8) Ap 78, p. 941.
  "The Has-Been." __DeKalb__ (11:1/2) Aut-Wint 77-78, p. 47.
  "The Head at the Desk." __MidwQ__ (19:2) Wint 78, p. 130.
  "The Leper." __Poem__ (33) Jl 78, p. 46.
  "Peacock Chair." __SouthwR__ (63:2) Spr 78, p. 132.

"Placed Objects in an Autumn Light." Poem (33) Jl 78, p. 45.
"The Weight of the Mastiff." Poem (33) Jl 78, p. 44.

EBERHARDT, Burgess
"The Solitary Goose." SoDakR (16:2) Sum 78, p. 47.

EBERHART, Richard
"Death in a Taxi." AmerPoR (7:5) S-O 78, p. 34.
"Hour." PoNow (19) 78, p. 5.
"In Situ." Atl (242:3) S 78, p. 62.
"A Loon Call." NewEngR (1:2) Aut 78, p. 140.
"A Rich Kiss." AmerPoR (7:5) S-O 78, p. 34.
"A Whack at Empson." NewEngR (1:1) Aut 78, p. 47.

EBNER, Hans, Jr.
"Just for Fun...." Smudge (2) Sum 78, p. 15.

ECKMAN, Frederick
"Aka." NewL (45:2) Wint 78, p. 76.
"The Crocuses." CentR (22:3) Sum 78, p. 320.
"The Enforcer." NewL (45:2) Wint 78, p. 77.

ECONOMOU, George
"Philodemos I. v. 112" (tr.). Pequod (2:4) 78, p. 60.

EDDY, Darlene
"Drifting." GRR (9:2) 78, p. 102.
"Fine Woods." GRR (9:2) 78, p. 103.
"Impressions." GRR (9:2) 78, p. 101.

EDDY, Gary
"High Field--First Day of Winter." GeoR (32:4) Wint 78, p. 857.

EDELMAN, Elaine
"Losing Your Voice." SoDakR (16:2) Sum 78, p. 20.
"a moment ago." AmerPoR (7:3) My-Je 78, p. 42.
"My Other Country." AmerPoR (7:3) My-Je 78, p. 42.
"Sleet." AmerPoR (7:3) My-Je 78, p. 42.

EDELMAN, Sandra Prewitt
"Beyond Night." SouthwR (63:3) Sum 78, p. 293.
"A Run of Very Poor Sibyls." SouthwR (63:1) Wint 78, p. 26.

EDER, Mari K.
"Fruit Stand." CarouselQ (3:2) Sum 78, p. 25.

EDSON, Russell
"The Doorway Trap." Field (18) Spr 78, p. 9.
"The Fainting." MissouriR (2:1) Aut 78, p. 24.
"The Falling Out of Bed Stories." Field (18) Spr 78, p. 5.
"The King's Windup Toy." Agni (8) 78, p. 93.
"The Old Woman Who Is Let Out of a Window." PoNow (19)
    78, p. 30.

"The Terrible Infant." PoNow (19) 78, p. 30.
"The Traffic." Field (18) Spr 78, p. 8.
"The Unforgiven." Field (18) Spr 78, p. 7.
"The Wounded Breakfast." Field (18) Spr 78, p. 6.

EDWARDS, Paul
from Hávamál: "Words from Up Top" (tr. of Old Norse, w.
    Hermann Palsson). LittleM (11:3) Aut 77, p. 60.

EGEMO, Constance
"Chatelaine." DacTerr (15) Wint-Spr 77-78, p. 35.
"The Keeper." DacTerr (15) Wint-Spr 77-78, p. 34.
"Three Ways of Looking at Birds." DacTerr (15) Wint-Spr 77-
    78, p. 35.

EHRHART, W. D.
"Eighteen Months in Chicago." Smudge (3) Aut 78, p. 19.
"Empire." Sam (64) 78, p. 43.
Empire (For Donaldo & Sam, & for my nephew, Harry). Sam
    (66) 78. Entire issue.
"Letter" (to a North Vietnamese soldier whose life crossed paths
    with mine in Hue City on February 5th, 1968). Wind (29)
    78, p. 19.
"Vietnamese-Cambodian Border War." Sam (64) 78, p. 42.
"Waiting for Rain." Wind (29) 78, p. 20.

EHRLICH, Shelly
"Elegy" (for AE, psychoanalyst). Nor (8) Aut 78, p. 20.

EIDUS, Janice
"Hoo-Doo Nature Poem." Epoch (27:2) Wint 78, p. 153.

EIGNER, Larry
"bird top." PoNow (19) 78, p. 32.
"Snow Sequence." ChiR (30:3) Wint 79, p. 117.

EIKENBERRY, G. L.
"Mountain Songs." Sam (65) 78, p. 42.

EISENBERG, Phil
"News of the Death of an Old Aunt." StoneC (78:1) Wint 78,
    p. 30.

EKELÖF, Gunnar
"Ghazal" (tr. by Rika Lesser). Poetry (131:6) Mr 78, p. 339.
"The Hypnogogue" (tr. by Rika Lesser). Poetry (131:6) Mr 78,
    p. 340.
"Losses" (tr. by Rika Lesser). Poetry (131:6) Mr 78, p. 342.
"Oecus" (tr. by Rika Lesser). Poetry (131:6) Mr 78, p. 338.

ELDER, Karl
"Sentiment." DacTerr (15) Wint-Spr 77-78, p. 42.

ELKIND, Sue
"Commemoration of a War." Wind (28) 78, p. 15.
"Fear." Wind (28) 78, p. 15.

ELLINGSON, Nancy
"Poem for a Nephew." PoNow (20) 78, p. 7.

ELLIOTT, George P.
"Sayer." NewL (45:2) Wint 78, p. 74.

ELLIOTT, Harley
"Going Bump in the Night." HangL (32) Spr 78, p. 10.
"In the Heart of Darkness" (for Mona). HangL (32) Spr 78,
    p. 11.
"Mailing Letters at Midnight." HangL (32) Spr 78, p. 12.
"Poets in Schools." HiramPoR (25) Aut-Wint 78, p. 20.
"The Teeth of Small Children." HangL (34) Wint 78-79, p. 15.
"Watch Out Your Life Is Coming True." HangL (34) Wint 78-79,
    p. 16.

ELLIOTT, William D.
"February Thaw." SouthernPR (18:2) Aut 78, p. 59.
"Refrigerator Gothic." SouthernPR (18:2) Aut 78, p. 60.

ELLIOTT, William I.
"Toying with a Buzzard." ChrC (95:18) 17 My 78, p. 532.
"Written at 14 E. 28th Street, New York City" (tr. of Shuntaro
    Tanikawa). SoDakR (16:4) Wint 78-79, p. 66.

ELLIS, Edward
"White Swans on Harvest Gold." Wind (31) 78, p. 59.

ELLIS, Rebecca
"The Mountain." PikeF (1) Spr 78, p. 12.
"To Hansel." HangL (32) Spr 78, p. 13.

ELLIS, Reuben
"A Gravitational Sound." EnPas (7) 78, p. 39.

ELLIS, Ron
"The Power of the Doe." PikeF (1) Spr 78, p. 14.

ELLISON, George
"7 March 77." Wind (28) 78, p. 16.
"Lituus of Augurs." Wind (28) 78, p. 16.
"The Taste in Yr Mouth." Wind (28) 78, p. 17.
"Without Metaphor." Wind (28) 78, p. 16.

ELLISON, Jessie T.
"The Coin Silver Spoon." Ascent (3:3) 78, p. 24.
"Crossings." Epos (27:2) 77, p. 6.
"Definitive." WindO (31) Wint-Spr 78, p. 36.

"Le Grand Mal. " <u>WindO</u> (33) Aut-Wint 78-79.
"Letter from the Rest Home. " <u>WindO</u> (31) Wint-Spr 78, p. 37.

ELLMAN, Dennis
"Some Common Dreams. " <u>Bachy</u> (13) Aut-Wint 78-79, p. 37.

ELMORE, Jeff
"Poet. " <u>SeC</u> (5:2) 78, p. 14.

ELMSLIE, Kenward
"Communications Equipment. " <u>SunM</u> (5) Aut 78, p. 22.
"Porn Dream" (for Patty on her 40th birthday). <u>SunM</u> (5) 78,
    p. 19.
"Time Study. " <u>SunM</u> (5) Aut 78, p. 20.

ELON, Florence
"Monica Dugall. " <u>Salm</u> (42) Sum-Aut 78, p. 126.
"New Orders. " <u>Salm</u> (40) Wint 78, p. 95.

ELSEY, David
"The Stars. " <u>PoNow</u> (20) 78, p. 8.

ELSON, Virginia
"Admission. " <u>SouthwR</u> (63:3) Sum 78, p. 257.
"Odd Hour. " <u>Epos</u> (27:2) 77, p. 35.
"Receptor. " <u>PoetryNW</u> (19:4) Wint 78-79, p. 9.

ELSTER, Charles
"Smoke. " <u>AmerPoR</u> (7:3) My-Je 78, p. 13.
"Underground. " <u>AmerPoR</u> (7:3) My-Je 78, p. 13.

ELUARD, Paul
"Between the Moon and the Sun" (tr. by Marilyn Kallet).
    <u>SlowLR</u> (1/2) 78, p. 20.
"From Peace Poems" (tr. by R. Sieburth and S. W. DeRache-
    wiltz). <u>St.AR</u> (5:1) Aut-Wint 78, p. 63.
"Here" (tr. by Marilyn Kallet). <u>SlowLR</u> (1/2) 78, p. 21.
"The Lover" (tr. by R. Sieburth and S. W. DeRachewiltz).
    <u>St.AR</u> (5:1) Aut-Wint 78, p. 62.
"Perspective" (tr. by R. Sieburth and S. W. DeRachewiltz).
    <u>St.AR</u> (5:1) Aut-Wint 78, p. 63.
"Seascape. " <u>SlowLR</u> (1/2) 78, p. 19.

ELYTIS, Odysseus
"The Garden Sees. " <u>ChiR</u> (30:2) Aut 78, p. 20.
"The Garden Sees" (tr. by Athan Anagnostopoulos). <u>ChiR</u> (30:2)
    Aut 78, p. 21.

EMANS, Elaine V.
"Carrier Pigeon. " <u>Epos</u> (27:2) 77, p. 33.
"Delicacy. " <u>Epos</u> (27:2) 77, p. 33.
"Mistakable Identity. " <u>SmPd</u> (42) Wint 78, p. 16.
"The Shredders. " <u>KanQ</u> (10:2) Spr 78, p. 38.

EMANUEL, Lynn
"Cow Poem." SlowLR (1/2) 78, p. 39.
"Crazy Quilt." SlowLR (1/2) 78, p. 38.
"Enormous Leisure" (for Jeffrey). SlowLR (1/2) 78, p. 40.
"Hallowmass." SlowLR (1/2) 78, p. 36.
"Sepia" (for Jon Anderson). SlowLR (1/2) 78, p. 42.

EMBLEN, D. L.
"A Long Diagonal." CalQ (13/14) Spr-Sum 78, p. 112.
"Shelter." CalQ (13/14) Spr-Sum 78, p. 112.

EMENHISER, JeDon
"Communion." ChrC (95:23) 5-12 Jl 78, p. 677.

EMERSON, Dorothy
"Come Soon." Poetry (132:2) My 78, p. 77.

EMRICK, Ernestine Hoff
"Mirror Twin." ChrC (95:36) 8 N 78, p. 1073.

ENGELS, John
"After Ten Years." Antaeus (30/31) Sum-Aut 78, p. 74.
"At Night on the Lake, in the Eye of the Hunter." NewEngR
    (1:1) Aut 78, p. 83.
"Bog Plants." VirQR (54:3) Sum 78, p. 488.
"Dreaming of the Natural History Museum at Notre Dame."
    VirQR (54:3) Sum 78, p. 487.
"The Geese." Nat (226:15) 22 Ap 78, p. 460.
"Ghosts" (for Donald Justice). Nat (226:18) 13 My 78, p. 575.
"The Great Crash." AmerPoR (7:1) Ja-F 78, p. 47.
"Muskrat." Antaeus (30/31) Sum-Aut 78, p. 80.
"Naming the Animals." Columbia (2) Aut 78, p. 40.
"Revisiting the Grave." Columbia (2) Aut 78, p. 58.

ENGLER, Robert Klein
"China Road." WindO (33) Aut-Wint 78-79.
"Epithalamium." WindO (33) Aut-Wint 78-79.
"The Velvet Cord." WindO (33) Aut-Wint 78-79, p. 9.

ENGLER, Robert L.
"Walking by the Moon." GRR (9:3) 78, p. 218.

ENGLISH, Maurice
"What Happens Is This." NewRep (179:20) 11 N 78, p. 30.

ENGMAN, John
"About the Deliverance of Men and Women from a Few Dark
    Buildings Overlooking Lowry Hill." AntR (36:4) Aut 78,
    p. 463.
"Alcatraz." AntR (36:4) Aut 78, p. 464.
"One Way of Looking at Wallace Stevens." AntR (36:4) Aut 78,
    p. 465.

"Photogravure of a Winter with Oranges: Confessions for Paul &
    Vanessa." PoetryNW (19:1) Spr 78, p. 42.

ENSLIN, Theodore
    "The Last Misfortune." Hand (2) 78, p. 17.
    "On such a windy afternoon." ChiR (30:3) Wint 79, p. 128.
    "The Planes in San Miguel" (for Keith Wilson). Northeast (3:5)
        Spr-Sum 78, p. 26.
    from Ranger: (CV). SunM (5) 78, p. 43.

ENTREKIN, Charles
    "Dream of Leaving You." US1 (11) Aut 78, p. 4.

EPLING, Kathy
    "A Birth Song for Garth." Kayak (48) Je 78, p. 47.
    "The Harbor Dweller." Kayak (48) Je 78, p. 49.
    "The Language of the Air." Kayak (48) Je 78, p. 48.
    "The Room with the Orange Screen" (for Victoria Serra). AndR
        (5:1) Spr 78, p. 80.

EPSKAMP, David
    "On Revolution." Smudge (1) Spr 78, p. 21.

EPSTEIN, Daniel Mark
    "The Catch." Atl (241:4) Ap 78, p. 117.
    "The Dance." VirQR (54:3) Sum 78, p. 484.
    "Easter." NewRep (178:9) 4 Mr 78, p. 33.
    "Poverty." VirQR (54:3) Sum 78, p. 484.

EPSTEIN, Elaine
    "Possessions: Randall Jarrell." Ploughs (4:2) 78, p. 39.

EPSTEIN, Judith
    "Family Pictures." HangL (32) Spr 78, p. 14.

ERAY, Nazli
    "The Eyes of the Dog." St.AR (4:3/4) 77-78, p. 17.

ERFORD, Esther
    "Sonata in Brown, for Woodwinds." DeKalb (11:1/2) Aut-Wint 77-
        78, p. 48.
    "Song: For a Little Girl." GRR (9:3) 78, p. 213.
    "Winter Lament." Wind (29) 78, p. 21.
    "The Wishing Hour." BallSUF (19:4) Aut 78, p. 18.

ERTESZEK, Christina
    "July 20th." SouthernHR (12:2) Spr 78, p. 139.
    "Notes on Mummy." SouthernHR (12:1) Wint 78, p. 42.

ESBENSEN, Barbara Juster
    "Two A.M.--Thirty Below Zero (Duluth)." PoNow (19) 78,
        p. 23.

ESHLEMAN, Clayton
"Elegy on the Death of a Friend" (tr. of Milan Exner, w. Jan
Benda). Montra (4) 78, p. 12.

ESPE, Cynthia Veach
"Minnesota Night." ChiR (29:4) Spr 78, p. 62.

ESPOSITO, Nancy
"Matins." SoDakR (16:2) Sum 78, p. 8.

ESPRIU, Salvador
"Hemeroskopeion" (tr. by Jan Pallister). SlowLR (1/2) 78,
p. 64.
"Sure Catch" (tr. by Jan Pallister). SlowLR (1/2) 78, p. 63.

ESSARY, Loris
Eight poems. LaB (10) 78, p. 5.
"Five Visual Poems." SunM (5) Aut 78, p. 48.
"wagon." Hills (5) 78, p. 54.
"X." Glass (3:1/2/3) 78, p. 56.

ESTEBAN, Claude
from Dieu Transparent: "Free the Path, Leave" (tr. by David
Cloutier). Durak (1) 78, p. 49.
from Dieu Transparent: "Less the Bird" (tr. by David Cloutier).
Durak (1) 78, p. 50.
from Dieu Transparent: "Stone" (tr. by David Cloutier). Durak
(1) 78, p. 48.

ETCHETO, John
"Love is a gorgeous/experience." SeC (5:2) 78, p. 15.

ETHIER, Mike
"The Cheshirebridge Massage Parlor." DeKalb (11:3/4) Spr-
Sum 78, p. 93.

ETTER, Dave
"Ardis Newkirk at the Charity Ball." MidwQ (19:4) Sum 78,
p. 376.
"Bluehawk." PoNow (19) 78, p. 34.
"Bright Mississippi." PoNow (19) 78, p. 34.
"Brother and Sister." PoNow (19) 78, p. 3.
"A Damned Pretty Rain." MidwQ (19:4) Sum 78, p. 375.
"Doing Nothing at Two in the Morning." MinnR (NS11) Aut 78,
p. 29.
"Empty Beer Can." MidwQ (19:4) Sum 78, p. 373.
"Hackensack." PoNow (19) 78, p. 34.
"The Inland Poet Dreams of Foreign Travel." AAR (28) 78,
p. 58.
"The Jesus Barn." PoNow (19) 78, p. 2.
"Late Night Thoughts." AAR (28) 78, p. 57.
"Murder." Northeast (3:5) Spr-Sum 78, p. 17.
"Nostalgia." PoNow (19) 78, p. 2.

"Off Minor. " PoNow (19) 78, p. 34.
"An Ohio Goodbye. " Focus (13:79) Ja-F 78, p. 31.
"On the School Bus. " MidwQ (19:4) Sum 78, p. 374.
"Poem on My Father's Eightieth Birthday. " Northeast (3:5) Spr-
    Sum 78, p. 16.
"Riding the Rock Island through Kansas. " PoNow (19) 78, p. 3.
"Robert. " PoNow (19) 78, p. 34.
"Second Honeymoon. " PoNow (19) 78, p. 34.
"Stuffy Turkey. " PoNow (19) 78, p. 34.
"Two Children in a Snowstorm. " Northeast (3:5) Spr-Sum 78,
    p. 18.
"Watermelons. " Northeast (3:5) Spr-Sum 78, p. 16.
"Worms. " PoNow (19) 78, p. 3.

EVANS, David
    "Sketch. " CalQ (13/14) Spr-Sum 78, p. 88.

EVANS, Martha
    "The Cage Alive with Vibrations. " BelPoJ (29:2) Wint 78-79,
        p. 1.
    "letter from Giuseppa Marsela to her mother after walking 2, 000
        miles. " NewL (45:1) Aut 78, p. 17.
    "surroundings. " NewL (45:1) Aut 78, p. 17.

EVATT, Julia
    "Copperhead at Cohutta. " BallSUF (19:4) Aut 78, p. 35.

EVERETT, Joanne Marie
    "The Struggle. " CarouselQ (3:4) Wint 78, p. 40.

EVERHARD, Jim
    "Henri Matisse. " HangL (34) Wint 78-79, p. 17.
    "I wear an orange dress. " HangL (34) Wint 78-79, p. 21.
    "Matisse, Again. " HangL (34) Wint 78-79, p. 19.
    "Orange. " HangL (34) Wint 78-79, p. 20.
    "Reasons Why I Love You" (for Richard Sawyer). HangL (34)
        Wint 78-79, p. 22.

EVERSON, William
    "Runoff. " Kayak (47) F 78, p. 28.

EWART, Gavin
    "The Moment. " Stand (19:2) 78, p. 3.

EWING, Patricia Renee
    "Cupping. " St. AR (4:3/4) 77-78, p. 121.

EXNER, Milan
    "Elegy on the Death of a Friend" (tr. by Clayton Eshleman and
        Jan Benda). Montra (4) 78, p. 12.

EXNER, Richard
    from A Book of Hours: "At Night, At the Tower of Babel" (tr.
        of Heinz Piontek). ChiR (30:2) Aut 78, p. 41.

FAGONE, Robert
  "Epidermal Things." NorthSR (8) Aut-Wint 78-79, p. 63.
  "Memo." NorthSR (8) Aut-Wint 78-79, p. 61.
  "Polemic." NorthSR (8) Aut-Wint 78-79, p. 60.
  "Spring." NorthSR (8) Aut-Wint 78-79, p. 62.

FAINLIGHT, Ruth
  "A Child Crying." MassR (19:3) Aut 78, p. 570.
  "Meeting." Nat (226:15) 22 Ap 78, p. 455.

FALK, Armand E.
  "Going on Sabbatical." AAUP (64:3) S 78, p. 276.
  "Office Burial." AAUP (64:3) S 78, p. 276.
  "On the Eve of Forty-Four." BelPoJ (28:4) Sum 78, p. 22.

FALK, Marcia
  "Alone" (tr. of T. Carmi). Hand (2) 78, p. 134.
  "Premonitions, Early Spring." Hand (2) 78, p. 23.
  "Swan Lake Rehearsal at the Ballet School." AndR (4:2) Aut 77,
     p. 39.
  "Then My Soul Cried Out" (tr. of Zelda). Hand (2) 78, p. 162.
  "Witnessing." Hand (2) 78, p. 22.

FALLIS, L. S.
  "Lighthouse Pointe." CarouselQ (3:1) Spr 78, p. 13.
  "Prairie du Chien." Pan (19) 77, p. 66.

FALLON, Peter
  "Fallow." LitR (22:2) Wint 79, p. 271.
  "It was not the day...." LitR (22:2) Wint 79, p. 273.
  "Victim." LitR (22:2) Wint 79, p. 272.

FANDEL, John
  "Late August Night." Comm (105:13) 7 Jl 78, p. 433.

FANNING, Charlie
  "Memorial Day in Eastham." Tendril (1) Wint 77-78.

FANTAUZZI, D. A.
  "My Father's Coronary." Bits (8) Jl 78.
  "Tall Ships." Bits (7) Ja 78.

FARALLO, Livio
  "Dormant Candles." CarouselQ (3:2) Sum 78, p. 5.

FARBER, Norma
  "Beekeeping." CentR (22:4) Aut 78, p. 419.
  "Capturing the Swarm." CentR (22:4) Aut 78, p. 420.
  "Even deep as I was." CentR (22:1) Wint 78, p. 70.
  "A Relict Joy." CentR (22:1) Wint 78, p. 70.

FAREWELL, Patricia
  "Keeping Company." LittleM (11:3) Aut 77, p. 64.

FARKAS, Andre
  "Murders in the Welcome Cafe." <u>Pig</u> (4) 78, p. 69.

FARRELL, Jim
  "The Last of April." <u>CarouselQ</u> (3:4) Wint 78, p. 27.
  "People Ask Us." <u>JnlONJP</u> (3:1) 78, p. 23.

FARRELL, Kate
  "River." <u>PartR</u> (45:1) 78, p. 11.

FAUCHER, Real
  "Adamant." <u>Smudge</u> (2) Sum 78, p. 14.
  "The Columnist." <u>Sam</u> (64) 78, p. 23.
  "the dancing girl." <u>Wind</u> (31) 78, p. 12.
  "Father's Funeral." <u>Vaga</u> (28) Aut 78, p. 57.
  "the last picture." <u>Tele</u> (13) 78.
  "Man with a Vision." <u>Wind</u> (31) 78, p. 12.
  "Mother's Funeral." <u>Vaga</u> (28) Aut 78, p. 57.
  "the poet's woman." <u>Smudge</u> (Supplement) Wint 78-79, p. 39.

FAULKNER, Margherita
  "Suppositions." <u>NewOR</u> (6:1) 78, p. 39.
  "Table Linen." <u>Northeast</u> (3:5) Spr-Sum 78, p. 22.

FAUTEUX, Robert
  "A Dream Beneath the Ice" (for Mary Larson). <u>DacTerr</u> (15)
      Wint-Spr 77-78, p. 20.
  "After Reading 'Intermission' by Louis Jenkins." <u>Wind</u> (29) 78,
      p. 23.
  "Breakfast" (for Marshall & Ann Moen). <u>Poem</u> (33) Jl 78, p. 20.
  "Jan Garbarek's Horn." <u>Wind</u> (29) 78, p. 14.
  "A Memory of Sparks" (for Gary O. Larson). <u>Poem</u> (33) Jl 78,
      p. 22.

FAVICCHIO, John
  "Rain." <u>CarouselQ</u> (3:1) Spr 78, p. 20.

FAY, Julie
  "Early Marriage: Burlington, Iowa, 1881." <u>CutB</u> (11) Aut-Wint
      78, p. 51.

FEDULLO, Mick
  "Trees" (for W. C. W.). <u>ChiR</u> (30:1) Sum 78, p. 103.

FEIN, Cheri
  "Blue." <u>GreenfieldR</u> (6:3/4) Spr 78, p. 152.
  "Lullaby." <u>PartR</u> (45:1) 78, p. 13.
  "Polio." <u>GreenfieldR</u> (6:3/4) Spr 78, p. 152.
  "The Silver Wires." <u>Nimrod</u> (22:2) Spr-Sum 78, p. 19.
  "The Unicorn Tapestry." <u>Nimrod</u> (22:2) Spr-Sum 78, p. 24.

FEIRSTEIN, Frederick
  "Written in a Tuscan Farmhouse." <u>CentR</u> (22:1) Wint 78, p. 75.

FELDMAN, Alan
"Plea." ColEng (39:8) Ap 78, p. 945.

FELDMAN, Irving
"Man of Letters." MichQR (17:4) Aut 78, p. 443.
"Three Tales." VirQR (54:4) Aut 78, p. 700.

FELDMAN, Jack
"Vox Semaphoric." PoNow (20) 78, p. 8.

FELDMAN, Ruth
"America" (tr. of Rocco Scotellaro, w. Brian Swann). GRR
    (9:1) 78, p. 37.
"Betrothed" (tr. of Rocco Scotellaro, w. Brian Swann). Paint
    (9/10) Spr-Aut 78, p. 42.
"Bormann" (tr. of Bartolo Cattafi, w. Brian Swann). MalR (46)
    Ap 78, p. 145.
"Christmas" (tr. of Rocco Scotellaro, w. Brian Swann). St. AR
    (4:3/4) 77-78, p. 107.
"Elephants as Elephants" (tr. of Mario Lunetta). ChiR (30:2)
    Aut 78, p. 43.
from Empedocles D'Artaud: "Fragment 57" (tr. of Giovanna
    Sandri, w. Brian Swann). Durak (1) 78, p. 56.
from Empedocles D'Artaud: "Fragment 61" (tr. of Giovanna
    Sandri, w. Brian Swann). Durak (1) 78, p. 57.
"Evening" (tr. of Rocco Scotellaro, w. Brian Swann). St. AR
    (4:3/4) 77-78, p. 107.
"Every Day Is Monday" (tr. of Rocco Scotellaro, w. Brian
    Swann). St. AR (4:3/4) 77-78, p. 106.
"Father Mine" (tr. of Rocco Scotellaro, w. Brian Swann). GRR
    (9:1) 78, p. 41.
"First Farewell to Naples" (tr. of Rocco Scotellaro, w. Brian
    Swann). GRR (9:1) 78, p. 39.
"A Friend" (tr. of Rocco Scotellaro, w. Brian Swann). Paint
    (9/10) Spr-Aut 78, p. 43.
"From Nyhavn" (tr. of Bartolo Cattafi, w. Brian Swann).
    Falcon (17) 78, p. 11.
"Guest." Glass (3:1/2/3) 78, p. 91.
"Homage to Cartier-Bresson." St. AR (4:3/4) 77-78, p. 118.
"Interior" (tr. of Bartolo Cattafi, w. Brian Swann). Falcon (17)
    78, p. 12.
from Ipotesi: "Jean Arp" (tr. of Murilo Mendes). GRR (9:2)
    78, p. 95.
from Ipotesi: "Klee" (tr. of Murilo Mendes). GRR (9:2) 78,
    p. 97.
from Ipotesi: "The Painting" (tr. of Murilo Mendes). GRR (9:2)
    78, p. 91.
"My Father" (tr. of Rocco Scotellaro, w. Brian Swann). St. AR
    (4:3/4) 77-78, p. 105.
"A New World" (tr. of Bartolo Cataffi, w. Brian Swann).
    Columbia (2) Aut 78, p. 80.
"On Cats' Paws" (tr. of Rocco Scotellaro, w. Brian Swann).
    St. AR (4:3/4) 77-78, p. 107.

"Peace" (tr. of Bartolo Cattafi, w. Brian Swann). MalR (46) Ap
    78, p. 144.
"Siege." Glass (3:1/2/3) 78, p. 92.
"Stalk" (tr. of Bartolo Cattafi, w. Brian Swann). MalR (46) Ap
    78, p. 144.
"They Stole You from Us" (tr. of Rocco Scotellaro, w. Brian
    Swann). GRR (9:1) 78, p. 35.
Twelve poems. GRR (9:3) 78, p. 165.

FELIPE, León
"Biography, Poetry and Destiny" (tr. by Electa Arenal). WebR
    (4:2) Aut 78, p. 15.
"Like a Flea" (tr. by Electa Arenal). AmerPoR (7:4) Jl-Ag 78,
    p. 15.
"Like You" (tr. by Electa Arenal). WebR (4:2) Aut 78, p. 16.
"XXIII Caption for the Child of Vallacas by Velázquez" (tr. by
    Electa Arenal). AmerPoR (7:4) Jl-Ag 78, p. 15.

FERACA, Jean
"Backstairs." AmerPoR (7:3) My-Je 78, p. 14.
"Botanical Gardens." AmerPoR (7:3) My-Je 78, p. 14.
"Ice-Storm in Armonk." AmerPoR (7:3) My-Je 78, p. 14.

FERGUSON, Barry G.
"Barefoot." CarouselQ (3:2) Sum 78, p. 20.

FERICANO, Paul F.
"On the Death of Moe Howard." WormR (68) 77, p. 91.
"Poet Arrested Here by Locals and Feds." WormR (68) 77,
    p. 91.
"Teddy Street." Zahir (9) 77, p. 49.

FERRARELLI, Rina
"Leaves Fill the Gutters." BallSUF (19:1) Wint 78, p. 62.

FERREIRO, Celso Emilio
"Nota Bene for Rafael Alberti" (tr. by Lucia Graves). MalR
    (47) Jl 78, p. 56.

FERRIL, Thomas Hornsby
"Set of Three." Aspen (6) Aut 78, p. 106.

FERRY, David
"Photographs from a Book." Poetry (131:4) Ja 78, p. 204.

FERRY, Dick
"A Shiny Place." PikeF (1) Spr 78, p. 13.

FEWELL, Richard
"Bamboo & Cotton Stalks." GreenfieldR (6:3/4) Spr 78, p. 159.
"Black Man in China." GreenfieldR (6:3/4) Spr 78, p. 162.
"Coming Home." Obs (4:2) Sum 78, p. 85.
"Dear Tom, Dear Uncle Tom (1863-1959)." GreenfieldR (6:3/4)

Spr 78, p. 160.
"The Death of an Oriental/Black." Obs (4:2) Sum 78, p. 88.
"The Hanging Tree." Obs (4:2) Sum 78, p. 84.
"Home." GreenfieldR (6:3/4) Spr 78, p. 161.
"King Joe (The 'Brown' Bomber)." Obs (4:2) Sum 78, p. 83.
"The Robin & the Rock." Obs (4:2) Sum 78, p. 89.

FIALKOWSKI, Barbara
"The Body-Snatchers." BallSUF (19:4) Aut 78, p. 54.
"Cartogram." PoNow (20) 78, p. 8.

FICKERT, Kurt J.
"Nobody Home." WindO (33) Aut-Wint 78-79, p. 4.
"Oblivion." Wind (31) 78, p. 14.
"This Morning at Breakfast." Wind (31) 78, p. 14.
"Virtue '77." SouthernHR (12:4) Wint 78, p. 338.

FIELD, B. S., Jr.
"Drips." BallSUF (19:4) Aut 78, p. 40.

FIELD, Matt
"The Fable of the Chickadee and the Cat" (tr. of Pierre Béarn).
    GRR (9:2) 78, p. 121.
"The Fable of the Untimely Fly" (tr. of Pierre Béarn). GRR
    (9:2) 78, p. 123.
"Sailors' Christmas" (tr. of Pierre Béarn). GRR (9:2) 78,
    p. 125.

FIFER, Ken
"Maple Street." Pig (5) 78, p. 91.

FILES, Meg
"Fire-Dance." Focus (12:78) N-D 77, p. 31.

FIMBINGER, Russ
"the tall father" (for carroll arnett). GreenfieldR (6:3/4) Spr
    78, p. 110.

FINALE, Frank
"Guinea Pig." Zahir (9) 77, p. 12.
"The House." SmPd (43) Spr 78, p. 15.
"Man and Wife." PoNow (20) 78, p. 8.

FINCHER, Jack
"The Day Walt Whitman's Brain Dropped on the Floor." EngJ
    (67:5) My 78, p. 55.

FINCKE, Gary
"Fire Drill." PoNow (20) 78, p. 9.
"I Am No Swimmer." SmPd (44) Aut 78, p. 19.
"The Room I Sit In Has Been Emptied." WormR (70) 78, p. 73.
"The Shallow Case." WormR (70) 78, p. 75.
"Shoes." WormR (70) 78, p. 74.

"Steak Dinner." WormR (70) 78, p. 74.
"Suspension." WormR (70) 78, p. 75.

FINK, Jon-Stephen
  "The Amarna Letters." SenR (9:2) Aut-Wint 78, p. 65.

FINKEL, Donald
  from Going Under: "Stephen" (Section 1). SenR (9:2) Aut-Wint
    78, p. 10.
  "The Party." Kayak (47) F 78, p. 51.
  "The Prodigal Son." PoNow (19) 78, p. 5.

FINKELSTEIN, Caroline
  "The Liberal Predicament." AntR (36:1) Wint 78, p. 86.
  "To Fairy Godmother." AntR (36:1) Wint 78, p. 87.

FINKELSTEIN, Miriam
  "Words to Say on Entering Rooms." Kayak (49) O 78, p. 38.

FINLEY, C. Stephen
  "Beans, Cowbirds, Grosbeaks." CarolQ (30:1) Wint 78, p. 110.
  "First Rain in Late Winter." CarolQ (30:1) Wint 78, p. 111.

FINLEY, Jeanne
  "I Dream I Write for the First Time." GreenfieldR (6:3/4) Spr
    78, p. 130.

FINLEY, Michael
  "The Audience." MoonsLT (2:4) 78, p. 43.
  "The Campaign." MidwQ (19:4) Sum 78, p. 378.
  "Eliminations." PoNow (20) 78, p. 8.
  "Enemies." DacTerr (15) Wint-Spr 77-78, p. 43.
  "How I Got My Good Luck Piece." MidwQ (19:4) Sum 78, p. 377.
  "Look What the Sun Has Lit Up." Falcon (17) 78, p. 15.
  "Miguel Hernandez." Sky (7/8) Spr 78, p. 21.
  "Parking Lot." Pan (19) 77, p. 31.
  "Rachel." Falcon (17) 78, p. 14.
  "The Secret." Pan (19) 77, p. 31.
  "Where Birds Fare Well." MoonsLT (2:4) 78, p. 45.
  "The Woman in Kensington Gardens." MoonsLT (2:4) 78, p. 44.

FINNELL, Dennis
  "Galileo." GreenfieldR (6:3/4) Spr 78, p. 111.
  "Just Outside Emporia, Kansas." PoNow (20) 78, p. 9.

FINUCANE, Martin
  "'The One I Shall Kiss Is the Man.'" HarvAd (111:3) Ap 78,
    p. 26.

FIORE, Peter
  "Dracula's Bolero." AmerPoR (7:4) Jl-Ag 78, p. 31.
  "New Year's Poem" (for leh). AmerPoR (7:4) Jl-Ag 78, p. 30.
  "Winter Night" (for c.). AmerPoR (7:4) Jl-Ag 78, p. 31.

FIRER, Susan
  "Comfort Me with Apples." Northeast (3:6) Wint 78-79, p. 19.
  "don't worry." MinnR (NS11) Aut 78, p. 24.

FIRESTONE, Catherine
  "Heroic Couple" (for AJM Smith). CentR (22:4) Aut 78, p. 422.
  "Whore." CentR (22:4) Aut 78, p. 422.

FISHER, David
  "Death of the Professor." Kayak (47) F 78, p. 42.

FISHER, Harrison
  "Bride of the Semaphore." Epoch (27:3) Spr 78, p. 216.
  "'Denial Made by Teacher of Brutality' (Dallas News)." Epoch
    (28:1) Aut 78, p. 40.
  "Kiss of Idols." Epoch (27:3) Spr 78, p. 217.
  "Ode to Gerbils." Epoch (27:3) Spr 78, p. 218.
  "Purity in What You Do." Epoch (27:3) Spr 78, p. 219.
  "Washer of Woe." Epoch (28:1) Aut 78, p. 41.

FISHER, Lenore Eversole
  "Kites ... and Kites." LadHJ (95:6) Je 78, p. P.S. 12.

FISHER, Roy
  from Handsworth Liberties: (1-3, 8, 19, 21, 22). Montra (4)
    78, p. 122.
  "Paraphrases" (for Peter Ryan). Stand (19:1) Wint 77-78, p. 45.
  "Staffordshire Red" (for Geoffrey Hill). Stand (19:1) 77-78,
    p. 44.

FISHER, Thomas Michael
  "Ditch, or the Way She Runs." Wind (29) 78, p. 22.
  "Our Rainbow Hills." Wind (29) 78, p. 22.

FISHER, Will
  "The Center." NorthSR (8) Aut-Wint 78-79, p. 96.

FISHMAN, Charles
  "Breaking-Out Ritual." GreenfieldR (6:3/4) Spr 78, p. 52.
  "Little Sister." Hand (2) 78, p. 184.
  "Salmon Return to the First, Perilous Stream." GreenfieldR
    (6:3/4) Spr 78, p. 51.
  "Savages." GreenfieldR (6:3/4) Spr 78, p. 50.
  "The Tallyers." HolCrit (15:2) Ap 78, p. 9.

FITZGIBBONS, Eleanor
  "On the Hardening of Arteries." Comm (105:11) 26 My 78,
    p. 333.

FIXEL, Lawrence
  "Slipping Away." Sky (7/8) Spr 78, p. 55.

FIXMER, Clyde
  "The Lover's Grammar & Composition Handbook." WormR (68)

77, p. 109.
"The Man Who Couldn't Say F." WormR (68) 77, p. 108.

FLANAGAN, Robert
"The Dream Children." KanQ (10:2) Spr 78, p. 52.

FLANDERS, Jane
"Before the Poem Begins." OhioR (19:3) Aut 78, p. 27.
"Bringing in the Plants." PoNow (20) 78, p. 9.
"Even the Grass." OhioR (19:3) Aut 78, p. 26.
"Fairy Tales." LitR (21:3) Spr 78, p. 338.
"Something the Leaves Do." Wind (30) 78, p. 10.
"Spring Fire." Nat (227:15) 4 N 78, p. 484.
"Stars Shine So Faithfully." 13thM (4:1) 78, p. 85.
"Stasis." Nat (227:10) 30 S 78, p. 324.

FLAVIN, Jack
"Genealogy." MidwQ (20:1) Aut 78, p. 92.
"In the Little Theatre I Am Seized with Weltschmerz." MidwQ
     (20:1) Aut 78, p. 93.

FLECK, Richard C., Jr.
"A Letter to Thoreau." Box (6) Aut 77, p. 4.

FLECK, Richard F.
"Story, Wyoming." Paint (9/10) Spr-Aut 78, p. 16.

FLEMING, Ray
"Failing by Flesh." Poem (32) Mr 78, p. 47.
"Having Concluded Prematurely." Poem (32) Mr 78, p. 50.
"Metaphysical Poem for Louise Bogan." Poem (32) Mr 78,
     p. 48.
"The Secrets of the Universe." Poem (32) Mr 78, p. 49.

FLEU, Richard
"The Debt." StoneC (78:2) Spr 78, p. 28.
"On Our Way." StoneC (78:2) Spr 78, p. 29.

FLINT, Roland
"Jog." OhioR (19:3) Aut 78, p. 24.
"Space." OhioR (19:3) Aut 78, p. 23.

FLOCK, Miriam
"All Through the Night." Poem (34) N 78, p. 62.
"Men Go on Voyages." Poem (34) N 78, p. 61.
"Mutable Water." WindO (31) Wint-Spr 78, p. 20.
"The Thing about Boys." WindO (31) Wint-Spr 78, p. 19.

FLORENCE, Michael
"Flight." SouthernHR (12:4) Aut 78, p. 324.

FLOTT, Phil, Jr.
"Buttoning Up the Belly." KanQ (10:2) Spr 78, p. 104.
"Carpenter Confessional." SmPd (44) Aut 78, p. 29.

FLYNN, Elizabeth
"Conjugation at Gull Point." LitR (21:3) Spr 78, p. 343.

FOERSTER, Richard
"The Musician." SouthernHR (12:3) Sum 78, p. 203.
"Street Scene." SouthernHR (12:2) Spr 78, p. 138.

FOGEL, Daniel Mark
"The People's Victory." SouthernR (14:1) Wint 78, p. 102.
"Pre-Birthday Poem." SouthernR (14:1) Wint 78, p. 101.

FOLKESTAD, Marilyn
"Kate's Place." CutB (10) Spr-Sum 78, p. 17.

FOLLAIN, Jean
"Wives of the Wind" (tr. by David Cloutier). WebR (4:1) Spr 78,
    p. 32.

FOLLY, Dennis W.
"sometimes at night." BlackF (2:2) Aut-Wint 78, p. 25.
"When i lay down." BlackF (2:2) Aut-Wint 78, p. 25.

FORCHE, Carolyn
"Before Morning" (para Maya). VirQR (54:1) Wint 78, p. 105.
"For the Stranger." NewYorker (54:38) 6 N 78, p. 183.
"The Island" (para Claribel Alegria). VirQR (54:1) Wint 78,
    p. 106.
"Reunion." AmerPoR (7:1) Ja-F 78, p. 48.
"San Onofre." VirQR (54:1) Wint 78, p. 104.
"Surrendering the Memory." AmerPoR (7:1) Ja-F 78, p. 48.

FORD, Frank B.
"Again Those Two." DeKalb (11:1/2) Aut-Wint 77-78, p. 49.

FORD, Michael C.
"Bulletin." Stonecloud (7) 78, p. 32.
"Timpanogos Mts/Provo, Utah." Stonecloud (7) 78, p. 58.
"the witch doctor succeeds in not being a marriage counselor."
    Stonecloud (7) 78, p. 29.

FORD, William
"Another Life at Fifteen." PoetC (10:2) 78, p. 21.

FORTINI, Franco
"In una strada di Firenze." NewOR (5:4) 78, p. 321.
"Per Pasolini." NewOR (5:4) 78, p. 320.
"'Quella era la montagna.'" NewOR (5:4) 78, p. 320.

FORTNER, Ethel
"Dialogue: Cloud and Sky." St. AR (5:1) Aut-Wint 78-79,
    p. 132.
"Later We Talked." St. AR (5:1) Aut-Wint 78, p. 131.
"Lifespring Breaking." St. AR (5:1) Aut-Wint 78, p. 133.

FOSTER, Carolyn
"Starting with Half of the Alphabet." StoneC (78:1) Wint 78, p. 18.

FOSTER, Don
"Because There Is Nothing Elemental or Accidental." StoneC
    (78:1) Wint 78, p. 16.

FOSTER, Susan
"Hush Fell Heavily." EngJ (67:5) My 78, p. 57.

FOURNIER, Donald N.
"The Light of the Wind." ArizQ (34:3) Aut 78, p. 229.

FOURTOUNI, Eleni
"Mother of the Bright Hollow." ConcPo (11:2) Aut 78, p. 90.

FOWLIE, Wallace
"Characters from Proust." SewanR (86:4) Aut 78, p. 514.
"Sensation" (tr. of Rimbaud). Montra (4) 78, p. 292.

FOX, Connie
"All Other Kinds of Watchers." Tele (14) 78.
"Black Toenails, Waterproof Wig." Tele (14) 78.
"Fiat." Tele (14) 78.
"What Concerns You." Tele (14) 78.

FOX, Hugh
from A Canticle for Liverwurst: "N. Philadelphia Penn Central."
    PikeF (1) Spr 78, p. 27.
"Spanish Journals." Zahir (9) 77, p. 69.

FOX, Ray
"Baptism of a Mad Dog." SouthernR (14:4) Aut 78, p. 749.
"Frogs." SouthernR (14:4) Aut 78, p. 747.
"Lines Written by a Reformed Male Chauvinist Pig after Recon-
    sidering the Earthshaking Significance of the Eagle Lunar
    Landing." Poem (34) N 78, p. 64.
"Sacred Pony." SouthernR (14:4) Aut 78, p. 745.
"Smoke Signal." Poem (34) N 78, p. 63.
"The Spit & Whittle Club." Poem (34) N 78, p. 65.

FOX, Robert R.
"Music." GreenfieldR (6:3/4) Spr 78, p. 143.

FOX, Siv Cedering
from Adirondack Note Book: "The snow is melting." Bits (7)
    Ja 78.
from Adirondack Note Book: "Tracks of jumping mouse." Bits
    (7) Ja 78.
"Five Stanzas for My Two Brothers." MassR (19:2) Sum 78, p. 293.

FRAHER, David J.
"Hand." AmerPoR (7:4) Jl-Ag 78, p. 31.

"Two Poems on Birth." AmerPoR (7:4) Jl-Ag 78, p. 31.

FRAIRE, Isabel
"City of Light" (tr. by Thomas Hoeksema). Nimrod (22:2) Spr-
Sum 78, p. 105.

FRANCIS, Pat-Therese
"Anniversary." Nor (8) Aut 78, p. 11.
"Each Poem." CimR (45) O 78, p. 6.
"From the Center of the Island." Sam (65) 78, p. 41.
"Giving It Away in the Fifties" (for M. J. M. 1941-1960). Chomo
(4:3) Spr 78, p. 27.
"Night in the Hospital." CimR (45) O 78, p. 18.
"The Second Wife's Lovesong." BelPoJ (28:3) Spr 78, p. 17.
"The Telephone Operator." BelPoJ (28:3) Spr 78, p. 16.

FRANCO, Lorraine
"President Ford." SeC (5:2) 78, p. 16.

FRANK, Peter
"Petrified Forest" (Ron Horning and Peter Frank). Tele (13) 77.
"The Travelogues IV: Lonely Bones" (for Kenneth Greenberg and
John Yohalem). SunM (5) Aut 78, p. 31.
"The Travelogues V: Musiques de Chambre" (for Greg Vitercik
and Leigh Landy). Tele (13) 77.

FRANKLIN, Tim
"The Lonely Tree." PikeF (1) Spr 78, p. 16.

FRANZ, William G.
"Two Meadows." Glass (3:1/2/3) 78, p. 116.

FRASER, Barbara B.
"Old Woman in the Park." DeKalb (11:3/4) Spr-Sum 78, p. 34.

FRASER, Kathleen
"Hit-and-Run." Madem (84:5) My 78, p. 234.
"Interior. With Mme. Vuillard and Son" (for M. A. F.). AntR
(36:3) Sum 78, p. 332.

FRAZEE, James
"The Boy." PoNow (20) 78, p. 9.

FRAZIER, Kitty B.
"Pattern." Poem (34) N 78, p. 60.
"Sometimes, Mother...." Poem (34) N 78, p. 59.

FREEDMAN, Diane P.
"Body Poem." Wind (31) 78, p. 15.
"A Young Man" (for SCD). Wind (31) 78, p. 16.

FREEDMAN, Howard
"My Body." CarouselQ (3:1) Spr 78, p. 16.
"Two Virgins." CarouselQ (3:1) Spr 78, p. 16.

FREEK, George A.
"Checking My Alternatives. " Wind (28) 78, p. 18.
"Just a Matter of Time. " Wind (28) 78, p. 18.
"Lately. " Stonecloud (7) 78, p. 29.
"Penchants. " WebR (4:1) Spr 78, p. 49.
"Sunrise. " Stonecloud (7) 78, p. 58.
"To Somewhere. " GreenfieldR (6:3/4) Spr 78, p. 64.

FREEMAN, Grace Beacham
"Feelings about the Color Gray. " St. AR (5:1) Aut-Wint 78,
    p. 70.
"Headline Story. " St. AR (5:1) Aut-Wint 78, p. 138.
"The Mathematics of It. " SoCaR (11:1) N 78, p. 117.

FREEMAN, Jean Todd
"Listening to Tchaikovsky. " LadHJ (95:11) N 78, p. P. S. 5.

FREEMAN, Richard
"Funny Money. " GreenfieldR (7:1/2) Aut 78, p. 9.
"Smitty. " Zahir (9) 77, p. 21.

FREMANTLE, Anne
"Sight Unseen. " Comm (105:25) 22 D 78, p. 813.

FRENCH, Gary
"The Sphinx. " Epoch (28:1) Aut 78, p. 24.

FREUND, Edith
"Symbiosis. " Wind (31) 78, p. 17.

FREY, Charles H.
"County Jail. " YaleR (67:3) Spr 78, p. 421.
"To Seek the Genius of These Shores. " YaleR (67:3) Spr 78,
    p. 422.
"Western Gents Westering. " KanQ (10:4) Aut 78, p. 98.

FRIAR, Kimon
Fourteen poems (tr. of Yannis Ritsos). Falcon (16) 78, pp. 55,
    59, 99, and 123.
"Liturgical" (tr. of Yannis Ritsos, w. Kostas Myrsiades). LitR
    (21:4) Sum 78, p. 457.
Seventeen poems (tr. of Yannis Ritsos, w. George Thaniel).
    Falcon (16) 78, p. 68.
Seventeen poems (tr. of Yannis Ritsos, w. Kostas Myrsiades).
    AmerPoR (7:4) Jl-Ag 78, p. 23.
"Simultaneously" (tr. of Yannis Ritsos, w. Kostas Myrsiades).
    LitR (21:4) Sum 78, p. 458.
"Small Sonata" (tr. of Yannis Ritsos, w. Kostas Myrsiades).
    LitR (21:4) Sum 78, p. 458.
"Stages of Ignorance" (tr. of Yannis Ritsos, w. Kostas Myrsiades).
    LitR (21:4) Sum 78, p. 459.
Ten poems (tr. of Yannis Ritsos, w. Kostas Myrsiades).
    Antaeus (28) Wint 78, p. 57.

"The Third Year" (tr. of Andonis Decavalles). LitR (21:4) Sum
     78, p. 392.
"To the Master-Builder" (to Pandelis Prevelakis) (tr. of Andonis
     Decavalles). LitR (21:4) Sum 78, p. 389.
Twenty poems (tr. of Yannis Ritsos, w. Kostas Myrsiades).
     Falcon (16) 78, p. 13.
"Way of Life" (tr. of Yannis Ritsos, w. Kostas Myrsiades).
     LitR (21:4) Sum 78, p. 457.
"Zoophoros" (tr. of Andonis Decavalles). LitR (21:4) Sum 78,
     p. 391.

FRIEBERT, Stuart
"Afternoon Movies" (tr. of Giovanni Raboni, w. Vinio Rossi).
     Field (18) Spr 78, p. 87.
"All He Meant." CutB (10) Spr-Sum 78, p. 24.
"Bad Year" (tr. of Giovanni Raboni, w. Vinio Rossi). Field
     (18) Spr 78, p. 84.
"Beyond Rjeka" (tr. of Rainer Brambach). Field (18) Spr 78,
     p. 34.
"Christmas Morning" (tr. of Giovanni Raboni, w. Vinio Rossi).
     Field (18) Spr 78, p. 85.
"The Colonial Error" (tr. of Giovanni Raboni, w. Vinio Rossi).
     Field (18) Spr 78, p. 86.
"The Effect of Chemistry" (tr. of Karl Krolow). CutB (11) Aut-
     Wint 78, p. 30.
"Every Year." CutB (10) Spr-Sum 78, p. 25.
"Every Year." CutB (11) Aut-Wint 78, p. 31.
"Going Home" (tr. of Rainer Brambach). Field (18) Spr 78,
     p. 31.
"Half a Melon" (tr. of Karl Krolow, w. Claudia Johnson). NewL
     (45:1) Aut 78, p. 47.
"Has Been Recorded." MassR (19:3) Aut 78, p. 462.
"How Dark It Is." MissouriR (2:1) Aut 78, p. 37.
"If the Egg's Not There." Agni (9) 78, p. 103.
"Let's Go" (tr. of Karl Krolow, w. Claudia Johnson). NewL
     (45:1) Aut 78, p. 45.
"Lumberjack's Bar" (tr. of Rainer Brambach). Tendril (2) Spr-
     Sum 78.
"More on the End of the Dock." MassR (19:3) Aut 78, p. 462.
"Obliged to You." QW (5) Wint 78, p. 72.
"Poor Prospects for Drinkers" (tr. of Rainer Brambach). Field
     (18) Spr 78, p. 32.
"Sung Landscape" (tr. of Rainer Brambach). Field (18) Spr 78,
     p. 33.
"Talking to Whitt." QW (5) Wint 78, p. 73.
"Theory" (tr. of Luis Suardiaz). Chowder (10/11) Aut-Wint 78-
     79, p. 52.
"Thinking You've Mastered the Problem of the World." CutB
     (10) Spr-Sum 78, p. 26.
"Under Appletrees" (tr. of Rainer Brambach). Field (18) Spr
     78, p. 33.
"We Were Young" (tr. of Karl Krolow). CutB (11) Aut-Wint 78,
     p. 29.
"Whispering to the Guard." NewRena (10) 78, p. 90.

FRIED, Philip
"The Death of the Watchman." PoetryNW (19:4) Wint 78-79,
    p. 18.
"In a Barbershop." PoetryNW (19:4) Wint 78-79, p. 19.
"More Things, Horatio!" ParisR (72) Wint 77, p. 28.
"Seeing He Was a Museum." ParisR (72) Wint 77, p. 29.

FRIEDMAN, Dorothy
"Celebration." HangL (33) Sum 78, p. 34.
"Ecology." PartR (45:1) 78, p. 14.
"Lady Poet." CentR (22:4) Aut 78, p. 417.
"Mother, Lover." HangL (33) Sum 78, p. 37.
"My bon-bon." HangL (33) Sum 78, p. 35.
"My Bon-Bon." Kayak (47) F 78, p. 43.
"The Rooms." CentR (22:4) Aut 78, p. 417.
"Some Myths about Lesbians." CalQ (13/14) Spr-Sum 78, p. 113.
"Taurus." HangL (33) Sum 78, p. 36.

FRIEDMAN, Edward
"Navacerrada, April" (tr. of Pedro Salinas). Paint (9/10) Spr-
    Aut 78, p. 48.

FRIEDMAN, Irene
"The Door." MalR (48) O 78, p. 27.
"Strategics for Treating a Tomcat." MalR (48) O 78, p. 26.

FRIEDMAN, Phyllys
"Summer's End." CarouselQ (3:2) Sum 78, p. 8.

FRIMAN, Alice R.
"Astronomy Lesson." SouthwR (63:3) Sum 78, p. 265.

FROELICH, Joey
"Heart-Field Fence." Wind (31) 78, p. 7.
"Wilderness Alley." Wind (31) 78, p. 46.

FROST, Carol
"Anemia." SouthernPR (18:2) Aut 78, p. 8.
"Baby." Chowder (10/11) Aut-Wint 78-79, p. 54.
"A Bed on the Floor." AntR (36:2) Spr 78, p. 187.
"Killing the Dog." VirQR (54:1) Wint 78, p. 110.
"Like His Mother." OhioR (19:3) Aut 78, p. 28.
"Mimicries." AntR (36:2) Spr 78, p. 186.
"The Paradise Zoo." Epoch (27:3) Spr 78, p. 279.
"The Quilt." Chowder (10/11) Aut-Wint 78-79, p. 55.
"Sovereign Bear." MissouriR (2:1) Aut 78, p. 32.
"This North." SouthernPR (18:2) Aut 78, p. 8.
"The Undressing." AmerPoR (7:5) S-O 78, p. 35.
"Weekend." BelPoJ (28:3) Spr 78, p. 33.

FROST, Kenneth
"Historian." SoDakR (16:2) Sum 78, p. 21.

FROST, Richard
"The Catholic Dance." AmerS (47:3) Sum 78, p. 300.

FRUHMAN, George J.
"The Anatomy Lesson." AAUP (64:4) D 78, p. 297.

FRUMKIN, Gene
"Correlating a Woman." ParisR (72) Wint 77, p. 52.
"The Hemophiliac." Paunch (52) O 78, p. 53.
"Without a Woman." Paunch (52) O 78, p. 54.

FUERTES, Gloria
"Autobiography" (tr. by Philip Levine). Anteaus (30/31) Sum-
   Aut 78, p. 86.
"Birds Nest" (tr. by Elaine Kerrigan Gurevitz). MalR (46) Ap
   78, p. 45.
"The Dawn Has Turned as Cold" (tr. by Philip Levine). Antaeus
   (30/31) Sum-Aut 78, p. 82.
"Doves" (tr. by Elaine Kerrigan Gurevitz). MalR (46) Ap 78,
   p. 45.
"A Drawing" (tr. by Elaine Kerrigan Gurevitz). MalR (46) Ap
   78, p. 44.
"Grammatical Sentences" (tr. by Philip Levine). Anteaus (30/31)
   Sum-Aut 78, p. 84.
"It's Useless" (tr. by Philip Levine). Anteaus (30/31) Sum-Aut
   78, p. 87.
"I've Slept" (tr. by Philip Levine). Anteaus (30/31) Sum-Aut 78,
   p. 85.
"A Man's Going" (tr. by Philip Levine). Anteaus (30/31) Sum-
   Aut 78, p. 83.

FULTON, Alice
"All Blankets Should Be White." GreenfieldR (6:3/4) Spr 78,
   p. 127.
"Forcing White Lilacs." Box (7) Spr 78, p. 16.
"The History of Dogs." SmPd (44) Aut 78, p. 20.
"Murder Mystery." GreenfieldR (6:3/4) Spr 78, p. 128.

FULTON, Robin
"From the Winter of 1947" (tr. of Tomas Tranströmer). Stand
   (19:4) 78, p. 54.

FUNK, Allison
"Italy." Iowa (9:1) Wint 78, p. 35.

GABBARD, G. N.
"Necromantis." TexQ (21:1) Spr 78, p. 33.

GABRIEL, Daniel
"Birth-Day." AmerPoR (7:3) My-Je 78, p. 42.
"Desert Scavenge." AmerPoR (7:3) My-Je 78, p. 42.
from Relations: (6). AmerPoR (7:3) My-Je 78, p. 42.

GAFFNEY, Maureen
   "Postcards from Wainscott, Long Island." CarolQ (30:1) Wint
      78, p. 106.

GAFFORD, Charlotte
   "About a Woman with Orange Hands." SouthernPR (18:1) Spr 78,
      p. 65.

GAGE, John
   "Insurance." Bits (8) Jl 78.

GAINLEY, Carole
   "A Molecule of Star." Epos (27:1) 77, p. 31.

GALANG, Deanna
   "one day after school." SeC (5:2) 78, p. 18.

GALARZA, Jaime
   "Geometry" (tr. by Roberto Márquez). MassR (19:2) Sum 78,
      p. 248.

GALASSI, Jonathan
   "Your Words." ThRiPo (11/12) 78, p. 36.

GALEF, Jack
   "Eating Rice." NewYorker (54:5) 20 Mr 78, p. 40.

GALLAGHER, Tess
   "As If It Happened." AmerPoR (7:2) Mr-Ap 78, p. 3.
   "Even After." AmerPoR (7:2) Mr-Ap 78, p. 3.
   "The Horse in the Drugstore." PoNow (20) 78, p. 20.
   "Kidnaper." PoNow (20) 78, p. 20.
   "Open Fire Near a Shed." AmerPoR (7:2) Mr-Ap 78, p. 3.
   "The Same Kiss After Many Years." AmerPoR (7:2) Mr-Ap 78,
      p. 4.
   "Second Language." AmerPoR (7:2) Mr-Ap 78, p. 4.
   "Under Stars." NewYorker (53:52) 13 F 78, p. 40.

GALLANT, Jill
   "When the World Was Flat." DacTerr (15) Wint-Spr 77-78,
      p. 66.

GALLANT, Suzanne
   "Living with Cats." AndR (5:2) Aut 78, p. 74.

GALVIN, Brenda
   "Fear of Nostalgia." MinnR (NS11) Aut 78, p. 45.

GALVIN, Brendan
   "Curse." PraS (52:1) Spr 78, p. 72.
   "Father Mapple Prepares a Sermon in Heaven." ThRiPo (11/12)
      78, p. 37.
   "Fear of Firewood." MinnR (NS10) Spr 78, p. 67.

"Fear of the Waldorf Cafeteria. " NewEngR (1:2) Wint 78,
    p. 208.
"Himself. " CalQ (13/14) Spr-Sum 78, p. 66.
"Homage to Henry Beston. " Chowder (10/11) Aut-Wint 78-79,
    p. 74.
"Hometown. " Chowder (10/11) Aut-Wint 78-79, p. 76.
"Little Solstice. " Chowder (10/11) Aut-Wint 78-79, p. 72.
"The Schoolmarms. " Chowder (10/11) Aut-Wint 78-79, p. 73.
"Stethoscope. " Poetry (133:1) O 78, p. 43.
"Tar. " ParisR (72) Wint 77, p. 144.
"Tautog. " Poetry (133:1) O 78, p. 41.
"Woodsmoke. " NewYorker (54:38) 6 N 78, p. 186.
"Young Owls. " NewYorker (54:12) 8 My 78, p. 125.

GALVIN, James
"Devotions. " NewYorker (54:3) 6 Mr 78, p. 34.
"Homesteader. " Iowa (9:1) Wint 78, p. 30.
"The Longest Distance Between Two Points. " Nat (227:9) 23 S
    78, p. 278.
"Making Hay and Funerals. " Iowa (9:1) Wint 78, p. 29.
"Ode to the Brown Paper Bag. " Columbia (2) Aut 78, p. 4.
"A Poem about Boulder Ridge. " Iowa (9:1) Wint 78, p. 28.

GANDER, Mac
"A Slight Deception, A Resting Place. " HarvAd (111:4) My 78,
    p. 24.

GANTZ, Jeffrey
"Burd Ellen. " StoneC (78:3) Aut 78, p. 19.
"December. " StoneC (78:3) Aut 78, p. 19.
"Your Soundless Foot" (tr. of Salvatore Quasimodo). Nimrod
    (22:2) Spr-Sum 78, p. 106.

GARDNER, Geoffrey
"Noah. " GreenfieldR (6:3/4) Spr 78, p. 114.

GARDNER, Isabella
"Are Poets Ball Players. " SoDakR (16:4) Wint 78-79, p. 63.
"Card Island or Cod Island?" NewL (45:1) Aut 78, p. 95.
"Cockchafer. " NewL (45:1) Aut 78, p. 96.
"Letter to Paul Robeson. " NewL (45:1) Aut 78, p. 91.
"The Moth Happened. " SoDakR (16:4) Wint 78-79, p. 65.
"Your Fearful Symmetries" (For Alice Neel). NewL (45:1) Aut
    78, p. 93.

GARDNER, Steve
"Waiting to Leave. " CimR (44) Jl 78, p. 18.

GARDNER, Thomas
"Joy. " Chowder (10/11) Aut-Wint 78-79, p. 45.
"Sprint. " PoetryNW (19:3) Aut 78, p. 29.

GARIN, Marita
"Dinner Party in Autumn. " Wind (30) 78, p. 11.

GARLAND, Max
"Coming Home, 1975." Wind (31) 78, p. 18.
"My Aunt Passes in a '68 Plymouth." Wind (31) 78, p. 18.
"Wet." Wind (31) 78, p. 19.
"Writing About It." SouthernPR (18:1) Spr 78, p. 57.

GARNER, William
"Compost." Wind (29) 78, p. 8.
"Obsequy." Wind (29) 78, p. 34.

GARRETT, Charlotte
"Meditation." SouthernR (14:3) Sum 78, p. 467.
"Nothing Is Yet in the Past." SouthernR (14:3) Sum 78, p. 466.

GARRETT, Matthew
"crossing over." SmPd (43) Spr 78, p. 8.

GARRISON, David
from Poemas de la consumación: "A Few Words" (tr. of Vicente
    Aleixandre, w. Willis Barnstone). Nat (226:8) 4 Mr 78,
    p. 248.
from Poemas de la consumación: "The Poet Remembers His
    Life" (tr. of Vicente Aleixandre, w. Willis Barnstone). Nat
    (226:8) 4 Mr 78, p. 248.

GARRISON, Joseph
"Collect Call." PoNow (20) 78, p. 47.
"Gravity." FourQt (27:3) Spr 78, p. 18.
"Hangings." NewRivR (2:2) 78, p. 9.
"In the Abdominal Cavity." WindO (32) Sum-Aut 78, p. 12.
"Love Song" (for Anne Sexton). WindO (32) Sum-Aut 78, p. 13.
"Morning: To a Friend." WindO (32) Sum-Aut 78, p. 12.
"Old Women." CarouselQ (3:3) Aut 78, p. 14.
"Sitting for a Sketch." WindO (32) Sum-Aut 78, p. 11.
"A Spell." SouthernPR (18:1) Spr 78, p. 40.

GARTLAND, Joan W.
"For Us the Living, Rather." ChrC (95:29) 20 S 78, p. 854.

GARTNER, Paul
"I could send a semi-bunch." Pig (5) 78, p. 10.

GARTON, Victoria
"The Beginning Ritual of My Grandmother's Day." CimR (43) Ap
    78, p. 33.
"The Flute Speaks." PraS (52:4) Wint 78-79, p. 321.

GARVER, Dan
from Hansel & Gretel: "The Witch, Finding Herself in Reduced
    Circumstances, Decides to Take a Cue from Her Captors
    and Make the Best of a Bad Situation." LittleM (11:3) Aut
    77, p. 69.
"I Wear a Mask." NewOR (5:4) 78, p. 359.
"My Father's Watch." Tendril (1) Wint 77-78.

GASS, William
"The Cuckold's Confusion." BosUJ (26:1) 78, p. 35.
"The First Elegy" (tr. of Rainer Maria Rilke). AmerPoR (7:2)
    Mr-Ap 78, p. 8.
"The Ninth Elegy" (tr. of Rainer Maria Rilke). AmerPoR (7:2)
    Mr-Ap 78, p. 10.

GASSER, Frederick
"Allhallows Again--Old October Magic." EngJ (67:5) My 78,
    p. 58.
"Honeycombs of Kitsch." CarouselQ (3:4) Wint 78, p. 14.
"Red Paraffin." CarouselQ (3:3) Aut 78, p. 21.

GASTON, Amparo
"Many Thanks" (to Rafael Alberti for the gift of Ora Maritima)
    (w. Gabriel Celaya, tr. by Lucia Graves). MalR (47) Jl 78,
    p. 110.

GATENBY, Greg
"The Alamo." SmPd (43) Spr 78, p. 7.
"On the Contemporary Surreal." LittleM (11:4) Wint 78, p. 25.

GAUGER, Jan
"Night Flying with a Single Engine." Tele (14) 78.

GELMAN, Juan
"The Heartache and Thousand Natural Shocks" (tr. by Roberto
    Márquez). Iowa (9:4) Aut 78, p. 77.

GENEGA, Paul
"A Giant Killer Legend." Epoch (27:3) Spr 78, p. 222.
"The Self-Made Man and the Moon." Epoch (27:3) Spr 78,
    p. 220.
"Times X 35521." Epoch (27:3) Spr 78, p. 224.

GENSER, Cynthia
"Heaven." Tele (13) 77.
"Hootchie Kootchie Man." Tele (13) 77.
"Shooting Star." Tele (13) 77.

GENSLER, Kinereth
"At Such Times of Divestiture" (for J.D.). MassR (19:2) Sum
    78, p. 364.

GEORGE, Emery
"Before Sleep" (tr. of Miklós Radnóti). Paint (9/10) Spr-Aut 77,
    p. 41.
"Chewing." ColEng (40:4) D 78, p. 421.
"Hymn" (tr. of Miklós Radnóti). ChiR (30:2) Aut 78, p. 13.
"Looking for Ezra Pound in Venice." GRR (9:2) 78, p. 149.
"Pirano Souvenir" (tr. of Miklós Radnóti). Paint (9/10) Spr-
    Aut 78, p. 40.
"Second Eclogue" (tr. of Miklós Radnóti). NewL (45:1) Aut 78,
    p. 44.

GEORGE, Stefan
  "Spread in the silence your soul" (tr. by Gerald Gillespie).
    Paint (7/8) Spr-Aut 77, p. 53.

GERBER, Dan
  "Once." PoNow (19) 78, p. 13.

GERMAN, Brad
  "Rabbis." Bits (7) Ja 78.

GERMANACOS, N. C.
  "The Fundamentals" (tr. of Yannis Ritsos). Falcon (16) 78,
    p. 44.
  "Imbecility" (tr. of Yannis Ritsos). Falcon (16) 78, p. 43.
  "Indiscriminately" (tr. of Yannis Ritsos). Falcon (16) 78, p. 45.
  "Inevitably" (tr. of Yannis Ritsos). Falcon (16) 78, p. 47.
  "In the Void" (tr. of Yannis Ritsos). Falcon (16) 78, p. 46.
  "The Same Meaning" (tr. of Yannis Ritsos). Falcon (16) 78,
    p. 48.
  "Scene" (tr. of Yannis Ritsos). Falcon (16) 78, p. 49.

GERSGOREN, Sid
  "Divisions of Labor." MoonsLT (2:4) 78, p. 17.
  "Late Afternoon." MoonsLT (2:4) 78, p. 20.
  "The Son Looking Up." MoonsLT (2:4) 78, p. 16.

GERSHUNY, Lee
  "Spirits of Beaujolais Wine." CarouselQ (3:2) Sum 78, p. 12.

GERY, John
  "Monks Compleynt." MichQR (17:3) Sum 78, p. 328.

GERYE, Robert
  "Other Poets." CarouselQ (3:4) Wint 78, p. 7.

GESSEL, Michael
  "Mexican Jesus Love." JnlONJP (3:1) 78, p. 11.
  "Sonnet." JnlONJP (3:1) 78, p. 10.
  "35th September 1." JnlONJP (3:1) 78, p. 10.

GETSI, Lucia Cordell
  "I Tried Floating." HiramPoR (25) Aut-Wint 78, p. 22.
  "Missing." PikeF (1) Spr 78, p. 12.

GHIGNA, Charles
  "Best Man." EngJ (67:5) My 78, p. 60.
  "Washington Hides America." KanQ (10:2) Spr 78, p. 77.

GHISELIN, Brewster
  "Ark." SewanR (86:3) Sum 78, p. 368.
  "Bittern." Poetry (132:5) Ag 78, p. 249.
  "Emblem: Aphrogeneia." WestHR (32:4) Aut 78, p. 337.
  "Explication of Evening." Poetry (132:5) Ag 78, p. 252.
  "Flower Mailed from a Forgotten Post Office." SewanR (86:3)

Sum 78, p. 368.
"For the Eighth Decade." Poetry (132:5) Ag 78, p. 252.
"Meridian." WestHR (32:4) Aut 78, p. 347.
"Of Shapes and Shadows." Poetry (132:5) Ag 78, p. 250.
"On the Loom of Light." Poetry (132:5) Ag 78, p. 253.
"On the Playas of Mazatlan: Vipers Out of the Sea." WestHR
       (32:3) Sum 78, p. 212.
"A View of Little Scope." Poetry (132:5) Ag 78, p. 251.

GHITELMAN, David
"Permission." Agni (9) 78, p. 93.
"The Secret." Agni (9) 78, p. 95.

GIAMMARINO, Jaye
"The Bull Fight." CarouselQ (3:1) Spr 78, p. 19.
"Crisis." CarouselQ (3:4) Wint 78, p. 23.
"A Matter of Directions." CarouselQ (3:4) Wint 78, p. 23.

GIBB, Robert
"At the End of Western Civilization Spring Still Comes to
       Emmaus." Wind (28) 78, p. 20.
from A Bestiary. ThRiPo (11/12) 78, p. 39.
"Hunting Crabs in Nag's Head." Wind (28) 78, p. 20.
"Nightwalk." Wind (28) 78, p. 19.
"Shelby, Nebraska, 1933." CutB (11) Aut-Wint 78, p. 69.

GIBBONS, Reginald
"Asturias." MinnR (NS10) Spr 78, p. 65.

GIBSON, Margaret
"Invisible Work." Tendril (3) Aut 78, p. 24.
"A Simple Elegy." MichQR (17:3) Sum 78, p. 296.
"Stories to Tell Children after the Destruction of the Earth by
       Fire." Tendril (3) Aut 78, p. 22.

GIBSON, Stephen M.
"The Peat-Cutters." Poetry (132:6) S 78, p. 326.

GILBERT, Celia
"Island Departure." MichQR (17:4) Aut 78, p. 495.
"Return." MichQR (17:4) Aut 78, p. 494.

GILBERT, Chris
"edges." Tele (14) 78.
"Now." BelPoJ (29:2) Wint 78-79, p. 40.
"Song for Living." BelPoJ (29:2) Wint 78-79, p. 40.

GILBERT, El
"Actually." Smudge (1) Spr 78, p. 25.

GILBERT, Sandra M.
"Anna La Noia." NewL (45:1) Aut 78, p. 18.
"Daguerreotype: Clergyman." PoetryNW (19:2) Sum 78, p. 44.

"Daguerreotype: 'Fallen' Woman-19th Century London. " Epos
    (27:2) 77, p. 19.
"Eurydice. " BelPoJ (28:4) Sum 78, p. 30.
"Minus Tide. " BelPoJ (28:4) Sum 78, p. 29.
"Scheherazade. " PoetryNW (19:2) Sum 78, p. 43.
"Sonnet: The Ladies' Home Journal. " PoetryNW (19:2) Sum 78,
    p. 45.
"Still Life: Man with Fur 'Cossack' Hat. " BelPoJ (28:4) Sum
    78, p. 31.

GILCHRIST, Ellen
    "The Carnival of the Stone Children/A Revolution Memoir, 1970"
        (for Frank Stanford). PoetryNW (19:3) Aut 78, p. 18.
    "Daphne. " Kayak (47) F 78, p. 54.
    "Elegy for Carolyn 1957-78. " PraS (52:2) Sum 78, p. 174.
    "Five Miles from the Grace P. O. " PraS (52:3) Aut 78, p. 257.
    "I Am Sleeping Again. " Kayak (48) Je 78, p. 62.
    "Mrs. Chaffe McCall Dreams During a Facelift. " CalQ (13/14)
        Spr-Sum 78, p. 31.
    "The Other Woman. " PoetryNW (19:3) Aut 78, p. 17.
    "Papyri. " Kayak (48) Je 78, p. 64.
    "Passion. " Kayak (48) Je 78, p. 63.
    "The Stepmother. " CalQ (13/14) Spr-Sum 78, p. 30.
    "Taboo. " CalQ (13/14) Spr-Sum 78, p. 30.
    "There Will Be Seven Fat Years" (For Don Lee Keith). Shen
        (29:2) Wint 78, p. 44.
    "The Van. " PoNow (20) 78, p. 10.

GILDNER, Gary
    "The Day before Thanksgiving, a Call Comes to Me Concerning
        Insulation. " PoetryNW (19:3) Aut 78, p. 3.
    "A Field Mouse at My Fishing Hole. " PoetryNW (19:3) Aut 78,
        p. 4.
    "Poem with Levels of Meaning. " PoetryNW (19:3) Aut 78, p. 7.
    "The Porch. " PoetryNW (19:3) Aut 78, p. 5.
    "This Was Supposed to Be about How the Gulls Hang. " MichQR
        (17:2) Spr 78, p. 211.

GILES, Dolores
    "Bray: Plangent. " SmPd (44) Aut 78, p. 9.

GILFILLAN, Merrill
    "Idée Fixe et Bonne. " NorthSR (8) Aut-Wint 78-79, p. 43.
    "Mont Joli, Que. " NorthSR (8) Aut-Wint 78-79, p. 42.
    "Written in Ferragus. " NorthSR (8) Aut-Wint 78-79, p. 43.

GILGUN, John
    "Gnat. " Pequod (2:4) 78, p. 1.

GILLAN, Maria
    "The Gift. " JnlONJP (2:2) 77, p. 10.

GILLESPIE, Gerald
    "Dark shadowing chestnut" (tr. of Conrad Ferdinand Meyer).

Paint (7/8) Spr-Aut 77, p. 53.
"Spread in the silence your soul" (tr. of Stefan George). Paint
(7/8) Spr-Aut 77, p. 53.

GILLESPIE, Jonathan
"Wendy's Complaint. " MidwQ (19:2) Wint 78, p. 131.

GILLETTE, Kathleen
"King of Nothing but Tears. " CarouselQ (3:1) Spr 78, p. 18.

GILLIAT, Penelope
"Dead Heat. " ParisR (72) Wint 77, p. 51.
"Gossip. " ParisR (72) Wint 77, p. 51.

GILLON, Joseph
"Pictures. " NewRivR (2:2) 78, p. 5.
"Scout Camp. " KanQ (10:2) Spr 78, p. 97.
"What I Learned. " NewRivR (2:2) 78, p. 7.

GINGERICH, Willard
"Point Park, Pittsburgh, July 4th. " SlowLR (1/2) 78, p. 79.

GINOCCHIO, F. L.
"His First Baseball Cap. " YellowBR (10) 78, p. 25.

GINSBERG, Allen
"Holy Ghost on the Nod over the Body of Bliss. " Some (9) 78,
p. 54.
"Lines for Creeley's Ear. " Bound (6:3/7:1) Spr-Aut 78, p. 445.
"On Neal's Ashes. " Some (9) 78, p. 53.

GINTER, Laurel
"Crescent Lake Snapshot. " Nimrod (22:2) Spr-Sum 78, p. 26.
"Saturday Morning at the State Hospital. " CimR (44) Jl 78,
p. 54.

GIORGI, Rubina
from Figure di Nessuno: "Avendo con questi occhi visto. "
Chelsea (37) 78, p. 160.

GIOVANNI, Nikki
"You Are There. " Madem (84:10) O 78, p. 228.

GIPSON, Nancy
"'A Daydream. '" DeKalb (11:3/4) Spr-Sum 78, p. 94.

GIRA, R. P.
"Mouth of the Amazon. " CarolQ (30:2) Spr-Sum 78, p. 110.

GITIN, Maria
"The Benediction" (for George Oppen). Pan (19) 77, p. 62.
"China Row. " Tele (14) 78.
"It's Not Over. " Tele (14) 78.

"Maureen Reminded Me." Tele (14) 78.
"nasturtiums climb." Pan (19) 77, p. 62.
"nothing gained." Tele (14) 78.

GITLIN, Todd
  "The Puritan Hacking Away at Oak." ChiR (30:3) Wint 79,
      p. 132.

GITZEN, Julian
  "Sunday Morning." MinnR (NS11) Aut 78, p. 54.
  "Watchfulness in Fountain Country." MinnR (NS11) Aut 78, p. 53.

GLASER, Elton
  "Blues at the Barbecue." CutB (11) Aut-Wint 79, p. 46.
  "Crescent City Blues." Wind (28) 78, p. 22.
  "Footnote to Shakespeare." Wind (28) 78, p. 23.
  "Nightwalker." PoetryNW (19:4) Wint 78-79, p. 4.
  "On the Relationship of Sex and Poetry." Wind (28) 78, p. 23.
  "Relics." PoetryNW (19:2) Sum 78, p. 3.
  "Rough Trade." Wind (28) 78, p. 22.
  "Saint Jerome." PoetryNW (19:4) Wint 78-79, p. 4.
  "State of the Art." Wind (28) 78, p. 23.
  "Table Talk." PoetryNW (19:4) Wint 78-79, p. 3.
  "Words for WCW." Wind (28) 78, p. 23.

GLASER, Isabel J.
  "Autumn Encounter: 1945." SouthernPR (18:1) Spr 78, p. 35.

GLASER, Michael S.
  "Flight." CarouselQ (3:1) Spr 78, p. 8.

GLASS, Marianne
  "Specific Ocean." SunM (5) Aut 78, p. 133.
  "This sweet glorious hour." SunM (5) Aut 78, p. 134.
  "To Greg, Tonight." SunM (5) 78, p. 135.

GLASSER, Carole
  "Towns." CentR (22:3) Sum 78, p. 319.

GLAZE, Andrew
  "Bus Driver Playing the Flute." PoNow (19) 78, p. 19.
  "Place." PoNow (19) 78, p. 19.

GLEN, Emilie
  "Dark." Wind (28) 78, p. 26.
  "Enough." Wind (28) 78, p. 25.
  "From Afraid." Wind (28) 78, p. 25.
  "Momentous." Wind (28) 78, p. 24.
  "Potato Stone." Wind (28) 78, p. 26.
  "Shouldn't Happen to a Great Grandmother." Wind (28) 78,
      p. 24.
  "String." Pig (4) 78, p. 28.
  "Summer of the tall ships." Wind (28) 78, p. 26.
  "Up through the Register." CarouselQ (3:2) Sum 78, p. 10.

GLENN, Barbara
"Anne Fairfax to Her Husband, the Lord General Thomas Fairfax
1645." SouthernR (14:1) Wint 78, p. 108.
"Weather." SouthernR (14:1) Wint 78, p. 107.

GLENN, Laura
"After Our Conversation Ended." AntR (36:1) Wint 78, p. 85.

GLOVER, Jon
"Away." Stand (19:1) 77-78, p. 63.
"Harvest." Stand (19:1) 77-78, p. 63.
"Islanders." Stand (19:1) 77-78, p. 62.
"On the Ship: Memories." Stand (19:1) 77-78, p. 62.
"To Quit." Stand (19:1) 77-78, p. 61.

GLOWNEY, John
"The Milk-Hauler." PoetryNW (19:4) Wint 78-79, p. 15.

GLÜCK, Louise
"The Clearing." Antaeus (28) Wint 78, p. 89.
Eleven poems. NewRep (178:24) 17 Je 78, p. 31.
"From the Japanese" (for K. and M.). Antaeus (28) Wint 78,
p. 91.
"Happiness." Antaeus (28) Wint 78, p. 88.
"The Logos." Antaeus (28) Wint 78, p. 92.
"The Return." Antaeus (28) Wint 78, p. 90.
"The Sick Child (Study in Oils)." NewYorker (53:49) 23 Ja 78,
p. 46.

GOBA, Ronald J.
"like father, like son." Tendril (1) Wint 77-78.

GODBEY, Geoffrey
"Remembrance." Nat (226:19) 20 My 78, p. 613.

GODDARD, Linda E.
"Leaving the Stone House" (for Sylvia Plath). Tendril (3) Aut 78,
p. 25.

GOEBEL, Ulf
"And This." Paunch (52) O 78, p. 97.
"Declarative Mode." HangL (33) Sum 78, p. 38.

GOEDICKE, Patricia
"The Arrival." MissouriR (1:1) Spr 78, p. 26.
"At the Dentist's." NoAmR (263:3) Aut 78, p. 30.
"Eating Radishes." MichQR (17:1) Wint 78, p. 37.
"The First Steps." Glass (3:1/2/3) 78, p. 39.
"In the Long Dangerous Light." QW (5) Wint 78, p. 102.
"Lightbulb." Iowa (9:3) Sum 78, p. 85.
"The Meaning of Life." PoetryNW (19:4) Wint 78-79, p. 11.
"The Opening." Glass (3:1/2/3) 78, p. 41.
"The Owner." Chowder (10/11) Aut-Wint 78-79, p. 48.

"Putting the Children to Bed." QW (5) Wint 78, p. 102.
"The Secret." Chowder (10/11) Aut-Wint 78-79, p. 50.
"The Suicide." PoetryNW (19:1) Spr 78, p. 28.
"To the River." Ascent (3:3) 78, p. 36.
"To Think We Can Hold On Forever." ThRiPo (11/12) 78,
    p. 42.
"Vacuum Cleaner." MichQR (17:1) Wint 78, p. 36.
"What Sign." MissouriR (1:1) Spr 78, p. 24.

GOETHE
  "Erotica Romana" (tr. by H. G. Haile). BosUJ (26:1) 78, p. 5.

GOFEN, Ethel
  "I Am Reminded of the Redskin." PartR (45:2) 78, p. 273.

GOGINS, Mike
  "2. 5. 76." Pig (5) 78, p. 13.
  "12. 12. 77." Pig (5) 78, p. 13.

GOGOL, John M.
  "Walls" (tr. of N. Ustinova). NorthSR (8) Aut-Wint 78-79,
    p. 30.

GOHLKE, Madelon
  "Fantasy." NorthSR (8) Aut-Wint 78-79, p. 49.
  "My Grandmother Was Always Giving Me Things." NorthSR (8)
    Aut-Wint 78-79, p. 50.

GOLD, Herman
  "They've Stopped Dancing in the Valley." Sam (69) 78, p. 72.

GOLDBARTH, Albert
  "America's Physics." CentR (22:1) Wint 78, p. 73.
  "August Lehman." Antaeus (30/31) Sum-Aut 78, p. 89.
  "Between Towns." Chowder (10/11) Aut-Wint 78-79, p. 59.
  "Calling the Horse." CutB (10) Spr-Sum 78, p. 80.
  "Covers for Books I Never Wrote." CarolQ (30:3) Aut 78, p. 61.
  "Definitions." CentR (22:1) Wint 78, p. 74.
  "Ellis." MissouriR (2:1) Aut 78, p. 28.
  "Esther." LittleM (11:3) Aut 77, p. 51.
  "From the Book." ThRiPo (11/12) 78, p. 43.
  "The Function of Popular Culture." Chowder (10/11) Aut-Wint
    78-79, p. 58.
  "The Harem Boy." Salm (41) Spr 78, p. 123.
  "How the Sky Counts Years." AntR (36:4) Aut 78, p. 469.
  "Marry." Falcon (17) 78, p. 17.
  "Motor." Bits (7) Ja 78.
  "Mute." Bits (8) Jl 78.
  "Orphan Boy, Fishing." Chowder (10/11) Aut-Wint 78-79,
    p. 60.
  "The Psychonaut Sonnets: Jones." LittleM (11:3) Aut 77, p. 48.
  "Schul." Shen (29:3) Spr 78, p. 22.
  "See." PoetryNW (19:4) Wint 78-79, p. 8.

"Song Across Millenia." Epos (27:1) 77, p. 11.
"Song: In the Garden." AntR (36:4) Aut 78, p. 468.
"The Story of Situation." Falcon (17) 78, p. 20.
"Toast Song." ModernPS (9:2) Aut 78, p. 85.
"Tonight." PoetryNW (19:4) Wint 78-79, p. 8.
"Versions." Antaeus (28) Wint 78, p. 198.
"Wash." CarolQ (30:3) Aut 78, p. 60.
"What to Tell Him." ThRiPo (11/12) 78, p. 44.
"'Yet Leaving Here a Name, I Trust, /That Will Not Perish in
    the Dust.'" CarolQ (30:1) Wint 78, p. 57.

GOLDEN, Renny
"The Coming of Winter in Chicago." ChrC (95:1) 4-11 Ja 78,
    p. 16.
"Dinny Murphy." LitR (21:3) Spr 78, p. 353.
"for a revolutionary returning to peru." LitR (21:3) Spr 78,
    p. 354.

GOLDENSOHN, Lorrie
"Elegy for Ann Green." SenR (9:1) Spr-Sum 78, p. 26.
"Writing a Novel." SenR (9:1) Spr-Sum 78, p. 27.

GOLDMAN, Beate
"Portrait of a Mother." ConcPo (11:1) Spr 78, p. 13.

GOLDMAN, Elizabeth
"Chopping Thoughts: Third Betrayal." CarolQ (30:2) Spr-Sum
    78, p. 21.

GOLDMAN, Michael
"In a Park." Antaeus (30/31) Sum-Aut 78, p. 94.

GOLDSTEIN, Joshua
"Grandfather." NewRep (179:5) 29 Jl 78, p. 27.

GOLDSTEIN, Laurence
"Still Stepping Westward." AAR (28) 78, p. 8.

GOLDSTEIN, Sanford
"Fifth Decade: A Tanka Sequence." NewL (44:3) Aut 78, p. 35.
"Masterless: A Tanka Sequence." NewL (44:3) Spr 78, p. 34.

GOLEMBIEWSKI, Alison
"Assertion." GeoR (32:2) Sum 78, p. 370.

GOLLUB, Christian-Albrecht
"In Praise of Vegetables." DeKalb (11:3/4) Spr-Sum 78, p. 35.
"Laughter Two Too." DeKalb (11:3/4) Spr-Sum 78, p. 35.

GONGORA Y ARGOTE, Luis de
from Polyphemus: (9, 12, 21, 22). Paint (7/8) Spr-Aut 77,
    p. 35.

GONNELLA, Joe
"A Debate between the Body and Heart of Villon" (tr. of Francois
    Villon). Chowder (10/11) Aut-Wint 78-79, p. 36.

GONTAREK, Leonard
"Beds. " AmerPoR (7:3) My-Je 78, p. 43.
"Sleepprayer. " AmerPoR (7:3) My-Je 78, p. 43.
"Tale. " AmerPoR (7:3) My-Je 78, p. 43.

GONZALEZ, Angel
"Acoma, New Mexico, December, 5:15 P.M. " (tr. by Allen
    Josephs). NewRep (178:20) 20 My 78, p. 26.
"Notes of a Voyager" (For José Ramón Marra-López) (tr. by
    Allen Josephs). NewRep (178:20) 20 My 78, p. 26.
"Oneiric Digression" (tr. by Allen Josephs). NewRep (178:20)
    20 My 78, p. 26.
"This Particular Moment" (tr. by Louis M. Bourne). AmerPoR
    (7:2) Mr-Ap 78, p. 35.

GOOCH, Brad
"Song. " LaB (11) 78, p. 15.
"Song. " LaB (11) 78, p. 16.
"Trying to Say It. " LaB (11) 78, p. 17.

GOODE, James B.
"Monument at Blackberry Fork. " BallSUF (19:4) Aut 78, p. 25.

GOODMAN, Jason
(10-12). WormR (70) 78, p. 73.

GOODMAN, Melinda
"Another Hysterical Woman Poem. " Box (6) Aut 77, p. 16.
"Count Down. " Box (6) Aut 77, p. 20.
"It's like I put my ear. " Box (7) Spr 78, p. 2.
"Untitled. " Box (7) Spr 78, p. 3.

GOODMAN, Miriam
"Industrial Park from the Air. " Aspect (71) Ap-Je 77, p. 19.

GOODMAN, Mitchell
"At Home. " Harp (256:1536) My 78, p. 77.

GOODPASTER, H. K.
"No Life Without Mirrors. " CarouselQ (3:2) Sum 78, p. 24.
"The Performer." CarouselQ (3:4) Wint 78, p. 16.

GORDON, Coco
"Discretely I. " Confr (16) Spr-Sum 78, p. 157.

GORDON, Don
"Light. " MinnR (NS10) Spr 78, p. 54.

GORDON, Leonore
"Translation. " Hand (2) 78, p. 10.

GORDON, Macdonnell
   "Elegy for the Whooping Cranes of Pawnee County, Kansas."
      GreenfieldR (6:3/4) Spr 78, p. 17.
   "Note to a Teacher." GreenfieldR (6:3/4) Spr 78, p. 16.

GOREN, Judith
   "At the Edge." GRR (9:3) 78, p. 207.
   "Snow White." GRR (9:3) 78, p. 208.

GORENBERG, Gershom
   "Escape." CalQ (13/14) Spr-Sum 78, p. 28.
   "Portrait of a Woman in Her Eighties" (for Malka Tussman).
      BelPoJ (29:1) Aut 78, p. 16.
   "This Moment Is the Knot." CalQ (13/14) Spr-Sum 78, p. 27.

GORHAM, Sarah
   "The Death of Saint Clare." Nat (227:11) 7 O 78, p. 354.
   "My Car Slides Off the Road." Antaeus (30/31) Sum-Aut 78,
      p. 95.

GORTON, Gregg
   "The Architect." Agni (9) 78, p. 106.

GOTTLIEB, Eli
   "Little Tim's Chimera." Box (7) Spr 78, p. 28.

GOUGH, Thomas H.
   "On Aging." CarouselQ (3:2) Sum 78, p. 1.

GOULD, Roberta
   "Wherever She Is." Wind (28) 78, p. 27.

GOUMAS, Yannis
   "Who Cares?" MalR (48) O 78, p. 28.

GRABILL, James
   "Almost Evening." Pan (19) 77, p. 21.
   "Got to Eat Less Meat." GreenfieldR (6:3/4) Spr 78, p. 100.
   "Hieroglyph: The ambulance." GreenfieldR (6:3/4) Spr 78,
      p. 98.
   "Hieroglyph: The Spaceless." GreenfieldR (6:3/4) Spr 78,
      p. 98.
   "Masses." GreenfieldR (6:3/4) Spr 78, p. 101.
   "Scaffolding." Pan (19) 77, p. 20.
   "Thin July." Pan (19) 77, p. 19.

GRABILL, Paul
   "The Golden Ladder." ChrC (95:25) 2-9 Ag 78, p. 733.
   "Hansel." ChrC (95:18) 17 My 78, p. 535.
   "Lazarus--Paradise or Bethany?" ChrC (95:21) 7-14 Je 78,
      p. 612.

GRADY, Naomi
   "Again in Darkness." Stonecloud (7) 78, p. 27.

"Coyote Hit by a Car." Stonecloud (7) 78, p. 142.
"Suite for Single Voices." Stonecloud (7) 78, p. 92.

GRAHAM, Jorie
    "Ambergris." Antaeus (30/31) Sum-Aut 78, p. 96.
    "Angels for Cezanne." Nat (227:13) 21 O 78, p. 418.
    "The Chicory Comes Out Late August in Umbria." Nat (227:10)
        30 S 78, p. 318.
    "Jackpot." GeoR (32:4) Wint 78, p. 798.
    "Mother's Sewing Box." PoetryNW (19:2) Sum 78, p. 25.
    "The Way Things Work." PoetryNW (19:2) Sum 78, p. 24.

GRAHAM, Philip
    "Appellation Contrôlée." VirQR (54:3) Sum 78, p. 500.
    "Handprints." VirQR (54:3) Sum 78, p. 500.

GRANATO, Carol
    "Afraid to Meet the Finale." CarouselQ (3:4) Wint 78, p. 8.

GRANT, Cheryl
    "Grandma." PikeF (1) Spr 78, p. 17.

GRANT, Susan
    "The Williamsburg Bus." Pan (19) 77, p. 44.

GRAPES, Marcus J.
    "And This Is My Father." Bachy (11) Spr 78, p. 100.
    "Cold Winter, Wet Streets, Dry Nerve." Bachy (11) Spr 78,
        p. 99.
    "Midnite in the Kitchen, 1946." Bachy (11) Spr 78, p. 100.
    "Someone in the Next Room Goes Mad, 1953." Bachy (11) Spr
        78, p. 99.
    "To My Father, the Captain." Bachy (11) Spr 78, p. 101.

GRASS, Günter
    "Fire-walls" (tr. by Paul T. Hopper). AmerPoR (7:4) Jl-Ag 78,
        p. 46.

GRAVES, Lucia
    "From Cordoba to Cadiz" (tr. of Blas de Otero). MalR (47) Jl
        78, p. 156.
    "Many Thanks" (to Rafael Alberti for the gift of Ora Maritima)
        (tr. of Amparo Gastón and Gabriel Celaya). MalR (47) Jl
        78, p. 110.
    "Nota Bene for Rafael Alberti" (tr. of Celso Emilio Ferreiro).
        MalR (47) Jl 78, p. 56.
    "Sonnet to Rafael Alberti" (tr. of José Bergamín). MalR (47) Jl
        78, p. 181.
    "A Tribute to Rafael Alberti" (tr. of Pablo Neruda). MalR (47)
        Jl 78, p. 57.
    "With Rafael Alberti the Poet" (tr. of Jorge Guillén). MalR (47)
        Jl 78, p. 54.

GRAVES, Steven
  "The Augury." <u>Shen</u> (29:2) Wint 78, p. 39.

GRAY, Don
  "The First Day of Camp." <u>EngJ</u> (67:5) My 78, p. 53.

GRAY, Patrick Worth
  "Birth." <u>SouthernPR</u> (18:2) Aut 78, p. 77.
  "Door" (For Joyce). <u>WebR</u> (4:2) Aut 78, p. 53.
  "Going to War." <u>Nimrod</u> (22:2) Spr-Sum 78, p. 29.
  "Haiku." <u>FourQt</u> (27:3) Spr 78, p. 34.
  "I Wake and Watch." <u>Poem</u> (32) Mr 78, p. 1.
  "I Watched My Father's Soul Take Flight." <u>Poem</u> (32) Mr 78,
      p. 4.
  "In a Wisconsin Cemetery Rows of Tombstones Reflect the Moon-
      light Like Silver Coins." <u>ColEng</u> (40:4) D 78, p. 424.
  "Juniper." <u>Poem</u> (32) Mr 78, p. 2.
  "My Office." <u>WindO</u> (31) Wint-Spr 78, p. 23.
  "Near the Washita." <u>KanQ</u> (10:2) Spr 78, p. 96.
  "The Romantic Poet's Nightmare." <u>PoetC</u> (10:2) 78, p. 14.
  "Roue." <u>SouthernHR</u> (12:1) Wint 78, p. 44.
  "Saturday Night at the Esquire." <u>NewRena</u> (10) 78, p. 63.
  "Sonnet for Janice." <u>Wind</u> (29) 78, p. 24.
  "State Meet." <u>WormR</u> (69) 78, p. 32.
  "Suburbia." <u>Smudge</u> (1) Spr 78, p. 31.
  "Sunrise in Nowata County." <u>Wind</u> (29) 78, p. 24.
  "Us." <u>PoetC</u> (10:2) 78, p. 12.
  "Vowels." <u>WormR</u> (69) 78, p. 32.
  "The Woman and the Snow." <u>ConcPo</u> (11:2) Aut 78, p. 66.

GRAZIANO, Frank
  "Edith. Danville, Virginia, 1968." <u>Chowder</u> (10/11) Aut-Wint
      78-79, p. 31.
  "Edith in Sandals & Corduroy Jacket, Danville, Virginia, 1966."
      <u>Chowder</u> (10/11) Aut-Wint 78-79, p. 33.
  "Edith in the Kitchen. Danville, Virginia, 1968." <u>Chowder</u>
      (10/11) Aut-Wint 78-79, p. 30.
  "The Potato Eaters." <u>BelPoJ</u> (28:4) Sum 78, p. 10.

GRECO, Stephen
  "Antarctica." <u>HangL</u> (32) Spr 78, p. 16.

GREEK
  Eight Songs (tr. by Anna Caraveli Chaves). <u>Montra</u> (4) 78,
      p. 68.

GREEN, Galen
  "The Old Folks." <u>Zahir</u> (9) 77, p. 65.
  "Snakesong of Suburbia." <u>KanQ</u> (10:1) Wint 78, p. 36.

GREEN, Kate
  "Farmhouse." <u>Nimrod</u> (22:2) Spr-Sum 78, p. 32.
  "Sauna." <u>Nimrod</u> (22:2) Spr-Sum 78, p. 32.

"To the Woman in the Snapshot." Nimrod (22:2) Spr-Sum 78,
    p. 31.

GREENBERG, Alvin
    "The Arts of the Midwest." DacTerr (15) Wint-Spr 77-78,
        p. 24.
    "Non Sequitur." DacTerr (15) Wint-Spr 77-78, p. 24.
    "Report from Cleveland" (For Charles Baxter). PoNow (19) 78,
        p. 23.

GREENBERG, Barbara L.
    "Cave Canem." LittleM (11:3) Aut 77, p. 27.
    "The Faithful Wife." PoetryNW (19:2) Sum 78, p. 31.
    "This Villanelle." LittleM (11:3) Aut 77, p. 26.

GREENBERG, Joyce
    "A Dream Retold to a Lover." JnlONJP (2:2) 77, p. 21.
    "Unexplored Man." StoneC (78:1) Wint 78, p. 26.

GREENE, Jeffrey
    "The Agreement." Iowa (9:3) Sum 78, p. 88.
    "Watch Hill." Iowa (9:3) Sum 78, p. 89.

GREENE, Jonathan
    "Dark Room at Night" (for Paul Celan). Montra (4) 78, p. 67.
    "Distraught Images." Montra (4) 78, p. 66.
    "Image-ing." Montra (4) 78, p. 65.

GREENWALD, Ted
    "Close Up." Tele (14) 78.
    "Each Sound Seems." Tele (14) 78.
    "Force of Habit." Tele (14) 78.
    "Getting a Breeze." LaB (10) 78, p. 13.
    "How Is It." PartR (45:3) 78, p. 435.
    "How Many Years Is It Now." LaB (10) 78, p. 15.
    "More" (for Miani Johnson). Hills (5) 78, p. 11.
    "Phone Rings." SunM (5) Aut 78, p. 58.
    "Room." LaB (10) 78, p. 16.
    "Solid Rain." Tele (14) 78.
    "Something Nice Happened." LaB (10) 78, p. 14.
    "Sun Comes in Windows Directly." SunM (5) Aut 78, p. 57.
    "This and." SunM (5) Aut 78, p. 56.
    "Warm Night." Tele (14) 78.

GREENWAY, William
    "I've Never Seen a Moor." Poem (32) Mr 78, p. 61.
    "Marriage Song." Poem (32) Mr 78, p. 60.

GREER, Michael
    "Tempo Changes." StoneC (78:2) Spr 78, p. 17.

GREGER, Debora
    "The Behavior of Solids." AmerPoR (7:3) My-Je 78, p. 15.

"Companions to Ships and the Sea." AntR (36:1) Wint 78, p. 77.
"Fall." AntR (36:1) Wint 78, p. 78.
"From This Angle." Nat (227:12) 14 O 78, p. 388.
"Going to Sleep." MassR (19:2) Sum 78, p. 380.
"Inventing a Childhood for Myself" (for Evan). MassR (19:2) Sum
    78, p. 379.
"Letter, on Whistling in This Weather." Nat (226:13) 8 Ap 78,
    p. 408.
"Myopia." AntR (36:1) Wint 78, p. 79.
"Natural Forces." AmerPoR (7:3) My-Je 78, p. 14.
"Pentimento." NewYorker (54:14) 22 My 78, p. 36.
"Pièce de Résistance." NoAmR (263:3) Aut 78, p. 53.
"Present Perfect." NewYorker (54:39) 13 N 78, p. 170.
"The Second Violinist's Son." GeoR (32:4) Wint 78, p. 820.
"Trompe-l'oeil." Antaeus (30/31) Sum-Aut 78, p. 97.

GREGG, Linda
    "Whole and without Blessing." Iowa (9:2) Spr 78, p. 78.

GREGOR, Arthur
    "Abundance, Now." MichQR (17:2) Spr 78, p. 157.
    "As Though in Pale Morning." PoNow (19) 78, p. 5.
    "Contours." SewanR (86:3) Sum 78, p. 370.
    "Crowd of Absences." Nat (227:14) 28 O 78, p. 446.
    "The Healing." Nat (227:5) 19-26 Ag 78, p. 150.
    "The Link." Harp (256:1536) My 78, p. 21.
    "The Power of Art." SouthernR (14:2) Spr 78, p. 318.
    "To Emily." MichQR (17:2) Spr 78, p. 158.
    "Val de Loire." SewanR (86:3) Sum 78, p. 369.

GREGORY, Carolyn Holmes
    "Excision." GreenfieldR (6:3/4) Spr 78, p. 135.
    "For Georgia O'Keefe." AAR (28) 78, p. 89.
    "Grandfather." AAR (28) 78, p. 90.

GREGORY, R. D.
    "Needed: Some Way of Moving." WindO (31) Wint-Spr 78,
    p. 16.
    "To the Memories That Are Listening." Wind (30) 78, p. 38.

GRENIER, Robert
    from Sentences: One hundred and thirty-six poems. Bound
    (6:3/7:1) Spr-Aut 78, p. 430.

GRENNAN, Eamon
    "Fox." OP (26) Aut-Wint 78, p. 30.
    "The Given." OP (26) Aut-Wint 78, p. 29.
    "Heady Weather." OP (26) Aut-Wint 78, p. 28.
    "In the National Library." OP (26) Aut-Wint 78, p. 34.
    "On the Train Home." OP (26) Aut-Wint 78, p. 32.

GREY, Robert Waters
    "Flight." SouthernPR (18:1) Spr 78, p. 74.

GRIERSON, Patricia
"Under the Influence." KanQ (10:1) Wint 78, p. 11.

GRIFFIN, Jonathan
"Before I Die." GRR (9:3) 78, p. 195.
"Cut." GRR (9:3) 78, p. 192.
Eight Sonnets and an Ode (tr. of Agrippa D'Aubigné). Montra
    (4) 78, p. 17.
"Holding." GRR (9:3) 78, p. 194.
"The Image of a Suicide God." GRR (9:3) 78, p. 196.
"Inshore from Above." GRR (9:3) 78, p. 193.
"Sensation" (tr. of Rimbaud). Montra (4) 78, p. 293.
"Stanzas" (tr. of DuBois Hus). Montra (4) 78, p. 111.
Ten poems. Montra (4) 78, p. 226.

GRIFFITH, D. W.
"Jam." PoetryNW (19:1) Spr 78, p. 26.

GRIFFITH, Jack
"To and For" (for John Natkie). GreenfieldR (7:1/2) Aut 78,
    p. 94.

GRIFFITHS, Steve
"Crossing Lady Stanley, Here, 1868." Stand (18:4) 77, p. 29.
"Getting It Wrong, Again." Stand (18:4) 77, p. 24.
"Hymns and Backward Glances." Stand (18:4) 77, p. 25.
"Under Mynydd-y-Twr." Stand (18:4) 77, p. 27.

GRIGSBY, Gordon
"Earth and the Night Sky, September 28, 1976." Stonecloud (7)
    78, p. 9.
"Grazing Horse." Stonecloud (7) 78, p. 13.

GRIGSON, Geoffrey
"Annotation." Poetry (132:5) Ag 78, p. 255.
"Fearing Invasion." Poetry (132:5) Ag 78, p. 255.
"Joan of Arc's Stone, Le Crotoy." Poetry (132:5) Ag 78,
    p. 254.

GRILLO, Paul
"Cubist Poem." Tele (13) 77.
"Sailor's Knot." Tele (13) 77.

GRINDAL, Gracia
"Vacation Bible School." ChrC (95:22) 21-28 Je 78, p. 642.

GRONOWICZ, Antoni
"Autumn Chord." Wind (30) 78, p. 12.
"Songs." HiramPoR (25) Aut-Wint 78, p. 24.
"There Is No Land" (tr. by Julian Tuwin). Confr (16) Spr-Sum
    78, p. 86.
"Two Brothers." Wind (30) 78, p. 13.
"Winter from the Top Floor." Wind (30) 78, p. 12.

GROSSBARDT, Andrew
  "Cabo San Lucas." Nat (226:20) 27 My 78, p. 644.
  "Fifty Below." PoetryNW (19:3) Aut 78, p. 22.
  "Heifetz." WestHR (32:1) Wint 78, p. 51.
  "The Mummies of Guanajuato." Poetry (132:6) S 78, p. 338.
  "No Good Reason." AmerS (47:1) Wint 77-78, p. 103.
  "Photo from Costa Rica." Poetry (132:6) S 78, p. 339.
  "The Ruins at Monte Albán." NewYorker (54:45) 25 D 78, p. 64.
  "Tracing" (for Brooke). DacTerr (15) Wint-Spr 77-78, p. 50.

GROSSMAN, Allen
  "A Pastoral." Salm (41) Spr 78, p. 124.

GROSSMAN, Elizabeth
  "The Forum." YaleLit (147:3) 78, p. 20.

GROSSMAN, Florence
  "Museum." Tele (13) 77.
  "On a Quiet Suburban Street." DacTerr (15) Wint-Spr 77-78,
    p. 51.
  "September Garden." DacTerr (15) Wint-Spr 77-78, p. 51.
  "Weather Report." Tele (13) 77.

GROSSMAN, Martin
  "How to Fall in Love." MichQR (17:3) Sum 78, p. 327.
  "Portrait." GRR (9:2) 78, p. 112.

GROSSMAN, Richard
  "Attack." ConcPo (11:1) Spr 78, p. 65.
  "Buffalo." MoonsLT (2:4) 78, p. 74.
  "Chimney Swift." DacTerr (15) Wint-Spr 77-78, p. 31.
  "Cricket." DacTerr (15) Wint-Spr 77-78, p. 30.
  "Difference." SouthernR (14:3) Sum 78, p. 480.
  "Fate." GreenfieldR (6:3/4) Spr 78, p. 60.
  "Hate." GreenfieldR (6:3/4) Spr 78, p. 59.
  "Hope." ParisR (73) Spr-Sum 78, p. 153.
  "Limitation." ConcPo (11:1) Spr 78, p. 66.
  "Literature." AndR (5:1) Spr 78, p. 51.
  "Morality." SouthernR (14:3) Sum 78, p. 481.
  "Owl." MoonsLT (2:4) 78, p. 72.
  "Oyster." MoonsLT (2:4) 78, p. 73.
  "Plants." ParisR (73) Spr-Sum 78, p. 153.
  "Pleasure." ParisR (73) Spr-Sum 78, p. 154.
  "Rat." DacTerr (15) Wint-Spr 77-78, p. 30.
  "Raven." SoDakR (16:4) Wint 78-79, p. 62.
  "Self-consciousness." SouthernR (14:3) Sum 78, p. 482.
  "Tenderness." GreenfieldR (6:3/4) Spr 78, p. 61.
  "Tissue." GreenfieldR (6:3/4) Spr 78, p. 59.
  "Wandering." Vaga (27) Spr 78, p. 8.
  "The Wastes." AndR (5:1) Spr 78, p. 51.

GROSZ, Joseph
  Eleven poems (tr. of Endre Ady). LitR (21:4) Sum 78, p. 490.

GRUE, Lee Meitzen
  "The Seaman's Wife." Poem (34) N 78, p. 28.
  "The Squall." Poem (34) N 78, p. 24.
  "Watching the Fish Die." Poem (34) N 78, p. 26.

GUAY, Cheri
  "crazy john used to sell comic books." SeC (5:2) 78, p. 19.

GUENTHER, Charles
  "Antonin Artaud" (tr. of René Guy Cadou). Bleb/Ark (13) 78,
    p. 19.
  "Behind the Curtains" (tr. of René Guy Cadou). Bleb/Ark (13)
    78, p. 18.
  "I Think about That Little Room" (tr. of René Guy Cadou).
    Bleb/Ark (13) 78, p. 17.
  "Poetic Art" (tr. of René Guy Cadou). Bleb/Ark (13) 78, p. 20.

GUIDO, Ann
  "The Farm." PoNow (20) 78, p. 46.
  "Mother Standing in Trees Near Water." Chomo (4:3) Spr 78,
    p. 15.
  "Onion." Chomo (4:3) Spr 78, p. 14.

GUILLEN, Jorge
  "With Rafael Alberti the Poet" (tr. by Lucia Graves). MalR
    (47) Jl 78, p. 54.

GULLANS, Charles
  "The Local." MichQR (17:3) Sum 78, p. 325.
  "'Philosopher Standing, Holding a Book.'" Poetry (132:3) Je 78,
    p. 158.
  "A Stranger in the Local." MichQR (17:3) Sum 78, p. 326.

GULLING, Dennis
  "New Jersey" (for Beth). Wind (31) 78, p. 53.

GUNDERSON, Andy
  "Thoughts on My Mother's Continuing Illness." Sam (69) 78,
    p. 62.

GUNN, Thom
  "The Cat and the Wind." NewYorker (54:41) 27 N 78, p. 188.

GUNSHANAN, Gail
  "Clarksburg, West Virginia." Tele (14) 78.
  "Persimmons from Zanzibar." Tele (14) 78.

GUNST, Mary
  "Calling Back." Durak (1) 78, p. 12.

GUNSTROM, Nickie
  "Birthday Poem 1978." SoDakR (16:2) Sum 78, p. 55.
  "The Clock Stopped by a False Sense." SoDakR (16:2) Sum 78,

p. 53.
"Four Notes on an Oboe." DacTerr (15) Wint-Spr 77-78, p. 68.
"New Year's Day Poem." SoDakR (16:2) Sum 78, p. 54.
"Wish for Snow." DacTerr (15) Wint-Spr 77-78, p. 68.

GUREVITZ, Elaine Kerrigan
"Birds Nest" (tr. of Gloria Fuertes). MalR (46) Ap 78, p. 45.
"Doves" (tr. of Gloria Fuertes). MalR (46) Ap 78, p. 45.
"A Drawing" (tr. of Gloria Fuertes). MalR (46) Ap 78, p. 44.

GURLEY, George H., Jr.
"Anchorman." DacTerr (15) Wint-Spr 77-78, p. 53.
"Fugues in the Plumbing." Nimrod (22:2) Spr-Sum 78, p. 34.
"Sharpshooter." KanQ (10:3) Sum 78, p. 16.
"Voyage Aboard the Kansas." Nimrod (22:2) Spr-Sum 78, p. 34.

GUSTAFSSON, Lars
"Calm Sequence from an Excited Film" (tr. by Robert R.
    Rovinsky). BosUJ (26:1) 78, p. 70.
"An Epigram of Sorts" (tr. by Robert R. Rovinsky). BosUJ
    (26:1) 78, p. 69.

HAAS, Jan E. M.
"Eating Darkness 2." Stonecloud (7) 78, p. 113.

HABERCOM, David
"Abraham's Discipline." GRR (9:2) 78, p. 147.
"How Many Women?" (for William Heyen). GRR (9:2) 78,
    p. 146.

HACKER, Marilyn
"Lines Declining a Transatlantic Dinner Invitation" (To Charlie
    and Tom). Poetry (132:2) My 78, p. 82.
"Rushing to press, it still would seem evasion." LittleM (11:3)
    Aut 77, p. 6.
"Third Snowfall." Poetry (133:3) D 78, p. 134.

HACKER, Neva
"Spring." DenQ (13:2) Sum 78, p. 133.

HACKMAN, Neil
"Afternoon." Tele (13) 77.
"Chelsea Spring" (for Alice Notley). Tele (13) 77.
"Twilight." Tele (13) 77.
"Why I Don't Eat Meat." Tele (13) 77.

HADAS, Pamela White
from All Isadora: "I. Always Moving." Madem (84:12) D 78,
    p. 194.
from All Isadora: "XI. Greek Positions Are Earth Positions."
    Madem (84:12) D 78, p. 194.

HADAS, Rachel
"Getting Up to Look at Charcoal." NewRep (179:5) 29 Jl 78,

p. 26.
"Moving Still. " GeoR (32:3) Aut 78, p. 530.
"Nostalgia. " PartR (45:1) 78, p. 16.
"Three-Finger Exercise. " PraS (52:1) Spr 78, p. 21.
"Villanelle in March. " Atl (241:3) Mr 78, p. 116.
"Wish Granted. " NewYorker (54:10) 24 Ap 78, p. 44.
"Woman. " Salm (40) Wint 78, p. 130.

HADEN-GUEST, Hadley
"Late Spring. " Tele (13) 77.
"Winter in the City" (To Pablo Neruda).   Confr (16) Spr-Sum 78,
   p. 41.

HADMAN, Ty
"Haiku. " WindO (32) Sum-Aut 78, p. 3.

HAGEN, Cecelia
"Eastern Shore. " Epoch (28:1) Aut 78, p. 23.

HAGIWARA, Sakutaro
"To Be a Girl" (tr. by Graeme Wilson). WestHR (32:1) Wint
   78, p. 37.
"Water Weed" (tr. by Graeme Wilson). WestHR (32:1) Wint 78,
   p. 36.
"White Cock" (tr. by Graeme Wilson). WestHR (32:1) Wint 78,
   p. 36.
"World of Bacteria" (tr. by Graeme Wilson). WestHR (32:1)
   Wint 78, p. 35.

HAGOOD, James
"Again Hesper. " Tele (13) 77.
"The Fairness and the Fading. " Tele (13) 77.
"Virulence. " Tele (13) 77.

HAHN, Kimiko
"Dance Instructions for a Young Girl. " Columbia (2) Aut 78,
   p. 27.
"Obon Oduri. " Columbia (2) Aut 78, p. 26.
"When You Leave" (for Tomie). Columbia (2) Aut 78, p. 25.

HAIGHT, Josepha M.
"Little 'david's' Song of Triumph. " CarouselQ (3:1) Spr 78,
   p. 12.

HAILE, H. G.
"Erotica Romana" (tr. of Goethe). BosUJ (26:1) 78, p. 5.

HAINES, John
from In a Dusty Light: "Missoula in a Dusty Light. " NewRep
   (179:5) 29 Jl 78, p. 28.
"One Rock on Another. " CornellR (4) Aut 78, p. 63.

HALDEMAN, Jill Breckenridge
"Ancient Sun Charms. " DacTerr (15) Wint-Spr 77-78,

p. 64.
"Ancient Sun Charms." YellowBR (10) 78, p. 28.

HALL, Donald
"The Black Faced Sheep." SenR (9:1) Spr-Sum 78, p. 5.
"Maple Syrup." SenR (9:1) Spr-Sum 78, p. 8.
"O Cheese." SenR (9:1) Spr-Sum 78, p. 10.
"Stone Walls" (for Jane Kenyon). OhioR (19:2) Spr-Sum 78,
    p. 6.

HALL, Gail
"Answering the Door." Pan (19) 77, p. 72.
"Information." Pan (19) 77, p. 73.
"Wedding." Pan (19) 77, p. 72.

HALL, H. Douglas
"July." PoNow (20) 78, p. 10.

HALL, James Baker
"The Fat Girl." NewL (44:3) Spr 78, p. 77.
"four year old brown & grey Ford family car, dirty." Poetry
    (132:2) My 78, p. 98.
"In the Terminal." SewanR (86:1) Wint 78, p. 35.
"Journals from the Ark." MalR (46) Ap 78, p. 88.
"A Suite for Hawkbells." MassR (19:3) Aut 78, p. 448.

HALL, Jim
"Come Here." Pan (19) 77, p. 68.
"Corral of Angels." WormR (70) 78, p. 44.
"Facts on File, July 4, 1947." WormR (70) 78, p. 44.
"Grandaddy Warns Me to Measure." ThRiPo (11/12) 78, p. 45.
"Live Studio Wrestling." PoNow (20) 78, p. 21.
"The Mating Reflex." BelPoJ (28:4) Sum 78, p. 2.
"The Nudist Park." PoNow (19) 78, p. 35.
"Reign of Terror." PoNow (20) 78, p. 21.
"Sic." WormR (70) 78, p. 45.
"Steps." PoNow (20) 78, p. 21.
"Year End Report." LittleM (11:4) Wint 78, p. 4.

HALL, Joan Joffe
"Arrivals and Departures." SouthernPR (18:1) Spr 78, p. 12.
"Courting the Muse." DenQ (13:2) Sum 78, p. 100.
"Eskimo Print Woman." SouthernPR (18:1) Spr 78, p. 11.
"The Feeder." SouthernPR (18:2) Aut 78, p. 14.
"Graffiti for Lovers." DenQ (13:2) Sum 78, p. 98.
"In the Family of Chinese Acrobats." DenQ (13:2) Sum 78,
    p. 97.
"Kvinnor." Falcon (17) 78, p. 8.
"Memorial Day." Falcon (17) 78, p. 9.
"On the Flats." DenQ (13:2) Sum 78, p. 95.
"She Approaches Men." DenQ (13:2) Sum 78, p. 92.
"That Year." DenQ (13:2) Sum 78, p. 99.

HALL, John
  "Fruit." NorthSR (8) Aut-Wint 78-79, p. 13.

HALL, Paul
  "Approximate Poem." ParisR (72) Wint 77, p. 150.

HALLA, R. C.
  "When the Flim Flam Man Came to Oshkosh." PoNow (20) 78,
    p. 47.

HALMAN, Talat Sait
  "Bone" (tr. of Bechet Necatigil, w. Brian Swann). St. AR
    (4:3/4) 77-78, p. 104.
  "Come come" (tr. of Rûmi, w. W. S. Merwin). ChiR (30:2)
    Aut 78, p. 9.
  "The Dagger" (tr. of Ülkü Tamer). Paint (7/8) Spr-Aut 77,
    p. 58.
  "Dead" (tr. of Bechet Necatigil, w. Brian Swann). St. AR
    (4:3/4) 77-78, p. 104.
  "The Death of the Vessel." St. AR (4:3/4) 77-78, p. 100.
  "Don't fall asleep tonight" (tr. of Rûmi, w. W. S. Merwin).
    ChiR (30:2) Aut 78, p. 11.
  "fly" (tr. of Bechet Necatigil, w. Brian Swann). St. AR (4:3/4)
    77-78, p. 103.
  "The Venus Line" (tr. of Bechet Necatigil, w. Brian Swann).
    St. AR (4:3/4) 77-78, p. 105.
  "the voice" (tr. of Bechet Necatigil, w. Brian Swann). St. AR
    (4:3/4) 77-78, p. 103.
  "What is the whirling dance" (tr. of Rûmi, w. W. S. Merwin).
    AmerPoR (7:1) Ja-F 78, p. 3.

HALPERIN, Mark
  "First Word of My Father's Death." Vaga (27) Spr 78, p. 74.
  "Florida." NewL (44:3) Spr 78, p. 33.
  "How You Died." Vaga (27) Spr 78, p. 73.
  "In the Nineteenth Century" (for Barbara Anderson). Chowder
    (10/11) Aut-Wint 78-79, p. 12.
  "In the Old Days." PoNow (19) 78, p. 19.
  "Kittitas Horses." Iowa (9:4) Aut 78, p. 40.
  "Two Lines from Paul Celan." Iowa (9:4) Aut 78, p. 42.

HALPERN, Daniel
  "The Apartment at 2 A.M." PoNow (19) 78, p. 12.
  "The Dance." VirQR (54:2) Spr 78, p. 285.
  "Letter" (for Louise). NewRep (178:9) 4 Mr 78, p. 31.
  "Life Among Others." MissouriR (1:1) Spr 78, p. 21.
  "Night Dance." PoNow (19) 78, p. 12.
  "Photograph" (I. D. H. 1921-1970). MissouriR (1:1) Spr 78,
    p. 20.
  "Sad Endings." PraS (52:2) Sum 78, p. 195.
  "Suspension." PoNow (19) 78, p. 12.
  "What Matters Is the Room Itself." PoetryNW (19:1) Spr 78,
    p. 21.

"White Contact." Salm (40) Wint 78, p. 41.
"White Tent." Salm (40) Wint 78, p. 40.
"White Train." Salm (40) Wint 78, p. 40.

HAMBURGER, Michael
"Dejection" (tr. of Georg Trakl). Stand (19:4) 78, p. 2.
"Enkidu" (tr. of Peter Huchel). Durak (1) 78, p. 13.

HAMILTON, Alfred Starr
"City." Glass (3:1/2/3) 78, p. 65.
"Glassworks." Glass (3:1/2/3) 78, p. 66.
"March Winds." NewL (44:3) Spr 78, p. 58.

HAMILTON, Steve
"Hommage to Tristan." Poetry (132:1) Ap 78, p. 20.

HAMLEN, Ann
"Bears." SlowLR (1/2) 78, p. 83.

HAMMER, Patrick, Jr.
"Message in a Bottle." StoneC (78:3) Spr 78, p. 6.

HAMMETT, Rita
"Eight Found Poems from the Journals of Emily Carr." MalR
    (45) Ja 78, p. 11.

HAMMOND, John G.
"2 A.M." SouthernPR (18:2) Aut 78, p. 32.

HAMMOND, Karla M.
"Design." ConcPo (11:1) Spr 78, p. 54.
"Fission." BallSUF (19:4) Aut 78, p. 8.
"From Shakespeare to Tate: Or What Books on a Shelf Might
    Say to Each Other." Pig (4) 78, p. 47.
"Resurrection." ConcPo (11:1) Spr 78, p. 53.
"Salad Days." CarouselQ (3:4) Wint 78, p. 18.
"Scene from Chardin." Glass (3:1/2/3) 78, p. 106.
"A Somber Season." BallSUF (19:4) Aut 78, p. 15.

HAMMOND, Mac
"Mappamundi II." AmerPoR (7:6) N-D 78, p. 18.

HAMPL, Patricia
"Charlotte's Web." AmerPoR (7:4) Jl-Ag 78, p. 16.
"Fire Engine." AmerPoR (7:4) Jl-Ag 78, p. 16.
"Hand, Eye." Antaeus (30/31) Sum-Aut 78, p. 98.
"Tired Of." ParisR (74) Aut-Wint 78, p. 86.
"Wild Rose" (for Carol Conroy and Chris Cinque). AmerPoR
    (7:4) Jl-Ag 78, p. 16.

HAMRICK, Lynda
"Release." DeKalb (11:3/4) Spr-Sum 78, p. 74.

HANDY, Nixeon Civille
"Dear Sister." Wind (29) 78, p. 25.
"Economies of Imagination." StoneC (78:2) Spr 78, p. 34.
"Lyric for a Long Song." Wind (29) 78, p. 25.

HANNERS, LaVerne
"Can of Sad." BallSUF (19:4) Aut 78, p. 14.

HANNIGAN, Paul
"Twenty Five Technical Careers You Can Learn in Two Years or
   Less." Some (9) 78, p. 77.
"Two Sonnets." Some (9) 78, p. 82.

HANSEN, Carol
"Clearing." MinnR (NS10) Spr 78, p. 64.

HANSEN, Jon
"Boy Found in Snow." SouthernPR (18:2) Aut 78, p. 70.

HANSEN, Joseph
"Richard Sheridan Ames" (1905-1977). Bachy (13) Aut-Wint 78-
   79, p. 102.
"Songs." Bachy (13) Aut-Wint 78-79, p. 101.
"Tynemouth." Bachy (13) Aut-Wint 78-79, p. 101.

HANSEN, R. Jackie
"Release." Smudge (Supplement) Wint 78-79, p. 29.

HANSEN, Tom
"Carved on the Air over the Nameless Dead." Kayak (49) O 78,
   p. 1.
"Doing It." KanQ (10:2) Spr 78, p. 57.
"Going Down." Focus (12:78) N-D 77, p. 31.
"My Shirt." Tele (13) 77.
"Pool Game." DacTerr (15) Wint-Spr 77-78, p. 32.
"Stones." DacTerr (15) Wint-Spr 77-78, p. 32.

HAN Shan
"am i this body or am i not" (tr. by Jim Hardesty and Arthur
   Tobias). GreenfieldR (6:3/4) Spr 78, p. 72.
"how cold it is on this mountain" (tr. by Jim Hardesty and
   Arthur Tobias). GreenfieldR (6:3/4) Spr 78, p. 72.
"i asked t'ien t'ai mountain" (tr. by Jim Hardesty and Arthur
   Tobias). GreenfieldR (6:3/4) Spr 78, p. 73.
"my resting place is deep in the woods now" (tr. by Jim
   Hardesty and Arthur Tobias). GreenfieldR (6:3/4) Spr 78,
   p. 73.
"when there's something to be happy about be happy" (tr. by
   Jim Hardesty and Arthur Tobias). GreenfieldR (6:3/4) Spr
   78, p. 72.
"yesterday i saw the trees along the river" (tr. by Jim Hardesty
   and Arthur Tobias). GreenfieldR (6:3/4) Spr 78, p. 73.

HANSON, Dereck
"Death." SeC (5:2) 78, p. 20.
"200 years ago." SeC (5:2) 78, p. 21.

HANSON, Elizabeth
"Delicious Poison" (tr. of Robert Sabatier). MassR (19:1) Spr
78, p. 128.

HANSON, Howard G.
"Meanwhile Ran a Gazelle." ArizQ (34:2) Sum 78, p. 100.
"The Return." LitR (22:1) Aut 78, p. 58.

HANZLICEK, C. G.
"The Naturalist." NoAmR (263:1) Spr 78, p. 83.
"The One Song." NewL (45:2) Wint 78, p. 30.

HARASYMOWICZ, Jerzy
"The House in March" (tr. by John Pijewski). NewYorker
(54:7) 3 Ap 78, p. 32.
"Sunday at My Aunts" (tr. by John Pijewski). NewYorker (54:7)
3 Ap 78, p. 32.

HARDESTY, Jim
"am i this body or am i not" (tr. of Han Shan, w. Arthur
Tobias). GreenfieldR (6:3/4) Spr 78, p. 72.
"how cold it is on this mountain" (tr. of Han Shan, w. Arthur
Tobias). GreenfieldR (6:3/4) Spr 78, p. 72.
"i asked t'ien t'ai mountain" (tr. of Han Shan, w. Arthur Tobias).
GreenfieldR (6:3/4) Spr 78, p. 73.
"my resting place is deep in the woods now" (tr. of Han Shan,
w. Arthur Tobias). GreenfieldR (6:3/4) Spr 78, p. 73.
"When there's something to be happy about be happy" (tr. of Han
Shan, w. Arthur Tobias). GreenfieldR (6:3/4) Spr 78,
p. 72.
"yesterday i saw the trees along the river" (tr. of Han Shan, w.
Arthur Tobias). GreenfieldR (6:3/4) Spr 78, p. 73.

HARDIE, Doris
"Without You." SouthernPR (18:1) Spr 78, p. 71.

HARDIE, Jack
"The Pallas Murre." ColEng (39:8) Ap 78, p. 946.

HARDIN, Glenn
"Leda." PoNow (20) 78, p. 21.
"Sloth." PoNow (20) 78, p. 21.
"Three Bears." PoNow (20) 78, p. 21.
"Uncle Ab." PoNow (20) 78, p. 21.

HARDMAN, James Llewellyn
"Waking in Place." Wind (30) 78, p. 15.
"Peripheries." Wind (30) 78, p. 15.

HARDY, Chris
"1916." Stand (19:4) 78, p. 10.

HARDY, Thomas
"The Photograph." Stand (19:1) 77-78, p. 48.

HARGREAVES, Anne
"Grandmother II." AAR (28) 78, p. 59.

HARKNESS, Edward
"In Celebration of the Sky's Old Age, Lewiston, Idaho" (for
    Jeanne & Leonard Woodall and for Linda). NowestR (17:1)
    78, p. 63.
"Letter from Danny." NowestR (17:1) 78, p. 62.
"Three Dreams." QW (5) Wint 78, p. 74.

HARMON, William
"Don't Let Aphasia." Agni (9) 78, p. 121.
"For the Present" (for R.D.R.). Agni (9) 78, p. 120.
"The Occidental Comedy of Domestication." CarolQ (30:2) Spr-
    Sum 78, p. 35.
"Our Contributors." Kayak (48) Je 78, p. 69.
"Wild Flowers: Remnants of a Field Guide." Kayak (47) F 78,
    p. 25.

HAROUTIOUNIAN, Artem
"Facing the Silence" (tr. by Diana der Hovanessian). CarolQ
    (30:2) Spr-Sum 78, p. 83.

HARRIGAN, Stephen
"Pecos Bill in Decline." DacTerr (15) Wint-Spr 77-78, p. 29.

HARRIS, Jana
"No." Tele (14) 78.

HARRIS, Joseph
"Edward Hopper's U.S.A." Epos (27:2) 77, p. 23.

HARRIS, Michael
"The Gamekeeper." Atl (242:6) D 78, p. 81.

HARRIS, Patricia Lee
"The Magician's Girl." EngJ (67:5) My 78, p. 59.

HARRISON, Howard
"To, Not About." EngJ (67:5) My 78, p. 53.

HARRISON, Jim
"Marriage Ghazal." PoNow (19) 78, p. 13.

HARRISON, Tony
from The School of Eloquence: "A Close One." Stand (19:2) 78,
    p. 66.

from The School of Eloquence: "Book Ends."   Stand (19:2) 78,
     p. 66.
from The School of Eloquence: "Rhubarbarians."   Stand (19:2)
     78, p. 65.
from The School of Eloquence: "Wordlists."   Stand (19:2) 78,
     p. 64.

HARROD, Lois Marie
"The Leopard Frog."   StoneC (78:1) Wint 78, p. 18.

HARROLD, William
"Clusters the Awaiting Years Can Handle."   ParisR (72) Wint 77,
     p. 31.
"The Moment of Decision."   WormR (69) 78, p. 4.
"The Strain."   Tele (13) 77.
"The Young Are a Pair of Scissors and Cut Their Way Off the
     Earth."   WormR (69) 78, p. 3.

HARROP, Leslie
"Epigrams of an Invalid."   Stand (18:4) 77, p. 40.
"Lymphoma."   Stand (18:4) 77, p. 40.

HARSHMAN, Marc
"Books."   PoetryNW (19:3) Aut 78, p. 35.

HART, Joanne
"Admonitions from a Winter."   DacTerr (15) Wint-Spr 77-78,
     p. 26.
"First Cold."   DacTerr (15) Wint-Spr 77-78, p. 26.
"When Your Parents Grow Old" (for Catherine Lupori).   DacTerr
     (15) Wint-Spr 77-78, p. 27.

HARTEIS, Richard
"The House-painter."   Ploughs (4:2) 78, p. 25.

HARTMAN, Charles O.
"The Cambridge Quakers."   PoNow (20) 78, p. 10.
"Daddy Long-Legs" (For Penelope Mesic).   Poetry (132:3) Je 78,
     p. 160.
"The Days."   PoNow (20) 78, p. 10.
"Double Mock Sonnet."   Poetry (132:3) Je 78, p. 159.
"Minnesota."   CarolQ (30:3) Aut 78, p. 59.

HARTMAN, Susan
"Wedding Signs."   KanQ (10:1) Wint 78, p. 66.

HARTMAN, Yuki
"Landscape."   EnPas (7) 78, p. 29.

HARTNETT, David
"I Want to Wake You Up."   Tendril (2) Spr-Sum 78.
"Instructions for Rubbing."   Tendril (3) Aut 78, p. 26.

HARTSFIELD, Larry
　　"Roadside Dreams." <u>BallSUF</u> (19:4) Aut 78, p. 20.

HARVEY, Gayle Elen
　　"it can't be otherwise" (for Marilyn Hacker). <u>HangL</u> (33) Sum
　　　　78, p. 42.
　　"radical." <u>HangL</u> (33) Sum 78, p. 39.
　　"Retarded Girl at the Lake." <u>CarouselQ</u> (3:4) Wint 78, p. 2.
　　"There's No Cure." <u>Paint</u> (9/10) Spr-Aut 78, p. 19.
　　"Where We 'Haven't Been Is Already Yesterday.'" <u>Paint</u> (9/10)
　　　　Spr-Aut 78, p. 18.

HARWOOD, Gwen
　　"The Lion's Bride." <u>Antaeus</u> (30/31) Sum-Aut 78, p. 261.
　　"Madame Esmerelda's Predictions." <u>Antaeus</u> (30/31) Sum-Aut
　　　　78, p. 262.

HASELOFF, Charles
　　"Sonnet 8.11., after Rilke" (In Memoriam: Egon von Rilke).
　　　　<u>PartR</u> (45:2) 78, p. 272.

HASKELL, Philip
　　"The Faces of Strangers." <u>Salm</u> (40) Wint 78, p. 129.
　　"Igor, the Plutonium." <u>Salm</u> (40) Wint 78, p. 127.
　　"Jonah and the Insomnia." <u>Salm</u> (40) Wint 78, p. 128.

HASS, Robert
　　Ten Poems. <u>Antaeus</u> (30/31) Sum-Aut 78, p. 9.

HASSE, Margaret
　　"Red." <u>NorthSR</u> (8) Aut-Wint 78-79, p. 14.

HASSELSTROM, Linda M.
　　"Spring." <u>SoDakR</u> (16:2) Sum 78, p. 41.
　　"Staying in One Place." <u>SoDakR</u> (16:2) Sum 78, p. 42.

HASSLER, Donald M.
　　"Sonnet for My Wife." <u>BallSUF</u> (19:4) Aut 78, p. 21.

HATHAWAY, Nancy
　　"The Death of Mothers." <u>13thM</u> (4:1) 78, p. 79.

HATHAWAY, William
　　"'The Gymnast of Inertia.'" <u>SouthernR</u> (14:3) Sum 78, p. 483.
　　"The Poet Hunts Doves with the Natchitoches Police" (for Jim
　　　　Dyson). <u>SouthernR</u> (14:3) Sum 78, p. 484.
　　"Walking with the Master." <u>SouthernR</u> (14:3) Sum 78, p. 487.
　　"Wandering Spirit." <u>SouthernR</u> (14:3) Sum 78, p. 486.

HATLEN, Burton
　　"A Letter to William Morris." <u>BelPoJ</u> (28:4) Sum 78, p. 6.
　　"March" (for Barbara). <u>BelPoJ</u> (28:4) Sum 78, p. 8.

HATTERSLEY, Michael
  "Citizenship in Several Words. " PoetryNW (19:4) Wint 78-79,
      p. 33.

HAUG, James
  "Dirty Money. " SmPd (44) Aut 78, p. 30.

HAUK, Barbara
  "Jupiter's Red Spot. " PikeF (1) Spr 78, p. 26.
  "Ten Questions Children Ask Their Mothers. " YellowBR (10) 78,
      p. 29.

HAWKINS, Hunt
  "The Complaint of a Househusband. " MinnR (NS10) Spr 78,
      p. 30.
  "My Cat Jack. " Poetry (133:3) D 78, p. 158.
  "New York. " MinnR (NS11) Aut 78, p. 46.

HAWKINS, Linda
  "Seven. " EngJ (67:5) My 78, p. 56.

HAWKINS, Tom
  "The Church Pianist at Home. " SoCaR (10:2) Ap 78, p. 11.
  "Needs, Deepening a Moment. " KanQ (10:1) Wint 78, p. 107.
  "Sunlight: A Study. " SenR (9:1) Spr-Sum 78, p. 28.
  "Thick as Smoke, Scenery Rolls By. " CarolQ (30:2) Spr-Sum 78,
      p. 23.

HAWKSWORTH, Marjorie
  "And Close the Window. " LitR (21:3) Spr 78, p. 337.
  "Another Way. " Bleb/Ark (13) 78, p. 68.
  "Catching Fire. " Wind (29) 78, p. 31.
  "Encounter. " Bleb/Ark (13) 78, p. 64.
  "The Fee. " Bleb/Ark (13) 78, p. 64.
  "A Free Ride. " SoCaR (10:2) Ap 78, p. 80.
  "In Ritual Against the Dark. " Bleb/Ark (13) 78, p. 67.
  "Likeness. " SoCaR (10:2) Ap 78, p. 80.
  "Our Informers. " PoetC (10:2) 78, p. 5.
  "Overturned. " Bleb/Ark (13) 78, p. 65.
  "Ploy. " SouthernPR (18:1) Spr 78, p. 62.
  "Sail On. " Bleb/Ark (13) 78, p. 66.
  "A Summer of Sand. " SouthernPR (18:1) Spr 78, p. 62.
  "Through the Tunnel. " Bleb/Ark (13) 78, p. 67.

HAWLEY, Beatrice
  "The Cleaning Lady Thinks of Lizzie Borden. " PoNow (20) 78,
      p. 22.
  "A Distance from Drowning. " PoNow (20) 78, p. 22.
  "Eggs. " PoNow (20) 78, p. 23.

HAWLEY, Richard A.
  "This Much I Can Say for Certain. " AndR (5:2) Aut 78, p. 22.

HAXTON, Brooks
"The Gravedigger and His Wife." SewanR (86:4) Aut 78, p. 516.

HAYES, Ann
"Chianti Classico." SouthernR (14:2) Spr 78, p. 336.
"The Penitent Magdalen." SouthernR (14:2) Spr 78, p. 337.
"The Smile of Reims." SouthernR (14:2) Spr 78, p. 339.

HAYES, Charles L.
"To the Metropole." Tele (13) 77.

HAYES, Diana
"Cayman at Hollows Marsh." MalR (45) Ja 78, p. 206.
"Message from Morpheus." MalR (45) Ja 78, p. 207.
"Pigeon on East Pender Street" (for Pat). MalR (45) Ja 78, p. 208.
"Sestina for Superior" (after the Edmund Fitzgerald). MalR (45)
    Ja 78, p. 210.

HAYES, Marilyn
"Postpartum: Burning the Pin Feathers." HiramPoR (25) Aut-
    Wint 78, p. 25.

HAYNES, John
"Night Song." Stand (19:4) 78, p. 39.
"Strangers." Stand (19:4) 78, p. 39.

HAYNES, Mary
"Ange Agenouille." Bachy (12) Aut 78, p. 32.
"Deep Water Creek." Bachy (12) Aut 78, p. 30.
"Flipper." Bachy (12) Aut 78, p. 31.
"Goose to Gander." Bachy (12) Aut 78, p. 31.
"Toward an Architecture of Bethlehem." Bachy (12) Aut 78,
    p. 32.

HAYS, H. R.
"Charles Fourier, Prophet of Passion." NorthSR (8) Aut-Wint
    78-79, p. 58.
"Target for Dictators." NorthSR (8) Aut-Wint 78-79, p. 59.

HAZO, Samuel
"In the Order of Disappearance." SlowLR (1/2) 78, p. 14.
"Mattering." SlowLR (1/2) 78, p. 17.
"Victorious Losses." AmerS (47:3) Sum 78, p. 354.

HEAD, Gwen
"Midas." Chowder (10/11) Aut-Wint 78-79, p. 39.
"Queen Conches" (for Allan). Chowder (10/11) Aut-Wint 78-79,
    p. 38.

HEALY, Eloise
"Edging." Stonecloud (7) 78, p. 101.
"For Tyler." Stonecloud (7) 78, p. 94.

"Iceberg Poems (2, 3, & 5)." Stonecloud (7) 78, p. 8.
"Learning to Read the Red Star Cafe" (for my mother). Bachy
(12) Aut 78, p. 52.
"A Preface." Bachy (12) Aut 78, p. 53.
"Things Happening on the Roads Going Fast." Bachy (12) Aut 78,
p. 52.

HEANEY, Seamus
"Field Work." NewEngR (1:1) Aut 78, p. 31.
"The Harvest Bow." LitR (22:2) Wint 79, p. 212.
"In Memoriam Francis Ledwidge." Stand (19:2) 78, p. 21.
"A Postcard from North Antrim" (In Memory of Sean Armstrong).
LitR (22:2) Wint 79, p. 213.

HEARST, James
"Bereaved." AmerS (47:3) Sum 78, p. 356.
"Birth Pains." NewRena (10) 78, p. 69.
"Change in Appetites." SoDakR (16:2) Sum 78, p. 46.
"The Inevitable Words Like Sign Posts." OhioR (19:2) Spr-Sum
78, p. 44.
"It Could Be Worse, Maybe." SlowLR (1/2) 78, p. 69.
"Modern Design." SlowLR (1/2) 78, p. 68.
"Penalty for Anger." SouthwR (63:4) Aut 78, p. 404.
"Virtue of Logic." NewRena (10) 78, p. 70.

HEATH, Jennifer
"Birds." Nimrod (22:2) Spr-Sum 78, p. 33.

HEBALD, Carol
"The Solitary Seal." Confr (16) Spr-Sum 78, p. 132.

HECHT, Anthony
"House Sparrows" (for Joe and U. T. Summers). Ploughs (4:3)
78, p. 27.
"The Lull" (for Allen Tate). Ploughs (4:3) 78, p. 29.
"Persistences." Ploughs (4:3) 78, p. 25.
"The Venetian Vespers." Poetry (133:1) O 78, p. 1.

HECHT, Roger
"After the Arrest." Hand (2) 78, p. 110.

HECKLER, Jonellen
"The Patience of Plants." LadHJ (95:6) Je 78, p. 88.
"Slow Recipes." LadHJ (95:11) N 78, p. 17.

HEDIN, Robert
"Waiting for Trains at Col d'Aubisque." Epoch (28:1) Aut 78,
p. 86.

HEFFERNAN, Michael
"February 1st." Poetry (132:2) My 78, p. 103.
"Kennedy." Chowder (10/11) Aut-Wint 78-79, p. 23.

HEFFERNAN, Thomas
  from The Liam Poems: "At the River." MidwQ (19:3) Spr 78,
    p. 274.
  from The Liam Poems: "His Dream at Noon." MidwQ (19:3)
    Spr 78, p. 272.
  from The Liam Poems: "His Dream of a Dream." MidwQ
    (19:3) Spr 78, p. 277.
  from The Liam Poems: "Liam Is Told by His Uncle." MidwQ
    (19:3) Spr 78, p. 271.
  from The Liam Poems: "Liam on the Fringe of the Dark Wood."
    MidwQ (19:3) Spr 78, p. 275.
  from The Liam Poems: "Liam's Fall into a Ditch." MidwQ
    (19:3) Spr 78, p. 278.
  from The Liam Poems: "Young Scholars Find a Dead Sparrow."
    MidwQ (19:3) Spr 78, p. 276.

HEGI, Ursula
  "Nobody Stocks Camellias Any More." Kayak (49) O 78, p. 54.

HEILIGER, William S.
  "Fall" (tr. of Srečko Kosovel). DenQ (13:3) Aut 78, p. 133.
  "Flowers on the Windowsill" (tr. of Srečko Kosovel). DenQ
    (13:3) Aut 78, p. 132.

HEIMER, Jackson W.
  "Dreams." WindO (31) Wint-Spr 78, p. 9.
  "On Taking Down the Christmas Tree." WindO (31) Wint-Spr 78,
    p. 10.
  "Pa." WindO (31) Wint-Spr 78, p. 9.

HEINE, Heinrich
  "Morphine" (tr. by Jerome Rothenberg). Hand (2) 78, p. 156.

HEINZELMAN, Kurt
  "Just Living." MassR (19:2) Sum 78, p. 273.
  "Proteus's Children." Poetry (131:4) Ja 78, p. 223.

HEJINIAN, Lyn
  "Later Grammar Rim (no. 3)" (for Ron Silliman). Hills (5) 78,
    p. 80.
  "Recollection." Hills (5) 78, p. 82.
  "Song #2 (also)." Hills (5) 78, p. 81.

HELENE, Alexandra
  "Carnation, never shared but mounted." DeKalb (11:3/4) Spr-
    Sum 78, p. 80.

HELLER, Michael
  "From a Note." Montra (4) 78, p. 116.
  "Leaving Grand Central" (for George Oppen). Montra (4) 78,
    p. 117.
  "With an Aging Father by Florida Waters." Montra (4) 78,
    p. 118.

HELMLING, Steven
"At the Museum, and After." Hudson (31:3) Aut 78, p. 463.
"The Snake." Hudson (31:3) Aut 78, p. 463.
"Two Weeks after an April Frost." Hudson (31:3) Aut 78,
    p. 464.
"With the Lights On." Hudson (31:3) Aut 78, p. 464.

HEMAN, Bob
"The Drama." WormR (68) 77, p. 95.
"The Silence." WormR (68) 77, p. 96.
"Those Remarkable Eyes." WormR (68) 77, p. 96.
"Unusually Dead." WormR (68) 77, p. 96.

HEMSCHEMEYER, Judith
"Poems" (tr. of Anna Akhmatova, w. Anne Wilkinson). Pequod
    (2:4) 78, p. 16.

HENDERSON, Archibald
"Death Will Not Come." NorthSR (8) Aut-Wint 78-79, p. 53.

HENDLER, Earl
"Resurrection." JnlONJP (3:1) 78, p. 4.

HENDLEY, Chuck
"Charlie's Angels." NewL (45:1) Aut 78, p. 62.
"Fire!" NewL (45:1) Aut 78, p. 62.

HENDRICKS, Betty Jean
"Rejection." Pan (19) 77, p. 40.

HENLEY, Patricia
"Slaughtering the Goat." GreenfieldR (6:3/4) Spr 78, p. 134.
"Slow Dance, Sure as Death." GreenfieldR (6:3/4) Spr 78,
    p. 133.

HENN, Sister Mary Ann
"Caribbean Recollections." Wind (31) 78, p. 20.
"My Mansion." Wind (31) 78, p. 20.

HENRY, Fran
"I've had to struggle...." Chomo (5:2) Aut-Wint 78, p. 71.

HENRY, Laura
"Remember Gloria?" Paint (9/10) Spr-Aut 78, p. 17.

HENRY, Sarah
"To D. H." HolCrit (15:5) D 78, p. 15.

HENSON, David
"Father to Son." Sam (65) 78, p. 45.
"Last Night's Storm." Tendril (2) Spr-Sum 78.

HENSON, Jim
"Acknowledgments." ParisR (72) Wint 77, p. 143.

"For My Wife to Say When They Ask." ParisR (72) Wint 77,
    p. 141.
"Things." ParisR (72) Wint 77, p. 139.

HENSON, Lance
Ten poems. GreenfieldR (6:3/4) Spr 78, p. 35.

HERAKLEITOS
One hundred and twenty-four poems (tr. by Guy Davenport).
    AmerPoR (7:1) Ja-F 78, p. 14.

HERBERT, Zbigniew
"Prayer of Mr Cogito-Traveller" (tr. by Adam Czerniawski).
    Stand (18:4) 77, p. 6.

HERBKERSMAN, Gretchen
"Cosmetic." Nowest (17:1) 78, p. 37.
"The Four-Color Problem." NowestR (17:1) 78, p. 36.

HERRINGTON, Neva Johnson
"Blue Stone." SouthwR (63:3) Sum 78, p. 216.
"Disappearances." SouthwR (63:4) Aut 78, p. 402.

HERRSTROM, David
"Beside Myself." US1 (11) Aut 78, p. 1.
"Mohammed in Pennsylvania." JnlONJP (2:1) 77, p. 28.

HERSHBERGER, Joan
"The Gods Have a Game. Listen:" Aspen (6) Aut 78, p. 11.

HERSHON, Elizabeth
"The Belltower." HangL (32) Spr 78, p. 58.
"The Box." HangL (32) Spr 78, p. 60.
"The dance." HangL (32) Spr 78, p. 62.
"The Gathering." HangL (32) Spr 78, p. 57.

HERSHON, Robert
"Learning from Artie Adler." PoNow (19) 78, p. 38.
"The Third of July." PoetryNW (19:2) Sum 78, p. 22.

HERZ, Robert
"Beautiful Women." AmerPoR (7:4) Jl-Ag 78, p. 17.
"Nights of Marriage." AmerPoR (7:4) Jl-Ag 78, p. 17.

HESTER, M. L.
"The Cartographer." NewRivR (2:2) 78, p. 44.
"The Escape Artist." AmerS (47:2) Spr 78, p. 230.
"Lucille." NewRivR (2:2) 78, p. 46.
"Pamphlet from a Seventh-Day Adventist." GRR (9:3) 78,
    p. 209.
"Sick Poem." NewRivR (2:2) 78, p. 45.
"Taking Bath with Aunt Gladys." SouthernPR (18:2) Aut 78,
    p. 64.

HESTER, M. L., Jr.
"E. C., Crumley, Pauline, & Me." PoNow (20) 78, p. 11.
"The Ice Man." PoNow (20) 78, p. 11.
"The Meditations of O. C. MacClean: Dependencies." DenQ
    (13:3) Aut 78, p. 75.
"Trains, Wives and Whistles." SouthernHR (12:1) Wint 78,
    p. 58.

HEULE, Sharon
"Tick Marks." Glass (3:1/2/3) 78, p. 105.

HEWITT, Christopher
"Autumn Signals." CalQ (13/14) Spr-Sum 78, p. 132.

HEWITT, Geof
"According to Latest Reports." NewL (45:2) Wint 78, p. 29.
"Dabbling in Oils." NorthSR (8) Aut-Wint 78-79, p. 51.
"Elm." Harp (256:1536) My 78, p. 84.
"Falling Asleep." PoNow (19) 78, p. 27.
"Half-Life." NewL (45:2) Wint 78, p. 29.

HEY, Phil
"Bait Shop." PoNow (19) 78, p. 35.
"Squirrel." Tendril (3) Aut 78, p. 28.
"Weather." Tendril (1) Wint 77-78.

HEYEN, William
"Anthem." Poetry (132:4) Jl 78, p. 194.
"The Crow." Poetry (133:3) D 78, p. 127.
"The Eternal Ash." Sky (7/8) Spr 78, p. 68.
"The Ewe." Iowa (9:1) Wint 78, p. 31.
"The Field." Poetry (133:3) D 78, p. 127.
"Lord Dragonfly." Poetry (132:4) Jl 78, p. 187.
"Nocturne: The Reichsführer at Stutthof." Sky (7/8) 78, p. 67.
"Plague Sermon." GeoR (32:1) Spr 78, p. 15.
"The Singer." Poetry (132:2) My 78, p. 95.
"To a Warplane." Poetry (132:4) Jl 78, p. 193.
"Witness." OhioR (19:1) Wint 78, p. 68.

HEYNEN, Jim
"Child Lost in Campus Coffee Shop." PoetryNW (19:4) Wint
    78-79.

HICKMAN, Leland
"Tiresias I: 9: B: Great Slave Lake Suite, Part One." Bachy
    (13) Aut-Wint 78-79, p. 139.

HICKS, John V.
"The Dragon in the Chimney." MalR (46) Ap 78, p. 147.

HIERRO, José
Nine poems (tr. by Louis M. Bourne). AmerPoR (7:2) Mr-Ap
    78, p. 30.

HIGGINS, Anne
  "Recipe." Comm (105:15) 4 Ag 78, p. 488.

HIGGINS, Dick
  "flight from italy." SunM (5) Aut 78, p. 87.
  "snowflake for ray johnson." SunM (5) Aut 78, p. 88.
  "what a day a day!" (w. Opal L. Nations). LaB (10) 78, p. 18.

HIGGINS, Frank
  "Drought Comes to Jackson County." DacTerr (15) Wint-Spr 77-
    78, p. 37.
  "Renting the Stud Horse." PoNow (20) 78, p. 11.
  "Showing Vacation Slides." PoNow (20) 78, p. 12.

HIGGINSON, William J.
  "It Is Not Death." JnlONJP (2:1) 77, p. 17.
  "Notes from the Paterson Dig." JnlONJP (2:2) 77, p. 23.
  "Paterson: Spring Morning." JnlONJP (2:1) 77, p. 16.
  "The Slide." JnlONJP (2:1) 77, p. 16.

HIGGS, Ted
  "The Dance of the Midnight Puppets." Wind (31) 78, p. 21.
  "Regeneration." Wind (31) 78, p. 21.

HIKMET, Nazim
  "Rubaiyat: Second Series" (tr. by Randy Blasing and Mutlu
    Konuk). LitR (21:4) Sum 78, p. 423.
  "Rubaiyat: Third Series" (tr. by Randy Blasing and Mutlu Konuk).
    AntR (36:3) Sum 78, p. 371.

HILBERRY, Conrad
  "A Christmas Poem." Poetry (133:3) D 78, p. 125.
  from House-marks: eight poems. Field (19) Aut 78, p. 5.
  "Logical Proof." ThRiPo (11/12) 78, p. 46.
  "Poem: Finally, the days let go." Bits (8) Jl 78.
  "The Sea." Poetry (132:6) S 78, p. 335.

HILDE, Don
  "Break Away." StoneC (78:2) Spr 78, p. 30.

HILDEBIDLE, John
  "Duty." SouthernPR (18:1) Spr 78, p. 61.
  "Jezebel." Aspect (71) Ap-Je 77, p. 38.

HILDEBRANDT, Gretchen
  "Dream." Box (7) Spr 78, p. 18.

HILL, Jeanne Foster
  "The Bones that Shape the Emptiness." Hudscn (31:1) Spr 78,
    p. 117.

HILL, Nellie
  "The Soil." DeKalb (11:3/4) Spr-Sum 78, p. 36.

HILL, Robert W.
"Museum Mummies Behind Glass." SouthernPR (18:2) Aut 78, p. 65.
"Of All Possible." SouthernR (14:4) Aut 78, p. 758.
"Purgatorio." Ascent (4:1) 78, p. 51.

HILL, Ronnie
"Oh God." DeKalb (11:3/4) Spr-Sum 78, p. 98.

HILLMAN, Brenda
"Anonymous Courtesan in a Jade Shroud." Field (19) Aut 78, p. 73.
"Coffee: 3 A.M." Madem (84:2) F 78, p. 38.
"Telescope." Field (19) Aut 78, p. 72.

HILLMAN, William S.
"August, 1934." CutB (11) Aut-Wint 78, p. 6.
"Climate." KanQ (10:4) Aut 78, p. 103.
"Owl Hymns." SoCaR (11:1) N 78, p. 80.

HILTON, David
"Desire." PoNow (19) 78, p. 45.
"Parfrey's Glen." HangL (32) Spr 78, p. 17.

HILTON, Jeremy
from An Orphan in the Cast: "how can you draw a person out." Montra (4) 78, p. 92.

HIND, Steven
"Leaving Together" (for Sam). MidwQ (19:2) Wint 78, p. 133.
"Song for Renetta at MacDonald's on 4th St." MidwQ (19:2) Wint 78, p. 134.

HINDLEY, Norman
"Long Walker." Tendril (3) Aut 78, p. 29.

HINDS, Art
"Currents." EngJ (67:5) My 78, p. 65.

HINE, Daryl
"After the Solstice." Poetry (131:4) Ja 78, p. 196.
"Codex." Poetry (131:4) Ja 78, p. 190.
"Coma Berenices." Poetry (131:4) Ja 78, p. 194.
"Copied in Camoes." Poetry (131:4) Ja 78, p. 193.
"Daylight Saving: A January Journal." Poetry (131:4) Ja 78, p. 187.
"Doctor Faustus' Welcome Home." Poetry (131:4) Ja 78, p. 191.

HINMAN, Sheryl
"A-V Lament." EngJ (67:5) My 78, p. 55.

HINRICHSEN, Dennis
"The Afterlife." PoNow (20) 78, p. 12.

"Autobiography." Iowa (9:1) Wint 78, p. 26.
"Babies from the Twenties & Thirties." SlowLR (1/2) 78, p. 47.
"Lines for the African Trader, A. Rimbaud." SlowLR (1/2) 78, p. 48.
"New York City." SlowLR (1/2) 78, p. 46.
"Pure Religion." Agni (9) 78, p. 104.

HIPPS, G. Melvin
"Helen." EngJ (67:5) My 78, p. 51.

HIRSCH, Edward
"And So It Begins Again." GeoR (32:3) Aut 78, p. 572.
"Denial." KanQ (10:1) Wint 78, p. 124.
"Dusk." NewYorker (54:2) 27 F 78, p. 87.
"Gerard de Nerval: Fairy Tale for a Whore." Agni (9) 78, p. 42.
"How to Get Back to Chester." Poetry (133:1) O 78, p. 37.
"Matisse." Iowa (9:3) Sum 78, p. 93.
"Prelude to Spring." NewYorker (54:9) 17 Ap 78, p. 36.

HIRSCHMAN, Jack
"Retour." Stonecloud (7) 78, p. 25.
"Selected Zaum Works" (tr. of Ilya Zdanevich, w. Alexander Kohav). SunM (5) Aut 78, p. 89.

HITCHCOCK, George
"At the Reef." PoetryNW (19:3) Aut 78, p. 19.
"The Collar." MoonsLT (2:4) 78, p. 8.
"Death of a Race Driver." MoonsLT (2:4) 78, p. 10.
"Eidolon." Durak (1) 78, p. 45.
"Enough of Numerals." Durak (1) 78, p. 42.
"Events of Our Epoch." Durak (1) 78, p. 46.
"Going Back There." Hudson (31:4) Wint 78-79, p. 635.
"Going Down." MalR (46) Ap 78, p. 106.
"The Hero." MalR (46) Ap 78, p. 108.
"How to Survive in the City of Dreadful Night." MoonsLT (2:4) 78, p. 9.
"Insert in the Dream a Pinch of Ivory." Durak (1) 78, p. 43.
"Nursery Rhyme." MoonsLT (2:4) 78, p. 7.
"The Picnic." CarolQ (30:1) Wint 78, p. 53.
"We Are Defined by the Absences Which Enclose Us." Durak (1) 78, p. 44.
"When I Came Back to Dancing Misery." PoetryNW (19:3) Aut 78, p. 20.

HITCHNER, John T.
"Remembering Apple Times." BallSUF (19:4) Aut 78, p. 24.

HIX, Hubert E.
"Full Moon." WindO (31) Wint-Spr 78, p. 10.

HOAG, Mae
"Sometimes It's Not Enough to Bring Camellias." Wind (30) 78, p. 58.

HOAG, Ron
"Crop Loss at Antietam." NewRivR (2:2) 78, p. 48.
"The End of the Oral Tradition; or, Stories My Grandfathers
Told Me That I Forgot." PoetryNW (19:3) Aut 78, p. 31.

HOAGLAND, Everett
"Blue Milk and Black Diamonds." BelPoJ (29:2) Wint 78-79,
p. 6.
"In Your Red Darkroom." BelPoJ (29:2) Wint 78, p. 7.
"Nia." BelPoJ (29:2) Wint 78-79, p. 8.
"NIA: A Celebration of Purpose" (for Alice). BelPoJ (29:2)
Wint 78-79, p. 5.

HOAGLAND, William
"His Lazy Neighbor." KanQ (10:2) Spr 78, p. 104.

HOBART, Jennifer
"Scandinavian Literature." HarvAd (111:3) Ap 78, p. 5.

HOBBS, Suzanne Marie
"Lullaby." Epos (27:2) 77, p. 29.
"Poem in Three Voices: By Any Other Name." St. AR (4:3/4)
77-78, p. 123.

HOBEN, Sandra
"The Great Salt Lake, July." QW (5) Wint 78, p. 86.
"Itele." QW (5) Wint 78, p. 87.
"New Moon." QW (5) Wint 78, p. 86.
"To Sleep." QW (5) Wint 78, p. 87.

HOBSON, Dale
"Nocturne." Wind (29) 78, p. 26.
"One Must Have a Mind of Winter." Wind (29) 78, p. 26.

HOBSON, Gerald
"Barbara's Land--May, 1974." GreenfieldR (6:3/4) Spr 78,
p. 172.

HODAPP, Marion
"Forgetfulness" (tr. of Alfonsina Storni, w. Mary Crow). WebR
(4:1) Spr 78, p. 12.
"Loneliness" (tr. of Alfonsina Storni, w. Mary Crow). WebR
(4:1) Spr 78, p. 11.
"The Moment" (tr. of Alfonsina Storni, w. Mary Crow). WebR
(4:1) 78, p. 10.
"Words to My Mother" (tr. of Alfonsina Storni, w. Mary Crow).
WebR (4:1) Spr 78, p. 9.

HODGE, Margaret
"How Aunt Margie Kept Her Umbrella." PoetryNW (19:3) Aut
78, p. 34.

HODGKINSON, Edith
"Abortion Set." HangL (34) Wint 78-79, p. 63.

"she must have been crazy." HangL (34) Wint 78-79,
    p. 68.

HOEFT, Robert D.
    "Almost a Sonnet." CarouselQ (3:4) Wint 78, p. 36.
    "The Mole." StoneC (78:1) Wint 78, p. 25.
    "Progress (As Photographed in Slow Motion)." StoneC (78:2)
        Spr 78, p. 23.
    "Uncle Billy on War." Wind (31) 78, p. 22.
    "We Are What We Eat." Wind (31) 78, p. 22.

HOEKSEMA, Thomas
    "City of Light" (tr. of Isabel Fraire). Nimrod (22:2) Spr-Sum
        78, p. 103.

HOEPPNER, Ed
    "From Garvey's Farm: Seneca, Wisconsin" (for Anna Marie).
        BelPoJ (28:4) Sum 78, p. 23.
    "Near Closing." SoDakR (16:2) Sum 78, p. 35.
    "One in Light and Water." NowestR (17:1) 78, p. 61.

HOEY, Allen
    "Fishing the Moon." Tendril (3) Aut 78, p. 30.

HOFFMAN, Daniel
    "At Don's Garage." AmerPoR (7:5) S-O 78, p. 47.
    "At the Roman Wall, 1956." Poetry (131:6) Mr 78, p. 328.
    "Crossing Walt Whitman Bridge." Shen (29:4) Sum 78, p. 77.
    "Folk Tale." Hudson (31:2) Sum 78, p. 273.
    "Haunted Houses." Poetry (131:6) Mr 78, p. 330.
    "Himself." Hudson (31:2) Sum 78, p. 274.
    "A Stillness." NewEngR (1:2) Wint 78, p. 134.
    "Witnesses." AmerPoR (7:5) S-O 78, p. 46.

HOFFMAN, Jill
    "Dumb Broad." GreenfieldR (6:3/4) Spr 78, p. 56.
    from Upper West Side: "General Studies." GreenfieldR (6:3/4)
        Spr 78, p. 56.
    "Your Triumph." GreenfieldR (6:3/4) Spr 78, p. 55.

HOFFNER, Christine
    "The Furthest Adventures of Nancy Drew." FourQt (27:4) Sum
        78, p. 17.

HOFSTADTER, Marc Elihu
    "Summer of Night" (tr. of Yves Bonnefoy). MalR (46) Ap
        78, p. 84.

HOGAN, Linda
    "Heritage." GreenfieldR (6:3/4) Spr 78, p. 29.
    "Land of Exile." Aspen (6) Aut 78, p. 60.
    "Leaving." GreenfieldR (6:3/4) Spr 78, p. 33.
    "Untitled." GreenfieldR (6:3/4) Spr 78, p. 31.

HOGAN, Michael
"Outside the North Wall." Hand (2) 78, p. 52.
"The Terrace, St. Tropez." ParisR (72) Wint 77, p. 54.

HOGUE, Cynthia
"Edging Winter." SenR (9:1) Spr-Sum 78, p. 64.
"What Is Given You." SenR (9:1) Spr-Sum 78, p. 66.

HOLAHAN, Susan
"A Woman, Moving." 13thM (4:1) 78, p. 5.

HOLDEN, Jonathan
"Blizzard." ThRiPo (11/12) 78, p. 47.
"Cutting Beetle-Blighted Ponderosa Pine." GeoR (32:4) Wint 78,
    p. 894.
"December Sunset." NewL (45:2) Wint 78, p. 99.
"'Early Sunday Morning': Edward Hopper." DenQ (13:3) Aut 78,
    p. 118.
"Ramanujan." PraS (52:2) Sum 78, p. 193.
"The Sequel." ConcPo (11:1) Spr 78, p. 74.
"What To Do with Time on Your Hands." DenQ (13:3) Aut 78,
    p. 120.
"Wrestling with My Son." NewL (45:2) Wint 78, p. 98.

HÖLDERLIN
from Drafts and Fragments (tr. by R. Sieburth and S. W.
    DeRachewiltz). St.AR (5:1) Aut-Wint 78, pp. 41-48.
"Remembrance" (tr. by R. Sieburth and S. W. DeRachewiltz).
    St.AR (5:1) Aut-Wint 78, p. 68.

HOLENDER, Barbara D.
"A Gift of Galtonia Princeps" (for Judy). LitR (21:3) Spr 78,
    p. 375.

HOLLAHAN, Eugene
"From Outer and Inner Space: Two Views of a Self."
    SouthernPR (18:1) Spr 78, p. 55.
"The Ohio River Breaks a Fine Swiss Watch." Wind (31) 78,
    p. 23.

HOLLAND, Barbara A.
"Clothesline." PoNow (19) 78, p. 32.

HOLLAND, Robert
"The Fisherman Casts His Line into the Sea." MidwQ (19:2)
    Wint 78, p. 136.
"The Unbeliever's Cross." MidwQ (19:2) Wint 78, p. 137.

HOLLANDER, Jean
"Rue Anemone." GRR (9:2) 78, p. 135.

HOLLANDER, John
"Baigneuse." NewYorker (54:5) 20 Mr 78, p. 34.

"The Four Ages." Iowa (9:3) Sum 78, p. 96.
"New Graveyard in New Jersey." NewYorker (54:36) 23 O 78,
    p. 36.
"Nox Regina." NewYorker (54:39) 13 N 78, p. 46.
"Ode to Landscape." NewYorker (54:10) 24 Ap 78, p. 40.
from Spectral Emanations: "under cancer." NewRep (179:11) 9
    S 78, p. 43.

HOLLANDER, Martha
    "The First View of Saturn." YaleLit (147:3) 77, p. 18.
    "Two Translations." YaleLit (147:3) 78, p. 19.

HOLLANDER, Robert
    "Roi Babtlto di Togbrattn & Gbamsoi." CimR (45) O 78, p. 27.

HOLLOWAY, Geoffrey
    "Caged." Stand (19:1) 77-78, p. 17.

HOLMAN, Bob
    "Detach your removable fangs & putty ugliness, Madness." Tele
        (14) 78.
    "Madness & I are sailing to Bongoland." Tele (14) 78.
    "The Return." Tele (14) 78.
    "The spy Madness winks." Tele (14) 78.

HOLMES, Jane
    "What About Tomorrow?" DeKalb (11:3/4) Spr-Sum 78, p. 99.

HOLMES, Zandra Diane
    "It Can't Be Love." BlackF (2:2) Aut-Wint 78, p. 24.
    "Never Saying Good-Bye." BlackF (2:2) Aut-Wint 78, p. 26.

HOLSCHER, Rory
    "A Beatitude." DacTerr (15) Wint-Spr 77-78, p. 69.

HOLSHOUSER, W. L.
    "Visits with Mr. John." SouthernPR (18:2) Aut 78, p. 28.

HOLZMAN, Dennis
    "A Thank You Note." GreenfieldR (6:3/4) Spr 78, p. 126.
    "Neck." GreenfieldR (6:3/4) Spr 78, p. 126.

HONECKER, George J.
    "Ode to My Liver." LittleM (11:3) Aut 77, p. 35.

HONIG, Edwin
    "Apollo in the Defeated Town." Columbia (2) Aut 78, p. 60.
    "Three Moments for George Sullivan." BosUJ (26:1) 78, p. 32.
    "When It Was Over You Thought." PoNow (19) 78, p. 12.

HOOKER, Jeremy
    "Mary Rose (1545)." Stand (18:4) 77, p. 5.

HOOPER, Patricia
"Reading a Poem." GRR (9:3) 78, p. 210.

HOORNIK, Ed.
"The Fish" (tr. by Koos Schuur). St. AR (5:1) Aut-Wint 78,
    p. 93.

HOOVEN, Evelyn
"Four After Nerval: Imitations." LitR (21:4) Sum 78, p. 436.
"Interview." LitR (21:3) Spr 78, p. 379.

HOOVER, Paul
"Confession." MassR (19:2) Sum 78, p. 318.
"Lesson of the Forgetful House." MassR (19:2) Sum 78, p. 317.

HOPES, David
"Admonition to the Shining Brother." PoetryNW (19:4) Wint 78-
    79, p. 40.
"Caliban Soliloquizes at the Vernal Equinox." EnPas (7) 78,
    p. 20.
"Land Eastward." HiramPoR (24) Spr-Sum 78, p. 18.
"The Sighting." HiramPoR (24) Spr-Sum 78, p. 20.

HOPPER, Paul T.
"Fire-walls" (tr. of Günter Grass). AmerPoR (7:4) Jl-Ag 78,
    p. 46.

HOPPING, Loraine
"Polaroid." HangL (32) Spr 78, p. 64.
"Walrus." HangL (32) Spr 78, p. 63.

HORNE, Lewis B.
"Never After." HiramPoR (24) Spr-Sum 78, p. 21.
"Waiting for Summer." SouthernPR (18:1) Spr 78, p. 44.

HORNUNG, Beth
"Translation." CalQ (13/14) Spr-Sum 78, p. 105.

HORSFIELD, Sue
"The Swan." PikeF (1) Spr 78, p. 16.

HORVATH, Lou
"Aphasia" (for John Acklin). ParisR (73) Spr-Sum 78, p. 139.
"The enemy was high." Tele (14) 78.
"Nouveau Conte Poem." ParisR (73) Spr-Sum 78, p. 140.

HOUCHIN, Ron
"In the Dark Hotel." SmPd (42) Wint 78, p. 20.
"The Ocean in Estrus." SmPd (42) Wint 78, p. 19.

HOUGAN, Jim
"Helmslet." Harp (256:1533) F 78, p. 64.

HOUGHTON, Elgar
"Wild Horses." HolCrit (15:3) Je 78, p. 17.

HOUSTON, Peyton
"The Death of the Minotaur." OP (26) Aut-Wint 78, p. 58.
"Difficulties of the Conchologist." OP (26) Aut-Wint 78, p. 60.
"In the Extraordinary Mazes." OP (26) Aut-Wint 78, p. 56.
"Oboe Concerto by Mozart." OP (26) Aut-Wint 78, p. 59.
"The Observation of Angels." OP (26) Aut-Wint 78, p. 62.
"Old Man Considering It." OP (26) Aut-Wint 78, p. 63.
"The Problem of Describing It." OP (26) Aut-Wint 78, p. 61.
"The Question We Come To." OP (26) Aut-Wint 78, p. 64.

HOUTS, Eric
"L'Idiot." AmerPoR (7:6) N-D 78, p. 37.

HOVDE, A. J.
"I Shall Never Go." KanQ (10:4) Aut 78, p. 83.

HOWARD, Ben
"Clarities." CarolQ (30:3) Aut 78, p. 77.
"Sluice." Poetry (131:5) F 78, p. 291.
"Span." CarolQ (30:3) Aut 78, p. 76.

HOWARD, Frances Minturn
"The Color Is Red." PoNow (19) 78, p. 45.

HOWARD, Jean C.
"Bed Side." Harp (257:1539) Ag 78, p. 28.

HOWARD, Richard
"Another Invitation." NewYorker (54:34) 9 O 78, p. 48.
"Charles Baudelaire." Nat (227:21) 16 D 78, p. 682.

HOWE, Fanny
"List." Tele (14) 78.

HOWE, Susan
"Sally." Tele (13) 77.

HOWELL, Gary A.
"Sometimes." CarouselQ (3:2) Sum 78, p. 13.

HOYEM, Andrew
"Alimentary." Poetry (131:5) F 78, p. 282.
"Eating the Afterbirth." Poetry (131:5) F 78, p. 285.

HOYT, Don A.
"Chem Plant by the River." Poem (32) Mr 78, p. 57.
"In the Ruins." Poem (32) Mr 78, p. 59.
"Letter from a Lunar Olympian." KanQ (10:4) Aut 78, p. 48.
"The Party." Poem (32) Mr 78, p. 58.

HRABAR, Linda
"Vanishing Wildlife." CarouselQ (3:2) Sum 78, p. 21.
"Waiting for the Hand." CarouselQ (3:4) Wint 78, p. 26.

HSINGTE, Nalan
"Sennin by the River" (tr. by Lenore Mayhew and William
    McNaughton). NewOR (6:1) 78, p. 57.

HUBERT, Jim
"Nobody's a One Man Band." DacTerr (15) Wint-Spr 77-78,
    p. 45.

HUBERT, Karen
"Beggar Rabbit." PoNow (20) 78, p. 12.

HUCHEL, Peter
"Enkidu" (tr. by Michael Hamburger). Durak (1) 78, p. 13.

HUDDLE, David
"Evening Services Every Fourth Sunday." Harp (256:1537) Je
    78, p. 85.

HUDDLESTON, Sheri
"If I had a kid." SeC (5:2) 78, p. 22.

HUDGINS, Andrew
"Bryce Hospital: The Old Cemetery." SenR (9:1) Spr-Sum 78,
    p. 82.
"Eastertime." KanQ (10:1) Wint 78, p. 50.
"Mine." SouthwR (63:2) Spr 78, p. 142.

HUDGINS, Arthur
"1933, Facism" (tr. of Boris Slutsky, w. James Naiden).
    NorthSR (8) Aut-Wint 78-79, p. 104.
"The Seed" (tr. of Boris Slutsky, w. James Naiden).   NorthSR
    (8) Aut-Wint 78-79, p. 106.
"Silhouette" (tr. of Boris Slutsky, w. James Naiden).   NorthSR
    (8) Aut-Wint 78-79, p. 105.

HUDSON, Marc
"Aeneas Valley, Summer." PoetryNW (19:1) Spr 78, p. 12.
"Elegy for Martin Heidegger." Poetry (131:4) Ja 78, p. 210.
"Home." Poetry (131:4) Ja 78, p. 209.
"Red Cedar." PoetryNW (19:1) Spr 78, p. 11.
"Winter, Aeneas Valley." Poetry (131:4) Ja 78, p. 208.

HUDSPITH, Vicki
"Bike Ride through Battery Park." Tele (14) 78.
"Dressing Up." Tele (14) 78.
"Dynamic." Tele (14) 78.
"Notes from Iran." Tele (14) 78.

HUDZIK, Robert
"The Infinite Monologue." SlowLR (1/2) 78, p. 33.

HUFF, Robert
"Lines for William Golding, 1975." Poetry (132:4) Jl 78, p. 202.
"While the Now Generation Basks in Its Brand New Milky Way"
  (for Tresa Hughes). Poetry (132:4) Jl 78, p. 201.

HUFF, Roland
"She Drinks No Wine." Poem (32) Mr 78, p. 17.

HUGHES, Austin
"David Rittenhouse Unveils His Orrery (College of Philadelphia,
  1771)." FourQt (28:1) Aut 78, p. 27.

HUGHES, Connie
"Silent Sentry." Wind (29) Aut 78, p. 49.

HUGHES, David
"tonight." Zahir (9) 77, p. 66.

HUGHES, Dorothy
"Cloudburst at Harvester Home." Vaga (27) Spr 78, p. 56.
"East." Vaga (27) Spr 78, p. 57.

HUGHES, Ted
"Birth of Rainbow." Antaeus (28) Wint 78, p. 82.
"Bridestones." Antaeus (30/31) Sum-Aut 78, p. 103.
"Cockcrow." Antaeus (28) Wint 78, p. 81.
"Heptonstall Cemetery." Antaeus (30/31) Sum-Aut 78, p. 101.
"March Morning Unlike Others." Atl (241:3) Mr 78, p. 90.
"Teaching a Dumb Calf." Antaeus (28) Wint 78, p. 84.
"Tractor." Antaeus (28) Wint 78, p. 79.
"(Untitled)." Antaeus (30/31) Sum-Aut 78, p. 102.
"Wycoller Hall." Antaeus (30/31) Sum-Aut 78, p. 99.

HUGO, Richard
"The Clearances." AmerPoR (7:6) N-D 78, p. 47.
"Druid Stones at Kensaleyre." Antaeus (30/31) Sum-Aut 78,
  p. 104.
"Fort Benton" (for Jan). OhioR (19:1) Wint 78, p. 91.
"Graves in Uig." Antaeus (30/31) Sum-Aut 78, p. 105.
"Greystone Cottage." NewYorker (54:30) 11 S 78, p. 34.
"Hawk in Uig." AmerPoR (7:6) N-D 78, p. 47.
"Kilmuir Cemetery: The Knight in Blue-Green Relief."
  AmerPoR (7:6) N-D 78, p. 48.
"Kilmuir Cemetery (Stone with Two Skulls and No Name)."
  AmerPoR (7:6) N-D 78, p. 47.
"Leaving the Dream." NewYorker (54:23) 24 Jl 78, p. 28.
"Museum of Cruel Days." NewYorker (54:35) 16 O 78, p. 42.
"Sneosdal." Field (18) Spr 78, p. 10.

HUHN, Luci
"For Your Sister." CutB (11) Aut-Wint 78, p. 73.

HULK, Gloria
"Oh Poet of Israel" (Yehuda Amachai). Wind (30) 78, p. 16.

HUMES, Harry
"Grandma Hex." <u>DacTerr</u> (15) Wint-Spr 77-78, p. 13.

HUMMER, T. R.
"Farewell Poem." <u>ParisR</u> (72) Wint 77, p. 36.
"The Genesis of Hands." <u>ParisR</u> (72) Wint 77, p. 36.
"Sage." <u>CarolQ</u> (30:1) Wint 78, p. 109.
"A Space <u>Warp</u> Appears, Right in the Middle of the Parlor
    Floor." <u>ParisR</u> (72) Wint 77, p. 33.
"Tides." <u>Wind (29)</u> 78, p. 28.
"Woodman." <u>Wind</u> (29) 78, p. 28.

HUMMER, Terry
"Bearing Gifts." <u>QW</u> (5) Wint 78, p. 38.
"The Myth of Being Born." <u>QW</u> (5) Wint 78, p. 40.
"A Poem for My Father, Written in the City." <u>QW</u> (5) Wint 78,
    p. 39.

HUMPHRIES, Dwight E.
"No Looking Back." <u>CarouselQ</u> (3:2) Sum 78, p. 27.

HUNT, Tim
"Cousin Diane." <u>Wind</u> (30) 78, p. 45.

HUNT, William
"No Longer May We Call." <u>NewL</u> (45:2) Wint 78, p. 91.

HUNTER, Paul
"What Is Given You Pour." <u>ConcPo</u> (11:1) Spr 78, p. 24.

HUNTINGTON, Cynthia
"Making a Place." <u>PoetryNW</u> (19:2) Sum 78, p. 23.
"On Thanksgiving Day." <u>PraS</u> (52:3) Aut 78, p. 276.
"Romance." <u>Iowa</u> (9:3) Sum 78, p. 86.
"Sleeping Alone with Others." <u>PraS</u> (52:3) Aut 78, p. 277.
"Sleeping in the Afternoon." <u>OhioR</u> (19:2) Spr-Sum 78, p. 46.
"The World Is On Fire." <u>OhioR</u> (19:3) Aut 78, p. 102.

HURWITZ, Sadie Wernick
"Invitation to an Old Friend." <u>Poem</u> (32) Mr 78, p. 13.

HUS, DuBois
Stanzas (1-7). <u>Montra</u> (4) 78, p. 110.

HUTCHINS, Elmer
"Fr. Berrigan." <u>GreenfieldR</u> (7:1/2) Aut 78, p. 23.
"Night Streets." <u>Zahir</u> (9) 77, p. 20.

HUTCHINSON, Debbie
"Beautician." <u>HolCrit</u> (15:1) F 78, p. 12.

HUTCHINSON, Robert
"The Apple Tree Again." <u>MichQR</u> (17:2) Spr 78, p. 133.
"Cain and Abel: Emblems." <u>ChrC</u> (95:1) 4-11 Ja 78, p. 17.

HUTCHISON, Alexander
  "'In Fire the Voice Goes Further.'" MalR (45) Ja 78, p. 202.
  "Riguarda." MalR (45) Ja 78, p. 204.

HUTCHISON, Joe
  "A Field of Pumpkins along the Willamette River." AAR (28)
      78, p. 85.
  "Harbinger." AAR (28) 78, p. 86.
  "Pneumonia." Aspen (5) Spr 78, p. 8.
  "Whale Songs." Aspen (5) Spr 78, p. 8.

HYDE, Lewis
  "After Love" (tr. of Vicente Aleixandre). ParisR (74) Aut-Wint
      78, p. 37.
  "Ants." NewL (45:2) Wint 78, p. 99.
  "The Comet" (tr. of Vicente Aleixandre). MoonsLT (2:4) 78,
      inside front cover.
  "The Eagles" (tr. of Vicente Aleixandre). ParisR (74) Aut-Wint
      78, p. 31.
  "Guitar or Moon" (tr. of Vicente Aleixandre, w. David Unger).
      ParisR (74) Aut-Wint 78, p. 33.
  "The Hands" (tr. of Vicente Aleixandre). ParisR (74) Aut-Wint
      78, p. 34.
  "Open Spaces." Aspect (71) Ap-Je 77, p. 16.
  "This Error Is the Sign of Love." MassR (19:2) Sum 78,
      p. 245.
  "We Feed on Shadow" (tr. of Vicente Aleixandre). ParisR (74)
      Aut-Wint 78, p. 35.
  "The Young and the Old" (tr. of Vicente Aleixandre). ParisR
      (74) Aut-Wint 78, p. 39.

HYLAND, Paul
  "Mark of a Master." Stand (19:1) 77-78, p. 16.
  "Terrorist." Stand (19:4) 78, p. 52.
  "Tomorrow Send Word." Stand (19:4) 78, p. 53.

IBANEZ, Edgardo
  "Grandpa is a/veteran." SeC (5:2) 78, p. 23.

IBATTO, Anna
  "Towards Istanbul." EngJ (67:5) My 78, p. 52.

IGNATOW, David
  "And To Live It." Hand (2) 78, p. 8.
  Eight poems. ParisR (72) Wint 77, pp. 123-27.
  "Epitaph for a Soldier." CentR (22:3) Sum 78, p. 323.
  "First Generation." CentR (22:3) Sum 78, p. 322.
  "'In this dream.'" Hudson (31:1) Spr 78, p. 107.
  "'I want to be buried.'" Hudson (31:1) Spr 78, p. 109.
  "The Life They Lead." Hudson (31:1) Spr 78, p. 108.
  "The Metamorphosis." Hudson (31:1) Spr 78, p. 107.
  "My Own House." ChiR (30:3) Wint 79, p. 122.
  "One Leaf." ChiR (30:3) Wint 79, p. 123.
  "The Question." Atl (241:1) Ja 78, p. 74.

"'The seasons doubt themselves.'" Hudson (31:1) Spr 78,
 p. 110.
"'There's the reality.'" Hudson (31:1) Spr 78, p. 108.

IKEMOTO, Takashi
 "Burning Oneself to Death" (tr. of Shinkichi Takahashi, w.
 Lucien Stryk). OhioR (19:2) Spr-Sum 78, p. 63.
 "Chinese Zen Poems of Enlightenment and Death" (tr., w. Lucien
 Stryk). QW (5) Wint 78, p. 36.
 "Four Poems" (tr. of Shinkichi Takahashi, w. Lucien Stryk).
 OhioR (19:2) Spr-Sum 78, p. 65.
 "Sparrow" (tr. of Shinkichi Takahashi, w. Lucien Stryk). OhioR
 (19:2) Spr-Sum 78, p. 60.

ILEY, Mollie
 "One Night Stand...." GreenfieldR (7:1/2) Aut 78, p. 38.

IMMERMAN, Jill
 "Dawn." Tendril (1) Wint 77-78.
 "Gestation." Tendril (1) Wint 77-78.

IMPEY, Michael
 "Alternative" (tr. of Gabriela Melinescu, w. Brian Swann).
 WebR (4:1) Spr 78, p. 3.
 "The Butterfly" (tr. of Gabriela Melinescu, w. Brian Swann).
 WebR (4:1) Spr 78, p. 6.
 "Fall" (tr. of Gabriela Melinescu, w. Brian Swann). WebR (4:1)
 Spr 78, p. 3.
 "John Climbing the Darkened Ladder" (tr. of Gabriela Melinescu,
 w. Brian Swann). WebR (4:1) Spr 78, p. 4.

INEZ, Colette
 "Implements." 13thM (4:1) 78, p. 87.
 "It Is an Irish Sea, O'Rourke." CalQ (13/14) Spr-Sum 78,
 p. 129.
 "Meeting in Germany." Poetry (132:3) Je 78, p. 136.
 "Orphanage Sisters." NowestR (17:1) 78, p. 21.
 "The Piano Tuner Elopes with a Chord as I Think of Capsized
 Love." NowestR (17:1) 78, p. 22.
 "Snapshot." Bleb/Ark (13) 78, p. 16.
 "To Take in the World as Waves Greet the Sand." AmerPoR
 (7:2) Mr-Ap 78, p. 34.
 "Western Time Concepts." PartR (45:1) 78, p. 9.

INGRAM, Alyce M.
 "Dobrovsky." SunM (5) Aut 78, p. 8.

INMAN, Robert
 "Elephant's Ears." SouthernPR (18:2) Aut 78, p. 43.

INMAN, Will
 "Dark Side of the Sun." Epos (27:1) 77, p. 28.
 "What, Truer Than Bereft Arms, Moves." Epos (27:2) 77,
 p. 5.

IRWIN, Mark
"Meditation on Bells" (for Philippe Denis). Bits (8) Jl 78.

ISAACS, Jay B.
"Come Spring." CarouselQ (3:1) Spr 78.

ISLAS, Arturo
"Drunk." Poetry (131:4) Ja 78, p. 203.
"Hostility." Poetry (131:4) Ja 78, p. 199.
"Motherfucker or the Exile." Poetry (131:4) Ja 78, p. 200.

ISON, Tawnya M.
"The After Dawn." Wind (30) 78, p. 18.

ITZIN, C.
"The Greyhounds of Comte de Cheiseul, 1866." LittleM (11:4)
    Wint 78, p. 6.

IVASK, Astrid
"Spring, Oklahoma." Nimrod (22:2) Spr-Sum 78, p. 29.

IVERSON, Carol Diane
"Grandmother Collected Elephants." JnlONJP (2:2) 77, p. 9.
"Photograph Exhibit of the City Through History." JnlONJP (2:2)
    77, p. 8.

IVES, Rich
"Interior Landscape" (1-5). MalR (46) Ap 78, p. 92.
"The Songs of the New Body." GreenfieldR (6:3/4) Spr 78,
    p. 20.
"Versions of the End." GreenfieldR (6:3/4) Spr 78, p. 23.

IZOARD, Jacquez
"J'assiste à l'union." Nimrod (22:2) Spr-Sum 78, p. 96.
"Voix sans écho, qui demeure." Nimrod (22:2) Spr-Sum 78,
    p. 96.

JACKSON, Dan
"Mermaid." CarouselQ (3:3) Aut 78, p. 20.

JACKSON, Haywood
"Education of a Honeydipper in the Trecento." SouthernPR
    (18:1) Spr 78, p. 22.
"I Do, You Have Done, Till Death Do Us." SouthernPR (18:1)
    Spr 78, p. 23.
"Reading 'The Ascent of Man' at Midnight, Alone with Uncombed
    Hair." Confr (16) Spr-Sum 78, p. 55.
"To Dream." SouthernPR (18:2) Aut 78, p. 54.
"'You Are Who You Dream.'" KanQ (10:4) Aut 78, p. 95.
"When the Little Story Began" (apologies to W. H. Auden).
    KanQ (10:4) Aut 78, p. 96.

JACKSON, Henry
"Miss Minnie Moss." Obs (4:2) Sum 78. p. 62.

JACKSON, Richard
"Holding On" (for his father, prematurely old).   PraS (52:4)
    Wint 78-79, p. 379.
"A Prayer for My Daughter after the Death of Martha Cashman. "
    PraS (52:4) Wint 78-79, p. 380.

JACKSON, William H.
"My Death Poem. "   DeKalb (11:1/2) Aut-Wint 77-78, p. 50.

JACOBS, Lucky
"Copyright. "   Smudge (1) Spr 78, p. 32.
"Daydream to Night. "   Bound (6:2) Wint 78, p. 547.
"Existential Night Baseball. "   PoNow (20) 78, p. 12.
"Great Dismal Swamp. "   Bound (6:2) Wint 78, p. 546.
"Leave of Absence. "   Bound (6:2) Wint 78, p. 544.

JACOBS, Sondra Dunner
"Leda's Soliloquy. "   Chomo (5:2) Aut-Wint 78, p. 5.

JACOBSEN, Josephine
"The Chinese Insomniacs. "   Nat (226:11) 25 Mr 78, p. 342.
"Country Drive-In. "   Nat (226:9) 11 Mr 78, p. 282.
"Notes Toward Time. "   CornellR (4) Aut 78, p. 70.
"Short Views in Africa. "   NewYorker (54:43) 11 D 78, p. 46.
"Simon. "   PoNow (19) 78, p. 9.
"Trial Run. "   SouthernPR (18:1) Spr 78, p. 16.

JACOBSON, Bonnie
"Marriage. "   Bits (7) Ja 78.

JACOBSON, Dale
"Refrain. "   MoonsLT (2:4) 78, p. 71.
"Short Elegy for John Berryman. "   MoonsLT (2:4) 78, p. 70.

JACOBY, Stan
"Oracle. "   PoetryNW (19:4) Wint 78-79, p. 37.

JACQUES, Ben
"Copper and Brass. "   WormR (72) 78, p. 129.
"Doug, Sitting in Mama's Truckstop. "   WormR (72) 78, p. 130.
"The Fall. "   WormR (72) 78, p. 131.
"In Her Shop Hang Pictures of Geronimo and Jesus. "   WormR
    (72) 78, p. 129.
"Tommy. "   WormR (72) 78, p. 130.
"Up in Maine. "   WormR (72) 78, p. 130.

JAECH, Stephen
"As I Watch Your House Come Down. "   PoNow (19) 78, p. 47.

JAEHNKE, Marilyn David
"The Deities. "   HiramPoR (25) Aut-Wint 78, p. 26.
"for an only son. "   HiramPoR (25) Aut-Wint 78, p. 27.
"Geese Moving North. "   CimR (44) Jl 78, p. 30.

JAHNS, T. R.
"A Weaning." BallSUF (19:4) Aut 78, p. 38.

JAMES, Billie Jean
"Bevel." SenR (9:1) Spr-Sum 78, p. 101.
"Near Searchlight." SoDakR (16:2) Sum 78, p. 60.

JAMES, David
"The Burning of Bridges." WormR (72) 78, p. 121.
"Drifting into Snow." CutB (11) Aut-Wint 78, p. 36.
"He Would Break the Mailbox." PoNow (20) 78, p. 12.
"Parenthood." Sky (7/8) Spr 78, p. 24.
"Running the Dogs." CarolQ (30:2) Spr-Sum 78, p. 58.
"Selfish Blue." Tele (13) 77.
"Some Nostalgia." Tele (13) 77.
"There Is Evidence." WormR (72) 78, p. 123.

JAMES, Nancy Esther
"My Mother in Dreams." YellowBR (10) 78, p. 42.

JAMES, Ronnie
"Grafitti to Confetti." GreenfieldR (7:1/2) Aut 78, p. 54.

JAMES, Sibyl
"Cycles of Homecoming." Tendril (3) Aut 78, p. 32.
"Harbor Meditations." Tendril (3) Aut 78, p. 33.

JAMES, Thomas
"Conditioning." NewRep (178:9) 4 Mr 78, p. 33.
"This Green Earth." Poetry (132:6) S 78, p. 336.

JANECZKO, Paul Bryan
"Poem for a Common Day" (for Elizabeth). EngJ (67:5) My 78,
    p. 62.

JANKIEWICZ, Henry
"Narcissus Bereft." FourQt (27:4) Sum 78, p. 16.

JANOWITZ, Phyllis
"Falling into the Moment." AndR (5:1) Spr 78, p. 39.
"Luncheon at the Marshalls." ParisR (73) Spr-Sum 78, p. 33.
"Their Town." AndR (5:2) Aut 78, p. 23.
"The Wait." Atl (242:3) S 78, p. 80.

JANUS, Pat
"Letters from an Inland Refuge." AmerPoR (7:4) Jl-Ag 78,
    p. 32.
"The Mail." Atl (241:4) Ap 78, p. 106.

JAPANESE
103 Tanka (tr. by Hiroaki Sato). Montra (4) 78, p. 152.

JARMAN, Mark
"Father, Son, and Ghost." Antaeus (30/31) Sum-Aut 78, p. 106.

"Kicking the Candles Out." Nat (226:16) 29 Ap 78, p. 516.
"Lullaby for Amy." Kayak (47) F 78, p. 58.
"Sedative." ThRiPo (11/12) 78, p. 48.
"Shepherd." ThRiPo (11/12) 78, p. 49.
"We Dare Not Go A-Hunting." Chowder (10/11) Aut-Wint 78-79,
     p. 26.

JARRETT, Emmett
"Listen." Hand (2) 78, p. 91.

JAUSS, David
"The Sixth Day." DacTerr (15) Wint-Spr 77-78, p. 43.

JAWORSKI, Jerry
"Associates." DeKalb (11:1/2) Aut-Wint 77-78, p. 54.

JELLEMA, Rod
"First Climb Up Three Surfers' Peak." ThRiPo (11/12) 78,
     p. 50.

JENDRZEJCZYK, L. M.
"Centering." GreenfieldR (6:3/4) Spr 78, p. 122.

JENKINS, Jay
"Brick Rows of Houses Attached." Bachy (11) Spr 78, p. 71.
"Brick Town." Bachy (11) Spr 78, p. 71.
"Graduation." Bachy (11) Spr 78, p. 70.
"Place St. Michel." Bachy (11) Spr 78, p. 71.
"Unconscionability in a Contract Is a Question of Law." Bachy
     (11) Spr 78, p. 67.

JENKINS, Paul
"The Apocalypse That Came and Went." Pan (19) 77, p. 69.
"November." ParisR (73) Spr-Sum 78, p. 26.
"A Party Near the Coast." ParisR (73) Spr-Sum 78, p. 28.

JENNERMANN, Donald L.
"Caption in Want of Aerial Perspective." SoDakR (16:2) Sum 78,
     p. 33.

JENNINGS, Cheryl
"Another New Caffeine Poem." Wind (30) 78, p. 19.
"Losing Touch." Wind (30) 78, p. 19.

JENNINGS, Elizabeth
"Ballad in Summer." SouthernR (14:1) Wint 78, p. 91.
"Better Than a Protest." SouthernR (14:1) Wint 78, p. 92.
"A Child in the Night." SouthernR (14:1) Wint 78, p. 91.

JENNINGS, Ernest L.
"The Escapist." SmPd (44) Aut 78, p. 29.

JENNINGS, Kate
"Divorce." CarolQ (30:3) Aut 78, p. 58.

"Men Laughing." CarolQ (30:3) Aut 78, p. 57.
"Rural Route." AmerS (47:1) Wint 77-78, p. 85.

JENSEN, Dana
    "Driving Home." NorthSR (8) Aut-Wint 78-79, p. 73.

JENSEN, Laura
    "At the End of the Workbook." Field (19) Aut 78, p. 68.
    "Bad Boats." PoNow (20) 78, p. 22.
    "Birthday." Field (19) Aut 78, p. 69.
    "The Complex Mechanism of the Up." PoNow (20) 78, p. 22.
    "The Moon Rises." Field (19) Aut 78, p. 71.
    "Redwing Blackbird." PoNow (20) 78, p. 22.
    "Some Kind of Poem." Antaeus (30/31) Sum-Aut 78, p. 108.
    "West Window." AndR (4:2) Aut 77, p. 77.

JESSE, Mildred
    "Allhallows Eve." PoetryNW (19:2) Sum 78, p. 37.

JESTER, Barbara A.
    "In the Same Place Where It Began." CarouselQ (3:4) Wint 78,
        p. 5.
    "Pale Virginia." EngJ (67:5) My 78, p. 58.

JEVREMOVIC, George
    "Dreaming of Beograd." Kayak (47) F 78, p. 65.
    "The Recital." Kayak (47) F 78, p. 64.
    Six poems (tr. of Vasko Popa). Kayak (49) O 78, p. 57.

JNANA
    "Aubade." Tele (14) 78.
    "Poem for Proctor & Gamble." Tele (14) 78.
    "Poem Protesting the High Price of Heat." Tele (14) 78.

JOHNSEN, Gretchen
    "Needlepoint." PoetC (10:2) 78, p. 25.

JOHNSON, Carol Eileen
    "The Awakening." CarouselQ (3:4) Wint 78, p. 24.
    "Elegy to my Grandfather." CarouselQ (3:2) Sum 78, p. 23.
    "An Experience in Loving." CarouselQ (3:3) Aut 78, p. 21.

JOHNSON, Claudia
    "All in One Breath" (tr. of Karl Krolow). NewL (45:1) Aut 78,
        p. 46.
    "Atlantis" (tr. of Wislawa Szymborska, w. Robin Behn). ThRiPo
        (11/12) 78, p. 69.
    "For You" (tr. of Bettina Schmeidel). MissouriR (2:1) Aut 78,
        p. 23.
    "Half a Melon" (tr. of Karl Krolow, w. Stuart Friebert). NewL
        (45:1) Aut 78, p. 47.
    "Let's Go" (tr. of Karl Krolow, w. Stuart Friebert). NewL
        (45:1) Aut 78, p. 45.
    "On the Street" (tr. of Karl Krolow). MissouriR (2:1) Aut 78,

p. 20.

"Seen from Above" (tr. of Wislawa Szymborska, w. Robin Behn).
ThRiPo (11/12) 78, p. 71.

"We Were Young" (tr. of Karl Krolow). NewL (45:1) Aut 78,
p. 46.

"Words in Winter" (tr. of Karl Krolow). MissouriR (2:1) Aut
78, p. 19.

JOHNSON, Conniesue
"Soledad. " GreenfieldR (6:3/4) Spr 78, p. 157.
"Someplace Not Here. " GreenfieldR (6:3/4) Spr 78, p. 158.
"Something in the Wind. " GreenfieldR (6:3/4) Spr 78, p. 157.

JOHNSON, Denis
"Heat. " AmerPoR (7:2) Mr-Ap 78, p. 16.
"Night. " AmerPoR (7:2) Mr-Ap 78, p. 16.
"Radio. " AmerPoR (7:2) Mr-Ap 78, p. 16.
"Tomorrow. " AmerPoR (7:2) Mr-Ap 78, p. 16.
"A Woman. " AmerPoR (7:2) Mr-Ap 78, p. 16.

JOHNSON, Don
"Abattoir. " Tendril (1) Wint 77-78.
"Metamorphosis. " Tendril (3) Aut 78, p. 34.
"On a New England Hill in Midwinter. " Tendril (1) Wint 77-78.

JOHNSON, Estelle
"Pregnancy. " JnlONJP (2:2) 77, p. 6.
"Wedding Anniversary. " JnlONJP (2:2) 77, p. 6.

JOHNSON, Evelyn P.
"Where Are My Songs. " Wind (29) 78, p. 29.

JOHNSON, Greg
"Sexton. " SouthwR (63:1) Wint 78, p. 79.

JOHNSON, Halvard
"St. Amour. " DacTerr (15) Wint-Spr 77-78, p. 50.

JOHNSON, J.
"Spinster. " DacTerr (15) Wint-Spr 77-78, p. 33.

JOHNSON, John
"News Report. " St. AR (5:1) Aut-Wint 78, p. 92.
"Poem: And what's the pt?" St. AR (5:1) Aut-Wint 78, p. 129.
"Poem: The numbers on the table. " St. AR (5:1) Aut-Wint 78,
p. 127.

JOHNSON, Kenneth E.
"Blind. " CarouselQ (3:1) Spr 78, p. 13.
"Silhouette. " CarouselQ (3:2) Sum 78, p. 9.

JOHNSON, Nan C.
"Hammering. " GreenfieldR (6:3/4) Spr 78, p. 131.

JOHNSON, Nate
"The Subject of the Blues." BelPoJ (29:2) Wint 78-79, p. 10.

JOHNSON, Nick
"Album" (for my mother). YellowBR (10) 78, p. 24.

JOHNSON, Paulette S.
"Artist" (for Charles Rowell). Obs (4:2) Sum 78, p. 77.
"Mello." Obs (4:2) Sum 78, p. 73.
"Self Portrait" (for Charles Rowell and other poets who feel).
    Obs (4:2) Sum 78, p. 78.
"White Fragment, #1." Obs (4:2) Sum 78, p. 78.

JOHNSON, Robert K.
"Medley." KanQ (10:1) Wint 78, p. 123.

JOHNSON, Robin
"Pas de Deux." SouthernHR (12:3) Sum 78, p. 284.

JOHNSON, Ronald
"Radi   os." Montra (4) 78, p. 291.

JOHNSON, Steve
"Rising." Wind (30) 78, p. 20.
"Wilderness." Wind (30) 78, p. 25.

JOHNSON, Thomas
"Kingfisher." PraS (52:1) Spr 78, p. 23.
"Ode to My Punishment." CarolQ (30:3) Aut 78, p. 20.
"Some Scribbles for a Lumpfish." NowestR (17:1) 78, p. 55.
"Song for One Voice in the Blue Ridge Passes." AmerPoR
    (7:1) Ja-F 78, p. 44.
"A Stanza for this Square of Light on My Desk." CarolQ (30:3)
    Aut 78, p. 21.
"Though You've Made Distance a Husband." PraS (52:1) Spr 78,
    p. 24.

JOHNSON, Tom
"The Fear of Oversleeping." Poetry (133:3) D 78, p. 138.
"How Plato Was Right." Poetry (132:3) Je 78, p. 153.
"John Singleton Mosby (1833-1916)." GeoR (32:3) Aut 78, p. 514.
"Wallace Stevens." Poetry (132:3) Je 78, p. 152.

JOHNSON, W. R.
"For Millay." LitR (21:3) Spr 78, p. 311.

JOHNSTON, Gordon
"A Conversation Designed for Two People About to." Wind (28)
    78, p. 28.
"Nativity." Wind (28) 78, p. 28.
"Remembrance, 1906." Wind (28) 78, p. 29.

JOHNSTON, Mark Evan
"Poem-Making: Negative Definitions." Tele (14) 78.

JOKL, Vivian
"The Cellar House." SoDakR (16:2) Sum 78, p. 9.
"Jam Cake." SoDakR (16:2) Sum 78, p. 10.
"Ready to Be Burned." SoDakR (16:2) Sum 78, p. 11.
"Sharp Shinned Hawk." Paint (9/10) Spr-Aut 78, p. 21.
"Sheets of Sand." Paint (9/10) Spr-Aut 78, p. 20.

JONAS, Ann
"Recovery." SouthernR (14:3) Sum 78, p. 511.

JONES, Cy Keith
"My Wild-Haired, Cluster-of-Whorls Sensation." JnlONJP (2:2)
77, p. 26.

JONES, Dave W.
"At One PM in a Wrestling Room." CarouselQ (3:2) Sum 78,
p. 29.
"The Divine Bicyclist." CarouselQ (3:4) Wint 78, p. 34.

JONES, Paula
"Cedrelatoona." PoetryNW (19:2) Sum 78, p. 35.
"The Clams." CutB (11) Aut-Wint 78, p. 28.
"'The Reason Forgets Itself.'" PoetryNW (19:2) Sum 78, p. 35.

JONES, Robert
"Life in a Theology Shop." ChrC (95:4) 1-8 F 78, p. 105.

JONES, Robert L.
"Before the Stone Settles Down for Good." Sky (7/8) Spr 78,
p. 57.
"Helplessness." BlackF (2:2) Aut-Wint 78, p. 27.
"Insulted Spirits." Sky (7/8) Spr 78, p. 56.

JONES, Stephen
"Future, Hopes the Boy." Wind (28) 78, p. 31.
"Setting Sail When Asleep." Wind (28) 78, p. 31.

JONES, Stephen Mack
"The Dream of Twenty Black Women." Atl (242:1) Jl 78, p. 44.

JONES, Tom
"Alexandrian Dialogue: The Death of Lightning Billy." YaleR
(68:2) Wint 79, p. 256.
"Art of the Fugue." Wind (28) 78, p. 34.
"Brother Rag." SouthernPR (18:2) Aut 78, p. 56.
"Boundaries." YaleR (68:2) Wint 79, p. 258.
"Earthworks" (i.m. Robert Smithson). SunM (5) Aut 78, p. 139.
"For a Book by Heidegger" (with Ed & Ka). Wind (28) 78,
p. 33.
"Invitation to the Crags." Wind (28) 78, p. 36.
"Maintenance." Wind (28) 78, p. 34.
"Narcissus in Oregon" (For Ed Corbin). Wind (28) 78, p. 33.
"The Seawall." HarvAd (111:4) My 78, p. 17.

"Stations of the Invisible" (for Ed McGowin). SunM (5) Aut 78,
     p. 140.
"Witness" (For Hart Crane). Wind (28) 78, p. 35.

JORDAN, Barbara
"Chang-O: The Chinese Moon Goddess." Pan (19) 77, p. 12.
"The Child." Pan (19) 77, p. 11.
"Sleeping on Water." Pan (19) 77, p. 11.

JORDAN, June
"Poem Towards the Bottom Line." LittleM (11:3) Aut 77,
     p. 105.

JOSE, Patricia
"Charon." MalR (45) Ja 78, p. 119.
"Death-Song." MalR (45) Ja 78, p. 118.
"Island/and Land." MalR (45) Ja 78, p. 123.
"Love Poem." MalR (45) Ja 78, p. 122.
"Stone Fish." MalR (45) Ja 78, p. 122.
"The Wandering Moon." MalR (45) Ja 78, p. 120.

JOSELOW, Beth
"Bijou." NewYorker (54:4) 13 Mr 78, p. 84.
"Walrus Factory." Epoch (27:3) Spr 78, p. 283.

JOSEPH, Jenny
"Against the Personality Cult." PartR (45:3) 78, p. 439.

JOSEPH, Lawrence
"Before Going Back." Stand (19:4) 78, p. 63.
"When You've Been Here Long Enough." Stand (19:4) 78, p. 62.

JOSEPHS, Allen
"Acoma, New Mexico, December, 5:15 P.M." (tr. of Angel
     González). NewRep (178:20) 20 My 78, p. 26.
"Notes of a Voyager" (For José Ramón Marra-López) (tr. of
     Angel González). NewRep (178:20) 20 My 78, p. 26.
"Oneiric Digression" (tr. of Angel González). NewRep (178:20)
     20 My 78, p. 26.

JOYCE, William
"'Connect, Connect.'" NewL (44:3) Spr 78, p. 40.
"The Great Mattress Poem." SouthernPR (18:2) Aut 78, p. 61.
"How a Protection Dog Came to Love Darkness." ThRiPo (11/12)
     78, p. 52.
"Money." GreenfieldR (6:3/4) Spr 78, p. 81.

JOZSEF, Attila
"In Fog, In Silence" (tr. by John Batki). Hand (2) 78, p. 20.
"My Mother" (tr. by Nicholas Kolumban). NewL (45:1) Aut 78,
     p. 42.
"Sleep Quietly Now" (tr. by John Batki). Hand (2) 78, p. 19.

JUDSON, John
    "Clock Dance-Song." <u>Confr</u> (16) Spr-Sum 78, p. 114.
    "Living on a Slant." <u>OhioR</u> (19:1) Wint 78, p. 33.

JUHASZ, Suzanne
    "Bistort." <u>Nimrod</u> (22:2) Spr-Sum 78, p. 39.
    "Coldbloom Saxifrage." <u>Nimrod</u> (22:2) Spr-Sum 78, p. 40.
    "Waiting." <u>Nimrod</u> (22:2) Spr-Sum 78, p. 36.

JULIA, Mary
    "April 23." <u>NewL</u> (45:1) Aut 78, p. 20.
    "Church Bells." <u>NewL</u> (45:1) Aut 78, p. 20.

JULIAN the Apostate
    "Long and Short" (tr. by Richard O'Connell). <u>Playb</u> (25:4) Ap
        78, p. 157.

JUNGER
    "New Wilderness" (tr. by R. Sieburth and S. W. DeRachewiltz).
        <u>St. AR</u> (5:1) Aut-Wint 78, p. 52.

JURADO, James
    "Canopeners." <u>Pig</u> (4) 78, p. 99.
    "Enema of a Rainbow." <u>Pig</u> (4) 78, p. 43.
    "The Greatest Prayer Is One Yawn." <u>Pig</u> (4) 78, p. 77.

JUSTICE, Donald
    "Angel Death Blues." <u>NewEngR</u> (1:2) Wint 78, p. 133.
    "In the Attic." <u>NewEngR</u> (1:2) Wint 78, p. 131.
    "The Silent World." <u>NewEngR</u> (1:2) Wint 78, p. 132.
    "The Sometime Dancer Blues." <u>Antaeus</u> (30/31) Sum-Aut 78,
        p. 109.
    "Two Memories of the Depression Years." <u>NewYorker</u> (54:41)
        27 N 78, p. 40.
    "Unflushed Urinals." <u>Antaeus</u> (30/31) Sum-Aut 78, p. 110.

KAHN, Hannah
    "Boy on a Merry-Go-Round." <u>LadHJ</u> (95:4) Ap 78, p. 144.
    "Seed Song." <u>LadHJ</u> (95:2) F 78, p. 140.

KAHN, Paul
    "I want to believe" (for John Yau). <u>Hand</u> (2) 78, p. 10.
    "The Moon and the Fan." <u>Aspect</u> (71) Ap-Je 77, p. 31.
    "On the Way to Jim & Peg's: The Poem for Today." <u>Aspect</u>
        (71) Ap-Je 77, p. 34.
    "The sun takes a slow warm slide thru Virgo." <u>Aspect</u> (71) Ap-
        Je 77, p. 32.

KAHONHES (John Fadden)
    "Kalakwa." <u>GreenfieldR</u> (6:3/4) Spr 78, p. 46.
    "My Sons." <u>GreenfieldR</u> (6:3/4) Spr 78, p. 46.

KALASZ, Marton
    "Hymn" (tr. by Jascha Kessler). <u>CalQ</u> (13/14) Spr-Sum 78, p. 63.

KALLET, Marilyn
"Between the Sun and the Moon" (tr. of Paul Eluard). SlowLR
    (1/2) 78, p. 20.
"Here" (tr. of Paul Eluard). SlowLR (1/2) 78, p. 21.
"Seascape" (tr. of Paul Eluard). SlowLR (1/2) 78, p. 19.

KALLSEN, T. J.
"Galveston." Wind (28) 78, p. 37.
"Intensive Care." KanQ (10:2) Spr 78, p. 106.
"My Daughter's Knowing." Wind (28) 78, p. 37.

KAMEI, Marlene
"buffalo pawing the moon." NewRena (10) 78, p. 64.
"I Can Hear/And Hear Her." LaB (10) 78, p. 24.
"i have learned exile & speaking." Bachy (11) Spr 78, p. 126.
"i proclaim the moon wild." Bachy (11) Spr 78, p. 127.
"I Think However Restore the Monarchy." LaB (10) 78, p. 21.
"onion mantra for male and female voices." NewRena (10) 78,
    p. 66.
"Sundial Ceremony." LaB (10) 78, p. 23.
"this is for our lady of kahiki." Bachy (11) Spr 78, p. 127.

KAMENETZ, Rodger
"Fountains." Shen (29:3) Spr 78, p. 36.

KAMINSKY, Daniel
"The Honor of the Quest." SmPd (42) Wint 78, p. 15.
"Lesson in Anthropology." SmPd (43) Spr 78, p. 3.
"The Protestant." Pig (5) 78, p. 11.

KAMINSKY, Mark
"A Man at Work." Hand (2) 78, p. 165.
"The West Side Senior Citizens Center." LittleM (11:4) Wint 78,
    p. 48.

KAMMEL, Edward P.
"Cat." Confr (16) Spr-Sum 78, p. 54.

KANE, Katherine
"Attics." Iowa (9:4) Aut 78, p. 32.

KANE, Paul
"Mr. Emerson Is Assisted on His Walk." Shen (29:2) Wint 78,
    p. 53.

KANFER, Allen
"The Analyst Who Got His Deserts." LitR (21:3) Spr 78, p. 377.

KAPLAN, Bob
"And Yet...." CarouselQ (3:2) Sum 78, p. 7.

KAPLAN, Marzi
"Known." LadHJ (95:1) Ja 78, p. 86.
"Metamorphosis." LadHJ (95:2) F 78, p. 182.

KAPLAN, Rebbekka
"Cyclamen." Tendril (2) Spr-Sum 78.
"My Hands." Tendril (1) Wint 77-78.

KAPLAN, Robin
"Flowering." Confr (17) Aut-Wint 78, p. 35.
"The Names Are Changed." PoNow (20) 78, p. 14.

KARLINS, Mark
"'But Negatives, my Love is so' (Donne)." Hand (2) 78, p. 50.

KARPOWICZ, Tymoteusz
"The Cloud" (tr. by John Pijewski). ChiR (29:4) Spr 78, p. 107.
"Feathers" (tr. by John Pijewski). ChiR (29:4) Spr 78, p. 106.
"The Hero" (tr. by John Pijewski). Durak (1) 78, p. 58.
"The Magic Mountain" (tr. by John Pijewski). ChiR (29:4) Spr
    78, p. 108.
"No One Knows" (tr. by John Pijewski). Durak (1) 78, p. 59.

KARR, Mary
"Vampire." CutB (10) Spr-Sum 78, p. 52.

KASE, Michael
"Divorced and Living Alone." CarouselQ (3:4) Wint 78, p. 20.
"Memories." Wind (30) 78, p. 21.

KASHNER, Samuel
"the closest living relative." PoNow (20) 78, p. 23.
"Jiggs." PoNow (20) 78, p. 23.
"letter." Tele (13) 77.
"The Owl." HangL (32) Spr 78, p. 18.
"when radio was a young kid just starting out." PoNow (20) 78,
    p. 23.

KASS, Andrew
"Returning to the Coast." Glass (3:1/2/3) 78, p. 19.

KASTNER, Ricky
"Led by Hazel-Rah." NewL (45:1) Aut 78, p. 63.

KATES, J.
"The Faucet" (for Helene). Stand (18:4) 77, p. 9.
"Musing, the Readiness Is All." Chowder (10/11) Aut-Wint 78-
    79, p. 157.
"Relict." Chowder (10/11) Aut-Wint 78-79, p. 158.
"Riddle." Aspect (71) Ap-Je 77, p. 35.

KATZ, Jeffrey
"He Looks for a Window in the World" (for my father). Aspect
    (71) Ap-Je 77, p. 14.
"The Suicide" (for F. L.). Aspect (71) Ap-Je 77, p. 13.

KATZ, Susan A.
"The Screaming." KanQ (10:2) Spr 78, p. 60.

KAUFFMAN, Janet
"Appetizer, for You." PoNow (20) 78, p. 13.
"The Distance, the Sorrow Now." PoNow (20) 78, p. 13.
"The Fall of Leaves." PoNow (20) 78, p. 13.
"Grapes." PoNow (20) 78, p. 13.
"Guerilla." PoNow (20) 78, p. 13.

KAUFMAN, Shirley
"Bunk Beds." Field (19) Aut 78, p. 14.
"Colors" (for Louis Comtois). OhioR (19:1) Wint 78, p. 35.
"From Here to There" (for the De Votis). OhioR (19:1) Wint 78,
     p. 34.
"Horseshoe Crabs." PoetryNW (19:2) Sum 78, p. 33.
"Lawrence at Taos." Field (18) Spr 78, p. 90.
"Shells." Field (18) Spr 78, p. 89.

KAUL, A. J.
"Intrusion." Wind (29) 78, p. 30.
"Marginalia." Wind (29) 78, p. 30.

KAY, John
"Everything is OK" (to Vera von Wuhlisch). Kayak (48) Je 78,
     p. 33.
"Fear." Kayak (48) Je 78, p. 33.
"A Formal Feeling." Kayak (48) Je 78, p. 34.
"Illusion." Kayak (48) Je 78, p. 32.
"An Offering." Kayak (48) Je 78, p. 30.
"Stepping Forward." Kayak (48) Je 78, p. 31.

KAYE, Edwin
"Dicky." CalQ (13/14) Spr-Sum 78, p. 142.

KEANE, Patrick
"Crossings: A Triptych for Robert Lowell, 1917-1977." Salm
     (41) Spr 78, p. 112.

KEARNEY, Lawrence
"The Cyclists." ParisR (74) Aut-Wint 78, p. 195.
"The Dead." MassR (19:1) Spr 78, p. 181.
"Delight." Poetry (132:4) Jl 78, p. 199.
"Joan's Woodcut." Box (6) Aut 77, p. 8.
"K-Mart." Poetry (132:4) Jl 78, p. 198.

KEELER, Marian
"Emil Nolde." WindO (32) Sum-Aut 78, p. 5.

KEELEY, Edmund
"Afternoon" (tr. of Yannis Ritsos). Iowa (9:2) Spr 78, p. 104.
"Autumn Expression" (tr. of Yannis Ritsos). Field (19) Aut 78,
     p. 21.
"Court Exhibit" (tr. of Yannis Ritsos). NewYorker (54:36) 23 O
     78, p. 42.
"Descent" (tr. of Yannis Ritsos). Antaeus (30/31) Sum-Aut 78,
     p. 190.

"Desk Calendar" (tr. of Yannis Ritsos). Iowa (9:2) Spr 78,
  p. 105.
"The Distant" (tr. of Yannis Ritsos). NewYorker (54:36) 23 O
  78, p. 42.
"Evening Profile" (tr. of Yannis Ritsos). Iowa (9:2) Spr 78,
  p. 104.
"Fever" (tr. of Yannis Ritsos). Iowa (9:2) Spr 78, p. 103.
"Final Agreement" (tr. of Yannis Ritsos). Antaeus (30/31) Sum-
  Aut 78, p. 191.
"Freedom" (tr. of Yannis Ritsos). Antaeus (30/31) Sum-Aut 78,
  p. 188.
"Inertia" (tr. of Yannis Ritsos). Iowa (9:2) Spr 78, p. 103.
"Marking" (tr. of Yannis Ritsos). Field (19) Aut 78, p. 22.
"Message" (tr. of Yannis Ritsos). Antaeus (30/31) Sum-Aut 78,
  p. 191.
"The Next Day" (tr. of Yannis Ritsos). Antaeus (30/31) Sum-
  Aut 78, p. 189.
"Preparing the Ceremony" (tr. of Yannis Ritsos). NewYorker
  (54:36) 23 O 78, p. 42.
"Red-Handed" (tr. of Yannis Ritsos). Field (19) Aut 78, p. 19.
"The Same Thorn" (tr. of Yannis Ritsos). Field (19) Aut 78,
  p. 20.
"Secretly" (tr. of Yannis Ritsos). Antaeus (30/31) Sum-Aut 78,
  p. 190.
"Security Deposits" (tr. of Yannis Ritsos). NewYorker (54:36)
  23 O 78, p. 42.
"Slowly" (tr. of Yannis Ritsos). Field (19) Aut 78, p. 18.
"Striding Over" (tr. of Yannis Ritsos). Antaeus (30/31) Sum-
  Aut 78, p. 189.
"Toward Saturday" (tr. of Yannis Ritsos). Field (19) Aut 78,
  p. 17.
Twelve poems (tr. of Yannis Ritsos). Falcon (16) 78, p. 106.
"Winter Sunshine" (tr. of Yannis Ritsos). NewYorker (54:36) 23
  O 78, p. 42.
"With Music" (tr. of Yannis Ritsos). Iowa (9:2) Spr 78, p. 105.

KEENAN, Deborah
  "Lessons from the Beach." SoDakR (16:2) Sum 78, p. 49.

KEENS, William
  "Rapture of the Deep." AmerPoR (7:6) N-D 78, p. 37.

KEIN, Sybil
  "Mo Oulé Mourri Dan Lac Lá." BelPoJ (29:2) Wint 78-79,
    p. 25.
  from Water Poems: "chestnut lilies." BelPoJ (29:2) Wint 78-
    79, p. 26.

KEIS, Vitalij
  "Atlantic Ocean" (tr. of Vladimir Mayakovsky, w. Harry Lewis).
    Pequod (2:4) 78, p. 19.

KEIZER, Garret
  "The Schedule." Poem (34) N 78, p. 68.

"Whales in the Sky." <u>Poem</u> (34) N 78, p. 67.

KELLEHER, Ann
 "Embryo." <u>Aspen</u> (5) Spr 78, p. 13.
 "Escarpment." <u>Aspen</u> (5) Spr 78, p. 14.
 "Knowing Song." <u>Aspen</u> (5) Spr 78, p. 15.
 "Northeaster." <u>Aspen</u> (5) Spr 78, p. 11.
 "Room." <u>Aspen</u> (5) Spr 78, p. 12.

KELLER, Anna
 "Zero Visibility." <u>Bachy</u> (13) Aut-Wint 78-79, p. 97.

KELLER, David
 "As Bad as the Past." <u>US1</u> (11) Aut 78, p. 9.
 "Before the Ceremony" (for Rod Tulloss). <u>US1</u> (11) Aut 78,
   p. 4.
 "Circling the Site." <u>US1</u> (11) Aut 78, p. 8.
 "From the Movie to the Corner" (for Robert Hass). <u>US1</u> (11)
   Aut 78, p. 8.
 "Getting Out of the Movies Alive." <u>US1</u> (11) Aut 78, p. 9.
 "Learning the Words." LittleM (11:4) Wint 78, p. 7.
 "Not Bad Looking, Really." WebR (4:2) Aut 78, p. 63.
 "Reading by Firelight." <u>DenQ</u> (13:1) Spr 78, p. 31.
 "Teaching It Cold." <u>DenQ</u> (13:2) Sum 78, p. 131.

KELLER, Pat
 "A Gift." <u>KanQ</u> (10:1) Wint 78, p. 77.

KELLEY, Tim
 "Very Tired in Detroit." <u>Stonecloud</u> (7) 78, p. 116.

KELLMAN, Steven G.
 "Villanelle." <u>KanQ</u> (10:2) Spr 78, p. 98.

KELLY, Dave
 "A Few Words." <u>AAR</u> (28) 78, p. 67.
 "Five Davids." <u>ThRiPo</u> (11/12) 78, p. 54.
 "Gargantua Walking." <u>NoAmR</u> (263:1) Spr 78, p. 26.
 "Gestures." <u>PoetryNW</u> (19:3) Aut 78, p. 12.
 "Voices." <u>ThRiPo</u> (11/12) 78, p. 55.
 "When." <u>AAR</u> (28) 78, p. 66.
 "The Writing Lesson." <u>AAR</u> (28) 78, p. 65.

KELLY, Robert A.
 "The Ocracoke Ferry." <u>Poem</u> (32) Mr 78, p. 36.

KELTY, Jean McClure
 "Bird Songs." <u>Poem</u> (33) Jl 78, p. 41.
 "Chance Meeting." <u>Poem</u> (33) Jl 78, p. 43.
 "Discovery." <u>Poem</u> (34) N 78, p. 23.
 "'For Only Evil Should Be Feared; Gods Should Be Loved.'"
   <u>Poem</u> (34) N 78, p. 22.
 "Points of View." <u>Poem</u> (34) N 78, p. 20.

KEMPHER, Ruth Moon
  "Having the Ex-Husband to Dinner in a New Place, Says Rutabaga
      Rose, Is Damned Disconcerting. " WindO (33) Aut-Wint 78-
      79.
  "Hilda Halfheart's Notes to the Milkman: #45. " FourQt (27:2)
      Wint 78, p. 16.
  "The Letters from Prattsburg ... The Ninth Letter, Sunday. "
      Epos (27:2) 77, p. 18.
  "The Lust Songs and Travel Diary of Sylvia Savage: XXVIII
      (Highway S19-N). " WindO (31) Wint-Spr 78, p. 28.
  "Speedometer, and Other Machinery. " Tele (13) 77.
  "Sylvia Savage Writes a P. S. to Adam about Hilda's Christmas
      Note. " WindO (31) Wint-Spr 78, p. 27.

KENDRICK, Dolores
  "Frustrated Genius. " BelPoJ (29:2) Wint 78-79, p. 47.
  "Josephine in the Jeu de Paume" (for Gaga). BelPoJ (29:2) Wint
      78-79, p. 46.

KENISON, Gloria
  Nine poems. WormR (68) 77, p. 115.
  Ten poems. WormR (72) 78, p. 126.

KENNEDY, Robert S.
  "I'm an arbitrary lover. " Tele (14) 78.

KENNEDY, Stephen
  "Marty Prepares the Kidneys. " NewL (44:3) Spr 78, p. 66.
  "poetry cant help it. " Tele (13) 77.

KENNEDY, Terry
  "Confession. " CarouselQ (3:3) Aut 78, p. 6.
  "The Pillow. " SouthernPR (18:1) Spr 78, p. 34.
  "The Price" (for Anne Sexton). SouthernPR (18:1) Spr 78, p. 33.

KENNEDY, X. J.
  "Jack and Jill. " Poetry (132:3) Je 78, p. 157.
  "On a Well-Dressed Man Much Married. " Poetry (132:3) Je 78,
      p. 157.
  "A Word from Hart Crane's Ghost. " Poetry (132:3) Je 78,
      p. 157.

KENNELLY, Brendan
  "It Is Failure. " LitR (22:2) Wint 79, p. 209.
  "The Joke. " LitR (22:2) Wint 79, p. 205.
  "A Man in Smoke Remembered. " LitR (22:2) Wint 79, p. 207.
  "A Man with the Good Word. " LitR (22:2) Wint 79, p. 206.

KENNEY, Richard
  "The Evolution of the Flightless Bird. " NewEngR (1:1) Aut 78,
      p. 40.
  "Night's La Brea. " AmerS (47:1) Wint 77-78, p. 86.
  "Notes from Greece" (For Jim Buchman). Poetry (131:5) F 78,
      p. 249.

KENNY, Maurice
"John Berryman. " GreenfieldR (6:3/4) Spr 78, p. 170.
"March Reserve: Long Island" (for Helen Rundell). GreenfieldR
(6:3/4) Spr 78, p. 168.
"Sand Creek, Colorado" (for Mary ... who was there). Green-
fieldR (6:3/4) Spr 78, p. 169.
"Sun. " Glass (3:1/2/3) 78, p. 29.
"Wejack. " GreenfieldR (6:3/4) Spr 78, p. 171.

KENT, Richard
"Incidental X. " Field (19) Aut 78, p. 25.
"A Secondary Character Collecting Trash. " Field (19) Aut 78,
p. 26.

KENYATTA, ibn
"Birthmark. " Harp (256:1535) Ap 78, p. 23.
"Fur Nature's Baby. " Harp (256:1535) Ap 78, p. 23.

KENYON, Jane
"American Triptych. " Iowa (9:3) Sum 78, p. 81.
"At the Feeder. " ParisR (72) Wint 77, p. 40.
"The Clothes Pin. " ParisR (72) Wint 77, p. 41.
"This Morning. " VirQR (54:1) Wint 78, p. 110.

KERCHER, Randy
"Farewell. " CarouselQ (3:3) Aut 78, p. 23.

KERLEY, Gary
"Opening Up the House After a Rain. " Confr (16) Spr-Sum 78,
p. 121.

KERNS, John
"The Meaning of Life. " EngJ (67:5) My 78, p. 53.

KERRIGAN, Anthony
"One Terse Line of Verse May Do.... " SewanR (86:4) Aut 78,
p. 517.

KERRIGAN, Thomas
"The Madmen. " StoneC (78:1) Wint 78, p. 29.
"Wordsworth. " StoneC (78:1) Wint 78, p. 28.

KERSHNER, Brandon
"Dream Poem. " AmerPoR (7:6) N-D 78, p. 33.

KESSLER, Jascha
"Afternoon of Grand Old Men" (tr. of Sándor Csoori). Nimrod
(22:2) Spr-Sum 78, p. 101.
"The Bird Cage. " Kayak (49) O 78, p. 60.
"Eschatology. " Kayak (49) O 78, p. 18.
"Going On Talking" (tr. of György Rába). Nimrod (22:2) Spr-
Sum 78, p. 98.
"Hymn" (tr. of Márton Kalász). CalQ (13/14) Spr-Sum 78, p. 63.

"Ports" (tr. of István Vas). Nimrod (22:2) Spr-Sum 78,
     p. 99.

KESSLER, Marion
  "A Mirror. " Glass (3:1/2/3) 78, p. 64.

KESSLER, Milton
  "Extreme Love. " ModernPS (9:2) Aut 78, p. 156.

KESSLER, Stephen
  "Delinquent Soliloquy with Switchblade. " Bleb/Ark (13) 78,
     p. 51.
  Eight poems (tr. of Vicente Aleixandre). Iowa (9:1) Wint 78,
     p. 53.
  "Hour of the Rush. " Bleb/Ark (13) 78, p. 50.
  "Loom. " Bleb/Ark (13) 78, p. 53.
  "Maps to the Stars Homes. " Stonecloud (7) 78, p. 52.
  "Urban Night. " Bachy (12) Aut 78, p. 54.
  "What You Have Gathered from Coincidence. " Bachy (12) Aut
     78, p. 56.

KESTENBAUM, Stuart
  "Solitude Poem. " GreenfieldR (6:3/4) Spr 78, p. 121.

KETZNER, John D.
  "Think of the Possibility. " GreenfieldR (7:1/2) Aut 78, p. 79.

KEYISHIAN, Marjorie
  "Sarah. " LitR (21:3) Spr 78, p. 356.

KEYS, Claire
  "Relic from Nantucket. " Tendril (3) Aut 78, p. 35.

KEYS, Kerry Shawn
  "Arctic Museum. " Nat (226:1) 7-14 Ja 78, p. 23.

KHATTAR, Chris
  "The Snow White Suzy Dwarfs. " HiramPoR (25) Aut-Wint 78,
     p. 28.
  "A Valentine Day's Poem. " HiramPoR (25) Aut-Wint 78, p. 29.

KHERDIAN, David
  "Garfield School. " ThRiPo (11/12) 78, p. 56.
  "Gustav Scheibach. " NewRivR (2:2) 78, p. 17.
  "Harold (Bobby) Vakos. " NewRivR (2:2) 78, p. 18.
  "Old Frogface of Washington Junior High. " ThRiPo (11/12) 78,
     p. 57.

KIEFER, Rita Brady
  "The Man from Kansas. " CimR (43) Ap 78, p. 22.
  "She Wore White Gloves. " ConcPo (11:2) Aut 78, p. 80.

KIKUCHI, Carl
  "From a Journal. " NorthSR (8) Aut-Wint 78-79, p. 7.

"Full-Length Mirror." NorthSR (8) Aut-Wint 78-79, p. 6.
"Saturday." NorthSR (8) Aut-Wint 78-79, p. 5.

KILGORE, James C.
"'The African'" (For Alex Haley). Obs (4:1) Spr 78, p. 77.
"Assignment for Alex Haley" (for Malcolm X). Obs (4:1) Spr 78,
      p. 75.
"I Shall Remember You." Obs (4:1) Spr 78, p. 78.
"Portrait." Obs (4:1) Spr 78, p. 76.
"Until I Met You." Obs (4:1) Spr 78, p. 79.

KILPATRICK, Nannette
"O the fluttering." DeKalb (11:3/4) Spr-Sum 78, p. 98.

KIMMEL, L. W.
"During a Change of Season." SmPd (43) Spr 78, p. 35.

KING, Bob
"Thursday Night." SoDakR (16:2) Sum 78, p. 33.

KING, Mary
"February." NewRena (10) 78, p. 35.
"if the silence." NewRena (10) 78, p. 36.

KING, Robert
"Celibacy, A Storm." CutB (11) Aut-Wint 78, p. 76.

KINGSLEY, Alyce W.
"I witness the fusion" (tr. of Jacquez Izoard). Nimrod (22:2)
      Spr-Sum 78, p. 96.
"Voice without echo, which lingers." Nimrod (22:2) Spr-Sum 78,
      p. 97.

KINLAW, Debra
"I Don't Want to Cry." Chomo (5:2) Aut-Wint 78, p. 77.
"March 19, 1978." Chomo (5:2) Aut-Wint 78, p. 76.

KINNELL, Galway
"Fergus Falling." NewYorker (54:28) 28 Ag 78, p. 34.

KINNICK, B. Jo
"Women's Wilderness." EngJ (67:5) My 78, p. 54.

KINSELLA, Thomas
from A Technical Supplement: (II, III, XVI, XIX, XXI). LitR
      (22:2) Wint 79, p. 147.

KINZIE, Mary
"The Childhood of Homer." Poetry (132:1) Ap 78, p. 26.
"Letter to Portsmouth Naval Prison." SouthernR (14:3) Sum 78,
      p. 475.
"Mélisande." Salm (40) Wint 78, p. 6.
"Minor Landscape." SouthernR (14:3) Sum 78, p. 477.
"The Muse of Satire." Poetry (132:1) Ap 78, p. 28.

"Nereid's Song." Poetry (132:1) Ap 78, p. 25.
"Superbia: A Triumph with No Train." Poetry (132:1) Ap 78,
    p. 29.
"The Tattooer." YaleR (68:2) Wint 79, p. 261.
"Venice Rising." SouthernR (14:3) Sum 78, p. 478.
"Vulcan." NewYorker (53:52) 13 F 78, p. 103.
"When We Turned Our Backs on It, the Ocean." Salm (40) Wint
    78, p. 4.
"Zeitblom: His Commentary on the Pictures." Salm (40) Wint
    78, p. 3.

KIPP, Allan F.
    "Arrival and Departure." ChrC (95:23) 5-12 Jl 78, p. 674.

KIRBY, David
    "Letter to Borges." SouthernPR (18:1) Spr 78, p. 64.
    "Sniper." CarolQ (30:2) Spr-Sum 78, p. 86.

KIRBY-SMITH, H. T.
    "The Commercial Traveler Remembers Lost Love." Poetry
        (132:3) Je 78, p. 134.
    "Eric on the Drums" (For Maudie). Poetry (132:3) Je 78,
        p. 132.

KIRK, Norman Andrew
    "Cleveland." Pan (19) 77, p. 33.

KIRKPATRICK, Sidney
    "At Newport." Box (6) Aut 77, p. 11.
    "His Reticence." Box (6) Aut 77, p. 12.

KIRKUP, James
    "Two Victorian Photographs." NewYorker (54:34) 9 O 78,
        p. 161.

KIRKWOOD, Judy
    "Considering." Chowder (10/11) Aut-Wint 78-79, p. 68.

KIRSCH, Phil
    "All Issues Are Clear If Kept Clear." JnlONJP (2:2) 77, p. 22.
    "J, J, & M (A Love Story)." JnlONJP (2:1) 77, p. 7.
    "The Poem I Was to Read Tonight." JnlONJP (2:1) 77, p. 5.
    "Real Magic" (for S. H.). JnlONJP (2:1) 77, p. 6.

KIRSCHEN, Mark
    "Before Sleep." Montra (4) 78, p. 58.
    "Christmas Eve." Montra (4) 78, p. 54.
    "From Where." Montra (4) 78, p. 56.
    "In Memoriam." Montra (4) 78, p. 59.
    "Radio." Montra (4) 78, p. 55.
    "Regret." Montra (4) 78, p. 57.

KIRWAN, Anna
    "Red Brother, Green Brother." Pan (19) 77, p. 16.

KISHKAN, Theresa
"Charm for Shelter." MalR (45) Ja 78, p. 218.
"Charm Gone Wrong." MalR (45) Ja 78, p. 218.
"Nausikaa, Vancouver Island." MalR (45) Ja 78, p. 216.
"Resting Song." MalR (45) Ja 78, p. 214.
"Womb Song." MalR (45) Ja 78, p. 212.

KITCHEN, Judith
"Tall Tales and Nightmares." PoNow (20) 78, p. 14.

KITZLER, Patricia O'Donnell
"The Ideal Lover." EngJ (67:5) My 78, p. 61.

KIWUS, Karin
"Splitting" (tr. by Almut McAuley). NewOR (6:1) 78, p. 26.
"Trapdoors" (tr. by Almut McAuley). NewOR (6:1) 78, p. 27.

KIZER, Carolyn
"Running Away from Home." Kayak (48) Je 78, p. 15.

KIZER, Gary
"Anthony Allan." GreenfieldR (7:1/2) Aut 78, p. 102.
"Some Nights I Dream in Chile" (for M. E.). GreenfieldR
    (6:3/4) Spr 78, p. 102.

KLAPPERT, Peter
from The Idiot Princess of the Last Dynasty: "Infectious
    Scotoma." Agni (9) 78, p. 21.
from The Idiot Princess of the Last Dynasty: "Patati et Patata."
    Agni (9) 78, p. 13.
from The Idiot Princess of the Last Dynasty: "The Subjects of
    Discontent (I)." Agni (9) 78, p. 16.
from The Idiot Princess of the Last Dynasty: "The Subjects of
    Discontent (II)." Agni (9) 78, p. 19.
from The Idiot Princess of the Last Dynasty: "The Subjects of
    Discontent (III)." Agni (9) 78, p. 23.

KLAUCK, Daniel L.
"My Grandmother." GreenfieldR (7:1/2) Aut 78, p. 19.

KLEIN, Binnie
"You Take a Lover." Tendril (3) Aut 78, p. 36.

KLEIN, James
"Greenhorns." JnlONJP (2:2) 77, p. 5.
"Gromer Wilkie." WormR (68) 77, p. 116.
"How to Wipe Your Two-Year-Old's Nose." WormR (68) 77,
    p. 117.
"Jaunty White Canes." PoNow (20) 78, p. 14.
"Monkeyshines" (for my sister, Judy). WormR (68) 77, p. 116.
"Night Baseball." PoNow (20) 78, p. 14.
"Poem about Making Rudolph the Red-Nosed Reindeer." WormR
    (68) 77, p. 117.

KLEIN, Simon L.
"Grandmother Flowers. " AAR (28) 78, p. 26.
"Hesitation. " AAR (28) 78, p. 25.
"Wasted Words." AAR (28) 78, p. 24.

KLEPFISZ, Irena
"Conditions. " CalQ (13/14) Spr-Sum 78, p. 143.

KLIEWER, Warren
"Halfway Measures. " JnlONJP (2:2) 77, p. 4.

KLINE, George L.
"(To E. R.)" (tr. of Joseph Brodsky). Paint (7/8) Spr-Aut 77,
    p. 27.

KLOEFKORN, William
"Homebody. " KanQ (10:1) Wint 78, p. 24.
from Leaving Town: "I am down at last from the mountain. "
    KanQ (10:1) Wint 78, p. 25.
from Leaving Town: "Today I have ten thumbs. " SoDakR (16:2)
    Sum 78, p. 34.

KLOSKO, Gregory
"A Confused Lazarus. " FourQt (27:3) Spr 78, p. 28.

KNAPP, Martha
"Poem of Kansas City. " Tendril (2) Spr-Sum 78.

KNAUTH, Stephen
"Amnesia. " SouthernPR (18:1) Spr 78, p. 46.
"North Carolina Life Cycle. " CarolQ (30:2) Spr-Sum 78, p. 20.

KNIES, Elizabeth
"Circles. " Hudson (31:3) Aut 78, p. 484.
"I Look Out." Hudson (31:3) Aut 78, p. 483.
"Legend. " Hudson (31:3) Aut 78, p. 483.

KNIGHT, Arthur Winfield
"Beer." Smudge (1) Spr 78, p. 30.
"Ode." PikeF (1) Spr 78, p. 12.
"The Return of the Electric Man. " Zahir (9) 77, p. 39.

KNIGHT, Kit
"A Valentine's Day Poem for Mark. " PoNow (20) 78, p. 14.

KNOEPFLE, John
"I offer you. " PikeF (1) Spr 78, p. 13.
"November. " BallSUF (19:3) Sum 78, p. 80.
"when you left. " PikeF (1) Spr 78, p. 13.

KNOTHE, Lisa
"Blackberrying. " Chowder (10/11) Aut-Wint 78-79, p. 35.

KNOX, Caroline
"The Fat Baby." Poetry (132:5) Ag 78, p. 284.
"The Foamy-Necked Floater." Poetry (132:5) Ag 78, p. 286.
"Herbert Smith." Poetry (132:5) Ag 78, p. 283.
"Hittites." Poetry (132:5) Ag 78, p. 287.
"I Have Met Freddy." Poetry (132:2) My 78, p. 105.
"Walden Remaindered." Poetry (132:5) Ag 78, p. 285.

KNUTSON, Nancy Roxbury
"La Vieja in the Sandia Mts." Iowa (9:4) Aut 78, p. 31.

KOCH, Claude
"The Gardener" (in memory of Raffaele Casale, 1881-1974).
    FourQt (27:3) Spr 78, p. 20.

KODAK, Cindy
"Sensation" (tr. of Rimbaud). Montra (4) 78, p. 293.

KOERTGE, Ronald
"Giving Directions." Wind (28) 78, p. 38.
"Happy Ending." WormR (72) 78, p. 135.
"I Went to the Movies Hoping That Just Once the Monster Would
    Get the Girl." PoNow (19) 78, p. 25.
"Karate." YellowBR (10) 78, p. 26.
"Let's Listen In on the Peacock Briefing Down at the Arboretum."
    Wind (28) 78, p. 38.
"Nares Moribundo." WormR (72) 78, p. 136.
"A Returning Student Takes Underwater Basket Weaving."
    WormR (72) 78, p. 136.
"Style." Wind (28) 78, p. 39.
"Victuals." Wind (28) 78, p. 39.

KOESTENBAUM, Phyllis
"Food." Bachy (13) Aut-Wint 78-79, p. 45.
"Hunger." Bachy (13) Aut-Wint 78-79, p. 40.

KOHAV, Alexander
"Selected Zaum Works" (tr. of Ilya Zdanevich, w. Jack Hirsch-
    man). SunM (5) Aut 78, p. 89.

KOHLER, Sandra
"After Adrienne Died." AmerPoR (7:1) Ja-F 78, p. 45.
"Nero Wolfe and His Young Boyfriend Goodwin." PoNow (20) 78,
    p. 15.

KOHN, Marjory
"Untitled Poem." AntR (36:4) Aut 78, p. 470.

KOLUMBAN, Nicholas
"Anniversary" (tr. of Sándor Csoóri). GreenfieldR (6:3/4) Spr
    78, p. 6.
"A Bullet" (tr. of Sándor Csoóri). GreenfieldR (6:3/4) Spr 78,

p. 7.
"The Death of a Starfish." StoneC (78:2) Spr 78, p. 6.
"Grandfather's Pocketwatch." GreenfieldR (6:3/4) Spr 78, p. 8.
"Imploring Words of Friendship to the Second Person" (tr. of
    Sándor Csoóri). NewL (45:1) Aut 78, p. 40.
"My Beast" (tr. of Sándor Csoóri). AntR (36:2) Spr 78, p. 195.
"My Mother" (tr. of Attila József). NewL (45:1) Aut 78, p. 42.
"Rejection Slip to the Editor of Chervil Review." Glass
    (3:1/2/3) 78, p. 118.
"Wait Until It's Evening" (tr. of Sándor Csoóri). NewL (45:1)
    Aut 78, p. 41.

KOMUNYAKAA, Yusef
"Blues Stomp Chant Hoodoo Revival." GreenfieldR (6:3/4) Spr
    78, p. 83.
"Captain Nobones' Threnody." BelPoJ (29:2) Wint 78-79, p. 36.
"False Leads." BelPoJ (29:2) Wint 78-79, p. 37.
from Family Tree: (1, 2, 6). BelPoJ (29:2) Wint 78-79,
    p. 39.
"Sunbather." PoNow (20) 78, p. 15.

KONUK, Mutlu
"Rubaiyat: Second Series" (tr. of Nazim Hikmet, w. Randy
    Blasing). LitR (21:4) Sum 78, p. 423.
"Rubaiyat: Third Series" (tr. of Nazim Hikmet, w. Randy
    Blasing). AntR (36:3) Sum 78, p. 371.

KOONTZ, Richard
"Distance Running." Box (7) Spr 78, p. 6.
"To My Mother." Box (7) Spr 78, p. 7.

KOOSER, Ted
"At the End of the Weekend." SouthernPR (18:2) Aut 78, p. 13.
"Carrie." PraS (52:3) Aut 78, p. 256.
"The Man with the Hearing Aid." PraS (52:3) Aut 78, p. 255.
"A Photograph." PraS (52:3) Aut 78, p. 254.
"Self-Portrait." SouthernPR (18:2) Aut 78, p. 12.
"The Skeleton in the Closet." DacTerr (15) Wint-Spr 77-78,
    p. 9.
"Thursday Night Blues." PraS (52:3) Aut 78, p. 255.
"Walking to Work." DacTerr (15) Wint-Spr 77-78, p. 9.

KOPROWICZ, George
"The Magazine Rack." Smudge (2) Sum 78, p. 46.

KORAN, Dennis
"For My Sister." PoNow (20) 78, p. 15.

KOSMICKI, Greg
"A Late Night in Row Crop Country." PoNow (20) 78, p. 15.
"Passing a Farm Going North." PoNow (20) 78, p. 16.

KOSOVEL, Srečko
"Fall" (tr. by William S. Heiliger). DenQ (13:3) Aut 78, p. 133.

"Flowers on the Windowsill" (tr. by William S. Heiliger). DenQ
(13:3) Aut 78, p. 132.

KOSTELANETZ, Richard
"Olympian Progress." Nimrod (22:2) Spr-Sum 78, p. 44.
"1024." Pan (19) 77, p. 38.
from Recyclings: "Self-Recycled." Zahir (9) 77, p. 35.
"Short Fiction." Nimrod (22:2) Spr-Sum 78, p. 45.

KOWIT, Steve
"Hero." PoNow (20) 78, p. 16.
"Invocation." Vaga (28) Aut 78, p. 58.
"No." Vaga (27) Spr 78, p. 69.
"Wanted--Sensuous Woman Who Can Handle 12 Inches of Man."
PoNow (20) 78, p. 16.
"The Words." Vaga (28) Aut 78, p. 58.

KRAMER, Aaron
"Kennedy Airport." ModernPS (9:2) Aut 78, p. 124.
"Nocturne." EngJ (67:5) My 78, p. 54.
"Two Visits." ModernPS (9:2) Aut 78, p. 125.
"Visiting Hour." ModernPS (9:2) Aut 78, p. 122.

KRAMER, Larry
"Overcoats." CalQ (13/14) Spr-Sum 78, p. 108.

KRAPF, Norbert
"Basketball Season Begins." PoNow (19) 78, p. 26.
"Dürer Sketches His Mother in Charcoal." AmerS (47:2) Spr 78,
p. 191.
"Harbor Hill in Snowstorm." PoNow (19) 78, p. 26.
"The Man Who Loved Books." WormR (68) 77, p. 88.

KRATT, Mary
"Homecoming." ChrC (95:7) 1 Mr 78, p. 204.
"Tuesday." SouthernPR (18:1) Spr 78, p. 31.

KRAUJA, Herta
"White Nights" (tr. by Inara Cedrins). FourQt (27:4) Sum 78,
p. 35.

KRAUS, Jim
"Body Surfing, the Lost Fin." Pequod (2:4) 78, p. 59.
"A Cycle of Tears." VirQR (54:3) Sum 78, p. 492.
"Poamoho Stream." Wind (31) 78, p. 24.
"A Short Geography of Oahu." Wind (31) 78, p. 24.
"Thinking About the Laundromat While Working in the Garden."
GreenfieldR (6:3/4) Spr 78, p. 71.
"Two Waterfalls." GreenfieldR (6:3/4) Spr 78, p. 71.

KRAUSS, Ruth
"lullabye." Tele (14) 78.
"Song Not for Annie." Tele (14) 78.

KREIGER, Ted
   "Buddy." PoNow (19) 78, p. 47.

KREINER, Peter
   "The Best Description of Bread Is a Description of Hunger."
       Bachy (12) Aut 78, p. 130.
   "River." PoetryNW (19:4) Wint 78-79, p. 27.
   "Windows." Bachy (12) Aut 78, p. 130.

KRESH, David
   "Face to Face with Death." SunM (5) Aut 78, p. 130.
   "A Note on Rembrandt's Late Landscape Drawings." SmPd (44)
       Aut 78, p. 30.
   "Since." CimR (42) Ja 78, p. 35.
   "Sketches after 'Pete's Beer.'" SouthernPR (18:2) Aut 78, p. 85.
   "Sketches after 'Pete's Beer' 7: Grace's Old-Fashioned Ideas:
       A Dance Tune." WebR (4:2) Aut 78, p. 57.

KRETZ, Thomas
   "Powerlessness in Appalachia." St. AR (5:1) Aut-Wint 78, p. 139.
   "Universal Love." ChrC (95:26) 16-23 Ag 78, p. 763.

KRIDLER, David
   "Morning After a Killing Frost." WindO (33) Aut-Wint 78-79.

KRIEGER, Ian
   "Another Planet." Wind (31) 78, p. 25.
   "Chanteuse" (for Marie Pascal). Tele (13) 77.
   "Echo Park." Tele (13) 77.
   "Heavens" (for Lynn). Wind (31) 78, p. 26.
   "Landforms" (for Sally). Wind (31) 78, p. 25.
   "1934." Tele (13) 77.
   "1936." Tele (13) 77.
   "Radio Tropism." Tele (13) 77.
   "Style" (for Carol Humiston). Tele (13) 77.

KROGFUS, Miles
   "Desert Vistas." CutB (10) Spr-Sum 78, p. 27.
   "An Infant's New October." CutB (10) Spr-Sum 78, p. 29.

KROHN, Pattie Leo
   "Letter of Resignation, 2." CarouselQ (3:4) Wint 78, p. 37.

KROK, Peter
   "The Trucker." Wind (30) 78, p. 54.

KROLL, Ernest
   "Apology to Lillian." SouthernHR (12:4) Aut 78, p. 352.
   "Brooklyn Bridge." CimR (44) Jl 78, p. 17.
   "Letter (New Jersey Turnpike)." SouthernHR (12:4) Aut 78,
       p. 350.
   "The Mexican Hairless." SouthernPR (18:1) Spr 78, p. 63.
   "Mt. Greylock Viewed from 'Arrowhead.'" ArizQ (34:4) Wint

78, p. 326.
"Noise." CimR (45) O 78, p. 64.
"'The Oeconomy of a Winter's Day.'" MichQR (17:1) Wint 78,
    p. 77.
"Pennsylvania Academy of Fine Arts (Summer Branch)."
    HolCrit (15:5) D 78, p. 14.
"Reno." Nor (8) Aut 78, p. 18.
"The Transmittal." BallSUF (19:2) Spr 78, p. 33.
"Upriver (Hydrojet Propulsion)." SouthernHR (12:4) Aut 78,
    p. 351.

KROLL, Judith
    "After Learning a Marriage Is Being Arranged for Your Brother."
        AntR (36:3) Sum 78, p. 362.
    "At Seven Thousand Feet" (Simla, India). NewYorker (54:32) 25
        S 78, p. 48.
    "Atlantis." YaleR (68:1) Aut 78, p. 82.
    "Dying in the Mountains." AntR (36:3) Sum 78, p. 365.
    "The Speed of Light." AntR (36:3) Sum 78, p. 364.

KROLOW, Karl
    "All in One Breath" (tr. by Claudia Johnson). NewL (45:1) Aut
        78, p. 46.
    "The Effect of Chemistry" (tr. by Stuart Friebert). CutB (11)
        Aut-Wint 78, p. 30.
    "Half a Melon" (tr. by Stuart Friebert and Claudia Johnson).
        NewL (45:1) Aut 78, p. 47.
    "Let's Go" (tr. by Stuart Friebert and Claudia Johnson). NewL
        (45:1) Aut 78, p. 45.
    "On the Street" (tr. by Claudia Johnson). MissouriR (2:1) Aut
        78, p. 20.
    "We Were Young" (tr. by Claudia Johnson). NewL (45:1) Aut 78,
        p. 46.
    "We Were Young" (tr. by Stuart Friebert). CutB (11) Aut-Wint
        78, p. 29.
    "Words in Winter" (tr. by Claudia Johnson). MissouriR (2:1)
        Aut 78, p. 19.

KRUCHKOW, Diane
    "Easter." Zahir (9) 77, p. 4.
    "Life & Death of Howard Hughes." Zahir (9) 77, p. 3.

KRUSOE, James
    "Civilization." Bachy (13) Aut-Wint 78-79, p. 11.
    "The Confessional Poem." PoNow (19) 78, p. 42.
    "Getting Through." Stonecloud (7) 78, p. 102.
    "The News." Bachy (13) Aut-Wint 78-79, p. 12.
    "Small Pianos." Aspen (5) Spr 78, p. 120.
    "Some Advice." Bachy (13) Aut-Wint 78-79, p. 11.
    "The Sun." Bachy (13) Aut-Wint 78-79, p. 12.
    "Thinking about Death." Bachy (13) Aut-Wint 78-79, p. 13.

KRYSL, Marilyn
    "Sestina" (for 119). LittleM (11:3)Aut 77, p. 90.

KUFFEL, Frances M.
"Kaddish for a Dead Child." CutB (10) Spr-Sum 78, p. 16.
"There Are No Masterpieces." CutB (10) Spr-Sum 78, p. 15.

KUHNER, Herbert
"Does Moonlight Suffice?" (tr. of Mubera Mujagic). MalR (46)
    Ap 78, p. 109.
"A Line" (tr. of Mubera Mujagic). MalR (46) Ap 78, p. 109.

KULLING, Monica
"Harbour Sequence." MalR (45) Ja 78, p. 143.
"Note Found in a Bottle." MalR (45) Ja 78, p. 142.
"Sketch." MalR (45) Ja 78, p. 141.

KUMAR, Shiv K.
"My First Love." SouthernPR (18:2) Aut 78, p. 79.

KUMIN, Maxine
"The Archaeology of a Marriage." Poetry (132:1) Ap 78, p. 3.
"Food Chain." Atl (241:6) Je 78, p. 81.
"In April, in Princeton." Poetry (132:1) Ap 78, p. 1.
"The Longing to Be Saved." NewYorker (53:48) 16 Ja 78, p. 34.
"Notes on a Blizzard." Madem (84:5) My 78, p. 240.

KUNERT, Gunter
"Answer to Question" (tr. by Agnes Stein). ModernPS (9:2) Aut
    78, p. 151.
"House Calls" (tr. by Agnes Stein). ModernPS (9:2) Aut 78,
    p. 148.
"Poem According to Benjamin" (tr. by Agnes Stein). ModernPS
    (9:2) Aut 78, p. 152.
"Sculpture of a Subjugated German" (tr. by Agnes Stein).
    ModernPS (9:2) Aut 78, p. 153.
"Signs, Berlin Style" (tr. by Agnes Stein). ModernPS (9:2) Aut
    78, p. 150.
"Venice II" (tr. by Agnes Stein). ModernPS (9:2) Aut 78,
    p. 152.

KUNITZ, Stanley
"The Lincoln Relics." NewYorker (53:52) 13 F 78, p. 32.
"Quinnapoxet." Antaeus (30/31) Sum-Aut 78, p. 111.

KURILIK, Norman
"Theban Pose." Sky (7/8) Spr 78, p. 69.

KUTCHINS, Laurie
"My Father in the Mountain." Hand (2) 78, p. 66.

KUZMA, Greg
"Advantages." LitR (21:3) Spr 78, p. 335.
"Cities." MinnR (NS10) Spr 78, p. 50.
"Drinking." CEACritic (41:1) N 78, p. 21.
Eight poems. PraS (52:2) Sum 78, p. 151.

"The Fire. " CEACritic (41:1) N 78, p. 19.
"The Grape. " CEACritic (41:1) N 78, p. 20.
"March, Two Houses. " DacTerr (15) Wint-Spr 77-78, p. 5.
"My Mother. " KanQ (10:1) Wint 78, p. 10.
"Okra" (for Wayne Dodd). CEACritic (41:1) N 78, p. 18.
"Poetry. " CarolQ (30:3) Aut 78, p. 22.
"Why I Do Not Go More to My Office. " CEACritic (41:1) N 78,
    p. 20.

KVAM, Wayne
"Cosmos. " DacTerr (15) Wint-Spr 77-78, p. 55.
"Homestead Auction" (for Mary, Wilma, and Alfred Larson).
    DacTerr (15) Wint-Spr 77-78, p. 55.

KWON, Paula
"The Balcony. " Tendril (2) Spr-Sum 78.
"Larimer Street. " Tendril (2) Spr-Sum 78.
"Ronin Samurai. " Tendril (2) Spr-Sum 78.

KYNELL, Kermit S.
"Dark Archeology. " ArizQ (34:2) Sum 78, p. 124.
"lines from an exiled alaskan on the streets of pittsburgh. "
    DeKalb (11:3/4) Spr-Sum 78, p. 37.

LaBARE, M.
"Going East. " Zahir (9) 77, p. 42.
"Meeting with a Soldier. " Zahir (9) 77, p. 42.
"We move one. " Zahir (9) 77, p. 42.

LaBOMBARD, Joan
"The Empress Dowager Builds a Navy. " PraS (52:2) Sum 78,
    p. 173.
"Morning, with Chinese Blue. " Nat (226:5) 11 F 78, p. 155.

LADDEN, Arlene
"Cezanne. " LaB (11) 78, p. 19.
"Leaving. " LaB (11) 78, p. 20.

LAGIER, Gary
"Awaiting Emma's Return from the Hospital with Our Baby. "
    Wind (30) 78, p. 22.

LAHEY-DOLEGA, Christine
"You Go to Vancouver: I'm Gonna Alienate in Detroit City. "
    Smudge (3) Aut 78, p. 17.

LAKE, Paul
"Ghetto. " Epos (27:2) 77, p. 28.
"Minoan Artifacts. " SouthernHR (12:4) Aut 78, p. 364.
"Today I would Rather Be Anything but a Poet. " Wind (30) 78,
    p. 23.

LAKIN, R. D.
"Gifts. " StoneC (78:2) Spr 78, p. 24.

"Learning to Travel." Northeast (3:5) Spr-Sum 78, p. 25.
"Night at MacDowell Colony." StoneC (78:1) Wint 78, p. 17.
"Return." Northeast (3:5) Spr-Sum 78, p. 24.

LALLY, Margaret
"landscape." Bits (7) Ja 78.

LALLY, Michael
"Bernadette." Tele (13) 77.
"Epitaph for Ralph Dickey." Tele (13) 77.
"On Turning 35." LaB (10) 78, p. 28.
"She's Funny That Way" (for R.W.). LaB (10) 78, p. 29.
"The Spirit." Tele (13) 77.
"Today" (for Ted Berrigan). LaB (10) 78, p. 25.
"Tomorrow" (for Ted Greenwald). LaB (10) 78, p. 27.
"Yesterday" (for Ted Hughes). LaB (10) 78, p. 26.

LALLY, Miles
"Snow." Tele (13) 77.

LAMB, Dorothy Shaw
"White Beauty." LadHJ (95:1) Ja 78, p. 109.

LAND, E. Waverly
Nine poems. St. AR (5:1) Aut-Wint 78, p. 32.

LANDY, Francis
"The Master of Prayer." Hand (2) 78, p. 135.

LANE, Erskine
"The astonishing reality of things" (tr. of Fernando Pessoa).
    Bleb/Ark (13) 78, p. 43.
"At times on days of exact and perfect light" (tr. of Fernando
    Pessoa). Bleb/Ark (13) 78, p. 38.
"If I should die young" (tr. of Fernando Pessoa). Bleb/Ark (13)
    78, p. 44.
"I'm not concerned with rhymes" (tr. of Fernando Pessoa).
    Bleb/Ark (13) 78, p. 45.
"On an unusually clear day" (tr. of Fernando Pessoa). Bleb/Ark
    (13) 78, p. 41.
"The Tagus is prettier than the river that flows by my village"
    (tr. of Fernando Pessoa). Bleb/Ark (13) 78, p. 37.

LANE, Gary
"Down." Wind (29) 78, p. 5.
"Inscape." QW (5) Wint 78, p. 71.

LANE, Mary
"I Was Afraid to Fall." Tele (14) 78.

LANE, Mervin
"Before Completion." Montra (4) 78, p. 236.
"The Clinging." Montra (4) 78, p. 232.

"Fellowship with Men." Montra (4) 78, p. 234.
"Holding Together." Montra (4) 78, p. 235.
"Possession in Great Measure." Montra (4) 78, p. 234.
"Rain on Gray Stone." StoneC (78:3) Aut 78, p. 5.

LANE, Patrick
   "At the edge of the/field." MalR (45) Ja 78, p. 38.
   "Day after day the sun hurts these hills into summer." MalR
      (45) Ja 78, p. 36.
   "Even though she has been pushed." MalR (45) Ja 78, p. 37.
   "How the heart stinks with its devotions" (for the brothers
      D'Amour and Johnny Gringo). MalR (45) Ja 78, p. 35.
   "Ice Storm." MalR (45) Ja 78, p. 38.

LANE, William
   "As the Sun Goes Down a Week Before Christmas." HangL (32)
      Spr 78, p. 22.
   "It Is November 29th and the First Day of Deer Season." HangL
      (32) Spr 78, p. 20.
   "Night Applies Pressure Water Boils in the Pan." HangL (34)
      Wint 78-79, p. 30.
   "Reality Is Like a Greased Flag Pole." HangL (34) Wint 78-79,
      p. 28.
   "13." Hand (2) 78, p. 109.

LANG, Doug
   "Fats Navarro Ode." LaB (11) 78, p. 22.

LANG, Jon
   "The Deal." Confr (16) Spr-Sum 78, p. 45.
   "The Other." Epos (27:2) 77, p. 8.
   "Sestina: A Letter in Winter from Erieville" (for Al). LittleM
      (11:3) Aut 77, p. 82.

LANG, Richard G.
   "the noises that come." JnlONJP (3:1) 78, p. 4.

LANG, Susanna
   "Rachel." SouthernPR (18:2) Aut 78, p. 55.
   "The River" (tr. of Yves Bonnefoy). ChiR (29:4) Spr 78, p. 88.

LANGE, Art
   from Composition: "Day grows rapidly suspended in time."
      PartR (45:2) 78, p. 265.
   "Sonnet." PartR (45:2) 78, p. 267.
   "Sonnet after Rilke." PartR (45:2) 78, p. 268.

LANGTON, Daniel J.
   "First Things." Poetry (133:1) O 78, p. 32.
   "This Year's Poem." SoDakR (16:3) Aut 78, p. 27.

LAPIDUS, Jacqueline
   from Family Portraits: "Daddy." HangL (32) Spr 78, p. 24.

"Lisboa. " HangL (32) Spr 78, p. 23.
"Yellow Poem. " HangL (32) Spr 78, p. 26.

LAPINGTON, S. C.
"A Pipit. " Stand (19:3) 78, p. 65.

LAPPIN, Linda
"Meditation. " Kayak (48) Je 78, p. 29.

LARKIN, Philip
"Aubade. " AmerPoR (7:5) S-O 78, p. 48.

LARSEN, Rich
"The American Highway. " ConcPo (11:1) Spr 78, p. 83.
"Lovers/Voyages. " BallSUF (19:4) Aut 78, p. 22.
"Western. " ConcPo (11:1) Spr 78, p. 82.

LARSON, R. A.
"Steelhead. " PoNow (20) 78, p. 16.

LaRUE, James
"Bearers of Light" (for Lisa). PikeF (1) Spr 78, p. 13.
"Song. " PikeF (1) Spr 78, p. 13.

LASKA, P. J.
"Grandmother Mary. " MinnR (NS10) Spr 78, p. 28.
"Intimation of Death in Arizona at the Hands of the Avenging
     Indian. " MinnR (NS10) Spr 78, p. 29.
"Reflections from the Shop Floor. " MinnR (NS10) Spr 78, p. 27.
"Uncle Frank's Death. " Wind (28) 78, p. 50.

LATTAK, Marjeanne
"Cleaning Woman in a Dormitory. " Wind (31) 78, p. 41.

LAU, Craig
"in the night. " SeC (5:2) 78, p. 24.

LAUGHLIN, J.
"In Another Country. " Harp (256:1532) Ja 78, p. 44.
"A Long Night of Dreaming. " Poetry (132:1) Ap 78, p. 5.

LAURIE, Peter
"Carmina Catulli IV, V, VI" (tr. of Catullus). St. AR (5:1) Aut-
     Wint 78, p. 123.
"Exile. " Poetry (133:3) D 78, p. 166.
"Noel. " Poetry (133:3) D 78, p. 160.
"Pomona. " Poetry (133:3) D 78, p. 164.

LAUTERBACH, Ann
"Between. " LaB (11) 78, p. 23.
"The Day After. " LaB (11) 78, p. 24.
"Romance (sans Rimbuad). " PartR (45:1) 78, p. 10.
"Single File. " LaB (11) 78, p. 23.

LAUTERMILCH, Steven
"for the Christ." CimR (42) Ja 78, p. 43.
from Sonnets to Orpheus (tr. of Rilke): (I, 3; I, 5; II, 8; and
    II, 29). CentR (22:1) Wint 78, p. 71.
"Sonnets to Orpheus, 1. 21" (tr. of Rainer Maria Rilke). HolCrit
    (15:4) O 78, p. 17.
"Sonnets to Orpheus, 2. 12" (tr. of Rainer Maria Rilke). HolCrit
    (15:4) O 78, p. 17.

LAUZON, Tracie P.
"Creases." Chomo (5:2) Aut-Wint 78, p. 74.
"Goodbye." Chomo (5:2) Aut-Wint 78, p. 55.

LAWDER, Donald
"Home and Abroad." Nat (226:12) 1 Ap 78, p. 382.

LAWN, Beverly
"Procession." StoneC (78:1) Wint 78, p. 11.

LAWNER, Lynne
"Fresh Snow." ParisR (74) Aut-Wint 78, p. 83.

LAWSON, Christopher
"Kansas Wind, Kansas Charity." EngJ (67:5) My 78, p. 61.

LAWTON, Susan
"Calipers." StoneC (78:2) Spr 78, p. 25.
"In Memoriam, Once Again." Wind (31) 78, p. 27.
"Portland To Pandleton." Wind (31) 78, p. 27.

LAX, Robert
"now." Comm (105:5) 3 Mr 78, p. 130.

LAZARD, Naomi
"'I Will Go to Israel,' Sadat Said to His Minister, November 15,
    1977." MassR (19:1) Spr 78, p. 167.

LAZARUS, A. L.
"And What of Helga?" CentR (22:3) Sum 78, p. 321.

LAZER, Hank
"But Then." Nat (227:7) 9 S 78, p. 214.

LEA, Sydney
"Duck Hunter." SouthernR (14:3) Sum 78, p. 489.
"Elegy at Peter Dana Point" (for Creston MacArthur, 1917-
    1976). SouthernR (14:3) Sum 78, p. 491.
"The Historical Sense of Miss Cambridge." LitR (21:3) Spr 78,
    p. 351.
"Night Message for Ted in the South." SouthernR (14:3) Sum 78,
    p. 488.
"Night Patrol: The Ancestral House." PoetryNW (19:4) Wint
    78-79, p. 36.
"Revision of the Seasons." Salm (41) Spr 78, p. 125.

LEAFSTRAND, Lisa
"Icon: St. Macarius Beside His Island Monastery of Unzen:
    Leaving England." Madem (84:9) S 78, p. 222.

LEALE, B. C.
"The Dance of Life." Stand (19:3) 78, p. 32.

LEARY, Bruce
"sad lady." Zahir (9) 77, p. 2.
"speed queen." Zahir (9) 77, p. 2.

LEARY, Lewis
"On Becoming All at Once." SouthernR (14:3) Sum 78, p. 471.

LEAVITT, Jean
"Crossings." FourQt (27:2) Wint 78, p. 44.
"Homecoming." FourQt (27:3) Spr 78, p. 22.
"Harvest." Chomo (4:3) Spr 78, p. 17.
"Morning in Zimbabwe." Chomo (4:3) Spr 78, p. 16.

LECHLITNER, Ruth
"The Best Remembered." PoNow (19) 78, p. 29.
"A Calendar of Green." Wind (31) 78, p. 28.
"Night Journey." SouthwR (63:1) Wint 78, p. 55.

LEDWITH, Delila M. J.
"Morning Poem." KanQ (10:1) Wint 78, p. 12.

LEE, Ann
"Sensical Blues." StoneC (78:3) Aut 78, p. 17.

LEE, John
"Abbott and Costello." SeC (5:2) 78, p. 48.

LEE, Li-Young
"My Father Sleeping." WindO (32) Sum-Aut 78, p. 14.

LEE, Paul Ching
"Memory of a Parting" (tr. of Li Yü). NewOR (6:1) 78, p. 51.
"The Pass" (tr. of Mao Tse-tung). NewOR (6:1) 78, p. 50.

LEE, Tom
"I Could Pluck You, Aster." CarouselQ (3:3) Aut 78, p. 18.

LEET, Judith
"Distraught, Alarmed, Uncomforted." Poetry (132:4) Jl 78,
    p. 213.

LEFCOWITZ, Barbara F.
"Ragged Island." LitR (21:3) Spr 78, p. 305.

LeFORGE, P. V.
"Mishima Commits Suicide Aboard a Burning Japanese Oil
    Tanker." Stonecloud (7) 78, p. 117.

"23 Straight Lines" (for Erica Jong). Stonecloud (7) 78, p. 115.

LEGLER, Philip
  "Birthday Dream: For Karen. " PoetryNW (19:1) Spr 78, p. 30.
  "March Storm. " MidwQ (19:2) Wint 78, p. 138.
  "Of Light and Water. " PoetryNW (19:1) Spr 78, p. 31.

LEHMAN, David
  "René Margritte. " SunM (5) Aut 78, p. 5.
  "The Thirty Nine Steps. " SunM (5) Aut 78, p. 3.

LEIGH, Michael Glover
  "Good. " WormR (69) 78, p. 35.

LEIGHT, Peter
  "The Business of Power. " ParisR (73) Spr-Sum 78, p. 30.
  "Manhattan. " SmPd (44) Aut 78, p. 17.

LEIGHTON, Daniel
  "The Warlock's Testament. " KanQ (10:1) Wint 78, p. 26.

LEISER, Wayne
  "Point Counterpoint. " ChrC (95:36) 8 N 78, p. 1060.

LEM, Carol
  "andermatt: a walking tour. " Bachy (12) Aut 78, p. 60.
  "Breakfast Time in Suburban Skokie. " Bachy (12) Aut 78, p. 59.
  "Henry Miller: a writer. " Bachy (12) Aut 78, p. 62.
  "Michelle Andrews, If You Can Hear Me Go Home (Helicopter
      Night Watch, 7/9/77). " Bachy (12) Aut 78, p. 61.
  "passing through. " Bachy (12) Aut 78, p. 59.

LeMIEUX, Dotty
  "Coffee. " Tele (14) 78.
  "Poem for David. " Tele (14) 78.
  "Railroad Jack. " Tele (14) 78.

LENAU, Nancy
  "Wallflower. " BallSUF (19:4) Aut 78, p. 13.

LEONTIEF, Estelle
  "42nd Street Library, 1936. " ConcPo (11:2) Aut 78, p. 48.
  "She. " ConcPo (11:2) Aut 78, p. 48.

LEPORE, Dominick J.
  "Litany of Sorrow. " ArizQ (34:2) Sum 78, p. 161.
  "A Sunday at the Family Plot. " ChrC (95:32) 11 O 78, p. 943.

LERER, Seth
  "No Trumpets: Robert Lowell. " SewanR (86:1) Wint 78, p. 101.

LERMONTOV, Mikhail
  "The Czar's Cadets at Peterhof" (tr. by Walter Arndt). Playb
      (25:1) 78, p. 198.

LERNER, Arthur
"On a Shopping Tour with Ben Franklin. " LitR (22:1) Aut 78,
    p. 73.
"Thomas Jefferson Getting a Message. " LitR (22:1) Aut 78,
    p. 72.

LERNER, Linda
"The Clock. " Confr (17) Aut-Wint 79, p. 96.
"Drinking Tea with an Archivist. " CentR (22:2) Spr 78, p. 184.
"Marriage Piece. " SouthernHR (12:2) Spr 78, p. 159.
"Posing. " SlowLR (1/2) 78, p. 44.
"Spoilage. " ColEng (40:1) S 78, p. 29.

LESLIE, Lynne
"The Schizophrenics' Bible Study Group. " ChrC (95:4) 1-8 F 78,
    p. 102.

LESNIAK, Rose
"Daybreak. " Tele (13) 77.
"On Eating Meat" (for Neil Hackman). Tele (13) 77.

LESSER, Rika
"Ghazal" (tr. of Gunner Ekelöf). Poetry (131:6) Mr 78, p. 339.
"The Hyponogogue" (tr. of Gunnar Ekelöf). Poetry (131:6) Mr
    78, p. 340.
"Joachim and Anna" (after Giotto). Shen (29:2) Wint 78, p. 23.
"Losses" (tr. of Gunnar Ekelöf). Poetry (131:6) Mr 78, p. 342.
"Oecus" (tr. of Gunnar Ekelöf). Poetry (131:6) Mr 78, p. 338.

LESSING, Karin
"Miniature. " Montra (4) 78, p. 61.
"Presage. " Montra (4) 78, p. 63.
"The Sculptor's Garden. " Montra (4) 78, p. 60.
"Turning. " Montra (4) 78, p. 64.
"Wind-Gathered. " Montra (4) 78, p. 62.

LEVANDOSKY, Charles
"the birth. " Hand (2) 78, p. 127.
"then. " Hand (2) 78, p. 199.

LEVERING, Donald
"Birdhouse. " Comm (105:3) 3 F 78, p. 71.
"Earl's Story. " StoneC (78:2) Spr 78, p. 8.
"The Groundskeeper. " StoneC (78:1) Wint 78, p. 13.

LEVERTOV, Denise
"Blake's Baptismal Font. " Field (18) Spr 78, p. 26.
"Death Psalm: O Lord of Mysteries. " HangL (33) Sum 78,
    p. 40.
"Emblem, I. " Bound (6:3/7:1) Spr-Aut 78, p. 451.
"Emblem, II. " Bound (6:3/7:1) Spr-Aut 78, p. 452.
"Kindness. " Bound (6:3/7:1) Spr-Aut 78, p. 450.
"Marta (Brazil, 1928). " ChiR (30:3) Wint 79, p. 129.
"Talking to Oneself. " Tendril (3) Aut 78, p. 38.

LEVIN, Amy
"Rock, Scissors, Paper." Aspen (6) Aut 78, p. 57.

LEVIN, Ileen
"My reasoning escapes." Tele (13) 77.

LEVIN, John
"privacy." Tele (13) 77.

LEVIN, Matt
"Homage to Picasso." Poem (34) N 78, p. 54.

LEVINE, Ellen
"Deer." SlowLR (1/2) 78, p. 97.
"Getting to Forbes Landing." PoNow (20) 78, p. 16.
"Provincial Museum, Victoria, B. C." MichQR (17:2) Spr 78,
    p. 159.

LEVINE, Philip
"Andorra." Antaeus (30/31) Sum-Aut 78, p. 115.
"Any Night." GeoR (32:2) Sum 78, p. 306.
"Ashes." Iowa (9:2) Spr 78, p. 87.
"Asking." NewL (45:1) Aut 78, p. 24.
"Autobiography" (tr. of Gloria Fuertes). Antaeus (30/31) Sum-
    Aut 78, p. 86.
"The Choice." MissouriR (1:1) Spr 78, p. 9.
"Common Objects." OhioR (19:1) Wint 78, p. 25.
"The Dawn Has Turned as Cold" (tr. of Gloria Fuertes). Antaeus
    (30/31) Sum-Aut 78, p. 82.
"Everything." GeoR (32:1) Spr 78, p. 13.
"The Face." NewYorker (54:20) 3 Jl 78, p. 35.
"Francisco, I'll Bring You Red Carnations." Harp (257:1543) D
    78, p. 20.
"Grammatical Sentences" (tr. of Gloria Fuertes). Antaeus
    (30/31) Sum-Aut 78, p. 84.
"The Gulf." Antaeus (30/31) Sum-Aut 78, p. 117.
"Hear Me." AmerPoR (7:1) Ja-F 78, p. 42.
"In the Dark." OhioR (19:1) Spr 78, p. 24.
"It's Useless" (tr. of Gloria Fuertes). Antaeus (30/31) Sum-Aut
    78, p. 87.
"I've Slept" (tr. of Gloria Fuertes). Antaeus (30/31) Sum-Aut
    78, p. 85.
"Last Song of the Angel of Bad Luck." GeoR (32:2) Sum 78,
    p. 307.
"Let Me Be." Iowa (9:2) Spr 78, p. 88.
"Let Me Begin Again." NewYorker (54:30) 11 S 78, p. 42.
"Lost and Found." Harp (256:1537) Je 78, p. 90.
"A Man's Going" (tr. of Gloria Fuertes). Antaeus (30/31) Sum-
    Aut 78, p. 83.
"Refusing to Serve--Dawn, 1952." NewYorker (54:44) 18 D 78,
    p. 42.
"The Secret of Their Voices." HarvAd (111:4) My 78, p. 7.
"Snow." NewYorker (54:39) 13 N 78, p. 52.
"Something Has Fallen." MissouriR (1:1) Spr 78, p. 6.

"Songs." Harp (257:1543) D 78, p. 26.
"Who." GeoR (32:4) Wint 78, p. 776.
"You Can Have It." Antaeus (30/31) Sum-Aut 78, p. 113.
"Your Life." MissouriR (1:1) Spr 78, p. 11.

LEVINSON, Margaret Ann
"Another Old Swede." Poem (34) N 78, p. 46.
"The Scarlet Ibis." Poem (34) N 78, p. 43.

LEVIS, Larry
"Adah." Iowa (9:3) Sum 78, p. 79.
"For a Ghost Who Once Placed Bets in the Park." AmerPoR
    (7:6) N-D 78, p. 9.
"García Lorca: A Photograph of the Granada Cemetery, 1966."
    Antaeus (30/31) Sum-Aut 78, p. 122.
"The Grass." Antaeus (30/31) Sum-Aut 78, p. 120.
"Lost Fan, Hotel California, Fresno, 1923." Antaeus (30/31)
    Sum-Aut 78, p. 118.
"The Map." PoNow (19) 78, p. 16.
"Near Ecuador." Sky (7/8) Spr 78, p. 14.
"Overhearing the Dollmaker's Ghost on the Riverbank." Antaeus
    (30/31) Sum-Aut 78, p. 124.
"The Ownership of the Night." Field (18) Spr 78, p. 105.
"A Poem of Horses." PoNow (19) 78, p. 16.
"Some Privacy for John Bowie, 1950-1977." SenR (9:1) Spr-Sum
    78, p. 75.
"Story." Sky (7/8) Spr 78, p. 15.

LEVITIN, Alexis
"That's Where I'm Going" (tr. of Clarice Lispector). WebR
    (4:2) Aut 78, p. 34.
"The Photographs" (tr. of Sophia de Mello Breyner Andresen).
    LitR (21:4) Sum 78, p. 456.
"The Young Girl and the Beach" (tr. of Sophia de Mello Breyner
    Andresen). LitR (21:4) Sum 78, p. 456.

LEVITT, Annabel
"Angers Castle." Tele (14) 78.
"Paris." Tele (14) 78.
"a page of salads." Tele (14) 78.
"soft verging brick." Tele (14) 78.
"2 chimes" (for Douglas). Tele (14) 78.
"Variety Shops." Tele (14) 78.

LEVITT, Peter
"At Sea" (for Paul Culberg). Bachy (11) Spr 78, p. 91.
"The Horse with Patched Blossoms." Bachy (11) Spr 78, p. 92.
"Nighthawk." Bachy (11) Spr 78, p. 91.
"Short Poem in Shadow." Bachy (11) Spr 78, p. 90.
"The Water Falls." Bachy (11) Spr 78, p. 92.

LEVY, James
"Chino and Cuba brought the bucket out." Smudge (3) Aut 78,
    p. 10.

LEVY, D. A.
  Kibbutz in the Sky. Sam (67) 78.   Entire issue.

LEWANDOWSKI, Steve
  "Anton & Marie Lewandowski. " GreenfieldR (6:3/4) Spr 78,
     p. 76.
  "Beyond the Equinox. " DacTerr (15) Wint-Spr 77-78, p. 23.
  "Ezra Pound. " Bachy (12) Aut 78, p. 134.
  "Looking into the Root Cupboard" (for Joe Bruchac). Bleb/Ark
     (13) 78, p. 73.
  "Meet the Ax. " Bleb/Ark (13) 78, p. 74.
  "The Nature of Meditation. " Bachy (12) Aut 78, p. 134.
  "Nothing Much. " GreenfieldR (6:3/4) Spr 78, p. 77.
  "One Lesson. " Bleb/Ark (13) 78, p. 75.
  "open the door. " Zahir (9) 77, p. 7.
  "Pillars" (for Richard Hugo). Paunch (52) O 78, p. 114.
  "Self-Defense. " Bachy (12) Aut 78, p. 134.
  "67 Plymouth Valiant. " Bleb/Ark (13) 78, p. 76.
  "Some Things Work. " Bleb/Ark (13) 78, p. 78.
  "Speaking English. " GreenfieldR (6:3/4) Spr 78, p. 75.
  "Spells" (for Michael Corr). Bachy (12) Aut 78, p. 134.
  "Thaw. " Bleb/Ark (13) 78, p. 77.
  "Thoughts on Fall Plowing. " Bachy (12) Aut 78, p. 133.

LEWIS, Harry
  "Atlantic Ocean" (tr. of Vladimir Mayakovsky, w. Vitalij Keis).
     Pequod (2:4) 78, p. 19.

LEWIS, Janet
  "The Ancient Ones: Betátakin. " SouthernR (14:2) Spr 78,
     p. 316.
  "The Ancient Ones: Water. " OhioR (19:3) Aut 78, p. 9.
  "Awátobi. " SouthernR (14:2) Spr 78, p. 310.
  "The Chord. " SouthernR (14:2) Spr 78, p. 314.
  "Garden Note, Los Altos, 1977. " SouthernR (14:2) Spr 78,
     p. 314.
  "Kayenta, May 12, 1977. " SouthernR (14:2) Spr 78, p. 314.
  "Lake George, on The Mohican. " SouthernR (14:2) Spr 78,
     p. 315.
  "March, Los Altos. " SouthernR (14:2) Spr 78, p. 315.

LEWTER, John
  Eleven poems. Poem (34) N 78, pp. 29-42.
  "The Pequod's Cabinboy. " Poem (32) Mr 78, p. 20.
  "Raw and Bleeding. " Poem (32) Mr 78, p. 18.
  "Sea Foam" (For Pauline). Poem (32) Mr 78, p. 21.

LIBBEY, Elizabeth
  "Come into the Night Grove. " NewYorker (54:24) 31 Jl 78,
     p. 68.
  "Déjà Vu. " Poetry (132:6) S 78, p. 314.
  "The Gesture. " Poetry (132:6) S 78, p. 311.
  "Girl Sitting Alone in Her Room. " Poetry (132:6) S 78, p. 315.
  "Juana Bautista Lucero, Circa 1926, To Her Photographer. "

Ascent (4:1) 78, p. 24.
"Love Poem." Poetry (132:6) S 78, p. 313.
"On Being Asked to Bring a Poem back from Montana." Epoch
(27:2) Wint 78, p. 174.
"Putting Things By" (For Bill Boggs). Poetry (132:6) S 78,
p. 316.

LIEBERMAN, David
"Geardagum." SmPd (42) Wint 78, p. 17.
"I am an egg." KanQ (10:1) Wint 78, p. 92.

LIEBERMAN, Laurence
"Cape Iro: The Stone Pillars" (for James Dickey). SoCaR
(10:2) Ap 78, p. 16.
"Kimono." NewYorker (54:15) 29 My 78, p. 93.
"Lockjaw." ModernPS (9:3) Wint 79, p. 161.

LIETZ, Robert
"For My Blood Relatives Who Suspect Joy." Epoch (28:1) Aut
78, p. 84.
"Furnished Rooms." DacTerr (15) Wint-Spr 77-78, p. 52.
"Getting Back, Getting On." Nimrod (22:2) Spr-Sum 78, p. 23.
"Sunday Morning." GreenfieldR (6:3/4) Spr 78, p. 119.

LIFSCHITZ, Leatrice
"Bringing Things Home." StoneC (78:3) Aut 78, p. 25.

LIFSHIN, Lyn
"Attic." PikeF (1) Spr 78, p. 6.
"Barre 1941." HangL (32) Spr 78, p. 27.
"Barre 1942." HolCrit (15:2) Ap 78, p. 15.
"Cape Cod." MoonsLT (2:4) 78, p. 13.
"Crumpled Photo." CalQ (13/14) Spr-Sum 78, p. 33.
"The Dead the No I Won't Pay Dried Tubers of the Stop Spending
Month." ChiR (30:1) Sum 78, p. 29.
"Diamond Ring." HolCrit (15:1) F 78, p. 6.
"The Dream of Going Back to Where I Was Jewish in a Small
Town." MoonsLT (2:4) 78, p. 15.
Eleven poems. Bleb/Ark (13) 78, p. 21.
"Fatimi." CalQ (13/14) Spr-Sum 78, p. 32.
"The Fifties." MoonsLT (2:4) 78, p. 11.
"Gigolo Madonna." MoonsLT (2:4) 78, p. 14.
"He Said He Was Patient That He Wanted To." WormR (72) 78,
p. 132.
"I'm Sitting in the Car When the Old Woman Comes Over."
WindO (33) Aut-Wint 78-79, p. 5.
"It Was Like." PikeF (1) Spr 78, p. 6.
"I've Written about My Mother's Gone Knife." HangL (34) Wint
78-79, p. 32.
"MLA Madonna." WormR (72) 78, p. 132.
"The Man Who Told Me I Was Cold." SoCaR (10:2) Ap 78,
p. 6.
"Martha Graham." LittleM (11:4) Wint 78, p. 37.

"More of the White Monday." WindO (33) Aut-Wint 78-79, p. 6.
"Mother and Daughter Photos." BelPoJ (29:1) Aut 78, p. 33.
"Mother's Song." HangL (34) Wint 78-79, p. 35.
"Mrs. Mokas." WormR (72) 78, p. 132.
"My Father Started To." WindO (33) Aut-Wint 78-79, p. 7.
"My Mother Covering the Carriage." YellowBR (10) 78, p. 8.
"My Mother Was Watching." PikeF (1) Spr 78, p. 6.
"My Mother's Knife." MassR (19:2) Sum 78, p. 363.
Nine poems. Stonecloud (7) 78, p. 37.
"1959 Silver Jaguar." HangL (34) Wint 78-79, p. 37.
"1945." WindO (32) Sum-Aut 78, p. 37.
"Photograph 1944." NorthSR (8) Aut-Wint 78-79, p. 57.
"A Pretty Boy with a / Hat." NorthSR (8) Aut-Wint 78-79, p. 56.
"Something about the Softest." HangL (34) Wint 78-79, p. 36.
"Today with the Bees Falling." SmPd (44) Aut 78, p. 32.
"When There's Food Around I'm Rarely Hungry and the Same
    with Men, Tho Alone I'm Starved for Both." Paunch (52) O
    78, p. 113.
"When What Seems the Nicest Is Sleeping." HangL (32) Spr 78,
    p. 28.
"White and Gold." HangL (32) Spr 78, p. 29.
"White Hair and Fleas." HangL (34) Wint 78-79, p. 34.
"The Why I'm Writing This in My Slash and Dash Handwriting
    and Not Typing It Clear and Big Like an Outlined Hot Hand
    in Snow." WindO (32) Sum-Aut 78, p. 37.
"Wormwood Madonna." WormR (72) 78, p. 132.

LIFSON, Martha
    "fingering along the walls in the dark." Bachy (11) Spr 78,
        p. 75.
    "how momentary the time." Bachy (11) Spr 78, p. 74.
    "in summer losing one I live with." Bachy (13) Aut-Wint 78-79,
        p. 84.
    "it's the taking of so goddamned many steps." Bachy (11) Spr
        78, p. 72.
    "quiet by hillsides in the afternoon." Bachy (11) Spr 78, p. 74.
    "short pieces." Bachy (11) Spr 78, p. 73.
    "Shyly she offered him" (for Sam Johnston). Bachy (13) Aut-
        Wint 78-79, p. 85.
    "sleeping somewhere not just in the smells of you." Bachy (11)
        Spr 78, p. 72.
    "The Blank Heroic Ones." Epoch (28:1) Aut 78, p. 67.
    "A Portrait." Epoch (28:1) Aut 78, p. 67.

LIGNELL, Kathleen
    "Calamity Jane Greets Her Dreams." CarolQ (30:2) Spr-Sum
        78, p. 19.
    "Jane on the Run." CarolQ (30:2) Spr-Sum 78, p. 18.

LILLARD, Charles
    "Circling the Avenue." MalR (45) Ja 78, p. 274.
    "Fec's Pool." MalR (45) Ja 78, p. 278.
    "Inscape." MalR (45) Ja 78, p. 275.

"Interlude. " MalR (45) Ja 78, p. 276.
"One View from the Kynoch. " MalR (45) Ja 78, p. 273.

LILLIBRIDGE, Sharon
"Afterthoughts. " StoneC (78:3) Aut 78, p. 30.

LILLY, Paul
"Bogie in Peru. " CalQ (13/14) Spr-Sum 78, p. 37.

LILLY, Paul R., Jr.
"Flight. " BelPoJ (28:3) Spr 78, p. 35.

LINDEMAN, Jack
"Plato. " SouthwR (63:2) Spr 78, p. 123.
"Tired. " BallSUF (19:2) Spr 78, p. 79.

LINDNER, Carl
"Advice to a Boy in a Schoolyard. " NewRivR (2:2) 78, p. 64.
"Conch. " SouthernHR (12:2) Spr 78, p. 132.
"I Am Thinking of Portals. " BelPoJ (28:3) Spr 78, p. 34.
"On Reports of Student Coupling in the Campus Woods. " KanQ
    (10:2) Spr 78, p. 105.
"When I Got It Right. " NewRivR (2:2) 78, p. 65.

LINDSAY, Frannie
"Learning to Hate You. " NewL (44:3) Spr 78, p. 72.
"The Possible First Edition. " GreenfieldR (6:3/4) Spr 78,
    p. 132.
"Still Ascending. " PoNow (20) 78, p. 17.

LINDSEY, Carol Chapin
"Ice Storm. " ChrC (95:13) 12 Ap 78, p. 381.

LINDSEY, Jim
"In Old Union. " Aspen (5) Spr 78, p. 59.
from The Lunatic Banns: "The Dead of Summer. " Aspen (5)
    Spr 78, p. 61.

LINEHAN, Moira
"In Boston. " PoetC (10:2) 78, p. 6.
"In Florence. " PoetC (10:2) 78, p. 6.
"Wintering. " Wind (31) 78, p. 29.

LINER, Tom
"Baptism. " Bachy (12) Aut 78, p. 135.
"Boar's Head. " Bachy (12) Aut 78, p. 137.
"Nocturne 6. " Bachy (12) Aut 78, p. 135.
"Salvation. " Bachy (12) Aut 78, p. 135.
"10th Street Hooker Chattanooga Memory. " EngJ (67:5) My 78,
    p. 54.
"when the darkness came. " Bachy (12) Aut 78, p. 135.

LINETT, Deena
"I'd Like to Watch a Government Dissolve. " JnlONJP (2:2) 77,

p. 25.
"Sounds from Cygnus A." StoneC (78:2) Spr 78, p. 19.
"Sunworks." StoneC (78:2) Spr 78, p. 19.

LING, Amy
"in/digestion." StoneC (78:3) Aut 78, p. 15.

LIPSINER, Sue
"Eulogy: To Nana." Box (6) Aut 77, p. 14.

LIPSITZ, Lou
"Evening." Kayak (47) F 78, p. 30.
"The Radical in the Alligator Shirt." CarolQ (30:2) Spr-Sum 78,
   p. 81.
"Seeking Sleep." Kayak (47) F 78, p. 30.
"The Sirens." SouthernPR (18:2) Aut 78, p. 92.

LISA J.
"Brighter Side of Darkness." BlackF (2:2) Aut-Wint 78, p. 24.

LISLE, Charles Leconte de
"Le Sommeil de Leïlah." SouthernR (14:2) Spr 78, p. 332.

LISOWSKI, Joseph
"Moving." StoneC (78:1) Wint 78, p. 27.

LISPECTOR, Clarice
"That's Where I'm Going" (tr. by Alexis Levitin). WebR (4:2)
   Aut 78, p. 34.

LISTMANN, Thomas
"Alameda." SoDakR (16:2) Sum 78, p. 62.
"Goodbye to Berkeley." SoDakR (16:2) Sum 78, p. 61.
"The Raisin Queen." CalQ (13/14) Spr-Sum 78, p. 130.
"Santa Cruz." PoNow (20) 78, p. 17.
"The Sixties." CalQ (13/14) Spr-Sum 78, p. 131.

LITT, Iris
"Love Poem." StoneC (78:2) Spr 78, p. 13.

LITTLE, Geraldine C.
"Helen: The Dark Interior." JnlONJP (3:1) 78, p. 5.
"Long Thoughts on a Lake in the Pine Barrens, New Jersey."
   JnlONJP (2:2) 77, p. 19.
"Pub: Belfast." PoetC (10:2) 78, p. 24.
"Summer's End." PoetC (10:2) 78, p. 22.
"Suzuki: After Years--Considerations on the Child." Shen
   (29:4) Sum 78, p. 80.

LITZ, Robert
"Refugees." Stonecloud (7) 78, p. 73.
"Snow." Stonecloud (7) 78, p. 100.

LIU Shen-hsu
"Untitled" (tr. by Robert Branham and Daniel Stevenson).
Nimrod (22:2) Spr-Sum 78, p. 108.

LIU, Stephen Shu Ning
"For David Wang (1931-1977)." GreenfieldR (6:3/4) Spr 78,
p. 3.
"I Lie on the Chilled Stones of the Great Wall." GreenfieldR
(6:3/4) Spr 78, p. 1.
"Snow Peas." GreenfieldR (6:3/4) Spr 78, p. 2.

LI Yü
"Memory of a Parting" (tr. by Paul Ching Lee). NewOR (6:1)
78, p. 51.

LOBERG, David
"Dear Mr. Smith." Stonecloud (7) 78, p. 114.
"A Speeding Station Wagon." Stonecloud (7) 78, p. 114.

LOCK, Norman
"The Friendship of Machines." Kayak (49) O 78, p. 70.
"The House Quieter." Kayak (49) O 78, p. 70.
"The Lechery of Neckties." Kayak (49) O 78, p. 71.
"The Treachery of Mirrors." Kayak (49) O 78, p. 71.

LOCKE, Duane
Foam on Gulf Shore. UTR (5:4) 78. Entire issue.
"Foam on Gulf Shore #1." AAR (28) 78, p. 20.

LOCKLIN, Gerald
"All Comparisons Are Invidious." PoNow (19) 78, p. 45.
"Chinatown." WormR (70) 78, p. 47.
"divorcée." AmerS (47:2) Spr 78, p. 231.
"His Handiwork." WormR (72) 78, p. 134.
"Late Registration." Smudge (3) Aut 78, p. 7.
"Modern Art in the Elementary Classroom." PoNow (19) 78, p. 44.
"mOm." YellowBR (10) 78, p. 10.
"my uncle hank." LitR (22:1) Aut 78, p. 56.
"Newlywed." WormR (72) 78, p. 135.
"A Plague Grew in Anaheim." WormR (72) 78, p. 134.
Pronouncing Borges. WormR (67) 77. Entire issue.
"Toad's Waterloo." WormR (70) 78, p. 47.

LODGE, John G.
"Toward Meeting." Poem (33) Jl 78, p. 10.
"Winterscapes." Poem (33) Jl 78, p. 9.

LOEB, Karen
"Home Births." YellowBR (10) 78, p. 5.

LOEWINSOHN, Ron
"Ovingdean Church" (for Lee & Judy Harwood). ChiR (30:3)
Wint 79, p. 127.
"The Sports Car." ChiR (30:3) Wint 79, p. 125.

LOGAN, Brent
 "Bombwalk." NorthSR (8) Aut-Wint 78-79, p. 65.
 "Double Vision." NorthSR (8) Aut-Wint 78-79, p. 66.
 "Traveler's Warning." NorthSR (8) Aut-Wint 78-79, p. 64.

LOGAN, John
 from Dublin Suite: "Homage to James Joyce." ModernPS (9:3)
      Wint 79, p. 188.

LOGAN, Thean
 "For Samson." NewL (45:2) Wint 78, p. 56.
 "Hecate." NewL (45:2) Wint 78, p. 57.
 "Lines for Anna Akhmatova." NewL (45:2) Wint 78, p. 56.

LOGAN, William
 "The Burning." SewanR (86:3) Sum 78, p. 372.
 "Children." SewanR (86:1) Wint 78, p. 37.
 "Dream of Dying." SewanR (86:3) Sum 78, p. 372.
 "Exercises from Latin." Shen (29:3) Spr 78, p. 16.
 "The Fog Night." AntR (36:2) Spr 78, p. 189.
 "Ice." NewYorker (53:46) 2 Ja 78, p. 28.
 "The Misbegotten." NoAmR (263:3) Aut 78, p. 46.
 "Observing Whales through Binoculars." Nat (227:21) 16 D 78,
      p. 678.
 "An Ode." GeoR (32:2) Sum 78, p. 388.
 "Odysseus Inland." SewanR (86:3) Sum 78, p. 371.
 "Sixteen Women Descending a Stairway." SewanR (86:1) Wint 78,
      p. 38.

LONDON, Jonathan
 "Grandma Sittenreich (1886-1960)." YellowBR (10) 78, p. 37.
 "Invitation to a Jailing." Zahir (9) 77, p. 26.
 "Moon Balanced on the Taut Wire." Zahir (9) 77, p. 27.

LONEY, Alan
 "As we supposed, the War Dance." Bound (6:2) Wint 78,
      p. 505.
 "Cook's wake." Bound (6:2) Wint 78, p. 506.
 "The Perishables." Bound (6:2) Wint 78, p. 508.
 "That." Bound (6:2) Wint 78, p. 504.
 "their Being broke." Bound (6:2) Wint 78, p. 509.
 "3 days." Bound (6:2) Wint 78, p. 510.

LONG, David
 "Maple Syrup." QW (5) Wint 78, p. 104.

LONG, Mike
 "Baby's Breath." AAR (28) 78, p. 71.

LONG, Robert
 "Harry and Patricia." Kayak (49) O 78, p. 63.
 "Scene." GreenfieldR (6:3/4) Spr 78, p. 153.
 "Teeth." GreenfieldR (6:3/4) Spr 78, p. 153.

LONGLEY, Michael
    Eight poems. LitR (22:2) Wint 79, p. 216.
    "On Hearing Irish Spoken" (for Ciarán Carson). LitR (22:2)
        Wint 79, p. 132.

LONGSTREET, Bruce
    "Harpo in Tiffany's" (for Susan). JnlONJP (2:2) 77, p. 15.
    "Hiatus #3." JnlONJP (2:2) 77, p. 15.

LONGWILL, James
    "My Father." Stand (18:4) 77, p. 4.

LOOBY, Georgette
    "Four Young Cowboys." SeC (5:2) 78, p. 49.

LOPATE, Phillip
    "August." SunM (5) Aut 78, p. 29.
    "Doing Crossword Puzzles." Pequod (2:4) 78, p. 57.
    "Hop and Roll." SunM (5) Aut 78, p. 27.
    "Inside the Bakery Shop." SunM (5) Aut 78, p. 28.
    "The Japanophiles." Pequod (2:4) 78, p. 54.
    "The Little Magazines Keep Coming." Some (9) 78, p. 48.
    "On Training for Emptiness." SunM (5) Aut 78, p. 30.

LOPES, Michael
    "Fishing." HangL (33) Sum 78, p. 44.
    "History." PoNow (20) 78, p. 23.
    "Saturday Morning Labor Day Weekend." PoNow (20) 78, p. 23.
    "Sketch from a Small Town." HangL (33) Sum 78, p. 43.
    "Three Memories Suddenly Come Together." PoNow (20) 78,
        p. 23.
    "Walking Away from the Road." PoNow (20) 78, p. 23.

LOPEZ, Rick
    "J'ai Apercu une Licorne." DeKalb (11:3/4) Spr-Sum 78,
        p. 104.

LOPEZ-PACHECO, José
    "Happy Ballads to Greet Rafael Alberti in My Absence" (tr. by
        Mario Angulo). MalR (47) Jl 78, p. 98.

LORDE, Audre
    "For Assata." 13thM (4:1) 78, p. 25.
    "Letter for Jan." 13thM (4:1) 78, p. 23.
    "Portrait." PoNow (19) 78, p. 17.
    "School Note." PoNow (19) 78, p. 17.
    "Touring." Some (9) 78, p. 71.

LOTT, Carolyn S.
    "Wind Change." Wind (31) 78, p. 31.

LOUCH, Elizabeth
    "I am absolutely fascinated." Zahir (9) 77, p. 67.

LOUCHHEIM, Katie
"About My Father." NewRep (179:5) 29 Jl 78, p. 27.
"Immutable." LadHJ (95:9) S 78, p. 102.

LOUIS, Helene
"After Granada." Poem (33) Jl 78, p. 16.
"A Cave, a Bed." Poem (33) Jl 78, p. 14.
"Drifts." Poem (33) Jl 78, p. 13.

LOURIE, Iven
"Noche Con Mimosas." HangL (34) Wint 78-79, p. 38.

LOUTHAN, Robert
"The Diary" (for Sue Owen). SlowLR (1/2) 78, p. 60.
"Love Poem." AntR (36:1) Wint 78, p. 81.
"No." SenR (9:1) Spr-Sum 78, p. 63.
"On December 25 of a Numberless Year." SenR (9:1) Spr-Sum
    78, p. 63.

LOVELL, Barbara
"At the Gate." SouthernPR (18:2) Aut 78, p. 24.

LOVINGTON, Ted, Jr.
"Song of Blake." Glass (3:1/2/3) 78, p. 115.

LOWELL, Robert
from The Oresteia: "From Agamemnon" (tr. of Aeschylus).
    AmerPoR (7:5) S-O 78, p. 22.
from The Oresteia: "From the Furies" (tr. of Aeschylus).
    AmerPoR (7:5) S-O 78, p. 23.

LOWENKRON, David
"Skiing." KanQ (10:1) Wint 78, p. 77.

LOWENSTEIN, Tom
"The Death of Dido" (For Grant Fisher). Poetry (131:4) Ja 78,
    p. 218.
"Excuse for the Exotic." Tele (13) 77.
"National Episode." Tele (13) 77.
"Questions to the Vedic Ugruk." Tele (13) 77.

LOWERY, Mike
"Changes." KanQ (10:1) Wint 78, p. 91.

LOWRY, John
"Earth Plates." PoNow (20) 78, p. 17.
"Micro Chips." WormR (69) 78, p. 33.

LUCAS, Cora
"A Gift of Arrangement." Wind (31) 78, p. 30.
"Prescription for Grief." Wind (31) 78, p. 30.

LUCAS, Henry N.
"May i Poet." GreenfieldR (7:1/2) Aut 78, p. 4.

LUCAS, Lawrence A.
  "Another Meeting." <u>BallSUF</u> (19:4) Aut 78, p. 32.

LUCEBERT
  "Brancusi." <u>GRR</u> (9:2) 78, p. 108.
  "Moore." <u>GRR</u> (9:2) 78, p. 104.
  "Rousseau Le Douanier." <u>GRR</u> (9:2) 78, p. 106.

LUCIAN
  "The Exorcist" (tr. by Richard O'Connell). <u>Playb</u> (25:4) Ap 78,
    p. 157.
  "Flagged" (tr. by Richard O'Connell). <u>Playb</u> (25:4) Ap 78,
    p. 157.

LUCILIUS
  "Holier Than Thou" (tr. by Richard O'Connell). <u>Playb</u> (25:4) Ap
    78, p. 157.
  "The Miser" (tr. by Richard O'Connell). <u>Playb</u> (25:4) Ap 78,
    p. 157.
  "Undergrad" (tr. by Richard O'Connell). <u>Playb</u> (25:4) Ap 78,
    p. 157.

LUCINA, Sister Mary
  "Beside the Night Pond." <u>Wind</u> (28) 78, p. 40.
  "The Scrubboard." <u>Wind</u> (28) 78, p. 40.

LUDVIGSON, Susan Bartels
  "After His Death." <u>QW</u> (5) Wint 78, p. 45.
  "The Arrival." <u>AndR</u> (5:1) Spr 78, p. 50.
  "The Artist to Her Patron." <u>SouthernPR</u> (18:2) Aut 78, p. 10.
  "How We Begin." <u>QW</u> (5) Wint 78, p. 45.
  "Next Time." <u>Nimrod</u> (22:2) Spr-Sum 78, p. 7.
  "Preparing for the Takeover." <u>GeoR</u> (32:1) Spr 78, p. 150.
  "The Psychiatrist Seeking Salvation." <u>GeoR</u> (32:1) Spr 78,
    p. 151.
  "Search Party." <u>SouthernPR</u> (18:2) Aut 78, p. 9.

LUDWIG, Tina
  "Gary Gilmore." <u>SeC</u> (5:2) 78, p. 51.
  "Madness." <u>SeC</u> (5:2) 78, p. 50.

LUHRMANN, Tom
  "Glimpses." <u>VirQR</u> (54:2) Spr 78, p. 284.
  "Moratorium." <u>VirQR</u> (54:2) Spr 78, p. 283.

LUKATCH, Neil
  "About What Is Said." <u>SouthernPR</u> (18:2) Aut 78, p. 82.
  "Boring." <u>SouthernPR</u> (18:2) Aut 78, p. 82.

LUMMIS, Suzanne
  "Finding Oneself." <u>Kayak</u> (47) F 78, p. 34.

LUNETTA, Mario
  "Elefanti Come Elefanti." <u>ChiR</u> (30:2) Aut 78, p. 42.

LUSK, Daniel
  "The Lion Tamer's Ring." Nimrod (22:2) Spr-Sum 78, p. 48.
  "One Last Love Poem." Nimrod (22:2) Spr-Sum 78, p. 46.
  "Two Marriage Songs." Nimrod (22:2) Spr-Sum 78, p. 47.

LUTTINGER, Abigail
  "After a Death." Nat (226:18) 13 My 78, p. 579.
  "Amagansett." Nat (226:12) 1 Ap 78, p. 380.
  "In Minnesota." PoNow (20) 78, p. 18.
  "My Mother Was Always Dressed." ParisR (72) Wint 77, p. 117.
  "The Palace for Teeth." Chowder (10/11) Aut-Wint 78-79,
      p. 71.
  "A True Story." ParisR (72) Wint 77, p. 116.

LUTZ, Gary
  "The Waiting Was All There Was." Wind (30) 78, p. 24.

LUX, Thomas
  "Capable as Hive" (for Carol). ParisR (74) Aut-Wint 78, p. 84.
  Eight poems. Antaeus (28) Wint 78, p. 117.
  "Flying Noises." Field (19) Aut 78, p. 63.
  "Next Image." AmerPoR (7:4) Jl-Ag 78, p. 32.
  "Poem Beginning with a Random Phrase from Coleridge."
      Poetry (132:2) My 78, p. 89.
  "This Is a Poem for the Fathers" (& for Michael Ryan).
      AmerPoR (7:4) Jl-Ag 78, p. 32.
  "View from a Porch." ParisR (74) Aut-Wint 78, p. 192.

LUXORIUS of Carthage
  "Epigrams" (tr. by Richard O'Connell). Playb (25:4) Ap 78,
      p. 157.

LYKE, Leo
  "The Big Monopoly Game." NewL (45:1) Aut 78, p. 65.

LYLES, Peggy Willis
  "All over." WindO (33) Aut-Wint 78-79.
  "Cold Snap in Georgia." StoneC (78:1) Wint 78, p. 10.
  "Love Affair." StoneC (78:1) Wint 78, p. 10.
  "Shorter Than the Cornstalks the Scarecrow." WindO (33) Aut-
      Wint 78-79.

LYMAN, Henry
  "On the Island of Ogygia" (tr. of Aleksis Rannit). Poetry
      (131:6) Mr 78, p. 321.

LYNN, Sandra
  "Anniversary." NewL (44:3) Spr 78, p. 68.
  "The Birth of Venus in the Gulf of Mexico." NewL (44:3) Spr
      78, p. 70.
  "Do-It-Yourself, Son of." NewL (44:3) Spr 78, p. 68.
  "The Fire Builder." NewL (44:3) Spr 78, p. 67.
  "No Poem." NewL (44:3) Spr 78, p. 69.

LYON, George Ella
"A Letter." CalQ (13/14) Spr-Sum 78, p. 86.
"Passage." SouthernPR (18:2) Aut 78, p. 39.
"The Syrup Bucket Lid." SouthernPR (18:2) Aut 78, p. 39.

LYONS, Richard
"Annunciation." Epoch (27:2) Wint 78, p. 173.
"Of Robert Lowell." DacTerr (15) Wint-Spr 77-78, p. 6.

LYONS, Tim
"Ebb Tide, Pacific." EnPas (7) 78, p. 15.

MAAS, Alberto
"I Have Journeyed Seeking Rain." SoDakR (16:4) Wint 78-79, p. 68.

McAFEE, Thomas
"The Actor." Wind (30) 78, p. 30.
"Back for the Last Funeral: The Accurate River." DacTerr
     (15) Wint-Spr 77-78, p. 14.
"Back for the Last Funeral: The Old Rugged Cross." DacTerr
     (15) Wint-Spr 77-78, p. 15.
"Back for the Last Funeral: The Stations." DacTerr (15) Wint-
     Spr 77-78, p. 14.
"The Children." PoNow (19) 78, p. 31.
"Introduction to the Drama." Wind (30) 78, p. 30.
"The Music." OhioR (19:1) Wint 78, p. 36.
"Running." PoNow (19) 78, p. 31.
"Sparrows and Zinnias." PoNow (19) 78, p. 31.
"Words for Hart Crane." MidwQ (19:3) Spr 78, p. 279.

McALEAVEY, David
"Baseball." NewRivR (2:2) 78, p. 47.
"Cecil." Chowder (10/11) Aut-Wint 78-79, p. 22.
"Day at the Beach of Naoussa (Paros)." CornellR (4) Aut 78,
     p. 43.
"Kiss of Fame." Wind (30) 78, p. 32.
"Transactions with Desire: A Chronology" (to my students,
     July 1978). Epoch (28:1) Aut 78, p. 79.
"Speech to Get Home." Wind (30) 78, p. 32.
"A True Story." Wind (30) 78, p. 33.

McALLISTER, Bruce
"Behavior During Plague." Chowder (10/11) Aut-Wint 78-78, p. 69.
"A Hymn." Chowder (10/11) Aut-Wint 78-79, p. 71.
"Life with Them." Chowder (10/11) Aut-Wint 78-79, p. 70.
"Poem on Your Teaching." Zahir (9) 77, p. 60.

McALLISTER, Byron L.
"Notes: Watching Bernstein's Mass on TV." DacTerr (15)
     Wint-Spr 77-78, p. 57.

McALPIN, Sandra
"Obituary for Otis Swain." CimR (44) Jl 78, p. 42.

McANALLY-KNIGHT, Mary
"The Day the Whales Committed Suicide." Nimrod (22:2) Spr-
Sum 78, p. 52.
"The Fat Lady Waits." NewL (44:3) Spr 78, p. 79.
"I Have Decided" (For every woman who has felt her life to be
empty without a man). Nimrod (22:2) Spr-Sum 78, p. 49.
"Now This Absence Cools." Nimrod (22:2) Spr-Sum 78, p.
50.
"Pieta, or Waiting at a Migrant Health Clinic." MoonsLT (2:4)
78, p. 37.
"Warning: Hitchhikers May Be Escaping Convicts." NewL (44:3)
Spr 78, p. 80.
"Winter Day at Leavenworth" (For Major Virgil P. McAnally).
MoonsLT (2:4) 78, p. 35.

MacANNA, Padraic
"Corn Dolly." Stand (18:4) 77, p. 64.

McAULEY, Almut
"Beautiful Rare Willow" (tr. of Rainer Malkowski). NewOR
(6:1) Aut 78, p. 25.
"I grind my watch into the sand" (tr. of Rainer Malkowski).
NewOR (6:1) 78, p. 25.
"Splitting" (tr. of Karin Kiwus). NewOR (6:1) 78, p. 26.
"Trapdoors" (tr. of Karin Kiwus). NewOR (6:1) 78, p. 27.

McAULEY, James J.
"The Exile Considers How His Life Is Spent." MalR (48) O 78,
p. 124.
"The Exile, En Famille." PoetryNW (19:1) Spr 78, p. 14.
"The Exile Takes Stock of His Surroundings." PoetryNW (19:1)
Spr 78, p. 13.
from Requiem: (IV, VI). NewOR (6:1) 78, p. 72.
"Studies for a Self-Portrait at Forty." MalR (48) O 78, p.
120.
"Timepiece." Poetry (133:1) O 78, p. 36.

McBRIDE, Mekeel
"At the Tables of the Famous." PoetryNW (19:2) Sum 78,
p. 26.
"The Climate of Paradox." Aspect (71) Ap-Je 77, p. 20.
Eight poems. Agni (8) 78, p. 78.
"The Fortune-Teller's Glass Hands." Kayak (47) F 78, p. 47.
"Mailmen at Dawn" (for Jeannie). Kayak (47) F 78, p. 48.
"Messages." PoetryNW (19:2) Sum 78, p. 27.
"People Who Deserve to Live in Light." Aspect (71) Ap-Je 77,
p. 22.
"Poem from a Typewriter Missing One Letter." Kayak (47) F
78, p. 50.
"A Series of Inward Turns." CalQ (13/14) Spr-Sum 78, p.
92.
"Sudden Attraction to Someone Not Quite a Stranger." Kayak

(47) F 78, p. 49.
"This October" (for Annie). Chowder (10/11) Aut-Wint 78-79, p. 44.
"The Whale Poem." Nat (227:12) 14 O 78, p. 383.

McCAFFERTY, H. W.
"A Nothingness of Time and A Time of Nothingness." DeKalb (11:1/2) Aut-Wint 77-78, p. 55.

McCAFFREY, Phillip
"The Aborigine." ColEng (40:3) N 78, p. 295.
"Moon Cast." ColEng (40:3) N 78, p. 296.
"The Tattoo Man." SouthernPR (18:2) Aut 78, p. 63.

McCALLION, Colleen
"Grace." Tele (14) 78.
"La Paz Bay." Tele (14) 78.
"Shirley." Tele (14) 78.

McCANN, Janet
"At the Travel Bureau." ChrC (95:18) 17 My 78, p. 532.
"Manet." Stonecloud (7) 78, p. 101.
"One Summer Morning." SouthernPR (18:2) Aut 78, p. 90.
"Poem with Alternate Lines Missing." NewL (45:2) Wint 78, p. 66.
"The Reason for Being Afraid of Witches." Stonecloud (7) 78, p. 33.
"Silence." Stonecloud (7) 78, p. 34.
"The Washing Up." SlowLR (1/2) 78, p. 76.

McCARTHY, Eugene
"Admiral Radford Crosses the Continental Divide." NewRep (179:5) 29 Jl 78, p. 28.

McCARTHY, Thomas
"The Word 'Silk.'" ParisR (74) Aut-Wint 78, p. 82.

McCARTY, Tom
"the machine and the other poet, at night." Smudge (1) Spr 78, p. 28.

McCLANAHAN, Tom
"Inspecting Whales on the Beach at Fripp Island, S. C." LitR (22:1) Aut 78, p. 125.

McCLANE, Kenneth A., Jr.
"Ithaca." Obs (4:1) 78, p. 82.
"Moosehead Lake." NowestR (17:1) 78, p. 49.
"No One May Rest." NowestR (17:1) 78, p. 51.
"On the Day of Ali's Retirement." Obs (4:1) Spr 78, p. 81.
"Saturday Night." Obs (4:1) Spr 78, p. 83.

McCLATCHY, J. D.
  "The Approach." Shen (29:2) Wint 78, p. 30.
  "Fetish." NewRep (179:20) 11 N 78, p. 28.

McCLELLAN, Jane
  "Scarcely Extinct." ColEng (39:8) Ap 78, p. 948.

McCLELLAN, Thomas
  "Dawn, the Two Marys." ChrC (95:10) 22 Mr 78, p. 303.

McCLELLAN, T. R.
  "Ascension." ChrC (95:16) 3 My 78, p. 462.

McCLOSKEY, Mark
  "Christmas." Poetry (19:4) Wint 78-79, p. 5.
  "Sixteen." PoetryNW (19:4) Wint 78-79, p. 6.

McCLURE, Michael
  "From Mount Tamalpais." Kayak (48) Je 78, p. 11.
  "Little Fantasies." Kayak (47) F 78, p. 15.

McCLUSKEY, Sally
  "A Good Trick, If You Can Keep It Up." Epos (27:2) 77, p. 7.
  "How We Passed the 'Danger Do Not Trespass' Sign and Climbed
    Widower's Hill." HiramPoR (24) Spr-Sum 78, p. 22.
  "To a Naturalist: Burning the Ticks." HiramPoR (24) Spr-Sum
    78, p. 23.
  "To a Rabbit, Dying Hard." Epos (27:1) 77, p. 12.

McCOMAS, Marilyn
  "Cleaning Lady." Wind (31) 78, p. 38.
  "That Summer." Wind (31) 78, p. 37.

McCOMBS, Judith
  "After the Surveyor's Death." ModernPS (9:2) Aut 78, p. 118.

McCORD, Howard L.
  "Backyard Outside." Hand (2) 78, p. 179.
  "Envoi." Hand (2) 78, p. 43.
  "Late Saturday." Hand (2) 78, p. 36.
  "Peach Mountain Smoke Out" (for Jennifer). Hand (2) 78, p. 37.

McCORMACK, Michael
  "The Great Composers Letters." Wind (28) 78, p. 46.

McCORQUONDALE, Robin
  "King Lion Two." Nor (8) Aut 78, p. 14.

McCOWN, Clint
  "Real-Life Romances." PoNow (20) 78, p. 25.
  "Sidetracks." PoNow (20) 78, p. 24.
  "Song of Experience." PoNow (20) 78, p. 25.
  "That's How It Was." PoNow (20) 78, p. 25.

McCOWN, Tom
    "Bombs." PoNow (20) 78, p. 31.
    "The Last Dinosaur." PoNow (20) 78, p. 31.
    "Roca's Dragon." PoNow (20) 78, p. 31.

McCULLAGH, James C.
    "For a Back-Sliding Cat." PoetC (10:2) 78, p. 8.
    "Prayer at the End of a Tomb." PartR (45:4) 78, p. 593.

McCULLEN, Kathleen
    "In the Varsity Bar." AmerPoR (7:6) N-D 78, p. 36.
    "Politics." AmerPoR (7:6) N-D 78, p. 36.
    "The Way Out at Deception Pass." AmerPoR (7:6) N-D 78,
        p. 36.

McCULLOUGH, Edward
    "Postcards." PikeF (1) Spr 78, p. 12.

McCULLOUGH, Ken
    "Amish Summer." PoNow (20) 78, p. 25.
    "Apparition." PoNow (20) 78, p. 25.
    "Cabin Fever." PoNow (20) 78, p. 25.
    "Montana: Midwinter." PoNow (20) 78, p. 25.

McCURDY, Harold
    "Emmaus." ChrC (95:10) 22 Mr 78, p. 293.
    "Galileo." Thought (53:208) Mr 78, p. 99.

McDERMOTT, Shirley A.
    "Relocated." Aspen (6) Aut 78, p. 58.

McDONALD, Barry
    "After the Freeze" (for C. C.). CutB (11) Aut-Wint 78, p. 57.

MacDONALD, Bernell
    "Old Photograph." Nimrod (22:2) Spr-Sum 78, p. 17.

MACDONALD, Cynthia
    "Francis Bacon, the Inventor of Spectacles Is the Ringmaster."
        Shen (29:4) Sum 78, p. 52.

McDONALD, Walter
    "Adapting" (for Jack Crocker). HiramPoR (24) Spr-Sum 78,
        p. 24.
    "Especially at Night." CarolQ (30:2) Spr-Sum 78, p. 87.
    "Filing System." GeoR (32:4) Wint 78, p. 796.
    "Great Expectations: A Short Story." GeoR (32:2) Sum 78,
        p. 340.
    "My Neighbor Who Kept Pigeons." CarolQ (30:2) Spr-Sum 78,
        p. 88.
    "On Teaching David to Shoot." SouthwR (63:4) Aut 78, p. 337.
    "Well I'll Be Damned." NoAmR (263:4) Wint 78, p. 14.

McDONOUGH, Paul
   "Diagenesis." ChiR (30:3) Wint 79, p. 136.
   "To Jane." ChiR (30:3) Wint 79, p. 137.

McDONOUGH, Thomas
   "Beneath the Abrupt Palisades." JnlONJP (2:2) 77, p. 13.

McDOWELL, Robert
   "Aardvark Bail Bonds." Kayak (49) O 78, back. Found poem.

McELROY, Colleen J.
   "Pulsing." SoDakR (16:3) Aut 78, p. 7.
   "This Is the Poem I Never Meant to Write." PoetryNW (19:3)
      Aut 78, p. 30.
   "Zeta and Xerosis." SoDakR (16:3) Aut 78, p. 5.

McELROY, Laurie
   "Nude with Chemise." Northeast (3:5) Spr-Sum 78, p. 23.

McELVEEN, Idris
   "Age." SouthernHR (12:3) Sum 78, p. 194.
   "Two at the Dock." SouthernPR (18:2) Aut 78, p. 38.

McENTEER, James
   "Getting Away from It All." MalR (48) O 78, p. 85.

McFARLAND, Ron
   "Ceramics Exhibit." SoDakR (16:2) Sum 78, p. 63.
   "Dialogues at the Bovill Tavern." WebR (4:1) Spr 78, p. 26.
   "Ted's Daughter." WebR (4:1) Spr 78, p. 27.

McFEE, Michael
   "St. Francis Receives the Stigmata from a Medieval Traveling
      Altar." SoCaR (11:1) N 78, p. 120.

McFERREN, Martha
   "Cutting Bread and Butter." Poem (33) Jl 78, p. 28.
   "The Piano in the Parlor." Poem (33) Jl 78, p. 26.

McGARTY, Ray
   "Brooklyn." GreenfieldR (6:3/4) Spr 78, p. 113.
   "Gloves." GreenfieldR (6:3/4) Spr 78, p. 113.

McGINLEY, Phyllis
   "Inland." Comm (105:7) 31 Mr 78, p. 194.

McGLOTHLIN, William J.
   "Perish, but Publish!" AAUP (64:1) Mr 78, p. 25.

McGOUGH, Roger
   "On Having No-One to Write a Love Poem About." NorthSR (8)
      Aut-Wint 78-79, p. 93.
   "Vandal." NorthSR (8) Aut-Wint 78-79, p. 94.

McGOWAN, James
"Beachclimbing at Seawall." HiramPoR (24) Spr-Sum 78, p. 26.
"'Cove's End.'" HiramPoR (24) Spr-Sum 78, p. 25.

McGRATH, Kristina
"If I Lay My Dreams on the Ground." Harp (257:1542) N 78, p. 104.
from Talking to the Back Parts of Light: (1, 2, 3, 4). ChiR
    (30:1) Sum 78, p. 24.
"The Visit." 13thM (4:1) 78, p. 32.

McGRATH, Thomas
"Higher Criticism." MinnR (NS10) Spr 78, p. 55.
"The Skull of the Horse." AmerPoR (7:1) 78, p. 47.

McGUINN, Rex
"A Lecture on Birth Control to the Book of the Month Club."
    St. AR (5:1) Aut-Wint 78, p. 139.

McGUIRE, Michael
"Nijinsky." Iowa (9:1) Wint 78, p. 39.

MACHADO, Antonio
"Fields of Soria" (tr. by William Zander). LitR (21:4) Sum 78,
    p. 475.
"The Flies" (tr. by William Zander). LitR (21:4) Sum 78,
    p. 474.

McHUGH, Heather
"Brightness." MoonsLT (2:4) 78, p. 24.
"Business." LittleM (11:3) Aut 77, p. 77.
"I Think." MoonsLT (2:4) 78, p. 22.
"Kindling." CornellR (3) Spr 78, p. 61.
"The Nymph to Narcissus." MoonsLT (2:4) 78, p. 21.
"The Nymph to Narcissus." Pequod (2:4) 78, p. 88.
"Retired Schoolteacher." NewYorker (54:40) 20 N 78, p. 210.
"Widow's Song." LittleM (11:3) Aut 77, p. 74.

McINERNEY, Brian
"Sounds." Hand (2) 78, p. 151.

MACK, Rick
"Coming Home." Wind (30) 78, p. 27.
"Huntington." Wind (30) 78, p. 26.
"Post-Consolidated Rock Creek School." Wind (30) 78, p. 27.
"While Waiting for a Train." Wind (30) 78, p. 26.

McKAIN, David
"Condemned." MinnR (NS11) Aut 78, p. 30.

McKAY, Anne
from when swans were blue: "and if i cannot bless." NewOR
    (6:1) 78, p. 74.

McKAY, Matthew

"Clearing." BallSUF (19:2) Spr 78, p. 54.
"The Kindness." PoNow (20) 78, p. 32.
"Kinship." CimR (43) Ap 78, p. 34.
"Nothing Has Changed but the Tree." StoneC (78:1) Wint 78, p. 12.

McKAY, Pamela
"To Mother Love." Chomo (5:2) Aut-Wint 78, p. 26.

McKEE, Carolyn
"Leukemia." NoAmR (263:4) Wint 78, p. 52.

McKEE, Louis
"Aesthetics." CarouselQ (3:2) Sum 78, p. 22.
"Lake Naomi." Tendril (2) Spr-Sum 78.
"A Matter of Style." StoneC (78:2) Spr 78, p. 34.
"The Secret." CarouselQ (3:2) Sum 78, p. 22.

MACKENZIE, Ginny
"Ars Amatoria." LittleM (11:4) Wint 78, p. 40.
"Provence Weekend." LittleM (11:3) Aut 77, p. 20.

McKEOWN, Tom
"Walking Peachtree Battle Avenue, Atlanta." NoAmR (263:1)
    Spr 78, p. 32.

McKERNAN, John
"My Name." Aspen (5) Spr 78, p. 53.
"The New Passport" (for a child beaten to death in Boston in
    January, 1975). Aspen (5) Spr 78, p. 55.
"Prayer Written After Burying a Pet Cat Killed While on a Win-
    ter Vacation in Massachusetts." Agni (8) 78, p. 101.

McKERNAN, Llewellyn
"A Cucumber." Aspen (5) Spr 78, p. 96.

McKEVITT, Garry
"Atrophy." MalR (45) Ja 78, p. 260.
"The Burial." MalR (45) Ja 78, p. 257.
"Dragons." MalR (45) Ja 78, p. 260.
"The Pride." MalR (45) Ja 78, p. 259.
"The Visitors." MalR (45) Ja 78, p. 258.

McKIM, Elizabeth
"Burning Through." Tendril (2) Spr-Sum 78.
"To Stay Alive." AndR (5:1) Spr 78, p. 82.
"Woman with Milkweed Meets Man from Deep Inside Whale."
    Tendril (2) Spr-Sum 78.

McKINLEY, James, Jr.
"Mallorca." NewL (45:1) Aut 78, p. 64.
"The Man Next Door." NewL (45:1) Aut 78, p. 64.

McKINNEY, Irene
"Nine Boxes." PoetryNW (19:3) Aut 78, p. 41.

McKINSEY, Martin
  "The Inexhaustible" (tr. of Yannis Ritsos). Falcon (16) 78,
      p. 122.
  "Insufficiency" (tr. of Yannis Ritsos). Falcon (16) 78, p. 120.
  "Old Men" (tr. of Yannis Ritsos). Falcon (16) 78, p. 104.
  "We Will Be Ready" (tr. of Yannis Ritsos). Falcon (16) 78, p. 103.

MACKLIN, Elizabeth
  "The Bird in the Dooryard." NewYorker (54:8) 10 Ap 78, p. 46.
  "Brooding." ParisR (73) Spr-Sum 78, p. 24.
  "A Woman Picks Up the Habit of Anger." NewYorker (54:40) 20
      N 78, p. 48.

McLAUGHLIN, Joseph
  "Capricorn." HiramPoR (24) Spr-Sum 78, p. 34.
  "Overtime." BallSUF (19:4) Aut 78, p. 10.

McLAUGHLIN, William
  "Jesus Freaks in Capitol Reef National Park." SmPd (43) 78, p. 35.

McLELLAND, Chris
  "Sections." AAR (28) 78, p. 68.

MacLOW, Jackson
  "1st Sharon Belle Mattlin Vocabulary Crossward Gatha." ChiR
      (30:3) Wint 79, p. 114.
  "Free Gatha 1." ChiR (30:3) Wint 79, p. 115.

McMAHON, Michael
  "1." Epos (27:1) 77, p. 16.
  "2." Epos (27:1) 77, p. 16.
  "3." Epos (27:1) 77, p. 16.
  "4." Epos (27:1) 77, p. 16.
  "Bosch." GreenfieldR (6:3/4) Spr 78, p. 123.
  "The Cars of the Rich." GreenfieldR (6:3/4) Spr 78, p. 125.
  "An Old Dandelion." GreenfieldR (6:3/4) Spr 78, p. 124.
  "Omens." GreenfieldR (6:3/4) Spr 78, p. 124.
  "Tomorrow, and Tomorrow, and Tomorrow." Epos (27:1) 77, p. 17.

McMULLEN, Richard E.
  "Bathrobes." Focus (13:79) Ja-F 78, p. 30.
  "My Grandmother's Anger." HangL (32) Spr 78, p. 37.

McNALLY, John
  "The Hundred Years War." Tele (13) 77.
  "In a New Year" (For Lee Enfield). Tele (13) 77.
  "Sunnybrook Farm." Tele (13) 77.

McNAMARA, Bob
  from Beatty, Oregon: (III). Zahir (9) 77, p. 47.

McNAMARA, Eugene
  "Hung Jury." StoneC (78:3) Aut 78, p. 27.
  "The Way Home." StoneC (78:3) Aut 78, p. 27.

McNAUGHTON, William
  "Sennin by the River" (tr. of Nalan Hsingte, w. Lenore Mayhew).
    NewOR (6:1) 78, p. 57.

McNEIL, Florence
  "The Miner." MalR (45) Ja 78, p. 293.
  "Pictures from Barkerville." MalR (45) Ja 78, p. 296.
  "To Julius H. Franklyn, Late of Barkerville 1847-1870." MalR
    (45) Ja 78, p. 298.

McNEILL, Julie
  "B. E. P." MalR (48) O 78, p. 118.

McNEILL, Patricia
  "Old Age." SeC (5:2) 78, p. 53.

McNITZKY, Michael
  "The Forest Route Toward Home." Wind (31) 78, p. 39.

McNULTY, Tim
  "Ice in Love." Kayak (47) F 78, p. 61.

MacPHEE, Rosalind
  "Coming to This." MalR (45) Ja 78, p. 135.

McPHERSON, Sandra
  "The Compound Eye." Antaeus (28) Wint 78, p. 97.
  "Dependence on Flowers." Field (18) Spr 78, p. 100.
  "For Neruda: Political Landscape." Poetry (131:6) Mr 78,
    p. 332.
  "The Memoir" (a fragment for the Emerson sisters). Antaeus
    (30/31) Sum-Aut 78, p. 133.
  "On a Picture of My Parents Together in the Second Grade."
    Antaeus (28) Wint 78, p. 99.
  "Orange Peels." Antaeus (28) Wint 78, p. 100.
  "Sensing." Field (18) Spr 78, p. 102.
  "Smoking: Notes." Poetry (131:6) Mr 78, p. 333.
  "The Steps." Antaeus (30/31) Sum-Aut 78, p. 131.
  "Umbra." Poetry (131:6) Mr 78, p. 335.

McWHINNEY, Norman N.
  "Elpenor." SlowLR (1/2) 78, p. 23.

McWHIRTER, George
  "A Journal for Don Caamano." MalR (45) Ja 78, p. 56.

MADDEN, David
  "Minimal Responses." WormR (70) 78, p. 46.
  "Monuments at the Last Moment." WormR (70) 78, p. 46.

MADDOX, Everette
  "Heard (Glider) Poem." NewRivR (2:2) 78, p. 42.
  "Late at Night." NewRivR (2:2) 78, p. 41.

MADIGAN, Brother
  "Upon Not Seeing My Poem Appear in the English Journal, May
    1977." EngJ (67:5) My 78, p. 50.

MADSEN, Rose Ann
  "Behold me; Hear me; Cherish me." DeKalb (11:3/4) Spr-Sum
    78, p. 105.

MAGEE, Cinda
  "The Hotel Warham." PikeF (1) Spr 78, p. 19.

MAGEE, Wes
  "On the Esplanade." Poetry (133:1) O 78, p. 33.

MAGNUSSON, Sigurdur A.
  "At a Deathbed." St. AR (4:3/4) 77-78, p. 120.
  "A Child Lost." St. AR (4:3/4) 77-78, p. 120.
  "Finale." St. AR (4:3/4) 77-78, p. 120.

MAGORIAN, James
  "Badly-Gored Explorer Reading Poetry at a Debutante Party."
    Smudge (3) Aut 78, p. 37.
  "Canada Lily." Sam (65) 78, p. 61.
  "The Day Before the Fourth of July." Tendril (3) Aut 78,
    p. 40.
  "The Edge of the Forest in November." Wind (28) 78, p. 21.
  "Sawed-Off Shotgun." Bits (7) Ja 78.
  "The Society for the Prevention of Poetry Workshops." Smudge
    (3) Aut 78, p. 33.
  "Trajectories." Wind (28) 78, p. 30.

MAGOWAN, Robin
  "At the Waltz." Kayak (47) F 78, p. 33.
  "Fog: Two Wings, One House" (with Michael Beard). Kayak
    (47) F 78, p. 32.
  "Lake." Kayak (47) F 78, p. 33.

MAGRATH, William T.
  "Thetis: After-Thoughts of a Shape-Shifter." BallSUF (19:4)
    Aut 78, p. 4.

MAGWAZA, C. R.
  "The Lifeguard." Poem (34) Jl 78, p. 11.
  "Lines Composed inside a Rubbish Heap Refrigerator." Poem
    (34) N 78, p. 13.
  "Nail Hook in Moon Light." Poem (34) N 78, p. 14.
  "Neighbors." CarolQ (30:2) Spr-Sum 78, p. 84.
  "The X-Rayed Zebra." Poem (34) Jl 78, p. 12.

MAHAPATRA, Jayanta
  "A Kind of Happiness." Poetry (131:4) Ja 78, p. 215.
  "Remembering." St. AR (4:3/4) 77-78, p. 108.
  "Shrines." St. AR (4:3/4) 77-78, p. 109.

"Song of the Past." Poetry (131:4) Ja 78, p. 211.
"The Storm." Poetry (131:4) Ja 78, p. 213.
"Sun Worshiper Bathing in the Ganga." St. AR (4:3/4) 77-78,
    p. 108.
"Violence." NewRep (178:9) 4 Mr 78, p. 31.
"The Wound." Poetry (131:4) Ja 78, p. 214.

MAHER, James
"Baltimore Morning." CarouselQ (3:3) Aut 78, p. 12.

MAHON, Derek
"Ford Manor." LitR (22:2) Wint 78, p. 231.
"Goodbye to the Trees." LitR (22:2) Wint 79, p. 231.
"Penshurst Place." LitR (22:2) Wint 79, p. 236.
"Sole." LitR (22:2) Wint 79, p. 236.
"Surrey Poems." LitR (22:2) Wint 79, p. 234.

MAHON, Robert Lee
"The Assignation." WebR (4:1) Spr 78, p. 61.
"On First Looking into John Keats: Koko the Great Ape Reflects
    for a Newsweek Reporter." WebR (4:1) Spr 78, p. 60.

MAHONY, Medb
"Fragment of a Letter from Anne O'Brian to Her Grandfather."
    Aspect (71) Ap-Je 77, p. 23.
"Fragment of a Letter from Patrick O'Brian to His Grand-
    daughter." Aspect (71) Ap-Je 77, p. 23.

MAILMAN, Leo
"the boar." PoNow (20) 78, p. 24.
"Kid Dracula." PoNow (19) 78, p. 25.
"omniDad." PoNow (20) 78, p. 24.
"picnic love." PoNow (20) 78, p. 24.
"Picnic Love." WormR (68) 77, p. 93.
"The Sears Caper." WormR (68) 77, p. 92.

MAINO, Jeannette
"First Parting." SouthwR (63:1) Wint 78, p. 9.

MAISNER, Kathleen A.
"To Heather." EngJ (67:5) My 78, p. 64.

MAJOR, Clarence
from Emergency Exit: "Al is standing naked." Obs (4:2) Sum
    78, p. 54.
"Night of the Amnesty" (tr. of Fazil Husnu Daglarca). Aspen
    (6) Aut 78, p. 37.
"Pencil Sketch." Aspen (6) Aut 78, p. 36.

MAKI, Victoria
"The Woman and the Child." YellowBR (10) 78, p. 12.

MAKUCK, Peter
"Depayse." Nat (227:8) 16 S 78, p. 251.

"Nights. " NewRivR (2:2) 78, p. 50.
"Pitt County, North Carolina. " SouthernPR (18:2) Aut 78, p. 25.

MALANGA, Gerald
  "Coda: Bringing Up Baby. " Glass (3:1/2/3) 78, p. 34.

MALKOWSKI, Rainer
  "Beautiful Rare Willow" (tr. by Almut McAuley). NewOR (6:1)
      78, p. 25.
  "I grind my watch into the sand" (tr. by Almut McAuley).
      NewOR (6:1) 78, p. 25.

MALLARME
  "Angst" (tr. by R. Sieburth and S. W. DeRachewiltz). St. AR
      (5:1) Aut-Wint 78, p. 62.

MALLEY, Kathleen
  "Confrontation" (one last time, for Betty). CarouselQ (3:1) Spr
      78, p. 14.
  "Flower of the Night. " Wind (30) 78, p. 9.
  "Under the Spell of the North Wind. " Wind (30) 78, p. 29.

MALON, Michael
  "The Advance Gardening Memoranda. " Epoch (28:1) Aut 78,
      p. 49.

MALONE, Hank
  "An Ageless Situation. " Smudge (3) Aut 78, p. 23.
  "Artists? ... Artists? ... We Don't Need No Stinkin' Artists. "
      Smudge (3) Aut 78, p. 22.
  "Few Write Antarctic" (for Daniel Hughes). Sam (69) 78, p. 28.
  "A Perfect American Life. " Smudge (2) Sum 78, p. 7.
  "Survivors, Rock and Roll Drop-Outs. " Smudge (2) Sum 78,
      p. 8.
  "What's the Use of Being a Poet Anymore?" Smudge (1) Spr 78,
      p. 11.

MALONEY, John
  "No Sonnet at the Ocean. " SouthernPR (18:2) Aut 78, p. 11.

MALONEY, Linda
  "The Siamese Fighting Fish. " Pan (19) 77, p. 35.
  "Wednesday. " Pan (19) 77, p. 35.

MANDEL, Charlotte
  "At the Home. " Iowa (9:4) Aut 78, p. 33.
  "The Grauballe Man. " JnlONJP (3:1) 78, p. 8.
  "I Wake Ignorant as Ever of the Mechanics of Things. " JnlONJP
      (3:1) 78, p. 9.
  "Soundings. " JnlONJP (2:2) 77, p. 7.
  "Stimulus at Nine A. M. " JnlONJP (3:1) 78, p. 7.
  "To a Suicide. " JnlONJP (2:2) 77, p. 7.
  "To the Ocean (Coney Island). " JnlONJP (2:1) 77, p. 18.

"Working with the Half-Dream. "   StoneC (78:3) Aut 78,
      p. 20.

MANDEL, Tom
   "Charles, A Date Ramble. "   Hills (5) 78, p. 119.

MANDELBAUM, Allen
   "The Ayre of All. "   DenQ (13:4) Wint 79, p. 79.
   "The Ayre of the Triste Chair. "   DenQ (13:4) Wint 79, p. 77.
   "Four Phantoms from the Far Savanna. "   DenQ (13:4) Wint 79,
      p. 81.

MANESS, Rhonda
   "Scratching at the Door. "   Poem (32) Mr 78, p. 35.

MANFRED, Freya
   "Dirt Road. "   PoNow (20) 78, p. 24.
   "Love on the Lake. "   PoNow (20) 78, p. 24.
   "My Basketball Brother Versus Windom. "   PoNow (19) 78, p. 40.
   "Moon Light. "   PoNow (20) 78, p. 24.

MANGAN, Kathy
   "Cold Snap. "   GeoR (32:1) Spr 78, p. 93.
   "Dead Letter. "   GreenfieldR (6:3/4) Spr 78, p. 136.
   "Proof. "   GeoR (32:1) Spr 78, p. 92.

MANLEY, Frank
   "Gloss. "   SewanR (86:1) Wint 78, p. 39.
   "Laughter. "   SewanR (86:1) Wint 78, p. 39.

MANNES, Marya
   "Canticles to Men--A Sonnet Sequence" (Nine sonnets).   NewL
      (45:2) Wint 78, p. 48.

MAO Tse-tung
   "The Pass" (tr. by Paul Ching Lee).   NewOR (6:1) 78, p. 50.

MAPLES, Evelyn
   "New Year. "   ChrC (95:43) 27 D 78, p. 1259.

MARABLE, Manning
   "Cuttin Cane. "   Wind (31) 78, p. 32.
   "deja vu. "   Wind (31) 78, p. 32.

MARCH, Katherine B.
   "Anticipation. "   CarouselQ (3:4) Wint 78, p. 27.

MARCHANT, Frederick
   "A baptismal photograph. "   Aspect (71) Ap-Je 77, p. 15.

MARCUS, Adrianne
   "Complimentary Close. "   PoNow (19) 78, p. 38.

MARCUS, Marne
"Desolation." BallSUF (19:4) Aut 78, p. 17.
"Disco Medicine." CarouselQ (3:2) Sum 78, p. 26.

MARCUS, Mordecai
"Archer and Bird and Girl." Wind (28) 78, p. 42.
"A Slow Saraband." Tele (13) 77.

MARCUS, Stanley
"Night." Epos (27:1) 77, p. 22.

MARCY, Sherry
"Couple." SoDakR (16:3) Aut 78, p. 107.

MARGOLIS, Gary
"Bearing Children." MidwQ (20:1) Aut 78, p. 95.
"Hitching Home I Strike a Mountain Underseas." ColEng (39:8)
    Ap 78, p. 949.
"Planting Asparagus." ColEng (40:4) D 78, p. 423.
"The Stroke." MidwQ (20:1) Aut 78, p. 98.
"Three Scenes." MidwQ (20:1) Aut 78, p. 96.

MARION, Jeff Daniel
"At the Wayside." NewRivR (2:2) 78, p. 24.
"Barsha Buchannan, 1858-1929." Epoch (27:2) Wint 78, p. 129.

MARKHAM, Robert
"Owl." Aspen (5) Spr 78, p. 122.

MARKS, S. J.
"Abandoned." AmerPoR (7:4) Jl-Ag 78, p. 33.
"Early One Sleepless." AmerPoR (7:4) Jl-Ag 78, p. 33.
"Happiness." AmerPoR (7:4) Jl-Ag 78, p. 32.

MARKS, Steven Dale
"Wurgen." CarouselQ (3:2) Sum 78, p. 5.

MARKS, Suzanne
"Swallows." Tele (13) 77.

MARLOW, M. D.
"The Heap." Smudge (2) Sum 78, p. 55.

MARQUEZ, Roberto
"A Fable" (tr. of Igor Calvo). Iowa (9:4) Aut 78, p. 76.
"Geometry" (tr. of Jaime Galarza). MassR (19:2) Sum 78,
    p. 248.
"The Heartache and Thousand Natural Shocks" (tr. of Juan
    Gelman). Iowa (9:4) Aut 78, p. 77.

MARRAFFINO, Elizabeth
"And afterwards we lay apart on the bed." Hand (2) 78, p. 123.

"Left here for a month. " Hand (2) 78, p. 124.
"You had left her earlier. " Hand (2) 78, p. 124.

MARSH, Carol
"Gas. " Bachy (12) Aut 78, p. 63.
"I give up your shoes. " Bachy (12) Aut 78, p. 64.
"Moving. " Bachy (12) Aut 78, p. 63.
"Someone's Hands Are Prepared. " Bachy (12) Aut 78, p. 64.

MARSHALL, Benjamin V.
"January. " Nimrod (22:2) Spr-Sum 78, p. 4.
"Proposal. " Nimrod (22:2) Spr-Sum 78, p. 5.
"To One Enclosed, a Letter. " Nimrod (22:2) Spr-Sum 78, p. 6.

MARSHALL, George
"Weary as Salmon." Nimrod (22:2) Spr-Sum 78, p. 4.

MARSHALL, John
"Knight Inlet Sky" (for R. K.). MalR (45) Ja 78, p. 309.

MARSHALL, Kathy
"one man's song is another man's poetry. " SeC (5:2) 78, p. 52.

MARTENS, Wayne
"Rain. " Poem (32) Mr 78, p. 40.
"Seasons--Winter. " Poem (32) Mr 78, p. 41.

MARTIN, James
"Leaving Arles. " Poetry (132:1) Ap 78, p. 15.

MARTIN, Jeanne Iacona
"Saint James Park. " CarouselQ (3:3) Aut 78, p. 28.

MARTIN, Jim
"The Ice Cream Maker. " Wind (30) 78, p. 28.
"We Are Not Each Other. " Wind (30) 78, p. 28.

MARTIN, Joan M.
"memories and rainy nights. " BelPoJ (29:2) Wint 78-79, p. 33.
"song for Noel Pointer. " BelPoJ (29:2) Wint 78-79, p. 33.

MARTIN, Robert A.
"At the Theatre on Opening Night. " JnlOPC (12:1) Sum 78,
    p. 10.

MARTIN, Stephanie
"By Their Voices Forced to Attend. " NowestR (17:1) 78, p. 65.
from 'the props assist the house': "the millyard house. "
    Epoch (28:1) Aut 78, p. 69.

MARTIN, Stephen H.
"Follow the Gleam. " Poem (32) Mr 78, p. 9.
"Lyric. " Poem (32) Mr 78, p. 8.

MARTINEZ, Juan Roque Domingo
"Metamorphose Sizing." Bachy (11) Spr 78, p. 32.

MARTINSON, David
"Canadian Flights." DacTerr (15) Wint-Spr 77-78, p. 28.
"The Plasma of Spacious Mind." DacTerr (15) Wint-Spr 77-78,
    p. 28.

MARTINSON, Harry
"No Name for It" (tr. by Robert Bly). MoonsLT (2:4) 78,
    p. 42.

MARTON, Alex B.
"Gone." Harp (256:1534) Mr 78, p. 27.

MARTY, Miriam
"Raku." CarolQ (30:2) Spr-Sum 78, p. 113.

MARY Marguerite, Sister
"Three Haiku." PikeF (1) Spr 78, p. 21.

MARZUKI, Marcy
"Amber Eyes." PikeF (1) Spr 78, p. 18.
"White Heat." PikeF (1) Spr 78, p. 18.

MASARIK, Al
from Broken Hips & Rusty Scooters: "dirge." Vaga (27) Spr
    78, p. 65.
"brush fire." Vaga (28) Aut 78, p. 32.
"chowder." Vaga (27) Spr 78, p. 43.
"every august." Vaga (27) Spr 78, p. 46.
"high rise." Vaga (27) Spr 78, p. 44.
"old woman on the pier." Vaga (28) Aut 78, p. 34.
"A Post Card from Al Masarik." Vaga (28) Aut 78, p. 50.
"sparrows." Vaga (28) Aut 78, p. 33.
"the wind sits in an empty white rocker opens a dusty black
    bible red rose petals fly up like frightened pigeons." Vaga
    (28) Aut 78, p. 35.

MASIELLO, Thomas
"Music" (for Joan Ravera). ParisR (74) Aut-Wint 78, p. 196.

MASKALERIS, Thanasis
"Chile" (for Allende and Neruda) (tr. of Yannis Ritsos). Falcon
    (16) 78, p. 12.

MASON, Chris
"on blue construction paper." Tele (14) 78.
"poem for Donna." Tele (14) 78.
"up & up mount fuji little snail" (for Marshall Reese). LaB (11)
    78, p. 25.

MASON, John
"I love a yarn." Hills (5) 78, p. 76.

MASON, Yvonne
"Lifeblood." St. AR (4:3/4) 77-78, p. 130.

MASSARO, S. A.
"At the Gates." Wind (29) 78, p. 32.
"Brief Companions." Wind (29) 78, p. 32.

MASSEY, Grace
"Graveyard." AndR (5:2) Aut 78, p. 60.

MASTERS, Carol
"Late." AAR (28) 78, p. 39.
"Pond Behind the Freeway." AAR (28) 78, p. 41.
"Two Oranges." AAR (28) 78, p. 40.

MASTERSON, Dan
"The Man Who Steals Thumbs." PoNow (19) 78, p. 42.
"Whatever You Say, Henry" (For Henry V. Larom 1903-1975).
    ParisR (72) Wint 77, p. 154.

MASUCCI, Janice
"My post and periodic lover wrote a poem." EngJ (67:5) My 78,
    p. 65.

MATASKER, Jill
"Man's Best Friend." JnlONJP (3:1) 78, p. 22.

MATCHETT, William H.
"Painting the Table." NewRep (179:5) 29 Jl 78, p. 26.

MATHIS, Cleopatra
"Family Life." DenQ (13:2) Sum 78, p. 25.
"Finding the Quarry: For Bill." DenQ (13:2) Sum 78, p. 24.
"Getting Out." NewYorker (54:9) 17 Ap 78, p. 115.
"Mimosa." GeoR (32:2) Sum 78, p. 387.
"Padre Island: A Sanctuary." Nat (227:2) 8-15 Jl 78, p. 54.
"Ruston, Louisiana: 1952." DenQ (13:2) Sum 78, p. 26.
"Snow." DenQ (13:2) Sum 78, p. 27.

MATSON, Clive
"Blocked in Contrasts." HangL (34) Wint 78-79, p. 39.

MATSUDA, Sumio
"Illusion." ConcPo (11:2) Aut 78, p. 11.
"Mad Song for Myself." Epos (27:1) 77, p. 14.
"Old Movies." ConcPo (11:2) Aut 78, p. 12.
"Only I Am Here." Epos (27:1) 77, p. 15.

MATTE, Robert, Jr.
"After the Sun Goes Down." Wind (31) 78, p. 34.
"Bent Hook, Broken Line, No Sinker." WormR (70) 78, p. 48.
"Fireworks and Ferris Wheel." WormR (70) 78, p. 49.
"Gauntlet." Wind (31) 78, p. 35.
"The Hunt." Wind (31) 78, p. 34.

"Laughing Stock" (for captain threshold).   WormR (70) 78, p. 50.
"Midway." Vaga (27) Spr 78, p. 87.
"Nevermore." WormR (70) 78, p. 49.
"Orphan." YellowBR (10) 78, p. 34.

MATTERN, Gracie
  "The Judgment." Chomo (5:2) Aut-Wint 78, p. 67.

MATTERN, Robert
  "Initiations." ModernPS (9:3) Aut 78, p. 218.
  "Perspectives on Love." ModernPS (9:2) Aut 78, p. 154.

MATTESON, George
  "Charles B. Wilcox." St. AR (5:1) Aut-Wint 78, p. 125.
  "Charlestown Pond." St. AR (5:1) Aut-Wint 78, p. 126.
  "Gulls at Sunset." St. AR (5:1) Aut-Wint 78, p. 125.
  "The Magic Man." St. AR (5:1) Wint 78, p. 40.
  "The Magic Man." St. AR (5:1) Aut-Wint 78, p. 116.
  "The price the same for silver as for coal" (To Timothy H.
      O'Sullivan who in 1868 set his camera at the mouth of the
      Savage Mine). Tele (14) 78.
  "Waiting for Snow." St. AR (5:1) Aut-Wint 78, p. 115.

MATTHAY, Camy
  "tonight please." Box (7) Spr 78, p. 30.

MATTHEW, Tonia
  "Too Late for Unicorns." CalQ (13/14) Spr-Sum 78, p. 106.

MATTHEWS, Jack
  "The Search." PoNow (19) 78, p. 36.

MATTHEWS, Lena Dale
  "Saint Valentine's Day Masque." Shen (29:3) Spr 78, p. 38.

MATTHEWS, William
  "A Hairpin Turn above Reading, Jamaica." MissouriR (2:1) Aut
      78, p. 26.
  "How to Kill Your Analyst." Bits (7) Ja 78.
  "In Memory of the Utah Stars." Iowa (9:1) Wint 78, p. 27.
  "Isla Mujeres." AmerPoR (7:5) S-O 78, p. 12.
  "Landmarks." Aspen (5) Spr 78, p. 121.
  "Long." Antaeus (28) Wint 78, p. 128.
  "The New Life." Bits (8) Jl 78.
  "A Roadside Near Ithaca, NY." Antaeus (30/31) Sum-Aut 78,
      p. 130.
  "Skin Diving." AmerPoR (7:5) S-O 78, p. 12.
  "A Small Room in Aspen." Antaeus (30/31) Sum-Aut 78,
      p. 128.
  "Snow Falling through Fog." OhioR (19:2) Spr-Sum 78, p. 69.
  "Spring Snow." Antaeus (28) Wint 78, p. 127.
  "Waking at Dusk from a Nap." Antaeus (30/31) Sum-Aut 78,
      p. 127.

MATTLIN, Sharon Belle
 "Tongue Poem." Tele (14) 78.
 "You." Tele (13) 77.
 "You Dance." Tele (14) 78.

MAURA, Sister
 "Little Elegy for Pope John Paul." ChrC (95:35) 1 N 78,
   p. 1039.
 "When She Came into Jerusalem." ChrC (95:5) 15 F 78, p. 162.

MAURER, Bonnie
 from Ms. Lilly Jane Babbitt before the 10 o'clock bus from
   Memphis ran her over: Eight poems. Northeast (3:6) Wint
   78-79, p. 23-29.
 "never take candy from strangers." BelPoJ (29:1) Aut 78,
   p. 45.

MAXSON, Gloria
 "Annunciation." ChrC (95:41) 13 D 78, p. 1203.
 "Denominational." ChrC (95:40) 6 D 78, p. 1174.
 "Ritualist." ChrC (95:5) 15 F 78, p. 160.
 "Squanto Plants the Corn." ChrC (95:39) 29 N 78, p. 1159.
 "Student." ChrC (95:33) 18 O 78, p. 979.
 "The Town Clock." ChrC (95:3) 25 Ja 78, p. 73.

MAXSON, H. A.
 "From: Walker in the Storm." JnlONJP (3:1) 78, p. 11.
 "Seabright, Shells, and a Woman Floating in the Moon." Nat
   (227:17) 18 N 78, p. 550.
 "Winter Apples." Confr (16) Spr-Sum 78, p. 77.

MAXWELL, Anne
 "Ballad." AmerPoR (7:4) Jl-Ag 78, p. 33.
 "the employer." FourQt (27:4) Sum 78, p. 19.
 "Indulgence." AmerPoR (7:4) Jl-Ag 78, p. 33.
 "Omen." AmerPoR (7:4) Jl-Ag 78, p. 33.

MAY, Connie
 "America: The Invitation and Rejection." AAR (28) 78, p. 43.
 "A Celebration of Nothingness." AAR (28) 78, p. 44.
 Fourteen poems. UTR (5:3) 77, pp. 19-32.
 "A Purity of Crabs." AAR (28) 78, p. 42.

MAY, Wong
 "Flowers in History" (Homage to Hilda Morley). Madem (84:6)
   Je 78, p. 110.

MAYAKOVSKY, Vladimir
 "Atlantic Ocean" (tr. by Harry Lewis and Vitalij Keis). Pequod
   (2:4) 78, p. 19.

MAYER, Bernadette
 "Baby Come Today, October 4th." SunM (5) Aut 78, p. 83.

"The Marble Faun." PartR (45:2) 78, p. 268.
"Nadja." Tele (14) 78.
"So I Spill the Ink." SunM (5) Aut 78, p. 85.
"Very Strong February." SunM (5) Aut 78, p. 78.
"What's Meant for Pleasure." SunM (5) Aut 78, p. 80.

MAYFIELD, Carl
"I Leave the Destruction of the Earth to Those Who Know How."
    Wind (31) 78, p. 36.
"Spring Storm." Wind (31) 78, p. 36.

MAYHALL, Jane
"As I Was Trying." PoNow (19) 78, p. 6.
"A Self-Taught, Contemplating Language." Humanists (38:3)
    My-Je 78, p. 60.

MAYHEW, Lenore
"Sennin by the River" (tr. of Nalan Hsingte, w. William
    McNaughton). NewOR (6:1) 78, p. 57.

MAZZARO, Jerome
"Aftermaths." Salm (42) Sum-Aut 78, p. 121.
"Blue Haze." Salm (42) Sum-Aut 78, p. 120.
"Buffalo/Stasis." Hudson (31:1) Spr 78, p. 113.
"Driving South." Hudson (31:1) Spr 78, p. 112.
"Jungle Gardens." Hudson (31:1) Spr 78, p. 111.
"Noon, Toronto." Hudson (31:1) Spr 78, p. 111.
"This Weather." Confr (16) Spr-Sum 78, p. 14.

MAZZOCCO, Robert
"Trader." NewYorker (53:51) 6 F 78, p. 34.
"Victory." NewYRB (25:20) 21 D 78, p. 47.

MBEMBE (Milton Smith)
"Doing Manhours in the Madhouse." GreenfieldR (6:3/4) Spr
    78, p. 68.
"Ralph." GreenfieldR (6:3/4) Spr 78, p. 67.
"Rocking Chair Therapy." GreenfieldR (6:3/4) Spr 78, p. 66.

MBERI, Antar Sudan Katara
"Deep and Resonant Clay." Obs (4:1) Spr 78, p. 85.
"The Insurgents." Obs (4:1) Spr 78, p. 86.

MEDER, Manfred
"Love." NewL (45:2) Wint 78, p. 68.
"Slapstick: The Art." NewL (45:2) Wint 78, p. 67.

MEDINA, Pablo
"For the End of Winter." US1 (11) Aut 78, p. 6.
"The Ivory Tower." US1 (11) Aut 78, p. 6.
"On the Death of a Spanish Poet." US1 (11) Aut 78, p. 6.

MEEK, Jay
"Child Molester." PoNow (20) 78, p. 26.

"The Farmhouse." Iowa (9:1) Wint 78, p. 32.
"Narrative Assumptions." DacTerr (15) Wint-Spr 77-78, p. 66.
"Rhapsody on a Theme." Confr (17) Aut-Wint 79, p. 164.
"Runaways." PoNow (20) 78, p. 26.
"The Week the Dirigible Came." PoNow (20) 78, p. 26.

MEINKE, Peter
    "The Artist." Poetry (133:3) D 78, p. 146.
    "Azaleas." Poetry (133:3) D 78, p. 144.
    "Elephant Tusks." Poetry (133:3) D 78, p. 147.
    "J Randall Randle." PoNow (20) 78, p. 26.
    "Momia." PoNow (20) 78, p. 26.
    "Playing Badminton: Sunday Afternoon 1968." Poetry (133:3) D
        78, p. 148.
    "The Night Train." PoNow (20) 78, p. 26.

MEIRELES, Cecília
    "Imaginary Bath" (For Dulce) (tr. by Nina Cascio). Paint (9/10)
        Spr-Aut 78, p. 45.
    "Sketches" (tr. by Nina Cascio). Paint (9/10) Spr-Aut 78,
        p. 44.

MEISSNER, Willaim
    "The Coal Mine Disaster's Last Trapped Man Contemplates Sal-
        vation." MidwQ (19:3) Spr 78, p. 280.
    "The Game." MidwQ (19:3) Spr 78, p. 281.
    "How to Avoid Being Struck by Lightning." NewL (45:2) Wint
        78, p. 58.
    "In Composition the Rules for Writing Good." EngJ (67:5) My
        78, p. 62.
    "The Lines in the Road Are Guesses." Northeast (3:5) Spr-Sum
        78, p. 48.
    "The Lip Collector." Box (7) Spr 78, p. 26.
    "Messages from A Found Bottle." GRR (9:2) 78, p. 143.
    "The Phantom of the Supermarket." PoetryNW (19:1) Spr 78,
        p. 44.
    "The UFO in Iowa." PoetryNW (19:1) Spr 78, p. 43.

MELINESCU, Gabriela
    "Alternative" (tr. by Michael Impey and Brian Swann). WebR
        (4:1) Spr 78, p. 3.
    "The Butterfly" (tr. by Michael Impey and Brian Swann). WebR
        (4:1) Spr 78, p. 6.
    "Fall" (tr. by Michael Impey and Brian Swann). WebR (4:1)
        Spr 78, p. 3.
    "John Climbing the Darkened Ladder" (tr. by Michael Impey and
        Brian Swann). WebR (4:1) Spr 78, p. 4.

MELLARD, Joan
    "Birthday Poem for a Student-Turned-Colleague." EngJ (67:5)
        My 78, p. 61.

MELLICK, Lee
    "A. M." PraS (52:1) Spr 78, p. 20.

"A Little Water, But No Fruit." PraS (52:1) Spr 78,
    p. 19.

MELLO, Bruce
"How Like Chagall's Lovers." Stonecloud (7) 78, p. 100.

MELLOTT, Leland
"A Kingdom of Sanctum" (for Chris). Wind (29) 78, p. 33.
"My Grandmother." Wind (29) 78, p. 34.

MELNYCZUK, Askold
"A Life of Surprises." Zahir (9) 77, p. 44.
"Swan Song." Ploughs (4:2) 78, p. 27.

MELTON, Keith
"Brother Nicholas and the Swans." Confr (17) Aut-Wint 79,
    p. 23.
"Thunderhead." DeKalb (11:3/4) Spr-Sum 78, p. 38.

MELTZER, David
"Rocks for AZ." Some (9) 78, p. 95.

MELVIN, Patricia
Found poem. Kayak (48) Je 78, p. 12.

MENDELSON, Chaim
"Deep Sleep." Epos (27:1) 77, p. 26.
"Lessons 10." ConcPo (11:1) Spr 78, p. 26.
"Lessons 12." ConcPo (11:1) Spr 78, p. 26.
"Lessons 15." ConcPo (11:1) Spr 78, p. 26.

MENDES, Murilo
from Ipotesi: "Jean Arp." GRR (9:2) 78, p. 94.
from Ipotesi: "Klee." GRR (9:2) 78, p. 96.
from Ipotesi: "Il Quadro." GRR (9:2) 78, p. 90.

MENEBROKER, Ann
"In the Half-Point Time of Night." Vaga (28) Aut 78, p. 68.

MEREDITH, Joseph E.
"Intimations of Closing on Opening Night." FourQt (27:4) Sum
    78, p. 15.

MEREDITH, William
"Parents." NewYorker (54:6) 27 Mr 78, p. 42.
"Remembering Robert Lowell." NewRep (178:9) 4 Mr 78, p. 30.

MERNIT, Susan
"for A Swan." Hand (2) 78, p. 211.
"The Old Woman's Song." Hand (2) 78, p. 210.
"The One We Call Complete-Death Comes." GreenfieldR (6:3/4)
    Spr 78, p. 65.
"Rahel." Hand (2) 78, p. 209.
"Seeking the Garden." Hand (2) 78, p. 56.

MERRIAM, Eve
"The Ballad of Baby Jane. " LittleM (11:3) Aut 77, p. 86.

MERRILL, James
"The Five Elemental Voices. " YaleR (67:4) Sum 78, p. 567.
"Their Fall. Akhnaton's Experiment." Antaeus (30/31) Sum-Aut
     78, p. 134.

MERRILL, Lee
"The Dancing Deer of the Marine Club Bar. " PoNow (20) 78,
     p. 45.
"Up Here Women Dance. " PikeF (1) Spr 78, p. 26.

MERWIN, W. S.
"Come come" (tr. of Rûmi, w. Talat Halman). ChiR (30:2) Aut
     78, p. 9.
"Don't fall asleep tonight" (tr. of Rûmi, w. Talat Halman).
     ChiR (30:2) Aut 78, p. 11.
"Going." Atl (242:2) Ag 78, p. 65.
"High Water." AmerPoR (7:1) Ja-F 78, p. 3.
"Sheep Clouds. " Field (18) Spr 78, p. 35.
"The Snow." NewYorker (54:10) 24 Ap 78, p. 35.
"Son. " Nat (226:8) 4 Mr 78, p. 246.
"Sound of Rapids of Laramie River in Late August." Harp
     (256:1536) My 78, p. 27.
"What is the whirling dance" (tr. of Rûmi, w. Talat Halman).
     AmerPoR (7:1) Ja-F 78, p. 3.

MESHAK, Mara
"Robert Schumann lying on a blue-covered couch" (w. John
     Moulder and Jack Collom). Tele (14) 78.

MESSENGER, Ruth
"Cumulus. " Wind (30) 78, p. 34.
"Delphiniums. " Wind (30) 78, p. 34.

METRAS, Gary
"Harsh Winter. " Sam (69) 78, p. 38.
from The Time of Birds: "Fall Scenes. " Wind (29) 78, p. 17.

METZ, Jerred
"Dill Seed. " Pig (4) 78, p. 26.
"Fennel. " Pig (4) 78, p. 26.
"The Sleepers. " NorthSR (8) Aut-Wint 78-79, p. 48.
"Wild Rue. " Pig (4) 78, p. 26.

METZ, Roberta
"bits & pieces. " Glass (3:1/2/3) 78, p. 86.
"The Minister Who Lived Next Door. " WebR (4:2) Aut 78, p. 62.
"Why She Didn't Marry the Butcher. " HangL (32) Spr 78, p. 38.

MEYER, Conrad Ferdinand
"Black-Shadow-Giving Chestnut" (tr. by John S. Anson). Poetry
     (131:6) Mr 78, p. 322.

"Dark shadowing chestnut" (tr. by Gerald Gillespie).   Paint (7/8)
    Spr-Aut 77, p. 53.
"Huss's Prison" (tr. by John S. Anson).   Poetry (131:6) Mr 78,
    p. 323.
"Sheet Lightning" (tr. by John S. Anson).   Poetry (131:6) Mr 78,
    p. 323.

MEYER, Deblea
"The Remembrance. " ConcPo (11:2) Aut 78, p. 24.

MEYER, Tom
"Pindar. "   St. AR (4:3/4) 77-78, p. 119.

MEYERS, Bert
"The Return. " Durak (1) 78, p. 60.
"Spleen. " Durak (1) 78, p. 61.

MEYERS, Bruce
"Montana Year. " Pig (4) 78, p. 24.
"This May Help. " Pig (4) 78, p. 46.

MEYERS, Christene Cosgriffe
"Grandmother with Iris at 85. " SlowLR (1/2) 78, p. 26.

MEZO, Richard
"Conversations. " Stonecloud (7) 78, p. 26.
"From a Line. " Stonecloud (7) 78, p. 12.
"Viking I. " Stonecloud (7) 78, p. 13.

MICHAEL, Vicki
"The Manager. " BallSUF (19:4) Aut 78, p. 42.

MICHALSKI, John
"Siblings. " PoNow (20) 78, p. 32.

MICHAUD, Rachael
"What Women Want. " Vaga (27) Spr 78, p. 71.

MICHELSON, Joan
"African Mask. " LittleM (11:3) Aut 77, p. 22.
"Faithful Lover. " KanQ (10:4) Aut 78, p. 67.

MICKLEBERRY, William
"Reservations. " FourQt (27:2) Wint 78, p. 14.

MIDDLETON, David
"Epithalamium: The Virgin of the Dead. " Poem (33) Jl 78,
    p. 38.
"Kew Gardens. " Poem (33) Jl 78, p. 35.
"Prothalamion of the Graves. " Poem (33) Jl 78, p. 40.

MIECZKOWSKI, Ron
"Bride Rides the Wind. " LittleM (11:4) Wint 78, p. 26.

MIKLITSCH, Robert
  "Dreaming of Egypt." Epoch (27:2) Wint 78, p. 178.

MILLAZZO, Richard
  from Denomisegninatura: "Destinegation" (tr. of Mario Diacono,
    w. Luigi Ballerini). Chelsea (37) 78, p. 57.
  from Indicta, Desunt: "both wouldst be saying apparition" (tr. of
    Nanni Cagnone). Chelsea (37) 78, p. 135.
  from 3 Ideologie da Piazza del Popolo/Senza L'Imprmatur:
    "Pythagoras' Hand" (tr. of Emilio Villa, w. Faust Pauluzzi).
    Chelsea (37) 78, p. 5.

MILES, Judith E.
  "Court." Chomo (5:2) Aut-Wint 78, p. 54.

MILLER, A. McA.
  "Birds Cannot Fly Over It." Tendril (2) Spr-Sum 78.
  "Extravaganza: From the Lens-Field." Epos (27:1) 77, p. 30.
  "My Soft Shoes Slick with Blood." NewRivR (2:2) 78, p. 49.
  "Obsession" [For Miss Paam (Bên Cát, Vietnam)]. SouthernPR
    (18:1) Spr 78, p. 51.
  "Reading the X-Rays, April." BelPoJ (28:3) Spr 78, p. 20.
  "Songs for the Sea-Cow--One. Becalmed (c. 1756)." StoneC
    (78:1) Wint 78, p. 14.
  "Songs for the Sea-Cow--Two. (c. 1974)." StoneC (78:1) Wint
    78, p. 15.

MILLER, Arthur
  "Dear Tarzan." PoNow (20) 78, p. 32.

MILLER, Bill
  "Waiting for her." WindO (31) Wint-Spr 78, p. 32.

MILLER, Brown
  "In the First of Morning." Zahir (9) 77, p. 33.
  "Poem to Begin April." Zahir (9) 77, p. 34.

MILLER, Carl
  "The Blackwing Damselfly." BallSUF (19:2) Spr 78, p. 37.

MILLER, Diane
  "Genetic Jumble." EngJ (67:5) My 78, p. 65.

MILLER, E. S.
  "Elegy for a Country Churchyard." OP (25) Spr-Sum 78, p. 55.
  "Rubbings." OP (25) Spr-Sum 78, p. 57.
  "Then and There." OP (25) Spr-Sum 78, p. 56.
  "Turnabout." OP (25) Spr-Sum 78, p. 53.
  "The Widow Jill." OP (25) Spr-Sum 78, p. 54.
  "The Years." OP (25) Spr-Sum 78, p. 55.

MILLER, Errol
  "At Control Point O." SumM (5) Aut 78, p. 145.

"Crystal Chandelier." SunM (5) Aut 78, p. 144.
"Tribal Business." Paint (9/10) Spr-Aut 78, p. 22.
"Waiting." StoneC (78:3) Aut 78, p. 11.

MILLER, J. L.
"Dirt Eater." PoNow (20) 78, p. 32.
"In a Rest Room at a State Park." SouthernPR (18:1) Spr 78,
    p. 49.

MILLER, Jane
"Bandits and White Sand, a Lament." Agni (9) 78, p. 47.
"Grandmother Seen as a Celestial Harbinger." Agni (9) 78,
    p. 46.
"Many Junipers, Heartbeats." Nat (226:18) 13 My 78, p. 576.
"Nettles." Antaeus (30/31) Sum-Aut 78, p. 143.
"One Radiant Morning." Iowa (9:1) Wint 78, p. 38.
"The Poem: 'There Are Many Black Barts but Only One Ginger
    Rogers.'" VirQR (54:3) Sum 78, p. 485.
"Summer." VirQR (54:3) Sum 78, p. 486.

MILLER, Jim Wayne
"The Brier before His Fireplace." SouthernPR (18:1) Spr 78,
    p. 68.
"The Brier Breathing." SouthernPR (18:1) Spr 78, p. 69.
"Living with Children." GRR (9:2) 78, p. 85.
"On the Wings of a Dove." CarolQ (30:2) Spr-Sum 78, p. 57.

MILLER, John N.
"Only in Passion." SouthernHR (12:2) Spr 78, p. 99.

MILLER, Karen
"Color." DeKalb (11:3/4) Spr-Sum 78, p. 39.
"Worthy of Record." DeKalb (11:3/4) Spr-Sum 78, p. 39.

MILLER, Leslie Adrienne
"Negative." NoAmR (263:1) Spr 78, p. 37.

MILLER, Marlene
"And Ain't I a Woman?" Chomo (5:2) Aut-Wint 78, p. 75.

MILLER, May
"Blazing Accusation." BelPoJ (29:2) Wint 78-79, p. 14.
"Love on the Cape." BelPoJ (29:2) Wint 78-79, p. 15.
"Nuptial Calendar." BelPoJ (29:2) Wint 78-79, p. 16.

MILLER, Pamela
"Fats Domino's Parents." ParisR (73) Spr-Sum 78, p. 37.
"The Speedreader." ParisR (73) Spr-Sum 78, p. 36.

MILLER, Raeburn
"Rereading an Early Poem." PoetryNW (19:3) Aut 78, p. 40.

MILLER, Rob Hollis
"Three Poems" (tr. of Hans Verhagen). St. AR (4:3/4) 77-78, p. 111.

MILLER, Vassar
"Fickle." PoNow (19) 78, p. 9.
"Germany, 1976." NewOR (5:4) 78, p. 313.
"Resolution." NewOR (5:4) 78, p. 313.
"With the Third Ear on Easter Even." Hand (2) 78, p. 152.

MILLETT, John
"A Small Man Talks Nonsense to His Daughter." HiramPoR
    (25) Aut-Wint 78, p. 30.

MILLIGAN, Estelle
"Fat Lady in the Circus." Epos (27:1) 77, p. 35.
"Robbing Peter to Pay Paul." SlowLR (1/2) 78, p. 81.
"Sunflower." SlowLR (1/2) 78, p. 82.

MILLIKEN, Patrick
"Photograph of Rain." Nat (227:21) 16 D 78, p. 680.

MILLS, Paul
"Long Distance." Stand (19:3) 78, p. 71.

MILLS, Ralph J., Jr.
"After New Year's." Poem (34) N 78, p. 4.
"A Bridge" (for Maurice English). Northeast (3:5) Spr-Sum 78,
    p. 19.
"Days to Come." Poem (34) N 78, p. 5.
"The Door" (for B.). NewEngR (1:2) Wint 78, p. 193.
"Four Songs" (For John Knoepfle). Poem (34) N 78, p. 2.
"Horse." NewEngR (1:2) Wint 78, p. 192.
"In February." Ascent (4:1) 78, p. 33.
"In This Attic." SlowLR (1/2) 78, p. 54.
"In This Hour." MidwQ (19:4) Sum 78, p. 379.
"March." MidwQ (20:1) Aut 78, p. 100.
"Mid-August." Ascent (4:1) 78, p. 34.
"Near Stonington." MidwQ (20:1) Aut 78, p. 99.
"The Second Life." SlowLR (1/2) 78, p. 57.
"Stumps." Northeast (3:5) Spr-Sum 78, p. 21.
"Variation on Apollinaire" (for Isabella Gardner). Northeast
    (3:5) Spr-Sum 78, p. 20.
"A Walk" (For Robert Bufalini). Poem (34) N 78, p. 1.
"Winter's End." SlowLR (1/2) 78, p. 55.
"With No Answer." Poem (34) Jl 78, p. 6.

MILLS, William
"Our Fathers at Corinth" (for William J. Mills, Co. A, 24th
    Mississippi Infantry Regiment. Died June 18, 1862. Buried
    in an unknown soldier's grave, Enterprise, Mississippi).
    SouthernR (14:4) Aut 78, p. 736.

MILNE, Ewart
"Haunted." Stand (19:2) 78, p. 20.

MILOSZ, Czeslaw
"Ars Poetica?" (tr. by Lillian Vallee, w. the author). Antaeus

(30/31) Sum-Aut 78, p. 148.
"A Magic Mountain" (tr. by Lillian Vallee, w. the author).
    Antaeus (30/31) Sum-Aut 78, p. 150.
"The Owners" (tr. by Lillian Vallee, w. the author).   Antaeus
    (30/31) Sum-Aut 78, p. 152.
"So Little" (tr. by Lillian Vallee, w. the author).   Antaeus
    (30/31) Sum-Aut 78, p. 154.
"Vandeaus" (tr. by Lillian Vallee, w. the author).   Antaeus
    (30/31) Sum-Aut 78, p. 153.

MILTON, John R.
    "After He Learned." NorthSR (8) Aut-Wint 78-79, p. 71.
    "Fragment Torn from a Newspaper--1971." NorthSR (8) Aut-
        Wint 78-79, p. 72.
    "How soon hath Time, the subtle thief of youth." CalQ (13/14)
        Spr-Sum 78, p. 105.

MILTON, Joyce
    "Hermit." CarolQ (30:2) Spr-Sum 78, p. 111.

MINARIK, John
    "The Poetry Pusher" (to Russ Palmer, Poet).   GreenfieldR
        (7:1/2) Aut 78, p. 72.

MINCZESKI, John
    "Mother." YellowBR (10) 78, p. 25.

MINER, Virginia Scott
    "Griefs." ArizQ (34:2) Sum 78, p. 173.

MINICH, Jan C.
    "Barn Mice." CutB (11) Aut-Wint 78, p. 7.
    "Cowboy Bar." StoneC (78:3) Aut 78, p. 29.
    "Each Passing Moment." KanQ (10:1) Wint 78, p. 110.
    "Time's Three." CutB (11) Aut-Wint 78, p. 8.

MINNS, Karen Marie Christa
    "The Colors of Potential." DeKalb (11:1/2) Aut-Wint 77-78,
        p. 57.
    "Remembrance." DeKalb (11:1/2) Aut-Wint 77-78, p. 57.

MINOCK, Dan
    "In Memory of a Stick." PoetryNW (19:1) Spr 78, p. 39.
    "Muhammad Speaks of Necessary Developments." PoetryNW
        (19:3) Aut 78, p. 21.
    "Sees All." PoetryNW (19:1) Spr 78, p. 40.

MINOR, James
    "White Buck." SoDakR (16:3) Aut 78, p. 11.

MINSHALL, Ellen
    "Camping." SeC (5:2) 78, p. 25.

MINTON, Helena
  "Morgue." Epos (27:1) 77, p. 21.
  "Persephone." BelPoJ (29:1) Aut 78, p. 10.
  "Pilgrimage to Lourdes, 1958." BelPoJ (29:1) Aut 78, p. 11.
  "The Swans." Chomo (4:3) Spr 78, p. 3.
  "Visit with My Mother." Chomo (4:3) Spr 78, p. 4.

MINTY, Judith
  "Finding a Depth: North Channel, Lake Huron." NewYorker
      (54:29) 4 S 78, p. 26.
  "Heights." MissouriR (2:1) Aut 78, p. 38.
  "Letters to My Daughters." GRR (9:1) 78, p. 5.
  "Wounds." MissouriR (2:1) Aut 78, p. 40.

MINX, Paul
  "The Crop." CalQ (13/14) Spr-Sum 78, p. 34.
  "Mt. Tamalpais, 'The Sleeping Woman.'" Nat (226:24) 24 Je 78,
      p. 767.
  "On Behalf of Persephone." CalQ (13/14) Spr-Sum 78, p. 35.

MIRANDA, Gary
  "Triptych" (for Marianne Von Zweck). SouthernR (14:3) Sum 78,
      p. 472.

MIRE, June
  "These Icy Sheets." EngJ (67:5) My 78, p. 64.

MISHKIN, Julia
  "You Show Me Your Slides of India." ParisR (74) Aut-Wint 78,
      p. 188.

MITCHELL, Daphna
  "To My Newborn Son in Intensive Care." YellowBR (10) 78,
      p. 6.

MITCHELL, John
  "December Hallucination." NorthSR (8) Aut-Wint 78-79, p. 55.
  "The Relativity of Love." NorthSR (8) Aut-Wint 78-79, p. 55.
  "Winter Dreams of Picasso." NorthSR (8) Aut-Wint 78-79,
      p. 54.

MITCHELL, Roger
  "Getting My Eyes Tested." WindO (31) Wint-Spr 78, p. 41.
  "Starting to Starve." WindO (31) Wint-Spr 78, p. 42.

MITCHELL, Susan
  "From the Journals of the Frog Prince." NewYorker (54:13) 15
      My 78, p. 40.
  "Woodcarving." Nat (227:12) 14 O 78, p. 386.

MITCHELL, Thomas
  "Home Again." NewL (45:1) Aut 78, p. 21.

"Hound of Heaven." NewOR (5:4) 78, p. 359.
"Small Craft Advisory." CutB (11) Aut-Wint 78, p. 78.
"Talking It Over." NewL (45:1) Aut 78, p. 22.

MITCHNER, Gary
"Photography." CarouselQ (3:4) Wint 78, p. 34.

MIZEJEWSKI, Linda
"The Stalking-Birds." SouthernR (14:3) Sum 78, p. 514.

MLADINIC, Peter
"Directions to Rutherford." Northeast (3:6) Wint 78-79, p. 9.

MOE, Rusty C.
"Pa-." GRR (9:1) 78, p. 50.
"II." GRR (9:1) 78, p. 51.
"III." GRR (9:1) 78, p. 51.

MOEBIUS, William
"The Last Obstacle" (for Judy M. /d. 4/29/77). Pan (19) 77,
     p. 24.

MOFFETT, Judith
"Mezzo Cammin." LittleM (11:3) Aut 77, p. 100.
"Souvenir: Sestina." LittleM (11:3) Aut 77, p. 98.
"Walk with the River." Iowa (9:4) Aut 78, p. 81.

MOFFI, Laurence
"Because Radio, Too, Is a Relic." PoNow (20) 78, p. 27.
"The Box Marked Patience." MalR (46) Ap 78, p. 132.
"Presence." MalR (46) Ap 78, p. 131.
"The Voyeur Directs an Ending." PoNow (20) 78, p. 27.
"What Is Noticeably Present." MalR (46) Ap 78, p. 130.
"The Word Man." CalQ (13/14) Spr-Sum 78, p. 109.

MOFFITT, John
"Who He Was." ChrC (95:42) 20 D 78, p. 1233.

MOHR, Joland
"On the Day My Friend Announces His Intentions by Phone and I
     Announce Mine Back in a Poem." DacTerr (15) Wint-Spr
     77-78, p. 54.

MOHR, William
"The Furnaces." Bachy (12) Aut 78, p. 22.

MOLESWORTH, Charles
"My Map of Paris." Salm (41) Spr 78, p. 119.

MOLL, Ernest G.
"de Senectute." NowestR (17:1) 78, p. 106. Correction.

MONAGHAN, Pat
"Christmas at Vail: On Staying Indoors." NoAmR (263:4) Wint

78, p. 63.
"Mothers and Amazons. " NoAmR (263:4) Wint 78, p. 62.

MONETTE, Paul
"A Man in Space" (For Walter). Shen (29:3) Spr 78, p. 47.

MONROE, Jonathan
"Shackleford Banks. " SouthernPR (18:1) Spr 78, p. 18.

MONTAG, Tom
from Mapping America: A Narrative of the Expedition: (1-4).
    NorthSR (8) Aut-Wint 78-79, p. 11.
"Re/Turns 3. " Northeast (3:6) Wint 78-79, p. 54.

MONTAGUE, John
"All Souls. " NorthSR (8) Aut-Wint 78-79, p. 20.
"Border Lake. " NorthSR (8) Aut-Wint 78-79, p. 19.
"Darkness. " LitR (22:2) Wint 79, p. 175.
"Hero's Portion. " NorthSR (8) Aut-Wint 78-79, p. 21.
"Killing the Pig. " NorthSR (8) Aut-Wint 78-79, p. 24.
"Lament. " Stand (19:2) 78, p. 19.
"The Massacre. " NorthSR (8) Aut-Wint 78-79, p. 23.
"Northern Express. " NorthSR (8) Aut-Wint 78-79, p. 25.
"She Walks Alone. " LitR (22:2) Wint 79, p. 178.
"Tearing. " LitR (22:2) Wint 79, p. 175.

MONTALE, Eugenio
"La Bufera. " StoneC (78:1) Wint 78, p. 22.
"Dear Life, I do not ask of you" (tr. by D. M. Pettinella).
    NewOR (6:1) 78, p. 76.
"For Un Omaggio a Rafael Alberti" (tr. by Anthony Burgess).
    MalR (47) Jl 78, p. 113.
"Happiness at Heart" (tr. by D. M. Pettinella). NewOR (6:1)
    78, p. 76.
Two poems (tr. by R. Sieburth and S. W. DeRachewiltz). St. AR
    (5:1) Aut-Wint 78, p. 66.

MONTGOMERY, George
"Poem from Atop a Purple Horse. " WormR (72) 78, p. 133.
"Supplies for the Hunting Lodge. " WormR (72) 78, p. 133.
"2 Rah-Rah's. " Tele (13) 77.

MONTGOMERY, John
"Bandidos!" DeKalb (11:3/4) Spr-Sum 78, p. 40.

MONTGOMERY, Ronald
"Prelude Black Baby. " BlackF (2:2) Aut-Wint 78, p. 25.
"To Nikki. " BlackF (2:2) Aut-Wint 78, p. 26.

MONTGOMERY, Vera
"Solidarity with Cataracts. " GreenfieldR (7:1/2) Aut 78, p. 55.

MOODY, W. V.
"Dream of the Rain Maker's Mistress. " Pan (19) 77, p. 46.

"The Man Who Loved Lime Pie." <u>Pan</u> (19) 77,
p. 46.

MOON, Clarice L.
"Dreams." <u>CarouselQ</u> (3:1) Spr 78, p. 5.

MOON, Samuel
"A Lake of Clear Water" (for Robert Creeley). <u>Bound</u> (6:3/7:1)
Spr-Aut 78, p. 460.

MOORE, Barbara
"Though we do not die your death, Miguel Hernandez." <u>Confr</u>
(16) Spr-Sum 78, p. 78.

MOORE, Jacqueline
"Handful of Thoughts." <u>AAR</u> (28) 78, p. 13.
"Reaching Desert Time." <u>AAR</u> (28) 78, p. 10.
"Sleeping in the North." <u>AAR</u> (28) 78, p. 13.

MOORE, James
"Dressed for the Visit to Cuzco." <u>NorthSR</u> (8) Aut-Wint 78-79,
p. 90.
"Prayer before Sleep." <u>NorthSR</u> (8) Aut-Wint 78-79, p. 91.
"The Freedom of History." <u>SenR</u> (9:2) Aut-Wint 78, p. 90.
"River." <u>NorthSR</u> (8) Aut-Wint 78-79, p. 91.
"Toward Objects." <u>NorthSR</u> (8) Aut-Wint 78-79, p. 89.

MOORE, Janice Townley
"Japonica." <u>SouthernPR</u> (18:2) Aut 78, p. 43.

MOORE, Marianne
"Old Tiger." <u>Antaeus</u> (30/31) Sum-Aut 78, p. 34.

MOORE, Robert
"Drifter." <u>KanQ</u> (10:3) Sum 78, p. 26.

MOORE, Todd
"Cars." <u>Wind</u> (30) 78, p. 35.
"Mother has." <u>YellowBR</u> (10) 78, p. 11.
"They Were Playing." <u>Wind</u> (30) 78, p. 35.
"Wild Dogs." <u>Wind</u> (30) 78, p. 36.

MOORE, Tom
"Dec. 4, 1968." <u>Aspen</u> (5) Spr 78, p. 76.

MOORMAN, Charles
"Epiphanies at Lux." <u>SouthernPR</u> (18:2) Aut 78, p. 68.

MOOS, Michael
"Before You Were Born." <u>HangL</u> (34) Wint 78-79, p. 40.
"In Your Eyes" (for Miriam Patchen). <u>NorthSR</u> (8) Aut-Wint
78-79, p. 103.
"Key." <u>NorthSR</u> (8) Aut-Wint 78-79, p. 102.

MOOSE, Ruth
"Hawk." GRR (9:2) 78, p. 126.

MORAFF, Barbara
"Briefly." WormR (68) 77, p. 114.
"For All the Women Who Sell Tupperware without Knowing the
    Meaning of 'Tup.'" WormR (72) 78, p. 148.
"hey, babe." WormR (68) 77, p. 114.
"love, you've uprooted me for the last time." WormR (72) 78,
    p. 149.

MORDENSKI, Janice E.
"The House and the Traveller." Hand (2) 78, p. 167.

MORENO, L.
"'The Color of Lonely.'" GreenfieldR (7:1/2) Aut 78, p. 11.
"Fear." GreenfieldR (7:1/2) Aut 78, p. 11.
"Third Fall." GreenfieldR (7:1/2) Aut 78, p. 10.

MORGAN, Frederick
"Ariettes Oubliées 111" (tr. of Verlaine). GreenfieldR (6:3/4)
    Spr 78, p. 4.
"Carmen Ci" (tr. of Catullus). GreenfieldR (6:3/4) Spr 78,
    p. 4.
"Carmen LXXV" (tr. of Catullus). SouthernR (14:2) Spr 78,
    p. 331.
"Catullus: Carmen XLI." Confr (16) Spr-Sum 78, p. 12.
"'Comes Often to My Memory.'" Confr (16) Spr-Sum 78, p. 12.
"Death Mother." Harp (257:1541) O 78, p. 86.
"The End of the Story." AntR (36:2) Spr 78, p. 188.
"Eternity, I." AmerS (47:1) Wint 77-78, p. 104.
"The Gate." PoNow (19) 78, p. 16.
"Here lies Archeanassa" (tr. of Asklepiades). GreenfieldR
    (6:3/4) Spr 78, p. 5.
"I played once with Hermione" (tr. of Asklepiades). GreenfieldR
    (6:3/4) Spr 78, p. 5.
"Legend." PoNow (19) 78, p. 16.
"Leilah Asleep" (tr. of Charles Leconte de Lisle). SouthernR
    (14:2) Spr 78, p. 333.
"Parisian Scenes XCIX" (tr. of Baudelaire). SouthernR (14:2)
    Spr 78, p. 331.
"The Path." NewEngR (1:1) Aut 78, p. 81.
"The Promise." VirQR (54:3) Sum 78, p. 489.
"Two Poems from the Latin." MichQR (17:1) Wint 78, p. 35.
"Two Riddles." Kayak (48) Je 78, p. 23.
"The Wedding of Cana in Galilee." SewanR (86:3) Sum 78,
    p. 374.
"'When it rained and rained.'" PoNow (19) 78, p. 16.

MORGAN, Jean
"Barn Fire." GeoR (32:2) Sum 78, p. 339.

MORGAN, John
"Air." Nimrod (22:2) Spr-Sum 78, p. 54.

"The Bone-Duster." NewYorker (54:18) 19 Je 78, p. 38.
"The Empty Universe Has a Temperature of 3 Degrees."
    Nimrod (22:2) Spr-Sum 78, p. 53.
"The Etiology of Angst." Nimrod (22:2) Spr-Sum 78, p. 53.
"The Refugee" (In memory of Roethke; in memory of Neruda).
    NoAmR (263:3) Aut 78, p. 57.

MORGAN, Robert
"Buffalo Trace." CarolQ (30:1) Wint 78, p. 22.
"Captain John." Epoch (27:2) Wint 78, p. 125.
"Chant Royal." Poetry (132:2) My 78, p. 63.
"Crop Dusting." CarolQ (30:1) Wint 78, p. 29.
"Fence." CarolQ (30:1) Wint 78, p. 21.
"Hypertension." NorthSR (8) Aut-Wint 78-79, p. 69.
"Mine." NorthSR (8) Aut-Wint 78-79, p. 68.
Nine poems. Poetry (133:2) N 78, p. 63.
"Sliding." CarolQ (30:1) Wint 78, p. 27.
"Visitation." CarolQ (30:1) Wint 78, p. 26.
"Watermelon Flower." NorthSR (8) Aut-Wint 78-79, p. 67.
"Yellowlight." CarolQ (30:1) Wint 78, p. 23.

MORGAN, Robin
"The Ruining of the Work" (for Kenneth Pitchford). NewEngR
    (1:2) Wint 78, p. 159.

MORGAN, Susan
"Amarillo." Chomo (4:3) Spr 78, p. 19.

MORIN, Edward
"Rapture of the Depths." SouthernHR (12:2) Spr 78, p. 120.

MORITZ, Albert Frank
"The Abnormal Labor" (tr. of Benjamin Peret, w. Jane Barnard).
    MalR (48) O 78, p. 78.
"Deaf as a Post." FourQt (28:1) Aut 78, p. 39.

MORLEY, Hilda
"Autumn." ChiR (30:3) Wint 79, p. 133.
"Scorched Earth." Harp (257:1543) D 78, p. 68.
"'So to suspend it.'" Hudson (31:2) Sum 78, p. 296.
"That Bright Grey Eye." Harp (256:1537) Je 78, p. 61.
"That Could Assuage Us." Hudson (31:3) Aut 78, p. 425.
"That One Could Say." Harp (257:1543) D 78, p. 68.
"Wheeling a cart down Amsterdam." ChiR (30:3) Wint 79,
    p. 134.
"The Women of New Guinea." Harp (256:1536) My 78, p. 18.

MORRIS, Captain
"Ambassador at Large." Playb (25:8) Ag 78, p. 149.

MORRIS, Harry
"Not Weighing Our Merits." SewanR (86:1) Wint 78, p. 40.

MORRIS, Herbert
   "At the Ravel Academy." Agni (9) 78, p. 52.
   "The End of Japan." Kayak (48) Je 78, p. 38.
   "Palm Beach, 1928." Shen (29:3) Spr 78, p. 18.
   "A Quiet Life" (for Michael Moriarty). Agni (9) 78, p. 48.
   "When the Silence Becomes Too Much to Bear." Antaeus (28)
      Wint 78, p. 201.

MORRIS, John N.
   "All He Knows." Poetry (132:5) Ag 78, p. 266.
   "Archaeology." Poetry (132:5) Ag 78, p. 263.
   "At the Death of Gulliver." Poetry (132:5) Ag 78, p. 267.
   "The Blacksnake in My Tree." OhioR (19:2) Spr-Sum 78, p. 70.
   "The End of the Rental." Poetry (132:5) Ag 78, p. 264.
   "Lost Things." OhioR (19:2) Spr-Sum 78, p. 71.
   "Man and Boy." Poetry (132:5) Ag 78, p. 265.
   "The Right to Life." NewEngR (1:2) Wint 78, p. 138.
   "The Will of the Children." NewEngR (1:2) Wint 78, p. 136.
   "Wintering Over." NewYorker (54:32) 25 S 78, p. 136.
   "Yearbooks." .NewEngR (1:2) Wint 78, p. 137.

MORRIS, Lois
   "There Are Five Quarts of Blood in the Human Body." Stone-
      cloud (7) 78, p. 28.

MORRIS, Marilyn A.
   "A Bar at the Follies Bergere, 1882." Box (6) Aut 77, p. 10.

MORRIS, Paul
   "The Occident" (For Else Lasker-Schuler, with admiration) (tr.
      of Georg Trakl). WebR (4:1) Spr 78, p. 33.

MORRIS, Peter
   "Talk to the Animals." PraS (52:3) Aut 78, p. 279.
   "Weak Eyes." PraS (52:3) Aut 78, p. 278.

MORRISON, Madison
   "Auction & Boutique." Tele (13) 77.

MORTON, Bruce
   "Afro Study." NegroHB (41:2) Mr-Ap 78, p. 819.

MOSBY, George, Jr.
   "as a young-un in my grandmother's house: sundays." Glass
      (3:1/2/3) 78, p. 50.

MOSES, W. R.
   "Emblem: Crossbills." Bits (8) Jl 78.
   "In the Beginning." SouthernPR (18:2) Aut 78, p. 44.
   "The Japanese Bit." SouthernPR (18:2) Aut 78, p. 44.
   "Rhapsody on a Bullhead." PoetryNW (19:1) Spr 78, p. 22.

MOSS, Howard
   "At the Café." NewYorker (54:16) 5 Je 78, p. 34.
   "Elegy for My Sister." NewYorker (54:12) 8 My 78, p. 39.
   "Impatiens." NewYorker (54:8) 10 Ap 78, p. 40.
   "Incomplete and Disputed Sonatas." NewYorker (53:46) 2 Ja 78,
      p. 23.
   "The Long Island Night." NewYRB (25:13) 17 Ag 78, p. 19.
   "Many Senses: Mexico City." NewYorker (54:41) 27 N 78, p. 44.
   "The Promissory Note." NewYorker (54:29) 4 S 78, p. 33.
   "Torso" (tr. of Joseph Brodsky). NewYorker (54:32) 25 S 78,
      p. 42.

MOSS, Stanley
   "The Debt." Nat (227:20) 9 D 78, p. 651.
   "Kangaroo." MichQR (17:2) Spr 78, p. 135.
   "Voice." MichQR (17:2) Spr 78, p. 136.

MOTT, Michael
   "Dragonflies have confused memories." Bits (7) Ja 78.

MOUL, Keith
   "Playing Catch" (for my father). Pig (5) 78, p. 92.

MOULDER, John
   "Robert Schumann lying on a blue-covered couch" (w. Mara
      Meshak and Jack Collom). Tele (14) 78.

MOYLES, Lois
   "Decent Formality." PartR (45:1) 78, p. 15.
   "Named Lazarus." PartR (45:3) 78, p. 438.

MUDD, Harvey
   "China Always Is Near." Stonecloud (7) 78, p. 12.
   "Death in Mexico." Stonecloud (7) 78, p. 143.
   "The Expulsion." Stonecloud (7) 78, p. 113.
   "Poem Addressed to My Father, which I Vowed Not to Publish."
      Stonecloud (7) 78, p. 75.
   "Song for the Angel." Stonecloud (7) 78, p. 140.

MÜHRINGER, Doris
   "'Let's Celebrate'" (tr. by Beth Bjorklund). Paint (9/10) Spr-
      Aut 78, p. 39.
   "Questions and Answers" (tr. by Beth Bjorklund). Paint (9/10)
      Spr-Aut 78, p. 38.

MUELLER, Lavonne
   "Phantom nerves." EngJ (67:5) My 78, p. 55.

MUELLER, Lisel
   "The Artist's Model, ca. 1912." Poetry (132:2) My 78, p. 71.
   "Eggs." MissouriR (2:1) Aut 78, p. 14.
   "Fenestration." OhioR (19:3) Aut 78, p. 10.
   "Fiction." OhioR (19:3) Aut 78, p. 10.
   "Found in the Cabbage Patch." Poetry (132:4) Jl 78, p. 206.

"The Need to Hold Still." MissouriR (1:1) Spr 78, p. 12.
"Night Song." OhioR (19:3) Aut 78, p. 11.
"One More Hymn to the Sun." MissouriR (2:1) Aut 78, p. 12.
"Picking Raspberries." MissouriR (2:1) Aut 78, p. 15.
"The Story." Poetry (132:4) Jl 78, p. 205.
"Why We Tell Stories" (For Linda Foster). Poetry (132:4) Jl 78,
    p. 203.

MUELLER, Melinda
    "Mute Naomi Sitting by the Lamp after Dark." PoetryNW (19:2)
    Sum 78, p. 7.

MUHICH, Marc
    "Vernal Necro." Tele (13) 77.

MUJAGIC, Mubera
    "Does Moonlight Suffice?" (tr. by Herbert Kuhner). MalR (46)
    Ap 78, p. 109.
    "A Line" (tr. by Herbert Kuhner). MalR (46) Ap 78, p. 109.

MULDOON, Paul
    "Grief." Stand (19:4) 78, p. 3.
    "Truce." Stand (19:4) 78, p. 3.

MULLER, Erik
    "The Browse." SouthernPR (18:1) Spr 78, p. 39.
    "Chicken Killing." PoNow (20) 78, p. 33.
    "Going to the Dump." EnPas (7) 78, p. 32.
    "Island Life." EnPas (7) 78, p. 34.

MULLETTE, Maurice
    "The Land of Moab." CimR (42) Ja 78, p. 27.

MULLIGAN, J. B.
    "All-Star." Sam (65) 78, p. 2.
    "Occurrence." CarouselQ (3:4) Wint 78, p. 5.
    "Windows in a New House." WebR (4:1) Spr 78, p. 30.

MUMFORD, Erika
    "Equinox." GRR (9:2) 78, p. 114.
    "obsessed by green." GRR (9:2) 78, p. 113.

MUMFORD, Marilyn R.
    "Found Poem." AndR (5:2) Aut 78, p. 54.

MUMM, Douglas
    "The Art Dept." Smudge (1) Spr 78, p. 35.
    "Basics." Smudge (2) Sum 78, p. 30.
    "i become." Smudge (1) Spr 78, p. 8.
    "People You Ought to Know." Sam (69) 78, p. 2.
    "Warm Weather." Smudge (2) Sum 78, p. 34.

MUNGIN, Horace
    "The City." BlackF (2:2) Aut-Wint 78.

MUQSIT, Hasib
"'Mom.'" CarouselQ (3:3) Aut 78, p. 8.
"Untitled." CarouselQ (3:3) Aut 78, p. 8.

MURATORI, Fred
"Almost an Elegy." SoDakR (16:2) Sum 78, p. 14.
"The Day of Open Sentiment." HiramPoR (24) Spr-Sum 78,
    p. 35.
"Low." SouthernPR (18:2) Aut 78, p. 34.
"November Elegy." FourQt (28:1) Aut 78, p. 2.
"Sunfish." Confr (16) Spr-Sum 78, p. 64.
"A Tale of Dangerous Men." Chowder (10/11) Aut-Wint 78-79,
    p. 56.

MURAWSKI, Elizabeth
"On the Island of Ocracoke." SouthernPR (18:1) Spr 78, p. 14.
"To its place my god." SouthernPR (18:1) Spr 78, p. 15.

MURCKO, Terry
"The Giant Metal 'E' Pome." Pig (4) 78, p. 44.

MURDY, Anne Elizabeth
"The Bar." PikeF (1) Spr 78, p. 16.
"Fog." PikeF (1) Spr 78, p. 16.

MURPHEY, Joseph Colin
"The Silver Racer." SouthwR (63:4) Aut 78, p. 384.

MURPHY, Brian
"When I told her." EngJ (67:5) My 78, p. 67.

MURPHY, George E., Jr.
"Fish Jokes." Aspect (71) Ap-Je 77, p. 36.

MURPHY, Kay
from The Cherry Tree: "The grafting was messy." Ascent
    (3:3) 78, p. 18.
"A Dream in Storm." Ascent (3:3) 78, p. 17.
"For My Husband Returning to His Lover." KanQ (10:1) Wint
    78, p. 38.

MURPHY, Kevin
"Ellen Tucker Emerson, 1811-1831." SenR (9:1) Spr-Sum 78,
    p. 76.

MURPHY, Rich
"From a Bunker." Tele (13) 77.
"Home." Tele (13) 77.

MURPHY, Sister Ellen
"Snowdrift." Comm (105:14) 21 Jl 78, p. 455.

MURRAY, Catherine
"Bio Graphy 26." Glass (3:1/2/3) 78, p. 59.

MURRAY, G. E.
  "Caitlin's Poem" (for my daughter). CutB (10) Spr-Sum 78,
      p. 60.
  "Catfishing in Natchez Trace." Ascent (4:1) 78, p. 49.
  "Fancy Machines." MinnR (NS10) Spr 78, p. 53.
  "The Hungarian Night." Ascent (4:1) 78, p. 50.
  "In Memory of a Coastal November." ChiR (30:1) Sum 78,
      p. 56.
  "When the Hills Became West Virginia." CutB (10) Spr-Sum 78,
      p. 57.

MURRAY, George
  "Airplane Poem #1." JnlONJP (3:1) 78, p. 18.
  "An Anonymous Note." JnlONJP (3:1) 78, p. 19.
  "The Knife-Thrower's Lady." JnlONJP (3:1) 78, p. 16.
  "On a Renaissance Painting." JnlONJP (3:1) 78, p. 16.
  "The Winter at the End of My Five-Year Plan to Learn How to
      Play the Piano and Talk to People." JnlONJP (3:1) 78,
      p. 18.

MURRAY, Joan
  "The Lovers." Atl (242:1) Jl 78, p. 46.

MURRAY, Les A.
  "The Buladelah-Taree Holiday Song Cycle." Antaeus (30/31)
      Sum-Aut 78, p. 273.

MURRAY, Rona
  "The Death of the Bear." MalR (45) Ja 78, p. 153.
  "For a Shade among the Dead." MalR (45) Ja 78, p. 158.
  "Snake Market." MalR (45) Ja 78, p. 156.

MUSGRAVE, Susan
  "The Angel Maker." MalR (45) Ja 78, p. 86.
  "Even in the Ordered World." MalR (45) Ja 78, p. 85.
  "A Marriage." MalR (45) Ja 78, p. 82.
  "Mourning Song." MalR (45) Ja 78, pp. 92-103. Includes manu-
      scripts and worksheets.
  "North Beach Birth" (for Jennie and Ghin). MalR (45) Ja 78,
      p. 90.
  "Without Title." MalR (45) Ja 78, p. 84.
  "Woodcutter, River-God and I." MalR (45) Ja 78, p. 88.

MUSKE, Carol
  "Ahimsa." Antaeus (30/31) Sum-Aut 78, p. 160.
  "Androgyny." VirQR (54:4) Aut 78, p. 697.
  "Chivalry." Antaeus (30/31) Sum-Aut 78, p. 162.
  "Choreography." VirQR (54:4) Aut 78, p. 696.
  "Coral Sea, 1945." AntR (36:1) Wint 78, p. 80.
  "Elocution: Touch" (for Tom). Pequod (2:4) 78, p. 73.
  "Fireflies" (for Edward Healton). Antaeus (30/31) Sum-Aut 78,
      p. 155.
  "Her Story: Leaving Eden." Antaeus (30/31) Sum-Aut 78,
      p. 158.

"The Invention of Cuisine." NewYorker (54:16) 5 Je 78, p. 42.
"Lines from the Private Eye." Columbia (2) Aut 78, p. 14.
"Moonlighting at the Embalmer's Parlor." Columbia (2) Aut 78,
    p. 16.
"Par." Pequod (2:4) 78, p. 71.
"Ransom." NewEngR (1:1) Aut 78, p. 42.
"Skylight" (for D. H.). Antaeus (30/31) Sum-Aut 78, p. 156.
"Trudy's Piano Bar: Tangier." SlowLR (1/2) 78, p. 72.
"Tuesday Again." SlowLR (1/2) 78, p. 71.

MUSTAJAB, Krishna
    "Serenade 77" (tr. by Elisavietta Ritchie and the author). AAR
        (28) 78, p. 47.
    "Shadow-Chase" (for Lisa) (tr. by Elisavietta Ritchie and the
        author). AAR (28) 78, p. 46.

MU'TAMID
    "Lament of an Exile" (tr. by Graham Ackroyd). Kayak (48) Je
        78, p. 68.

MWENEA, Jabari (E. L. Coleman)
    "Ellsii Attiba." Obs (4:1) Spr 78, p. 73.
    "Gave Us to Us" (For Rahsaan Roland Kirk after a concert in
        Phila. Jan. 21, 1977). Obs (4:1) Spr 78, p. 72.
    "Inside Out." Obs (4:1) Spr 78, p. 73.
    "Neon Blue." Obs (4:1) Spr 78, p. 71.
    "Poem of the Future Now." Obs (4:1) Spr 78, p. 74.
    "This Lady." Obs (4:1) Spr 78, p. 74.

MYERS, Alan
    "Brighton Rock" (tr. of Joseph Brodsky). NewYorker (53:51) 6
        F 78, p. 30.
    "December 24, 1971" (tr. of Joseph Brodsky). NewYRB (25:20)
        21 D 78, p. 4.
    "East Finchley" (tr. of Joseph Brodsky). NewYorker (54:14) 22
        My 78, p. 42.
    "Lithuanian Divertissement" (to Thomas Ventslova) (tr. of Joseph
        Brodksy). NewYRB (25:15) 12 O 78, p. 11.
    "Mexican Divertimento" (for Octavio Paz) (tr. of Joseph Brodsky).
        NewYRB (25:19) 7 D 78, p. 10.
    "To a Tyrant" (tr. of Joseph Brodsky). NewYorker (54:22) 17
        Jl 78, p. 26.
    "York: In Memoriam W. H. Auden" (tr. of Joseph Brodsky).
        NewYorker (54:18) 19 Je 78, p. 34.

MYERS, George, Jr.
    "1." Glass (3:1/2/3) 78, p. 99.

MYERS, Jack
    "Another Coil." Iowa (9:3) Sum 78, p. 87.
    "Ask Anyone." Tendril (2) Spr-Sum 78.
    "Being Alive." SouthernPR (18:1) Spr 78, p. 10.
    "The Butcher's Hand." SenR (9:1) Spr-Sum 78, p. 47.

"Louie the Fruitman." SenR (9:1) Spr-Sum 78, p. 46.
"Thanksgiving Day." Columbia (2) Aut 78, p. 75.
"Thoughts of a Scissors Sharpener." SenR (9:1) Spr-Sum 78,
    p. 48.

MYERS, Robert J.
    "bat." SouthernPR (18:1) Spr 78, p. 7.

MYLES, Eileen
    "Corialanus." Tele (14) 78.
    "'Me I'm More Electrical'"--John Godfrey. Tele (14) 78.

MYRSIADES, Kostas
    "Almost Complete" (tr. of Yannis Ritsos). Falcon (16) 78, p. 9.
    "Descent" (tr. of Yannis Ritsos). Falcon (16) 78, p. 9.
    "Exhibits" (tr. of Yannis Ritsos). Falcon (16) 78, p. 10.
    "Liturgical" (tr. of Yannis Ritsos, w. Kimon Friar). LitR
        (21:4) Sum 78, p. 457.
    Seventeen poems (tr. of Yannis Ritsos, w. Kimon Friar).
        AmerPoR (7:4) Jl-Ag 78, p. 23.
    "Simultaneously" (tr. of Yannis Ritsos, w. Kimon Friar). LitR
        (21:4) Sum 78, p. 458.
    "Sluggishly" (tr. of Yannis Ritsos). Falcon (16) 78, p. 10.
    "Small Dialogue" (tr. of Yannis Ritsos). Falcon (16) 78, p. 11.
    "Small Sonata" (tr. of Yannis Ritsos, w. Kimon Friar). LitR
        (21:4) Sum 78, p. 458.
    "Stages of Ignorance" (tr. of Yannis Ritsos, w. Kimon Friar).
        LitR (21:4) Sum 78, p. 459.
    Ten poems (tr. of Yannis Ritsos, w. Kimon Friar). Antaeus
        (28) Wint 78, p. 57.
    "Towards Saturday" (tr. of Yannis Ritsos). Falcon (16) 78,
        p. 11.
    Twenty poems (tr. of Yannis Ritsos, w. Kimon Friar). Falcon
        (16) 78, p. 13.
    "Way of Life" (tr. of Yannis Ritsos, w. Kimon Friar). LitR
        (21:4) Sum 78, p. 457.

NABOKOV, Vladimir
    "Who Will Drive Me Home?" (tr. by Djemma Bider).
        NewYorker (54:37) 30 O 78, p. 40.

NAGLE, Alice Connelly
    "question." SmPd (44) Aut 78, p. 15.

NAIDEN, James
    "Minneapolis Sonnet No. 67." SoDakR (16:2) Sum 78, p. 48.
    "1933, Fascism" (tr. of Borris Slutsky, w. Arthur Hudgins).
        NorthSR (8) Aut-Wint 78-79, p. 104.
    "Poem in William's Pub" (w. Jonathan Sisson). NorthSR (8)
        Aut-Wint 78-79, p. 101.
    "The Seed" (tr. of Boris Slutsky, w. Arthur Hudgins). NorthSR
        (8) Aut-Wint 78-79, p. 106.
    "Silhouette" (tr. of Boris Slutsky, w. Arthur Hudgins).
        NorthSR (8) Aut Wint 78-79, p. 105.

NALLEY, Richard
 "Agamemnon. " HarvAd (112:1) D 78, p. 9.

NANGLE, Julian
 "At Centrepond Point. " GRR (9:3) 78, p. 190.
 "Glider. " GRR (9:3) 78, p. 189.
 "Love Poem. " GRR (9:3) 78, p. 191.

NASH, Mildred J.
 "Cotton Mather, Meet Miss Duval. " LittleM (11:3) Aut 77,
    p. 70.

NASH, Valery
 "Mamma. " Epos (27:1) 77, p. 18.

NASIO, Brenda
 "batik maker" (for jodi and rich). ParisR (73) Spr-Sum 78,
    p. 38.
 "missed signals" (for barbara and bruce). ParisR (73) Spr-Sum
    78, p. 39.

NATHAN, Leonard
 "The Abandoned Orchard. " Epoch (27:2) Wint 78, p. 149.
 "Again. " Bits (7) Ja 78.
 "Airs" (for Miriam). OhioR (19:1) Wint 78, p. 48.
 "Chief Rain-in-the-Face Confesses He Lied to the Anthropologist. "
    PoetryNW (19:1) Spr 78, p. 38.
 "Going by Rain. " ThRiPo (11/12) 78, p. 58.
 "Keys. " Bits (8) Jl 78.
 "Near Relations. " Bits (7) Ja 78.
 "News from the Low Country. " Nat (226:15) 22 Ap 78, p. 485.
 "Results. " PoNow (19) 78, p. 17.
 "Seeing. " ThRiPo (11/12) 78, p. 59.
 "Something Happens and. " PoetryNW (19:1) Spr 78, p. 37.
 "Song. " Nat (227:16) 11 N 78, p. 506.
 "Spirit. " NewYorker (54:13) 15 My 78, p. 133.
 "The Summons. " NewL (44:3) Spr 78, p. 36.

NATHAN, Norman
 "from an airplane. " ConcPo (11:2) Aut 78, p. 70.
 "Hymn Written in the Country Churchyard of My Mind. " Epos
    (27:1) 77, p. 21.
 "Short Lived Phenomena. " CalQ (13/14) Spr-Sum 78, p. 140.
 "trauma. " SouthernHR (12:1) Wint 78, p. 43.

NATHANIEL, Isabel
 "Of a Cold Country. " LitR (22:1) Aut 78, p. 4.

NATIONS, Opal L.
 "Air Mail Letter Poem. " WormR (70) 78, p. 76.
 "The Use of Writing Cards with Designs. " WormR (70) 78,
    p. 77.
 "what a day a day!" (w. Dick Higgins). LaB (10) 78, p. 18.

NATKIE, John Leon
  "Antioch." GreenfieldR (7:1/2) Aut 78, p. 93.
  "Dear Cold Mountain." GreenfieldR (7:1/2) Aut 78, p. 80.

NAVROZOV, Andrei
  "A Grand Elegy for John Donne" (tr. of Joseph Brodsky).
    YaleLit (147:3) 78, p. 9.

NECATIGIL, Bechet
  "Bone" (tr. by Talat Halman and Brian Swann). St. AR (4:3/4)
    77-78, p. 104.
  "Dead" (tr. by Talat Halman and Brian Swann). St. AR (4:3/4)
    77-78, p. 104.
  "fly" (tr. by Talat Halman and Brian Swann). St. AR (4:3/4) 77-
    78, p. 103.
  "The Venus Line" (tr. by Talat Halman and Brian Swann). St. AR
    (4:3/4) 77-78, p. 105.
  "the voice" (tr. by Talat Halman and Brain Swann). St. AR
    (4:3/4) 77-78, p. 103.

NECKER, Robert
  "Bicycling." StoneC (78:2) Spr 78, p. 11.

NEELD, Judith Phillips
  "The Boy and the Catch." JnlONJP (2:1) 77, p. 13.
  "Cornwall." JnlONJP (2:1) 77, p. 12.
  "End Paper." SouthwR (63:2) Spr 78, p. 163.
  "The Fool." JnlONJP (2:1) 77, p. 13.

NEILL, Bert
  "Darlene Sees Tigers." PikeF (1) Spr 78, p. 12.

NELSON, Paul
  "Cellars." OhioR (19:3) Aut 78, p. 99.

NELSON, Warren
  "Loan." Bits (7) Ja 78.

NEMARICH, Patricia
  "Moonscaped." Wind (30) 78, p. 37.
  "Rejuvenation." Wind (30) 78, p. 37.

NEPO, Mark
  "The Darker Side of Stars." ColEng (40:3) N 78, p. 294.

NERUDA, Pablo
  "Ode to Poetry" (tr. by Alastair Reid). NewEngR (1:1) Aut 78,
    p. 25.
  "A Tribute to Rafael Alberti" (tr. by Lucia Graves). MalR (47)
    Jl 78, p. 57.

NESTI, Faith
  "To Recapitulate." CarouselQ (3:1) Spr 78, p. 15.

NETTELBECK, F. A.
  "Gun Magic." <u>Tele</u> (13) 77.
  "we ah thee." <u>Tele</u> (13) 77.

NEUFELDT, Leonard
  "Car Failure North of Nimes." <u>SewanR</u> (86:3) Sum 78, p. 375.

NEUMEYER, Peter
  "Difficult Letter." <u>Tendril</u> (1) Wint 77-78.
  "Kafka in West Virginia." <u>ThRiPo</u> (11/12) 78, p. 60.
  "Lashley St. Morgantown West Virginia." <u>Tendril</u> (1) Wint 77-78.

NEWCOMB, P. F.
  "Days Like This." <u>StoneC</u> (78:3) Aut 78, p. 25.

NEWMAN, Felice
  "Telephone: 1/20/78." <u>SlowLR</u> (1/2) 78, p. 87.

NEWMAN, P. B.
  "Horry County Eschatology." <u>SouthernPR</u> (18:1) Spr 78, p. 41.
  "Journey by Sea." <u>NewRivR</u> (2:2) 78, p. 15.
  "The Wretched of the Earth." <u>NewRivR</u> (2:2) 78, p. 16.

NEWTH, Rebecca
  "One for Hulda." <u>Tele</u> (13) 77.

NEY, Linda
  "At the Field." <u>Tendril</u> (1) Wint 77-78.
  "Iguana." <u>Tendril</u> (1) Wint 77-78.

NIATUM, Duane
  "Light Moments in February." <u>NowestR</u> (17:1) 78, p. 32.

NIBBELINK, Cynthia
  Nine poems. <u>GRR</u> (9:1) 78, p. 15.

NICHOLAS
  "Rory." <u>CarouselQ</u> (3:3) Aut 78, p. 27.

NICHOLS, Fred J.
  "The Tomb of Rosa, a Girl Dead before Her Time" (tr. of
      Giovanni Pontano). <u>Paint</u> (7/8) Spr-Aut 77, p. 33.
  "The Tomb of Sanzia, a Neopolitan Girl/She Speaks to Her Hus-
      band, a Painter" (tr. of Giovanni Pontano). <u>Paint</u> (7/8) Spr-
      Aut 77, p. 34.

NICHOLS, Jeanne Moffatt
  "Addie Hall." <u>Epos</u> (27:1) 77, p. 34.

NICHOLSON, Joseph
  "Fort Earth." <u>WormR</u> (70) 78, p. 41.
  "Jo-Jo, the Dog-Faced Boy." <u>WormR</u> (70) 78, p. 43.

"Sabotage. " WormR (70) 78, p. 42.
"The Twenty-One Movie. " WormR (70) 78, p. 43.

NICKLES, Patricia
"Gonna Fly Now. " NewL (45:1) Aut 78, p. 58.

NICOLET, Patt
"On the Function of the Humanities at the Present Time. " AAUP
(64:1) Mr 78, p. 35.

NIDITCH, B. Z.
"Kierkegaard. " ChrC (95:11) 29 Mr 78, p. 330.
"Kierkegaard. " StoneC (78:2) Spr 78, p. 18.
"Minnesota. " StoneC (78:2) Spr 78, p. 18.
"Stud. " NorthSR (8) Aut-Wint 78-79, p. 95.

NIMMO, Kevin
"Descendence. " Smudge (1) Spr 78, p. 33.

NIMMO, Kurt
"Final Stop. " Smudge (1) Spr 78, p. 9.
"humanity has yet to find. " Smudge (3) Aut 78, p. 12.
"in a subterranean world. " Smudge (3) Aut 78, p. 14.
"in a twenty year old suit. " Smudge (3) Aut 78, p. 13.
"village woman. " Smudge (3) Aut 78, p. 15.
"walls. " Smudge (3) Aut 78, p. 11.

NIMNICHT, Nona
"August Wedding. " PoNow (20) 78, p. 33.

NIMS, John Frederick
"Back to Basics: On Rhythm and Rhyme. " LittleM (11:3) Aut
77, p. 25.
"Design: A Further Word. " NewRep (179:20) 11 N 78, p. 28.

NIMTZ, Steven R.
"A Map. " SmPd (44) Aut 78, p. 13.

NISCHAN, Gerda
"The Watchtowers. " SouthernPR (18:1) Spr 78, p. 42.

NIST, John
"Into a Lesser Thing. " Poem (33) Jl 78, p. 11.
"Song to the Man of the People: Charlie Chaplin" (tr. of Carlos
Drummond De Andrade). AmerPoR (7:2) Mr-Ap 78, p. 23.
"Still-Born. " DeKalb (11:3/4) Spr-Sum 78, p. 40.
"You, William Butler Yeats, May Sing. " Poem (33) Jl 78,
p. 12.

NITZSCHE, Jane C.
"Wasp Bite. " LitR (21:3) Spr 78, p. 348.

NIXON, Colin
"Sacred Percentage. " ChrC (95:3) 25 Ja 78, p. 75.

NIXON, John, Jr.
"Across the Hall." SouthernPR (18:1) Spr 78, p. 45.
"August." EngJ (67:5) My 78, p. 56.

NOBLE, Jeanne
"Let the Sky Have a Place in This." Wind (29) 78, p. 37.

NOLAN, Pat
"California Split." LaB (10) 78, p. 31.
"Domestique" (for Steven Paul LaVoie). LaB (10) 78, p. 36.
"St. Pat's Day." LaB (10) 78, p. 34.
"Slippery but Wet." LaB (10) 78, p. 35.

NORD, CarolAnn Russell
"Carrousel." Nimrod (22:2) Spr-Sum 78, p. 51.

NORD, Julie
"The Mask Becomes the Face." Smudge (2) Sum 78, p. 10.

NORDEEN, Steve
"Furrow Poem" (for William Kloefkorn). DacTerr (15) Wint-Spr
77-78, p. 41.
"The Reaper's Harvest." DacTerr (15) Wint-Spr 77-78, p. 40.

NORDHAUS, Jean
"Gift." CentR (22:2) Spr 78, p. 181.
"Lily as Landscape." HiramPoR (25) Aut-Wint 78, p. 31.

NORRIS, Gunilla B.
"Giving In." SouthernPR (18:2) Aut 78, p. 91.

NORRIS, Kathleen
"Dust." VirQR (54:1) Wint 78, p. 112.
"The Little Mermaid." MissouriR (2:1) Aut 78, p. 27.

NORRIS, Leslie
"Cave Paintings." NewYorker (54:3) 6 Mr 78, p. 40.
"Hyperion." Atl (242:2) Ag 78, p. 66.

NORRIS-SZANTO, Gillian
"Ode on the Death of a Favorite Squirrel." NewRena (10) 78,
p. 52.

NORSE, Harold
"Gas Station." PoNow (19) 78, p. 15.
"Green Ballet" (For W. I. Scobie). PoNow (19) 78, p. 15.
"Stratagems." PoNow (19) 78, p. 15.
"Tantalus." PoNow (19) 78, p. 15.
"To Mohammed at the Height." PoNow (19) 78, p. 15.
"You Must Have Been a Sensational Baby." PoNow (19) 78,
p. 15.

NORTH, Charles
"Drawing 1970." Tele (14) 78.

"Poem 1970." Tele (14) 78.
"To David Schubert 1969." Tele (14) 78.

NORTH, Susan
  "Counting." GreenfieldR (6:3/4) Spr 78, p. 107.
  "1400 Lake Shore Drive, Nineteen Floors Up and No Closer to
      Heaven." Aspen (5) Spr 78, p. 118.
  "January." GreenfieldR (6:3/4) Spr 78, p. 106.
  "Juxtaposition." Aspen (5) Spr 78, p. 118.

NORTHNAGEL, E. W.
  "Going Along with the Lie." CarouselQ (3:2) Sum 78, p. 26.

NORTHSUN, Nila
  "la raza." Vaga (27) Spr 78, p. 70.

NORTHUP, Harry E.
  Fourteen poems. Bachy (11) Spr 78, p. 11.

NORTON, Rachel
  "Claude's Wife." 13thM (4:1) 78, p. 75.
  "Middle Name." PoNow (20) 78, p. 33.

NOVACK, Estelle Gershgoren
  "Hunger." CalQ (13/14) Spr-Sum 78, p. 138.

NOVAK, Robert
  "suddenly one day the sun." WindO (31) Wint-Spr 78, p. 47.

NOVEMBER, Sharyn
  "At Dinner." SmPd (43) Spr 78, p. 18.
  "Carving." SmPd (43) Spr 78, p. 19.

NOVET, Harriet
  "cold coffee." Tele (13) 77.
  "sky." Tele (13) 77.

NOWELL, Bob
  "Conspiracy." BallSUF (19:4) Aut 78, p. 33.

NYBERG, Morgan
  "A Brother's Clock." ChiR (29:4) Spr 78, p. 60.

NYHART, Nina
  "Anniversary Quilt." LittleM (11:3) Aut 77, p. 52.
  "Squares: Portrait of a Carpenter." PoetryNW (19:2) Sum 78,
      p. 32.

NYREN, Eve Alison
  "Free Translation of a Stanza by Su Shih (Sung Dynasty)." Pan
      (19) 77, p. 22.

NYSTEDT, Bob
  "Sounds." CarouselQ (3:2) Sum 78, p. 9.

OANDASAN, William
  "Acoma." GreenfieldR (6:3/4) Spr 78, p. 167.

OATES, Joyce Carol
  "Appetite. Terror." TexQ (21:1) Spr 78, p. 6.
  "F" (for Robert Phillips). Iowa (9:3) Sum 78, p. 94.
  "Feast-Day." NewL (45:2) Wint 78, p. 31.
  "Fever Song." TexQ (21:1) Spr 78, p. 8.
  "Giant Sunday Rats." TexQ (21:1) Spr 78, p. 8.
  "Holy Saturday" (For Milton White). MissouriR (1:1) Spr 78,
      p. 17.
  "Psalm." TexQ (21:1) Spr 78, p. 6.
  "Query." MissouriR (1:1) Spr 78, p. 16.
  "Rising to Trees." CentR (22:4) Aut 78, p. 415.
  "The River." NewL (45:2) Wint 78, p. 31.
  "Sweetest Gloomsday." TexQ (21:1) Spr 78, p. 7.
  "There Are Northern Lakes...." Madem (84:3) Mr 78, p. 86.
  "Upon Being Asked 'What Is It Your Practice To Do on Christ-
      mas' by a Mass-Market Women's Magazine with a Circula-
      tion of 75 Billion Readers." CentR (22:4) Aut 78, p. 415.
  "Winter Landscape: Children Teasing Death." NewL (45:2) Wint
      78, p. 33.

OBERTO, Martino (OM)
  from Anaphilosophia: "Ana dell'Esserialismo." Chelsea (37) 78,
      p. 78.
  from Anaphilosophia: "Ana Ars Philosophica." Chelsea (37) 78,
      p. 108.

OBSTFELD, Raymond
  "Patient." CalQ (13/14) Spr-Sum 78, p. 139.

OCHESTER, Ed
  "Panties." WormR (70) 78, p. 71.

O'CONNELL, George
  "Black Clothes at Night" (for Randall Jarrell). AmerPoR (7:6)
      N-D 78, p. 33.

O'CONNELL, Richard
  "About Zoë" (tr. of Palladas). Playb (25:4) Ap 78, p. 157.
  "Complaint" (tr. of Philodemus). Playb (25:4) Ap 78, p. 157.
  "Epigrams" (tr. of Luxorius of Carthage). Playb (25:4) Ap 78,
      p. 157.
  "The Exorcist" (tr. of Lucian). Playb (25:4) Ap 78, p. 157.
  "Flagged" (tr. of Lucian). Playb (25:4) Ap 78, p. 157.
  "Holier Than Thou" (tr. of Lucilius). Playb (25:4) Ap 78,
      p. 157.
  "Long and Short" (tr. of Julian the Apostate). Playb (25:4) Ap
      78, p. 157.
  "The Miser" (tr. of Lucilius). Playb (25:4) Ap 78, p. 157.
  "Revelation" (tr. of Anonymous). Playb (25:4) Ap 78, p. 157.
  "Stiff" (tr. of Antipater of Thessalonica). Playb (25:4) Ap 78,

p. 157.

"Two Against One" (tr. of Dionysius of Andros). Playb (25:4)
    Ap 78, p. 157.

"Undergrad" (tr. of Lucilius). Playb (25:4) Ap 78, p. 157.

ODAM, Joyce
    "Chewing Water. " CimR (45) O 78, p. 36.
    "Elegy for Right Decisions. " Epos (27:1) 77, p. 32.
    "Octave for a Grain of Sand. " Epos (27:1) 77, p. 33.
    "These Days, Coming Like Accusations. " Stonecloud (7) 78,
        p. 68.

O'DONOGHUE, Gregory
    "Aisling. " LitR (22:2) Wint 79, p. 277.
    "Anna Akhmatova. " LitR (22:2) Wint 79, p. 277.
    "A Nomad" (for Sean Lucy). LitR (22:2) Wint 79, p. 276.
    "Nuair chómhnocas an t-iolar ar an ngleann. " LitR (22:2) Wint
        79, p. 277.
    "Rest in Youghall Abbey. " LitR (22:2) Wint 79, p. 278.

O HEHIR, Diana
    "Anger. " Kayak (47) F 78, p. 12.
    "Are You Concerned for Your Safety, Alone in the House?"
        PoetryNW (19:1) Spr 78, p. 5.
    "Exorcising Ghosts. " PoetryNW (19:1) Spr 78, p. 6.
    "Four AM. " PoetryNW (19:1) Spr 78, p. 5.
    "An Isthmus in the Bay. " Kayak (47) F 78, p. 14.
    "Metamorphosis. " Kayak (47) F 78, p. 11.
    "The Power to Change Geography. " Kayak (47) F 78, p. 10.
    "Waiting. " PoetryNW (19:1) Spr 78, p. 4.
    "Watching. " PoetryNW (19:1) Spr 78, p. 3.
    "Waterfall. " Kayak (47) F 78, p. 13.
    "The Worst Motel. " PoetryNW (19:1) Spr 78, p. 3.

O'KEEFE, Richard R.
    "The 'Chinese Exhibition. ' " Chowder (10/11) Aut-Wint 78-79,
        p. 51.
    "Little Feet. " PoetryNW (19:2) Sum 78, p. 19.
    "Postponing Suicide to Buy the Groceries. " PoetryNW (19:2)
        Sum 78, p. 18.

OLACK, Frances Grace
    "Old Man Zelenok. " JnlONJP (2:1) 77, p. 11.
    "Oxheart Bonanza. " JnlONJP (2:1) 77, p. 10.

OLD NORSE
    from Hávamál: "Words from Up Top" (tr. by Paul Edwards and
        Hermann Palsson). LittleM (11:3) Aut 77, p. 60.

OLDKNOW, Antony
    "Cow in a Green Field Charm. " LittleM (11:3) Aut 77, p. 39.
    "Margot. " Nat (226:19) 20 My 78, p. 614.

OLDS, Sharon
"The Daughter Comes Home. " PoNow (20) 78, p. 33.
"The Eye. " Nat (227:19) 2 D 78, p. 615.
"The Feat. " PraS (52:1) Spr 78, p. 89.
"The Guild. " Poetry (133:1) O 78, p. 35.
"Ideographs" (A Photograph of China, 1905). Poetry (133:1) O
    78, p. 34.
"Poem for My Neighbor" (G. T. , -1975). DacTerr (15) Wint-Spr
    77-78, p. 48.
"The Sisters of Sexual Treasure. " ParisR (74) Aut-Wint 78,
    p. 81.
"The Woman at the Sink. " DacTerr (15) Wint-Spr 77-78, p. 48.

OLEAF, Jerry
"Solitude. " Zahir (9) 77, p. 68.

O'LEARY, Dawn
"Another Photo. " JnlONJP (2:2) 77, p. 26.

O'LEARY, Tomas
"Pornographic, for Nathaniel Hawthorne. " MidwQ (19:2) Wint 78,
    p. 142.
"Waking Up Naked on Mother's Day. " MidwQ (19:2) Wint 78,
    p. 140.

OLES, Carole
"Confirmation. " PraS (52:2) Sum 78, p. 172.
"Domestica. " PraS (52:2) Sum 78, p. 170.
"Familiars. " PraS (52:2) Sum 78, p. 170.
"Francestown Suite" (For Jabez Holmes, d. May 11, 1824,
    Francestown, New Hampshire). Poetry (133:2) N 78, p. 82.
"From Outside the Last Room. " QW (5) Wint 78, p. 106.
"Gate in Snow. " PraS (52:2) Sum 78, p. 169.
"The Loneliness Factor. " PraS (52:2) Sum 78, p. 168.
"On an Airplane, Considering Night. " Poetry (133:2) N 78,
    p. 85.
"One Page in The American Heritage Dictionary. " Poetry
    (133:2) N 78, p. 83.
"Rain the Rememberer. " Poetry (132:2) My 78, p. 96.

OLIVER, Mary
"Aerialists. " AmerS (47:4) Aut 78, p. 448.
"Fall Days. " WestHR (32:4) Aut 78, p. 302.
"How She Travels. " WestHR (32:3) Sum 78, p. 268.
"Last Week of Winter. " Comm (105:6) 17 Mr 78, p. 166.
"Messages. " YaleR (67:3) Spr 78, p. 423.
"Night on the Train. " PoetryNW (19:4) Wint 78-79, p. 39.
from The Night Traveler: "Blackleaf Swamp. " NewRep (179:24)
    9 D 78, p. 29.
"Raccoons. " WestHR (32:1) Wint 78, p. 38.
"Sharks. " AndR (5:1) Spr 78, p. 13.
"Sleeping in the Forest. " OhioR (19:1) Wint 78, pp. 49-60.
    Twelve poems.

"Sunday Morning, High Tide." WestHR (32:2) Spr 78, p. 137.
"Walking through the Woods to Pasture Pond, and Back."
    WestHR (32:3) Sum 78, p. 267.

OLIVER, Michael Brian
"Christmas Past." MalR (48) O 78, p. 30.

OLIVER, Raymond
"Sprache als Zuflucht und Doppelgänger to Myself." SouthernHR
    (12:1) Wint 78, p. 30.

OLIVER, William
"Saturday Night/intentions." BlackF (2:2) Aut-Wint 78, p. 25.
"Upon the Backs of Women a Nation Stands." BlackF (2:2) Aut-
    Wint 78, p. 26.

OLIVEROS, Chuck
"Dialectic." CalQ (13/14) Spr-Sum 78, p. 136.
"Diving." CimR (42) Ja 78, p. 16.
"What Do You Do?" CalQ (13/14) Spr-Sum 78, p. 137.
"Flying Blind." Sky (7/8) Spr 78, p. 26.
"Long Johns." PoNow (20) 78, p. 33.
"The Patron Saint of Gimp." SmPd (44) Aut 78, p. 14.
"Suicide." SouthernPR (18:2) Aut 78, p. 84.
"Sunning." WindO (32) Sum-Aut 78, p. 6.

OLMSTEAD, Jane
"Our Shadows Race Lengthwise." PoetryNW (19:2) Sum 78,
    p. 38.

OLSEN, Susan
"Mitch's hard, furrowed hands." Nor (8) Aut 78, p. 2.

OLSEN, William
"Conoco Station and House." CutB (11) Aut-Wint 78, p. 12.
"Ephemera: After the War." SouthernPR (18:2) Aut 78, p. 7.
"Migrant Workers Asleep by the Pacific at Twilight." Falcon
    (17) 78, p. 13.
"Rest Home, Kearney, Nebraska." CutB (11) Aut-Wint 78,
    p. 11.

OLSON, Elder
"Rottenrock Mountain" (For James Dickey). SoCaR (10:2) Ap 78,
    p. 4.

OLSON, Toby
"Aesthetics-31." Hand (2) 78, p. 122.
"Standard-7, an Austere Song for Sal Mineo." Hand (2) 78,
    p. 180.
"Yellow Bird." Hand (2) 78, p. 121.

OLSZONOWICZ, Kathryn
"I am chasing racing clouds." Wind (29) 78, p. 35.

O'MALLEY, Sister Emanuela
"To Our Unborn. " KanQ (10:2) Spr 78, p. 39.

O'NEIL, Susan Breen
"Drowning Naked. " HolCrit (15:3) Je 78, p. 16.

O'NEILL, Laurence T.
"Composition. " Wind (31) 78, p. 40.
"A Monologue. " Wind (31) 78, p. 40.

O'NEILL, Patrick
"The Maternal Pros. " YellowBR (10) 78, p. 36.

OPALOV, Leonard
"Far Away Vision. " Wind (31) 78, p. 44.

OPPEN, George
"Gold on Oak Leaves. " Montra (4) 78, p. 237.
"Gold on Oak Leaves Said Young. " AmerPoR (7:3) My-Je 78,
    p. 19.
"The Natural. " Montra (4) 78, p. 241.
"Neighbors. " Montra (4) 78, p. 238.
"Probity. " Montra (4) 78, p. 240.
"The Whirl Wind Must. " AmerPoR (7:3) My-Je 78, p. 19.

OPPENHEIMER, Joel
"Houses. " ChiR (30:3) Wint 79, p. 89.

ORCHOFF, Marilyn
"A Suburbanite Talks to William Wordsworth. " EngJ (67:5) My
    78, p. 64.

ORLEN, Steve
"Aegean. " SenR (9:1) Spr-Sum 78, p. 72.
"Disguise. " Antaeus (30/31) Sum-Aut 78, p. 163.
"Family Cups. " AntR (36:3) Sum 78, p. 373.
"Letter from a Saint. " Antaeus (30/31) Sum-Aut 78, p. 167.
"Love and Memory. " Antaeus (30/31) Sum-Aut 78, p. 165.
"The Magic of the Pale Event: Transsexual. " SenR (9:1) Spr-
    Sum 78, p. 70.

ORLOVITZ, Gil
Twelve poems. AmerPoR (7:6) N-D 78, p. 23.

ORMSBY, Frank
"Being Walked by a Dog. " LitR (22:2) Wint 79, p. 261.
"Interior Decorating. " LitR (22:2) Wint 79, p. 260.
"A Memory of Summer. " LitR (22:2) Wint 79, p. 262.
"Sightings. " LitR (22:2) Wint 79, p. 259.
"A Small Town in Ireland. " LitR (22:2) Wint 79, p. 260.
"Walking Home at Night. " LitR (22:2) Wint 79, p. 263.
"Walking Home at Night. " Stand (19:2) 78, p. 15.
"A Wet Hour in Belfast. " LitR (22:2) Wint 79, p. 263.

O'ROURKE, Michael
"Retreat." BallSUF (19:1) Wint 78, p. 56.

ORR, Gregory
"A Buoyant Song." Antaeus (30/31) Sum-Aut 78, p. 169.
"Interrogation." Antaeus (30/31) Sum-Aut 78, p. 171.
"Lullaby Elegy Dream." Antaeus (30/31) Sum-Aut 78, p. 172.
"Song." Antaeus (30/31) Sum-Aut 78, p. 171.
"Song of the Invisible Corpse in the Field." Antaeus (30/31)
     Sum-Aut 78, p. 170.
"The Wall." Box (6) Aut 77, p. 9.

OSAKI, M. S.
"The Photograph." SoCaR (10:2) Ap 78, p. 99.

OSTRIKER, Alicia
"Becky and Benny in Far Rockaway." CalQ (13/14) Spr-Sum 78,
     p. 64.
"The Courage." US1 (11) Aut 78, p. 3.
"The Exchange." US1 (11) Aut 78, p. 2.
"For the Daughters." CalQ (13/14) Spr-Sum 78, p. 65.
"In Spring Rain." MidwQ (19:4) Sum 78, p. 381.
"Moon and Earth." US1 (11) Aut 78, p. 2.
"My Lecture to the Writing Students." MidwQ (19:4) Sum 78,
     p. 382.
"Once More Out of Darkness." SenR (9:2) Aut-Wint 78, p. 32.
"The Singing School." MidwQ (19:4) Sum 78, p. 380.
"The Waiting Room." US1 (11) Aut 78, p. 3.

OSTROFF, Anthony
"The Altar at Teotihuacán." PoNow (19) 78, p. 10.
"Jumping Bean." PoNow (19) 78, p. 10.
"Monte Albán." PoNow (19) 78, p. 10.
"Village Morning." PoNow (19) 78, p. 10.

OSTROM, Hans
"Sea Monster." Wind (28) 78, p. 52.

OSWALD, Roy
"Vagabond." CarouselQ (3:1) Spr 78, p. 15.

OTERO, Blas de
"From Cordoba to Cadiz" (tr. by Lucia Graves). MalR (47) Jl
     78, p. 156.

OTT, Tom
"The Basic Two by Four." Nimrod (22:2) Spr-Sum 78, p. 55.

OUTRAM, Richard
"Nine Poems from Guise." MalR (48) O 78, p. 128.

OVIATT, Phil
"The Glacier." YaleLit (147:3) 78, p. 17.
"The Slime Mold." YaleLit (147:3) 78, p. 16.

OWEN, Sue
   "About My Bones." SlowLR (1/2) 78, p. 65.
   "The Fear." Epos (27:1) 77, p. 36.
   "Journey." PoetryNW (19:4) Wint 78-79, p. 35.
   "Lullaby" (for Robert Louthan). Iowa (9:3) Sum 78, p. 90.
   "The Obscure." CalQ (13/14) Spr-Sum 78, p. 87.
   "Trouble." SlowLR (1/2) 78, p. 67.

OWENS, George
   "1 Purple heard near Ohio, You All, Poem." Tele (14) 78.
   "West-bound." Tele (14) 78.

OWENS, Rochelle
   from The Joe Chronicles, Part 2: (4, 5). 13thM (4:1) 78, p. 27.

OWER, John
   "A la Recherche." Poem (34) Jl 78, p. 15.
   "Canadian Homecoming." SoDakR (16:2) Sum 78, p. 25.
   "The Legacy." Epos (27:1) 77, p. 10.
   "Moths." QW (5) Wint 78, p. 49.
   "Perspectives." Poem (34) N 78, p. 17.
   "Temptation." Poem (34) Jl 78, p. 16.
   "Trans-Canada Train." SoDakR (16:2) Sum 78, p. 27.

OZAROW, Kent Jorgensen
   "Low Down." StoneC (78:1) Wint 78, p. 10.

PACERNICK, Gary
   "The Diver." PoNow (19) 78, p. 14.

PACK, Robert
   "The Meeting." Poetry (132:2) My 78, p. 102.
   "Rondo of the Familiar." Chowder (10/11) Aut-Wint 78-79,
      p. 62.
   "Rules." Poetry (132:5) Ag 78, p. 281.
   "The Vase." NewEngR (1:1) Aut 78, p. 46.

PADDOCK, Nancy
   "The Pay-Off." MoonsLT (2:4) 78, p. 47.
   "Rapunzel." MoonsLT (2:4) 78, p. 46.

PADILLA, David
   "Pinto Viejo." GreenfieldR (7:1/2) Aut 78, p. 21.

PADILLA, Heberto
   "Just by Opening Your Eyes" (tr. by Alastair Reid). NewYRB
      (25:18) 23 N 78, p. 10.
   "Techniques of Pursuit" (tr. by Alastair Reid). NewYRB (25:18)
      23 N 78, p. 10.

PAGANELLI, Marilyn J.
   "Small, Yet Peace." Wind (28) 78, p. 27.

PAGE, P. K.
  "About Death. " MalR (45) Ja 78, p. 197.
  "Evening Dance of the Grey Flies" (For Chris).   MalR (45) Ja
      78, p. 196.
  "Message. " MalR (45) Ja 78, p. 199.
  "On Brushing My Hair in the Static-Filled Air. " MalR (45) Ja
      78, p. 199.
  "Sestina for Pat Lane after Reading 'Albino Pheasants.'" MalR
      (45) Ja 78, p. 200.
  "Song ... Much of It Borrowed. " MalR (45) Ja 78, p. 198.

PAGE, William
  "A Blister of Paint. " SouthernPR (18:2) Aut 78, p. 35.
  "The Contact. " SlowLR (1/2) 78, p. 74.
  "A Fable. " Wind (28) 78, p. 47.
  "Gallagher. " Wind (28) 78, p. 47.
  "On My 50th Birthday. " Zahir (9) 77, p. 67.

PAGNUCCI, G.
  "The Death of an Elephant. " Northeast (3:6) Wint 78-79, p. 8.

PALADINO, Tom
  from Behind Narcissus: "Museumed Lung. " Tele (13) 77.
  from Behind Narcissus: "Night-Grin at the UN Diner. " Tele
      (13) 77.
  from Behind Narcissus: "Valencia Hotel '66. " Tele (13) 77.

PALAZZOLA, Benedette
  "Eleven-Thirty. " HangL (34) Wint 78-79, p. 57.

PALCHI, Alfredo de
  "The Storm" (tr. of Eugenio Montale, w. Sonia Raiziss).   StoneC
      (78:1) Wint 78, p. 23.

PALEN, John
  "Missouri Town. " PoetryNW (19:3) Aut 78, p. 43.

PALEY, Grace
  "Stanzas: Old Age and the Conventions of Retirement Have
      Driven My Friends From the Work They Love. " Field (19)
      Aut 78, p. 57.

PALEY, Morton
  "Six Days of Creation at Middleton Cheney. " MichQR (17:2) Spr
      78, p. 196.

PALLADAS
  "About Zoë" (tr. by Richard O'Connell).   Playb (25:4) Ap 78,
      p. 157.

PALLANT, Marilee Lehman
  "Joy. " Wind (31) 78, p. 42.

PALLISTER, Jan
"Hemeroskopeion" (tr. of Salvador Espriu). SlowLR (1/2) 78,
    p. 64.
"Sure Catch" (tr. of Salvador Espriu). SlowLR (1/2) 78, p. 63.

PALMER, Jeremy
"Shadow Piece." StoneC (78:31) Aut 78, p. 13.

PALMER, Leslie
"Few Chords and Sad and Low: Sing We So." BallSUF (19:2)
    Spr 78, p. 55.

PALMER, Michael
"November Talks." Hills (5) 78, p. 84.
"Portrait Now Before Then." Hills (5) 78, p. 84.

PALMER, William
"Drinking from a Pond." Bits (8) Jl 78.
"The Mirror of the Dove." Stand (19:3) 78, p. 44.
"Walking from the House of the Dead." Stand (19:3) 78, p. 45.

PALSSON, Hermann
from Hávamál: "Words from Up Top" (tr. of Old Norse, w.
    Paul Edwards). LittleM (11:3) Aut 77, p. 60.

PAPADAKIS, Miro
"Four Poems" (tr. by Frank Polite). Paint (9/10) Spr-Aut 78,
    p. 49.

PARINI, Jay
"Beginning the World." Hudson (31:4) Wint 78-79, p. 618.
"Illimitable Kingdom." Hudson (31:4) Wint 78-79, p. 619.
"Playing in the Mines." GeoR (32:3) Aut 78, p. 610.
"Seasons of the Skin." ParisR (74) Aut-Wint 78, p. 80.
"Tanya." Hudson (31:4) Wint 78-79, p. 618.
"Walking the Trestle." Atl (242:3) S 78, p. 46.

PARINS, Jim
"John Coons Pursued and Taken." NewOR (6:1) 78, p. 69.

PARISH, Barbara S.
"Discontent." SmPd (43) Spr 78, p. 14.

PARKER, Douglass
"Ars Poetica I: Beginning" (for Lili). Hudson (31:4) Wint 78-
    79, p. 631.

PARKS, Patricia
"Wandering Still." GRR (9:3) 78, p. 222.

PARLETT, Jim
"The Absence of Light." Atl (241:1) Ja 78, p. 57.

PARNELL, Wayne
  "Can't We Just." GreenfieldR (7:1/2) Aut 78, p. 68.

PARRISH, Wendy
  "A Heavy Feeling." Paunch (52) O 78, p. 4.
  "Last Weather Poem." AntR (36:2) Spr 78, p. 196.
  "A Poem without You." Paunch (52) O 78, p. 5.
  "Sick Bed." Northeast (3:5) Spr-Sum 78, p. 13.
  "Speaking to Herself." Paunch (52) O 78, p. 3.
  "Visions." Northeast (3:5) Spr-Sum 78, p. 12.

PARSON, Tom
  "After the Party." Tele (14) 78.
  "The End of Apartheid." Tele (14) 78.

PASTAN, Linda
  "Bird of Paradise." Glass (3:1/2/3) 78, p. 26.
  "Blizzard." Poetry (133:3) D 78, p. 136.
  "Elegy." Hudson (31:1) Spr 78, p. 123.
  "Elsewhere." NewEngR (1:1) Aut 78, p. 29.
  "Excursion." Poetry (132:5) Ag 78, p. 273.
  "Friday's Child." Nat (226:17) 6 My 78, p. 548.
  "In Back Of." NewYorker (54:6) 27 Mr 78, p. 42.
  "Lot's Wife." Confr (17) Aut-Wint 79, p. 85.
  "McGuffey's First Eclectic Reader." Field (19) Aut 78, p. 23.
  "On Hearing the Testimony of Those Revived after Cardiac Ar-
      rest." Poetry (132:2) My 78, p. 80.
  "On the Road to Delphi." Confr (17) Aut-Wint 79, p. 85.
  "Pain." Poetry (132:5) Ag 78, p. 274.
  "Pears." OhioR (19:2) Spr-Sum 78, p. 48.
  "Petit Dejeuner." Bits (7) Ja 78.
  "Presbyopia." Nat (227:2) 8-15 Jl 78, p. 56.
  "Sabbatical" (for Ira). Glass (3:1/2/3) 78, p. 26.
  "Waiting for My Life." Hudson (31:1) Spr 78, p. 123.

PASTERNAK, Boris
  Eight poems (tr. by Mark Rudman and Bohdan Boychuk). VirQR
      (54:4) Aut 78, p. 601.
  "How Life Lulls Us" (tr. by Mark Rudman and Bohdan Boychuk).
      Pequod (2:4) 78, p. 12.

PATERNOSTER, Linda T.
  "Erotic." CarouselQ (3:2) Sum 78, p. 15.
  "Longing to Be Me." CarouselQ (3:4) Wint 78, p. 14.
  "Neptune's Daughter." CarouselQ (3:2) Sum 78, p. 15.

PATRICK, W. B.
  "Companion" (for my grandmother). SlowLR (1/2) 78, p. 52.
  "May, 1864: Two Photographs." SlowLR (1/2) 78, p. 50.

PATTEN, Karl
  "Anecdote of Two Poets: How Supervielle's Forgetfulness Made

Either Truth Truer or Truer Truth: Or, How to Get from
the Real to the Really Unreal. " NewL (44:3) Spr 78, p. 41.

PATTERSON, J. Hunter
"For Jeannette. " St. AR (4:3/4) 77-78, p. 126.
"Tutankhamun in Washington. " St. AR (4:3/4) 77-78, p. 125.

PATTERSON, Raymond R.
"Dearest Phillis. " BelPoJ (29:2) Wint 78-79, p. 27.

PATTERSON, Tom
"The Age of Reptiles. " St. AR (4:3/4) 77-78, p. 122.
"The Chosen Notes, the Chimes in China. " St. AR (5:1) Aut-
Wint 78, p. 136.
"One Walks. " St. AR (5:1) Aut-Wint 78, p. 14.
"Sapelo Island--Dec. 31, 1976. " St. AR (4:3/4) 77-78, p. 122.

PATTERSON, Veronica
"Dying Down. " Wind (29) 78, p. 7.
"Reading Little House on the Prairie to You. " SmPd (44) Aut
78, p. 8.

PATTON, Rob
"Accident. " GreenfieldR (6:3/4) Spr 78, p. 156.
"Born in Chicago. " GreenfieldR (6:3/4) Spr 78, p. 155.

PAUL, James
"The Mouths of the Year. " NewRep (179:20) 11 N 78, p. 28.

PAUL, Jay S.
"Heirloom Cups. " Wind (28) 78, p. 49.

PAULIN, Tom
"Still Century. " Stand (19:2) 78, p. 22.
"Trotsky in Finland. " Stand (19:2) 78, p. 23.

PAU-LLOSA, Ricardo
"Dive. " Epos (27:2) 77, p. 24.

PAULUZZI, Faust
from Figure di Nessuno: "Having with these eyes seen" (tr. of
Rubina Giorgi). Chelsea (37) 78, p. 161.
from 3 Ideologie da Piazza del Popolo/Senza L'Imprimatur:
"Pythagoras' Hand" (tr. of Emilio Villa, w. Richard Milazzo).
Chelsea (37) 78, p. 5.

PAYACK, Paul J. J.
"Doe or Zho?" NewL (44:3) Spr 78, p. 62.
"The Face of His Father. " NewL (44:3) Spr 78, p. 63.
"A Little Known Fact IV. " NewL (44:3) Spr 78, p. 62.

PAYACK, Peter
Rainbow Bridges (for Monica and Mary). Sam (70) 78.   Entire

issue.
"Stone Cold." <u>PoNow</u> (20) 78, p. 34.

PAYNE, Gerrye
"The Returning" (for my daughter). <u>Wind</u> (29) 78, p. 36.

PAZ, Octavio
"La caverna" (a Donald Sutherland) (tr. by Leland H. Chambers).
    <u>DenQ</u> (13:3) Aut 78, p. 4.
"Distant Neighbor" (tr. by Eliot Weinberger). <u>Montra</u> (4) 78,
    p. 184.
"Exclamation" (tr. by Eliot Weinberger). <u>Montra</u> (4) 78, p. 183.
"Flame, Speech" (tr. by Mark Strand). <u>Nat</u> (227:6) 2 S 78,
    p. 182.
"Stars and Cricket" (tr. by Eliot Weinberger). <u>Montra</u> (4) 78,
    p. 184.

PEACOCK, Molly
"A Kind of Parlance." <u>Shen</u> (29:2) Wint 78, p. 40.
"Matisse: Two Girls." <u>Epoch</u> (27:3) Spr 78, p. 288.

PEACOCK, Nancy Been
"Three Examples of Death in the Same Room." <u>GreenfieldR</u>
    (6:3/4) Spr 78, p. 164.

PEAKE, Richard
"Sails from the Orient." <u>Wind</u> (28) 78, p. 51.

PEARLBERG, Gerry
"Boxes." <u>HangL</u> (34) Wint 78-79, p. 60.
"City Shorts." <u>HangL</u> (34) Wint 78-79, p. 58.
"Dream #1." <u>HangL</u> (34) Wint 78-79, p. 59.
"In a Dream." <u>HangL</u> (34) Wint 78-79, p. 59.
"Seven Snows." <u>HangL</u> (34) Wint 78-79, p. 58.

PEARLMAN, Robert
"Lacustrine." <u>Pan</u> (19) 77, p. 61.

PEARLMAN, Tish
"Fragments from a Shattered Summer." <u>CarouselQ</u> (3:3) Aut 78,
    p. 2.

PEARSON, Carol Lynn
"Good Ground." <u>LadHJ</u> (95:2) F 78, p. P.S.3.

PEARSON, Stephen
"Northern General Hospital, Sheffield, April 1977." <u>Stand</u> (19:3)
    78, p. 11.

PEASE, Deborah
"Chivalry." <u>Confr</u> (17) Aut-Wint 79, p. 21.
"Coquette." <u>BelPoJ</u> (28:4) Sum 78, p. 16.
"A New Home." <u>SoDakR</u> (16:2) Sum 78, p. 6.
"A Toll of Industry." <u>Ploughs</u> (4:2) 78, p. 36.

PEASE, Roland
  "Strike." PoNow (20) 78, p. 34.

PECK, Gail
  "Restraints." SouthernPR (18:2) Aut 78, p. 19.

PEERY, Pamela Jane
  "Hands grasp wooden handles." Tele (13) 77.
  "my eye can see the lint." Tele (13) 77.

PEFFER, Randall
  "Daughter." AndR (5:2) Aut 78, p. 37.

PELLETIER, Cathie
  "Stonehenge." BelPoJ (28:4) Sum 78, p. 28.

PELLETIER, Gus
  "A Vertical Arrangement of Horizontal Lines." CarouselQ (3:4)
    Wint 78, p. 39.

PENCE, Susan
  "Earth Song." CarouselQ (3:3) Aut 78, p. 19.
  "Kauai (Hawaii)." CarouselQ (3:4) Wint 78, p. 36.

PENFOLD, Gerda
  "After the Last Scene." Vaga (27) Spr 78, p. 23.
  "The Atom Bomb Finally Went Off." Vaga (27) Spr 78, p. 22.
  "Nada Sweet Nada." Vaga (27) Spr 78, p. 20.
  "Nothing Bath Oil Sweet Here." Vaga (27) Spr 78, p. 16.
  "Peeling." Vaga (27) Spr 78, p. 19.
  "She Insists." Stonecloud (7) 78, p. 93.
  "They're Starting to Hatch Again." Vaga (27) Spr 78, p. 21.

PENNES, Rickey
  "My Brothers." SeC (5:2) 78, p. 26.

PENTRE, Barbara
  "Desperate Prattle." Tendril (3) Aut 78, p. 41.

PERCHAN, Bob
  "The Coming of Spring III." Zahir (9) 77, p. 62.

PERCHIK, Simon
  "Antiqued to show damage." Bleb/Ark (13) 78, p. 31.
  "Arrayed, pitted, opened, my coat." Bleb/Ark (13) 78, p. 30.
  "*." MassR (19:2) Sum 78, p. 407.
  "*." Pig (5) 78, p. 63.
  "*." SlowLR (1/2) 78, p. 59.
  "*." Tele (14) 78.
  "*." Tele (14) 78.

PERELMAN, Bob
  "The Earth." Tele (13) 77.

"Lovemaking." Tele (13) 77.
"Outlines." Hills (5) 78, p. 87.
"the standard subjects." Tele (13) 77.

PERET, Benjamin
  "The Abnormal Labor" (tr. by Jane Barnard and Albert Frank
    Moritz). MalR (48) O 78, p. 78.

PERKINS, D. N.
  "The Caretaker." PraS (52:3) Aut 78, p. 274.
  "The Prisoners." PraS (52:3) Aut 78, p. 275.

PERKINS, Mark
  "The Young Arsonist." SouthwR (63:1) Wint 78, p. 40.

PERLBERG, Mark
  "The Leap." Hudson (31:2) Sum 78, p. 302.

PERLMAN, Anne S.
  "Summer Hillside." Nat (226:13) 8 Ap 78, p. 414.

PERMENTER, Amy
  "Along the Seashore." DeKalb (11:3/4) Spr-Sum 78, p. 41.

PERREAULT, George
  "Nearing the Winter Solstice." Tele (13) 77.

PERROTTA, Raffaele
  "Corpus." Chelsea (37) 78, p. 198.
  "Verso Opus." Chelsea (37) 78, p. 206.

PERRY, Thelma D.
  "Inheritance." NegroHB (41:1) Ja-F 78, p. 786.

PERRY, Thomas A.
  "Dioptric" (tr. of Ion Barbu). Paint (7/8) Spr-Aut 77, p. 61.

PERSON, Tom
  "Paper Airplane." Tele (14) 78.
  "Summer 1910." Tele (14) 78.

PESEROFF, Joyce
  "The Captive." Aspect (71) Ap-Je 77, p. 7.
  "Cripples from Brueghel." PoNow (20) 78, p. 27.
  "Florida." Aspect (71) Ap-Je 77, p. 8.
  "Fuck Poem." PoNow (20) 78, p. 27.
  "Layover." VirQR (54:2) Spr 78, p. 286.
  "Rain." PoNow (20) 78, p. 27.
  "Winter in New England." AndR (5:2) Aut 78, p. 61.

PESSOA, Fernando
  "The astonishing reality of things" (tr. by Erskine Lane).
    Bleb/Ark (13) 78, p. 43.

"At times on days of exact and perfect light" (tr. by Erskine
Lane). Bleb/Ark (13) 78, p. 38.
"If I should die young" (tr. by Erskine Lane). Bleb/Ark (13) 78,
p. 44.
"I'm not concerned with rhymes" (tr. by Erskine Lane).
Bleb/Ark (13) 78, p. 45.
"On an unusually clear day" (tr. by Erskine Lane). Bleb/Ark
(13) 78, p. 41.
"The Tagus is prettier than the river that flows by my village"
(tr. of Erskine Lane). Bleb/Ark (13) 78, p. 37.

PETACCIA, Mario A.
"Play Dylan for Sally." GreenfieldR (7:1/2) Aut 78, p. 58.
"Six Days." SouthernPR (18:2) Aut 78, p. 15.

PETERFREUND, Stuart
"Solstice Letter" (for my father). Epoch (27:2) Wint 78, p. 172.

PETERS, Nancy
"New Scent." Comm (105:9) 28 Ap 78, p. 265.
"A Woman in Her Room." Comm (105:1) 6 Ja 78, p. 12.

PETERS, Robert
"Ikagnak: The North Wind." Kayak (49) O 78, p. 10.

PETERSEN, Gail
"blown cool." Tele (13) 77.
"Flight 66." Tele (13) 77.

PETERSON, James
"Blackhawk." KanQ (10:3) Sum 78, p. 75.

PETERSON, Jim
"Never." StoneC (78:3) Aut 78, p. 24.

PETERSON, Margaret
"Setting Chrysanthemums" (for Kris, age 9). SouthernR (14:1)
Wint 78, p. 114.

PETERSON, Marsha
"The Camellia." DacTerr (15) Wint-Spr 77-78, p. 36.

PETESCH, Donald A.
"An Early Kodak." PoNow (20) 78, p. 35.
"The Poet Visits Indiana State University Looking for a Job."
SlowLR (1/2) 78, p. 70.

PETRIE, Paul
"Handstand." AmerS (47:3) Sum 78, p. 328.
"The Pause." Atl (241:5) My 78, p. 47.

PETROSKI, Henry
"Chairs." LittleM (11:3) Aut 77, p. 72.

PETROSKY, Anthony
  "The Storm." OhioR (19:2) Spr-Sum 78, p. 45.

PETTINELLA, Dora M.
  "Dear Life, I do not ask of you" (tr. of Eugenio Montale).
      NewOR (6:1) 78, p. 76.
  "Finale" (tr. of Giuseppe Ungaretti). MalR (46) Ap 78, p. 146.
  "Happiness at Heart" (tr. of Eugenio Montale). NewOR (6:1) 78,
      p. 76.

PETTEE, Dan
  "Halfway Between." ChiR (30:1) Sum 78, p. 60.

PETTIT, Michael
  "Coastal Bermuda Hay." BelPoJ (28:3) Spr 78, p. 23.
  "Peace and Quiet are Not the Same Thing." BelPoJ (28:3) Spr
      78, p. 22.
  "Storm Watch." BelPoJ (28:3) Spr 78, p. 23.

PEYSTER, Steven
  Eight poems. Tele (14) 78.

PFINGSTON, Roger
  "Cracking Under the Weight of Snow." Bits (7) Ja 78.
  "Early History." NewRivR (2:2) 78, p. 60.
  "From the Heartland." NewRivR (2:2) 78, p. 61.
  "The Gardener's Wife Speaks of Fire." NewRivR (2:2) 78,
      p. 62.
  Nesting. Sparrow (36) 78. 28pp. A Sparrow Poverty Pamphlet.

PFISTERER, Ruth
  "Untitled." CarouselQ (3:1) Spr 78, p. 14.

PHELPS, Dean
  "Parma." SoDakR (16:2) Sum 78, p. 65.
  "Under Water Sound." SoDakR (16:2) Sum 78, p. 64.
  "A View from Another Churchyard." SoDakR (16:2) Sum 78,
      p. 67.

PHILBRICK, Stephen
  "'Let's Pants Him.'" PoNow (19) 78, p. 43.
  "Two Boys Went." PoNow (19) 78, p. 43.

PHILIPPS, Roxanne
  "A Broken Doll." CarouselQ (3:2) Sum 78, p. 19.

PHILLIPS, Dennis
  from The Frontier: "Part One (Historical) Funeral, Continuance,
      Depth-perception, and Recognition of Perimeters." Bachy
      (11) Spr 78, p. 21.
  from The Frontier: "Part Two (Mythological)-first half." Bachy
      (12) Aut 78, p. 94.
  from The Frontier: "Part Two (Mythological)-second half."

Bachy (13) Aut-Wint 78-79, p. 123.
from Two Cross: "We were left safe on the beach." ChiR
(30:1) Sum 78, p. 62.

PHILLIPS, Frances
"Carried to Wear the Frosty Light." HangL (32) Spr 78, p. 39.
"Everywhere on Palm Avenue Custom Throws Glitter." HangL
(32) Spr 78, p. 40.
"In Which Libby Gets Her Rock." HangL (32) Spr 78, p. 44.

PHILLIPS, Jayne Anne
"Rhyming." PoetryNW (19:3) Aut 78, p. 28.

PHILLIPS, L. C.
"Gone." BelPoJ (29:1) Aut 78, p. 17.

PHILLIPS, Louis
"Disaster Films in Los Angeles." DeKalb (11:1/2) Aut-Wint 77-
78, p. 60.
"For the Man Who Built His Own Life Out of Spare Automobile
Parts." CentR (22:3) Sum 78, p. 323.
"In Friendship Our Lives Come Around." CentR (22:1) Wint 78,
p. 76.
"Mare Imbrium." CimR (43) Ap 78, p. 46.
"The Meaning of Astronomy." DeKalb (11:1/2) Aut-Wint 77-78,
p. 61.
"The Musings of a Solitary Bus Traveller." DeKalb (11:1/2)
Aut-Wint 77-78, p. 62.

PHILLIPS, Robert
"Burchfield's World" (for John I. H. Baur). Hudson (31:2) Sum
78, p. 271.
"Decks." Hudson (31:2) Sum 78, p. 270.
from The Pregnant Man: "The Married Man." NewRep
(179:24) 9 D 78, p. 27.
"Soft and Hard." Hudson (31:2) Sum 78, p. 272.
"The Stone Crab: A Love Poem." Hudson (31:2) Sum 78,
p. 269.

PHILLIS, Yannis
"He Said." StoneC (78:3) Aut 78, p. 22.

PHILODEMUS
"Complaint" (tr. by Richard O'Connell). Playb (25:4) Ap 78,
p. 157.
"I. v. 112" (tr. by George Economou). Pequod (2:4) 78, p. 60.
"Thrice Blessed" (tr. by Philodemus). Playb (25:4) Ap 78,
p. 157.

PICCIONE, Anthony
"By a Pond in Winter." SlowLR (1/2) 78, p. 10.
"For My Wife: Poem with Whitman Standing Nearby." AmerPoR
(7:4) Jl-Ag 78, p. 33.

"For Rachel: Talking to Frogs in Winter." SlowLR (1/2) 78,
    p. 11.
"Late Night, World of Croaks." SlowLR (1/2) 78, p. 12.
"Like the Siberian Mammoth." AmerPoR (7:4) Jl-Ag 78, p. 33.
"Poem Touching the Feet." AmerPoR (7:4) Jl-Ag 78, p. 33.

PICCIONE, Sandi
    "After a Long Time Waiting." AmerPoR (7:4) Jl-Ag 78, p. 34.
    "In March, Longing for Bees." AmerPoR (7:4) Jl-Ag 78, p. 34.
    "Polar Sun." SlowLR (1/2) 78, p. 98.
    "Snake Skin" (for Kay). SlowLR (1/2) 78, p. 99.
    "Watching Friends on an Empty Beach." AmerPoR (7:4) Jl-Ag
        78, p. 34.
    "With You at Blakelock Pond." AmerPoR (7:4) Jl-Ag 78, p. 34.

PICHASKE, David R.
    "Reflections." BallSUF (19:4) Aut 78, p. 39.

PIERCE, Edith Lovejoy
    "Bells." ChrC (95:21) 7-14 Je 78, p. 604.
    "Salute to Pope John Paul II." ChrC (95:35) 1 N 78, p. 1037.

PIERCY, Marge
    "Aries and Capricorn." Tendril (3) Aut 78, p. 42.
    "Excursions, Incursions." OP (26) Aut-Wint 78, p. 42.
    "Michigan Jenny." Tendril (1) Wint 77-78.
    "Nothing You Can Have." MassR (19:1) Spr 78, p. 89.
    "Sentimental Poem" (for Woody). Bits (8) Jl 78.
    "September Afternoon at Four O'Clock." OP (26) Aut-Wint 78,
        p. 47.
    "Waiting Outside." Tendril (1) Wint 77-78.

PIERSON, Philip
    "Bagworms." SlowLR (1/2) 78, p. 6.
    "The Bat Tree." SlowLR (1/2) 78, p. 4.
    "The Catch." SlowLR (1/2) 78, p. 8.
    "Deer on the Stillrun River." SouthernPR (18:1) Spr 78, p. 29.
    "The Good Life." NewOR (5:4) 78, p. 332.
    "The Junkyard Tractor-Driver Defies His Death." SoCaR (10:2)
        Ap 78, p. 63.
    "My Grandmother Rises from the Grave." SewanR (86:3) Sum
        78, p. 376.
    "My Mother Rehearses Her Funeral." MassR (19:2) Sum 78,
        p. 335.
    "Technique." Chowder (10/11) Aut-Wint 78-79, p. 34.
    "To a Child Bride at the Rose Lane Tourist." OhioR (19:3) Aut
        78, p. 6.

PIES, Ronald
    "Voices." LitR (21:3) Spr 78, p. 339.

PIETRI, Pedro Juan
    "Traffic Violations." AmerPoR (7:4) Jl-Ag 78, p. 21.

PIJEWSKI, John
  "The Cloud" (tr. of Tymoteusz Karpowicz). <u>ChiR</u> (29:4) Spr 78,
    p. 106.
  "Fathers." <u>PoetryNW</u> (19:1) Spr 78, p. 47.
  "Feathers" (tr. of Tymoteusz Karpowicz). <u>ChiR</u> (29:4) Spr 78,
    p. 106.
  "Growing Potatoes." <u>CentR</u> (22:2) Spr 78, p. 186.
  "The Hero" (tr. of Tymoteusz Karpowicz). <u>Durak</u> (1) 78, p. 58.
  "The House in March" (tr. of Jerzy Harasymowicz). <u>NewYorker</u>
    (54:7) 3 Ap 78, p. 32.
  "Hunger." <u>ParisR</u> (72) Wint 77, p. 138.
  "In the Bag." <u>PoetryNW</u> (19:1) Spr 78, p. 46.
  "The Magic Mountain" (tr. of Tymoteusz Karpowicz). <u>ChiR</u>
    (29:4) Spr 78, p. 108.
  "Mushrooms." <u>CentR</u> (22:2) Spr 78, p. 185.
  "No One Knows" (tr. of Tymoteusz Karpowicz). <u>Durak</u> (1) 78, p. 59.
  "The Partitioning of My Father." <u>PoetryNW</u> (19:1) Spr 78,
    p. 45.
  "Sunday at My Aunt's" (tr. of Jerzy Pijewski). <u>NewYorker</u>
    (54:7) 3 Ap 78, p. 32.

PILKINGTON, Kevin
  "The Beach Club." <u>PoNow</u> (20) 78, p. 34.
  "The Emergency Room." <u>PoNow</u> (19) 78, p. 47.

PILLIN, William
  "Akriel's Consolation." <u>Bachy</u> (12) Aut 78, p. 35.
  "All of My Cities." <u>LitR</u> (21:3) Spr 78, p. 328.
  "Ascensions." <u>Durak</u> (1) 78, p. 14.
  "The Blue Candle." <u>LitR</u> (21:3) Spr 78, p. 333.
  "Canzone for My Grandma." <u>LitR</u> (21:3) Spr 78, p. 329.
  "Dawn." <u>Kayak</u> (48) Je 78, p. 35.
  "A Few Minutes of Dying." <u>Bachy</u> (12) Aut 78, p. 36.
  "Gerontic Sequence" (for Felix Pollak). <u>Bachy</u> (12) Aut 78,
    p. 33.
  "Greedy Birds." <u>Durak</u> (1) 78, p. 16.
  "Holy Beggars." <u>LitR</u> (21:3) Spr 78, p. 327.
  "The Lost Song." <u>LitR</u> (21:3) Spr 78, p. 330.
  "Neighborhood II." <u>Bachy</u> (12) Aut 78, p. 34.
  "Night Poem with Important Thoughts." <u>LitR</u> (21:3) Spr 78,
    p. 331.
  "On Saying No to Retirement." <u>Bachy</u> (12) Aut 78, p. 36.
  "Realities." <u>Durak</u> (1) 78, p. 18.

PINES, Paul
  "Blackburn." <u>Confr</u> (16) Spr-Sum 78, p. 91.
  "Time Piece." <u>HangL</u> (32) Spr 78, p. 48.

PINK, David
  "Tattooed Lady." <u>DacTerr</u> (15) Wint-Spr 77-78, p. 60.

PINSKER, Sanford
  "Acting Up." <u>SmPd</u> (42) Wint 78, p. 25.

"Amazed by Science, I Salute the Bisexual Hag." KanQ (10:2)
    Spr 78, p. 58.
"Busted Lives, for Dinner." GreenfieldR (6:3/4) Spr 78, p. 54.
"Garage Sale." GreenfieldR (6:3/4) Spr 78, p. 54.
"The Godfather II$\frac{1}{4}$." KanQ (10:2) Spr 78, p. 56.
"Hunting Indians with My Son." SouthernPR (18:2) Aut 78, p. 52.
"On Air-Conditioned Nights." SouthernPR (18:2) Aut 78, p. 52.
"Rodeo-Going in New Jersey." PoNow (19) 78, p. 23.

PINSKY, Robert
    from An Explanation of America (a poem to my daughter):
        "Horace, Epistulae I, xvi." NewEngR (1:1) Aut 78, p. 92.
    from An Explanation of America: "A Poem to My Daughter."
        Poetry (132:3) Je 78, p. 125.
    "Dreaming of Deafness." Hudson (31:1) Spr 78, p. 127.
    from An Explanation of America: "A Love of Death." AmerPoR
        (7:5) S-O 78, p. 20.
    from An Explanation of America: "Braveries" (to my daughter).
        ChiR (30:2) Aut 78, p. 64.
    "Memorial." Nat (226:12) 1 Ap 78, p. 378.

PIONTEK, Heinz
    In einem Stuudenbuch: "Nachts, beim Turmbau zu babel." ChiR
        (30:2) Aut 78, p. 40.

PISARETZ, Jim
    "Aunt Betty." Wind (29) 78, p. 41.

PISTILLI, Lorraine
    "The Flower Beheld." Glass (3:1/2/3) 78, p. 112.

PITCHFORD, Kenneth
    "The Uniting of the Opposites" (to the artifex mystica of this
        work). NewEngR (1:2) Wint 78, p. 165.

PITKIN, Anne
    "The Homes." PraS (52:4) Wint 78-79, p. 335.

PIZINGER, NT
    "Party-line." Wind (29) 78, p. 37.

PLANTEEN, Pete
    "The Dead Won't Disappoint." Sam (65) 78, p. 60.

PLANTENGA, Bart
    "irreverent literature." Smudge (Supplement) Wint 78-79, p. 36.
    "Local Poetry Scene 2/78." Smudge (3) Aut 78, p. 44.
    "Nite Lites 3/77 (in Ann Arbor)." Smudge (2) Sum 78, p. 9.

PLASTRIK, Marilyn
    "... And we." EngJ (67:5) My 78, p. 57.

PLATH, Sylvia
    "Stings (2)." Antaeus (30/31) Sum-Aut 78, p. 41.

"Words Heard, By Accident, Over the Phone." Antaeus (30/31) Sum-Aut 78, p. 42.

PLEASANTS, Ben
"Pleasantries" (Eight poems). WormR (72) 78, pp. 137-144.

PLIMPTON, Sarah
"blackened skies." PartR (45:1) 78, p. 19.
"the eyes." PartR (45:1) 78, p. 19.
"a face turning over." PartR (45:1) 78, p. 19.

PLUMLY, Stanley
"Another November." Antaeus (30/31) Sum-Aut 78, p. 173.
"Blossom." GeoR (32:2) Sum 78, p. 427.
"Wildflower." Antaeus (30/31) Sum-Aut 78, p. 174.

PLYMELL, Charles
"Hey Ray" (for Ray Bremser [in the mood of Chet Baker]). Tele (14) 78.

POBO, Kenneth
"Between Past and Present." DeKalb (11:3/4) Spr-Sum 78, p. 42.
"Billions of Lit Cigarettes." Tendril (2) Spr-Sum 78.

POE, John T.
"The Next Time It Rains." CutB (11) Aut-Wint 78, p. 80.

POLACK, Frank
"Brave Like Their Fathers." PoNow (20) 78, p. 35.

POLCOVAR, Carol
"Les Fauves." PartR (45:1) 78, p. 18.

POLITE, Frank
"Four Poems" (tr. of Miro Papadakis). Paint (9/10) Spr-Aut 78, p. 49.

POLLAK, Felix
"The Funeral Home." PoNow (19) 78, p. 38.
"Old Woman." PoNow (19) 78, p. 38.

POLLETT, Sylvester
"Approaching a Mountain." BelPoJ (29:1) Aut 78, p. 34.

POLLITT, Katha
"Discussion of the Vicissitudes of History under a Pine Tree." NewYorker (54:4) 13 Mr 78, p. 40.
"Eggplant." Poetry (132:3) Je 78, p. 154.
"Midwinter Thaw." Atl (241:2) F 78, p. 76.
"Sonnet." Atl (242:1) Jl 78, p. 74.

POLLOCK, Estill
"The Face in the Water." StoneC (78:3) Aut 78, p. 6.

"Pendragon. " <u>Wind</u> (30) 78, p. 39.

POLLY, Allison R.
 "Before she asked to go. " <u>HangL</u> (34) Wint 78-79, p. 61.

POLLY, Natale S.
 "The Day After. " <u>Glass</u> (3:1/2/3) 78, p. 17.
 "Dream Tableau with Three Voices. " <u>13thM</u> (4:1) 78, p. 50.
 "Observing the Planets Venus & Jupiter, An Exploration of
   Polarities. " <u>Glass</u> (3:1/2/3) 78, p. 15.

PONSOT, Marie
 "Faithful. " <u>LittleM</u> (11:3) Aut 77, p. 44.
 "Summer Sestina for Rosemary. " <u>LittleM</u> (11:3) Aut 77, p. 42.

PONTANO, Giovanni
 "Tumulus Rosae puellae ante diem mortuae. " <u>Paint</u> (7/8) Spr-
   Aut 77, p. 33.
 "Tumulus Sanctiae puellae Neopolitanae/Ipse virum suum
   pictorem alloquitur. " <u>Paint</u> (7/8) Spr-Aut 77, p. 34.

POOLE, Francis
 "Arrowmaker. " <u>SouthernPR</u> (18:1) Spr 78, p. 32.

POPA, Vasko
 "Earthbound Constellation" (tr. by Charles Simic). <u>Durak</u> (1) 78,
   p. 6.
 "Eyes of a Wolf" (tr. by Charles Simic). <u>Durak</u> (1) 78, p. 7.
 "In the Village of My Ancestors" (tr. by Charles Simic). <u>Durak</u>
   (1) 78, p. 8.
 Six poems (tr. by George Jevremovic). <u>Kayak</u> (49) Je 78, p. 57.
 "Unknown Citizen" (tr. by Charles Simic). <u>Durak</u> (1) 78, p. 9.

POPE, Alan
 "Fire and Ivory. " <u>EnPas</u> (7) 78, p. 36.

POPE, Deborah
 "Undressed Man with a Beard. " <u>CimR</u> (43) Ap 78, p. 64.

POPPINO, Kathryn
 "The Prodigal Son. " <u>HangL</u> (32) Spr 78, p. 49.

PORETZ, Doraine
 "A Bracelet of Hair" (for my daughter). <u>Bachy</u> (13) Aut-Wint
   78-79, p. 55.
 "In the Eighth House. " <u>Bachy</u> (13) Aut-Wint 78-79, p. 56.
 "Sepulchre. " <u>Bachy</u> (13) Aut-Wint 78-79, p. 54.
 "This Woman in America" (for Edith). <u>Bachy</u> (13) Aut-Wint 78-
   79, p. 51.
 "This Woman in America" (for Kate). <u>Bachy</u> (13) Aut-Wint 78-
   79, p. 50.
 "This Woman in America" (for Lily). <u>Bachy</u> (13) Aut-Wint 78-
   79, p. 52.

"This Woman in America" (for Lyla).   Bachy (13) Aut-Wint 78-
     79, p. 53.

PORSENA, L.
     "Death on the TV Screen."   Zahir (9) 77, p. 22.

PORTER, Sharon
     "The Chipmunk."   PikeF (1) Spr 78, p. 17.
     "The Season Tree."   PikeF (1) Spr 78, p. 17.
     "The Waterfall."   PikeF (1) Spr 78, p. 17.

PORTUGILL, Jestyn
     "Agricultural Award Ceremonies, Tigre Province, 1971."
          NewRep (178:9) 4 Mr 78, p. 31.

POSAMENTIER, Evelyn
     "Attack."   AmerPoR (7:3) My-Je 78, p. 45.
     "Counting Backwards."   AmerPoR (7:3) My-Je 78, p. 45.
     "Immigration."   AmerPoR (7:3) My-Je 78, p. 45.

POSNER, David
     "Dionysiou."   Poetry (132:3) Je 78, p. 155.
     "The Earthquake."   Kayak (48) Je 78, p. 3.
     "Leaves."   NewYorker (53:50) 30 Ja 78, p. 95.
     "Lessons in Natural History" (for Peter Nathan).   MalR (46) Ap
          78, p. 124.
     "A Poem for My Wife Strictly about the Weather."   MalR (46) Ap
          78, p. 129.
     "Timepiece for Lily."   PoetryNW (19:2) Sum 78, p. 39.
     "Weasel."   Poetry (132:3) Je 78, p. 156.

POSTER, Carol
     "Composition Francaise" (tr. of Jacques Prévert).   WebR (4:1)
          Spr 78, p. 31.
     "Flat Fall."   Wind (30) 78, p. 43.

POTTLE, Kathy
     "Whale-oil."   AntR (36:4) Aut 78, p. 471.

POULIN, A., Jr.
     "The Angel of Confusion."   Bound (6:2) Wint 78, p. 578.
     "The Angel of Imagination."   Bound (6:2) Wint 78, p. 580.
     "The Angel of the Gate."   Bound (6:2) Wint 78, p. 581.
     "The Angels of Reincarnation."   Bound (6:2) Wint 78, p. 579.
     "The Nameless Garden."   Salm (40) Wint 78, p. 92.
     "Shadows."   SoCaR (10:2) Ap 78, p. 55.
     "Snowstorm: Biddeford Pool."   ColEng (39:8) Ap 78, p. 940.
     "The Voices."   NewEngR (1:2) Wint 78, p. 205.

POUND
     "Canto XLVII" (tr. by R. Sieburth and S. W. De Rachewiltz).
          St. AR (5:1) Aut-Wint 78, p. 66.

POUND, Omar
"Kano." Montra (4) 78, p. 38.
"Last night I dreamt you brought me wine" (tr. of Amir Khusrow
     Dehlavi). Montra (4) 78, p. 41.
"A Witch." Montra (4) 78, p. 40.

POWELL, Bruce
"Leaving." Tendril (1) Wint 77-78.

POWERS, Jeffrey
"Mistress." Pan (19) 77, p. 14.
"This Never Was Our Town." Pan (19) 77, p. 14.

POWERS, William
"Over in Chompion." CentR (22:3) Sum 78, p. 325.
"Saturday night." CentR (22:3) Sum 78, p. 324.

POYNER, Kenneth
"Liberties." Zahir (9) 77, p. 23.

PRAAMSA, Petrus
"Room 109." ChrC (95:3) 25 Ja 78, p. 76.

PRADO, Holly
"At Ninety: The Woman Near the Door." ThRiPo (11/12) 78,
     p. 61.
"At the Bottom." Stonecloud (7) 78, p. 129.
"A Fairy Tale for Middle Age." Bachy (12) Aut 78, p. 21.
"For Another Birthday." Stonecloud (7) 78, p. 131.
"The Heart." Stonecloud (7) 78, p. 130.
"Introductions: 15 Morning Love Stories" (for Harry E. North-
     up). Bachy (12) Aut 78, p. 15.
"Lemon Seed." ParisR (72) Wint 77, p. 50.
"To a Young Woman Going Mad." Bachy (12) Aut 78, p. 19.
"Venice Beach Before My Birthday." Bachy (12) Aut 78, p. 19.

PRATER, Larry A.
"An Act of Grief." CarouselQ (3:1) Spr 78, p. 2.

PRATER, Larry Coe
"Of Both Worlds." KanQ (10:2) Spr 78, p. 106.

PRATT, Charles
"The Poet Attempts to Console His Wife, Who Has Just Put His
     Wallet Through the Washing Machine." HiramPoR (24) Spr-
     Sum 78, p. 36.

PRESCOTT, Edgar A.
"The Thompson River Rampage" (for Howard). Wind (31) 78,
     p. 43.

PRESS, John
"The Workhouse" (to Michael and Bridget Riviere). SouthernR
     (14:1) Wint 78, p. 111.

PRESS, Marcia
  "The Magician. " JnlONJP (3:1) 78, p. 12.
  "Refusal to Mourn the Death by Decay of Just Another Four-Let-
      ter Word. " JnlONJP (3:1) 78, p. 13.
  "The Writers Consider a Quick Change in the Lineup. " JnlONJP
      (3:1) 78, p. 14.

PREVERT, Jacques
  "Composition Francaise" (tr. by Carol Poster).   WebR (4:1) Spr
      78, p. 31.

PRICE, Joseph L.
  "Elegy for a Baptist Steeple. " ChrC (95:12) 5 Ap 78, p. 357.

PRITCHARD, Leigh
  "Offering. " CarolQ (30:3) Aut 78, p. 56.

PRIVETT, Katharine
  "A Time of Weavers. " CarouselQ (3:3) Aut 78, p. 10.

PROCTOR, James W.
  "Refugees. " Wind (31) 78, p. 45.

PROPERTIUS
  "I. 1, II. 4, II. 9, II. 33, and III. 23" (tr. by Michael West).
      Nimrod (22:2) Spr-Sum 78, pp. 87-92.
  "3. 21" (tr. by Michael West).   Iowa (9:4) Aut 78, p. 82.

PROSER, Maria A.
  "Curfew" (tr. of Teresa De Jesus, w. Arlene & James Scully).
      MinnR (NS11) Aut 78, p. 6.
  "'I Am a Small Woman'" (tr. of Teresa De Jesus, w. Arlene &
      James Scully). MinnR (NS11) Aut 78, p. 8.
  "It Makes Me Furious!" (tr. of Teresa De Jesus, w. Arlene &
      James Scully). MinnR (NS11) Aut 78, p. 7.
  "Mistrust" (tr. of Teresa De Jesus, w. Arlene & James Scully).
      MinnR (NS11) Aut 78, p. 9.

PROVOST, Sarah
  "Corrigan's Wife. " GreenfieldR (6:3/4) Spr 78, p. 129.

PRUITT, Bill
  "Wedding at Black Creek Park. " PoNow (20) 78, p. 36.

PRUNTY, Wyatt
  "Capt. Dennis Morgan. " ModernPS (9:1) Spr 78, p. 52.
  "A Doctor's Note on His Newborn. " Poem (31) N 77, p. 43.
  "Horse Laughter and a Saxophone. " SouthernPR (18:2) Aut 78,
      p. 58.
  "Soliloquies of Ships. " GRR (9:3) 78, p. 187.
  "Towards Atlanta. " GRR (9:3) 78, p. 186.
  "Winter on the Piedmont. " SoCaR (11:1) N 78, p. 107.

PURSER, Ralph
"Metamorphosis." StoneC (78:1) Wint 78, p. 4.

PYLE, Patricia
"Snow Geese." SoDakR (16:2) Sum 78, p. 40.

QUAGLIANO, Tony
"Get the poets out of the schools." Kayak (48) Je 78, p. 27.

QUART, Pere
"A Postcard for Rafael Alberti" (tr. by Mario Angulo). MalR
    (47) Jl 78, p. 154.

QUASIMODO, Salvatore
"Il Tuo piede silenzioso." Nimrod (22:2) Spr-Sum 78, p. 106.

QUATRALE, Donald
"Joe Presto." SunM (5) Aut 78, p. 136.
"Mask Quencher" (for Giorgio de Chirico). SunM (5) Aut 78,
    p. 138.

QUENEAU, Jean
"To William Carlos Williams." Aspen (6) Aut 78, p. 59.

QUINN, John
"Awaiting Game." CutB (10) Spr-Sum 78, p. 22.
"Congenitalia." CutB (11) Aut-Wint 78, p. 48.
"The Pika" (for Jennifer). CutB (10) Spr-Sum 78, p. 21.

QUINTANA, Leroy V.
"Eulogio." GreenfieldR (6:3/4) Spr 78, p. 95.
"Legacy II." GreenfieldR (6:3/4) Spr 78, p. 96.
"Leroy and Quintana." GreenfieldR (6:3/4) Spr 78, p. 97.
"Sister Concepta...." GreenfieldR (6:3/4) Spr 78, p. 97.

QUINTANAR, Raymond
"The Thief." CalQ (13/14) Spr-Sum 78, p. 36.

RAAB, Lawrence
"Empire of Lights." Antaeus (30/31) Sum-Aut 78, p. 180.
"The Moon Murders." Antaeus (30/31) Sum-Aut 78, p. 176.
"Small Stories." AmerPoR (7:6) N-D 78, p. 7.
"While You Were Sleeping." NewEngR (1:2) Wint 78, p. 207.

RABA, György
"Going On Talking" (tr. by Jascha Kessler). Nimrod (22:2) Spr-
    Sum 78, p. 98.

RABBITT, Thomas
"Researching Lost Time." Antaeus (28) Wint 78, p. 192.

RABONI, Giovanni
"Afternoon Movies" (tr. by Vinio Rossi and Stuart Friebert).

Field (18) Spr 78, p. 87.
"Bad Year" (tr. by Vinio Rossi and Stuart Friebert). Field (18)
    Spr 78, p. 84.
"Christmas Morning" (tr. by Vinio Rossi and Stuart Friebert).
    Field (18) Spr 78, p. 85.
"The Colonial Error" (tr. by Vinio Rossi and Stuart Friebert).
    Field (18) Spr 78, p. 86.
"The Dead and the True" (tr. by Vinio Rossi). Field (18) Spr
    78, p. 82.
"Pontius P. " (tr. by Vinio Rossi). Field (18) Spr 78, p. 83.

RACHEL, Naomi
"Kitchen Composition. " YellowBR (10) 78, p. 40.

RACHFORD, Fred
"The Rousing. " Zahir (9) 77, p. 50.

RACINES, Anthony
"Old Age. " SeC (5:2) 78, p. 27.

RADAVICIUS, Marian
"found poem /a letter. " Tele (14) 78.
"Living on a Suburban Farm" (song for a Storybook). Tele (13)
    77.
"living on a suburban farm" (song for a storybook). Tele (14)
    78.

RADIN, Doris
"Study in Black and White. " Zahir (9) 77, p. 53.
"The winter is life. " SouthernPR (18:2) Aut 78, p. 89.

RADLEY, Gail
"Circus Tent. " Confr (16) Spr-Sum 78, p. 156.

RADNOTI, Miklós
"Before Sleep" (tr. by Emery George). Paint (9/10) Spr-Aut 78,
    p. 41.
"Himnusz. " ChiR (30:2) Aut 78, p. 12.
"Pirano Souvenir" (tr. by Emery George). Paint (9/10) Spr-Aut
    78, p. 40.
"Second Eclogue" (tr. by Emery George). NewL (45:1) Aut 78,
    p. 44.

RAFFEL, Burton
"Thinking about Death. " Pan (19) 77, p. 56.

RAGAIN, Maj
"Illinois Oyster /Pushing Upward. " PoNow (20) 78, p. 36.

RAGAN, James
"Umbrella Man. " Box (7) Spr 78, p. 29.

RAHMMINGS, Keith
"Qwertuiop. " Glass (3:1/2/3) 78, p. 107.

RAIL, DeWayne
"For You." SouthernPR (18:2) Aut 78, p. 40.
"Photographs of Greece & Images of War." BelPoJ (28:4) Sum
    78, p. 32.

RAINE, Kathleen
"Cloud." SouthernR (14:1) Wint 78, p. 84.
Eight poems. MalR (48) O 78, p. 24.
"High Summer." MalR (48) O 78, p. 117.
"November Dream." SouthernR (14:1) Wint 78, p. 86.
"Record Player." SouthernR (14:1) Wint 78, p. 88.
"Tir n'an Oge." SouthernR (14:1) Wint 78, p. 89.
"Turner's Seas." SouthernR (14:1) Wint 78, p. 87.
"Winter Paradise." SouthernR (14:1) Wint 78, p. 85.

RAINES, Charlotte A.
"The Game, The Dance." Epos (27:2) 77, p. 26.

RAIZIS, M. Byron
"There Is No Solitude" (tr. of Nikephoros Vrettakos). BallSUF
    (19:2) Spr 78, p. 50.

RAIZISS, Sonia
"The Storm" (tr. of Eugenio Montale, w. Alfredo de Palchi).
    StoneC (78:1) Wint 78, p. 23.

RAKOSI, Carl
"In Situ." Montra (4) 78, p. 74.
"Meditation." ChiR (30:3) Wint 79, p. 23.
"The Menage." Montra (4) 78, p. 71.
"The Poet, XXIX." Montra (4) 78, p. 76.

RALEIGH, Michael
"On the Difficult Lot of a Prophet." KanQ (10:1) Wint 78, p. 37.

RAMBO, Beth
"African Coast." CarouselQ (3:3) Aut 78, p. 9.
"Mockingbirds." St.AR (4:3/4) 77-78, p. 131.

RAMIREZ, Orlan
"I'm bored." SeC (5:2) 78, p. 29.
"life is good." SeC (5:2) 78, p. 28.

RAMKE, Bin
"Eclipse." GeoR (32:2) Sum 78, p. 334.
"The Mother of the Bride." AmerPoR (7:4) Jl-Ag 78, p. 34.
"Poems for a Tall, Sad Lady." SouthernR (14:1) Wint 78,
    p. 95.
"Revealing Oneself to a Woman." Madem (84:4) Ap 78, p. 142.
"Sex Therapy." Agni (9) 78, p. 85.

RAMOS, Judith
"Still Life." MichQR (17:3) Sum 78, p. 345.

RAMPERSAD, Smokey
"Robert." PoNow (20) 78, p. 47.

RAMSEY, Jarold
"Ontogeny." Shen (29:4) Sum 78, p. 56.
"Waking Up First." PoetryNW (19:2) Sum 78, p. 36.

RANDALL, Margaret
"Where October comes seventeen times" (for Gregory). Falcon
(17) 78, p. 6.

RANK, Duke
"Myths." EngJ (67:5) My 78, p. 67.

RANKIN, Paula
"At the Wharf, Yorktown: For All Tracks Made in Sand." Nat
(226:12) 1 Ap 78, p. 375.
"Wrestling with the Angels of Intention." ThRiPo (11/12) 78,
p. 62.

RANKIN, Rush
"Sigmund Freud." AntR (36:2) Spr 78, p. 190.

RANNIT, Aleksis
"On the Island of Ogygia" (tr. by Henry Lyman). Poetry (131:6)
Mr 78, p. 321.

RANSOM, W. M.
"Medicine Wheel Song" (for Tree Swenson, Menesihkta).
DacTerr (15) Wint-Spr 77-78, p. 25.

RANSON, Nicholas
"Registration." Bits (8) Jl 78.

RAS, Barbara
"On the Lawn, Surrounded by Snails." Pan (19) 77, p. 65.
"Something Burning." NowestR (17:1) 78, p. 53.

RASCH, Bill
"gentle court with its surprises." Tele (13) 77.
"gleam of cobbled streets greased." Tele (13) 77.
"lethargy." Tele (13) 77.
"you must eat." Tele (13) 77.

RASNIC, Steve
"Snapping Turtle." Tendril (3) Aut 78, p. 43.

RATCLIFF, Carter
"The Dossier: What You Were." LaB (11) 78, p. 28.
"Theater of the Terrific." LaB (11) 78, p. 33.

RATCLIFFE, Stephen
from A Book of Hours: "A Book of Hours." SouthernR (14:1)

Wint 78, p. 116.
from A Book of Hours: "Conclusions." SouthernR (14:1) Wint
78, p. 119.
from A Book of Hours: "Gioconda." SouthernR (14:1) Wint 78,
p. 117.
from A Book of Hours: "Surf Cottage, Bolinas." SouthernR
(14:1) Wint 78, p. 116.
"Readings from John Muir's Journal." Poetry (131:5) F 78,
p. 272.
"Rustic Diversions." Poetry (131:5) F 78, p. 275.

RATINER, Steven
"the ballet master." Tendril (1) Wint 77-78.
"the fox mask." HangL (32) Spr 78, p. 50.
"Hearts of Gravity." CalQ (13/14) Spr-Sum 78, p. 90.
"hearts of gravity." HangL (34) Wint 78-79, p. 41.
"marriage at midnight." Tendril (1) Wint 77-78.
"palomas" (for Kathy). Tendril (2) Spr-Sum 78.

RATNER, Rochelle
"Cradle." Glass (3:1/2/3) 78, p. 71.
"The Discharge" (for Rose). HangL (34) Wint 78-79, p. 44.
"The Far Bedroom." GreenfieldR (6:3/4) Spr 78, p. 149.
"The Gift." GreenfieldR (6:3/4) Spr 78, p. 148.
"Kaiemsenuwy's Tomb." HangL (32) Spr 78, p. 52.
"Madonna and Child." HangL (33) Sum 78, p. 46.
"The Maze." LaB (10) 78, p. 39.
"Memory." Hand (2) 78, p. 184.
"Nightmare." Glass (3:1/2/3) 78, p. 72.
"No Man Can Hear the Mermaids' Song and Live." HangL (33)
Sum 78, p. 45.
"The Poor Beadle of Berditchev." Hand (2) 78, p. 186.
"Reply to the Loudspeaker." Some (9) 78, p. 89.
"Revenge at Knockdolion." HangL (33) Sum 78, p. 49.
"Singing Lessons" (for Niels). HangL (33) Sum 78, p. 50.
"Some Nights." HangL (34) Wint 78-79, p. 43.
"Speech, Historical Tribute." LaB (10) 78, p. 38.
"Steps." NorthSR (8) Aut-Wint 78-79, p. 92.
"Swansong." Hand (2) 78, p. 185.
"Taunting." HangL (33) Sum 78, p. 52.
"Trying to Love Once More." HangL (32) Spr 78, p. 51.
"Virginia." LaB (10) 78, p. 40.
"Woman Tossing Her Infant Son in the Pool." HangL (34) Wint
78-79, p. 42.

RATTI, John
"Autobiographical Poem." Glass (3:1/2/3) 78, p. 73.
"More or Less." Glass (3:1/2/3) 78, p. 76.
"Stargazer." Glass (3:1/2/3) 78, p. 74.

RAVIKOVITCH, Dahlia
"Deep Calleth Unto Deep." ChiR (30:2) Aut 78, p. 50.

RAY, David
"The Castaways." PoNow (19) 78, p. 9.
"A Christmas Tale." LitR (21:3) Spr 78, p. 313.
"The Goal." Nat (226:2) 21 Ja 78, p. 54.
"Hymn to Aunt Edris." Hudson (31:2) Sum 78, p. 300.
"The Night Sam and Wes Stayed in Their Own Hotel Room in
     Osceola." PoNow (19) 78, p. 9.
"Nightingales in Sussex." Epoch (27:3) Spr 78, p. 280.
"On the Photograph 'Yarn Mill,' by Lewis W. Hine" (for Samuel
     Cyrus David Ray). NewYorker (54:40) 20 N 78, p. 44.
"Waking to Music." GeoR (32:3) Aut 78, p. 644.

RAY, Robert
"Lady Behind the Gate." EngJ (67:5) My 78, p. 52.

RAY, Samuel
"My Car." NewL (45:1) Aut 78, p. 65.

RAYMOND, Kathy
"Chainging Tune." CarouselQ (3:2) Sum 78, p. 7.
"The Persistence of Memory." CarouselQ (3:4) Wint 78, p. 12.

RAYMOND, Monica
"twice in my life." Tendril (1) Wint 77-78.

RAYMOND, Richard C.
"Conversation Piece." Tele (14) 78.
"Fafnir in New England." Tele (14) 78.
"O Tempora, O Mores." StoneC (78:3) Aut 78, p. 15.
"Subway Rimas." Tele (14) 78.

REA, Susan Irene
"Property Line." FourQt (27:4) Sum 78, p. 34.

READ, Frances
"Message from Edouard." ChrC (95:12) 5 Ap 78, p. 358.

READ, Linda
"via new york." Stonecloud (7) 78, p. 72.

REBELSKY, Freda
"At a Meeting." StoneC (78:2) Spr 78, p. 14.
"Pro-Busing." StoneC (78:2) Spr 78, p. 14.

REDDALL, Dave
"The Mall." Vaga (27) Spr 78, p. 47.

REDSHAW, Thomas Dillon
"Milk Snake." SewanR (86:4) Aut 78, p. 519.
"Mistress Bat." DacTerr (15) Wint-Spr 77-78, p. 61.

REED, Ishmael
"St. Louis Woman." NewL (45:1) Aut 78, p. 33.

REED, James
"Death and Sex." Bits (8) Jl 78.

REED, John R.
"Como." ModernPS (9:2) Aut 78, p. 82.
"Dante's Tomb: Ravenna." ModernPS (9:2) Aut 78, p. 83.
from The Detroit Song Book: "City Cemetery." MichQR (17:1)
    Wint 78, p. 22.
from The Detroit Song Book: "Detroit River." MichQR (17:1)
    Wint 78, p. 23.
from The Detroit Song Book: "From the Windsor Side" (for
    Joyce and Ray). KanQ (10:4) Aut 78, p. 104.
from The Detroit Song Book: "Wildemere St.: Cardinal at the
    Feeder." MichQR (17:1) Wint 78, p. 21.
"Foreign Languages: Padua." ModernPS (9:2) Aut 78, p. 82.
"Piero della Francesca." SewanR (86:2) Spr 78, p. 268.
"Piero the Unfortunate." SewanR (86:2) Spr 78, p. 267.
"Savonarola." SewanR (86:2) Spr 78, p. 266.
"Wilderness" (for Ed Chielens). ModernPS (9:2) Aut 78, p. 81.

REES, Richard
"Orion." HangL (34) Wint 78-79, p. 46.

REEVE, F. D.
"Botany Lesson." AmerPoR (7:2) Mr-Ap 78, p. 47.
"Flies swarm on the living." NewOR (6:1) 78, p. 31.

REGAN, Jennifer
"Summer/Omens." PoNow (20) 78, p. 36.

REID, Alastair
"A History of Night" (tr. of Jorge Luis Borges). NewYRB
    (25:21/22) 25 Ja 79, p. 26.
"Just by Opening Your Eyes" (tr. of Heberto Padilla). NewYRB
    (25:18) 23 N 78, p. 10.
"Ode to Poetry" (tr. of Pablo Neruda). NewEngR (1:1) Aut 78,
    p. 25.
"Techniques of Pursuit" (tr. of Heberto Padilla). NewYRB
    (25:18) 23 N 78, p. 10.
"Weathering." NewRep (178:9) 4 Mr 78, p. 33.

REID, Robert Sims
"Directions for the Day." Iowa (9:2) Spr 78, p. 85.

REID, Wanda J.
"Here in my garden." WorldO (12:1) Aut 77, p. 18.

REILLY, Robert T.
"Sparrowfall." StoneC (78:2) Spr 78, p. 22.

REINELT, Carl
"The Dark." SmPd (43) Spr 78, p. 30.
"Harbour." SmPd (43) Spr 78, p. 31.

REINEMAN, Earl
"Adaptation. " PoetryNW (19:4) Wint 78-79, p. 22.

REISS, James
"Anna's Song. " Hudson (31:1) Spr 78, p. 125.
"Approaching Washington Heights. " NewYorker (53:49) 23 Ja 78,
    p. 34.
"God Knows Many Stories. " Antaeus (28) Wint 78, p. 200.

REITER, Lora K.
"Growing Up Female. " KanQ (10:2) Spr 78, p. 50.

REITER, Thomas
"Autograph Session. " PoNow (20) 78, p. 36.
"The Other Side. " OhioR (19:2) Spr-Sum 78, p. 17.
"The Other Side. " OhioR (19:3) Aut 78, p. 70.
"The Season's Bluebottle Hatch. " ModernPS (9:2) Aut 78, p. 83.

RELLACK, Joan
"For Borges. " CentR (22:2) Spr 78, p. 180.

RENDLEMAN, Danny
"The Vealer. " Epoch (28:1) Aut 78, p. 26.

RENNER, Bruce
"Here. " SunM (5) Aut 78, p. 131.
"The Word. " SunM (5) Aut 78, p. 132.

REPETTO, Joanne
"Crazy Jane. " SeC (5:2) 78, p. 54.

REPLANSKY, Naomi
"Death of the Fugitive. " MissouriR (1:1) Spr 78, p. 18.

RETALLACK, Joan
"Circumstantial Evidence. " Epoch (27:2) Wint 78, p. 150.
"Oh Mother Goose Oh Yin Oh Yang. " Epoch (28:1) Aut 78,
    p. 70.
"Southern Liebeslieder. " LittleM (11:3) Aut 77, p. 92.

RETALLACK, John
"English Snapshots in America. " SoDakR (16:4) Wint 78-79, p. 69.

REVELL, Donald
"Aesthete's Complaint. " Antaeus (28) Wint 78, p. 135.
"Augustine in Paphos. " Bound (6:2) Wint 78, p. 554.
"Central Park South. " Antaeus (30/31) Sum-Aut 78, p. 186.
"In Lombardy. " Antaeus (30/31) Sum-Aut 78, p. 184.
"Maestro. " Antaeus (30/31) Sum-Aut 78, p. 183.
"Mignonette. " Antaeus (28) Wint 78, p. 131.
"Odette. " Antaeus (28) Wint 78, p. 133.
"Odille. " Antaeus (28) Wint 78, p. 134.
"Theriot Cove. " Poetry (133:2) N 78, p. 91.

REVERE, Elizabeth
"I Should Be Proper." SmPd (43) Spr 78, p. 17.

REWAK, William J.
"Technique." ArizQ (34:3) Aut 78, p. 238.

REXROTH, Kenneth
Eleven poems (tr. of Yosano Akiko). GreenfieldR (6:3/4) Spr 78,
    p. 9.

REYNOLDS, Brad
"Harmony." NewOR (5:4) 78, p. 323.
"When Someone Good Is Gone." AmerS (47:2) Spr 78, p. 244.

REYNOLDS, Diane
"In Spite of Resolve I Am Always Thanks to Charles Bukowski."
    Nimrod (22:2) Spr-Sum 78, p. 72.

REZMERSKI, John Calvin
"Monster Story." PoNow (19) 78, p. 41.

REZNIKOFF, Charles
from The North, part V, Domestic Difficulties: (16, 17). ChiR
    (30:3) Wint 79, p. 24.
from Testimony: The United States (1911-1915): "V. Family
    Difficulties." Montra (4) 78, p. 30.

RICE, David L.
"And Walter Cronkite Wishes Us All a Happy New Year." Obs
    (4:2) Sum 78, p. 58.
"Erasing Interstate 80." Obs (4:2) Sum 78, p. 58.
"King Konk." Obs (4:2) Sum 78, p. 56.
"Proletariat." Obs (4:2) Sum 78, p. 59.

RICH, Adrienne
"The Lioness." ColEng (39:6) F 78, p. 689.
"Origins and History of Consciousness." ColEng (39:6) F 78,
    p. 690.
"Toward the Solstice." ColEng (39:6) F 78, p. 686.
"A Woman Dead in Her Forties." 13thM (4:1) 78, p. 53.

RICHARDS, Brian
"morning first." Hand (2) 78, p. 50.

RICHARDS, I. A.
"Nothing at All" (for Roman Jakobson). AmerS (47:1) Wint 77-
    78, p. 14.

RICHARDS, Melanie
"The Gift." Epos (27:1) 77, p. 37.

RICHARDSON, Barbara
"Sandgrass." QW (5) Wint 78, p. 101.

"You lie a breath away like stone." QW (5) Wint 78,
    p. 101.

RICHARDSON, Deborah
"the play went on the road years ago." BallSUF (19:4) Aut 78,
    p. 47.

RICHMOND, Steve
"Demons Dance" (Twenty-seven poems). WormR (70) 78,
    pp. 53-68.
"Gagaku" (Three poems). WormR (72) 78, p. 152.

RICHSTONE, May
"Happily Ever After." LadHJ (95:7) Jl 78, p. 128.

RIDGLEY, Sylvia
"Advice." MalR (48) O 78, p. 116.
"Papaya Island." MalR (48) O 78, p. 113.
"Riddle." MalR (48) O 78, p. 115.
"Synthesis." MalR (48) O 78, p. 112.
"Trying to Simplify You." MalR (48) O 78, p. 114.

RIDL, Jack
"The Sun." PoNow (20) 78, p. 36.

RIDLAND, John
"Merrick and Treves: An Essay on Ugliness." MichQR (17:3)
    Sum 78, p. 321.

RIEMER, Ruby
"Orphic Transformations." StoneC (78:2) Spr 78, p. 24.

RIGGS, Dionis Coffin
"First Ballet." StoneC (78:2) Spr 78, p. 31.

RILEY, Robin
"Whores." Pan (19) 77, p. 67.

RILKE, Rainer Maria
from Book for the Hours of Prayer: "2" (tr. by Robert Bly).
    Field (18) Spr 78, p. 95.
from Book for the Hours of Prayer: "7" (tr. by Robert Bly).
    Field (18) Spr 78, p. 96.
from Book for the Hours of Prayer: "11" (tr. by Robert Bly).
    Field (18) Spr 78, p. 97.
from Book for the Hours of Prayer: "18" (tr. by Robert Bly).
    Field (18) Spr 78, p. 98.
from Book for the Hours of Prayer: "20" (tr. by Robert Bly).
    Field (18) Spr 78, p. 99.
"Bridge of the Carousel" (tr. by John Drury). DenQ (13:4) Wint
    79, p. 52.
"The First Elegy" (tr. by William Gass). AmerPoR (7:2) Mr-
    Ap 78, p. 8.

"My Life Is Not This Steep and Turning Hour" (tr. by John
   Drury).   DenQ (13:4) Wint 79, p. 53.
"Nike" (tr. by R. Sieburth and S. W. De Rachewiltz).   St. AR
   (5:1) Aut-Wint 78, p. 53.
"The Ninth E'egy" (tr. by William Gass).   AmerPoR (7:2) Mr-Ap
   78, p. 10.
from Sonnets to Orpheus (tr. by Steven Lautermilch):   (I, 3;
   I, 5; II, 8; and II, 29).   CentR (22:1) Wint 78, p. 71.
"Sonnets to Orpheus, 1. 21" (tr. by Steven Lautermilch).   HolCrit
   (15:4) O 78, p. 17.
"Sonnets to Orpheus, 2. 12" (tr. by Steven Lautermilch).   HolCrit
   (15:4) O 78, p. 17.
from Sonnets to Orpheus: twenty-six poems.   Field (19) Aut 78,
   p. 75.

RIMBAUD
   "Sensation. "   Montra (4) 78, p. 292.

RINALDI, Nicholas
   "Hauling in the Nets off the Costa Del Sol. "   BallSUF (19:4) Aut
      78, p. 28.

RIND, Sherry
   "Imagine Yourself. "   PoetryNW (19:4) Wint 78-79, p. 13.

RINEHART, Becky
   "I dreamt you came. "   GreenfieldR (7:1/2) Aut 78, p. 81.

RIOS, Alberto
   "The Arroyo, Sergio, and Me. "   LittleM (11:3) Aut 77, p. 89.
   "Returning to the Cat. "   NoAmR (263:4) Wint 78, p. 61.
   "Sailing Directions. "   PraS (52:3) Aut 78, p. 227.
   "A Stranger's Plates. "   PraS (52:3) Aut 78, p. 226.

RIOS, Rykardo Rodriguez
   "Hurricane, the Stallion" (tr. by D. B. Brink).   Paint (9/10)
      Spr-Aut 78, p. 46.
   "Litany to Levu" (tr. by D. B. Brink).   Paint (9/10) Spr-Aut
      78, p. 47.

RIPPY, Bob
   "The Pedestrian. "   Wind (28) 78, p. 53.
   "Sitting in Church. "   Nimrod (22:2) Spr-Sum 78, p. 74.
   "Teaching My Son to Bat. "   Northeast (3:5) Spr-Sum 78, p. 59.

RISTAU, Harland
   "Evening Scene 7:45 P. M. "   ChrC (95:37) 15 N 78, p. 1103.

RISTEEN, Eleanor
   "Canterbury Cathedral" (to Geoffrey Chaucer).   Poem (33) Jl 78,
      p. 47.
   "Greetings. "   Poem (33) Jl 78, p. 48.

RITCHIE, Elisavietta
  "May Day Moon." AAR (28) 78, p. 84.
  "Mushroom Merchant: Korea." AAR (28) 78, p. 82.
  "A Prodigal Cycle" (tr. of Alfredo Navarro Salanga). AAR (28)
      78, p. 49.
  "Pumpkin Children." StoneC (78:1) Wint 78, p. 8.
  "Resurgo." AAR (28) 78, p. 81.
  "Serenade 77" (tr. of Krishna Mustajab, w. the author). AAR
      (28) 78, p. 47.
  "Shadow-Chase" (for Lisa) (tr. of Krishna Mustajab, w. the
      author). AAR (28) 78, p. 46.
  "Sleeper's Song." AAR (28) 78, p. 83.
  "Villagers" (tr. of Muhammud haji Salleh). AAR (28) 78, p. 48.

RITSOS, Yannis
  "Afternoon" (tr. by Edmund Keeley). Iowa (9:2) Spr 78, p. 104.
  "Almost Complete" (tr. by Kostas Myrsiades). Falcon (16) 78,
      p. 9.
  "Autumn Expression" (tr. by Edmund Keeley). Field (19) Aut
      78, p. 21.
  "Chile" (for Allende and Neruda) (tr. by Thanasis Maskaleris).
      Falcon (16) 78, p. 12.
  "Court Exhibit" (tr. by Edmund Keeley). NewYorker (54:36) 23
      O 78, p. 42.
  "Descent" (tr. by Edmund Keeley). Antaeus (30/31) Sum-Aut 78,
      p. 190.
  "Descent" (tr. by Kostas Myrsiades). Falcon (16) 78, p. 9.
  "Desk Calendar" (tr. by Edmund Keeley). Iowa (9:2) Spr 78,
      p. 105.
  "The Distant" (tr. by Edmund Keeley). NewYorker (54:36) 23 O
      78, p. 42.
  Eleven poems (tr. by Andonis Decavalles). Falcon (16) 78,
      p. 32.
  "Evening Profile" (tr. by Edmund Keeley). Iowa (9:2) Spr 78,
      p. 104.
  "Exhibits" (tr. by Kostas Myrsiades). Falcon (16) 78, p. 10.
  "Fever" (tr. by Edmund Keeley). Iowa (9:2) Spr 78, p. 103.
  "Final Agreement" (tr. by Edmund Keeley). Antaeus (30/31)
      Sum-Aut 78, p. 191.
  Fourteen poems (tr. by Kimon Friar). Falcon (16) 78, pp. 55,
      59, 99, and 123.
  "Freedom" (tr. by Edmund Keeley). Antaeus (30/31) Sum-Aut
      78, p. 188.
  "The Fundamentals" (tr. by N. C. Germanacos). Falcon (16) 78,
      p. 44.
  "Imbecility" (tr. by N. C. Germanacos). Falcon (16) 78, p. 43.
  "In the Void" (tr. by N. C. Germanacos). Falcon (16) 78,
      p. 46.
  "Indiscriminately" (tr. by N. C. Germanacos). Falcon (16) 78,
      p. 45.
  "Inertia" (tr. by Edmund Keeley). Iowa (9:2) Spr 78, p. 103.
  "Inevitably" (tr. by N. C. Germanacos). Falcon (16) 78, p. 47.
  "The Inexhaustible" (tr. by Martin McKinsey). Falcon (16) 78,

p. 122.

"Insufficiency" (tr. by Martin McKinsey). <u>Falcon</u> (16) 78,
p. 120.

"Liturgical" (tr. by Kimon Friar and Kostas Myrsiades). <u>LitR</u>
(21:4) Sum 78, p. 457.

"Preparing the Ceremony" (tr. by Edmund Keeley). <u>NewYorker</u>
(54:36) 23 O 78, p. 42.

"Marking" (tr. by Edmund Keeley). <u>Field</u> (19) Aut 78, p. 22.

"Message" (tr. by Edmund Keeley). <u>Antaeus</u> (30/31) Sum-Aut
78, p. 191.

"The Next Day" (tr. by Edmund Keeley). <u>Antaeus</u> (30/31) Sum-
Aut 78, p. 189.

"Old Men" (tr. by Martin McKinsey). <u>Falcon</u> (16) 78, p. 104.

"Red-Handed" (tr. by Edmund Keeley). <u>Field</u> (19) Aut 78, p. 19.

"The Same Meaning" (tr. by N. C. Germanacos). <u>Falcon</u> (16)
78, p. 48.

"The Same Thorn" (tr. by Edmund Keeley). <u>Field</u> (19) Aut 78,
p. 20.

"Scene" (tr. by N. C. Germanacos). <u>Falcon</u> (16) 78, p. 49.

"Secretly" (tr. by Edmund Keeley). <u>Antaeus</u> (30/31) Sum-Aut 78,
p. 190.

"Security Deposits" (tr. by Edmund Keeley). <u>NewYorker</u> (54:36)
23 O 78, p. 42.

Seventeen poems (tr. by Kimon Friar and George Thaniel).
<u>Falcon</u> (16) 78, p. 68.

Seventeen poems (tr. by Kimon Friar and Kostas Myrsiades).
<u>AmerPoR</u> (7:4) Jl-Ag 78, p. 23.

"Simultaneously" (tr. by Kimon Friar and Kostas Myrsiades).
<u>LitR</u> (21:4) Sum 78, p. 458.

Sixteen poems (tr. by Minas Savvas). <u>Falcon</u> (16) 78, pp. 50
and 86.

"Slowly" (tr. by Edmund Keeley). <u>Field</u> (19) Aut 78, p. 18.

"Sluggishly" (tr. by Kostas Myrsiades). <u>Falcon</u> (16) 78, p. 10.

"Small Dialogue" (tr. by Kostas Myrsiades). <u>Falcon</u> (16) 78,
p. 11.

"Small Sonata" (tr. by Kimon Friar and Kostas Myrsiades).
<u>LitR</u> (21:4) Sum 78, p. 458.

"Stages of Ignorance" (tr. by Kimon Friar and Kostas Myrsiades).
<u>LitR</u> (21:4) Sum 78, p. 459.

"Striding Over" (tr. by Edmund Keeley). <u>Antaeus</u> (30/31) Sum-
Aut 78, p. 189.

Ten poems (tr. by Kimon Friar and Kostas Myrsiades). <u>Antaeus</u>
(28) Wint 78, p. 57.

"Toward Saturday" (tr. by Edmund Keeley). <u>Field</u> (19) Aut 78,
p. 17.

"Towards Saturday" (tr. by Kostas Myrsiades). <u>Falcon</u> (16) 78,
p. 11.

Twelve poems (tr. by Edmund Keeley). <u>Falcon</u> (16) 78, p. 106.

Twenty poems (tr. by Kimon Friar and Kostas Myrsiades).
<u>Falcon</u> (16) 78, p. 13.

"Unaccomplished" (tr. by Ann Rivers). <u>StoneC</u> (78:2) Spr 78,
p. 21.

"Way of Life" (tr. by Kimon Friar and Kostas Myrsiades). <u>LitR</u>

(21:4) Sum 78, p. 457.
"We Will Be Ready" (tr. by Martin McKinsey). Falcon (16) 78,
    p. 103.
"Winter Sunshine" (tr. by Edmund Keeley). NewYorker (54:36)
    23 O 78, p. 42.
"With Music" (tr. by Edmund Keeley). Iowa (9:2) Spr 78,
    p. 105.

RIVERS, Ann
"'Hiroshima, Mon Amour'" (tr. of Stelios Yeranis). StoneC
    (78:2) Spr 78, p. 20.
"Unaccomplished" (tr. of Yannis Ritsos). ·StoneC (78:2) Spr 78,
    p. 21.   .

RIVERS, J. W.
"From a Mulberry Tree Branch in Jackson Park." HiramPoR
    (25) Aut-Wint 78, p. 32.
"To Most of My Family, Dead of Lung Cancer." SoCaR (10:2)
    Ap 78, p. 100.
"Wine." Sam (69) 78, p. 63.

RIZZA, Peggy
"Côte d'Or." ParisR (74) Aut-Wint 78, p. 107.
"Four Chinese Screens." ParisR (74) Aut-Wint 78, p. 106.
"The Joyful Mysteries." NewRep (179:20) 11 N 78, p. 29.

RIZZUTO, Helen Morrissey
"Elephant Nuts and Broken Dolls." Zahir (9) 77, p. 44.

ROAZEN, Donna
"Hail Mary." Sam (64) 78, p. 64.

ROBBINS, Anthony J.
"Andalusia." Wind (31) 78, p. 46.

ROBBINS, Martin
"Chant against the Winter Solstice." GRR (9:2) 78, p. 115.
"Communique from North of Eden." GRR (9:2) 78, p. 117.
"Footnote to the Trustees." StoneC (78:1) Wint 78, p. 35.
"Interior (with Street Corner)." SouthernPR (18:2) Aut 78, p. 33.
"Lodestar." GRR (9:2) 78, p. 116.
"Old Connecticut Farmhouse." StoneC (78:1) Wint 78, p. 35.
"On My Bride's Wedding Dress." St. AR (5:1) Aut-Wint 78,
    p. 118.
"Starscape." SouthernPR (18:2) Aut 78, p. 33.
"To a House in Winter." GRR (9:2) 78, p. 117.
"To the Pilots at Christmas." St. AR (4:3/4) 77-78, p. 22.

ROBBINS, Rick
"Coming Home." NoAmR (263:1) Spr 78, p. 35.
"Island in Oregon." CalQ (13/14) Spr-Sum 78, p. 62.

ROBERTS, A. F.
"The Fifth Season." PartR (45:4) 78, p. 592.

ROBERTS, George
"Andrew Talks to Gulls." NorthSR (8) Aut-Wint 78-79, p. 100.
"The Armored Car Is a Resumption of the Snail Shell." NorthSR
    (8) Aut-Wint 78-79, p. 97.
"If I Meet You in My Sleep." NorthSR (8) Aut-Wint 78-79,
    p. 100.
"News from Home." NorthSR (8) Aut-Wint 78-79, p. 98.
"Writing Poems." NorthSR (8) Aut-Wint 78-79, p. 99.

ROBERTS, Hortense Roberta
"Early Snow." Wind (31) 78, p. 51.
"Gulls and Fog." Wind (31) 78, p. 44.

ROBERTS, Laurence H., III
"Protective Medicine." Box (6) Aut 77, p. 6.
"Stilled Life." Box (6) Aut 77, p. 7.

ROBERTS, Len
"After." Tele (13) 77.
"Cat Nap." GreenfieldR (6:3/4) Spr 78, p. 92.
"Five-Year Wheat." Wind (28) 78, p. 54.
"Nails." GreenfieldR (6:3/4) Spr 78, p. 91.
"Thinking About Hands." Tele (13) 77.

ROBERTS, Sheila
"Thoughts on the Nazi Extermination Camps and the Coming
    South African Revolution." CentR (22:4) Aut 78, p. 418.

ROBERTSON, Brian
"Praise." Wind (28) 78, p. 55.

ROBERTSON, Howard
"Yucca, Joshuah tree." Glass (3:1/2/3) 78, p. 49.

ROBERTSON, Kell
from Regular Grinding: "Ken Maynard." Vaga (27) Spr 78,
    p. 68.

ROBERTSON, Kirk
"Crossroads." GreenfieldR (6:3/4) Spr 78, p. 80.
"Momma in Movieland." YellowBR (10) 78, p. 30.
"a note of exit signs." Tele (13) 77.
"Shovel Off to Buffalo" (Twenty-five poems). WormR (69) 78,
    pp. 13-28.
"snowing & in the dark." Tele (13) 77.

ROBIN, Ralph
"Dragon." SouthernHR (12:1) Wint 78, p. 44.
"Old Age." AmerS (47:3) Sum 78, p. 381.

ROBINS, Natalie
"For Eleven New Priests." OP (26) Aut-Wint 78, p. 14.
"Shadow." OP (26) Aut-Wint 78, p. 17.
"Waiting for Rain." OP (26) Aut-Wint 78, p. 18.

ROBINSON, Andy
"Well Texans." DeKalb (11:1/2) Aut-Wint 77-78, p. 64.

ROBINSON, Catherine
"Cats are Clouds with Teeth." MalR (45) Ja 78, p. 312.
"It Rained on Sunday." MalR (45) Ja 78, p. 313.

ROBINSON, Frank K.
"how dull." WindO (33) Aut-Wint 78-79.
"sheet lightning." WindO (33) Aut-Wint 78-79.
"stepping out of the creek." WindO (33) Aut-Wint 78-79.

ROBINSON, Kit
"1811." Hills (5) 78, p. 95.
"The Separateness of the Fingers in Trance." Hills (5) 78,
    p. 96.

ROBINSON, Lee M.
"November." SoCaR (11:1) Ap 78, p. 95.
"The White Door and the Wall." SoCaR (11:1) N 78, p. 94.

ROBINSON, Peter
"Poem from 'The Benefit Forms.'" Stand (19:3) 78, p. 10.

ROBISON, Margaret
"Water." Pan (19) 77, p. 1.

ROBSON, Ros
"Journey in the Attic." Wind (31) 78, p. 33.

ROCHE, David
"Recreation." Wind (31) 78, p. 47.

ROCHE, Paul
"The House Ants (Tangier)." Confr (17) Aut-Wint 79, p. 22.

RODDEY, Bill
"Burning." Sam (65) 78, p. 57.

RODGERS, Joan
"Amethyst--Against Drunkenness." MalR (45) Ja 78, p. 219.
"A Bearded Man, in Profile." MalR (45) Ja 78, p. 220.
"Birth Place." MalR (45) Ja 78, p. 220.
"Talisman." MalR (45) Ja 78, p. 221.

RODGERS, Katherine J.
"Sea of Disillusion." CarouselQ (3:4) Wint 78, p. 21.

RODITI, Edouard
"Confessions of a Prodigal Son." Kayak (49) O 78, p. 31.

RODNEY, Janet
from Alashka: "July 4, 1976: Sevuokuk" (w. Nathaniel Tarn).

Hand (2) 78, p. 57.
"Crystal XI. " Hand (2) 78, p. 18.

RODRIGUES, Manolo
"sitting here alone. " SeC (5:2) 78, p. 30.

RODRIGUEZ, Aleida
"Caesar. " Pig (4) 78, p. 95.

RODRIGUEZ, Shawn
"Crazy John was a true character. " SeC (5:2) 78, p. 32.
"My Grandmother. " SeC (5:2) 78, p. 31.

RODRIGUEZ-ALCALA, Guido
"Farewell" (tr. by C. R. Carlisle). Nimrod (22:2) Spr-Sum 78,
p. 94.

RODRIGUEZ-ALCALA, Hugo
"The Exile" (tr. by C. R. Carlisle). Nimrod (22:2) Spr-Sum 78,
p. 95.

ROGERS, Alice Ray
"Policeman in the New Orange World. " St. AR (5:1) Aut-Wint 78,
p. 137.

ROGERS, Jill
"Arithmetic Progression. " MalR (45) Ja 78, p. 52.
"End of the world comes early. " MalR (45) Ja 78, p. 53.
"Memorial. " MalR (45) Ja 78, p. 50.
"Touchstone. " MalR (45) Ja 78, p. 52.
"The Women. " MalR (45) Ja 78, p. 55.
"Writer of Legends. " MalR (45) Ja 78, p. 51.

ROGERS, Mary Bee
"One Thought on Madness. " Wind (29) 78, p. 27.
"Predator. " Wind (29) 78, p. 38.

ROGERS, Pattiann
"Crocodile God. " PoetC (10:2) 78, p. 20.
"In Order to Perceive. " PraS (52:3) Aut 78, p. 272.
"The Literary Adventure. " Poetry (132:6) S 78, p. 331.
"Our Children Are Drifting Downriver. " PoetC (10:2) 78, p. 18.
"Portrait. " Poetry (132:6) S 78, p. 333.

ROGERS, Ronald
"Sand Hill Crane: Montana, 1977. " GreenfieldR (6:3/4) Spr 78,
p. 39.
"Scape. " GreenfieldR (6:3/4) Spr 78, p. 39.

ROGERS, W. E.
"Easter. " BallSUF (19:2) Spr 78, p. 66.
"The Gulls. " Poem (33) Jl 78, p. 60.
"Harlequin in the Tropics. " Poem (33) Jl 78, p. 59.

"Proverbs." <u>Poem</u> (33) Jl 78, p. 58.
"Resurrection." <u>Poem</u> (33) Jl 78, p. 57.
"Seasons." <u>BallSUF</u> (19:4) Aut 78, p. 3.

ROGOFF, Jay
    "Greyhound Lullaby." <u>Wind</u> (29) 78, p. 39.
    "In Hospitals." <u>Wind</u> (29) 78, p. 39.

ROGOW, Zack
    "Let Your Fingers Do the Walking." <u>Tele</u> (14) 78.
    "Surfaces." <u>Tele</u> (14) 78.

ROJCEWICZ, Peter
    "Of Death and Dreams" (for Carol Brady). <u>Tendril</u> (2) Spr-Sum
        78.

ROKWAHO (Daniel Thompson)
    "Clickstone." <u>GreenfieldR</u> (6:3/4) Spr 78, p. 44.
    "From 'The Poet's Analyst.'" <u>GreenfieldR</u> (6:3/4) Spr 78,
        p. 45.

ROLLINGS, Alane
    "The Life." <u>SenR</u> (9:1) Spr-Sum 78, p. 24.
    "Light Years and the Love Lost in the Oleanders." <u>SenR</u> (9:1)
        Spr-Sum 78, p. 22.
    "Silkwood." <u>WindO</u> (31) Wint-Spr 78, p. 12.

ROMAN, Howard
    "Trees at Winter Solstice." <u>StoneC</u> (78:3) Aut 78, p. 23.

ROMER, Stephen
    "Nenuphars, Nympheas." <u>HarvAd</u> (112:1) D 78, p. 21.

ROMERO, Leo
    "Drawing and Poem." <u>SoDakR</u> (16:2) Sum 78, p. 50.
    "The First Ever Picked by Eve." <u>GreenfieldR</u> (6:3/4) Spr 78,
        p. 94.
    "Mentiras." <u>GreenfieldR</u> (6:3/4) Spr 78, p. 93.
    "The Miracle." <u>GreenfieldR</u> (6:3/4) Spr 78, p. 93.

ROMOND, Edwin
    "A Poem for Jake." <u>EngJ</u> (67:5) My 78, p. 52.

ROMTVEDT, David
    "Arson." <u>AmerPoR</u> (7:6) N-D 78, p. 20.
    "Breathing." <u>Wind</u> (30) 78, p. 56.
    "Feathers Are Tied in the Manner of a Hand." <u>Ascent</u> (3:3) 78,
        p. 25.
    "Man up North." <u>Ascent</u> (3:3) 78, p. 26.

RONAN, John J.
    "The Guard at Sunset: Arlington." <u>Epos</u> (27:2) 77, p. 14.
    "The Hospital." <u>Poem</u> (33) Jl 78, p. 19.

"Mountain Poem." WindO (31) Wint-Spr 78, p. 29.
"On the Street." WindO (31) Wint-Spr 78, p. 29.

RONAN, Richard
  "Embers." US1 (11) Aut 78, p. 1.
  "I don't know what it's like really." AmerPoR (7:3) My-Je 78,
    p. 20.
  "moving west." AmerPoR (7:3) My-Je 78, p. 20.
  "The Pickerel." US1 (11) Aut 78, p. 10.

ROOSEVELT, Glenn
  "For Thomas Merton." ChrC (95:40) 6 D 78, p. 1180.

ROOT, William Pitt
  "Leveling" (for K.K.). Atl (242:6) D 78, p. 87.
  "Sweat." QW (5) Wint 78, p. 90.
  "Teaching Among the Children of Chief Plenty Coups." QW (5)
    Wint 78, p. 88.
  "White Horse of the Father, White Horse of the Son." Chowder
    (10/11) Aut-Wint 78-79, p. 24.

ROSE, George
  "Coming Out of Oceans after Dark." PoetryNW (19:3) Aut 78,
    p. 37.

ROSE, Judith
  "I would like to adopt...." Chomo (5:1) Sum 78, p. 3.

ROSE, Lynne Carol
  "Grandma." GRR (9:2) 78, p. 98.
  "Harvest Moon." Epos (27:2) 77, p. 28.
  "Night Watch." GRR (9:2) 78, p. 100.
  "One Woman's Resurrection" (for Anne Sexton [1928-1974]). GRR
    (9:3) 78, p. 211.
  "Psalm." GRR (9:2) 78, p. 99.

ROSE, Wendy
  "Academic Squaw." GreenfieldR (6:3/4) Spr 78, p. 42.
  "Going in...." GreenfieldR (6:3/4) Spr 78, p. 40.
  "How I Came to Be a Graduate Student." GreenfieldR (6:3/4)
    Spr 78, p. 43.

ROSELIEP, Raymond
  "Before Vatican II." Bits (7) Ja 78.
  "Blow, Winds, and Crack Your Cheeks." SlowLR (1/2) 78,
    p. 100.
  "Five Haiku." PikeF (1) Spr 78, p. 21.
  "Haiku." WindO (32) Sum-Aut 78, p. 3.
  "'In Love, Ther Is But Litel Reste'--Troilus and Criseyde."
    SlowLR (1/2) 78, p. 102.
  "Love's Not Time's Fool." SlowLR (1/2) 78, p. 106.
  "Monarch." ChrC (95:25) 2-9 Ag 78, p. 724.
  "O Little Town." ChrC (95:42) 20 D 78, p. 1233.

"Siesta. " WindO (33) Aut-Wint 78-79.
"Telephone Wire. " Bits (8) Jl 78.
"Walk. " ChrC (95:43) 27 D 78, p. 1252.
"White Child to Black. " PoNow (19) 78, p. 12.

ROSEN, Amy
"1968 Volvo. " Paunch (52) O 78, p. 96.

ROSEN, Michael
"Passover. " Hand (2) 78, p. 68.
"Praxis from a Lifeboat. " Hand (2) 78, p. 104.
"Wintering. " PoNow (20) 78, p. 37.

ROSENBERG, D. M.
"The Painted Caves. " BallSUF (19:2) Spr 78, p. 2.

ROSENBERG, Paul
"The Aftermath. " WindO (31) Wint-Spr 78, p. 24.
"The Final Corner. " Epos (27:1) 77, p. 20.

ROSENBERG, Robert
"The Burial of Tomorrow: The Lost Boys. " Epos (27:1) 77,
    p. 6.
"A Medley for a Few of the Living Dead. " ThRiPo (11/12) 78,
    p. 63.

ROSENBERGER, Francis Coleman
"The Jade Box. " SouthernPR (18:2) Aut 78, p. 78.
"Zebu, Zed, Zen. " SouthwR (63:1) Wint 78, p. 73.

ROSENFELD, Rita
"Deus Misereatur. " Sam (65) 78, p. 32.
"The Hills of Lebanon. " Sam (69) 78, p. 41.
"Life in the Universe. " Sam (65) 78, p. 33.
"Poem: Self contemplates. " Smudge (Supplement) Wint 78-79,
    p. 16.

ROSENHEIM, Andrew
"Blue Is Not Your Dying. " PartR (45:2) 78, p. 274.

ROSENTHAL, Abby
"The Discontent. " Paint (9/10) Spr-Aut 78, p. 23.
"The Sailboat. " SouthernPR (18:1) Spr 78, p. 19.
"Warning to History's Children. " CarolQ (30:2) Spr-Sum 78,
    p. 85.

ROSENZWEIG, Phyllis
"Avant le Cinema. " Tele (14) 78.
"For Bernie. " Tele (14) 78.
"There's a little beast. " LaB (10) 78, p. 41.

ROSS, Bob
"Land. " PraS (52:3) Aut 78, p. 290.

ROSS, Carolyn
  "Days Alone." Salm (40) Wint 78, p. 68.
  "The Image, the Idea" (for Susan Yeh, after her clay miniature).
      Salm (40) Wint 78, p. 67.

ROSS, Lynn Edgar
  "Around Walnut." Pig (4) 78, p. 86.

ROSSI, Vinio
  "Afternoon Movies" (tr. of Giovanni Raboni, w. Stuart Friebert).
      Field (18) Spr 78, p. 87.
  "Bad Year" (tr. of Giovanni Raboni, w. Stuart Friebert). Field
      (18) Spr 78, p. 84.
  "Christmas Morning" (tr. of Giovanni Raboni, w. Stuart Friebert).
      Field (18) Spr 78, p. 85.
  "The Colonial Error" (tr. of Giovanni Raboni, w. Stuart Frie-
      bert). Field (18) Spr 78, p. 86.
  "The Dead and the True" (tr. of Giovanni Raboni). Field (18)
      Spr 78, p. 82.
  "Pontius P." (tr. of Giovanni Raboni). Field (18) Spr 78, p. 83.

ROSSINI, Frank
  "hello." YellowBR (10) 78, p. 3.
  "rain again." SmPd (44) Aut 78, p. 28.
  "Success." PoNow (20) 78, p. 37.

ROTH, Paul
  "Pacific." Hand (2) 78, p. 69.

ROTHENBERG, Jerome
  from Abulafia's Circles. Montra (4) 78, p. 222.
  "Morphine" (tr. of Heinrich Heine). Hand (2) 78, p. 156.

ROVINSKY, Robert R.
  "Calm Sequence from an Excited Film" (tr. of Lars Gustafsson).
      BosUJ (26:1) 78, p. 70.
  "An Epigram of Sorts" (tr. of Lars Gustafsson). BosUJ (26:1)
      78, p. 69.

ROWELL, Charles H.
  "For Ann Beard-Grundy." Obs (4:2) Sum 78, p. 93.
  "For Lolita Burns." Obs (4:2) Sum 78, p. 93.
  "Green Bottles" (for --------). Obs (4:2) Sum 78, p. 93.
  "Seadiver" (for Robert Hayden). Obs (4:2) Sum 78, p. 92.

ROWLAND, Sidney
  "Three Bouncing Boys." StoneC (78:1) Wint 78, p. 16.

ROYSTER, Phillip M.
  "Autumn." Obs (4:2) Sum 78, p. 72.
  "Photo for Sara" (from one Fabio to another). Obs (4:2) Sum
      78, p. 72.
  "Sunday Afternoon." Obs (4:2) Sum 78, p. 71.

ROZEWICZ, Tadeusz
"Anonymous Voice" (tr. by Victor Contoski). Hand (2) 78, p. 91.
"Chestnut" (tr. by Adam Czerniawski). Stand (18:4) 77, p. 8.
"Whoever Sees" (tr. by Adam Czerniawski). Stand (18:4) 77,
     p. 8.

RUARK, Gibbons
"The Goods She Can Carry." Poetry (133:1) O 78, p. 26.

RUBENSTEIN, Carol
"Cradle Song" (tr.). Hand (2) 78, p. 86.
"Cradle Song for Female Child" (tr.). Hand (2) 78, p. 86.
"I Lack Voice to Sing" (tr.). Hand (2) 78, p. 89.
from Orang Utan in Subway Subtitled: "Part I--Trip." Tele (13)
     77.
from Orang Utan in Subway Subtitled: "Part 1--Trip." Tele
     (14) 78.

RUBENSTEIN, Elaine
"Summertime." SouthernPR (18:2) Aut 78, p. 36.

RUBIN, Larry
"Growing Up on the Beach." SouthernR (14:3) Aut 78, p. 516.
"The Tagalong." SewanR (86:2) Spr 78, p. 269.
"Telling Time at Sea." SewanR (86:2) Spr 78, p. 269.

RUBIN, Mark
"Avenues on the Elm." Nat (226:18) 13 My 78, p. 576.
"A Form of Asking." Nat (226:22) 10 Je 78, p. 704.
"Three Portraits of a Lightning Bug." Antaeus (30/31) Sum-Aut
     78, p. 193.
"Two Bird Oppositions." Antaeus (30/31) Sum-Aut 78, p. 192.

RUBIN, Stan Stanvel
"Marriage." SouthernPR (18:2) Aut 78, p. 16.

RUBY, Michael
"Possible Worlds." HarvAd (111:3) Ap 78, p. 29.

RUDMAN, Mark
Eight poems (tr. of Boris Pasternak, w. Bohdan Boychuk).
     VirQR (54:4) Aut 78, p. 601.
"How Life Lulls Us" (tr. of Boris Pasternak, w. Bohdan Boy-
     chuk). Pequod (2:4) 78, p. 12.

RUDNIK, Raphael
"Dream." Poetry (131:6) Mr 78, p. 337.
"Now That Your Body." Poetry (131:6) Mr 78, p. 337.

RUDOLF, Anthony
"The Last Poem of Karl Kraus." Hand (2) 78, p. 136.
"The Remembrancer/The Survivor." Hand (2) 78, p. 136.

RUDY, D. L.
  "Mortality's Wounding Wings." Wind (30) 78, p. 18.
  "You-Me." Poem (32) Mr 78, p. 15.

RUESCHER, Scott
  "Chicory." PraS (52:3) Aut 78, p. 224.
  "Cumberland Gap." PraS (52:3) Aut 78, p. 225.
  "Lake Hope." Nat (227:16) 11 N 78, p. 525.
  "Late in July." PraS (52:3) Aut 78, p. 223.
  "Preface to Luther's 95 Theses." Nat (227:13) 21 O 78, p. 420.

RUFFIN, Paul
  "The Practice Is Over, Tom Hardy." NewOR (5:4) 78, p. 322.
  "To a Student on the Front Row." MichQR (17:1) Wint 78,
      p. 76.

RUGGLES, Eugene
  "God." PoNow (19) 78, p. 33.
  "The Lifeguard in the Snow." PoNow (19) 78, p. 33.
  "An Old Man on the Bum Sitting in an All-Night Detroit Diner."
      PoNow (19) 78, p. 33.
  "The Water Trough." PoNow (19) 78, p. 33.

RUGO, Mariève
  "Beatrice Remembers." 13thM (4:1) 78, p. 8.
  "Borders." PraS (52:4) Wint 78-79, p. 360.
  "The Cave Called My Body." SouthernPR (18:2) Aut 78, p. 21.
  "Circus Lady." PoetryNW (19:1) Spr 78, p. 15.
  "Expatriot." PoetryNW (19:1) Spr 78, p. 15.
  "In the Season of Wolves and Names." PraS (52:4) Wint 78-79,
      p. 359.
  "The Pedestrian." SouthernPR (18:2) Aut 78, p. 21.
  "Il Salto Mortale." PraS (52:4) Wint 78-79, p. 358.
  "Warning to Swimmers." Tendril (2) Spr-Sum 78.
  "A Woman at Middle Age." Tendril (2) Spr-Sum 78.

RUIZ, Anita
  "A hundred years from now." SeC (5:2) 78, p. 56.

RUIZ, Dolly
  "Bubble Gum." SeC (5:2) 78, p. 58.
  "A hundred years from now." SeC (5:2) 78, p. 57.

RUKAVINA, Joanne
  "Signs." DacTerr (15) Wint-Spr 77-78, p. 49.

RUKEYSER, Muriel
  "Blue Spruce." PoNow (19) 78, p. 8.
  "Islands." PoNow (19) 78, p. 8.
  "Ms. Lot." PoNow (19) 78, p. 8.

RUMI
  "Come come." ChiR (30:2) Aut 78, p. 8.

"Don't fall asleep tonight." ChiR (30:2) Aut 78, p. 8.
"What is the whirling dance" (tr. by W. S. Merwin and Talat
    Halman). AmerPoR (7:1) Ja-F 78, p. 3.

RUNCIMAN, Lex
    "Journal Entry." QW (5) Wint 78, p. 118.

RUSCH, Frederick L.
    "Elephant Poem." ParisR (73) Spr-Sum 78, p. 150.

RUSS, Lawrence
    "After a Cold Spell." GreenfieldR (6:3/4) Spr 78, p. 87.
    "Night in Fog." GreenfieldR (6:3/4) Spr 78, p. 87.
    "The Wedding Poem" (for Mary). BelPoJ (29:1) Aut 78, p. 7.

RUSSELL, CarolAnn
    "Called Sleeping." CutB (10) Spr-Sum 78, p. 77.
    "Crossing the Lake." CutB (10) Spr-Sum 78, p. 78.
    "Into the Forest, into the Heart" (for my brother, John).
        PoetryNW (19:3) Aut 78, p. 12.
    "Outcast." CutB (10) Spr-Sum 78, p. 76.
    "Photo of Women Plowing (circa 1850)." Columbia (2) Aut 78,
        p. 28.
    "Walking at Night." CutB (11) Spr-Sum 78, p. 10.

RUSSELL, R. Stephen
    "The Egg." ParisR (73) Spr-Sum 78, p. 148.
    "How Michael Was Conceived." ParisR (73) Spr-Sum 78, p. 148.

RUSSELL, Richard
    "Outsiders." StoneC (78:1) Wint 78, p. 24.
    "Peace." Wind (30) 78, p. 44.

RUST, Gary
    "State Fair: Hutchinson Kansas." PoNow (20) 78, p. 46.

RUTCOSKY, Cindy
    "Sweet mood come down on me." NewL (45:1) Aut 78, p. 60.

RUTSALA, Vern
    "Building the House." SouthernR (14:1) Wint 78, p. 120.
    "By the Willamette." PoNow (19) 78, p. 28.
    "Eagle Squadron." Iowa (9:2) Spr 78, p. 75.
    "The House at Night." PoNow (19) 78, p. 28.
    "Killing Time." PoNow (19) 78, p. 30.
    "The Mill Back Home." Bits (8) Jl 78.
    "Other Lives." PoNow (19) 78, p. 28.
    "The Perfect Stranger." GeoR (32:4) Wint 78, p. 842.
    "The Public Lecture." PoNow (19) 78, p. 30.

RYAN, Heather A.
    "Love Poem." HangL (33) Sum 78, p. 69.
    "A Man Walks with a Woman." HangL (33) Sum 78, p. 68.

RYAN, Kay
    from Face Up: "Temperance." PikeF (1) Spr-Sum 78, p. 3.
    from Face Up: "The Devil." PikeF (1) Spr 78, p. 3.
    from Face Up: "The Hanged Man." PikeF (1) Spr 78, p. 3.
    from Face Up: "Wheel of Fortune." PikeF (1) Spr 78, p. 3.

RYAN, Michael
    "The Past." Poetry (133:2) N 78, p. 88.
    "Waking at Night." Poetry (133:2) N 78, p. 89.
    "When I Was Conceived." Poetry (132:2) My 78, p. 78.

RYAN, William E., II
    "Eulogy for the Lone Ranger." SoDakR (16:3) Aut 78, p. 111.
    "Gleaner." SoDakR (16:3) Aut 78, p. 112.

RYERSON, Alice
    "Tornado Warning." WindO (32) Sum-Aut 78, p. 9.

SABATIER, Robert
    "Delicious Poison" (tr. by Elizabeth Hanson). MassR (19:1) Spr
        78, p. 128.

SABINES, Jaime
    "At the Station" (tr. by Ameen Alwan). AmerPoR (7:2) Mr-Ap
        78, p. 29.
    "Here's What's Happening" (tr. by Ameen Alwan). AmerPoR
        (7:2) Mr-Ap 78, p. 28.
    "I'm Happy" (tr. by Ameen Alwan). AmerPoR (7:2) Mr-Ap 78,
        p. 28.
    "Like Lost Birds" (tr. by Ameen Alwan). AmerPoR (7:2) Mr-
        Ap 78, p. 28.
    "Poem: It's said ..." (tr. by Ameen Alwan). AmerPoR (7:2)
        Mr-Ap 78, p. 29.
    "Something About the Death of Major Sabines" (tr. by Ameen
        Alwan). AmerPoR (7:2) Mr-Ap 78, p. 29.

SABUKEWICZ, Charles
    "A Winter Night." Epos (27:1) 77, p. 26.

SADOFF, Ira
    "The Execution of the Rosenbergs." VirQR (54:1) Wint 78.
    "First Light." Antaeus (30/31) Sum-Aut 78, p. 196.
    "The McCarthy Hearings." Poetry (132:5) Ag 78, p. 260.
    "Nathaniel Hawthorne." Poetry (132:2) My 78, p. 72.
    "Street Scene by Hopper." Antaeus (30/31) Sum-Aut 78, p. 195.
    "While Watching 'Young and Innocent' I Think of My Mother."
        Poetry (132:5) Ag 78, p. 261.

SAGAN, Miriam
    "Mantra." Tendril (3) Aut 78, p. 44.
    "Montage for Houdini." JnlONJP (2:2) 77, p. 26.
    Vision's Edge. Sam (63) 78. Entire issue.

SAGSTETTER, Karen
"Lying." Bits (7) Ja 78.

SAIGYO
Sixty-four poems. Montra (4) 78, p. 164.

ST. CLAIR, Philip
"An Honest Prayer." Pig (5) 78, p. 21.

ST. CYR, Napoleon
"batterups." SmPd (42) Wint 78, p. 3.

ST. JOHN, David
"Blue Waves." NewYorker (54:26) 14 Ag 78, p. 89.
"Elegy." Poetry (132:1) Ap 78, p. 13.
"Guitar." NewYorker (54:44) 18 D 78, p. 63.
"Song Without Forgiveness." Antaeus (30/31) Sum-Aut 78,
    p. 225.
"Welcome." MissouriR (1:1) Spr 78, p. 19.

SAISER, Marjorie
"Lying on the Driveway Studying Stars" (for my sister Kathy).
    PraS (52:4) Wint 78-79, p. 357.
"Man at the Derby Star." Aspen (5) Spr 78, p. 89.
"Morning." PraS (52:4) Wint 78-79, p. 356.
"Rancher." Aspen (5) Spr 78, p. 90.
"Shroud." Aspen (5) Spr 78, p. 90.

SALAMON, Russell
"Below the midnight." Stonecloud (7) 78, p. 11.
"I Move as Blood." Stonecloud (7) 78, p. 11.

SALAMONE, Rosa Maria
from Anaphilosophia: "Ana Ars Philosophia" (tr. of Martino
    Oberto). Chelsea (37) 78, p. 109.
from Anaphilosophia: "Ana of Esserialism" (tr. of Martino
    Oberto). Chelsea (37) 78, p. 79.

SALANGA, Alfredro Navarro
"A Prodigal Cycle" (tr. by Elisavietta Ritchie). AAR (28) 78,
    p. 49.

SALINAS, Pedro
"Navacerrada, April (tr. by Edward Friedman). Paint (9/10)
    Spr-Aut 78, p. 48.

SALISBURY, Ralph
"Aeons of Wishes." CutB (10) Spr-Sum 78, p. 84.
"All He Will Feel." NewL (44:3) Spr 78, p. 60.
"Some Music" (For Carl Dolmetsch). PoNow (19) 78, p. 38.

SALKEY, Andrew
"Caribbea's Wall." NewL (45:1) Aut 78, p. 98.

"Mountains, Rivers, and Caribbea" (For Eliot and Jason). NewL
   (45:1) Aut 78, p. 97.

SALLEH, Mahammud haji
   "Villagers" (tr. by Elisavietta Ritchie). AAR (28) 78, p. 48.

SALTER, Mary Jo
   "England. " Atl (242:1) Jl 78, p. 45.

SALTMAN, Benjamin
   from Deck: fourteen poems. Bachy (11) Spr 78, p. 57.
   "Deck: King of Clubs. " PoetryNW (19:1) Spr 78, p. 23.

SALVATIERRA, Estella
   "(Across the Table). " CarouselQ (3:2) Sum 78, p. 29.

SALZMANN, Jerome
   "Marquis de Sade. " DeKalb (11:3/4) Spr-Sum 78, p. 43.
   "Mathematician. " DeKalb (11:3/4) Spr-Sum 78, p. 43.
   "Turtle. " Tele (13) 78.

SAMMANS, Virgie McCoy
   "Colors. " CarouselQ (3:4) Wint 78, p. 22.

SAMPSON, Dennis
   "Fault of the Phenomenal. " SoDakR (16:2) Sum 78, p. 28.

SANCHEZ, Sonia
   Eight poems. BelPoJ (29:2) Wint 78-79, p. 35.

SANDEEN, Ernest
   "How Time Is Kept. " Poetry (132:5) Ag 78, p. 268.
   "In the Cage. " Poetry (132:5) Ag 78, p. 268.

SANDERS, Barry
   "Parable of the Stone. " Atl (242:1) Jl 78, p. 44.

SANDERS, Mark
   "A Girl's Woman Desires. " HiramPoR (25) Aut-Wint 78, p. 33.

SANDERS, Scott Patrick
   "The Fisherman Considers His Life's Work. " Aspen (6) Aut 78,
      p. 105.
   "There's a Bar in Salome, Arizona. " Aspen (6) Aut 78, p. 104.

SANDRI, Giovanna
   from Empedocles D'Artaud: "Fragment 57" (tr. by Ruth Feldman
      and Brian Swann). Durak (1) 78, p. 56.
   from Empedocles D'Artaud: "Fragment 61" (tr. by Ruth Feldman
      and Brian Swann). Durak (1) 78, p. 57.

SANDY, Stephen
   "Near Pamet Marsh. " Hudson (31:2) Sum 78, p. 277.
   "Riding to Greystone. " Salm (42) Sum-Aut 78, p. 113.

SANER, Reg
"All-Purpose Military Epitaph." MinnR (NS11) Aut 78, p. 54.
"Ancient Fragment from the Edge of the Empire." MinnR (NS11)
    Aut 78, p. 55.
"Ancient History." MinnR (NS11) Aut 78, p. 56.
"And So We Climb Higher." Aspen (6) Aut 78, p. 10.
"Eastward from Somewhere: San Vitale, Ravenna." Poetry
    (133:3) D 78, p. 129.
"Ghiberti's Baptistery Doors Revisited." Poetry (133:3) D 78,
    p. 130.
"In the Iron Trough of the Year." Poetry (133:3) D 78, p. 128.
"Knowing Me Well." Aspen (6) Aut 78, p. 9.
"Mango." NowestR (17:1) 78, p. 24.
"Moon." Atl (242:2) Ag 78, p. 72.
"Mountain of the Holy Cross: San Juan Range." Poetry (133:3)
    D 78, p. 131.
"Scene for an Early October to Come." Aspen (6) Aut 78, p. 8.
"Why I Marvel at Certain Noises." NowestR (17:1) 78, p. 23.

SANESI, Roberto
"On a Photograph of Machado, Thinking of Pablo, for Rafael"
    (tr. by Mario Angulo). MalR (47) Jl 78, p. 114.

SANGE, Gary
"Among Frogs." ThRiPo (11/12) 78, p. 64.
"Sudden Country." ThRiPo (11/12) 78, p. 65.

SANGE, Sally Harris
"Kate's Poem." AmerS (47:3) Sum 78, p. 396.

SANTOS, Sherod
"Ancient Lamentation." Nat (226:18) 13 My 78, p. 576.
"Fear of the Dark." ParisR (73) Spr-Sum 78, p. 146.
"Madame Orchidée." Antaeus (30/31) Sum-Aut 78, p. 197.
"Memory." Antaeus (30/31) Sum-Aut 78, p. 204.
"Sarah Coleridge at Greta Hall." Antaeus (30/31) Sum-Aut 78,
    p. 200.
"Stages of a Man Waking in the Afternoon." Columbia (2) Aut
    78, p. 2.
"The Summer Privacy of Things." ParisR (73) Spr-Sum 78,
    p. 147.
"Summer Vacation." Antaeus (30/31) Sum-Aut 78, p. 202.
"W. C. W.'s Moment of Suspense." Iowa (9:4) Aut 78, p. 78.

SAPORITA, Jay
"She does not wait for a response." JnlONJP (3:1) 78, p. 15.

SARGENT, Robert
"The Identity of 'They' in 'They Flee Me.'" ColEng (39:8) Ap
    78, p. 942.

SASLOW, Helen
"Late Afternoon." Glass (3:1/2/3) 78, p. 62.
"Villanelle: Night Watch." Glass (3:1/2/3) 78, p. 63.

SATO, Hiroaki
    103 Tanka (tr.).   Montra (4) 78, p. 152.

SATTLER, Joel
    "LSD Elevator."   Stonecloud (7) 78, p. 50.

SAULS, Roger
    "Letter to Wisconsin."   PoNow (19) 78, p. 21.

SAUNDERS, Geraldine
    "Double Time."   GreenfieldR (6:3/4) Spr 78, p. 139.
    "Fire."   GreenfieldR (6:3/4) Spr 78, p. 140.
    "'Willow Weep for Me.'"   GreenfieldR (6:3/4) Spr 78, p. 137.

SAUNDERS, Josephine
    "Ending. Beginning."   Kayak (47) F 78, p. 31.

SAVAGE, Tom
    "Gossip at the Sink."   Tele (14) 78.
    "Hitting the Road."   Tele (14) 78.

SAVITT, Lynne
    "Love Poem to My Son."   13thM (4:1) 78, p. 77.
    "On the Hospitalization of My Daughter for Diabetes."   YellowBR
        (10) 78, p. 27.

SAVORY, Teo
    "'... In Other Mountains.'"   WebR (4:2) Aut 78, p. 61.

SAVVAS, Minas
    Sixteen poems (tr. of Yannis Ritsos).   Falcon (16) 78, pp. 50
        and 86.

SAWYER, Mary
    "The Valley."   NewL (45:1) Aut 78, p. 55.

SAX, Boria
    "Bestiary."   PoetC (10:2) 78, p. 11.

SAXON, Sonia
    "Poem to a Young Student."   HangL (34) Wint 78-79, p. 48.
    "Screaming and Squealing at 14."   HangL (34) Wint 78-79, p. 47.
    "Sunday."   HangL (34) Wint 78-79, p. 49.
    "Swimming at the Y Pool."   HangL (34) Wint 78-79, p. 50.

SAYRE, Rose
    "Teaberry Grandma Conquers Nature."   Pig (4) 78, p. 25.

SAYRES, William
    "Mazar."   Sam (64) 78, p. 2.
    "Mazar."   Zahir (9) 77, p. 32.

SCANLON, Daniel
    "Corpus" (tr. of Raffaele Perrotta).   Chelsea (37) 78, p. 199.

"Verso Opus" (tr. of Raffaele Perrotta). Chelsea (37) 78, p. 207.

SCANNELL, Vernon
"A Partial View." Stand (19:4) 78, p. 36.

SCARPATO, T.
"Impregnation. " CarouselQ (3:4) Wint 78, p. 21.

SCATES, Maxine
"Garden Movements. " CalQ (13/14) Spr-Sum 78, p. 83.

SCHADE, Richard
"Dreams Which Never Die." CarouselQ (3:3) Aut 78, p. 24.
"Parallel." CarouselQ (3:4) Wint 78, p. 30.

SCHAEFER, Ted
"The Canary Song. " NewL (44:3) Spr 78, p. 76.
"The Summer People. " Glass (3:1/2/3) 78, p. 54.

SCHAEFFER, Susan Fromberg
"The Child. " Stonecloud (7) 78, p. 15.
"The Creature Asks Advice." Salm (42) Sum-Aut 78, p. 128.
"Jacks." Epos (27:2) 77, p. 12.
"Landscape. " Pan (19) 77, p. 63.
"Postcards from the Country." Salm (42) Sum-Aut 78, p. 129.
"Seeing Snow. " SoDakR (16:2) Sum 78, p. 23.
"Silences." Paint (9/10) Spr-Aut 78, p. 24.
"Things To Do." Confr (17) Aut-Wint 79, p. 189.
"Two People at Christmas." Stonecloud (7) 78, p. 16.
"The Vanity." Stonecloud (7) 78, p. 17.

SCHAEFFER, Terry T.
"I Saw You Take My Measure." JnlONJP (2:2) 77, p. 16.

SCHAFFER, Ariel
"Out of Mind. " AmerS (47:4) Aut 78, p. 458.

SCHEDLER, Gilbert
"This I Believe." ChrC (95:38) 22 N 78, p. 1130.

SCHEELE, Roy
"Poppies." Comm (105:17) 1 S 78, p. 552.
"The Sparrows Way." Comm (105:13) 7 Jl 78, p. 423.
"Wild Pear. " Comm (105:18) 15 S 78, p. 590.

SCHEIBLI, Silvia
"Arm in Arm/Federico, the Sun and the Sea." Stonecloud (7) 78, p. 114.
"Desiré." Stonecloud (7) 78, p. 100.
"Doves from Desiré." Stonecloud (7) 78, p. 95.
"Elder Blossoms" (tr. of Johannes Bobrowski). Stonecloud (7) 78, p. 119.

"For Desiré." Stonecloud (7) 78, p. 95.
"Gertrud Kolmar" (tr. of Johannes Bobrowski). Stonecloud (7)
    78, p. 118.
"Home of the Painter, Chagall" (tr. of Johannes Bobrowski).
    Stonecloud (7) 78, p. 119.

SCHENKER, Donald
"I Make My Bed." WormR (68) 77, p. 82.
"Juggernaut." WormR (68) 77, p. 81.
"Miss Hurryback." WormR (68) 77, p. 84.
"War Movie." WormR (68) 77, p. 83.

SCHEVILL, James
"Three Women Bending over a Blue Cape." ThRiPo (11/12) 78,
    p. 66.

SCHJELDAHL, Peter
"Draft Dodger." LaB (11) 78, p. 40.
"Face." LaB (11) 78, p. 43.
"Poem with Ada." LaB (11) 78, p. 41.
"Verses Reply." LaB (11) 78, p. 39.

SCHMEIDEL, Bettina
"For You" (tr. by Claudia Johnson). MissouriR (2:1) Aut 78,
    p. 23.

SCHMID, Vernon
"For the Children." ChrC (95:8) 8 Mr 78, p. 228.
"Shepherd's Poem." ChrC (95:42) 20 D 78, p. 1233.

SCHMIDT, Paul
"Feelings" (tr. of Rimbaud). Montra (4) 78, p. 292.

SCHMITT, Ronnie
"The Night Before Christmas." GreenfieldR (7:1/2) Aut 78,
    p. 105.

SCHMITZ, Dennis
"Auto-." NewL (45:1) Aut 78, p. 23.
"Dog." Antaeus (30/31) Sum-Aut 78, p. 208.
"The Feast of Tabernacles." Field (18) Spr 78, p. 27.
"Homing." Iowa (9:4) Aut 78, p. 75.
"How to Build a Wall." Antaeus (30/31) Sum-Aut 78, p. 208.
"In Bosch's World." Iowa (9:4) Aut 78, p. 73.
"Infinitives." Field (18) Spr 78, p. 29.
"Like Children We Sing." NewL (45:1) Aut 78, p. 22.
"Mile Hill." Field (18) Spr 78, p. 30.
"The Other Side." Antaeus (28) Wint 78, p. 96.
"Planting Trout in the Chicago River." Antaeus (28) Wint 78,
    p. 94.
"Revival." QW (5) Wint 78, p. 76.
"String." Antaeus (28) Wint 78, p. 93.
"Trying to Remember Paradise." Antaeus (30/31) Sum-Aut 78,

p. 209.
"Wings." <u>Antaeus</u> (30/31) Sum-Aut 78, p. 207.

SCHNEIDER, Nina
"The Certainty of Bees." <u>Nat</u> (227:1) 1 Jl 78, p. 25.

SCHNEIDER, Steven
"Lao Tzu's Sister's Dream." <u>BelPoJ</u> (28:4) Sum 78, p. 34.

SCHNEIDERMAN, Leo
"A Boat from the Steamer Glides Toward the Beach." <u>ArizQ</u>
    (36:4) Wint 78, p. 292.
"The Sacred Landscape Number 123." <u>ArizQ</u> (34:2) Sum 78,
    p. 131.

SCHNELL, David
"Paranoia." <u>CarouselQ</u> (3:4) Wint 78, p. 24.

SCHNELL, Hartmut
"The African" (tr. of Rolf Dieter Brinkmann). <u>NewL</u> (45:1) Aut
    78, p. 37.
"Journey to the Northern Gardens" (tr. of Rolf Dieter Brink-
    mann). <u>NewL</u> (45:1) Aut 78, p. 38.

SCHOENBERGER, Nancy
"After Camille." <u>SouthernR</u> (14:3) Sum 78, p. 469.
"From the Glass House." <u>Antaeus</u> (30/31) Sum-Aut 78, p. 210.
"I Have No Memory." <u>Poem</u> (34) N 78, p. 52.
"Lady of the Cups." <u>Poem</u> (34) N 78, p. 50.
"Musselshell Woman." <u>Poem</u> (34) N 78, p. 53.
"This Is Missoula." <u>SouthernR</u> (14:3) Sum 78, p. 468.

SCHOFIELD, Don
"Howling Man and His Young." <u>CutB</u> (10) Spr-Sum 78, p. 54.
"Rain on the Face Is a Bad Dream." <u>CutB</u> (11) Aut-Wint 78,
    p. 47.
"We Men Weep." <u>CutB</u> (10) Spr-Sum 78, p. 56.

SCHOLNICK, Michael
"And On Top of This America." <u>Tele</u> (13) 77.

SCHORB, E. M.
"Insect Song." <u>KanQ</u> (10:3) Sum 78, p. 28.
"The Loss." <u>YaleR</u> (67:4) Sum 78, p. 571.
"The Orphaned." <u>YaleR</u> (67:4) Sum 78, p. 571.
"Travelling Child." <u>Confr</u> (17) Aut-Wint 79, p. 153.

SCHORR, Miriam
"Table." <u>PoetryNW</u> (19:2) Sum 78, p. 39.

SCHRADER, Allen
"Defined, Refined, and Dismissed." <u>SouthwR</u> (63:3) Sum 78,
    p. 228.

SCHREIBER, Ron
"picnicking in Sitka." Aspect (71) Ap-Je 77, p. 18.

SCHUCHAT, Simon
"After Dante." Tele (14) 78.
"Appealing to the Eye." LaB (11) 78, p. 45.
"Journey to the East." Tele (14) 78.
"Morning Poem" (to Bob Rosenthal). Tele (14) 78.
"Ode to the Confederate Dead" (An Ecloque in honor of the
    Memory of Robert Lowell). LaB (11) 78, p. 46.
"Stanzas." Tele (14) 78.
"Tom Brown's School Days." Tele (14) 78.
"Yellow Flowers." Tele (14) 78.

SCHULER, Robert
from Bits of Maya for Martha: (II). PikeF (1) Spr 78, p. 20.
from Gypsy Bands Lost in the Plains: "Weather Report from
    Lusitanos." PikeF (1) Spr 78, p. 20.
"Old Testament" (to Peter and Linda Hamm). DacTerr (15)
    Wint-Spr 77-78, p. 19.
from Wakarusha Creek Notebook: "Dawn at Benton's Curve."
    PikeF (1) Spr 78, p. 20.

SCHULER, Ruth Wildes
"A Frail Golden Tale." BallSUF (19:2) Spr 78, p. 51.
"In Memoriam, Alex Klushkin." Sam (69) 78, p. 40.
"The Social Hour." Tele (14) 78.
"To Ernest Hemingway." Tele (14) 78.

SCHULMAN, Grace
"Blessed Is the Light." Poetry (132:3) Je 78, p. 140.

SCHULTZ, Philip
"Cezanne." Nat (227:11) 7 O 78, p. 350.
"Darwin, Tortoises, Galapagos Archipelago & New Hampshire"
    (For John & Mary Cheever). Poetry (132:6) S 78, p. 318.
"For My Father" (Samuel Schultz, 1903-1963). Poetry (132:6) S
    78, p. 321.
"The Gift" (For Ralph Dickey 1945-1972). NewYorker (53:47) 9
    Ja 78, p. 30.
"Laughter." Nat (227:14) 28 O 78, p. 450.
"Savage Feelings." Poetry (132:6) S 78, p. 320.

SCHULTZ, Robert
"Cascadilla Place." GreenfieldR (6:3/4) Spr 78, p. 123.

SCHUUR, Koos
"The Fish" (tr. of Ed. Hoornik). St.AR (5:1) Aut-Wint 78,
    p. 93.

SCHUYLER, James
"En Route to Southampton." NewYorker (54:42) 4 D 78, p. 197.
from Payne Whitney Poems: "Arches." NewYRB (25:13) 17 Ag

78, p. 12.
from Payne Whitney Poems: "February 15th, 1975." NewYRB
(25:13) 17 Ag 78, p. 12.
from Payne Whitney Poems: "Sleep." NewYRB (25:13) 17 Ag
78, p. 12.
from Payne Whitney Poems: "Trip." NewYRB (25:13) 17 Ag 78,
p. 12.
from Payne Whitney Poems: "What." NewYRB (25:13) 17 Ag
78, p. 12.

SCHWARTZ, Hillel
"The Elements." Agni (8) 78, p. 92.
"In the Climb in the Hanging." Pig (4) 78, p. 27.
"Knelt at Your Grave." CarolQ (30:2) Spr-Sum 78, p. 60.
"Old Woman, Hopping." Pig (4) 78, p. 23.
"Pennsylvania Life." Epoch (28:1) Aut 78, p. 19.
"Personals." CalQ (13/14) Spr-Sum 78, p. 91.
"Potter's Field." SouthernHR (12:2) Spr 78, p. 110.
"Tracks." HolCrit (15:1) F 78, p. 11.
"Transfers." Pig (4) 78, p. 22.

SCHWARTZ, Jeffrey
"Contending with the Dark." Aspect (71) Ap-Je 77, p. 11.
"Florida (Land of Flowers)." Aspect (71) Ap-Je 77, p. 9.
"The Landlady's Scars." HangL (32) Spr 78, p. 53.
"Note Left after Being Recognized in a Crowded Cafe." Aspect
(71) Ap-Je 77, p. 10.
"On a Mountain at Night." HangL (32) Spr 78, p. 54.
"Tree Dream." HangL (32) Spr 78, p. 55.

SCHWARTZ, Lloyd
"Apparitions." Shen (29:2) Wint 78, p. 42.
"Hannah." Ploughs (4:2) 78, p. 29.
"On the Recent Deaths of His Friend Colonna and His Lady Laura
(Petrarch)." PartR (45:4) 78, p. 585.
"Swimming." PoNow (19) 78, p. 44.
"The Wanderer." PartR (45:4) 78, p. 580.

SCHWARTZE, Karen
"Metastasis." NewL (45:1) Aut 78, p. 56.

SCHWERNER, Armand
"the joy of Sven Hedin." AmerPoR (7:1) Ja-F 78, p. 6.

SCIBETTA, Susan
"Home Movies of Yourself as a Child." PoNow (20) 78, p. 37.

SCIRROTTO, Gregory
"Prayer: To Burn." FourQt (27:4) Sum 78, p. 26.

SCOTELLARO, Robert
from Blinded by Halos: "He's Read Them All." Vaga (27) Spr
78, p. 64.

SCOTELLARO, Rocco
"America. " GRR (9:1) 78, p. 36.
"Betrothed" (tr. by Ruth Feldman and Brian Swann). Paint
    (9/10) Spr-Aut 78, p. 42.
"Christmas" (tr. by Ruth Feldman and Brian Swann). St. AR
    (4:3/4) 77-78, p. 107.
"Evening" (tr. by Ruth Feldman and Brian Swann). St. AR
    (4:3/4) 77-78, p. 107.
"Every Day Is Monday" (tr. by Ruth Feldman and Brian Swann).
    St. AR (4:3/4) 77-78, p. 106.
"A Friend" (tr. by Ruth Feldman and Brian Swann). Paint
    (9/10) Spr-Aut 78, p. 43.
"My Father" (tr. by Ruth Feldman and Brian Swann). St. AR
    (4:3/4) 77-78, p. 105.
"On Cats' Paws" (tr. by Ruth Feldman and Brian Swann). St. AR
    (4:3/4) 77-78, p. 107.
"Padre mio. " GRR (9:1) 78, p. 40.
"Il primo addio a Napoli. " GRR (9:1) 78, p. 38.
"Ti rubarono nio come una spiga. " GRR (9:1) 78, p. 34.

SCOTT, Herbert
"Elegy for Hilltop Farm, Condemned for Use as a Cemetery. "
    QW (5) Wint 78, p. 23.
"Refusals. " NowestR (17:1) 78, p. 66.
"The Woman Who Loves Old Men. " QW (5) Wint 78, p. 22.

SCOTT, Louise
"Spring's Last Storm. " Wind (29) 78, p. 41.

SCOTT, Nancy
"Martha's Vineyard. " PoNow (20) 78, p. 37.

SCOTT, Shirley R.
"Breaking New Ground. " ChiR (30:1) Sum 78, p. 57.

SCRANTON, Neil
"Introduction & Fanfare. " FourQt (27:4) Sum 78, p. 28.

SCULLY, Arlene
"Curfew" (tr. of Teresa De Jesus, w. Maria A. Proser and
    James Scully). MinnR (NS11) Aut 78, p. 6.
" 'I Am a Small Woman' " (tr. of Teresa De Jesus, w. Maria A.
    Proser and James Scully). MinnR (NS11) Aut 78, p. 8.
"It Makes Me Furious!" (tr. of Teresa De Jesus, w. Maria A.
    Proser & James Scully). MinnR (NS11) Aut 78, p. 7.
"Mistrust" (tr. of Teresa De Jesus, w. Maria A. Proser and
    James Scully). MinnR (NS11) Aut 78, p. 9.

SCULLY, James
"Curfew" (tr. of Teresa De Jesus, w. Maria A. Proser and
    Arlene Scully). MinnR (NS11) Aut 78, p. 6.
" 'I Am a Small Woman' " (tr. of Teresa De Jesus, w. Maria A.
    Proser and Arlene Scully). MinnR (NS11) Aut 78, p. 8.

"It Makes Me Furious!" (tr. of Teresa De Jesus, w. Maria A. Proser and Arlene Scully). MinnR (NS11) Aut 78, p. 7.
"Mistrust" (tr. of Teresa De Jesus, w. Maria A. Proser and Arlene Scully). MinnR (NS11) Aut 78, p. 9.

SCHWERNER, Armand
"Old Dog Sermon" (for Jackson Mac Low). Some (9) 78, p. 86.

SEARS, Peter
"The Color of Air." PoNow (20) 78, p. 28.
"The Lady Who Got Me to Say Solong Mom." PoNow (20) 78, p. 28.
"A Place for Four-Letter Words." PoNow (20) 78, p. 28.
"Recovery." PoNow (20) 78, p. 28.

SEAY, James
"Where Our Voices Broke Off." CarolQ (30:2) Spr-Sum 78, p. 78.

SEBENTHALL, R. E.
"Courage." Northeast (3:5) Spr-Sum 78, back cover.

SECRIST, Margaret
"Unbelievable Earth." BelPoJ (29:1) Aut 78, p. 47.

SEDWICK, Angie
"Reasonable Facsimile." JnlONJP (2:2) 77, p. 25.

SEGER, Jeffrey
"I Feel Your Warm Clammy." CarouselQ (3:3) Aut 78, p. 15.

SEIDEL, Frederick
"1968." NewYRB (25:16) 26 O 78, p. 12.

SEILER, Barry
"Ancestors." PoetryNW (19:3) Aut 78, p. 33.
"My Grandfather's Table." PoetryNW (19:3) Aut 78, p. 33.

SELLERS, Bettie M.
"Beth in White." GRR (9:2) 78, p. 118.
"Dog." GRR (9:3) 78, p. 214.
"For Charles, Who Touched the Sun." GRR (9:2) 78, p. 119.
"In the Counselor's Waiting Room." Chomo (5:2) Aut-Wint 78, p. 19.
"Mountain Circuit." Chomo (5:2) Aut-Wint 78, p. 18.
"The Season of Cicadas." GRR (9:3) 78, p. 215.
"Sonnet in Stained Glass." GRR (9:3) 78, p. 216.

SELTZER, Joanne
"Almost Saved: A Parable of Liberation." CimR (42) Ja 78, p. 26.
"Expensive Poems." DeKalb (11:1/2) Aut-Wint 77-78, p. 65.
"A Sonnet for the Beast." PoNow (19) 78, p. 24.
"The Traveling Companions." CimR (42) Ja 78, p. 51.

SELVAGGIO, Leni
"The Catch." SmPd (43) Spr 78, p. 14.

SEMENOVICH, Joseph
"My Latest Conceit." WebR (4:2) Aut 78, p. 55.
"The Real Bird." WebR (4:2) Aut 78, p. 56.

SEMONES, Charles
"Adagio" (for J. L. R.). Wind (31) 78, p. 48.
"The Barns of Autumn." Wind (31) 78, p. 48.
"A Summer Trilogy" (for P. N. R.). Wind (31) 78, p. 49.

SERCHUK, Peter
"Bent Tree." Hudson (31:2) Sum 78, p. 298.
"Last Words at Marblehead." Hudson (31:2) Sum 78, p. 299.
"Summer on Green Lake." Hudson (31:2) Sum 78, p. 298.
"What the Animals Said." ParisR (73) Spr-Sum 78, p. 143.

SERIN, Judith
"Homes of the Stars" (for Irene Borger). Bachy (11) Spr 78,
    p. 63.

SEVERY, Bruce
"Lost in the Storm." PoNow (20) 78, p. 38.

SEXTON, Anne
"The Death King." Antaeus (30/31) Sum-Aut 78, p. 46.
"Dr. Y." Madem (84:8) Ag 78, p. 126.
"Speaking Bitterness." Antaeus (30/31) Sum-Aut 78, p. 43.
"To Like, To Love." Antaeus (30/31) Sum-Aut 78, p. 47.
"The Twelve-Thousand-Day Honeymoon." Antaeus (30/31) Sum-
    Aut 78, p. 45.
"Yellow." Madem (84:8) Ag 78, p. 126.

SEYFRIED, Robin H.
"Divining." PoetryNW (19:2) Sum 78, p. 17.
"Elegy for a Flight Instructor." PoetryNW (19:2) Sum 78, p. 16.

SHABO, Gary
"From the Scraps of Blank Paper." Poetry (132:6) S 78, p. 317.

SHACKLEFORD, Ruby P.
"We Learn the Canyonlands." Wind (30) 78, p. 43.

SHAFARZEK, Susan
"It Isn't Enough to Be Lonely." HangL (34) Wint 78-79, p. 51.

SHAFER, Margaret
"After an Argument." PoNow (20) 78, p. 38.
"Homecoming." CalQ (13/14) Spr-Sum 78, p. 58.
"Shame." Confr (16) Spr-Sum 78, p. 149.
"Untitled Poem." CalQ (13/14) Spr-Sum 78, p. 57.

SHAFFER, I. D.
"Muerta." FourQt (27:4) Sum 78, p. 27.

SHAKESPEARE
"Sonnet 53." NewYRB (25:5) 6 Ap 78, p. 35.
"Sonnet 98." NewYRB (25:5) 6 Ap 78, p. 36.
"Sonnet 109." NewYRB (25:5) 6 Ap 78, p. 34.
"Sonnet 116." NewYRB (25:5) 6 Ap 78, p. 33.
"Sonnet 151." NewYRB (25:5) 6 Ap 78, p. 36.

SHALOM, Shin
"The Man" (tr. by Ada Aharoni). WebR (4:2) Aut 78, p. 35.

SHANGE, Ntozake
"We Are Just Kinda That Way." BelPoJ (29:2) Wint 78-79,
    p. 22.

SHANKEN-SKWERSKY, Serena
"Belly Full of Sighs." CarouselQ (3:4) Wint 78, p. 4.

SHANNON, Susan
"Outlook." StoneC (78:2) Spr 78, p. 9.

SHAPIRO, Daniel E.
"Hive." CutB (11) Aut-Wint 78, p. 56.

SHAPIRO, E. B.
"that the poem." SmPd (43) Spr 78, p. 5.

SHAPIRO, Harvey
"In the Broad Street." PoNow (19) 78, p. 13.

SHAPIRO, Karl
"Evangelist." Kayak (47) F 78, p. 9.
"Girls Working in Banks." PoNow (19) 78, p. 7.
"Jefferson's Greeting." PoNow (19) 78, p. 7.
"Nō Mask." Kayak (47) F 78, p. 8.

SHARBROUGH, David
"Frank Zarbb, energy chief for the U.S." Tele (13) 77.
"To anyone who knew Edward McGarry as a child." Tele (14)
    78.

SHARP, Constance
"I Show the Daffodils to the Retarded Kids." SouthernPR (18:1)
    Spr 78, p. 8.

SHARP, David Joshua
"Casting Off." Poetry (132:1) Ap 78, p. 22.
"Did You Die Inside, Woman?" ChiR (30:1) Sum 78, p. 58.

SHARP, Virginia
"If God Were a Mare, If I Rode Her." CarouselQ (3:1) Spr 78,

p. 10.
"Love Poem: The Carpenter & the Wood." CarouselQ (3:3) Aut
78, p. 4.
"Smeared Mirror, Sated Mirror, If Only You Could Taste."
StoneC (78:2) Spr 78, p. 27.

SHARPE, David
from Unions: "Momentum." GRR (9:2) 78, p. 129.

SHAUGER, Carol
"Afterall." WindO (32) Sum-Aut 78, p. 18.

SHAW, Martha
"A Little Less Than Love." LadHJ (95:2) F 78, p. 74.

SHAW, Robert B.
"The Invention of Zero." NewRep (178:9) 4 Mr 78, p. 32.

SHECK, Laurie
"Continuum." Columbia (2) Aut 78, p. 64.
"Natural History." CutB (11) Aut-Wint 78, p. 54.

SHEEHAN, Marc J.
"Divining Water." GRR (9:2) 78, p. 137.
"restoration." GRR (9:2) 78, p. 139.
"War Movies." Sky (7/8) Spr 78, p. 22.

SHEEHY, Donald G.
"Driving through Kansas Mid-December." Wind (29) 78, p. 43.
"Overnight in a Midwest Motel." Wind (29) 78, p. 43.
"Three Postures: A Woman Becomes a Spring Afternoon."
Wind (29) 78, p. 42.

SHEFF, Norma Russell
"This Is the Way to Meet the Knives." EngJ (67:5) My 78,
p. 59.

SHEGOLEFF, Vera
"Gary Gilmore." SeC (5:2) 78, p. 62.

SHEPHERD, J. Barrie
"All Hallows." ChrC (95:34) 25 O 78, p. 1011.
"Corkscrew." ChrC (95:10) 22 Mr 78, p. 299.
"Crashing." ChrC (95:32) 11 O 78, p. 940.
"Thanksgiving, Family-Style." ChrC (95:38) 22 N 78, p. 1132.

SHEPPARD, Patricia
"Advertisement." Hudson (31:1) Spr 78, p. 122.
"The Whistling Swans." Hudson (31:1) Spr 78, p. 122.

SHEPPERD, Walt
"8:07 AM--Draper, Utah" (for Gary Gilmore). GreenfieldR
(7:1/2) Aut 78, p. 96.

"The Free-Lance Recidivist." GreenfieldR (7:1/2) Aut 78, p. 116.

SHERIDAN, Michael
"Caves." PoNow (20) 78, p. 38.
"Days." OhioR (19:2) Spr-Sum 78, pp. 19-32. Ten poems.
"In America" (for my mother). AmerPoR (7:4) Jl-Ag 78, p. 34.
"Postcard from Nebraska" (for Dan Wakefield). AmerPoR (7:4) Jl-Ag 78, p. 34.

SHERMAN, R. H.
"unidentified." EngJ (67:5) My 78, p. 66.

SHEROD, Santos
"The Professor." Antaeus (30/31) Sum-Aut 78, p. 205.

SHERRY, Pearl Andelson
"Hallucination of Bird of Paradise Plant vs. Hummingbird." SouthernR (14:1) Wint 78, p. 93.
"Pitcher Plant." SouthernR (14:1) Wint 78, p. 94.

SHERWIN, Judith Johnson
"The Lives of Rain." MidwQ (19:3) Spr 78, p. 283.
"Omne Animale...." LittleM (11:3) Aut 77, p. 84.
"the Reckoning." MidwQ (19:3) Spr 78, p. 285.
"Relic." Nimrod (22:2) Spr-Sum 78, p. 70.
"Schroedinger's Cat." MidwQ (19:3) Spr 78, p. 284.
"Some Far Place." LittleM (11:3) Aut 77, p. 85.
"The Spoilers and the Spoils." Poetry (132:1) Ap 78, p. 10.

SHETTERLY, Susan
"For Aran." BelPoJ (29:1) Aut 78, p. 4.

SHEVCHENKO, Tony
"Presidents." SeC (5:2) 78, p. 17.

SHIDELER, Ross
"What My Father Knows." ParisR (72) Wint 77, p. 110.

SHIELDS, Barry
"An Old Black Couple I Know." EngJ (67:5) My 78, p. 66.

SHIELDS, James W.
"December Song." JnlONJP (3:1) 78, p. 15.

SHIHAB, Naomi
"The Indian in the Kitchen." Vaga (28) Aut 78, p. 8.
"Missing the Boat." ParisR (72) Wint 77, p. 56.
"On the Road to Chichicastenango." Vaga (28) Aut 78, p. 6.
"The True Picture." Vaga (28) Aut 78, p. 4.

SHIRAZ, Hovaness
"Gazel for Semiramis" (tr. by Diana Der Hovanessian). Nimrod (22:2) Spr-Sum 78, p. 86.

SHIVELY, Bill
    "I don't give jack-shit." Wind (31) 78, p. 52.

SHOEMAKER, Lynn
    "Aunt Louise." DacTerr (15) Wint-Spr 77-78, p. 63.
    "1974: Three Children in Bangladesh." GreenfieldR (6:3/4) Spr
        78, p. 108.
    "The Sum." GreenfieldR (6:3/4) Spr 78, p. 108.
    "Wall Painter." GreenfieldR (6:3/4) Spr 78, p. 109.

SHOHER, Jessica
    "A Set of Four." NewRep (178:9) 4 Mr 78, p. 30.

SHOLL, Betsy
    "High Tide." HangL (34) Wint 78-79, p. 52.
    "My Mother Stops Going to Movies." YellowBR (10) 78, p. 14.
    "What Is Happening to Us?" Aspect (71) Ap-Je 77, p. 43.

SHORB, Michael
    "A Case of Free Will in the Late 40's." Pig (4) 78, p. 8.
    "Instructions for a Celebration." Sam (69) 78, p. 40.

SHORE, Jane
    "Iowa Spring Viewed from a Plane." PoNow (20) 78, p. 28.
    "The Lifeguard." PoNow (20) 78, p. 28.
    "Witness." PoNow (20) 78, p. 28.

SHORT, Clarice
    "Comment on a Tapestry." ConcPo (11:2) Aut 78, p. 3.
    "Herakles and Persephone." ConcPo (11:2) Aut 78, p. 3.
    "The Widows." ConcPo (11:2) Aut 78, p. 2.

SHORT, Frank
    "Afternoon Kitchen." Bits (8) Jl 78.
    "Baggage." PoNow (20) 78, p. 38.
    "Chain Saw." Bits (8) Jl 78.

SHUTTLEWORTH, Paul
    "Doc Holliday Recalls Meeting Kate Elder." PoNow (20) 78,
        p. 29.
    Poems to the Memory of Benny Kid Paret. Sparrow (37) 78.
        26 pp. A Sparrow Poverty Pamphlet.
    "Take the Children Home to the Mountains." PoNow (20) 78,
        p. 29.
    "Tornado Watch." PoNow (20) 78, p. 29.

SIDERS, V. Hodgson
    "Pieta." BelPoJ (29:1) Aut 78, p. 46.

SIDOR, Ellen
    "porch love." Aspect (71) Ap-Je 77, p. 43.

SIEBURTH, R.
    "Angst" (tr. of Mallerme, w. S. W. De Rachewiltz). St. AR

(5:1) Aut-Wint 78, p. 62.
"Canto XLVII" (tr. of Pound, w. S. W. De Rachewiltz). St. AR
     (5:1) Aut-Wint 78, p. 66.
"Chopin" (tr. of Benn, w. S. W. De Rachewiltz). St. AR (5:1)
     Aut-Wint 78, p. 54.
from Drafts and Fragments (tr. of Hölderlin, w. S. W. De
     Rachewiltz). St. AR (5:1) Aut-Wint 78, pp. 41-48.
"From Peace Poems" (tr. of Eluard, w. S. W. De Rachewiltz).
     St. AR (5:1) Aut-Wint 78, p. 63.
"The Lover" (tr. of Eluard, w. S. W. De Rachewiltz). St. AR
     (5:1) Aut-Wint 78, p. 62.
"Make Room" (tr. of Supervielle, w. S. W. De Rachewiltz).
     St. AR (5:1) Aut-Wint 78, p. 65.
"Morning" (tr. of Theophile de Viau, w. S. W. De Rachewiltz).
     St. AR (5:1) Aut-Wint 78, p. 60.
"Movement" (tr. of Supervielle, w. S. W. De Rachewiltz). St. AR
     (5:1) Aut-Wint 78, p. 64.
"New Wilderness" (tr. of Junger, w. S. W. De Rachewiltz).
     St. AR (5:1) Aut-Wint 78, p. 52.
"Night" (tr. of Supervielle, w. S. W. De Rachewiltz). St. AR
     (5:1) Aut-Wint 78, p. 64.
"Nike" (tr. of Rilke, w. S. W. De Rachewiltz). St. AR (5:1) Aut-
     Wint 78, p. 53.
"Other America" (tr. of Supervielle, w. S. W. De Rachewiltz).
     St. AR (5:1) Aut-Wint 78, p. 65.
"Perspective" (tr. of Eluard, w. S. W. De Rachewiltz). St. AR
     (5:1) Aut-Wint 78, p. 62.
"Psalm" (tr. of Trakl, w. S. W. De Rachewiltz). St. AR (5:1)
     Aut-Wint 78, p. 51.
"Recuillement" (tr. of Baudelaire, w. S. W. De Rachewiltz).
     St. AR (5:1) Aut-Wint 78, p. 61.
"Remembrance" (tr. of Holderin, w. S. W. De Rachewiltz).
     St. AR (5:1) Aut-Wint 78, p. 68.
from Schneepart (tr. of Celan, w. S. W. De Rachewiltz). St. AR
     (5:1) Aut-Wint 78, p. 55.
"To Childe Elis" (tr. of Trakl, w. S. W. De Rachewiltz).
     St. AR (5:1) Aut-Wint 78, p. 51.
Two poems (tr. of Montale, w. S. W. De Rachewiltz). St. AR
     (5:1) Aut-Wint 78, p. 66.
"Untitled" (tr. of Supervielle, w. S. W. De Rachewiltz). St. AR
     (5:1) Aut-Wint 78, p. 64.

SIEDLECKI, Peter
     "Barrier." StoneC (78:1) Wint 78, p. 32.
     "Highway Study." StoneC (78:1) Wint 78, p. 33.

SIEGEL, Lois
     "Arena." St. AR (5:1) Aut-Wint 78, p. 111.

SIEGEL, Robert
     "Hans and His Wife." PraS (52:2) Sum 78, p. 156.
     "Now They Stand Still." NewEngR (1:2) Wint 78, p. 206.
     "Sir Roger De Trumpington." BallSUF (19:3) Sum 78, p. 28.
     "Sow's Ear." BelPoJ (28:4) Sum 78, p. 37.

SIEGFRIED, Rodney
"First Great Grandchild." WormR (70) 78, p. 72.
"Heard Weidman Read." WormR (70) 78, p. 72.
"Oakland Laundromat." WormR (70) 78, p. 72.
"Ten Yr. Reunion." WormR (70) 78, p. 70.

SILKIN, Jon
"The old version." BosUJ (26:1) 78, p. 51.
"The uses of man and poetry." BosUJ (26:1) 78, p. 50.

SILLIMAN, Ron
from 2197: "Turk Street News." LaB (10) 78, p. 43.

SILVA, Jeff
"Little Gothic." SlowLR (1/2) 78, p. 92.
"The Longer Dead" (after a painting by & then for Bunny Harvey).
    SenR (9:1) Spr-Sum 78, p. 35.
"No Wind to Speak Of." SenR (9:1) Spr-Sum 78, p. 37.

SILVERSTEIN, Shel
"The Smoke Off." Playb (25:1) Ja 78, p. 172.

SIMIC, Charles
"Baby Pictures of Famous Dictators." Iowa (9:2) Spr 78, p. 73.
"Bedtime Story." Antaeus (30/31) Sum-Aut 78, p. 215.
"Earthbound Constellation" (tr. of Vasko Popa). Durak (1) 78,
    p. 6.
"Elegy." GeoR (32:4) Wint 78, p. 774.
"Empire of Dreams." Field (19) Aut 78, p. 53.
"An Evening with the Master." Antaeus (30/31) Sum-Aut 78,
    p. 212.
"Eyes of a Wolf" (tr. of Vasko Popa). Durak (1) 78, p. 7.
"Great Infirmities." Antaeus (30/31) Sum-Aut 78, p. 216.
"Grocery." Field (19) Aut 78, p. 52.
"In the Village of My Ancestors" (tr. of Vasko Popa). Durak
    (1) 78, p. 8.
"Navigator." NewEngR (1:1) Aut 78, p. 80.
"Overcoat." VirQR (54:2) Spr 78, p. 283.
"Roll Call." VirQR (54:2) Spr 78, p. 282.
"Symmetry." Antaeus (30/31) Sum-Aut 78, p. 214.
"Unknown Citizen" (tr. of Vasko Popa). Durak (1) 78, p. 9.
"Vermin." Antaeus (30/31) Sum-Aut 78, p. 213.

SIMMER, Scott
"Looking for Gas on New Year's." NewOR (5:4) 78, p. 330.
"Mrs. G." NewOR (5:4) 78, p. 331.

SIMMONS, James
"At the Post Office." LitR (22:2) Wint 79, p. 193.
"Interior Decorating." LitR (22:2) Wint 79, p. 187.
"Knocking On." LitR (22:2) Wint 79, p. 191.
"The Liberator." LitR (22:2) Wint 79, p. 188.
"Rogation Day: Portrush." LitR (22:2) Wint 79, p. 187.

SIMON, Jane
"Addicts. "   Zahir (9) 77, p. 13.

SIMON, John Oliver
"Excavating the Great Mother Shrine #33. "   YellowBR (10) 78,
    p. 10.
"I make a ceremony for you. "   HangL (33) Sum 78, p. 55.
"I went to you for your wisdom & blessing. "   HangL (33) Sum
    78, p. 54.

SIMON, Shelley
"Vegetarian. "   PoNow (20) 78, p. 38.

SIMPSON, Grace P.
"Remembering Polyphemus' Cave. "   HiramPoR (25) Aut-Wint 78,
    p. 34.

SIMPSON, Louis
"Basic Blues. "   MissouriR (2:1) Aut 78, p. 5.
"A Bower of Roses. "   MissouriR (2:1) Aut 78, p. 9.
"On the Ledge. "   MissouriR (2:1) Aut 78, p. 7.
"The Pawnshop. "   NewYorker (54:20) 3 Jl 78, p. 28.

SIMPSON, Mark
"Marriage. "   QW (5) Wint 78, p. 21.

SIMPSON, Tobey A.
"For Mariella, in Antrona. "   NewEngR (1:2) Wint 78, p. 139.

SIMS, Elizabeth
"Breasts. "   Smudge (2) Sum 78, p. 16.
"Dream. "   Smudge (3) Aut 78, p. 5.
"For My Father. "   Smudge (2) Sum 78, p. 17.
"Looking into a Store Mirror. "   Smudge (3) Aut 78, p. 21.
"Weekend. "   Smudge (2) Sum 78, p. 33.

SISSMAN, L. E.
"Tras os Montes. "   Atl (241:5) My 78, p. 48.

SISSON, Jonathan
"Poem in William's Pub" (w. James Naiden).   NorthSR (8) Aut-
    Wint 78-79, p. 101.

SKEEN, Anita
"theory of evolution. "   PraS (52:3) Aut 78, p. 242.

SKEETER, Sharyn Jeanne
"On Planes and Other Gadgets" (To Beverly De Monde, St.
    Thomas).   GreenfieldR (6:3/4) Spr 78, p. 154.

SKELTON, Robin
"In the Gulf. "   Kayak (49) O 78, p. 24.
"Invocation. "   Kayak (49) O 78, p. 22.

"Last Song." Kayak (49) O 78, p. 26.
"Raven's Island." Kayak (49) O 78, p. 23.
"Skin." Kayak (49) O 78, p. 25.
"The Visitant." MalR (45) Ja 78, p. 109.

SKILES, Don
  "The Cactus." Stonecloud (7) 78, p. 14.
  "Feeling a Peach." WindO (32) Sum-Aut 78, p. 15.
  "The Five." WindO (32) Sum-Aut 78, p. 16.
  "Old Floors." WindO (32) Sum-Aut 78, p. 15.
  "Raku (Baien, 18th c. Japanese Potter)." Stonecloud (7) 78,
      p. 10.

SKLAR, Morty
  "All American." YellowBR (10) 78, p. 31.

SKLOOT, Floyd
  "Background Work." SouthwR (63:4) Aut 78, p. 403.
  "Camping in August." KanQ (10:2) Spr 78, p. 12.
  "The Getting There." Poem (32) Mr 78, p. 5.
  "Giftsong." SouthernPR (18:2) Aut 78, p. 73.
  "Hold." Poem (32) Mr 78, p. 6.
  "The Leavers." Wind (28) 78, p. 48.
  "A Morning in Southern Illinois." Northeast (3:6) Wint 78-79,
      p. 45.
  "Picture Taking at Hunting Island." GreenfieldR (6:3/4) Spr 78,
      p. 120.
  "Working through the Night." StoneC (78:2) Spr 78, p. 32.

SKLORENKO, Artelle G.
  "Indecision." BelPoJ (28:4) Sum 78, p. 9.

SKOBLE, Marty
  "The Big Game." Tele (13) 77.

SKOYLES, John
  Fourteen poems. ArkRiv (4:2) 78, p. 5.

SKRATZ, G. P.
  "Mother's Day" (for Cece). YellowBR (10) 78, p. 15.

SLATE, Ron
  "At the Experimental Pig Farm." PoNow (19) 78, p. 29.
  "Bed." CutB (10) Spr-Sum 78, p. 83.
  "The Conversion." Northeast (3:5) Spr-Sum 78, p. 54.
  "Traffic." ThRiPo (11/12) 78, p. 67.
  "Walking Papers." Northeast (3:5) Spr-Sum 78, p. 52.

SLATER, Michael
  "The Bus Driver." Tele (13) 77.
  Eight poems. Tele (14) 78.
  "Up North." Tele (13) 77.

SLAVITT, David R.
"Poster." Poetry (132:4) Jl 78, p. 196.

SLEBODA, Steve
Fourteen poems. UTR (5:3) 77, pp. 5-18.
"While Bird Songs Drown." AAR (28) 78, p. 15.

SLEGMAN, Ann
"The People Are Half the Show." PoNow (20) 78, p. 38.

SLUTSKY, Boris
"1933, Fascism" (tr. by Arthur Hudgins and James Naiden).
    NorthSR (8) Aut-Wint 78-79, p. 104.
"The Seed" (tr. by Arthur Hudgins and James Naiden). NorthSR
    (8) Aut-Wint 78-79, p. 106.
"Silhouette" (tr. by Arthur Hudgins and James Naiden). NorthSR
    (8) Aut-Wint 78-79, p. 105.

SMALL, Judith
"If This Song Is for You." PoetryNW (19:3) Aut 78, p. 38.

SMALLWOOD, Randy
"Drinking at Twilight." Wind (31) 78, p. 54.
"Return to the Homeland." Wind (31) 78, p. 55.

SMETZER, Michael
"Report to the Air." HangL (34) Wint 78-79, p. 53.

SMITH, Annick
"Dead Calf" (June 1974--First Poem for David). PoetryNW
    (19:1) Spr 78, p. 20.

SMITH, Arthur H.
"The Hat Dance." Tele (13) 77.
"Love Poem." Tele (13) 77.

SMITH, Bruce
"Dream of First Labor." SoCaR (11:1) N 78, p. 121.
"Proposal for an Irresponsible Poem." PoetryNW (19:2) Sum 78,
    p. 40.
"Three Shakings" (for Laurel Zimmerman). CarolQ (30:3) Aut
    78, p. 63.

SMITH, Court
"Form Poem." WindO (32) Sum-Aut 78, p. 10.

SMITH, Dave
"Chinaberry Tree." Nat (227:15) 4 N 78, p. 480.
"The Collector of the Sun." NewYorker (54:41) 27 N 78, p. 180.
"Greenheart Fern" (for Helen Vendler). WestHR (32:3) Sum 78,
    p. 226.
"Having Seen This, the Day Ends." NowestR (17:1) 78, p. 28.
"In the Yard, Late Summer." Hudson (31:4) Wint 78-79, p. 594.

"In Snow, a Possible Life. " WestHR (32:2) Spr 78, p. 136.
"Messenger. " NewYorker (54:31) 18 S 78, p. 40.
"The Mind Hawk. " WestHR (32:2) Spr 78, p. 122.
"Oak Leaf, a Midnight Dream. " WestHR (32:2) Spr 78, p. 178.
"Pine Cones. " GeoR (32:4) Wint 78, p. 807.
"Portrait of a Woman. " NewYorker (54:37) 30 O 78, p. 44.
"Raw Light, Mountain Lake. " Hudson (31:4) Wint 78-79, p. 593.
"Rain Forest. " NewYorker (54:44) 18 D 78, p. 38.
"Season of Light, Season of Sickness. " Antaeus (30/31) Sum-Aut
    78, p. 218.
"Snow Owl. " Antaeus (30/31) Sum-Aut 78, p. 217.
"Under the Scrub Oak, a Red Shoe. " Iowa (9:2) Spr 78, p. 76.
"Utah Prospective. " WestHR (32:2) Spr 78, p. 121.
"Waving. " NewYorker (54:1) 20 F 78, p. 106.
"The White Holster. " Hudson (31:4) Wint 78-79, p. 591.

SMITH, David M.
"Course Description. " AndR (4:2) Aut 77, p. 10.

SMITH, Francis J.
"Mary Tracy McLoughlin (cum laude, '53). " Sam (69) 78,
    p. 48.

SMITH, Gary
"In the Distance, a Boy Crashing Down a Steeply Graded Hill. "
    PoNow (20) 78, p. 39.

SMITH, Iain Crichton
"On Meeting in Ireland Some Young Poets Who Write in English. "
    Stand (19:2) 78, p. 25.

SMITH, Jared
"Conewango Creek. " Tele (14) 78.
"Mood in Grays. " DacTerr (15) Wint-Spr 77-78, p. 22.
"Of Moons. " GreenfieldR (6:3/4) Spr 78, p. 142.
"Passage from Home. " DacTerr (15) Wint-Spr 77-78, p. 22.
"Taking What's There. " Tele (13) 77.
"The Wedding Night. " Tele (13) 77.

SMITH, Joan
"As Sweet as That. " WormR (68) 77, p. 95.
"Listening to the Radio. " PoNow (20) 78, p. 39.
"Next Summer. " WormR (68) 77, p. 94.
"Sadie Thompson Lives on Elm Street. " WormR (68) 77, p. 93.

SMITH, Jordan
"Kossow's, the Cottage Hotel, and the Rock. " Shen (29:3) Spr
    78, p. 56.
"Self-Portrait with Burning Cigarette (after the painting by
    Edvard Munch). " Epoch (28:1) Aut 78, p. 22.
"Self Portrait with Wine Bottle. " OhioR (19:1) Wint 78, p. 70.

SMITH, Lawrence R.
"Something Precise" (tr. of Bartolo Cattafi). ParisR (74) Aut-

Wint 78, p. 110.
"Wingspan" (tr. of Bartolo Cattafi).   ParisR (74) Aut-Wint 78,
    p. 109.

SMITH, Margoret
"Creative Writing I. "   PoetryNW (19:4) Wint 78-79, p. 46.
"Dark Reverse. "   PoetryNW (19:4) Wint 78-79, p. 47.
"Oven Watch. "   PoetryNW (19:4) Wint 78-79, p. 44.
"Roon. "   BosUJ (26:2) 78, p. 64.

SMITH, Michael C.
"The Neighbor Lady's Testimony. "   Iowa (9:4) Aut 78, p. 38.
"Our Christmas Carol. "   Iowa (9:4) Aut 78, p. 39.

SMITH, Michael W.
"A Pot Roast (Slightly) Burnt. "   EngJ (67:5) My 78, p. 51.

SMITH, Mike
"How Did It Sound?"   NewL (45:1) Aut 78, p. 59.

SMITH, R. T.
"Bernini's 'The Ecstasy of St. Theresa.'"   Poem (33) Jl 78,
    p. 54.
"Brimming. "   GRR (9:3) 78, p. 227.
"Dying Elm. "   GRR (9:3) 78, p. 224.
"From the High Dive in Late August. "   Wind (30) 78, p. 46.
"Shadow. "   Poem (33) Jl 78, p. 55.
"Tactic. "   ConcPo (11:2) Aut 78, p. 89.
"To James Dickey: On His Blindness. "   SouthernHR (12:4) Aut
    78, p. 312.
"Wish. "   SouthernPR (18:1) Spr 78, p. 47.
"Young Woman Discovering Her Curse (II). "   Poem (33) Jl 78,
    p. 56.

SMITH, Ray
"August. "   NorthSR (8) Aut-Wint 78-79, p. 32.
"Northern Fall. "   NorthSR (8) Aut-Wint 78-79, p. 32.
"Stone. "   NorthSR (8) Aut-Wint 78-79, p. 31.

SMITH, Rick
"distance. "   Stonecloud (7) 78, p. 103.
"Earth Watch. "   Stonecloud (7) 78, p. 74.
"804: Head Trauma Ward. "   Bachy (11) Spr 78, p. 125.
"From the Wren Notebook. "   Bachy (11) Spr 78, p. 123.
"Jumping Off. "   Stonecloud (7) 78, p. 115.
"Mural of a Lake, N. Y. C. "   Stonecloud (7) 78, p. 34.
"A Picnic in Downey, California (6/76). "   Stonecloud (7) 78,
    p. 25.

SMITH, Robert L.
"Three Stages. "   GRR (9:1) 78, p. 46.

SMITH, Ronald
"During a Study of Aragon's Matisse. "   Kayak (49) O 78, p. 27.

"New Hampshire" (for Charles Simic). Kayak (49) O 78, p. 29.
"The Wall Behind the Windows. " Kayak (49) O 78, p. 28.

SMITH, Virginia E.
"Sculptress. " StoneC (78:2) Spr 78, p. 30.

SMYTH, Gjertrud Schnackenberg
from Laughing with One Eye: "Walter Charles Schnackenberg,
    Professor of History (1917-1973). " Poetry (132:3) Je 78,
    p. 161.

SMYTH, Paul
"Day Moon. " Poetry (132:4) Jl 78, p. 223.
"Of Scholarship, Divorce, and Lunch. " Poetry (132:4) Jl 78,
    p. 221.
"Timing. " Poetry (132:4) Jl 78, p. 219.
"Two Lovers in the Late Triassic. " NorthSR (8) Aut-Wint 78-
    79, p. 27.

SNELLER, Del
"Into Darkness I Will Work. " StoneC (78:1) Wint 78, p. 20.

SNEYD, Steve
"Incantation. " WindO (31) Wint-Spr 78, p. 16.

SNIDER, Clifton
"Billy Budd. " Stonecloud (7) 78, p. 144.
"Ten Weeks. " StoneC (78:3) Aut 78, p. 18.

SNOW, Don
"The Coal-Strike at Consumers, Utah: 1933. " CutB (11) Aut-
    Wint 78, p. 50.

SNOW, Karen
"Clover. " BelPoJ (29:1) Aut 78, p. 35.
"Whelping. " BelPoJ (29:1) Aut 78, p. 40.
"Whitey. " BelPoJ (28:3) Spr 78, p. 25.

SOBIN, A. G.
"Brittle January, Absolute Zero. " MidwQ (19:2) Wint 78, p. 146.
"The Children. " PoetryNW (19:3) Aut 78, p. 32.
"King René at the Spring. " AmerPoR (7:4) Jl-Ag 78, p. 45.
"Propping Up Bodies to Fool the Indians. " AmerPoR (7:4) Jl-Ag
    78, p. 46.
"Snow Camp. " BelPoJ (28:4) Sum 78, p. 25.
"Theodora's Dream. " MidwQ (19:2) Wint 78, p. 144.
"Thin Air Camp, the La Sal Range. " BelPoJ (28:4) Sum 78,
    p. 26.

SOBIN, Gustaf
"Breath's Reflections. " Montra (4) 78, p. 213.
"Dominion. " Montra (4) 78, p. 204.
"Hold Flowing Polyphonous. " Montra (4) 78, p. 209.
"Making the Mirror. " Kayak (48) Je 78, p. 20.

"Notes on Sound, Speech-Crystals and the Celestial Echo."
    Montra (4) 78, p. 206.
"Signs." Montra (4) 78, p. 205.
"Terra Alba." Montra (4) 78, p. 212.
"The Turban." Kayak (48) Je 78, p. 22.
"Two." Montra (4) 78, p. 211.

SOCOLOW, Liz
"The Neighbors Kept Roosters." US1 (11) Aut 78, p. 2.

SOFIELD, David
"That Moment Long." NewYorker (54:11) 1 My 78, p. 38.

SOFINETI, Vasile
"The Attack 1." St. AR (5:1) Aut-Wint 78, p. 131.
"Nenuphar." St. AR (5:1) Aut-Wint 78, p. 132.

SOFRANKO, Michael
"Tarpey's Junction." PoNow (20) 78, p. 39.

SOHN, Sally Ann
"A Tribute to Greek Food." PikeF (1) Spr 78, p. 12.

SOLAN, Miriam
"Directions." Confr (16) Spr-Sum 78, p. 24.
"A Woman Combing." Glass (3:1/2/3) 78, p. 9.

SOLHEIM, David
"Sandstorm." DacTerr (15) Wint-Spr 77-78, p. 67.

SOLLARS, Trina
"Matrix." Smudge (1) Spr 78, p. 29.

SOLOMON, A. J.
"Minks." KanQ (10:2) Spr 78, p. 51.

SOLONCHE, J. R.
"Incan Mummy." WindO (33) Aut-Wint 78-79, p. 8.

SOLYN, Paul
"The Poet in the Studio of Jan Breughel the Elder 1568-1625."
    MinnR (NS11) Aut 78, p. 28.

SOMOZA, Joseph
"Franklin Discovers the Harmonica." BelPoJ (28:4) Sum 78,
    p. 36.

SONDE, Susan
"Modular Piece." Epoch (28:1) Aut 78, p. 52.

SONIAT, Katherine
"A Comparable Season." Nat (226:4) 4 F 78, p. 120.
"Departures." NewRep (179:20) 11 N 78, p. 28.

"Holding Pattern." Nat (226:7) 25 F 78, p. 218.
"Still Life with Grass, Fur and Air at the Museum of Natural
    History." Nat (226:21) 3 Je 78, p. 678.

SONNEMANN, Margaret
    "Calliope." CarouselQ (3:1) Spr 78, p. 9.

SOOS, R., Jr.
    "The Surf." Wind (29) 78, p. 50.

SORRELL, John Edward
    "Complaint Against Three Words on a Bath Mat." DeKalb
    (11:3/4) Spr-Sum 78, p. 45.

SORRENTINO, Gilbert
    "Crool Time." PartR (45:2) 78, p. 275.

SOTO, Gary
    "Blanco." Nat (227:8) 16 S 78, p. 252.
    "Salt" (For Juan Rodriguez). Poetry (132:3) Je 78, p. 139.
    "The Shepherd." NewYorker (54:22) 17 Jl 78, p. 34.
    "The Soup." SlowLR (1/2) 78, p. 86.
    "The Tracks." SlowLR (1/2) 78, p. 84.
    "The Years." Nat (227:7) 9 S 78, p. 216.

SOUTHWICK, Marcia
    "Insomnia." PoNow (20) 78, p. 39.
    "Landscape." Poetry (132:1) Ap 78, p. 12.
    "A Song of Drowning." NoAmR (263:3) Aut 78, p. 23.
    "Thaisa." OP (26) Spr-Sum 78, p. 8.
    "Witch." OP (26) Aut-Wint 78, p. 12.

SOURS, John Appling
    "Portofino." Tele (13) 77.

SPACKS, Barry
    "Bags." Salm (42) Sum-Aut 78, p. 127.
    "The Brief Art of Streaking (1974)." Bits (7) Ja 78.
    "A Dream: Crossing the Border." PoetryNW (19:1) Spr 78,
        p. 17.
    "Elegy." CalQ (13/14) Spr-Sum 78, p. 59.
    "Gliding" (In Memory of Timothy Holm 1954-1973). SewanR
        (86:2) Spr 78, p. 270.
    "In the Fields." Bits (7) Ja 78.
    "The Last Fish." KanQ (10:4) Aut 78, p. 19.
    "Old-Time Stereopticon." CentR (22:3) Sum 78, p. 319.
    "Playing the Uncle." CentR (22:3) Sum 78, p. 319.
    "Rehearsal." NewRep (179:5) 29 Jl 78, p. 27.
    "The Warm Connection." NewYorker (54:17) 12 Je 78, p. 38.

SPARER, Laurie T.
    "Kerosene Dream." DacTerr (15) Wint-Spr 77-78, p. 59.
    "Wolves in Como Park." SouthernPR (18:1) Spr 78, p. 28.

SPAULDING, John
"Country." Bleb/Ark (13) 78, p. 13.
"Forest Fire (1851)." Bleb/Ark (13) 78, p. 11.
"Letter from Mexico." Glass (3:1/2/3) 78, p. 98.
"Love Letter." Bleb/Ark (13) 78, p. 14.
"Neighbor." Wind (29) 78, p. 28.
"November." Bleb/Ark (13) 78, p. 15.
"Refugees." Bleb/Ark (13) 78, p. 12.
"Wheat Fields." Bleb/Ark (13) 78, p. 10.

SPEAKES, Richard
"Father." PoetryNW (19:2) Sum 78, p. 30.
"Harvesting Leaves." PoetryNW (19:2) Sum 78, p. 29.
"The La Brea Tarpits in a Requiem for Clarence Seven Years
    after His Death." PraS (52:4) Wint 78-79, p. 319.
"A Present for My Brothers and Sisters." PoetryNW (19:2) Sum
    78, p. 29.

SPEAR, Jean
"Girl with a Burning Torch." Pig (5) 78, p. 64.

SPEER, Laurel
"Blowout." WindO (33) Aut-Wint 78-79, p. 11.
"The Famous Greyhound Bus Hijack." PikeF (1) Spr 78, p. 26.
"Interesting English Anecdotes." CarouselQ (3:4) Wint 78, p. 32.

SPENCE, Michael
"Epitaph on a Millionaire." PoNow (20) 78, p. 39.
"The Swamp." StoneC (78:3) Aut 78, p. 17.

SPENCER, Brent
"Old Hills in Pennsylvania and What I Would Have Told You."
    PoetC (10:2) 78, p. 4.
"Two Lancaster Poems." PoetC (10:2) 78, p. 2.

SPIELBERG, Peter
"Nostalgia." KanQ (10:2) Spr 78, p. 95.

SPILMAN, Richard
"Directions for Installing Coldwater Brass Co. 'Superior Brass
    Ballcock.'" Kayak (48) Je 78, p. 13. Found poem.

SPIRES, Elizabeth
"After Three Japanese Drawings." ParisR (74) Aut-Wint 78,
    p. 87.
"Bertram at Fat Camp." ThRiPo (11/12) 78, p. 68.
"Chiaroscuro." YaleR (68:2) Wint 79, p. 255.
"Death Dress" (For A. S.). Poetry (133:1) O 78, p. 38.
"Globe." Poetry (133:1) O 78, p. 40.
"Snowfall." Antaeus (30/31) Sum-Aut 78, p. 220.
"Wake." YaleR (68:2) Wint 79, p. 256.
"Widow's Walk." NewYorker (54:2) 27 F 78, p. 38.

SPIVACK, Kathleen
  "I Want to Tell You." ParisR (72) Wint 77, p. 152.
  "The Porch." Kayak (48) Je 78, p. 51.
  "Swimmer in the Spreading Dawn." Kayak (48) Je 78, p. 52.
  "Swimming Through." Durak (1) 78, p. 47.

SQUIRES, Radcliffe
  "The Garden of Aphrodite." Shen (29:2) Wint 78, p. 29.

STACH, Carl
  "For the Illinois Dying." DacTerr (15) Wint-Spr 77-78, p. 46.
  "Only October." DacTerr (15) Wint-Spr 77-78, p. 47.
  "Reading the Mail: Her Lover Wins Forgiveness." CarolQ
      (30:3) Aut 78, p. 19.

STAFFORD, Kim
  "fossil." MalR (48) O 78, p. 87.
  "Promises to the Dead." NowestR (17:1) 78, p. 29.
  "Proposal." MalR (48) O 78, p. 86.
  "Vigilance." NowestR (17:1) 78, p. 30.

STAFFORD, William
  "After Arguing Against Stanley's and Diane's Contention That
      Poetry Must Come from Discontent." Tendril (3) Aut 78,
      p. 45.
  "Assurance." Hand (2) 78, p. 33.
  "A Certain Bend." MissouriR (1:1) Spr 78, p. 37.
  "All Changing." WestHR (32:1) Wint 78, p. 22.
  "At the Falls: A Birthday Picture." Nimrod (22:2) Spr-Sum 78,
      p. 2.
  "Brother Wind." WestHR (32:1) Wint 78, p. 76.
  "The Child You Were." Tendril (1) Wint 77-78.
  "Down on the Warm Springs Reservation." QW (5) Wint 78,
      p. 5.
  "An Evening Walk." NewYorker (54:25) 7 Ag 78, p. 32.
  "Gasoline." Poetry (132:5) Ag 78, p. 262.
  "Giving You Something." QW (5) Wint 78, p. 5.
  "Hinge in the Wind." MissouriR (1:1) Spr 78, p. 36.
  "The Next Room." Nimrod (22:2) Spr-Sum 78, p. 2.
  "An Old Pickerel in Walden Pond." ChiR (30:1) Sum 78, p. 102.
  "Our Cave." ChiR (30:1) Sum 78, p. 101.
  "Passing Our Playground." SouthernPR (18:2) Aut 78, p. 6.
  "Pegleg Lookout." VirQR (54:3) Aut 78, p. 502.
  "Resolutions." Poetry (132:2) My 78, p. 76.
  "Scenes That Escaped from James Dickey Poems." SoCaR (10:2)
      Ap 78, p. 47.
  "School Days." Field (18) Spr 78, p. 88.
  "Smoke." ThRiPo (11/12) 78, p. 69.
  "Something Has Happened to Us." Nimrod (22:2) Spr-Sum 78,
      p. 28.
  "Sonnet 747." Nimrod (22:2) Spr-Sum 78, p. 3.
  "Staging the Real." SouthernPR (18:2) Aut 78, p. 5.

"Things That Happen Where There Aren't Any People." WestHR
(32:1) Wint 78, p. 50.
"Thinking about Being Called Simple by a Critic." ChiR (30:3)
Wint 79, p. 124.
"Three Stories from Inside James Dickey's Guitar." SoCaR
(10:2) Ap 78, p. 47.
"Through the Junipers." WestHR (32:1) Wint 78, p. 44.
"Ways to Say 'Wind.'" AmerS (47:1) Wint 77-78, p. 51.
"When You Close Your Eyes." Nimrod (22:2) Spr-Sum 78, p. 1.

STAINTON, Albert
"The First and Only Patented Elephant Hotel." WormR (70) 78,
p. 69.
"The Prodigy." WormR (70) 78, p. 70.
"Wallet." WormR (70) 78, p. 69.

STALLWORTHY, Jon
from A Familiar Tree: Thirteen poems. CornellR (3) Spr 78,
p. 46.

STANDING, Sue
"A Blind Woman in the Wood." Salm (41) Spr 78, p. 122.
"New Habits." Bits (8) Jl 78.

STANFORD, Ann
"Andromeda." PoNow (19) 78, p. 6.
"The Center of the Garden." Atl (242:5) N 78, p. 85.
"Perseus." PoNow (19) 78, p. 6.

STANGE, Ken
"Towards the Limit." Smudge (1) Spr 78, p. 27.

STANLEY, George
"Donatello's David." LittleM (11:3) Aut 77, p. 46.

STANTON, Joseph
"At the Window." SmPd (42) Wint 78, p. 16.

STANTON, Maura
"Alcestis" (for Stanley Kunitz). Columbia (2) Aut 78, p. 62.
"Anna." AmerPoR (7:6) N-D 78, p. 4.
"Atlantis." AmerPoR (7:6) N-D 78, p. 3.
"At the North Pole." AmerPoR (7:6) N-D 78, p. 3.
"Breath." Columbia (2) Aut 78, p. 76.
"Dialogue." AmerPoR (7:6) N-D 78, p. 4.
"Fathers." AmerPoR (7:6) N-D 78, p. 4.
"Hitchhiker." AmerPoR (7:6) N-D 78, p. 3.
"Poem." PoNow (19) 78, p. 27.
"Visibility." AmerPoR (7:6) N-D 78, p. 3.

STANTON, Will
"Patches." LadHJ (95:4) Ap 78, p. 158.

STAPLETON, Wilson
"... before fall." SmPd (42) Wint 78, p. 12.
"a butcher's love." Paunch (52) O 78, p. 102.

STARBUCK, George
"On Reading John Hollander's Poem 'Breadth. Circle. Desert.
    Monarch. Month. Wisdom. (For Which There Are No
    Rhymes).'" Agni (8) 78, p. 11.
"On Reading John Hollander's Poem 'Breadth. Circle. Monarch.
    Month. Wisdom. (For Which There Are No Rhymes).'"
    Agni (9) 78, p. 123.
"On Reading John Hollander's Poem 'Breadth. Circle. Desert.
    Monarch. Month. Wisdom. (For Which There Are No
    Rhymes)' Part Two." Agni (8) 78, p. 13.
"The Passion of G. Gordon Giddy." SenR (9:1) Spr-Sum 78,
    p. 29.
"Sonnet in the Shape of a Potted Christmas Tree." Poetry
    (133:3) D 78, p. 168.
"Tuolomne." Agni (8) 78, p. 5.

STARK, David
"Bicentennial." SouthernPR (18:1) Spr 78, p. 50.

STATHATOS, John
"'These Were the Mountains of My Dreams.'" Stand (19:3) 78,
    p. 31.

STAZER, Lawrence
"Ten poems." HangL (32) Spr 78, p. 65.

STEDINGH, R. W.
"Yellowhead." MalR (45) Ja 78, p. 124.

STEELE, Peter
"New Orleans (An Australian Villanelle)." NewOR (6:1) 78,
    p. 66.

STEFANIK, Ernest
"Leaf and Star." SlowLR (1/2) 78, p. 27.

STEFANILE, Felix
"The Americanization of the Immigrant." Kayak (47) F 78,
    p. 45.
"How I Spent My Youth." Kayak (47) F 78, p. 47.
"Museum." PoNow (19) 78, p. 29.
"Remembering the Forties." Kayak (47) F 78, p. 45.

STEIN, Agnes
"Answer to Question" (tr. of Gunter Kunert). ModernPS (9:2)
    Aut 78, p. 151.
"House Calls" (tr. of Gunter Kunert). ModernPS (9:2) Aut 78,
    p. 148.

"Poem According to Benjamin" (tr. of Gunter Kunert). ModernPS
(9:2) Aut 78, p. 152.
"Sculpture of a Subjugated German" (tr. of Gunter Kunert).
ModernPS (9:2) Aut 78, p. 153.
"Signs, Berlin Style" (tr. of Gunter Kunert). ModernPS (9:2) Aut
78, p. 150.
"Venice II" (tr. of Gunter Kunert). ModernPS (9:2) Aut 78,
p. 152.

STEIN, Dona
"The Little Horses of the Cave (Lascaux)." DenQ (13:3) Aut 78,
p. 144.
"Tom." AndR (4:2) Aut 77, p. 90.
"Van Gogh, Painting His Way Out of the Asylum." DenQ (13:3)
Aut 78, p. 143.
"The Wing Factory." DenQ (13:3) Aut 78, p. 145.

STEIN, Joel
"Self-Portrait." KanQ (10:2) Spr 78, p. 39.

STEIN, Mary Kathryn
"Rain in Arkansas Makes People Go Crazy." EngJ (67:5) My 78,
p. 54.

STEINBERG, Alan L.
"St. John's Place: November 28." Nimrod (22:2) Spr-Sum 78,
p. 77.

STEINBERG, Suzanne
"Exhibition." Chomo (5:1) Sum 78, p. 33.

STEINGASS, David
"First Fish." Chowder (10/11) Aut-Wint 78-79, p. 46.
"How Are You Feeling in Ancient September." Northeast (3:5)
Spr-Sum 78, p. 11.
"Meditation in Maine." Northeast (3:5) Spr-Sum 78, p. 9.
"The Sea Creatures' Buryness: A Map." Chowder (10/11) Aut-
Wint 78-79, p. 47.
"Two Poems of Pure Place." NoAmR (263:1) Spr 78, p. 81.
"The Woman at the Fountain in Altaya." QW (5) Wint 78, p. 77.

STEINGESSER, Martin
"The Three" (for Miroslav Košek, 12, Hanuš Löwy, 13, and one
Bachner, three children who died in German death camps).
AmerPoR (7:4) Jl-Ag 78, p. 22.

STEINKE, Russell
"In Maple Country." SouthernPR (18:2) Aut 78, p. 51.

STEINMAN, Lisa
"Foolish Grace Defines Her Hero with Malice; Leaves Him High
& Dry." Epoch (27:2) Wint 78, p. 169.
"Foolish Grace Gets Ambition; Lectures the Moon." Epoch
(27:2) Wint 78, p. 171.

"Foolish Grace, Seduced by Wit." Epoch (27:2) Wint 78,
    p. 170.

STEINWAY, Frederick E.
  "The Change." Tele (13) 77.
  "Matins." Tele (13) 77.

STEPANCHEV, Stephen
  "January Wind." PoNow (19) 78, p. 27.
  "Junk." Glass (3:1/2/3) 78, p. 97.
  "The Knife." AmerPoR (7:6) N-D 78, p. 16.
  "Kodak Snapshot." PoNow (19) 78, p. 27.
  "Matter." Glass (3:1/2/3) 78, p. 96.
  "Pain." AmerPoR (7:6) N-D 78, p. 16.
  "The Quaker Dead in Flushing." Glass (3:1/2/3) 78, p. 95.
  "Sweet Eleanor." AmerPoR (7:6) N-D 78, p. 16.

STEPHENS, Carolyn
  "His Mother loved him." SeC (5:2) 78, p. 60.
  "Poetry." SeC (5:2) 78, p. 59.

STEPHENSON, Brett
  "A tree standing alone." DeKalb (11:3/4) Spr-Sum 78, p. 105.

STEPHENSON, Shelby
  "Azel Browning." Wind (31) 78, p. 56.
  "Backhouse." Wind (31) 78, p. 56.
  "Bladder Balloons." PoNow (20) 78, p. 40.
  "Hog Eyes." Bits (7) Ja 78.
  "Taking Stock." KanQ (10:1) Wint 78, p. 100.
  "Uncle Alton, Stella, and Night." Bits (8) Jl 78.

STERN, Gerald
  "The Drunk." PoNow (19) 78, p. 37.
  "Elaine Comparone." ParisR (74) Aut-Wint 78, p. 113.
  "The Faces I Love." MissouriR (1:1) Spr 78, p. 34.
  "Ice, Ice." Antaeus (30/31) Sum-Aut 78, p. 224.
  "Immensity." ParisR (74) Aut-Wint 78, p. 114.
  "Lobelia." PoNow (19) 78, p. 37.
  "Modern Love." AmerPoR (7:5) S-O 78, p. 4.
  "Pick and Poke." Antaeus (30/31) Sum-Aut 78, p. 222.
  "Rotten Angel." AmerPoR (7:5) S-O 78, p. 4.
  "The Sacred Spine." MissouriR (1:1) Spr 78, p. 33.
  "The Shirt Poem." AmerPoR (7:5) S-O 78, p. 3.
  "Swan Song." ParisR (74) Aut-Wint 78, p. 112.
  "The War Against the Jews." Iowa (9:2) Spr 78, p. 74.

STERN, Robert
  "Noah's Ark." Pig (4) 78, p. 9.
  "the stars walk across my chest." Wind (29) 78, p. 47.
  "Where." Wind (29) 78, p. 40.

STERNBERG, Ricardo
  "Ana Louca." Poetry (133:2) N 78, p. 75.

"The Bee." AmerPoR (7:3) My-Je 78, p. 14.
"Dancer." Agni (9) 78, p. 112.
"Double Root." AmerPoR (7:3) My-Je 78, p. 13.
"Exigencies of the Poem." Poetry (133:2) N 78, p. 73.
"Francis's Barn" (For Paul & Harriet). Poetry (133:2) N 78, p. 76.
"Santa Cruz." AmerPoR (7:3) My-Je 78, p. 13.
"The Snail." AmerPoR (7:3) My-Je 78, p. 14.

STESSEL, Harry
"Child." St. AR (5:1) Aut-Wint 78, p. 134.
"Cycles." St. AR (5:1) Aut-Wint 78, p. 134.
"Letter to Accompany a Grade of F." St. AR (5:1) Aut-Wint 78, p. 80.
"Night Ride." St. AR (5:1) Aut-Wint 78, p. 106.
"Picture History." Focus (13:79) Ja-F 78, p. 31.
"Pillow Talk." Focus (13:79) Ja-F 78, p. 31.
"The Point." St. AR (5:1) Aut-Wint 78, p. 120.
"These Are Your Assignments." St. AR (5:1) Aut-Wint 78, p. 79.

STETLER, Margaret
"before i fell asleep." Zahir (9) 77, p. 25.
"In Answer to Nicole's Poem." Tele (14) 78.
"Poem for My Mother, Thanksgiving 1973." Zahir (9) 77, p. 24.

STEVENS, Alex
"Capital Meeting." Epoch (27:3) Spr 78, p. 238.
"Clubs." Epoch (27:3) Spr 78, p. 242.
"Diamonds." Epoch (27:3) Spr 78, p. 243.
"Hearts." Epoch (27:3) Spr 78, p. 240.
"Oblique Man, Essential Text." GeoR (32:2) Sum 78, p. 317.
"Spades." Epoch (27:3) Spr 78, p. 240.
"Spider Dissertation." NewYorker (54:2) 27 F 78, p. 34.
"Vespers." NewYorker (54:33) 2 O 78, p. 40.

STEVENS, Elisabeth
"Water in the Woods." Confr (17) Aut-Wint 79, p. 121.

STEVENS, May
"Night in a Motel." Confr (17) Aut-Wint 79, p. 67.

STEVENSON, Anne
"Views from Parnassus." NewEngR (1:1) Aut 78, p. 44.

STEVENSON, Daniel
"Recluse Unfound" (tr. of Chia Tao, w. Robert Branham). Nimrod (22:2) Spr-Sum 78, p. 108.
"Staying with Wang Ch'ang-Ling" (tr. of Ch'ang Chien, w. Robert Branham). Nimrod (22:2) Spr-Sum 78, p. 109.
"Untitled" (tr. of Liu Shen-hsu, w. Robert Branham). Nimrod (22:2) Spr-Sum 78, p. 108.

STEVENSON, Diane
"The Birthday." SlowLR (1/2) 78, p. 90.

STEVENSON, Richard
"Landscape Interrupted by Three Ideas" (for Bert Devink).   MalR
    (45) Ja 78, p. 308.

STEWART, Frank
"The Poet's End: From Cocteau's Posthumous Letters."   LittleM
    (11:3) Aut 77, p. 96.
"The Waiting."   PoNow (20) 78, p. 40.

STEWART, Marie Vogl
"Who Holds the Key?"   EngJ (67:5) My 78, p. 60.

STEWART, Pamela
"Autopsy."   Antaeus (28) Wint 78, p. 141.
"The Bloom."   SenR (9:1) Spr-Sum 78, p. 54.
"Central Park, 1916."   SenR (9:1) Spr-Sum 78, p. 55.
"Dark Markings: 1974."   Salm (42) Sum-Aut 78, p. 117.
"Eleanor Roosevelt."   AmerPoR (7:2) Mr-Ap 78, p. 17.
"A Father's Walk in the Water-Meadow."   Salm (42) Sum-Aut 78,
    p. 116.
"Harvest" (for S. Z. R., 1947-1978).   Chowder (10/11) Aut-Wint
    78-79, p. 17.
"Niebelungenleid."   Salm (42) Sum-Aut 78, p. 118.
"The Pears."   Antaeus (28) Wint 78, p. 139.
"The Sergeant's Gardenia."   AmerPoR (7:2) Mr-Ap 78, p. 17.

STEWART, Robert
"Boss Told Me."   PoNow (20) 78, p. 40.
"The Point Coupee Funeral Home."   PoNow (20) 78, p. 40.

STEWART, Susan
"The Carnival at the End of the Parade."   ParisR (73) Spr-Sum
    78, p. 112.
"The Doves Are Swallowing Wind."   Kayak (47) F 78, p. 6.
"Every True Miracle."   Kayak (47) F 78, p. 3.
"Four Questions Regarding the Dreams of Animals."   BelPoJ
    (29:1) Aut 78, p. 14.
"Wish You Were Here."   Kayak (47) F 78, p. 4.

STIBER, Alex
"Leaving Them."   Poem (32) Mr 78, p. 65.
"Shadow Painting" (for Amy).   Poem (32) Mr 78, p. 64.

STIEBER, Ruth
"Untitled."   CarouselQ (3:3) Aut 78, p. 10.

STILL, Gloria
"Summer Storm Highway 37."   WindO (32) Sum-Aut 78, p. 47.

STILLWELL, Mary Kathryn
"Afternoons."   LittleM (11:4) Wint 78, p. 42.

STILWELL, Elizabeth
"A Walk Down Any Street."   Wind (31) 78, p. 57.

STILWELL, Robert
"Cold Raging Stones of Many Winter Constellations above
     Abandoned Back Woods Burial Grounds at Night." AAR (28)
     78, p. 5.
"Ernst's Late Studio." AAR (28) 78, p. 7.
"Fishing with Jars of Dynamite." AAR (28) 78, p. 4.
"Rabbit Hunting Season." AAR (28) 78, p. 6.

STIVER, Mary Weeden
"'I Sing the Body Electric'--W. W." CarouselQ (3:2) Sum 78,
     p. 6.

STIX, Judith Saul
"Abishag." WebR (4:2) Aut 78, p. 64.

STOCK, Bud
"Electric July." CarouselQ (3:3) Aut 78, p. 6.

STOCK, Robert
"Epistle to Spencer Holst." LittleM (11:3) Aut 77, p. 57.
"Frost Warnings." SewanR (86:1) Wint 78, p. 41.
"The Incomplete Angler" (for Alex Comfort). WebR (4:1) Spr 78,
     p. 50.
"The Last Resort." Poem (32) Mr 78, p. 29.
"No Graven Image." Poem (32) Mr 78, p. 30.
"Revenants of a Village Smaller Than Wherever." StoneC (78:2)
     Spr 78, p. 11.
"The Stroke" (for John & Marianne). Glass (3:1/2/3) 78,
     p. 101.

STOKELY, Jim
"Scaphiopus Couchii." AndR (4:2) Aut 77, p. 55.

STOKES, Frank
"Quipus." BallSUF (19:4) Aut 78, p. 55.

STOKES, Terry
"& What If." Confr (17) Aut-Wint 79, p. 53.
"Speaking of Poetry Readings." Some (9) 78, p. 85.

STOKESBURY, Leon
"Beef." PoNow (19) 78, p. 33.
"California." PoNow (19) 78, p. 33.
"Little Keats' Soliloquy." PoNow (19) 78, p. 33.
"Reynaldo in Paris." PartR (45:3) 78, p. 440.
"The True Meaning of Life Revealed." PoNow (19) 78, p. 33.

STOLOFF, Carolyn
"A Letter from Dick." Agni (8) 78, p. 103.
"Moon." SouthernPR (18:1) Spr 78, p. 43.
"Twilight." LittleM (11:4) Wint 78, p. 8.

STONE, Arlene
"Brief (Of the Mother)." Chomo (5:2) Aut-Wint 78, p. 24.

from Son Sonnets: Eleven poems. LittleM (11:3) Aut 78,
    p. 12.

STONE, Carole
"The Night of the Fireworks." SmPd (42) Wint 78, p. 4.
"Witness." Sam (64) 78, p. 54.

STONE, Ed
"Such as You." StoneC (78:1) Wint 78, p. 19.

STONE, Jennifer
"The Lunch Wagon at San Francisco State." Vaga (28) Aut 78,
    p. 39.

STONE, Joan
"Alchemy." GRR (9:2) 78, p. 136.
"A Letter to Myself to Water." SoDakR (16:2) Sum 78, p. 51.
"Part of an Answer." SoDakR (16:2) Sum 78, p. 52.
"The Way Up." PoetryNW (19:4) Wint 78-79, p. 20.

STONE, John
"Epitaph: The Auctioneer." Bits (7) Ja 78.
"Fugue." NewEngR (1:2) Wint 78, p. 194.
"The Parable of the Instruments." NewOR (6:1) 78, p. 38.

STORNI, Alfonsina
"Forgetfulness" (tr. by Marion Hodapp and Mary Crow). WebR
    (4:1) Spr 78, p. 12.
"Loneliness" (tr. by Marion Hodapp and Mary Crow). WebR
    (4:1) Spr 78, p. 11.
"The Moment" (tr. by Marion Hodapp and Mary Crow). WebR
    (4:1) Spr 78, p. 10.
"Words to My Mother" (tr. by Marion Hodapp and Mary Crow).
    WebR (4:1) Spr 78, p. 9.

STOTT, William R., Jr.
"Feely and Griffin's." BallSUF (19:4) Aut 78, p. 29.

STOUT, Liz
"Clean, Like a Fool." PraS (52:1) Spr 78, p. 62.
"Cripple's Eulogy" (for Anne Sexton). AmerPoR (7:1) Ja-F 78,
    p. 43.
"Making It Count." PraS (52:4) Wint 78-79, p. 377.
"Too Short, Even in a Sleep." AmerPoR (7:1) Ja-F 78, p. 43.

STOUT, Robert Joe
"Anger." Zahir (9) 77, p. 37.
"Late at Night: We Talk Civil Rights." Zahir (9) 77, p. 36.
"Missing Her" (For Lynne). Poem (32) Mr 78, p. 46.
"Tornado at the Carnival." ChrC (95:33) 18 O 78, p. 972.
"The Way." Sam (65) 78, p. 18.

STOUTENBURG, Adrien
"Before We Drown." Durak (1) 78, p. 5.

STOVALL, John Thomas
"Vox Hoops." DeKalb (11:1/2) Aut-Wint 77-78, p. 66.

STRAHAN, B. R.
"The White Woman." CarouselQ (3:2) Sum 78, p. 3.

STRAND, Mark
"Flame, Speech" (tr. of Octavio Paz). Nat (227:6) 2 S 78,
    p. 183.
"Night Piece." VirQR (54:1) Wint 78, p. 114.
"An Old Man Awake in His Own Death." VirQR (54:2) Spr 78,
    p. 281.
"Poem after Leopardi." Antaeus (30/31) Sum-Aut 78, p. 226.
"Poems of Air." VirQR (54:2) Spr 78, p. 282.
"Poor North." Antaeus (28) Wint 78, p. 86.
"The Story." Antaeus (28) Wint 78, p. 87.

STRAZEWSKI, Len
"The Poetry Teacher Meets Dr. J." PikeF (1) Spr 78, p. 25.
"To Brothers John." PikeF (1) Spr 78, p. 26.

STREETER, Barbara
"Bone Cancer." JnlONJP (2:2) 77, p. 4.

STRICKLAND, Stephanie
"When I Get There." Iowa (9:3) Sum 78, p. 91.

STRIPLING, Kathryn
"The Carpenter." VirQR (54:4) Aut 78, p. 698.
"Search Party." ThRiPo (11/12) 78, p. 17.

STROBLAS, Laurie
"Filament." StoneC (78:1) Wint 78, p. 4.
"Moving." Chomo (5:1) Sum 78, p. 34.

STROMBERG, Scott
"The Amputation." Wind (30) 78, p. 48.
"Pogrom." Wind (30) 78, p. 49.
"The Settling of My Mother's Estate." Wind (30) 78, p. 48.
"Verticalness." Wind (30) 78, p. 49.

STRYK, Dan
"Birdfeeder." Poem (32) Mr 78, p. 63.
"Malaise." Poem (32) Mr 78, p. 62.
"An Old Woman Gardens the Summit of Galena." BallSUF (19:4)
    Aut 78, p. 43.
"Swelter." SouthernPR (18:1) Spr 78, p. 38.

STRYK, Lucien
"Burning Oneself to Death" (tr. of Shinkichi Takahashi, w.
    Takashi Ikemoto). OhioR (19:2) Spr-Sum 78, p. 63.
"Cherries." Poetry (132:3) Je 78, p. 138.
"Chinese Zen Poems of Enlightenment and Death" (tr., w.

Takashi Ikemoto). QW (5) Wint 78, p. 36.
"Four Poems" (tr. of Shinkichi Takahashi, w. Takashi Ikemoto).
    OhioR (19:2) Spr-Sum 78, p. 65.
"Juggler." Nat (226:23) 17 Je 78, p. 738.
"Old Folks Home. " GeoR (32:2) Sum 78, p. 420.
"Sparrow" (tr. of Shinkichi Takahashi, w. Takashi Ikemoto).
    OhioR (19:2) Spr-Sum 78, p. 60.

STUART, Floyd C.
"Asparagns Is of Deceptive Sex. " PoNow (20) 78, p. 40.
"Geese Again. " Nimrod (22:2) Spr-Sum 78, p. 75.
"The Portland Cobbles. " CimR (43) Ap 78, p. 63.

STUART, Jane
"Memorial Day 1975. " BallSUF (19:2) Spr 78, p. 80.

STUDEBAKER, William
"The Magicians. " SoDakR (16:2) Sum 78, p. 59.

STYLE, Colin
"Coffins in Capetown. " Stand (19:4) 78, p. 38.

SUARDIAZ, Luis
"Theory" (tr. by Stuart Friebert). Chowder (10/11) Aut-Wint
    78-79, p. 52.

SUDERMAN, Elmer F.
"A Fifty-Year Old Husband on Kissing His Wife for at Least the
    Ten Thousandth Time. " Zahir (9) 77, p. 43.
"South Dakota Wind. " DacTerr (15) Wint-Spr 77-78, p. 62.
"Space Trip. " Zahir (9) 77, p. 43.

SUK, Julie
"For Now. " PoNow (20) 78, p. 41.
"Remnants. " St. AR (5:1) Aut-Wint 78, p. 135.
"Seeds. " SouthernPR (18:1) Spr 78, p. 25.
"You Sit There Staring. " PoNow (20) 78, p. 41.
"Where We Meet. " St. AR (5:1) Aut-Wint 78, p. 136.

SUKENICK, Lynn
"The Fire Pond. " CalQ (13/14) Spr-Sum 78, p. 133.

SULKIN, Sidney
"Eye. " Confr (16) Spr-Sum 78, p. 115.

SULLIVAN
"December 21, 1968. " BallSUF (19:4) Aut 78, p. 57.

SULLIVAN, Anne McCrary
"Albert. " DeKalb (11:1/2) Aut-Wint 77-78, p. 67.

SULLIVAN, Chuck
"Young Goodman Brown: What You See Is What You Get. "
    SoCaR (10:2) Ap 78, p. 89.

SULLIVAN, Francis
"A Waking Dream." LittleM (11:4) Wint 78, p. 38.

SULLIVAN, J. P.
"The Garden." ModernPS (9:1) Spr 78, p. 50.
"First Light." ModernPS (9:1) Spr 78, p. 51.

SULLIVAN, James
"To Margaret, on Reaching Forty." Comm (105:4) 17 F 78,
    p. 106.

SULLIVAN, William P.
"Storm Warning." Comm (105:8) 14 Ap 78, p. 247.

SUMMERS, Hollis
"Ace in the Hole, if That Is Where Aces Hide." KanQ (10:4)
    Aut 78, p. 20.
"An Afternoon in the Life Of." PoNow (19) 78, p. 18.
"Again, Well." KanQ (10:4) Aut 78, p. 19.
"Blind Song." PoNow (19) 78, p. 19.
"George M. Pullman (1831-1897)." PoNow (19) 78, p. 18.
"Invitation." PoNow (19) 78, p. 18.
"Notes for a Coffin Lid." AAR (28) 78, p. 72.
"On Having Loved Not Wisely or Too Well." PoNow (19) 78,
    p. 18.
"Twelve Gray Gulls." Bits (7) Ja 78.

SUNDERLAND, Tom
"Rio Shanty Town at Carnival." Nor (8) Aut 78, p. 17.

SUNWALL, James
"After the War." KanQ (10:1) Wint 78, p. 49.
"Voltaire's Villanelle." StoneC (78:1) Wint 78, p. 30.

SUPERVIELLE
"Make Room" (tr. by R. Sieburth and S. W. De Rachewiltz).
    St. AR (5:1) Aut-Wint 78, p. 65.
"Movement" (tr. by R. Sieburth and S. W. De Rachewiltz).
    St. AR (5:1) Aut-Wint 78, p. 64.
"Night" (tr. by R. Sieburth and S. W. De Rachewiltz). St. AR
    (5:1) Aut-Wint 78, p. 64.
"Other America" (tr. by R. Sieburth and S. W. De Rachewiltz).
    St. AR (5:1) Aut-Wint 78, p. 65.
"Untitled" (tr. by R. Sieburth and S. W. De Rachewiltz). St. AR
    (5:1) Aut-Wint 78, p. 64.

SUPRENANT, Dominic
"Ghost Poem" (for Mary). PikeF (1) Spr 78, p. 1.

SU SHI SU Tung-P'o
"Mid-Autumn Moon" (tr. by Jonathan Chaves). VirQR (54:2)
    Spr 78, p. 333.

SUSSMAN, Margaret
"Bears are sound asleep." Wind (28) 78, p. 5.
"To balance the blue." Wind (28) 78, p. 5.

SUSSMAN, S. W.
"Hissing of the Fire." Pan (19) 77, p. 59.
"Shades of Light." Pan (19) 77, p. 58.

SUTHERLAND-SMITH, James
"Chinese Considerations." Kayak (48) Je 78, p. 43.
"Dream." Kayak (48) Je 78, p. 44.
"The Ghost." Kayak (48) Je 78, p. 42.
"Nightowl." Kayak (48) Je 78, p. 45.
"Whodunnit." Kayak (48) Je 78, p. 46.

SUTTER, Barton
"Homing." PoNow (20) 78, p. 29.
"Night Out." PoNow (20) 78, p. 29.
"Talking to Grandpa Eastman." PoNow (20) 78, p. 29.

SVOBODA, Robert J.
"Maid in Hollywood." SmPd (42) Wint 78, p. 14.
"Sexual Hang-Ups." Tele (13) 77.

SVOBODA, Terese
"End of Bass." PraS (52:2) Sum 78, p. 190.
"The girls' hearts soften" (tr. of Anonymous). Antaeus (28)
   Wint 78, p. 205.
"Go heap dung on the hearth" (tr. of Anonymous). Antaeus (28)
   Wint 78, p. 204.
"The old-fashioned girls" (tr. of Anonymous). Antaeus (28) Wint
   78, p. 206.

SWAIM, Alice Mackenzie
"Deeper into Silence." CarouselQ (3:4) Wint 78, p. 9.
"To Make Allowances." CarouselQ (3:1) Spr 78, p. 8.

SWANDER, Mary
"Swift." Iowa (9:2) Spr 78, p. 82.

SWANGER, David
"The Horse Dies." Tendril (1) Wint 77-78.
"The Mistake." Tendril (1) Wint 77-78.

SWANN, Brian
"All Done By Mirrors." Falcon (17) 78, p. 10.
"Alternative" (tr. of Gabriela Melinescu, w. Michael Impey).
   WebR (4:1) Spr 78, p. 3.
"America" (tr. of Rocco Scotellaro, w. Ruth Feldman). GRR
   (9:1) 78, p. 37.
"Among the Urdos" (tr. of J. J. Arreola). WebR (4:2) Aut 78,
   p. 14.

"Another Departure. " ConcPo (11:1) Spr 78, p. 64.
"Betrothed" (tr. of Rocco Scotellaro, w. Ruth Feldman). Paint
(9/10) Spr-Aut 78, p. 42.
"Blank Sequence." NoAmR (263:1) Spr 78, p. 73.
"Bone" (tr. of Bechet Necatigil, w. Talat Halman). St. AR
(4:3/4) 77-78, p. 104.
"Bormann" (tr. of Bartolo Cattafi, w. Ruth Feldman). MalR
(46) Ap 78, p. 145.
"The Butterfly" (tr. of Gabriela Melinescu, w. Michael Impey).
WebR (4:1) Spr 78, p. 6.
"Christ Is Risen. " WebR (4:2) Aut 78, p. 12.
"Christmas" (tr. of Rocco Scotellaro, w. Ruth Feldman). St. AR
(4:3/4) 77-78, p. 107.
"Circumstantial. " ConcPo (11:1) Spr 78, p. 64.
"Dead" (tr. of Bechet Necatigil, w. Talat Halman). St. AR
(4:3/4) 77-78, p. 104.
"The Death of the Vessel. " St. AR (4:3/4) 77-78, p. 100.
from Empedocles D'Artaud: "Fragment 57" (tr. of Giovanna
Sandri, w. Ruth Feldman). Durak (1) 78, p. 56.
from Empedocles D'Artaud: "Fragment 61" (tr. of Giovanna
Sandri, w. Ruth Feldman). Durak (1) 78, p. 57.
"Et In Arcadia Ego. " SouthernPR (18:2) Aut 78, p. 88.
"The Eternal City. " ColEng (40:2) O 78, p. 162.
"Evening" (tr. of Rocco Scotellaro, w. Ruth Feldman). St. AR
(4:3/4) 77-78, p. 107.
"Every Day Is Monday" (tr. of Rocco Scotellaro, w. Ruth Feld-
man). St. AR (4:3/4) 77-78, p. 106.
"Fairy Tale. " PartR (45:3) 78, p. 437.
"Fall" (tr. of Gabriela Melinescu, w. Michael Impey). WebR
(4:1) Spr 78, p. 3.
"Father Mine" (tr. of Rocco Scotellaro, w. Ruth Feldman). GRR
(9:1) 78, p. 41.
"First Farewell to Naples" (tr. of Rocco Scotellaro, w. Ruth
Feldman). GRR (9:1) 78, p. 39.
"fly" (tr. of Bechet Necatigil, w. Talat Halman). St. AR
(4:3/4) 77-78, p. 103.
"A Friend" (tr. of Rocco Scotellaro, w. Ruth Feldman). Paint
(9/10) Spr-Aut 78, p. 43.
"From Nyhavn" (tr. of Bartolo Cattafi, w. Ruth Feldman).
Falcon (17) 78, p. 11.
"The Grass Seen from the Point of View of the Roots. " Aspen
(5) Spr 78, p. 77.
"Greek Sequence/Waking to White. " WebR (4:2) Aut 78, p. 11.
"Hens. " WebR (4:2) Aut 78, p. 13.
"Hiding. " NewYorker (54:15) 29 My 78, p. 113.
"Interior" (tr. of Bartolo Cattafi, w. Ruth Feldman). Falcon
(17) 78, p. 12.
"Istanbul. " MinnR (NS11) Aut 78, p. 47.
"John Climbing the Darkened Ladder" (tr. of Gabriela Melinescu,
w. Michael Impey). WebR (4:1) Spr 78, p. 4.
"Legend. " Nat (226:1) 7-14 Ja 78, p. 27.
"Living Phonetically. " Northeast (3:6) Wint 78-79, p. 18.
"Living Time. " NewYorker (54:19) 26 Je 78, p. 36.

"Manitou. " PoetryNW (19:1) Spr 78, p. 32.
"Migrant Worker. " ColEng (40:2) O 78, p. 161.
"Moths. " Confr (17) Aut-Wint 79, p. 140.
"My Father" (tr. of Rocco Scotellaro, w. Ruth Feldman). St. AR
    (4:3/4) 77-78, p. 105.
"The Names" (for Mike Keeley). SouthernPR (18:2) Aut 78,
    p. 86.
"A New World" (tr. of Bartolo Cattafi, w. Ruth Feldman).
    Columbia (2) Aut 78, p. 80.
"On Cats' Paws" (tr. of Rocco Scotellaro, w. Ruth Feldman).
    St. AR (4:3/4) 77-78, p. 107.
"Peace" (tr. of Bartolo Cattafi, w. Ruth Feldman). MalR (46)
    Ap 78, p. 146.
"Piazza S. Egidio, 9. " NewYorker (54:12) 8 My 78, p. 44.
"Rocks. " Nat (226:6) 18 F 78, p. 185.
"Six Pious Pieces and Some Not So" (Nine poems). WormR (68)
    77, pp. 97-104.
"Stalk" (tr. of Bartolo Cattafi, w. Ruth Feldman). MalR (46)
    Ap 78, p. 144.
"They Stole You from Us" (tr. of Rocco Scotellaro, w. Ruth
    Feldman). GRR (9:1) 78, p. 35.
"The Venus Line" (tr. of Bechet Necatigil, w. Talat Halman).
    St. AR (4:3/4) 77-78, p. 105.
"the voice" (tr. of Bechet Necatigil, w. Talat Halman). St. AR
    (4:3/4) 77-78, p. 103.
"The Wives. " ColEng (40:2) O 78, p. 163.
"Zero at the Bone. " Pequod (2:4) 78, p. 62.

SWARTS, Helene
"A Dream. " PoNow (20) 78, p. 41.
"Evidence. " ChrC (95:6) 22 F 78, p. 188.

SWARTS, William
"Cabin Fever. " PikeF (1) Spr 78, p. 13.
"Toward the End of a Line. " SmPd (44) Aut 78, p. 16.

SWEENEY, Kevin
"For Glee Knight. " Zahir (9) 77, p. 40.

SWEENEY, Matthew
"Empty Trains. " GRR (9:3) 78, p. 179.
"Forbidden Fruit. " GRR (9:3) 78, p. 184.
"Hometrip to Freiburg. " GRR (9:3) 78, p. 182.
"House of Cards. " GRR (9:3) 78, p. 185.
"The Roads. " GRR (9:3) 78, p. 181.
"The Unable. " GRR (9:3) 78, p. 180.

SWENSON, Karen
"The Chinese Laundryman. " Poetry (133:3) D 78, p. 157.
"Composing the Album. " DenQ (13:4) Wint 79, p. 110.
"Grave Clothes. " DenQ (13:4) Wint 79, p. 109.
"Kaleidoscope. " SoDakR (16:2) Sum 78, p. 12.
"The Nazi Hygienist. " Aspen (5) Spr 78, p. 97.

"Pockets." ParisR (73) Spr-Sum 78, p. 25.
"60 to 70." Epos (27:1) 77, p. 7.

SWENSON, May
"Digging in the Garden of Age I Uncover a Live Root" (for E. W.).
    Poetry (132:4) Jl 78, p. 211.
"Ending." Poetry (132:4) Jl 78, p. 212.
"Fashion in the 70's." Poetry (132:2) My 78, p. 94.
"Going to the Whitney and Walking on the Floor." Poetry (132:4)
    Jl 78, p. 207.
"How Everything Happens (Based on a Study of the Wave)."
    AmerPoR (7:4) Jl-Ag 78, p. 42.
"Night Visits with the Family." Shen (29:2) Wint 78, p. 27.
"Old No. 1." LittleM (11:3) Aut 77, p. 11.
"Overboard." AmerPoR (7:2) Mr-Ap 78, p. 39.
"Scroppo's Dog." AmerPoR (7:2) Mr-Ap 78, p. 39.
"Survey of the Whole." Nat (226:16) 29 Ap 78, p. 511.
"Teeth." Nat (226:9) 11 Mr 78, p. 278.
"That the Soul May Wax Plump." Atl (241:6) Je 78, p. 46.

SWERB, Candy
"public---the." Tele (14) 78.

SWETS, R. D.
"the commentaries." Zahir (9) 77, p. 45.
"Stoffel the printmaker pulls a proof." BallSUF (19:4) Aut 78,
    p. 48.
"walking into the light." Zahir (9) 77, p. 46.

SWIFT, Joan
"Narrows." PoNow (19) 78, p. 44.
"Wake." PoetryNW (19:1) Spr 78, p. 41.

SWILKY, Jody
"Affection." PoNow (20) 78, p. 41.
"Animation and Ego." GeoR (32:3) Aut 78, p. 633.
"The Curious Cold." GeoR (32:3) Aut 78, p. 632.

SWISS, Thom
"Man Waxing Car. 1953." QW (5) Wint 78, p. 92.

SWIST, Wally
"The Book of Love Rewritten According to Hoyle." Tele (14) 78.
"Communication." SmPd (44) Aut 78, p. 32.
"Hurricane." Tele (13) 77.
"Poem: I'd like to think we convinced you." Paint (9/10) Spr-
    Aut 78, p. 25.
"Poem: The sky, when you laugh." Tele (14) 78.

SYRKIN, Marie
"Of Age." NewRep (179:20) 11 N 78, p. 27.

SZYMBORSKA, Wislawa
"Atlantis" (tr. by Robin Behn, w. Claudia Johnson). ThRiPo

(11/12) 78, p. 69.
"Seen from Above" (tr. by Robin Behn, w. Claudia Johnson).
ThRiPo (11/12) 78, p. 71.

TABLADA, José Juan
Ten poems (tr. by Eliot Weinberger). Montra (4) 78, p. 182.

TAGGART, John
from Dodeka: "a second plait, a bracelet." Bound (6:2) Wint
78, p. 443.
"Giant Steps." ChiR (30:3) Wint 79, p. 144.

TAGLIABUE, John
"Blake says 'All deities reside in the human breast.'" BelPoJ
(29:1) Aut 78, p. 44.
"Debussy and Proust." NewL (44:3) Spr 78, p. 70.
"Harp as Instrument of Conquest." NewL (45:2) Wint 78, p. 97.
"June Thoughts." CarolQ (30:1) Wint 78, p. 51.
"Three Poems." Kayak (47) F 78, p. 62.

TAGRIN, Barry
"The Fruit Tree." StoneC (78:2) Spr 78, p. 10.

TAKACS, Nancy
"Blaming the Heat." CutB (10) Spr-Sum 78, p. 12.
"Near the Covered Bridge." CutB (11) Aut-Wint 78, p. 75.

TAKAHASHI, Shinkichi
"Burning Oneself to Death" (tr. by Lucien Stryk and Takashi
Ikemoto). OhioR (19:2) Spr-Sum 78, p. 63.
"Four Poems" (tr. by Lucien Stryk and Takashi Ikemoto). OhioR
(19:2) Spr-Sum 78, p. 65.
"Sparrow" (tr. by Lucien Stryk and Takashi Ikemoto). OhioR
(19:2) Spr-Sum 78, p. 60.

TAKARO, Gedeon
"For a Friend Buried at Sea." CarouselQ (3:4) Wint 78, p. 17.

TALARICO, Ross
"Taking a Punch" (for Phil Levine). Epoch (27:3) Spr 78, p. 286.
"To the Girl I Loved." Iowa (9:4) Aut 78, p. 79.

TAMBUZI, Jitu
"I Betcha Ain't Never...." GreenfieldR (7:1/2) Aut 78, p. 36.
"My Poolroom Buddy." GreenfieldR (7:1/2) Aut 78, p. 104.

TAMER, Ülkü
"The Dagger" (tr. by Talat Sait Halman). Paint (7/8) Spr-Aut
77, p. 58.

TANGREDI, Sam J.
"Misfire/Broken Correspondence." SmPd (43) Spr 78, p. 6.

TANIKAWA, Shuntaro
"Written at 14 E. 28th Street, New York City" (tr. by William I.
Elliott). SoDakR (16:4) Wint 78-79, p. 66.

TAPSCOTT, Stephen
"Genetics. " CornellR (3) Spr 78, p. 67.
"The Man Who Stutters. " GreenfieldR (6:3/4) Spr 78, p. 117.
"A Secret. " ThRiPo (11/12) 78, p. 72.
"Sixty Second Raga. " ThRiPo (11/12) 78, p. 74.
"To Sherlock Holmes. " CarolQ (30:1) Wint 78, p. 55.

TARACHOW, Michael
"Portrait of a Dead Sparrow. " PoNow (20) 78, p. 42.

TARN, Nathaniel
from Alashka: "July 4, 1976: Sevuokuk" (w. Janet Rodney).
Hand (2) 78, p. 57.

TATE, James
"Blank Stare Encounter. " PoNow (19) 78, p. 30.
"Experience & Tradition. " Kayak (47) F 78, p. 57.
"The Gentle Beckendorfs. " PoNow (19) 78, p. 8.
"Heatstroke. " AmerPoR (7:3) My-Je 78, p. 10.
"The Human Eraser. " AmerPoR (7:3) My-Je 78, p. 10.
"The Life of Poetry. " Durak (1) 78, p. 21.
"The Major Cleft. " Antaeus (30/31) Sum-Aut 78, p. 229.
"Nature Poem: Demanding Stiff Sentences. " MissouriR (1:1) Spr
78, p. 28.
"The Old Man's Young Wife. " QW (5) Wint 78, p. 35.
"On to the Source. " Antaeus (30/31) Sum-Aut 78, p. 227.
"The Prince at Amherst. " Durak (1) 78, p. 20.
"Pythons Kill Trainer. " Antaeus (30/31) Sum-Aut 78, p. 230.
"Return. " PoNow (19) 78, p. 8.
"Riven Doggeries. " MissouriR (1:1) Spr 78, p. 29.
"Schizophrenic Kiss. " PoNow (19) 78, p. 8.
"She Squatted Alongside. " Durak (1) 78, p. 19.
"Time X. " Kayak (47) F 78, p. 56.
"Tomb of Secrets. " QW (5) Wint 78, p. 34.
"With a Child All Day. " Poetry (132:5) Ag 78, p. 275.

TAYLOR, Alexander
"Atmosphere" (tr. of Benny Andersen). MoonsLT (2:4) 78,
p. 81.
"The Last Poem in the World" (tr. of Benny Andersen).
MoonsLT (2:4) 78, p. 79.
"Women" (tr. of Benny Andersen). MoonsLT (2:4) 78, p. 76.

TAYLOR, Benjamin
"Neoptolemus Puts to Sea" (for JHT). Shen (29:2) Wint 78,
p. 77.

TAYLOR, Brian
"December on the Esterel. " AntR (36:1) Wint 78, p. 82.

"Henut in the Bridal Salon. " AntR (36:1) Wint 78, p. 84.
"Place de la Poste. " ModernPS (9:2) Aut 78, p. 84.

TAYLOR, I. P.
"Edge. " SewanR (86:4) Aut 78, p. 521.
"Ironstone Miners 1874. " SewanR (86:4) Aut 78, p. 520.
"White Owl. " SewanR (86:4) Aut 78, p. 523.

TAYLOR, Jeffrey
"As Graveyards Die. " KanQ (10:3) Sum 78, p. 27.

TAYLOR, Joan Imig
"The Witch of Devil's Canyon. " WorldO (12:4) Sum 78, p. 32.

TAYLOR, John
"About Songs. " PoetryNW (19:4) Wint 78-79, p. 42.
"Abyssus Invocat Abbysums. " BallSUF (19:2) Spr 78, p. 11.
"Caritas. " PoetryNW (19:1) Spr 78, p. 27.
"Dissolving. " PoetryNW (19:4) Wint 78-79, p. 41.
"First Lesson. " PoetryNW (19:4) Wint 78-79, p. 43.
"The Laureate. " PoetryNW (19:4) Wint 78-79, p. 42.
"Princeps Tenebrarum. " BallSUF (19:3) Sum 78, p. 79.
"With a Cool Eye. " PoetryNW (19:1) Spr 78, p. 26.

TAYLOR, K. P. A.
"The Brass Ring. " SewanR (86:4) Aut 78, p. 524.
"Tin Wedding. " SewanR (86:4) Aut 78, p. 523.

TAYLOR, Kent
"autumn. " Vaga (27) Spr 78, p. 58.
"1-2-78. " Vaga (27) Spr 78, p. 42.
"3-17-78. " Vaga (27) Spr 78, p. 41.

TAYLOR, Laurie
"The Seekers Are No Longer Among Us. " Sam (69) 78, p. 71.

TAYLOR, Leah
"Quickly. " YellowBR (10) 78, p. 17.

Ten HARMSEL, Larry
"Brancusi" (tr. of Lucebert). GRR (9:2) 78, p. 109.
"A Breughel" (tr. of Anthonie Donker). GRR (9:2) 78, p. 111.
"Henry Moore" (tr. of Lucebert). GRR (9:2) 78, p. 105.
"Rousseau Le Douanier" (tr. of Lucebert). GRR (9:2) 78,
    p. 107.
"Tourist in Amsterdam. " GRR (9:3) 78, p. 188.

Ter MEULEN, Leith
"Husband. " Glass (3:1/2/3) 78, p. 100.

TERRANOVA, Elaine
"Piano Lesson. " Northeast (3:6) Wint 78-79, p. 7.
"3. " Northeast (3:6) Wint 78-79, p. 7.

TERRILL, Kathryn
"In the Powerhouse." AmerPoR (7:1) Ja-F 78, p. 36.

TERRIS, Virginia R.
"Flash." Hand (2) 78, p. 151.
"Ghost." PoNow (20) 78, p. 30.
"Neighbor." DacTerr (15) Wint-Spr 77-78, p. 64.
"Night Sound." Confr (16) Spr-Sum 78, p. 158.
"Not Knowing." PoNow (20) 78, p. 30.
"Tracking." PoNow (20) 78, p. 30.
"We Wear Ugly Hats." PoNow (20) 78, p. 30.

TESZLEWICZ, Jane
"Hardwood and Crystal." EngJ (67:5) My 78, p. 58.

THACKER, Julia
"At the Marina." Madem (84:7) Jl 78, p. 146.
"Crosstown" (for Paul Laurence Dunbar). MassR (19:2) Sum 78,
    p. 276.

THADDEUS, Janice
"A Cry to the Country." StoneC (78:1) Wint 78, p. 6.
"Old in This Time." StoneC (78:1) Wint 78, p. 7.

THALMAN, Mark
"Born in Oregon." PoNow (20) 78, p. 42.
"Long Distance." PoNow (20) 78, p. 42.
"The Peasant Dance." CutB (10) Spr-Sum 78, p. 10.
"Shelter Cove." CarolQ (30:3) Aut 78, p. 75.

THANIEL, George
Seventeen poems (tr. of Yannis Ritsos, w. Kimon Friar).
    Falcon (16) 78, p. 68.

THARP, Roland
"Along the Road to the Ruins." PraS (52:2) Sum 78, p. 150.
"Obligations." CarolQ (30:2) Spr-Sum 78, p. 109.

THERSON-COFIE, Larweh
"The Late-Comer" (to Lartey's first born). MalR (46) Ap 78,
    p. 43.
"Recipe for Thunder." MalR (46) Ap 78, p. 42.

THOMAS, D. M.
"The Dreaming Game." AmerS (47:1) Wint 77-78, p. 49.

THOMAS, F. Richard
"Nikstlitslepmur." PoNow (19) 78, p. 44.

THOMAS, Kirk
"Free Spirit." EngJ (67:5) My 78, p. 58.

THOMAS, Lisa
"Oscar." KanQ (10:4) Aut 78, p. 47.

THOMAS, Lorenzo
"Changes." LaB (10) 78, p. 50.
"Sketches of Susan." LaB (10) 78, p. 51.

THOMAS, Maurice
"Front Porch Summer." Poem (33) Jl 78, p. 3.
"Straw Gathering." Poem (33) Jl 78, p. 2.
"To the Lady Among the Iris." Poem (33) Jl 78, p. 1.
"The Winter Man." Poem (33) Jl 78, p. 4.

THOMAS, Richard
"In the Moment." PartR (45:3) 78, p. 444.
"A Small Hand." PartR (45:3) 78, p. 444.

THOMPSON, Daniel (see ROKWAHO)

THOMPSON, Don
"Listening to Wild Dogs at Buena Vista Lake." SoDakR (16:2)
   Sum 78, p. 69.

THOMPSON, Gary
"Like Being at Home." NewL (45:1) Aut 78, p. 32.
"This Morning's Shiver." NewL (45:1) Aut 78, p. 31.
"To Cover You." NewL (45:1) Aut 78, p. 32.

THOMPSON, Jeanie
"The Black Venus. Paris: 1842." SouthernHR (12:4) Aut 78,
   p. 325.
"Rapunzel." SouthernHR (12:4) Aut 78, p. 326.
"Whittle." SouthernHR (12:4) Aut 78, p. 326.

THOMPSON, Joanna
"The Boy with Surprised Eyes." WindO (31) Wint-Spr 78, p. 23.
"Geometric Solution." FourQt (28:1) Aut 78, p. 12.
"Lover." WindO (31) Wint-Spr 78, p. 22.
"Mother." CalQ (13/14) Spr-Sum 78, p. 134.
"A Personal History." WindO (31) Wint-Spr 78, p. 21.
"Target." NewOR (5:4) 78, p. 304.

THOMPSON, Nance E.
"Refrigerated." Sam (69) 78, p. 2.

THOMPSON, Phyllis Hoge
"Banyan Roots." Paunch (52) O 78, p. 116.
"Moloka'i." Paunch (52) O 78, p. 115.

THORNBURG, Thomas R.
"Ancient Letters." BallSUF (19:4) Aut 78, p. 34.
"Matthew Paris." BallSUF (19:3) Sum 78, p. 2.

THORNE, Evelyn
"Kaleidoscope." Wind (28) 78, p. 57.
"A Meditation." Wind (28) 78, p. 56.
"The Recluses." Wind (28) 78, p. 56.

THORPE, Dwayne
"The Bride Approaches the Kansas Border." PoetryNW (19:4)
 Wint 78-79, p. 27.

TIDLER, Charles
"Living the Right Life." Vaga (27) Spr 78, p. 72.

TIFFT, Ellen
"Introduction." WormR (72) 78, p. 149.
"The Last Days." WormR (72) 78, p. 149.
"We Travel a Contour Map." WormR (72) 78, p. 149.

TILLINGHAST, Richard
"Hearing of the End of the War." NewRep (179:5) 29 Jl 78,
 p. 25.
"Return." MissouriR (2:1) Aut 78, p. 16.

TINKLE, Harold
"Earning a Drink." Bits (7) Ja 78.

TINSLEY, Bonnie
"Love Song to a Sculptor." PikeF (1) Spr 78, p. 13.
"The Old." PikeF (1) Spr 78, p. 13.

TINSLEY, Molly Best
"Soundings." Epos (27:2) 77, p. 27.

TISDALE, Charles
"My Childhood's Bedroom." CimR (43) Ap 78, p. 52.
"These Dependencies." ChiR (30:2) Aut 78, p. 68.

TISDALE, Elizabeth
"Analogy of Harry." DeKalb (11:3/4) Spr-Sum 78, p. 106.
"If Only ... (That Would Solve Everything!)." DeKalb (11:3/4)
 Spr-Sum 78, p. 107.
"Lost Love." DeKalb (11:3/4) Spr-Sum 78, p. 106.

TITONE, Margaret
"The Jesse Tree." BallSUF (19:4) Aut 78, p. 10.

TOBIAS, Arthur
"am i this body or am i not" (tr. of Han Shan, w. Jim
 Hardesty). GreenfieldR (6:3/4) Spr 78, p. 72.
"how cold it is on this mountain" (tr. of Han Shan, w. Jim
 Hardesty). GreenfieldR (6:3/4) Spr 78, p. 72.
"i asked t'ien t'ai mountain" (tr. of Han Shan, w. Jim
 Hardesty). GreenfieldR (6:3/4) Spr 78, p. 73.
"Letter to Steve." GreenfieldR (6:3/4) Spr 78, p. 74.
"my resting place is deep in the woods now" (tr. of Han Shan,
 w. Jim Hardesty). GreenfieldR (6:3/4) Spr 78, p. 73.
"when there's something to be happy about be happy" (tr. of Han
 Shan, w. Jim Hardesty). GreenfieldR (6:3/4) Spr 78,
 p. 72.

"yesterday i saw the trees along the river" (tr. of Han Shan, w.
Jim Hardesty). GreenfieldR (6:3/4) Spr 78, p. 73.

TOMLINSON, K.
"for judyl on her birthday." HangL (33) Sum 78, p. 57.
"instinct." HangL (33) Sum 78, p. 56.

TOMLINSON, Russanne
"Just last night." SeC (5:2) 78, p. 61.

TOMPKINS, B.
"Bull Baiting." KanQ (10:1) Wint 78, p. 98.

TOMSKY, James
"The Porch." MoonsLT (2:4) 78, p. 65.
"Soliloquy." MoonsLT (2:4) 78, p. 67.
"Vigil Light." Tendril (2) Spr-Sum 78.

TONER, M. P.
"Lady Kay." FourQt (27:4) Sum 78, p. 24.

TORYFTER, Michael
"Forest Fire." CarouselQ (3:1) Spr 78, p. 3.
"Inner Voyage." CarouselQ (3:1) Spr 78, p. 3.
"Misfit." CarouselQ (3:1) Spr 78, p. 3.
"Saints and Sinners." CarouselQ (3:1) Spr 78, p. 3.

TOWLE, Barbara Bloom
"Naming Poem." SoDakR (16:2) Sum 78, p. 58.

TOWNSEND, Marion
"The Difference Between Male Writers and Female Writers."
LitR (21:3) Spr 78, p. 381.

TOY, Suey Ping
"Poem Found in a Dark Basement." Kayak (47) F 78, p. 55.

TRACHMAN, William Brian
"flat broke airport." Tele (13) 77.
"I sometimes." Tele (13) 77.
"valerie." Tele (13) 77.

TRACHTENBERG, Paul
"Birds in Riptide Winds." PoNow (20) 78, p. 42.
"Grace." PoNow (20) 78, p. 42.

TRAKL, Georg
"Dejection" (tr. by Michael Hamburger). Stand (19:4) 78, p. 2.
"The Occident" (For Else Lasker-Schuler, with admiration) (tr.
by Paul Morris). WebR (4:1) Spr 78, p. 33.
"Psalm" (tr. by R. Sieburth and S. W. De Rachewiltz). St.AR
(5:1) Aut-Wint 78, p. 51.
"To Childe Elis" (tr. by R. Sieburth and S. W. De Rachewiltz).
St.AR (5:1) Aut-Wint 78, p. 51.

TRANSTRÖMER, Tomas
"From the Winter of 1947" (tr. by Robin Fulton).   Stand (19:4)
    78, p. 54.

TRANTHAM, Ann Caldwell
"Miranda in the Mirror."   EngJ (67:5) My 78, p. 60.

TRAWICK, Leonard
"Severed Parts."   Poetry (132:3) Je 78, p. 141.
"The Underworld."   Poetry (132:3) Je 78, p. 143.
"Wood Fires."   Poetry (132:3) Je 78, p. 142.

TREFETHEN, Florence
"A Host to Spanish Moss."   LitR (21:3) Spr 78, p. 349.
"Moving Up One at the Good Samaritan Hospital."   LitR (21:3)
    Spr 78, p. 350.
"Recycling."   StoneC (78:1) Wint 78, p. 5.

TREITEL, Margot
"Carolyn's Blues."   Chomo (4:3) Spr 78, p. 28.
"Culture Shock."   CarolQ (30:1) Wint 78, p. 105.
"The Dutch Have Four Words for Horizon."   ChiR (29:4) Spr 78,
    p. 8.
"The Geography of this Place."   CarolQ (30:1) Wint 78, p. 104.
"Lunch in the Land of Plenty."   Northeast (3:5) Spr-Sum 78,
    p. 56.
"Paint Yourself into the Corner."   NewRivR (2:2) 78, p. 51.
"The Unfinished Still Life in My Mother's Closet."   Northeast
    (3:5) Spr-Sum 78, p. 55.

TREJO, Ernesto
"E. Is in Love."   Kayak (48) Je 78, p. 41.
"E. Curses the Rich."   Kayak (48) Je 78, p. 41.

TREMBLAY, Bill
"Fall."   MassR (19:1) Spr 78, p. 92.
"Little Miracles."   ThRiPo (11/12) 78, p. 75.

TREMMEL, Robert
"Koala."   HiramPoR (25) Aut-Wint 78, p. 35.

TRETHEWAY, Eric
"In the Traces."   SewanR (86:3) Sum 78, p. 378.
"Sunday Outing at Grand Lake."   SewanR (86:3) Sum 78, p. 378.

TRIEM, Eve
"Midsummer Rites."   PoetryNW (19:3) Aut 78, p. 46.

TRIFILIO, Jim
"The Essential House."   Wind (30) 78, p. 51.

TRIGGS, Jeffery Alan
"Attic Stele on a Child's Tomb."   LitR (21:3) Spr 78, p. 347.

TRIVELPIECE, Laurel
"The Dear Departed." AmerPoR (7:2) Mr-Ap 78, p. 12.
"Report from Dorothy Wordsworth." AmerPoR (7:2) Mr-Ap 78,
     p. 12.

TROLL, Tim
"The View from Pamela's Hollow." StoneC (78:3) Aut 78, p. 4.

TROWBRIDGE, Virginia M.
"Untitled." CarouselQ (3:1) Spr 78, p. 12.
"Untitled." CarouselQ (3:4) Wint 78, p. 10.

TROWBRIDGE, William
"Crone." Wind (30) 78, p. 50.
"Headline from History: Normandy, June 6, 1944." KanQ
     (10:1) Wint 78, p. 109.
"Nostalgia." DeKalb (11:3/4) Spr-Sum 78, p. 46.
"A Rose for Mistress Hibbins." DeKalb (11:3/4) Spr-Sum 78, p. 46.

TROY, Sheila
"Drought." AmerPoR (7:6) N-D 78, p. 36.

TRUDELL, Dennis
"Father." NoAmR (263:1) Spr 78, p. 13.
"My Old Playmates." Bits (7) Ja 78.
"What You Already Know." GeoR (32:3) Aut 78, p. 607.

TRUSCOTT, Robert Blake
"The Anniversary." LitR (22:4) Aut 78, p. 22.
"The Mad Children Among the Navaho Trees." GreenfieldR
     (6:3/4) Spr 78, p. 47.
"Sand Creek." GreenfieldR (6:3/4) Spr 78, p. 48.

TRUSTMAN, Deborah
"Dinner at the Neighbors'." Atl (242:1) Jl 78, p. 45.

TUCKER, David
"Columbus Discovers Niggerhill, Linden, Tennessee." HangL
     (33) Sum 78, p. 58.
"The Bankrupt Farm." CarolQ (30:3) Aut 78, p. 73.
"Monday Morning." CarolQ (30:3) Aut 78, p. 74.

TUCKER, Liza
"It Was Frightful ..." (tr. of Anna Akhamtova). Field (18) Spr
     78, p. 21.
"Northern Elegies"(tr. of Anna Akhmatova). Field (18) Spr 78, p. 15.

TUCKER, Robert
"June Rain '72" (for my colleagues & MR). MassR (19:3) Aut
     78, p. 569.

TUDOR, Stephen
"Home Tune-up." SouthernPR (18:1) Spr 78, p. 67.
"The Mystery." AmerPoR (7:6) N-D 78, p. 34.

TULLOSS, Rod
"Homage to Vallejo." JnlONJP (2:1) 77, p. 15.
Nine poems. US1 (11) Aut 78, p. 5.
"A Nose Is a Pigeon." JnlONJP (2:1) 77, p. 14.
"Watching the Mammoths Die." JnlONJP (2:1) 77, p. 14.
"The Wonder Bread Horror." JnlONJP (2:2) 77, p. 27.

TURCO, Lewis
"The College (Massachusetts, 1700s)." SewanR (86:1) Wint 78,
    p. 42.
"The Covered Bridge." ModernPS (9:3) Wint 79, p. 166.
"The Compleat Malancholick." Wind (28) 78, p. 58.
"Frost and Amaranth." KanQ (10:1) Wint 78, p. 23.
"The Girl You Thought You Loved." ModernPS (9:3) Wint 79,
    p. 165.
"The High Priestess." Wind (28) 78, p. 58.
"The Homestead." ModernPS (9:3) Wint 79, p. 167.
"The Indian Stockade (Rhode Island, 17th century)." SoCaR
    (11:1) N 78, p. 43.
"The Lighthouse." ModernPS (9:3) Wint 79, p. 167.
"The Shipyard." ConcPo (11:1) Spr 78, p. 58.
"The Tobacco Shed (Virginia, 1800s)." SewanR (86:1) Wint 78,
    p. 43.
"The Walking Tree." Nat (226:8) 4 Mr 78, p. 253.

TURELL, Jane Colman
"An Invitation into the Country, in Imitation of Horace." 13thM
    (4:1) 78, p. 68.
"Lines on Childbirth." 13thM (4:1) 78, p. 70.
"On Reading the Warning by Mrs. Singer." 13thM (4:1) 78,
    p. 67.
"To My Muse, December 29, 1725." 13thM (4:1) 78, p. 67.

TURGEON, Gregoire
"The Four Kinds of Discourse" (for my students). PoetryNW
    (19:4) Wint 78-79, p. 16.
"Mrs. Anderson." CarolQ (30:1) Wint 78, p. 108.

TURNER, Alberta
"Necessary Magic." MissouriR (2:1) Aut 78, p. 25.

TURNER, Jamie
"America." SeC (5:2) 78, p. 34.

TURNER, Keith
"War Photograph." Stand (19:4) 78, p. 16.

TUTEUR, Mary
"Everything Has a Name." AndR (4:2) Aut 77, p. 64.

TUWIN, Julian
"There Is No Land" (tr. of Antoni Gronowicz). Confr (16) Spr-
    Sum 78, p. 86.

TWEED, Robert J.
  "Phaedra." EngJ (67:5) My 78, p. 57.

TWICHELL, Chase
  "Watercress & Ice" (for Rick Knupfer). Antaeus (30/31) Sum-
    Aut 78, p. 231.

TWISS, Dorothy
  "Rondelet." SouthernHR (12:2) Spr 78, p. 121.
  "Workshop Truck Stop Blues." SouthernHR (12:2) Spr 78, p. 100.

TYLER, Robert L.
  "Then This Atom Bomb Exploded and Melted the Polar Ice Cap."
    PoNow (19) 78, p. 41.

UKSTINS, R. A.
  "Avalon Mary: A 'Poim.'" BallSUF (19:4) Aut 78, p. 45.

ULLMAN, Leslie
  Fourteen poems. ArkRiv (4:2) 78, p. 21.
  "In Barcelona You Tried to Scream." AntR (36:2) Spr 78,
    p. 191.
  "Shade." SenR (9:1) Spr-Sum 78, p. 39.
  "The Voyeurs." SenR (9:1) Spr-Sum 78, p. 40.

UNGARETTI, Giuseppe
  "Finale" (tr. by Dora M. Pettinella). MalR (46) Ap 78, p. 146.

UNGER, Barbara
  "Corn Maiden." PoetC (10:2) 78, p. 15.
  "In Reply." Wind (29) 78, p. 45.
  "Libra." PoetC (10:2) 78, p. 16.
  "Making Phone Calls from the Drugstore." PoNow (20) 78,
    p. 45.
  "Making Phone Calls from the Drugstore." Zahir (9) 77, p. 48.
  "A Wild One." Wind (29) 78, p. 44.
  "Woman Poet." 13thM (4:1) 78, p. 86.
  "Woman Professor." MinnR (NS11) Aut 78, p. 27.

UNGER, David
  "Guitar or Moon" (tr. of Vicente Aleixandre, w. Lewis Hyde).
    ParisR (74) Aut-Wint 78, p. 33.

UNTERECKER, John
  "Bas-Relief at Banyuls." Salm (42) Sum-Aut 78, p. 122.
  "Bruises." VirQR (54:3) Sum 78, p. 497.
  "Dark Song." PraS (52:1) Spr 78, p. 108.
  "Falling." Pequod (2:4) 78, p. 61.
  "January Fragment." Pequod (2:4) 78, p. 59.
  "Letter: October." LittleM (11:4) Wint 78, p. 10.
  "Long Light at Evening." WestHR (32:3) Sum 78, p. 253.
  "Portrait." Kayak (48) Je 78, p. 36.
  "Toward." Pequod (2:4) 78, p. 60.
  "Unidentified" (for Susan Weston). VirQR (54:3) Sum 78, p. 498.

UPDIKE, John
"Ohio." AmerS (47:3) Sum 78, p. 325.
"Spanish Sonnets." NewYorker (54:23) 24 Jl 78, p. 25.
"Travel Tips." Bits (8) Jl 78.

UPTON, John
from Polyphemus: (9, 12, 21, 22) (tr. of Luis de Gongora y
Argote). Paint (7/8) Spr-Aut 77, p. 35.

UPTON, Lee
"The Ceremony of Small Girls." CalQ (13/14) Spr-Sum 78,
p. 84.
"Lust for the Lazy Sloe-Eyed." FourQt (27:2) Wint 78, p. 34.
"The Pickpocket." HiramPoR (25) Aut-Wint 78, p. 36.

URDANG, Constance
"The Absence of a Tradition." OP (25) Spr-Sum 78, p. 17.
"Daughters." OP (25) Spr-Sum 78, p. 24.
"Déjà Vu." OP (25) Spr-Sum 78, p. 18.
"Driving to Mexico." Nat (226:10) 18 Mr 78, p. 310.
"How to Make a Prairie." OP (25) Spr-Sum 78, p. 19.
"The Lone Woman of San Nicolas Island." OP (25) Spr-Sum 78,
p. 20.
"Walking Papers." Ascent (4:1) 78, p. 13.

USTINOVA, N.
"Walls" (tr. by John M. Gogol). NorthSR (8) Aut-Wint 78-79,
p. 30.

UYEHARA-HOFFMAN, Avron
"On Becoming a Canadian Citizen." WormR (70) 78, p. 52.
"Quasi-Political Lunch Hour." WormR (70) 78, p. 51.
"Speech Given at Lunchtime to a Convention of Bums, Hoboes &
Termagants." WormR (70) 78, p. 51.
"Spontaneous Juxtaposition No. 2." WormR (70) 78, p. 52.

UYENO, Keith
"Angling Form for 30 Foot Piers." Zahir (9) 77, p. 16.
"The Draftsman." Zahir (9) 77, p. 16.

VALENTINE, Jean
"December 21st." Field (18) Spr 78, p. 39.
"Letter from a Stranger." Nat (227:20) 9 D 78, p. 646.
"The Messenger." NewYorker (54:28) 28 Ag 78, p. 29.
"Robert Lowell (1917-1977)." Nat (226:5) 11 F 78, p. 153.
"Silences: A Dream of Governments." Field (18) Spr 78,
p. 38.

VALLEE, Lillian
"Ars Poetica?" (tr. of Czeslaw Milosz, w. the author). Antaeus
(30/31) Sum-Aut 78, p. 148.
"A Magic Mountain" (tr. of Czeslaw Milosz, w. the author).
Antaeus (30/31) Sum-Aut 78, p. 150.

"The Owners" (tr. of Czeslaw Milosz, w. the author). <u>Antaeus</u>
(30/31) Sum-Aut 78, p. 152.
"So little" (tr. of Czeslaw Milosz, w. the author). <u>Antaeus</u>
(30/31) Sum-Aut 78, p. 154.
"Vandeans" (tr. of Czeslaw Milosz, w. the author). <u>Antaeus</u>
(30/31) Sum-Aut 78, p. 153.

Van BRUNT, H. L.
"A Fable." <u>PoNow</u> (19) 78, p. 36.
"Fireflies." <u>PoNow</u> (19) 78, p. 36.
"Genesis." <u>Confr</u> (17) Aut-Wint 79, p. 37.
"Visitations." <u>GeoR</u> (32:3) Aut 78, p. 606.

VANCE, Ronald
"New Yet to Be" (for Ray Johnson). <u>SunM</u> (5) Aut 78, p. 15.

VANDER MOLEN, Robert
"Cricket Poem." <u>NowestR</u> (17:1) 78, p. 60.
"Sunny." <u>NewL</u> (45:2) Wint 78, p. 94.
"Suspicion." <u>Epoch</u> (27:3) Spr 78, p. 249.

VANDERSEE, Charles
"Fragment from a Travel Journal." <u>PoNow</u> (20) 78, p. 42.
"Horizon." <u>OP</u> (25) Spr-Sum 78, p. 31.
"Low Tide, Beachmont, 1897, by Maurice Prendergast." <u>OP</u>
(25) Spr-Sum 78, p. 25.
"The Poem about the Critics and New Jersey." <u>OP</u> (25) Spr-
Sum 78, p. 28.
"Poem Painted on a Birthday." <u>OP</u> (25) Spr-Sum 78, p. 26.
"Three Halves." <u>OP</u> (25) Spr-Sum 78, p. 30.

Van DUYN, Mona
"Caring for Surfaces." <u>LittleM</u> (11:3) Aut 77, p. 53.
"Goya's 'Two Old People Eating Soup.'" <u>Ploughs</u> (4:3) 78, p. 51.
"Letters from a Father." <u>Ploughs</u> (4:3) 78, p. 45.
"Letters from a Father." <u>PoNow</u> (19) 78, p. 4.
"Madrid, 1977." <u>Ploughs</u> (4:3) 78, p. 49.
"Ringling Brothers, Barnum and Bailey." <u>AmerPoR</u> (7:4) Jl-Ag
78, p. 22.
"Speak, Memory!" <u>Ploughs</u> (4:3) 78, p. 53.

Van HOUTEN, Lois
"Diminishments." <u>StoneC</u> (78:3) Aut 78, p. 12.
"Wild Strawberries." <u>Epos</u> (27:2) 77, p. 13.

Van SPANCKEREN, Kathryn
"The Pregnant Woman." <u>13thM</u> (4:1) 78, p. 74.
"The Time in Baja California." <u>Aspect</u> (71) Ap-Je 77, p. 40.
"The Time in Baja California." <u>CarolQ</u> (30:2) Spr-Sum 78,
p. 24.

Van WINCKEL, Nance
Fifteen poems. <u>ArkRiv</u> (4:2) 78, p. 38.
"How to Shoot Your Lover." <u>MidwQ</u> (19:2) Wint 78, p. 148.

VARGAS, R.
"Eleven Ways of Looking at a Tequila Bird." WormR (69) 78,
    p. 29.
"1/7/77: For the Father of My Fathers." WormR (69) 78,
    p. 31.
"3/6/77: The 'African Queen' Revisited." WormR (69) 78,
    p. 31.

VAS, István
"Ports" (tr. by Jascha Kessler). Nimrod (22:2) Spr-Sum 78,
    p. 99.

VASQUE, Francois
"My happiness." SmPd (42) Wint 78, p. 13.

VAZAKAS, Byron
"The Disciplines of Baudelaire." NewL (45:2) Wint 78, p. 26.
"The Enigmatic Traveler." NewL (45:2) Wint 78, p. 28.
"The Marble Distances." NewL (45:2) Wint 78, p. 28.
"'Valse Noble et Sentimentale.'" NewL (45:2) Wint 78, p. 27.

VEAZEY, Mary
"Sleeping with Thoreau." WindO (32) Sum-Aut 78, p. 7.
"Storing Books." WindO (32) Sum-Aut 78, p. 7.
"To My Purse." WindO (32) Sum-Aut 78, p. 8.

VECCHARELLI, Ann
"Owners' Manual." SmPd (44) Aut 78, p. 15.

VEENENDAAL, Cornelia
"The Serpent Moves On." Aspect (71) Ap-Je 77, p. 52.

VEGA, Janine Pommy
"The Birds" (for Armando). Falcon (17) 78, p. 5.
"The Lover." Tele (14) 78.
"November Landscape" (for Maureen Owen). Tele (14) 78.
"Promise of a Day" (for Irene Pommy). Tele (14) 78.
"Serenade" (for Jacquie Davis). Falcon (17) 78, p. 3.
"Song for César." Falcon (17) 78, p. 4.
"Trainride" (for Hugh). Tele (14) 78.

VENCLOVA, Tomas
"Three Poems" (tr. by Jonas Zdanys). Poetry (132:6) S 78,
    p. 342.

VENN, George
"Forgive Us...." PoetryNW (19:2) Sum 78, p. 21.

VENTADOUR, Fanny
"The Day Everything Stopped in Caucusville." Epos (27:2) 77,
    p. 15.
"Linguistics and the Open Road." Wind (29) 78, p. 46.

VERDERY, Daniel
"These Dolls." SewanR (86:2) Spr 78, p. 272.

VERHAGEN, Hans
"Three Poems." St. AR (4:3/4) 77-78, p. 110.

VERLAINE
"Ariettes Oubliées 111" (tr. by Frederick Morgan).   GreenfieldR
(6:3/4) Spr 78, p. 4.

VERZONI, David
from CLAUDIO COSTA sintomi di un lavoro: "'a,' in other
words 'b'" (tr. of Nanni Cagnone). Chelsea (37) 78, p. 117.

VIANT, William
"You had been drinking, Li Po." StoneC (78:2) Spr 78, p. 26.

VIAU, Theophile de
"Morning" (tr. by R. Sieburth and S. W. De Rachewiltz).   St. AR
(5:1) Aut-Wint 78, p. 60.

VICKERS, Zann
"Country Winter." CarouselQ (3:4) Wint 78, p. 9.

VICKERY, James
"Widow's Walk." SoDakR (16:3) Aut 78, p. 106.

VIDIKSIS, Pat
"On How She Burnt Herself Out." Glass (3:1/2/3) 78, p. 46.

VIERECK, Peter
"La Condition Humaine." PoNow (19) 78, p. 5.
"Progress, Anti-Classical (for Philipp and Raina Fehl).   Nat
(227:12) 14 O 78, p. 381.

VIGIL, Carmen
"Post Card." Tele (13) 77.
"To the Reader." Tele (13) 77.

VILLA, Emilio
from Attirbuti Dell'Arte Odierna: "Cy Twombly." Chelsea (37)
78, p. 43.
from Brunt H: "and." Chelsea (37) 78, p. 35.
from Heurarium: "Apoklypse." Chelsea (37) 78, p. 30.
from Heurarium: "Eructavit Cor Verbum." Chelsea (37) 78,
p. 23.
from Heurarium: "Homoioteleuton." Chelsea (37) 78, p. 27.
from Heurarium: "Hymnenee Pour." Chelsea (37) 78, p. 25.
from Heurarium: "Tour de Pouces." Chelsea (37) 78, p. 31.
from 3 Ideologie da Piazza del Popolo/Senza L'Imprimatur:
"La Mano di Pitagora." Chelsea (37) 78, p. 4.

VILLON, Francois
"A Debate between the Body and Heart of Villon" (tr. by Joe

Gonnella). Chowder (10/11) Aut-Wint 78-79, p. 36.

VINCENT, John Clark
"Bread." KanQ (10:1) Wint 78, p. 48.

VINES, Jay
"Misled." Wind (31) 78, p. 58.

VINZ, Mark
"Along the Way." GreenfieldR (6:3/4) Spr 78, p. 19.
"Anthology Piece." MinnR (NS10) Spr 78, p. 56.
"Changing the Guard." SlowLR (1/2) 78, p. 93.
"Contingency Plans." OhioR (19:3) Aut 78, pp. 73-88. Eleven
  poems.
"Dear Friend." SlowLR (1/2) 78, p. 94.
"Endangered Species." GreenfieldR (6:3/4) Spr 78, p. 18.

VIOLI, Paul
"Slump." PartR (45:3) 78, p. 440.

VIRGO, Sean
"Deathwatch on Skidegate Narrows" (for the bright covers).
  MalR (45) Ja 78, pp. 224-56.

VIVANTE, Arturo
"A Bowl of Kale Soup." NewL (44:3) Spr 78, p. 64.
"To a Victim of Radiation" (Cecil W. Kelly, died Jan. 1, 1959
  at Los Alamos). NewL (44:3) Spr 78, p. 65.

VIZENOR, Gerald
"Creation Fires." MoonsLT (2:4) 78, p. 49.

VOGELSANG, Arthur
"Circles and Waves." Antaeus (28) Wint 78, p. 130.
"Indian Summer in North America." ParisR (74) Aut-Wint 78,
  p. 89.
"Letter to Shakespeare." Iowa (9:2) Spr 78, p. 80.
"Poem: Here on Mars, it's simple." Antaeus (28) Wint 78,
  p. 129.
"Poem: Sometimes if you've been in and out of them a lot for
  you." ParisR (74) Aut-Wint 78, p. 111.
"Proletariat." ThRiPo (11/12) 78, p. 77.
"Saturday." ThRiPo (11/12) 78, p. 76.
"What to Say" (to M.S.). Iowa (9:2) Spr 78, p. 81.

VOIGT, Ellen Bryant
"Bamboo." Nat (226:15) 22 Ap 78, p. 480.
"The Diviner." Nat (226:22) 10 Je 78, p. 706.
"The Medium." OhioR (19:1) Wint 78, p. 94.
"Prey." Poetry (133:2) N 78, p. 90.
"The Starveling." Poetry (132:2) My 78, p. 79.

VOLK, Craig
"red bear and red fish." SoDakR (16:3) Aut 78, p. 110.

"winnie no ears." SoDakR (16:3) Aut 78, p. 108.

VOZNESENSKY, Andrei
"At the Glass-Blowing Factory" (tr. by Guy Daniels). Pequod
(2:4) 78, p. 25.

VRETTAKOS, Nikephoros
"There Is No Solitude" (tr. by M. Byron Raizis). BallSUF
(19:2) Spr 78, p. 50.

WADDELL, Sarah
"that bum is late." HangL (34) Wint 78-79, p. 62.
"working." HangL (34) Wint 78-79, p. 62.

WADE, Cory
"The End of Barnum & Bailey." SouthernR (14:1) Wint 78,
p. 82.
"Milk, Honey." SouthernPR (14:1) Wint 78, p. 81.

WADE, John Stevens
"Fingers." Confr (16) Spr-Sum 78, p. 113.
"A Penny's Worth." Poem (32) Mr 78, p. 14.
Some of My Best Friends Are Trees. Sparrow (35) 78. 28pp.
A Sparrow Poverty Pamphlet.

WAGNER, Linda
"Elegy, On the Drowning of the Children." Bleb/Ark (13) 78,
p. 57.
"Finale." Bleb/Ark (13) 78, p. 59.
"Flower Poem." Bleb/Ark (13) 78, p. 55.
"'I'd prefer the sea....'" Bleb/Ark (13) 78, p. 58.
"My space." Bleb/Ark (13) 78, p. 56.

WAGNER, Maryfrances
"So You Think You Want to Travel East." HiramPoR (25) Aut-
Wint 78, p. 37.

WAGONER, David
"Book Sale (Five Cents Each)." Hudson (31:2) Sum 78, p. 276.
"The Boy Who Became Sky." Antaeus (30/31) Sum-Aut 78,
p. 234.
"The Burial of Salmon-Flying." Salm (41) Spr 78, p. 115.
"Burial Song." Poetry (132:1) Ap 78, p. 9.
"Climbing Alone." GeoR (32:1) Spr 78, p. 61.
"Crossing a River." Poetry (132:1) Ap 78, p. 6.
"For a Woman Who Dreamed All the Horses Were Dying."
PraS (52:4) Wint 78-79, p. 355.
"How Canoe-maker Fought with Southeast." Antaeus (30/31)
Sum-Aut 78, p. 236.
"How Lies-in-the-Water Became Seaweed." VirQR (54:2) Spr
78, p. 287.
"How Owl Won Back His Father." SenR (9:1) Spr-Sum 78,
p. 41.
"How Raven Came to the Feast." Antaeus (30/31) Sum-Aut 78,

p. 237.
"How Raven Stole Beaver's Pond." SenR (9:1) Spr-Sum 78,
    p. 43.
"Into the Nameless Places." Field (19) Aut 78, p. 59.
"The Junior High School Band Concert." ParisR (72) Wint 77,
    p. 42.
"Love Song after a Nightmare." Hudson (31:2) Sum 78, p. 275.
"Lying Awake in A Desert." Salm (42) Sum-Aut 78, p. 111.
"The Man Who Ate Himself." Kayak (47) F 78, p. 22.
"The Man Who Killed Too Many." SenR (9:1) Spr-Sum 78, p. 44.
"Reading the Landscape." Salm (42) Sum-Aut 78, p. 112.
"Return to the River." Atl (242:2) Ag 78, p. 58.
"Salmon Boy." Antaeus (30/31) Sum-Aut 78, p. 232.
"Seeing Things." Poetry (132:1) Ap 78, p. 8.
"Songs My Mother Taught Me." PraS (52:4) Wint 78-79, p. 354.
"Trapline." SouthernR (14:2) Spr 78, p. 334.
"Walking in Broken Country." OhioR (19:1) Wint 78, p. 97.
"Watching the Harbor Seals." PraS (52:4) Wint 78-79, p. 353.
"Wood-Carver and Cedar Woman." OhioR (19:1) Wint 78, p. 96.

WAH, Fred
"Poem: outside its snowing." MalR (45) Ja 78, p. 61.

WAHLE, F. Keith
"The Deer." SenR (9:1) Spr-Sum 78, p. 78.
"Letter from South America." SenR (9:1) Spr-Sum 78, p. 80.
"Secrets." ParisR (73) Spr-Sum 78, p. 105.
"The Tax Collector." ThRiPo (11/12) 78, p. 78.

WAIN, John
"Enobarbus." SenR (9:2) Aut-Wint 78, p. 41.

WAINWRIGHT, Jeffrey
Nine poems. Stand (19:1) 77-78, p. 5.

WAITE, Wendy
"A Dolphin Here." LadHJ (95:11) N 78, p. 62.

WAITS, Tom
"Small Change." Stonecloud (7) 78, p. 87.
"Tom Traubert's Blues." Stonecloud (7) 78, p. 88.

WAKOSKI, Diane
"Searching for the Canto Fermo" (for Norman Hindley).
    MissouriR (1:1) Spr 78, p. 30.

WALCOTT, Derek
"Egypt, Tobago." Antaeus (30/31) Sum-Aut 78, p. 238.
"Forest of Europe" (For Joseph Brodsky). NewYorker (54:25)
    7 Ag 78, p. 28.
"Koenig of the River." NewYorker (54:21) 10 Jl 78, p. 27.
"R. T. S. L. (1917-1977)." ParisR (74) Aut-Wint 78, p. 119.
"Sabbaths." AmerPoR (7:3) My-Je 78, p. 3.

"The Saddhu of Couva." AmerPoR (7:3) My-Je 78, p. 6.
"The Sea Is History." ParisR (74) Aut-Wint 78, p. 115.
"The Star-Apple Kingdom." AmerPoR (7:3) My-Je 78, p. 3.

WALD, Diane
"The Blue Season." Kayak (47) F 78, p. 36.
"Employment on the Coast." WormR (68) 77, p. 111.
"For April." Kayak (47) F 78, p. 38.
"Green Shoulderpad." AntR (36:1) Wint 78, p. 88.
"I Don't Even Ask to Write Them Down." MassR (19:1) Spr 78,
   p. 200.
"In My Fashion." WormR (68) 77, p. 112.
"Initial Meeting." WormR (68) 77, p. 111.
"Privileged Information." Kayak (47) F 78, p. 37.
"Secrecy." MassR (19:1) Spr 78, p. 199.
"The Unattainable." Kayak (47) F 78, p. 37.

WALD, Eva
"The Hot Line." Kayak (47) F 78, p. 39. Found poem.

WALDEN, William
"Areal Warfare." Atl (242:5) N 78, p. 68.

WALDMAN, Anne
"Mauve Flowers of the Ubiquitous Wisteria." PartR (45:3) 78,
   p. 445.

WALDROP, Keith
"Covering." ColEng (39:7) Mr 78, p. 828.
"Like a Vanity." ColEng (39:7) Mr 78, p. 830.
"Scape." ColEng (39:7) Mr 78, p. 829.

WALDROP, Rosmarie
"Regaining the Day." Epoch (27:3) Spr 78, p. 245.
"The Senses Briefly: A Letter." PartR (45:1) 78, p. 23.
"The Senses Inevitably: A Davy Crockett Hat." ColEng (39:7)
   Mr 78, p. 831.

WALKER, Christina Lynne
"Amagansett, Late Winter." AmerPoR (7:1) Ja-F 78, p. 45.

WALKER, Daniel
"Dying Harvest." FourQt (27:4) Sum 78, p. 25.

WALKER, David
"Interlude with René Char." AntR (36:3) Sum 78, p. 367.

WALKER, Jeanne Murray
"Ariadne." Poetry (132:6) S 78, p. 323.
"The B Movie." Poetry (132:6) S 78, p. 325.
"Observations of a Woman at Needlepoint, Listening to a Man
   Who Can Talk." PoetC (10:2) 78, p. 25.
"There Conveys Meaning" (For Bill Pepicello). Poetry (132:6) S
   78, p. 324.

WALKER, Joseph
"My Friend Is Buried in the Garden." CarouselQ (3:3) Aut 78,
    p. 16.

WALKER, Lawrie
"War Effort." Stand (19:1) 77-78, p. 47.

WALKER, Lois V.
"Afterclaps." Hand (2) 78, p. 212.
"Inland." CarouselQ (3:4) Wint 78, p. 35.

WALKER, Stephen Robert
"Van Meter, 1958, 1972." Wind (29) 78, p. 12.

WALKER, Ted
"Mountain Ponies." NewYorker (54:26) 14 Ag 78, p. 38.

WALLACE, Jon
"In April." Wind (30) 78, p. 53.
"The Poet, Older and Far from Home, Turns Melancholy."
    Wind (30) 78, p. 53.

WALLACE, Robert
"Spare the Pickle and Spoil the Child." PoetryNW (19:3) Aut 78,
    p. 39.

WALLACE, Ronald
"At the St. Louis Institute of Music." ParisR (73) Spr-Sum 78,
    p. 42.
"Cleaning House." Northeast (3:5) Spr-Sum 78, p. 51.
"Doing the Laundry." HiramPoR (24) Spr-Sum 78, p. 37.
"Drought." PoetryNW (19:3) Aut 78, p. 8.
"Drowned Children." CarolQ (30:2) Spr-Sum 78, p. 59.
"Extracting the Honey." ParisR (73) Spr-Sum 78, p. 43.
"Fat." PoNow (19) 78, p. 40.
"First Love." Poem (33) Jl 78, p. 6.
"Insulation." MidwQ (19:2) Wint 78, p. 143.
"Making Bread." NewOR (5:4) 78, p. 360.
"Old Times." Kayak (48) Je 78, p. 61.
"Potatoes." Nimrod (22:2) Spr-Sum 78, p. 78.
"Prayer for Fish." NowestR (17:1) 78, p. 54.
"Second Coming." Poem (33) Jl 78, p. 5.
"Sisters." Poem (33) Jl 78, p. 7.
"Tossa: Diagnosis." Nimrod (22:2) Spr-Sum 78, p. 79.

WALLIN, Stephen
"Autobiographical" (for Michael Harper). OP (26) Aut-Wint 78,
    p. 25.
"Daddy Flex." OP (26) Aut-Wint 78, p. 20.
"Your Dimple" (for Trisha). OP (26) Aut-Wint 78, p. 26.

WALLING, Donovan R.
"John and Kurt and the Rest." WindO (33) Aut-Wint 78-79.

"The Stars Are Always There." WindO (33) Aut-Wint 78-79.
"To the Student in the First Row." WindO (33) Aut-Wint 78-79.

WALSH, Charlie
"Hymn #40." Tele (14) 78.
"Hymn #72." Tele (14) 78.

WALSH, Donald D.
"Biography for the Use of Birds" (tr. of Jorge Carrera
   Andrade). AmerPoR (7:4) Jl-Ag 78, p. 20.

WALSH, Dorothy
"Untitled." CarouselQ (3:2) Sum 78, p. 2.

WALSH, Marty
"Hansel." HiramPoR (24) Spr-Sum 78, p. 38.

WALTER, Linda G.
"Mirror Image." Obs (4:1) Spr 78, p. 80.
"Through the Windows." Obs (4:1) Spr 78, p. 80.

WALTER, Nina Willis
"Shock Treatment." Wind (28) 78, p. 10.

WANBERG, C. G.
"Because the Mexican Gardener Noticed." SenR (9:1) Spr-Sum
   78, p. 68.
"Markings." SenR (9:1) Spr-Sum 78, p. 69.

WANG, Buster K.
"Clairvoyance." PoNow (20) 78, p. 42.

WANG, Karl
"Climate." GreenfieldR (6:3/4) Spr 78, p. 166.
from Unfinished Letters of an Opium Smoker. Zahir (9) 77,
   p. 64.

WANIEK, Marilyn
"Animals Who Remember." GeoR (32:4) Wint 78, p. 866.
"I Decide Not to Have Children." GeoR (32:1) Spr 78, p. 44.
"I Imagine Driving Across Country." Hudson (31:1) Spr 78,
   p. 114.
"My Grandfather Walks in the Woods." Hudson (31:1) Spr 78,
   p. 115.
"Other Women's Children." GeoR (32:1) Spr 78, p. 45.

WARD, Candice
"Eyrie." Pan (19) 77, p. 49.
"Gazelle." Pan (19) 77, p. 49.
"Landscapes of Lexica." Pan (19) 77, p. 48.

WARD, Diane
from Citizens Band: "Staircase fanfare comes across the night."

LaB (11) 78, p. 49.
"Even If" (for Tad Wanveer). LaB (10) 78, p. 56.
"Intensive Care." LaB (11) 78, p. 53.

WARD, Frank
"Prune." BallSUF (19:4) Aut 78, p. 50.

WARD, J. P.
"Calvin." Poetry (131:5) F 78, p. 288.
"The Guards." Poetry (131:5) F 78, p. 286.
"The Word-Hoard." Poetry (131:5) F 78, p. 289.

WARD, Robert
"The San Francisco Rowing Club." NoAmR (263:2) Sum 78,
    p. 10.

WARD, Robert R.
"Killing Time." KanQ (10:2) Spr 78, p. 59.

WARDEN, Marine Robert
"Lyrics from Two Lands." Bachy (13) Aut-Wint 78-79, p. 87.
"No One Asked." Bachy (13) Aut-Wint 78-79, p. 87.
"October." Bachy (13) Aut-Wint 78-79, p. 86.

WARDLEY, Lynn
"Chinook." Madem (84:10) O 78, p. 234.

WARE, Kathy
"The Dump Lady." Chomo (5:1) Sum 78, p. 35.

WARGO, Allen
"In November the President Waits for the Prophet's Return."
    SouthernHR (12:3) Sum 78, p. 242.

WARMBROD, Nancy Compton
"Thanksgiving Day." EngJ (67:5) My 78, p. 60.

WARREN, Rebecca
"Eggplant." GRR (9:2) 78, p. 150.

WARREN, Robert Penn
"An Argument for Prayer." SouthernR (14:2) Sum 78, p. 306.
"Better Than Counting Sheep." NewYRB (25:17) 9 N 78, p. 27.
"Boyhood in Tobacco Country, at Sunset." Antaeus (30/31) Sum-
    Aut 78, p. 241.
"The Cross." NewYorker (54:33) 2 O 78, p. 36.
"Diver." SouthernR (14:2) Spr 78, p. 303.
"Evening Hour." GeoR (32:2) Sum 78, p. 282.
"Function of Blizzard." Antaeus (30/31) Sum-Aut 78, p. 242.
"Heart of the Backlog." NewYorker (53:50) 30 Ja 78, p. 34.
"Inevitable Frontier." NewYorker (54:4) 13 Mr 78, p. 36.
"Last Laugh." NewYorker (54:17) 12 Je 78, p. 34.
"Not Quite Like a Top." NewYRB (25:2) 23 F 78, p. 36.

from Now and Then: Poems 1976-1978: "Last Laugh." NewRep
   (179:14) 30 S 78, p. 35.
"Praise." Atl (241:6) Je 78, p. 45.
"Rather Like a Dream." SouthernR (14:2) Spr 78, p. 304.
"Somewhere." SouthernR (14:2) Spr 78, p. 305.
"Star Fall." YaleR (67:3) Spr 78, p. 419.
"Truth-Seeker, Half-Naked, At Night, Running Down Beach South
   of San Francisco." Atl (242:6) D 78, p. 64.
"Waking to Tap of Hammer." YaleR (67:3) Spr 78, p. 418.

WARROCK, Anna M.
"Monet." Aspect (71) Ap-Je 77, p. 48.

WASSERMAN, E. H.
"Ananke." AmerPoR (7:6) N-D 78, p. 38.
"The Rowers." AmerPoR (7:6) N-D 78, p. 38.

WATERHOUSE, Elizabeth
"Somnambulism." HarvAd (111:3) Ap 78, p. 22.

WATERMAN, Cary
"Flight." SoDakR (16:2) Sum 78, p. 30.
"Getting Old." Northeast (3:6) Wint 78-79, p. 6.
"Matins" (for Carol and Robert). Northeast (3:6) Wint 78-79,
   p. 6.
"Pilgrimage" (for Charlie). Tendril (3) Aut 78, p. 46.

WATERS, Michael
"Black Leaves." MissouriR (1:1) Spr 78, p. 22.
"The Blind." GeoR (32:1) Spr 78, p. 169.
"Dachau Moon." AmerPoR (7:4) Jl-Ag 78, p. 35.
"The Dead." AmerPoR (7:4) Jl-Ag 78, p. 35.
"Drunk with Cavafy." Aspen (5) Spr 78, p. 75.
"Leaving Tracks." PoNow (19) 78, p. 46.
"Locomotive." SouthernPR (18:1) Spr 78, p. 24.
"One Degree." NewOR (5:4) 78, p. 322.
"Salad" (for my grandmother). MissouriR (1:1) Spr 78, p. 23.
"The Scent of Apples." GeoR (32:1) Spr 78, p. 171.
"The Scent of White Roses." Aspen (5) Spr 78, p. 74.
"The Wax Apple." SlowLR (1/2) 78, p. 43.
"Wedding Poem." AmerPoR (7:4) Jl-Ag 78, p. 35.

WATKINS, Barbara
"Josefa Kankovska." 13thM (4:1) 78, p. 7.

WATSON, Burton
from Man'yōshū: Twenty poems (tr.). Montra (4) 78, p. 143.
Sixty-four poems (tr. of Saigyō). Montra (4) 78, p. 164.

WATSON, Celia
from Memories from Out of the Mouth of God: (9-11). NewRivR
   (2:2) 78, p. 19.

WATSON, Ellen
"Easter Sunday." Nimrod (22:2) Spr-Sum 78, p. 80.

WATSON, Tamara
"You May As Well Know." PoNow (20) 78, p. 43.

WATTEN, Barrett
"Protection." LaB (11) 78, p. 54.

WAX, Judith
"That Was the Year That Was." Playb (25:1) Ja 78, p. 122.
"To a Designer of Women's Fashions." Playb (25:12) D 78,
    p. 233.
"To a TV Programer." Playb (25:12) D 78, p. 232.
"To the King of the Dance Floor." Playb (25:12) D 78, p. 232.
"To the New Literary Luminaries." Playb (25:12) D 78, p. 233.
"To the Queen of the Orgy." Playb (25:12) D 78, p. 233.

WAYMAN, Tom
"A Chilean Incident." MalR (48) O 78, p. 77.

WAYNE, Jane
"Outpatient." WebR (4:1) Spr 78, p. 29.
"Refuge." WebR (4:1) Spr 78, p. 28.

WAYNE, Jane O.
"Interval." WindO (33) Aut-Wint 78-79.
"A Physical Examination." WindO (33) Aut-Wint 78-79.

WEATHERS, Ed
"Seven Months." SouthernHR (12:1) Wint 78, p. 6.

WEATHERS, Winston
"The Red Jugs." Comm (105:16) 18 Ag 78, p. 524.

WEBB, Charles
"Ambition." Pan (19) 77, p. 43.
"Breakfast of Champions." WormR (68) 77, p. 107.
"Directions." Zahir (9) 77, p. 19.
"Encountering the Soul Mate." WormR (68) 77, p. 105.
"The Find." Zahir (9) 77, p. 18.
"I'm in the Kitchen When the Phone Rings." WindO (31) Wint-
    Spr 78, p. 39.
"Just Passing Through, Webb Hits Reno, Navada." WormR (68)
    77, p. 106.
"Long Distance, 8 A.M." WormR (68) 77, p. 107.
"Marking Time." Zahir (9) 77, p. 19.
"Mostly You're Doing Great to Manage." WindO (31) Wint-Spr
    78, p. 40.
"Needing a File." GreenfieldR (6:3/4) Spr 78, p. 89.
"A Situation of Extreme Hopelessness." WormR (68) 77, p. 105.
"Swinging the River." GreenfieldR (6:3/4) Spr 78, p. 88.
"Webb, Cowering in a Corner of the Sundance Inn." DacTerr

(15) Wint-Spr 77-78, p. 56.
"Winged Victory." WormR (68) 77, p. 106.
Zinjanthropus Disease. Madrona (15/16) 78. Entire issue.

WEBB, Phyllis
"Free Translations." MalR (45) Ja 78, p. 316.
"Socrates." MalR (46) Ap 78, p. 62.
"Still there are wars and crimes of war." MalR (45) Ja 78,
    p. 318.

WEBB, Rhonda
"Ode to Niel." NewL (45:1) Aut 78, p. 55.

WEBBER, Jan Farnum
"Bones of the Fire." NowestR (17:1) 78, p. 35.
"Free." Nowest (17:1) 78, p. 34.

WEBBER, Joan
"After a Year." HiramPoR (25) Aut-Wint 78, p. 38.
"Shadowless." PraS (52:4) Wint 78-79, p. 320.

WEBBER, Malory
"Jealousy as a Children's Game." PoetryNW (19:1) Spr 78,
    p. 19.
"Losing Time." PoetryNW (19:1) Spr 78, p. 18.

WEBER, Ron
"Afterlight" (for Helen Frankenthaler). Tele (14) 78.
"Out." PoNow (20) 78, p. 43.
"Water Color." Tele (14) 78.

WEBSTER, Anne
"Sunday Prayer." SouthernPR (18:1) Spr 78, p. 60.

WEEDEN, Craig
"Heron, Grazing." SouthernPR (18:1) Spr 78, p. 59.
"Love: Another Twist." NewOR (5:4) 78, p. 357.
"Mugging in a Small Park." SmPd (42) Wint 78, p. 13.
"The Neighborly Thing." EnPas (7) 78, p. 25.
"Since." SouthernPR (18:1) Spr 78, p. 59.
"What Warren's Wife Said." PoNow (20) 78, p. 43.

WEEKS, Ramona
"Abortions." BallSUF (19:4) Aut 78, p. 9.
"Drinking in a White Field with a Boll Weevil." PoetryNW
    (19:3) Aut 78, p. 26.
"Ladypoem." BallSUF (19:4) Aut 78, p. 44.

WEIANT, Ted
"Sunday Afternoon." SouthernPR (18:1) Spr 78, p. 66.

WEIDMAN, Phil
"Choices." WormR (68) 77, p. 115.

"East Area Rapist." WormR (68) 77, p. 116.
"House Sitter." WormR (68) 77, p. 115.
"Protege." WormR (68) 77, p. 115.
"Suburban Types." WormR (68) 77, p. 116.
Twelve poems. WormR (72) 78, p. 150.

WEIGEL, Tom
"Beau Monde." Tele (14) 78.
"Exile." ParisR (73) Spr-Sum 78, p. 111.

WEIGL, Bruce
"Elegy for Charles Sonny Liston 1932-1970." QW (5) Wint 78,
   p. 47.
"For Raskolnikov." Zahir (9) 77, p. 31.
"I Have Had My Time Rising and Singing." QW (5) Wint 78,
   p. 46.
"If You Forgive Me." Zahir (9) 77, p. 31.
"Passive Resistance." PoNow (20) 78, p. 43.
"Strawberries." PoNow (20) 78, p. 43.

WEIL, James L.
"Portrait of the Artist Painting Her Son." Hand (2) 78, p. 147.

WEINBERGER, Eliot
"Distant Neighbor" (tr. of Octavio Paz). Montra (4) 78, p. 184.
"Exclamation" (tr. of Octavio Paz). Montra (4) 78, p. 183.
"Stars and Cricket" (tr. of Octavio Paz). Montra (4) 78,
   p. 184.
Ten poems (tr. of Homero Aridjis). Montra (4) 78, p. 184.
Ten poems (tr. of José Juan Tablada). Montra (4) 78, p. 182.
"Two Airs." Montra (4) 78, p. 88.
from 212: "love at last sight." Montra (4) 78, p. 89.

WEINER, Hannah
"May 4." Tele (13) 77.

WEINERMAN, Chester
"Mount Morris Baths, New York." PoNow (20) 78, p. 44.

WEINGART, S. L.
"Good Friday 1976 at the Sailing Ship Mayflower." SewanR
   (86:4) Aut 78, p. 525.
"The Season in Connecticut." SewanR (86:4) Aut 78, p. 526.

WEINGARTEN, Roger
"The Tale of the Green Rose." SenR (9:1) Spr-Sum 78, p. 83.

WEINLEIN, Gregg Thomas
"Outside the Circle." CarouselQ (3:1) Spr 78, p. 21.

WEINMAN, Paul
"My Grandmother Had Knobby Knees." Pig (5) 78, p. 73.
"Trying to Find Something to Warm Old." Wind (28) 78, p. 60.
"Where Family Picnics Were Celebrated." Wind (28) 78, p. 60.

WEISS, David
"Broken Twig, Colorado" (for Jim Galvin).   GreenfieldR (6:3/4)
     Spr 78, p. 116.
"To My Right Hand Pulling in a Circle of Thresher of Nouns and
     Verbs. " PoetryNW (19:4) Wint 78-79, p. 34.

WEISS, Mark
"it was the coldest day of my paper-route. " Some (9) 78, p. 41.
"A Meditation on Charles Ives. " Hand (2) 78, p. 99.

WEISS, Sigmund
"The Pause Between. " CarouselQ (3:4) Wint 78, p. 14.

WEISS, Theodore
"Art in America. " AmerPoR (7:5) S-O 78, p. 35.
"The Quarrel. " AmerPoR (7:5) S-O 78, p. 35.
"The Rapture" (for Katy). AmerPoR (7:5) S-O 78, p. 35.

WEISSBORT, Daniel
"Autumn in Novenskaya" (tr. of Joseph Brodsky, w. the author).
     Iowa (9:4) Aut 78, p. 2.
"Part of Speech" (tr. of Joseph Brodsky). Poetry (131:6) Mr 78,
     p. 311.
"The Rustle of Acacias" (tr. of Joseph Brodsky, w. the author).
     Iowa (9:4) Aut 78, p. 1.

WEITZEL, Allen Field
"bird song. " SmPd (43) Spr 78, p. 16.
"Pinnacle. " CarouselQ (3:1) Spr 78, p. 22.
"The Successful Marriage. " CarouselQ (3:1) Spr 78, p. 22.

WELCH, Don
"The Coyote. " BallSUF (19:4) Aut 78, p. 30.
"Deer, at Night. " KanQ (10:3) Sum 78, p. 102.
"Old Dick. " KanQ (10:3) Sum 78, p. 94.

WELCH, Jim
"Meeting. " KanQ (10:2) Spr 78, p. 16.
"Opera on the Adriatic. " DeKalb (11:1/2) Aut-Wint 77-78,
     p. 68.
"Response. " Shen (29:3) Spr 78, p. 17.

WELCH, Lillane
"Life of Two Clowns. " StoneC (78:3) Aut 78, p. 7.

WELCH, Marie de L.
"Interrealiste. " AmerPoR (7:3) My-Je 78, p. 47.

WELCH, Michael Irene
"Winter Water Song. " Tele (13) 77.
"You ... Rain. " Tele (13) 77.

WELISH, Marjorie
"Careers. " PartR (45:4) 78, p. 586.

"Greenhouses and Gardens." PartR (45:1) 78, p. 21.

WELLS, Nigel
from Three Snow Poems: "Stjernstedt in yellow." Stand (19:3)
    78, p. 30.

WELLS, Will
"Cicada Husk on a Fencepost." SouthernPR (18:1) Spr 78, p. 53.
"Counting Coup." GRR (9:1) 78, p. 32.
"Filthy Rich." BelPoJ (28:3) Spr 78, p. 2.
"The Fisherman" (for my father). BelPoJ (28:3) Spr 78, p. 3.
"A Photo of My Grandfather Reuben." GRR (9:1) 78, p. 31.
"The Retriever" (for Jim Smith). BelPoJ (28:3) Spr 78, p. 2.
"Sleep" (for Ronda). GRR (9:1) 78, p. 31.
"Vertigo." SouthernPR (18:1) Spr 78, p. 52.

WELT, Bernard
"Adagietto for Tim Dlugos." SunM (5) Aut 78, p. 26.
"Grace" (for Tim Dlugos). SunM (5) Aut 78, p. 24.
"The Tomb of Edgar Poe." FourQt (27:3) Spr 78, p. 19.

WERTMAN, Carl
"Lovers #10." BallSUF (19:4) Aut 78, p. 21.

WEST, Anthony
"Median Strip." PoetryNW (19:2) Sum 78, p. 41.

WEST, Charles L., Jr.
"Two Points." EngJ (67:5) My 78, p. 64.

WEST, Michael
"Propertius I.1, II.4, II.9, II.33, and III.23" (tr.). Nimrod
    (22:2) Spr-Sum 78, pp. 87-92.
"3.21" (tr. of Propertius). Iowa (9:4) Aut 78, p. 83.

WESTBROOK, Donna
"Somewhere within you, live I." BlackF (2:2) Aut-Wint 78,
    p. 15.

WESTERFIELD, Nancy
"The Lawn Swing." FourQt (27:2) Wint 78, p. 33.
"Truck Plaza: Daybreak." FourQt (27:2) Wint 78, p. 32.
"The Man Who Saw UFO's." Comm (105:5) 3 Mr 78, p. 140.
"The Philatelist." ChrC (95:9) 15 Mr 78, p. 276.
"Time Piece." Confr (16) Spr-Sum 78, p. 144.
"'And Here the Soldiers Have Come Rapidly to Hastings.'"
    ColEng (39:8) Ap 78, p. 943.
"Rememberers." AAUP (64:1) Mr 78, p. 18.

WESTWOOD, Norma J.
"Rain." ChrC (95:19) 24 My 78, p. 565.

WHEATCROFT, John
"Breakfast in the Dining Room." BelPoJ (28:4) Sum 78, p. 17.

"49 + 5 Months." SoDakR (16:3) Aut 78, p. 104.
"The Habitues." Epos (27:2) 77, p. 9.
"How Metaphor Exposes." Poem (34) N 78, p. 18.
"The Intangibles." SoDakR (16:3) Aut 78, p. 102.

WHISLER, Robert F.
"Attraction." CarouselQ (3:2) Sum 78, p. 8.
"Biography II, Philadelphia." Wind (29) 78, p. 47.
"Biography IV, an American Poet." Wind (29) 78, p. 47.
"love." CarouselQ (3:3) Aut 78, p. 3.
"The Potter's Hand." CarouselQ (3:1) Spr 78, p. 11.

WHITCOMB, Kathy
"Shadow-black man." PikeF (1) Spr 78, p. 17.

WHITE, Claire Nicolas
"The Legend of St. Ursula." ParisR (72) Wint 77, p. 37.
"The Roses of Queens." NewYorker (54:35) 16 O 78, p. 139.
"To Sylvia Rediscovered." ParisR (72) Wint 77, p. 39.

WHITE, Gail
"The Fishers." SouthernHR (12:4) Aut 78, p. 363.
"Happy Endings." Poem (34) N 78, p. 10.
"In Their Deep Chambers." Pan (19) 77, p. 32.
"The Reason." Wind (29) 78, p. 29.
"A Refutation." Poem (34) N 78, p. 8.
"'You Can't See the Forest for the Trees.'" Poem (34) N 78,
   p. 9.

WHITE, Gina
"Solstice" (for my husband). NewRep (179:5) 29 Jl 78, p. 28.

WHITE, J. P.
"In Pursuit of Wings." Pan (19) 77, p. 77.
"Inside the Movie Palace." Pan (19) 77, p. 78.

WHITE, James L.
"Before the Birds." NorthSR (8) Aut-Wint 78-79, p. 45.
"Catholic Hill" (for John Shevlin). NorthSR (8) Aut-Wint 78-79,
   p. 46.
"Excerpts from a Juarez Journal, 1973" (for Ken and Burney).
   NorthSR (8) Aut-Wint 78-79, p. 47.
"5th and Hennepin." NorthSR (8) Aut-Wint 78-79, p. 46.
"The Salt Ecstasies." ParisR (74) Aut-Wint 78, p. 85.

WHITE, John L.
"late night horror shows." GreenfieldR (7:1/2) Aut 78, p. 92.
"The surgeon general recently." GreenfieldR (7:1/2) Aut 78,
   p. 37.

WHITE, Kenneth S.
"Of Cells and Breath." StoneC (78:3) Aut 78, p. 13.
"The Powers of a Conic Hat from Martinique." StoneC (78:1)
   Wint 78, p. 21.

WHITE, Kristin
"Christina's World." EngJ (67:5) My 78, p. 61.

WHITE, Mary Jane
"To Jeannie, On Losing the Farm: 1929." Iowa (9:4) Aut 78,
    p. 34.

WHITE, Roger
"Everybody's Writing Haiku: Why Not You?" WorldO (12:4) Sum
    78, p. 6.
"Mark Tobey: A Letter and Two Snapshots." WorldO (12:3) Spr
    78, p. 34.

WHITE, Sharon
from The Tana Poems: Eleven poems. Northeast (3:5) Spr-Sum
    78, pp. 27-35.

WHITE, Steven
"The Silent Sequence." Zahir (9) 77, p. 5.

WHITE, William M.
"Gold Record." NewRivR (2:2) 78, p. 66.
"Susan Awakes." Paint (9/10) Spr-Aut 78, p. 27.
"Susan's Birthday Party." Paint (9/10) Spr-Aut 78, p. 26.

WHITEHEAD, James
"Doing Bidness" (for William Harrison). SouthernR (14:4) Aut
    78, p. 741.
"His Slightly Longer Story Song." SouthernR (14:4) Aut 78,
    p. 740.
"Some Local Men after Their Election" (for President Jimmy
    Carter). SouthernR (14:4) Aut 78, p. 742.

WHITEMAN, John M., Jr.
"The Rider." GreenfieldR (7:1/2) Aut 78, p. 101.

WHITMAN, Cedric
"Voyage from Sudbury." NewRep (179:20) 11 Mr 78, p. 29.

WHITMAN, Ruth
"Seven Variations on Robert Schumann." Ploughs (4:2) 78,
    p. 30.
"Word." Agni (8) 78, p. 94.

WHITTEMORE, Reed
"The Whodunit Shaggy." Harp (256:1533) F 78, p. 22.

WHITTEN, Hubert N.
"Guilt." ChrC (95:27) 30 Ag-6 S 78, p. 790.

WICKE, R.
"Balance." JnlONJP (2:2) 77, p. 16.

WICKELHAUS, Martha
"Searching for Worms." QW (5) Wint 78, p. 8.

WICKERT, Max
"Born Lucky" (for Esther Swartz). AmerPoR (7:4) Jl-Ag 78,
    p. 22.

WICKLESS, Robert
"For the Old Men Asleep by the Waters." Shen (29:4) Sum 78,
    p. 75.

WIEGAND, Ronn
"Anemone." Kayak (49) O 78, p. 66.
"Artist with Seven Lives." Kayak (49) O 78, p. 67.
"Musee Des Beaux Arts." Kayak (49) O 78, p. 66.
"Piano Player." Kayak (49) O 78, p. 67.

WIEGNER, Kathleen K.
"In from the Cold." MinnR (NS10) Spr 78, p. 32.
"Seven Years Bad Luck." MinnR (NS10) Spr 78, p. 31.

WIENERS, John
"My Ownly Father in Heaven." Some (9) 78, p. 64.

WIENS, Paul
"Time for Dreams." NewWR (46:2) Mr-Ap 78, p. 27.

WIER, Dara
"The Contortionist." PoNow (20) 78, p. 30.
"Lucille Conceives." NewL (44:3) Spr 78, p. 38.
"Lucille Enters the Meat Market." NewL (44:3) Spr 78, p. 38.
"She Has This Phantom Limb." PoNow (20) 78, p. 30.
"Toad Suck Ferry." PoNow (20) 78, p. 30.
"Watering the Snakes." PoNow (20) 78, p. 30.

WIEZELL, Elsa
"I Have" (tr. by C. R. Carlisle). Nimrod (22:2) Spr-Sum 78,
    p. 102.
"Small Account" (tr. by C. R. Carlisle). Nimrod (22:2) Spr-
    Sum 78, p. 102.

WILBUR, Richard
"A Black Birch in Winter." PoNow (19) 78, p. 7.
"Cottage Street, 1953." PoNow (19) 78, p. 7.
"Shad-Time." NewYorker (54:15) 29 My 78, p. 30.

WILCOX, Patricia
"A Public and Private Hearth." Poem (32) Mr 78, p. 54.
    Selections.

WILD, Peter
"California." CutB (10) Spr-Sum 78, p. 14.

"Catholics." PoNow (19) 78, p. 14.
"Confidence." CutB (10) Spr-Sum 78, p. 13.
"Cristades Saguaros." AmerPoR (7:4) Jl-Ag 78, p. 37.
"Cycads." AAR (28) 78, p. 3.
"Dawn." AmerPoR (7:4) Jl-Ag 78, p. 37.
"Edward C. Pulaski." CutB (11) Aut-Wint 78, p. 77.
"Elijah." GreenfieldR (6:3/4) Spr 78, p. 58.
"Folding Candle Lanterns." Glass (3:1/2/3) 78, p. 12.
"Forest Ranger." NewOR (6:1) 78, p. 40.
"Frontier." LittleM (11:4) Wint 78, p. 46.
"Heretics." Epoch (27:2) Wint 78, p. 151.
"Jeanne D'Arc." NoAmR (263:4) Wint 78, p. 41.
"Natural Gas." Bits (8) Jl 78.
"Ouray." Glass (3:1/2/3) 78, p. 13.
"Photographer." Bits (8) Jl 78.
"Squirrels." PraS (52:2) Sum 78, p. 192.
"Whales." Agni (9) 78, p. 108.
"Wind River Mountains." Epoch (27:2) Wint 78, p. 152.

WILEY, Eddie
    "She Is Still the Same." GreenfieldR (7:1/2) Aut 78, p. 57.

WILEY, Harold
    "The Changeling." SoCaR (11:1) N 78, p. 69.
    "Edges." SoCaR (10:2) Ap 78, p. 65.

WILK, Melvin
    "Hart Crane." KanQ (10:4) Aut 78, p. 39.

WILKINS, W. R. "Bill"
    "Mediiiiccc!" PikeF (1) Spr 78, p. 26.
    "Seagulls Flying Patrol." Wind (31) 78, p. 71.

WILKINSON, Anne
    "Poems" (tr. of Anna Akhmatova, w. Judith Hemschemeyer).
        Pequod (2:4) 78, p. 16.

WILKINSON, Constance
    "Gathering In." Nimrod (22:2) Spr-Sum 78, p. 81.
    "Outside my window, the rivers are broken." Nimrod (22:2)
        Spr-Sum 78, p. 82.

WILL, Frederic
    "For There Was Wind, Max." MassR (19:2) Sum 78, p. 274.
    "The German Fellow." ParisR (73) Spr-Sum 78, p. 116.
    "In the Hollow Provided." ParisR (73) Spr-Sum 78, p. 116.
    "Max Plays with Textures of Words and Things." MassR (19:2)
        Sum 78, p. 275.
    "Tom and the Rebellion of the Carrots." ParisR (73) Spr-Sum
        78, p. 114.
    "Tom Washes the Minerals." ParisR (73) Spr-Sum 78, p. 114.
    "Tom's Military Career." ParisR (73) Spr-Sum 78, p. 115.

WILLARD, Nancy
"The Ceremony of the Coconut." OP (25) Spr-Sum 78, p. 40.
"Fairy Tale." PoNow (19) 78, p. 36.
"Family Picnic with Wine and Water." MassR (19:3) Aut 78,
    p. 474.
"Lovely Anna, Crazy Anna." OP (25) Spr-Sum 78, p. 41.
"My Life on the Road with Bread and Water." Kayak (49) O 78,
    p. 42.
"My Life on the Road with Bread and Water." MissouriR (2:1)
    Aut 78, p. 42.
"Old Old Story." OP (25) Spr-Sum 78, p. 42.
"The Photographer." OP (25) Spr-Sum 78, p. 38.
"Psalm for the Ear Drum." OP (25) Spr-Sum 78, p. 44.
"Questions My Son Asked Me, Answers I Never Gave Him."
    Field (19) Aut 78, p. 50.
"The Sleep of the Painted Ladies." MassR (19:3) Aut 78, p. 473.
"Two from the Sports Page." Kayak (47) F 78, p. 20.

WILLEMS, J. Rutherford
"Ten (a fugue)." Hand (2) 78, p. 106.

WILLIAMS, Beryle
"The Night Flute." MoonsLT (2:4) 78, p. 68.

WILLIAMS, Evan Gwyn
"Poems from Machynlleth." Stand (18:4) 77, p. 63.

WILLIAMS, Julie
"Close Out." NewL (45:1) Aut 78, p. 57.

WILLIAMS, Margaret Edwards
"Empowerment in Ebony." NegroHB (41:1) Ja-F 78, p. 786.

WILLIAMS, Miller
"And I Have Witnesses" (tr. of Giuseppe Gioachino Belli).
    SouthernR (14:3) Sum 78, p. 465.
"Beauty" (tr. of Giuseppe Gioachino Belli). SouthernR (14:3)
    Sum 78, p. 461.
"Evening: A Studio in Rome." Poetry (132:5) Ag 78, p. 280.
"For Pasolini" (tr. of Franco Fortini). NewOR (5:4) 78,
    p. 320.
"For Rebecca, for Whom Nothing Has Been Written Page after
    Page." Poetry (132:5) Ag 78, p. 276.
"Green Mansions." SouthernR (14:4) Aut 78, p. 744.
"In a Street in Florence" (tr. of Franco Fortini). NewOR (5:4)
    Aut 78, p. 321.
"Judgment Day" (tr. of Giuseppe Gioachino Belli). SouthernR
    (14:3) Sum 78, p. 463.
"Love and How It Becomes Important in Our Day to Day Lives."
    Poetry (132:5) Ag 78, p. 279.
"Main Street." SouthernR (14:4) Aut 78, p. 743.
"Martha and Magdalene" (tr. of Giuseppe Gioachino Belli).

WestHR (32:4) Aut 78, p. 315.
"Memphis, 2:00 P.M." PoNow (19) 78, p. 13.
"Sometimes You Stand There Waiting for the Paper to Be De-
    livered." SouthernR (14:4) Aut 78, p. 743.
"Style." Poetry (132:5) Ag 78, p. 277.
"'That Was the Mountain'" (tr. of Franco Fortini). NewOR
    (5:4) 78, p. 320.
"Why I Go to Roger's Pool Hall." PoNow (19) 78, p. 13.
"The Woman in the Room." Poetry (132:5) Ag 78, p. 278.

WILLIAMS, Patricia J.
"Caged Marriage." CarouselQ (3:3) Aut 78, p. 13.
"The Day Beth Froze in Old Ed's Pond." CarouselQ (3:3) Aut
    78, p. 13.

WILLIAMS, Peter
"Possible Migration in Pennsylvania." US1 (11) Aut 78, p. 3.

WILLIAMS, R. B.
"January in Salt Lake." SoCaR (11:1) N 78, p. 59.

WILLIAMS, Sherley
"Soul Saga." AmerPoR (7:3) My-Je 78, p. 15.

WILLIAMS, William Carlos
Eight poems. Antaeus (30/31) Sum-Aut 78, p. 26.

WILLIAMSON, Alan
"Childless Couple." Poetry (132:3) Je 78, p. 148.
"For My Grandfather" (F. A. Bächer, 1874-1968). VirQR (54:3)
    Sum 78, p. 496.
"Heaven." VirQR (54:3) Sum 78, p. 495.
"Sandy." Poetry (132:3) Je 78, p. 150.

WILLIAMSON, Craig
"A Riddle-Song for Duke Ellington." ColEng (39:8) Ap 78,
    p. 944.

WILLIAMSON, John
"Letter from Japan." St. AR (5:1) Aut-Wint 77-78, p. 29.
"Marriage." St. AR (4:3/4) 77-78, p. 22.
"Patricia." St. AR (5:1) Aut-Wint 78, p. 26.

WILLIS, Irene
"Antigone at the Morgue." BallSUF (19:4) Aut 78, p. 52.

WILLITTS, Martin, Jr.
"Father Would Like to Hear the Universe." Hand (2) 78, p. 67.
"The Train Station." Wind (31) 78, p. 35.

WILLSON, John
"Dream." Box (7) Spr 78, p. 25.

WILSON, Austin
"Snake Season. " <u>Wind</u> (31) 78, p. 2.

WILSON, David
"The Coffee. " St. AR (5:1) Aut-Wint 78, p. 121.
"The Line. " St. AR (5:1) Aut-Wint 78, p. 119.

WILSON, Edward
"Aubade. " <u>Epos</u> (27:2) 77, p. 25.
"August. " AmerPoR (7:6) N-D 78, p. 36.
"Henry. " PoNow (19) 78, p. 35.
"The Living Corpse. " Poetry (132:5) Ag 78, p. 256.
"The Miner. " SoCaR (10:2) Ap 78, p. 71.
"A Photograph of Mandelstam at 31. " SoCaR (10:2) Ap 78,
    p. 70.
"The Weekend Our Team Won. " Poetry (132:5) Ag 78, p. 258.

WILSON, Emily Herring
"Ann Eliza Young. " PoNow (20) 78, p. 44.
"The Bluebird of Happiness. " Wind (30) 78, p. 55.
"Driving Home. " Wind (30) 78, p. 55.

WILSON, Graeme
"To Be a Girl" (tr. of Sakutaro Hagiwara). WestHR (32:1) Wint
    78, p. 37.
"Water Weed" (tr. of Sakutaro Hagiwara). WestHR (32:1) Wint
    78, p. 36.
"White Cock" (tr. of Sakutaro Hagiwara). WestHR (32:1) Wint
    78, p. 36.
"World of Bacteria" (tr. of Sakutaro Hagiwara). WestHR (32:1)
    Wint 78, p. 35.

WILSON, Joseph
"The Return. " Tendril (2) Spr-Sum 78.

WILSON, Miles
"Last Spring. " CimR (44) Jl 78, p. 60.

WILSON, Norma
"The Hester Hoedown. " SoDakR (16:3) Aut 78, p. 9.

WILSON, Robley, Jr.
"The Islands. " Poetry (132:1) Ap 78, p. 23.
"Moving Out. " GeoR (32:3) Aut 78, p. 542.

WINANS, A. D.
"For My Critics. " PikeF (1) Spr 78, p. 27.
"How to Make It in the Small Press World. " Smudge (3) Aut
    78, p. 42.
"notes on a rainy day. " Confr (17) Aut-Wint 79, p. 150.
"Visiting Folsom Prison. " GreenfieldR (7:1/2) Aut 78, p. 117.
"The Would Be Assassins. " Smudge (3) Aut 78, p. 48.

WINDER, Barbara
"Lexicons: In Celebration of Word-Magic." ColEng (40:1) S 78,
p. 30.
"Medicine Bow National Park." ColEng (40:1) S 78, p. 31.
"Perjuries." Chomo (5:2) Aut-Wint 78, p. 69.

WINK, Johnny
"After Having Read Malcolm Cowley's Account of Hart Crane's
Midnight Visit to His Bed." KanQ (10:4) Aut 78, p. 39.

WINN, Howard
"Fragment 90: 'Dogs Bark at Strangers.'" GRR (9:3) 78,
p. 217.
"Schools of Poetry." Wind (29) 78, p. 48.
"Wife and Mother of Children Nearly Grown." Wind (29) 78,
p. 48.

WINNER, Robert
"The Youth Ghost." Confr (17) Aut-Wint 79, p. 191.

WINNING, Rebecca
"Sister." BallSUF (19:4) Aut 78, p. 16.

WINSLOW, Hall
"To a Laconian Graveyard." Epoch (28:1) Aut 78, p. 20.

WIRTZ, Lynda LaRocca
"I toppled the vase." JnlONJP (3:1) 78, p. 5.

WISE-MARTIN, Malva
"O. T. B." Glass (3:1/2/3) 78, p. 117.

WISKER, Alistair
"Tortoise." Stand (18:4) 77, p. 30.

WISOFF, Ellen
"The Opposite of a Still Life." PartR (45:1) 78, p. 20.

WISTEY, John
"Iowa Landscape." NoAmR (263:1) Spr 78, p. 42.

WITCHEL, John
"A Star." Epos (27:2) 77, p. 22.

WITHERUP, William
"Crows." PoNow (19) 78, p. 17.

WITSCHEL, John
"After the Storm." Glass (3:1/2/3) 78, p. 88.
"Falcons." Epos (27:1) 77, p. 13.
"In Desert Air." Poem (32) Mr 78, p. 26.
"The Isolation Tank" (for John Lilly). PraS (52:4) Wint 78-79,
p. 369.

"Pictures of the Next Life." Glass (3:1/2/3) 78, p. 87.
"Seeing." Poem (32) Mr 78, p. 28.
"Turtles." Epos (27:1) 77, p. 13.

WITT, Harold
"Again Odysseus." PoetryNW (19:4) Wint 78-79, p. 26.
"The Bat in Slow Motion." SouthwR (63:2) Spr 78, p. 149.
"Eratomania." WindO (31) Wint-Spr 78, p. 15.
"Henry Thinnes." GreenfieldR (6:3/4) Spr 78, p. 90.
"Love Poems." WindO (31) Wint-Spr 78, p. 14.
"Narcissus." NewL (44:3) Spr 78, p. 32.
"Now, Voyager." PoetryNW (19:4) Wint 78-79, p. 24.
"Obsessed with Sex." WindO (31) Wint-Spr 78, p. 15.
"Orville Kettle, Organist." GreenfieldR (6:3/4) Spr 78, p. 90.
"Sonnet." WindO (31) Wint-Spr 78, p. 14.
"Touched with Fairness." NewL (44:3) Spr 78, p. 32.

WITTE, John C.
"The Crotch Island Quarry, Maine." NewYorker (54:19) 26 Je
    78, p. 32.
"From Memory." GreenfieldR (6:3/4) Spr 78, p. 151.
"Terrified at the Family Reunion in Mendota, Illinois."
    GreenfieldR (6:3/4) Spr 78, p. 150.

WITTENBERG, Rudolf
"Beach." DeKalb (11:1/2) Aut-Wint 77-78, p. 70.

WITTLINGER, Ellen
"For the Girl Drowned Off the Provincetown Breakwater, March
    1975." Aspect (71) Ap-Je 77, p. 47.
"Her Name Might Be Magdelena." MassR (19:1) Spr 78, p. 22.

WIXON, Vincent
"Pete's Drive In, Logan, Utah." EngJ (67:5) My 78, p. 59.

WOESSNER, Warren
"Hard Winter." CutB (11) Aut-Wint 78, p. 49.
"Parvin State Park." Chowder (10/11) Aut-Wint 78-79, p. 28.

WOJAHN, David
"Distance." Iowa (9:3) Sum 78, p. 92.
"Driving Blind." DacTerr (15) Wint-Spr 77-78, p. 10.
"Wine." DacTerr (15) Wint-Spr 77-78, p. 11.

WOLF, Howard
"Of Her Silent Pressure." Nimrod (22:2) Spr-Sum 78, p. 83.

WOLFE, Benjamin
"Moonflower." CarouselQ (3:1) Spr 78, p. 7.
"Tortoise." CarouselQ (3:3) Aut 78, p. 23.

WOLFE, Kary Kilpatric
"There Will Be No Solace." StoneC (78:3) Aut 78, p. 32.

WOLFERT, Helen
"Letter to Rabbi Akiba." AmerPoR (7:3) My-Je 78, p. 43.

WOLIVER, Robbie
"The Monster, the Child." Zahir (9) 77, p. 52.

WOLVEN, Fred
"Studying Magritte." AAR (28) 78, p. 61.

WOOD, Jim
"Enigmas of Nature." Pan (19) 77, p. 41.

WOOD, John A.
"Afternoon with an Aesthete." Poetry (132:4) Jl 78, p. 200.
"Elegiac Stanza on a Photograph of Ethel Rosenberg in Her
   Kitchen." Poetry (132:4) Jl 78, p. 200.

WOOD, Krissy
"Going Home." NewL (45:1) Aut 78, p. 27.
"learning to keep quiet about it" (for Mary). NewL (45:1) Aut
   78, p. 27.

WOOD, Randy
"The Parting." QW (5) Wint 78, p. 48.

WOOD, Susan
"The Disappearance." Antaeus (30/31) Sum-Aut 78, p. 244.
"The Names of the Dead." Antaeus (30/31) Sum-Aut 78, p. 243.

WOODRUFF, Robin
"Aftermath." Paint (9/10) Spr-Aut 78, p. 7.

WOODS, Carl
"Alameda Park." Wind (29) 78, p. 4.
"Alba." Epos (27:2) 77, p. 31.
"Chinese River Village: Summer." Epos (27:2) 77, p. 31.
"Rock Out-Crop." Tele (14) 78.
"Round Dance." Wind (29) 78, p. 50.
"Sunday." CarouselQ (3:3) Aut 78, p. 7.
"Wet Spell." Epos (27:2) 77, p. 30.

WOOD-THOMPSON, Susan
"Generation." KanQ (10:2) Spr 78, p. 40.
"The Name." KanQ (10:2) Spr 78, p. 40.
"Prehistoric Pottery Design." ArizQ (34:3) Aut 78, p. 254.

WOOLFOLK, Ann
"Water Cress." US1 (11) Aut 78, p. 4.

WOOLSON, Peter
"The Crooked Man." Zahir (9) 77, p. 25.
"The Maryland Museum of Fire." WormR (72) 78, p. 145.
"Portrait." WormR (72) 78, p. 145.

WORKMASTER, S. C.
"The Second Civil War." DeKalb (11:1/2) Aut-Wint 77-78,
　　p. 71.

WORLEY, James
"Before My Very Eyes." ChrC (95:14) 19 Ap 78, p. 419.
"Continuum." ChrC (95:35) 1 N 78, p. 1035.
"Guineapig." ChrC (95:4) 1-8 F 78, p. 95.

WORTH, Valerie
"Body." NewL (45:2) Wint 78, p. 89.

WORTSMAN, Peter
"Overhearing Moosehead" (for Susanne). Zahir (9) 77, p. 61.

WOSTER, Kevin
"Tourists in Summer." SoDakR (16:2) Sum 78, p. 45.

WRAY, Ron
"The Midnight Department Store." Glass (3:1/2/3) 78, p. 33.

WRIGHT, C. D.
"Obedience of the Corpse." Field (19) Aut 78, p. 63.
"Trance." Field (19) Aut 78, p. 61.

WRIGHT, Carolyne
"Choosing My Name." Poetry (132:6) S 78, p. 340.
"The Trestle Bridge." AmerPoR (7:1) Ja-F 78, p. 47.

WRIGHT, Charles
"Called Back." ParisR (74) Aut-Wint 78, p. 105.
"Holy Thursday." Antaeus (30/31) Sum-Aut 78, p. 248.
"Self-Portrait." Antaeus (30/31) Sum-Aut 78, p. 247.
"Self Portrait." MissouriR (1:1) Spr 78, p. 15.
"Self-Portrait." NewEngR (1:1) Aut 78, p. 30.
"Virginia Reel." Antaeus (30/31) Sum-Aut 78, p. 244.

WRIGHT, Franz
"Autumn on West Lorain Street." AntR (36:2) Spr 78, p. 184.
"The Cemetery." Kayak (47) F 78, p. 53.
"End of Autumn, 1973." AntR (36:2) Spr 78, p. 183.
"Hand." Kayak (47) F 78, p. 53.
"Looking at My Own Face in a Tidepool." Durak (1) 78, p. 10.
"Return." Durak (1) 78, p. 11.
"The Sniper." Kayak (47) F 78, p. 52.
"The Wish." AntR (36:2) Spr 78, p. 182.
"Your Last Poem." AntR (36:2) Spr 78, p. 185.

WRIGHT, Fred W., Jr.
"Primal." DeKalb (11:3/4) Spr-Sum 78, p. 45.

WRIGHT, G. T.
"Lines Written a Few Miles Above Three Turkey Rain." DacTerr

(15) Wint-Spr 77-78, p. 65.
Nine poems. NorthSR (8) Aut-Wint 78-79, p. 33.
"Poker." PoetryNW (19:1) Spr 78, p. 24.

WRIGHT, James
  "Dawn Near an Old Battlefield, in a Time of Peace." Antaeus
    (30/31) Sum-Aut 78, p. 250.
  "Small Wild Crabs Delighting on Black Sand." NewYorker
    (54:1) 20 F 78, p. 44.
  "To the Cicada." GeoR (32:4) Wint 78, p. 755.

WRIGHT, Katharine
  "Flight." Epoch (28:1) Aut 78, p. 51.
  "Virgins Wading Toward the Sea." Epoch (28:1) Aut 78, p. 50.

WRIGHT, Rebecca
  "The economics of the calendar." Tele (14) 78.
  "Rapid Poems." Tele (14) 78.
  "Seven Days." Tele (14) 78.
  "Swept Away." Tele (14) 78.
  "Up the Earth." Tele (14) 78.
  "Wednesday Poem" (for John Godfrey). Tele (14) 78.

WRIGHT, Terry
  "Macho Scherzo." WindO (31) Wint-Spr 78, p. 17.
  "Nothing to Eat." WindO (31) Wint-Spr 78, p. 17.
  "Seven Sins." Pig (4) 78, p. 36.

WRIGLEY, Robert
  "Coroner's Report." PoetryNW (19:1) Spr 78, p. 36.
  "Oh Yeah, the Mine Talks." PoetryNW (19:1) Spr 78, p. 35.
  "Song of the Trapped Miners." PoetryNW (19:1) Spr 78, p. 36.
  "Yard Work." Chowder (10/11) Aut-Wint 78-79, p. 29.

WROBEL, Sylvia
  "For Gabriel." YellowBR (10) 78, p. 4.

WUEST, Barbara
  "Abandoned House in West Virginia." Wind (30) 78, p. 57.
  "Aunt." CarouselQ (3:2) Sum 78, p. 11.

WURSTER, Michael
  "Seasonal Elegy." Epos (27:2) 77, p. 23.

WYATT, David
  "Helix, Unger, Mendelssohn, the Cat." HiramPoR (25) Aut-
    Wint 78, p. 39.
  "Listening, in Late Spring, to Handel's Messiah." HiramPoR
    (25) Aut-Wint 78, p. 40.
  "Sailing the Missouri to Iowa." SmPd (43) Spr 78, p. 13.

WYGRA, Ripa
  "Aspects of the Blackstone Hotel." WindO (33) Aut-Wint 78-79.

"Despair at the Blackstone Hotel." NewRena (10) 78, p. 42.
"Letter." WindO (33) Aut-Wint 78-79.
"Monday Evening, Another Beginning." WindO (33) Aut-Wint
    78-79.

WYLY, Ron
    "Epiphany." Wind (30) 78, p. 59.

WYNAND, Derk
    "Nebulous Love Poem." MalR (45) Ja 78, p. 285.
    "Poem for Herbert." MalR (45) Ja 78, p. 292.
    "Reconstruction" (for my brother). MalR (45) Ja 78, p. 286.

WYNDHAM, Harald
    "After the Battle." MinnR (NS10) Spr 78, p. 26.
    "The End." MinnR (NS10) Spr 78, p. 24.
    "Killed in Action." MinnR (NS10) Spr 78, p. 26.
    "March of the Weavers." MinnR (NS10) Spr 78, p. 24.
    "Woman with Folded Hands." MinnR (NS10) Spr 78, p. 25.

WYSZOMIERSKI, Donna
    "These childrens." HangL (34) Wint 78-79, p. 54.

YATES, James
    "Sex in Poetry." SouthernPR (18:1) Spr 78, p. 20.

YATES, Jamie
    "The Point of Departure." Pan (19) 77, p. 57.

YAU, John
    "After Moving." Pan (19) 77, p. 5.
    "A Bottle." Pan (19) 77, p. 7.
    "The Construction Crew." Pan (19) 77, p. 5.
    "Moll Flanders." SunM (5) Aut 78, p. 6.
    "Night." SunM (5) Aut 78, p. 7.
    "The Return of the Hunters." Pan (19) 77, p. 6.

YERANIS, Stelios
    "'Hiroshima, Mon Amour'" (tr. by Ann Rivers). StoneC (78:2)
        Spr 78, p. 20.

YOTS, Michael
    "Checking In." Wind (30) 78, p. 60.

YOUMANS, Marlene
    "History Report." SoCaR (11:1) N 78, p. 93.

YOUNG, Al
    "In a Mist." BelPoJ (29:2) Wint 78-79, p. 12.
    "Jungle Strut." BelPoJ (29:2) Wint 78-79, p. 12.

YOUNG, David
    "How Music Began." MissouriR (1:1) Spr 78, p. 35.

YOUNG, Ellen R.
  "Ruth to Orpah." ChrC (95:13) 12 Ap 78, p. 391.
  "Shallow Water." ChrC (95:28) 13 S 78, p. 820.

YOUNG, Gary
  "Eating Wild Mushrooms." Antaeus (30/31) Sum-Aut 78, p. 251.
  "February Morning." Nat (226:24) 24 Je 78, p. 772.
  "First Rain." Antaeus (30/31) Sum-Aut 78, p. 252.
  "My Brother." SlowLR (1/2) 78, p. 22.
  "My Wife." NewOR (6:1) 78, p. 8.

YOUNG, Jim
  "The Elk Horn." NewL (45:1) Aut 78, p. 30.
  "In the Poet's World." NewL (45:1) Aut 78, p. 30.
  "Reno Journal." NewL (45:1) Aut 78, p. 29.

YOUNG, Thomas
  "Introductory." Smudge (Supplement) Wint 78-79, p. 34.

YOUNG BEAR, Ray A.
  "For the Rain in March: The Blackened Hearts of Herons."
      AmerPoR (7:2) Mr-Ap 78, p. 41.
  "I Can Still Picture the Caribou." AmerPoR (7:2) Mr-Ap 78,
      p. 40.

YOURGRAU, Barry
  "Marvels." Tele (13) 77.
  "Pathos." Tele (13) 77.
  "Shaman." Tele (13) 77.
  "Two Bears." ParisR (72) Wint 77, p. 113.

YÜAN Hung-tao
  "I Get Up from My Sickbed and Sit by Myself" (tr. by Jonathan
      Chaves). VirQR (54:2) Spr 78, p. 335.
  "Pei-Mang Cemetery" (tr. by Jonathan Chaves). VirQR (54:2)
      Spr 78, p. 335.
  "On Hearing That a Girl" (tr. by Jonathan Chaves). VirQR
      (54:2) Spr 78, p. 336.
  "A Record of My Trip to Mount Shê" (tr. by Jonathan Chaves).
      VirQR (54:2) Spr 78, p. 337.
  Ten poems and a letter (tr. by Jonathan Chaves). Montra (4)
      78, p. 43.
  "Twenty-First Day of the Seventh Month" (tr. by Jonathan Chaves)
      VirQR (54:2) Spr 78, p. 334.

YÜN Shou-p'ing
  Nine poems (tr. by Jonathan Chaves). Hudson (31:4) Wint 78-79,
      p. 605.

YUSON, Alfred
  "Father." Iowa (9:4) Aut 78, p. 36.
  "Midlandfall." Iowa (9:4) Aut 78, p. 37.

ZACK, David
"Buddha University Meeting." SouthwR (63:3) Sum 78,
    p. 256.

ZADE, Wayne
"First Child." NoAmR (263:3) Aut 78, p. 49.
"Thirtieth Birthday." AntR (36:3) Sum 78, p. 370.

ZADRAVEC, Katharine
"Skating the Canal." SmPd (44) Aut 78, p. 18.

ZAMORA, Sheila
"Belongings." Chowder (10/11) Aut-Wint 78-79, p. 15.
"Claudette." AntR (36:4) Aut 78, p. 473.
"For Jody." Chowder (10/11) Aut-Wint 78-79, p. 16.
"Landscape for the Witch." AntR (36:4) Aut 78, p. 474.
"Weight Drawings." Chowder (10/11) Aut-Wint 78-79, p. 14.

ZANCANELLA, Don
"Coalminers' Wives in Hanna, Wyo." QW (5) Wint 78, p. 24.
"Night Terrors." QW (5) Wint 78, p. 24.

ZANDER, William
"Fears" (for Alex and Josh). PoetryNW (19:4) Wint 78-79,
    p. 30.
"Fields of Soria" (tr. of Antonio Machado). LitR (21:4) Sum 78,
    p. 475.
"The Flies" (tr. of Antonio Machado). LitR (21:4) Sum 78,
    p. 474.

ZARANKA, William
"The Fisherman and His Wife." HiramPoR (24) Spr-Sum 78,
    p. 39.
"Introducing My Wife." KanQ (10:4) Aut 78, p. 40.
"Moose Head." SoDakR (16:2) Sum 78, p. 13.

ZATURENSKA, Marya
"Girl and Scarecrow." ModernPS (9:1) Spr 78, p. 47.
"Song." ModernPS (9:1) Spr 78, p. 49.
"Strange Captivity." ModernPS (9:1) Spr 78, p. 48.
"The Unsepulchred 1914-1918" (For Bryher). ModernPS (9:1)
    Spr 78, p. 46.

ZAURIAN, Suzanne Ostro
"Pupa." Hand (2) 78, p. 44.

ZAWADIWSKY, Christine
"Before Sleep Grabs Me." Pan (19) 77, p. 9.
"Limbo." GeoR (32:3) Aut 78, p. 578.
"Living in the Shadow." Pan (19) 77, p. 9.
"Riddles and Lies." Iowa (9:2) Spr 78, p. 83.
"Where Flowers Are Not Flowers." EnPas (7) 78, p. 14.

ZBORNIK, Richard Carl
"On Stealing Paterson I from the Cincinnati Public Library. "
<u>NewL</u> (45:1) Aut 78, p. 105.

ZDANEVICH, Ilya
"Selected Zaum Works" (tr. by Jack Hirschman and Alexander
Kohav). <u>SunM</u> (5) Aut 78, p. 89.

ZDANYS, Jonas
"Three Poems" (tr. of Tomas Venclova). <u>Poetry</u> (132:6) S 78,
p. 342.

ZEIDNER, Lisa
"Directions. " <u>Epoch</u> (27:3) Spr 78, p. 290.

ZEIGER, David
"Climbing Mt. Washington. " <u>Tele</u> (14) 78.

ZEIGER, L. L.
"Dracula. " <u>PoNow</u> (19) 78, p. 41.
"Furs" (for my children, who feel it is immoral to wear them--).
<u>Confr</u> (17) Aut-Wint 79, p. 54.

ZEIS, Gabriel
"Finding It to Be the Hour. " <u>ChrC</u> (95:25) 2-9 Ag 78, p. 736.
"A Prayer at the Death of One's Friend. " <u>ChrC</u> (95:35) 1 N 78,
p. 1042.

ZEKOWSKI, Arlene
from The Sudden Testimony: (III-V). <u>Kayak</u> (49) O 78, p. 51.

ZELDA
"Then My Soul Cried Out" (tr. by Marcia Falk). <u>Hand</u> (2) 78,
p. 162.

ZELVIN, Elizabeth
"In the Closet" (for M.). <u>13thM</u> (4:1) 78, p. 19.

ZIMMER, Paul
"Alphonse Tells of Wanda and the Storm. " <u>ThRiPo</u> (11/12) 78,
p. 79.
"The Curse of the Frogs. " <u>Chowder</u> (10/11) Aut-Wint 78-79,
p. 41.
"Death of the Hired Zimmer. " <u>PoNow</u> (19) 78, p. 39.
"Letter to Hugo from Pittsburgh. " <u>ThRiPo</u> (11/12) 78, p. 90.
"Zimmer Envying Elephants. " <u>PoNow</u> (19) 78, p. 39.
"Zimmer in Grade School. " <u>PoNow</u> (19) 78, p. 39.
"Zimmer Stunned by Rancor. " <u>PoetryNW</u> (19:3) Aut 78, p. 37.
"Zimmer to His Students. " <u>GeoR</u> (32:1) Spr 78, p. 198.

ZIMMERMAN, Caroline Saenz
"Lone Love. " <u>Poem</u> (34) N 78, p. 57.
"Scarcely. " <u>Poem</u> (34) N 78, p. 58.

ZINNES, Harriet
"Log." <u>Confr</u> (17) Aut-Wint 79, p. 52.

ZIVKOVIC, Peter D.
"Catechism." <u>SouthwR</u> (63:2) Spr 78, p. 164.

ZOGLIN, Janet
"To a Very Possibly Someday Fine Potter." <u>Tele</u> (13) 77.

ZORN, Marilyn
"For Advent." <u>ChrC</u> (95:39) 29 N 78, p. 1155.

ZU-BOLTON, Ahmos, II.
"Bedtime Story." <u>Tele</u> (14) 78.
"Black Skin for John" (On the death of a friend).   <u>Obs</u> (4:2) Sum
    78, p. 90.
"Black Skin for John" (on the death of a friend).   <u>Tele</u> (14) 78.
"Vegetarian Blues." <u>NewOR</u> (5:4) 78, p. 361.

ZUCKERMAN, Marilyn
"Women as Friends" (for Louise) (for Cynthia).   <u>LittleM</u> (11:3)
    Aut 77, p. 45.

ZULAUF, Sander
"Group Therapy." <u>BallSUF</u> (19:4) Aut 78, p. 12.

ZWEIG, Paul
"A Fly on the Water." <u>AmerPoR</u> (7:6) N-D 78, p. 14.
"The Other Side." <u>AmerPoR</u> (7:6) N-D 78, p. 14.
"The Taking Away." <u>NewYorker</u> (54:24) 31 Jl 78, p. 36.

ZWICKY, Fay
"Kaddish" (for my father).   <u>Antaeus</u> (30/31) Sum-Aut 78, p. 263.

ZYDEK, Fredrick
"Beyond Straw and Fire" (for DW).   <u>ConcPo</u> (11:2) Aut 78,
    p. 17.
"The Death of Ralph Lawrence Finger." <u>StoneC</u> (78:3) Aut 78,
    p. 31.
"The Morning After." <u>BallSUF</u> (19:1) Wint 78, p. 30.